# COMING FROM HOME
## Readings for Writers

# Coming from Home

## Readings for Writers

MARJORIE FORD ❧ JON FORD ❧ ANN WATTERS

Stanford University  College of Alameda  Stanford University

**McGraw-Hill, Inc.**
New York  St. Louis  San Francisco  Auckland  Bogotá
Caracas  Lisbon  London  Madrid  Mexico City  Milan
Montreal  New Delhi  San Juan  Singapore
Sydney  Tokyo  Toronto

COMING FROM HOME
*Readings for Writers*

Acknowledgments appear on pages 551–555, and on this page by reference.

4 5 6 7 8 9 0 *AGM AGM* 9 0 9 8 7 6 5 4

ISBN 0-07-021510-3

*This book was set in Plantin Light by The Clarinda Company.*
*The editors were Lesley Denton and Scott Amerman;*
*the designer was Joan Greenfield;*
*the production supervisor was Al Rihner.*
*The photo editor was Barbara Salz.*
*The cover photograph was taken by Jim Finlayson.*
**Arcata Graphics/Martinsburg was printer and binder.**

*Chapter Opening Photo Credits*

*Chapter 1:* Olive R. Pierre/Stock, Boston    *Chapter 2:* Eastcott/Momatiuk/The Image Works    *Chapters 3, 4 and 5:* Joel Gordon    *Chapter 6:* Michal Heron/Woodfin Camp & Associates    *Chapter 7:* Catherine Allport/The Image Works    *Chapter 8:* Jerry Howard/Stock, Boston    *Chapter 9:* Joel Gordon

*Library of Congress Cataloging-in-Publication Data*

Ford, Marjorie (Marjorie A.)
    Coming from home: readings for writers/Marjorie Ford, Jon Ford, Ann Watters.
        p.        cm.
    Includes index.
    ISBN 0-07-021510-3
    1. College readers.    2. English language—Rhetoric.    I. Ford, Jon.    II. Watters, Ann.    III. Title.
PE1417.F62        1993
808'.042—dc20                                        92-31039

This book is printed on acid-free paper.

# ABOUT THE AUTHORS

*MARJORIE FORD* graduated from the University of California at Berkeley and is currently a lecturer in English at Stanford University. This is her third year as the editor of the composition program's newsletter, *Notes in the Margins*. Marjorie Ford has taught freshman composition at San Jose State University and at a number of the community colleges in the Bay Area. *Coming From Home* is the third freshman English text that she has collaborated on. Along with Jon Ford, she has written *Dreams and Inward Journeys* (1990) and *Writing as Revelation* (1991).

*JON FORD* graduated with a B.A. in English from the University of Texas and completed a Master's Degree in comparative literature at the University of Wisconsin, where he was a Woodrow Wilson Fellow. He also studied creative writing at San Francisco State University and started the successful poetry newsletter, *Poetryflash,* now in its twentieth year. Currently Jon Ford is chairman of English programs at the College of Alameda. *Coming From Home* is the third freshman English text that he has collaborated on. Along with Marjorie Ford, he has written *Dreams and Inward Journeys* (1990) and *Writing as Revelation* (1991).

*ANN WATTERS* graduated from the University of California at Berkeley and did graduate work at Washington University in St. Louis, where she took a Master's Degree in English literature. She has taught at the college level since 1977 at several state, private, and community colleges. She is currently a lecturer in English at Stanford University, where she has directed the freshman writing program. Ann Watters instituted a number of innovative projects at Stanford and has authored academic software, including *The Art of Persuasion* (1990), an interactive, multimedia program for teaching rhetoric.

*For Sylvia, Barbara, and Marian;*
*for Tom, Andy, and Mike*

# CONTENTS

# CHAPTER 3: MYTHS AND RITUALS 119

## *CHAPTER 4:*
## *THE MASS-PRODUCED FAMILY*     170

# CHAPTER 5: THE FAMILY IN A MULTICULTURAL SOCIETY 239

# CHAPTER 6:  TENSIONS                                           303

## CHAPTER 7: BREAKING THE MOLD   379

## CHAPTER 9: FAMILY AND COMMUNITY    481

# INSTRUCTORS' PREFACE

*D*uring any new relationship, adventure, or educational experience to which we bring our hopes, our values, our personalities, we also reflect a bit on our home life, on our core of family relationships and experiences. Early memories of family and home are permanently etched in our minds, although our estimation of our families may change over time. For example, a young child may see his or her home as the center of the universe, while a college student returning home from school may be surprised at how undistinguished his or her home and neighborhood appear. While our bodies and minds grow older, the people we were as children remain an important part of us—vulnerable, vibrant, determined, demanding. Like a web, or a wheel with spokes emanating from a center, memories of family and home stay with us even as we move, grow, and change. Perhaps we are always—if sometimes only figuratively—*coming from home.*

*Coming from Home* is intended for the first or second semester or quarter course in composition. It is a single-theme reader focusing on the modern American family as it has been explored by men and women from different cultural, ethnic, and professional backgrounds. The principal modes of writing are represented: the reflective memoir, fiction and poetry, expository writing, causal analysis and argumentation, proposal and research writing. Each of the nine chapters reflects a different aspect of the theme as well as a particular rhetorical focus.

*Coming from Home* includes an extensive teaching apparatus that features a thorough introduction to journal keeping and the reading/writing process. Each selection is accompanied by a journal entry topic and a set of questions for discussion of themes and structure, as well as by suggestions for writing. A student essay and additional writing activities conclude each chapter; a glossary of rhetorical and thematically related terms is included. Also available is an instructor's manual containing advice on presenting the reading and writing assignments.

The thematic emphasis on the family creates both a strong focus and a diversity of perspective through which a broad range of issues are linked to the central theme of the family. Among these issues are the function of memory in the life of the individual (Chapter One), the nature of myth and ritual (Chapter Three), the impact of the mass media (Chapter Four), cultural diversity (Chapter Five) and community involvement (Chapter Nine).

Along with the traditional apparatus, *Coming from Home* integrates a mixture of innovative teaching approaches, including reader-based response theory; a focus on journal keeping and creativity; and an emphasis on audience awareness, critical thinking, collaborative learning, and computer applications. The book also aims for an increased understanding and appreciation of our society's diversity in terms of culture, class, and ethnicity.

## Themes

In organizing this text, we have focused first on the foundation of family life: how people come to make meaning of their early years and the recollections they have of the bonds formed in childhood. The readings in Chapter One ("Memories") present various perspectives on childhood recollections, while each of the selections in Chapter Two ("Relationships") reflects on a different kind of family relationship and how that relationship significantly influences the individuals involved.

Chapters Three, Four, and Five examine ways in which the family is defined and extended by social conventions and realities. The selections in "Myths and Rituals" show how a family's traditions continue to influence the present. "The Mass-Produced Family" offers evidence and interpretations of the media's impact as a shaper of new roles, new needs, pastimes, and values for family members. Each of the readings in "The Family in a Multicultural Society" presents a unique view of how the cultural diversity within communities affects family life.

While many people still look to the past to define "family values" and have an image of the traditional family as a model or ideal, the realities of family life in today's world necessitate compromise and change. Chapter Six, "Tensions," focuses on problems that families often have to face, including economic concerns, divorce, working and/or single parents, physical abuse, and substance abuse. Chapter Seven, "Breaking the Mold," presents alternative forms of family life, each of which seems to meet some of the emerging needs, expectations, and values of contemporary society.

The two concluding chapters of *Coming from Home* focus on new connections that individuals can make as they develop beyond the immediate world of the family. The readings in Chapter Eight, "Growing Away," explore a variety of ways that children and parents separate and then work together to establish new connections with one another during adolescence and as a result of the changes brought about by loss and death. The selections in Chapter Nine, "The Family and Community," show how the skills learned within families are translated into the ways in which individuals relate to and help to shape the communities they live in and the ways that those communities in turn dictate the political, educational, environmental, and social conditions affecting our personal and public lives.

## Modes of Writing

In addition to emphasizing a particular theme, each chapter's reading selections have been chosen to emphasize progressively more complex modes of writing as the text moves the reader's attention from private concerns outward to increasingly public issues.

The readings in Chapter One, "Memories," are primarily autobiographical, presenting examples of *narrative* and *descriptive* techniques of writing. In Chapter Two, "Relationships," many of the selections are organized according to *comparative* strategies that invite the reader to examine the complex patterns of family relationships. A number of the readings in "Myths and Rituals," Chapter Three, clarify through *process analysis* the way in which family stories and rituals shape the identities of family members. Chapter Four, "The Mass-Produced Family," provides examples of particular media programs and fictional portraits to *illustrate* the impact of the all-pervasive television medium on family life. The essays in Chapter Five, "The Family in a Multicultural Society," illustrate a variety of ways to develop *definitions* that can help clarify the nature of culture and family heritage.

The readings in Chapter Six, "Tensions," present different strategies of *causal analysis,* focusing on the influence of social change on the family and on the individual. "Breaking the Mold," Chapter Seven, presents a variety of *argumentative* techniques, including essays that make a case for different kinds of new and emerging family life-styles. In "Growing Away," Chapter Eight, the selections are primarily *reflective* and contemplative. Here the writers take time to examine the new patterns and insights that emerge as families grow apart and adolescents come to define themselves both as individuals and as members of a family network. *Proposal and research* writing are the strategies modeled in the final chapter, "Family and Community." While particular rhetorical strategies are emphasized in each chapter, all the selections included are richly composed and offer the reader helpful ideas and models for organizing writing that is creative, moving, and persuasive.

## Thinking and Writing Activities

Along with the readings on the family, we have included suggestions for thinking and writing to stimulate reflection on the concepts embodied in the theme. These activities are designed not only to help you examine how writers use different strategies to clarify and develop the ideas explored in the essays, fiction, and poetry in the text, but also to suggest, in response to the chapter readings, many different projects for writing and research.

The Journal Entry writing topic that prefaces each selection is included to encourage your students to think about issues that may emerge in the reading. Following each of the selections is a set of discussion questions that should help students to shape and share both individual and collaborative answers to issues raised by the particular reading.

The discussion topics following each selection are divided into four categories. The questions under Looking at Ideas encourage students to read carefully and reflect on the writer's themes and ideas. The questions following Looking at Strategies are designed to help students analyze how the author has used rhetorical or organizational strategies to create and clarify meaning in his or her writing. The Looking at Connections topics will help your students to find parallels between the themes and meanings of the selection they have just read and the themes in one or two of the other readings in the chapter. Each reading has at least three different suggestions for ways that students might develop essays related to the reading's themes; these are listed under Suggestions for Writing.

At the end of each chapter are Reaching Out Activities; these assignments extend the ideas presented in the Suggestions for Writing and reinforce the importance of student collaboration and a sense of connection with different communities. We have included computer-based writing projects to inform students about some of the remarkable new possibilities that computers make available to writers, both as individuals and (through networking) as group members. Finally, for individual or group viewing and discussion, we provide a list of films on video related to the theme of each chapter. The instructor's manual provides sample essays and advice on presenting the nontraditional writing assignments suggested in the Reaching Out Activities.

## Acknowledgments

As the three of us worked together and with our students and our editor to shape this text, we gained valuable and reassuring insights into the way bonds of community are built within families, friendships, classrooms, and the workplace. We are especially grateful to Brian Gore, who encouraged us to present our proposal to McGraw-Hill and who kept in touch with us during the long composing process; to all our many students who worked with diligence and care to help us to create this text; and to our colleagues at the College of Alameda and Stanford University who provided a supportive community of listeners with insightful responses and advice. We have special thanks for our editor, Lesley Denton, who believed in the concept behind the project from the very start, who was instrumental in making sure that this project came to have a life of its own, and who helped us to realize our vision. We would also like to acknowledge our reviewers for their detailed reports, for their helpful suggestions, and for their words of encouragement: Ken Autrey, Francis Marion College; Anne Barrows, University of San Francisco–Ignatian Heights; Michael P. Berberich, Galveston College; Liz Buckley, East Texas State University; Beverly Connor, The University of Puget Sound; Susan X. Day, Illinois State University; Paula Gibson, Cardinal Stritch College; Sandra Baker Holt,

California State University–Fullerton; Kate Kiefer, Colorado State University; Lyle W. Morgan, Pittsburg State University; Jon F. Patton, University of Toledo; Randall Wells, University of South Carolina; Elizabeth Wheeler, Nassau Community College; and Jacqueline S. Wilson, Western Illinois University.

Finally, we are thankful to our families, who shared their love and kept us in touch with the realities of our lives. Our last acknowledgement is to Marjorie Ford's mother, Sylvia Klein Title, whose struggle to survive a cancer diagnosed when she was in her early eighties reaffirmed the strength and courage of the human spirit. Her faith and hope speak to us, reminding us to cherish our blessings on our daily journeys as travelers *coming from home*.

Marjorie Ford
Jon Ford
Ann Watters

# STUDENTS' INTRODUCTION

## STUDENTS TO STUDENTS: WHAT TO EXPECT FROM COMING FROM HOME

*A*s students who have already used this book, we wanted to share some of our insights about *Coming from Home* with you. *Coming from Home* focuses on the home and the community, and that is exactly what your class will become: a community of other students who, like yourselves, will be experiencing the fears and anxieties as well as the challenges and rewards that will inevitably occur as you develop your identities as writers.

Approaching a book such as this one, one that gives you the opportunity to reflect upon your family, your cultural heritage, your emotions, and your experiences, you will learn that a one-sided argumentative position will not always work in the writing assignments for this text. Nor are you likely to find one good, conclusive solution to the problems and issues that each chapter presents. This book was designed to make you think and reflect; it will encourage you to put your thoughts down on paper with emotion, character, and purpose.

*Coming from Home* asks you to experience writing as a process that can lead to greater self-understanding. We realize that this approach may be new to a number of you within the setting of an English class. So here's a little advice: relax and say what you mean.

—From the Students of the Coming from Home class
Freshman English, Fall 1991
Stanford University

# AUTHORS TO STUDENTS

*A*s a college student you may have already become aware of the emphasis on the family in higher education; many of the subjects you will be studying focus on the family as a fundamental unit of society. In such fields as literature, anthropology, psychology, sociology, political science, business, economics, nutrition, and genetics, students and their professors read and learn about the family. It is a lively topic for research and theory as well as for interpretation through the creative arts.

In an even broader sense, as a citizen in a democracy you are learning to make political and social decisions that affect the family. As a voter or member of social organizations within your community, you continually face questions and make decisions that relate to the family. Does the government have a responsibility to attempt to preserve the traditional nuclear family and the values it represents? Should the government or private business fund child care and maternity leave for employees? Should the government provide a social welfare "safety net" to prevent families, particularly those with young children, from living lives of economic deprivation and hunger? Should unmarried "domestic partners" be given health care benefits? Should the schools provide moral or religious education? Should educators help their students explore the issues of sexuality and birth control, or should these matters be left for parents to discuss with their children as they see fit?

As you come to know the other students in your class, as you reflect on the readings in the text, as you discuss and write about the various themes related to the family and community presented in the readings, we hope you will begin to see your classroom as a new kind of family or community, one that can help you better understand and express yourself as an individual and as a member of the various communities of which you are a part. We hope that this text will encourage you to embark on many new journeys *coming from home,* and that these journeys will help you discover and create meaningful connections with your past while building bridges to the future.

## Focus on the Reading/Writing Process

Despite the fact that most of the readings we have selected relate to the central theme of the family, the diversity will be both stimulating and challenging to you, both as a reader and as a writer. You will need to take a systematic approach to understanding the variety of reading selections you encounter in this textbook. However, the more you read and the more you write in response to reading, the more both of these related skills will improve, and the more natural and fluid your reading/writing process will become.

## Keeping a Reading/Writing Journal

Often your lives as students are busy, and a reading included in this text that is not directly related to your day-to-day realities may not seem relevant to you until you take a few moments to write and think about the issue in your journal. You may feel freer to express yourself in a journal than in classroom essays, since you know you are the primary audience and that you need not concern yourself with the formal expectations of an assigned essay, such as correct punctuation, grammar, or topic ideas for paragraphs. On the other hand, the entries and observations you make in your reader's journal can become the seeds for later, more developed and audience-oriented writing.

In this text we emphasize several approaches to journal writing. As a prereading activity, journal keeping will help you clarify your own thoughts and feelings on the issues about which you will be reading. Another way to develop your reader's journal is to write yourself questions about passages in the readings that you find difficult, and then try to work out answers in your writing. This application of journal keeping will help you develop your critical thinking skills. You can also use the journal productively by seeing it as a place to capture periodically your reflections on your learning process. What did you learn this week about the theme of the family? About your writing process? About how you read and interpret texts? Finally, the journal can be a place to store ideas and preliminary drafts for future essays. As the term progresses and you can look back through the pages of your journal, you are likely to realize that you have come to understand your writing, your reading, and yourself better through the journal-keeping process.

The following passage from a student's journal analyzes what keeping a journal has meant to her and how the journal has helped her develop her talents as a writer.

I write in my journal about memories, values, morals, or thoughts and ideas which have taken me by surprise and have stayed with me. Some thoughts stay at the back of my mind and continue to grow until I write them down and fully explore them. I feel my thoughts and ideas becoming organized as I am writing in my journal. In writing journals in a free-flowing style, I often discover in the finished entry new ideas and viewpoints. Although I begin a journal entry by listing the topic and knowing my intention before I write, when I begin writing, I let everything come onto the paper without correcting ideas or grammar.

—Tami Koval

Although the text and your instructor may suggest specific journal entries, it is up to you to develop entries and to make productive use of your journal. The journal can be an ideal place to link reading, writing, experience, and thought by serving as a place to record your personal responses to the readings. One such entry was completed by a student who was writing in response to the journal entry suggestion for Alice Walker's "Father" in Chapter One: "Write a sketch of a relative whose values influenced you." Notice how the details that the student captures in his journal entry give a clear sense of the meaning that this student's relationship with his grandmother has continued to hold for him.

Nonna Carolina, I have a photograph of her, looking small and fragile as she is knitting a pair of socks, while standing in front of an enormous oak tree. She always knitted. With two balls of yarn in each pocket of her apron, and the cat purring on her knees; she would relax by knitting.

During the summer, when on vacation from boarding school, I would go and stay with her. My grandparents had a farm up in the hills near Florence. She would tend to the cows; I would help Nonna prune the vineyards, and cultivate the vegetable and flower gardens. Tuesdays and Fridays she would make bread. Those were special days. Nonna would start a gigantic fire in the oven outside near the house. Once the fire had died down, she would swipe the hot glowing carbon to the side of the oven with a broom. When the bread was ready to be baked, with a long wooden spatula she would make neat rows of white uncooked bread inside the hot oven. I don't remember the taste of that bread anymore, but I can still remember the fragrance of it. Sometimes, when in Italy vacationing, the same fragrance will come out of a bakery and rekindle my childhood memory.

Looking at her in the photograph, I realize that the gigantic oak tree seems to dwarf her. With her apron on she looks like one of those Italian folklore pictures that foreigners are fond of. In my childhood and my memory Nonna was my oak tree, she symbolized stability and provided me with comfort and shelter.

—Sauro Mangaelli

Sauro Mangaelli's attention to detail in sketching his memory of his grandmother gives a clear image of the activities as well as the feelings that they shared. His exercise in journal writing gave him insight into the impact his grandmother had on his life while helping him to make his writing more vivid and more powerful.

## Reading: Preparing for the Journey

One use for your reading and writing journal is to keep notes on your reading process, which will help you become a more systematic and thoughtful reader. Rather than simply regarding reading as a matter of moving through a text, of getting the main idea and preparing for a class assignment, it is helpful to envision the act of reading as a way of increasing your awareness: of a particular subject, of the act of reading itself, of yourself, and of your values. Consider, above all, that you bring to life the texts you read, completing the circle of meaning that encompasses the world of the writer, his or her arrangement of language in the text, and your own experiences and ideas.

*Prereading*

Reading is a process with several overlapping stages. Initially, the act of reading involves entering several new worlds—the private universe of the writer's own voice and experience, as well as the more public worlds of subject, issue, and the discipline or genre that the writer has chosen to write within. To ease your passage into the writer's worlds, you need to make some advance preparations. First, you can begin to make personal associations with the text's basic subject matter. This can involve making a brainstorming list in your journal of all the ideas that come to mind when you notice an intriguing title or subject. Or it can involve narrating a personal experience that seems to fit with the topic or title you are reading, as Sauro Maengelli did in the journal entry about his grandmother.

After writing a quick preliminary response to your reading selection, reflect on any feelings, ideas, or questions that come to your mind. With some awareness of your own background knowledge and preconceptions on the subject of the selection, you will be better prepared to begin reading. Scan the selection to determine the overall shape and purpose of the reading: to inform, to tell a story, to persuade or argue, to reflect philosophically on an experience. Examine special features like the headnote, major headings and subheadings, and explicit topic sentences. For each of these features, write down a question:

1. What do I expect the writer to accomplish in this selection?
2. What is my perspective on the issue raised in the main headings?
3. What do I know already about this subject?
4. What questions do I have that I hope the reading will answer?

Reflecting on the main issues of a reading selection can help you anticipate major turns of an argument or prepare yourself emotionally to respond to a narrative.

*Reading Different Forms of Writing*

Each form of writing has its own purposes and makes special kinds of demands on the reader. For example, when you read informational or expository material, such as Judith Wallerstein's "On the Brow of the Hill" (Chapter Six), which discusses the impact of divorce and provides statistics and case histories, you need to look at the main points made by the writer and make a brief mental or written summary of the major facts that support each point. Depending on your familiarity with the subject matter, you should be able to read expository material fairly rapidly, but don't forget to look closely to see what questions the selection as a whole raises about its subject. In contrast, argumentative essays, such as Keenan Peck's "When Family Is Not a Household Word" (Chapter Seven) call for a slow pace of reading. Peck's essay requires that you pay careful attention to his central issue—community laws against cohabitation by nonrelated groups of individuals—noting each new supporting argument as well as taking a highly critical, active stance, formulating answers or rebuttals to points with which you may find yourself in disagreement.

Many forms of writing, particularly longer essays, combine an argumentative thesis with exposition and narration, using narrative in longer examples and case histories, exposition to explain complex ideas and processes. In a reading built on diverse of forms of writing, you need to be especially flexible, slowing down to focus on major points and transitions within the larger argument. See the glossary on writing strategies at the end of the book for a fuller discussion of the different types of essays and organizational strategies you will encounter in your reading.

On the other hand, reflective, personal essays like Michael Dorris's "Moving Out" (Chapter Eight) call upon you to read in an engaged manner that matches the author's own reflective stance, slowing down to empathize or identify with the narrator as he or she shares personal experiences, drawing parallels to events in your own life. In a similar manner, literature demands a slow reading pace, as well as an intense involvement of your physical senses and feelings, your mind and your imagination. Literature asks that you pay close attention, both to subtle choices and shadings of meaning in words, and to the conventions of stories or poetry. Among these literary conventions are stages of the plot (exposition, introduction of conflict, rising action, climax, and resolution); major and supporting or antagonistic characters; setting and symbolic objects. See the Glossaries at the end of the book for a fuller explanation of literary strategies and conventions.

Literature also differs from other types of reading, such as a personal memoir or the reflective, first-person essay, in that the story, poem, or play you are reading and its narrator or central characters are frequently considered ironically, that is, in a way contrary to the beliefs and intentions of the characters themselves. A character who is narrating a story may attempt to deceive or may be unsure of what is really going on, as is the case with the confused father in Malamud's "My Son the Murderer" (Chapter Eight). Indeed, part of the pleasure of reading literature is deciding for yourself how much of what a narrator says can be taken seriously and how much is revealed about a character's confusion and self-deception. Finally, and perhaps most importantly, because the author of a fictional work does not directly reveal the meaning through thesis statement and straightforward logical or factual supports, literature allows us the greatest room of all forms of reading to make meaning from a selection through active, imaginative interpretations of the text.

## Reading and Marking the Text

After preparing to read a text, you will be ready to do a complete read-through of the selection. Make simple marginal notes, but don't let your marking impede your progress, as it's important to get an overall perception of the work. Use your pen or pencil as an extension of the reading act, expressing yourself in abbreviations: bracketing crucial passages, using question marks or exclamation marks; writing "no" or "yes" to indicate disagreement or agreement, putting in the letters "MS" for main support or "SS" for secondary support. You should develop whatever notation system best fits your needs. As you read, try to remember the major conventions of the form, looking for relevant patterns of support, key senses, examples and images, and noting any repeated words and phrases that reveal special emphasis. If you are reading poetry, be sure to read the poem aloud, listening to the way the sounds and rhythms of the words contribute to the overall feeling or mood of the work.

## Responding to the Whole Reading

After you have read the text carefully, you will be ready to write a brief response. The goal of this type of writing, which can be kept in your reading journal, is to react to the selection as a whole rather than just to one or two points as you do when you are answering study questions. In your reading response, you might consider questions such as the following:

1. Did you like or dislike the selection as a whole?
2. Did the selection achieve its purpose?
3. Did the writer offer evidence in support of the conclusions drawn?
4. Were there any ambiguities or contradictions in the text?
5. Do you have any information that might cast doubts on the writer's conclusions?

Notice how in the following response to Freud's "Interpretation of *Oedipus Rex*" a student shares her feelings about the subject matter as well as some reservations about Freud's ideas:

> I'm not an authority on Freud, but the parental sexuality theory, I believe to be very extreme. I don't believe that all women want to kill their mothers so that they can be with their fathers or vice versa. As far as the sexuality goes, of course, it is going to start in the home because the first human contact of an infant is with his or her parents. However, I don't see how the story of Oedipus, who didn't even know his father and mother before his crime, supports such a far-reaching theory. I would really like to learn more about Freud's theories and do some more research into psychology to learn if anyone has updated or disproved anything he has said or claimed to be true.

Although the student realized that she didn't have quite enough knowledge to fully evaluate Freud's theories on child sexuality, she has started to form an opinion about her reading as well as to seek a direction for further reading and study. Another, closer reading of the selection would be helpful at this point, along with some research to learn more about Freud's ideas. Reading the text again reflectively, the student could begin to make some more particular points in criticism of Freud's essay, or she might even change her mind and come to accept some of the ideas she had previously resisted. Like writing, reading is a process that requires "multiple drafts" or revisions of early impressions to create a strong, unified perspective on a work.

## Making the Transition: From Reading to Writing Essays

In her journal entry about Freud's ideas on *Oedipus Rex,* the student wrote to develop a tentative response to what she had read; her notes weren't intended to stand up as independent, audience-oriented creations, as essays usually are. An *essay* (from the French word *essai,* or attempt) is an exploration of ideas, a fully developed statement in which you express, for an audience of readers, a point of view of your own on a text or other subject. Classroom essays frequently have clear divisions, such as the attention-getting introduction, the clear thesis statement that indicates your stance on an issue, and the "body" section that develops your ideas thoroughly, often with personal examples and references to relevant texts. Essays usually end with an emphatic conclusion. Thus, moving from reading to writing involves transforming your experiences and your reflections on your reading into clear, well-developed communication. At this point you might skim over some of the student essays included in *Coming from Home* to get an idea of the different ways that students emphasize, develop, and organize their experiences and ideas for their readers.

The essays you will write in this course will probably take many forms and may be directed at different audiences. Some of your essays will follow the forms of your readings. For example, you may be asked to write a narrative, an expository essay, an argument, or a research paper in response to a reading in your textbook. See the Glossaries for a fuller explanation of these and other strategies of essay writing. Whatever form your essays take, your writing will need to move through several stages: *prewriting, drafting,* and *revising* your drafts; and then *rewriting* and *proofreading* the final version of your paper.

### From Private to Public Writing: Prewriting
A variety of writing activities can help you move from reading and journal responses, through the drafting stage, to an essay that communicates effectively with an audience. In addition to the active reading and note-taking techniques described above, a variety of prewriting strategies can help you develop your own response to the readings. Use your prewriting notes to stretch your vision and ideas, to restate issues that a reading raises, to explore related personal experiences and observations, to capture ideas for further reflection and development.

*Brainstorming* and *freewriting* are helpful techniques for generating and recording ideas in preparation for developing an essay. Such techniques can help you silence the internal critic who may block your writing by expecting a perfect product immediately. To brainstorm, jot down a list, on paper or computer screen, of whatever comes into your mind about a topic: an idea that a reading raised, an issue, a character, an assertion, a vivid image. After developing your list is complete, you can group related ideas, do further brainstorming on interesting groups of ideas, or delete information that seems irrelevant or repetitious. The following brainstorming list was done on the subject of "family." Which items on the list might be grouped together? What might be areas for further brainstorming?

| | |
|---|---|
| family members | dealing with the pain |
| brother/sisters | nothing like your family |
| grandparents/parents | love |
| importance of parents | support |
| guidance—growing up | crisis |
| birth/death | family gatherings |
| pain of death, loss | motherly love |

While brainstorming tends to be "linear" and to evolve as a list down the page, freewriting involves writing rapidly without stopping for brief periods of time (five to ten minutes) in a continuous flow on the page. Freewriting will help you to get in touch with what you really want to say about a subject, with what your underlying feelings about a topic may be. After freewriting you can reread what you have written and circle fresh, insightful ideas and expressions. Then you can try further freewriting using these discoveries as points of departure. Following is a student's freewriting in response to "family." What areas seem to indicate possible directions for further freewriting and development?

> The word family means love, love between parents, grandparents, brothers and sisters. It means dealing with a whole range of emotions between the joy of birth to the pain of losing a loved one. Family also means guidance from those who love and know you counting on your family for guidance on things you need help on because they know and have been through the same thing before. Family also means getting together with loved ones, especially around the holidays and being together, enjoying one another's company. Christmas and Thanksgiving are holidays I especially look forward to Family means celebrating birthdays with each other. But it also means growing up, graduating from high school, going off to college, and eventually moving out, starting a family of your own, bringing children of your own into the world and weatching them grow and making our own memories.

Computer users can take advantage of *invisible writing,* a type of freewriting in which you cannot see what you have written until you have finished the prewriting exercise. To write invisibly, turn down the screen brightness on your computer or turn off the monitor and let your mind and fingers work unattended by critical consciousness. Use invisible writing to develop ideas, explore connections, take positions on issues, and reach for images to develop into later drafts.

*Clustering or mapping* also can be effective in developing and making connections between ideas. Try putting a key word or short phrase or image in the center of a page. Draw a balloon around it and develop offshoots from your original word or phrase like spokes from a wheel or blossoms from the central stem of a plant; each of these major associations can in turn become the point of origin for a further cluster of associations.

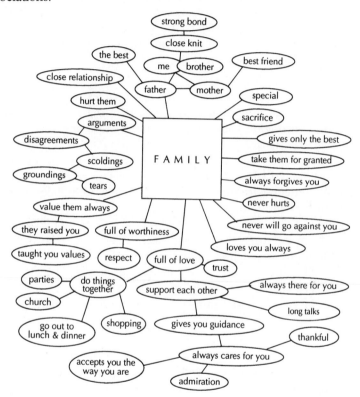

*Outlining* is a strategy that works better for some writers than for others. Some writers rely on just a few words and notes as a guideline for a draft; others work from a "scratch" outline similar to a brainstorming list or a clustering with a few key points and phrases included; others work best when they use their rough notes and prewritings to develop a full, formal outline before attempting to draft an essay. Whatever techniques of prewriting or outlining you choose to use, it is important to gradually develop the threads, the images, the ideas, that come to mind as you reflect on your readings and on your own feelings, experiences, and ideas.

**Authors to Students**

After collecting journal entries, notes, and prewritings for your essay, look over your material and select a particular idea or notion raised in your prewriting and freewrite on that more limited selection. Search for other ideas or examples that relate to the limited topic you have drawn from your early prewriting. Through thinking and active reading, through reflection and consistent prewriting, you can focus on the aspects of the topic you want to develop into a full essay.

As you review and reflect on material generated in your prewriting, you will need to consider your purpose in writing, your audience, and your subject. As you begin to draft, keep the purpose for your writing in mind and try to select a major strategy or *mode* of writing for your paper. Before you decide on a dominant mode or writing strategy, ask yourself the following questions:

1. Are you trying primarily to explain, to tell a story, or to argue?
2. Do you want to approach the subject from a personal perspective, reflecting on your topic or issue in the context of your personal experience?
3. Can you illustrate a concept with a narrative, such as a case history? Should you describe a scene, a person, an object?
4. Can you compare two readings, characters, techniques, in order to understand both of them better?
5. Should you analyze or break down a reading, topic, issue, or problem into parts through a process analysis, a cause and effect analysis, or an extended definition?
6. Should you present a cause and then discuss effects? Or should you take an effect, and then trace back to the causes?
7. Should you analyze a problem and propose a solution, either in an expository problem-solution essay or a researched proposal which argues for a particular position or course of action?

In drafting your essay, you will also need to think carefully about the audience for your writing, your intended readers. One way to pay special attention to your audience is to ask yourself some questions:

1. For whom is the writing intended? For peers? An instructor? Advisors or deans on campus? People in the community? A general audience or an audience with whom you share specialized knowledge in the field in which you are writing?
2. What is the bias or predisposition of the audience on the issue of your paper? Is your audience receptive or skeptical, neutral or committed?
3. What does your audience already know about your subject?
4. What does your audience need to know?
5. How much and what kinds of evidence do you need to convince

your audience that your argument, interpretation, or proposal should be accepted?

Asking these questions will also guide your method of developing the essay and help you make crucial decisions about word choice and about facts and arguments to include or exclude. Selecting topics and issues according to your own interest and knowledge, prewriting extensively on the selected issue, letting purpose and audience guide the assertions you make and the mode of development you use—all these will help you to develop a rough draft that you can then review, reflect on, and refine through the revision process.

*From Draft to Revision*

Just as you need to revise your vision of the past through reexamining your childhood as you grow older and as your values and beliefs evolve, so you will want to revise and reconsider your writing as you move from the insights of prewriting and drafting in the direction of a clear and convincing statement of position. As you share your paper, working through it with friends, classmates, and instructors, your writing will go through several transformations. You may retain only a small part of the original draft of the paper, possibly none of the initial wording at all, perhaps only a thought or direction of mind. We recommend that you save your early drafts, keeping all your possibilities open as you revise, so that you may go back to an earlier version of your paper if you choose, to reinsert a strong, original image or phrase you might have originally deleted in your efforts to shape the essay.

The process of revision can be divided into several steps or stages, which in practice overlap. First, re-examine your original draft after putting it aside for a period of time. Begin by asking yourself questions about the overall shape or form of the essay:

1. Does your main idea or thesis seem clear?
2. Are there major contradictions or inconsistencies in your argument?
3. Do you stick with your thesis throughout the paper, or do you stray into other, unrelated ideas? If so, perhaps you need to change the original thought behind your paper or possibly narrow or broaden your focus to include or exclude emerging thoughts.
4. Could you benefit from outlining or reoutlining your original draft? Even if you tried outlining before drafting your paper, your ideas may have changed so much in the course of your draft that it may be worthwhile to outline once again, perhaps leaving out sections of your original outline or developing other sections so that your essay seems to be following a satisfactory pattern that clearly develops and divides your core idea.

*From Revision to Editing*

Writers frequently follow up their initial overview of a draft with a closer scrutiny of the paragraphs that make up their composition. Paragraphs are like the floors of a building: each must be solidly constructed, well secured to the the floor immediately before it and the one just beyond it, and reflective of the goals and design of the whole structure. The introductory paragraph is like the entry way of a home you want your reader to enter and linger in; the body paragraphs are like the rooms that a good floor plan naturally leads us through, while the conclusion is like the peak of a roof, a natural culmination of the structure that often points beyond the limits of what's already been said, to suggest the future, to reflect on the implications of your thesis. Test your paragraphs for solid supporting ideas and examples—the "beams" of your structure—as well as for repetitions that lead the reader back to your thesis idea. Make sure that you've nailed the paragraph together, phrase to phrase, sentence to sentence, and paragraph to paragraph with repetitions of key words, consistent pronoun use and verb tense, as well as transitional expressions, such as *in contrast to, therefore, however, nevertheless* or *next,* to ensure an overall unity and flow of ideas.

The final stages of revision—editing and proofreading—include careful attention to language. Using a thesaurus or dictionary, check and replace any words or expressions that seem vague or unclear in order to assure vividness and precision. Fine-tune your sentences for variety, length, and rhythm, reading them aloud to feel the flow or choppiness of the language. As you perform your editing and proofreading of the essay, check carefully for grammatical clarity and correctness, punctuation, and spelling. By the time you have finished the revision process, you will probably have completed a number of drafts of your paper and will have made a great many minor corrections and improvements.

*Peer Review and the Revision Process*
Student writers often benefit from sharing even early drafts with their peers. If peer review happens frequently in your writing classroom, usually in small groups of four or five students, you may come to experience your writing group as a community with shared interests and concerns. Just as in family life, there are obstacles to be overcome for peer review to function successfully. Peer group participants need to listen to one another's work, to make both supportive and constructive comments on one another's writing. Just as families often gather to discuss responsibilities and procedures for accomplishing shared work, so does your peer writing group need to be conscious of its patterns of group interaction and develop consistent guidelines and rituals, such as agreeing to read papers aloud and to go over a set of prepared questions that will help direct discussion in a productive way.

Although we have found that most students enjoy peer review, some individuals are more accustomed to working alone. The following passage was written by a student who, for personal reasons, found it difficult to share her writing with her peers. Do you share any of her reservations? What advice would you have for her about participating in classroom sharing and critiques?

I always remember that those who give away too many pieces of themselves end up like the "Giving Tree" that was too selfless to save itself. That old tree gave bits and leaves and branches of itself away until it had nothing left but a stump. Becoming a "Giving Tree" is what I feel like I'm being asked to do when I write for a group. I feel pressured to bare my soul for a group of people who are, if not strangers, still only acquaintances. The obvious advice here is, "If you don't want to share something, don't write about it." The problem is that all of my writing feels like a part of me. I believe that when we write, try as we may to resist it, we reveal ourselves. I never escape the feeling that writing is like a hole in the fabric of myself, just waiting to bleed everything away if given the chance. We all helplessly stain our papers with who we are.

That's why I'm so sensitive to peer reviews. I always get the impression that my peers are sitting there like a panel of august judges to determine if what I have to say, if who I am, is interesting enough. I don't like to be that vulnerable, not for a grade, not "to get in touch with my fellow humanity." With my writing I entertain, inform, and maybe even teach, but always I remain jealously myself. I freely admit that I don't take criticism as well as I probably should, and I never like to give it. Perhaps my subconscious mind cannot tell the difference between good and bad criticism. To the inner self, it is all damaging, and when the criticism is given in front of a group, embarrassment is added to the wound. It is always too easy for a group to gang up against a paper. I've witnessed the phenomenon many times. The review always begins positively, ". . . liked the description," ". . . ideas are really good." ". . . interesting point," but many times as soon as the group feels that it's done its duty to make the writer feel good, it starts to rip the paper apart. It is done in sympathetic tones, but it is still painful to watch. It would be much kinder simply to write down any comments on the paper itself so that the writer can go over it in private.

I realize that my opinions on peer sharing are not popular opinions, but I am only myself, and so speak only for myself. For me, peer reviews open a tunnel to the past through which the whispered shouts of childhood rumble threateningly forward. The criticism of my peers today echos too similarly the sibilant whispers of old. Group reviews are simply not something that I can enjoy, and the only excuse that I can offer is that my need for isolation in childhood became a habit of solitude as I grew up, and now it is a need again.

—Lida Chaipatanakarn

In contrast, student writer Carlos Perez, whose essay is included in Chapter Three, "Myths and Rituals," wrote several drafts of his essay on the Thanksgiving celebration, and shared each of his drafts with his peer group. In the draft version of his introduction, Perez evoked the "fairytale" image of the first Thanksgiving dinner. He wrote:

Once upon a time, a group of oppressed people made a perilous voyage across a great ocean to a land where they could be free from persecution and where they could practice democracy. They landed at a

xxxvii

place called Plymouth Rock and settled nearby to build their town. Due to their intrepidness and bravery, these people were able to survive countless unknown dangers and harsh, starving winters. These people, whose fortitude is here briefly described, were the Pilgrims, the first Americans.

Peer reviewers in Perez's writing group commented on this draft, providing positive feedback about the "once upon a time" beginning and its ironic implications that echo throughout the paper. The reviewers made a number of suggestions about the writing style and the content of the essay. For instance, the peer critics suggested that Perez cut the phrase, "whose fortitude is here briefly described." They pointed out that the phrase is passive and unnecessarily announces and calls attention to the presentation of the paper rather than moving directly to the argument of the paper, thus adding unnecessary words and diluting the emphasis of the ideas Perez needs to emphasize. After listening to the suggestions of his reviewers, Perez wrote, "These hardy pioneers were the first Americans." In making this choice, he made his paragraph more concise and direct. In giving him feedback on content and style, Perez's peer critics were able to suggest both what to keep and what to revise in the essay.

Although the end result of your efforts at revision should be an essay you can take pride in, it is difficult to know when your essay is at last finished. As Carlos Perez puts it: "Even after having written what seemed like the final draft of the essay, I found new things to change and new ways to improve the writing. . . . There is no such thing as a final draft. We use this term only because of time limits and deadlines that must end the rewriting process."

Like the wheel of family relationships that move with us on our journey through life, the process of reading, thinking, and writing, of rereading, rethinking, and revising can lead us closer to clarifying, refining, and understanding who we are, how we feel, what we think. Both writing about and understanding ourselves within our family constellation are spiraling processes that offer extraordinary challenges. Working through this text, we hope that you will discover and shape your own definition of *coming from home*. We believe that this journey will help you write more effectively and better understand yourself and your world.

Marjorie Ford
Jon Ford
Ann Watters

# COMING FROM HOME
## *Readings for Writers*

CHAPTER ONE

# *Memories*

*I remember my mother from the time I was five years old, the day my father passed away and I was brought home from school. My mother, whom I had never seen cry, was sobbing in pain and friends took her away from all nine of her children to rest. She pulled herself together at once and showed a great interest in all of her children, watching carefully over the weakest. Mother was also a wonderful cook; every Friday night was a great occasion with the lighting of candles and the prayers over the bread. We all worked and helped her. She had our love and devotion always. Although my mother died over 35 years ago, my sisters and I still feel the power of her strength helping us through our sorrows.* —Sylvia Klein Title, interview

*The writer of memoir takes us back to a corner of his or her life that was unusually vivid or intense. . . . By narrowing the lens, the writer achieves a focus that isn't possible in autobiography; memoir is a window into life.*
—Russell Baker, "Inventing the Truth"

*Who knows where inspiration comes from? Perhaps it arises from desperation. Perhaps it comes from the flakes of the universe, the kindness of the muses. Whatever the case, one day I found myself asking, "But why is my narrator telling this story?" And I realized: a story should be a gift. She needs to give her story to someone.*
—Amy Tan, interview, *Publishers Weekly* (5/91)

When you think about your childhood, what do you remember? Like the older student, Sylvia Title, who recalls her mother's response to the death of her father 35 years earlier, many people find themselves reflecting on important moments or events, filled with joy or with sorrow, that were shared with family members. Each person has a storehouse of family memories that have helped to shape his or her self-concept and world view.

Reading through the selections in this chapter may encourage or even inspire you to begin to record those memories and grasp more fully the importance of your changing relationships with family members (and with yourself). Russell Baker captures the ways in which writing about his mother's illness helped him understand their changing relationship and the importance of the writing process: "What finally prompted the book to become a book was what I came to think of as the living death of my mother. . . . Gradually it seemed to me that the way to deal with it was to write about the times that the two of us had passed through together."

Just as you can come to understand your experiences better through writing about them, you are also likely to write best about what you know from experience. While your childhood memories may be buried in the recesses of your mind, through prewriting activities you will be able to uncover them so that you can explore and express them more fully in your own words. Good writing is also often rooted in strong feelings, and your most powerful attitudes, ideas, and feelings may be related to experiences you had as a child, with your mother or father, grandparents, brothers, or sisters. As you write about your child-hood memories, you will not only discover important insights about yourself; you will also begin to realize that you have the potential to be a writer. You will discover an inner self with meaningful and vivid ideas and memories to recount and analyze, as well as a unique voice, a writ-er's identity, that can help make your inner experiences a part of the public world of language.

While you write about your past to develop self-understanding and a writer's voice, at the same time this writing process can help you clar-ify your values, which were first encountered and then shaped within the world of your family. Writing about childhood memories will help you see more clearly what your family's values were, whom you re-spected and emulated, whom you rebelled against and for what rea-sons, how you came to create your own particular identity. You may find a deeper understanding of your family's beliefs and struggles as you come to understand the social and political implications of key events and decisions in your family's past. As you begin to define your family structure, its social class, economic status, cultural rituals, and religion, you will also be better able to see its special strengths—its uniqueness and value. As poet and essayist Patricia Hampl has pointed out: "If we refuse to do the work of creating this personal version of the past, someone else will do it for us. . . . What is remembered is what *becomes* reality."

The memoirs we have selected for this chapter explore a range of parent-child relationships and a variety of fundamental issues that you are likely to have encountered, or possibly will face, as a family mem-ber. We have included a poem, "The Child," by George Keithley, that involves the reader in the paradoxical parental expectations; two mem-oirs of sons who write about the ways in which their mothers' lives in-fluenced them ("Life with Mother" by Russell Baker and "In Mother's Kitchen" by Alfred Kazin); and readings in which women examine their relationships with their mothers and/or grandmothers. In "Beginnings," Sarah Lawrence Lightfoot describes her experience of growing up as the daughter of a new pioneer, a woman with legendary status in her community, while in "Scar," An-mei Hsu, a fictional char-acter in Amy Tan's *The Joy Luck Club*, writes of the memory of her mother's humiliating departure and then her return to An-mei's grand-mother's deathbed.

The next two selections, a short story, "The National Pastime," by John Cheever, and an essay, "Father," by Alice Walker, focus on the ways in which children find themselves living out the legacy of their fa-thers, needing their fathers' approval, and striving to understand and resolve or accept the double meanings and disappointments they expe-rienced in their father-child relationships.

The final selections for this chapter explore the ways in which the memories of childhood and important family members are often em-bedded in images of childhood homes. In "On Going Home," Joan Didion explores the conflicts she experiences when she returns to her childhood home to celebrate her daughter's first birthday. In this chapter's student essay, "My Grandfather's Memories," Amy Marx discusses the ways in which her grandfather's life and values have helped shape her self-concept and create the legacy of her home and family life.

As you read the selections focusing on family memories in the pages to follow, we hope that you will begin to retrace your own literal, imagined, and inward journeys as adventurers *coming from home*.

**GEORGE KEITHLEY: "The Child"**    George Keithley was born in Chicago in 1935 and raised in Illinois. He earned his B.A. at Duke University (1957), did graduate study at Stanford, and then completed his M.F.A. at the University of Iowa (1960). Keithley has worked as a free-lance writer, as an editorial consultant, and as a professor of American literature and poetry. Currently he lives in Chico, California, with his wife and three sons. His poetry has appeared in national magazines and literary journals, including *Harper's, Yale Review,* the *New York Times,* and *American Poetry Review.* "The Child" was originally published in the *Iowa Review* and is included in *Nineteen New American Poets of the Golden Gate* (1984). As you read Keithley's poem, notice how the speaker's self-concept and values have been shaped by his family.

GEORGE KEITHLEY

# The Child

In my dream the brooding child
I was ten years ago leans back
far, tilting his kitchen chair,
to hear the Chicago Symphony
of the Air. No one else is home
until the strings and horns grow still.
How soon my family fills the room—
Grey-eyed uncles and aunts, and father
and mother. My sister, Julia, too.
It might be every holiday reunion.
If I were younger I would guess
my First Communion. It's not,
though someone has invited Father Tein,
who thought he was a friend of mine.

Each face is flame. The gleam or glow
of flesh without its weight of guilt.
All their voices know my name—
"Gerhardt!" they cry. Or simply
"Gary!" if it's my sister. Always
I look as if I'm listening.
Now they command my attention
their mouths form an important shape—

5

"You can be anyone you want.
Anyone at all!"

          I smile.
They blaze into ordinary air.
Why should they stay? I recall
their message vividly. They dare
not fester in restless sleep
like some hallucination out of hell.
Mostly they're my family, you see.

And because I was taught every dream
is a delusion, telling you this
just now I smiled. Still
in the dream I understand they mean
what they say: "Be anyone at all"

but not that child.

## QUESTIONS

*Looking at Ideas:*

1. What does the image "each face is flame" suggest?

2. In the speaker's dream his family says: "You can be anyone you want./ Anyone at all!" In what ways did the speaker's waking life with his family contradict the message delivered in his dream?

3. How many definitions of a dream are implied in the poem? Refer to the text to support your response. Why would the poet create multiple meanings of the word *dream?* How does this affect the poem's meaning?

4. The speaker of the poem asks, "Why should they stay? I recall/ their message vividly." Does the speaker answer his own question in this poem? How would you answer his question?

*Looking at Strategies:*

1. Which of the details and images that the poet includes seem dreamlike? Why does Keithley draw on dream imagery?

2. Why is the poem entitled "The Child"? What images or words in the poem make you think that the poet is trying to universalize the meaning of the memory presented in the poem?

3. As the speaker develops his memory, he seems to be trying to find a positive meaning in it. Does he succeed? What is the effect of the final line, with its warning, "but not that child"?

*Looking at Connections:*

1. Compare and contrast the parental expectations conveyed in Keithley's poem with those described in the essay "Beginnings" by Sara Lawrence Lightfoot in this chapter.

2. Compare the power of family memories in "The Child" to the power of family memories in Amy Tan's story "Scar" in this chapter.

*Suggestions for Writing:*

1. Develop your journal writing into an essay in which you recount the dream or memory in as much detail as you can. Then discuss what the dream or memory reflects about your relationship to your family and the influence that your family has had on you. How has it helped to shape your self-concept and values?

2. Develop a vivid image, memory, or dream about your family from your childhood into a story or a poem. When you are finished, write about what you think your story or poem reflects about your relationship to your family, about your roots, about "coming from home," and about your future.

3. Write an essay in which you discuss why you think that memories from childhood continue to influence, to haunt, many people, even as they grow older and move away from their immediate families. Refer to your own experiences, readings, observations, or films to provide evidence for your explanation.

**JOURNAL ENTRY**
If you were going to write your own memoir, who would you include as
important to you when you were growing up? Why?

**RUSSELL BAKER: "Life with Mother"**  Russell Baker was born in Virginia in
1925. He grew up in a large extended family; in his writing he reflects on the
ways his family life helped prepare him to be a journalist, columnist, and
memoir writer. Baker completed his B.A. at Johns Hopkins University (1947)
and then began his career working as a newspaper reporter for the *Baltimore
Sun.* After writing for the *New York Times* in London and Washington, D.C., in
1962 he was given a syndicated column, "The Observer," which he continues
to produce. Russell Baker has won the Pulitzer Prize twice, in 1979 for distinguished commentary and in 1982 for his memoir *Growing Up* (1989), which
tells the story of his family life. The following selection was originally given as
a talk at the New York Public Library in the winter of 1986 and was included
in *Inventing the Truth* (1987), a collection of essays by authors of memoirs
about their craft. As you read Baker's essay, take account of the many different
ways in which his family life and his vivid memories have influenced his career as a writer.

RUSSELL BAKER

# Life with Mother

I'm primarily a journalist, a commercial writer, and I find it odd to be
talking as a memoirist. Memoirs are for remembrance. And the remem-
brances of journalists, when they take book form, are what I think of as
"and then I met" books. In my time as a journalist I have met many
what we call great men—at least celebrated men. But in *Growing Up* I
was not interested in doing an "and then I met" book. My prime interest was to celebrate people whom nobody had ever heard of. And
whom I was terribly fond of, for the most part, and thought deserved
to be known.

Why did I write this book? I asked my daughter the other day,
"What should I say when I talk at the Public Library next week?" And
she said, "You should say why you thought you had something so interesting to say that a large number of people would want to read it."
And I said I hadn't anticipated that any number of people would want
to read it; what I'd wanted was to write a book that I felt I had to write.
It grew out of a number of things that had been happening in my life,
perhaps starting at birth. As a writer I was blessed from the cradle, be-

cause I had the good fortune to be born into two very large, some people would say immense, families. The sort they don't make anymore.

My father was one of thirteen children, twelve of whom were boys. My mother was one of nine children, seven of whom were boys. So I came into the world well equipped with uncles. Twenty of them—that is, if you count my uncle Emil and my uncle Harold, who married Aunt Sally and Aunt Sister, respectively. What's more, a lot of these uncles got married, and this has provided me with a healthy supply of aunts. Now if you're destined to have a not very interesting life—and I was so destined—the next best thing, if you're going to be a writer, is to have a huge family. It gives you a chance to learn a lot about humanity from close-up observation.

I worry about people who get born nowadays, because they get born into such tiny families—sometimes into no family at all. When you're the only pea in the pod, your parents are likely to get you confused with the Hope Diamond. And that encourages you to talk too much. Getting into the habit of talking too much is fine if you're destined to be a lawyer or a politician or an entertainer. But if you're going to be a writer, it's death. We have many writers nowadays who don't realize this. Writers have to cultivate the habit early in life of listening to people other than themselves. And if you're born into a big family, as I was, you might as well learn to listen, because they're not going to give you much chance to talk. With twenty uncles and a dozen aunts, all old enough to have earned the right to speak whenever they wanted to open their mouths, there was not a great demand for us three children to put in our oar and to liven up the discussion.

I've never been able to complete an accurate count of the number of cousins I have. But I have cousins to the utmost degree. In addition to first cousins, I have second, third and fourth cousins, plus cousins many times removed. I have first cousins who are old enough to be my parents, and I have first cousins young enough to be my children. I'm constantly discovering cousins who were born when my attention was diverted somewhere else. Just recently I learned that the star of the Johns Hopkins lacrosse team is the great-grandson of my first cousin Myrtle, which I suppose makes him my great-grandcousin.

Now I cite these battalions of relatives not to boast about the fertility of my blood line, but to illustrate why I spent most of my childhood learning to listen. When the grown-ups in a family that big said that children were born to be seen and not heard, they weren't just exercising the grown-up right to engage in picturesque speech and tired old maxims. Nor were they trying to stifle children's right to creative expression. For them holding down the uproar was a question of survival. And it was wonderful training if you are going to be a writer: having to give up the right to show off and be a childhood performer and just sit there, quietly watching and listening to the curious things grown-ups did and said.

Out of this experience, at least in my family, there grew a kind of home folklore tradition, which was sustained among those of us who had been children together—a habit of reminiscent storytelling, whenever we got together, about what we remembered from childhood. About the lives, deeds, sayings and wisdom of elders. About aunts, uncles, grandparents, great-aunts, strangers who would come courting, women who—as the phrase always went—put up with an awful lot.

Putting up with an awful lot was what women seemed to do in the days of my childhood. My cousin Lillian, who was nearly eighty when I interviewed her for *Growing Up* about my mother's relationship with my father, said, "Well, Russell, people said Betty was hard to get along with. But she had to put up with an awful lot." Indeed she did. I had my own stock of these family tales and was fond, when dining out and the wine was flowing a little too generously, of telling the company about the time my grandmother Baker scolded a visiting delegation of the Ku Klux Klan for making a mess of their mothers' bed sheets. Or the time the Jersey City cops arrested Uncle Jim for running a red light and took away his shoelaces so he wouldn't try to hang himself in the cell. With that many uncles you had a great variety of material.

My editor, Tom Congdon, was present at a few of these dinners when I was telling old stories, and after a while he began cajoling me to put them into some kind of book about what it was like growing up in an antique time in a big family. He began referring to it as "the growing up book." Of course I had no intention of writing it. I was already turning out a newspaper column three times a week, which meant grinding out a hundred thousand words a year for my job. Spending my leisure writing another couple of hundred thousand words was hardly my idea of amusement.

But long before Tom started stirring the creative waters, something had begun to bother me. To wit, middle age. My children arrived at adolescence in the 1960s—that slum of a decade—and the 1970s, not one of the vintage decades either. And I was dismayed to observe, as elderly folk usually do when the children hit adolescence, that the values I'd been bred to cherish and live by were now held in contempt by people of my children's age. What was even worse, those values were regarded as squalid—remnants of the despicable, social-political system that my generation had connived in creating for the suppression of freedom.

It seemed to me that these views came out of a profound ignorance of history. Not uncommon among adolescents. As I vaguely recalled from my own experience, adolescence was a time when you firmly believed that sex hadn't been invented until the year you started high school, when the very idea that anything interesting might have happened during your parents' lifetime was unthinkable. I knew because I had been an adolescent myself. I remembered how ludicrous I thought it was that anybody could have tolerated spending their youth in the dreary decades of Theodore Roosevelt, Woodrow Wilson and World War I, as my parents had.

With my children in this insufferable phase of life it became harder and harder to speak with them as a father ought to speak to his children. When I corrected them and undertook to advise them on how to do things right, I took my example from the way things were done in my days. Which produced a great deal of invisible but nevertheless palpable sneering. Adolescence was finishing its nasty work of turning them from dear sweet children into the same ornery people you meet every day as you go through life. The kind of people who insist on disagreeing with you. And behaving like people.

In the hope of breaking through that communications blackout I tried writing a few letters to them. Just a few. For I soon realized that these were the kind of letters that bore the eyes right out of an adolescent. They were long descriptions of my own childhood, in which I tried to convey to them some sense of how different and remote was the world that I had come from; to tell them about their own forebears, who had lied and died before they were born, so they might glean at least a hint that life was more than a single journey from the diaper to the shroud. I wanted my children to know that they were part of a long chain of humanity extending deep into the past and that they had some responsibility for extending it into the future.

Going through the carbons of some old correspondence recently, I was astonished to come across a couple of these letters that I had written the kids a long time ago and to recognize long blocks of writing that would appear again, not much changed, in *Growing Up*, which I wrote ten years later. And I realized that I'd been writing that book to my children long before Tom Congdon heard me writing it over the wine at dinner.

But what finally prompted the book to become a book was what I came to think of as the living death of my mother—whose mind went out one day as though every circuit in the city had been blown. I was in Key West at the time; my sister Doris called me and told me what had happened, and I flew up to Baltimore and went to the hospital—completely unprepared for what I was going to encounter. And I started talking to my mother, and she was completely gone. I was speechless. She was suffering from something that I have since come to recognize as very common to elderly folks but that I had never seen before and certainly had never thought would happen to my mother. I was so astonished that my only reaction was to start taking notes on what she was saying. I had stopped at the hospital gift shop, as people sometimes do, to take some knicknack up to her, not realizing what I was going to find, and I tore the paper bag open so that I could write on the back of it. And I started making a record of our conversation. It's a reporter's reflex. What I was hearing was so amazing that I instinctively began recording it on the back of this bag. When I left I stuffed it in a raincoat pocket and forgot about it. I found it many weeks later and put it in a desk drawer and again I forgot it for a long time. And that turned out to be the conversation that appears in the first chapter of *Growing Up*—that disjointed conversation.

When I realized what had happened to my mother I was in a kind of intellectual shock, and I didn't know how to deal with it for a long time. Gradually it seemed to me that the way to deal with it was to write about the times that the two of us had passed through together. And I began to do that. But being the good reporter, I had no concept of how to write a memoir. I knew nothing about it; I only knew how to report a magazine piece. So I took my tape recorder out and I interviewed many of my relatives, those who were still living—people in their eighties, one or two in their nineties—about the family, things I had never been interested in before. And my wife Mimi and I began doing the genealogy. Who were these people? I had no notion of who they were or where they had come from. And in the process I began to learn how interesting they were. They were people who would be extremely boring to read about in the newspaper, but they were fascinating. And I transcribed all these interviews and notes. I reported everything very carefully: a long piece of newspaper reportage. Then I started writing, and what I wrote was a reporter's book in which I quoted these elderly people talking about what life was like long ago in that time and place. I was reporting my own life and, being the good journalist, I kept myself out of it. And because I was uneasy about what had always been an awkward relationship with my mother and because she wasn't there to testify for herself, I kept *her* out of it. And I wrote a rather long book. I think it ran to four hundred and fifty pages in manuscript.

I was very pleased with it and I sent it off to my agent and my editor and I thought, "Well, I'll give them twenty-four hours to sit up all night and read it and they'll phone me back tomorrow." You always have that feeling of euphoria just about having finished anything. Well, there was no phone call the next day, nor the day after. Nobody called the next week, nor the week after that. A month passed and nobody called. By then Tom Congdon had his own publishing company, and I knew he was in financial trouble, and I told myself, "Tom is too busy trying to raise money to bother reading this great manuscript." And I put it in the drawer and forgot it.

Eventually I began to sense that there was something wrong, and one night I took it out of the drawer and sat down in my office and started to read. I nodded off on about page 20. And I thought, "If I can't read this thing. . . ." But it was an intensely responsible book. Everything in it was correct, the quotations were accurate, everything had been double-checked. Finally, Tom, in despair, asked for a conference. Tom and I had worked together a long time, but he has never quite figured out how to tell me something is no good, and to tell somebody that a whole book is no good is tough for any editor, I guess.

But by that time I had made a second judgment myself that the book was in terrible shape and I knew what was wrong with it: my mother wasn't in it. There were all these interesting relatives, the uncles and the aunts and people talking from the present about the old days, but it was really nothing but journalism—reminiscences of today about yesterday. I had lunch with Tom and I said that I knew what was wrong with the book and that I would rewrite the whole thing. I said it was a book about a boy and his mother. It was about the tension between a child and his mother, and everything had to hinge on that. And Tom said he thought that was right—that I had made a grievous mistake in trying to write a book about myself in which I didn't appear. He didn't realize the strength of the mother character as I did, and I knew that if I brought the mother in and made her the hinge on which everything swung, the book would be a story. It would work as a book. I told Tom that's what I intended to do.

Now at one point Tom gave me a piece of advice, and I pass it on to any of you who are tempted someday to write your memoir. As I say, I had given Tom this manuscript of faithfully reported history of what people remembered of the '20s and '30s, and in it I had written what I thought was a good chapter about my uncle Harold. It's the one that begins: "Uncle Harold was famous for lying." And I knew that was a good chapter because I "got" Uncle Harold—I turned him into a character. I hadn't reported him; I made him the man whose memory lived inside me. At some point in the book I made a conclusion about him: I said that Uncle Harold, an uneducated and an unread man, was famous for being a great liar. But he wasn't really a liar; he just wanted life to be more interesting than it was. He lived a very dull life—he was a gravedigger at that time—and he liked to tell stories, but he didn't tell them very well. I said that in his primitive way Uncle Harold had perceived that the possibilities of achieving art lie not in reporting, but in fiction. And Tom Congdon sent that page back to me underlined in red, and he wrote on it, "I honor Uncle Harold."

Well, the problem that I knew, and that Tom didn't know at the time I resolved to rewrite the book, was that I had been dishonest about my mother. What I had written, though it was accurate to the extent that the reporting was there, was dishonest because of what I had left out. I had been unwilling to write honestly. And that dishonesty left a great hollow in the center of the original book.

Funny things happen to you when you really start to research something like this. I made a couple of serendipitous discoveries. One was that . . . well, my mother kept a trunk. I knew that. All good Southern ladies kept a trunk that they carried with them through life, and my mother was no exception. When she became incompetent, my sister took custody of this trunk, but my sister has no interest in that sort of thing, and she called my younger son, who was a pack rat, and told him to come over and take anything he was interested in out of it.

He was delighted. He went through the trunk and he came back with, among other things, a series of love letters that had been sent to my mother in the years 1932 and 1933, the depths of the Depression, by an immigrant Dane named Oluf. I had never known that she was in love with this man. It was obviously an unconsummated love affair because he was away most of the time. He moved to western Pennsylvania and they never saw each other after the most casual encounters.

Now I knew that what I was writing was a book about the Depression, and yet I dreaded having to write about it. Writing about the Depression is extremely dull—everybody knows the statistics, and I

13

couldn't figure out any way to make this interesting. And yet the Depression was the very essence of the setting of this book. I kept worrying about how I was going to handle the Depression chapter. I made several passes at it, writing in terms of statistical reports. Then my son went through my mother's trunk and found Oluf's letters. They were almost illegible—he wrote in a fractured English that was hard to read, in a big flowing script, and there were many of these letters. I gave them to my wife. I said, "Read these and tell me if there's anything in them," and I went off to work. That evening when I got home she was visibly moved. She said, "This is the story of a man who was destroyed by the Depression."

So I read them, and it was the most moving story. It was a self-contained story. And while I was moved, I was also delighted, because it had solved my Depression problem. Here was what the Depression meant to one man. That made a chapter which cleared up a lot of problems and some mysteries about my mother.

The second serendipitous discovery that came from that trunk was my mother's marriage certificate, which my son brought me in Nantucket. He paid me a surprise call. One summer day I was sitting in the backyard sunning myself, and my son came in the yard grinning. "You won't guess what I've got," he said. It was my mother's marriage certificate. And I looked at it: she was married in March of the year in which I was born in August. I was fifty-four years old and I realized I was a love child.

Well, it made me feel a little more interesting than I was. And it also cleared up a number of things—mysteries that I hadn't been able to solve in the first version of the book. Why my mother and my grandmother (my father's mother) detested each other so deeply. Why my mother left that part of the world so rapidly after my father died. The morning she learned that he was dead, she called her brother in New Jersey and announced that she was going to come live with him.

All of these things that had left me utterly baffled suddenly fell into place. And then I realized, too, why she had opposed so deeply my own relationship with the woman who was ultimately to be my wife. Everything fell into place, made a story. The question was, Could I write this? I hadn't written it in the book, and it made that first book a lie. So, in revising, I determined I would write that story. I thought, "If I want to honor my mother in this book I must be truthful." But I did it with great trepidation. Because you could be accused of vulgarity, of airing dirty linen and exploiting your dying mother for commercial purposes. And yet I felt that it dishonored her to lie about it.

So I decided to do it. I decided that although nobody's life makes any sense, if you're going to make a book out of it you might as well make it into a story. I remember saying to my wife, "I am now going upstairs to invent the story of my life." And I started writing, on the days when I wasn't doing my column, and I rewrote that whole book—almost the entire thing, with the exception of a couple of chapters—in about six months. That was the book that was eventually published.

But first I took the manuscript to my sister Doris—the two of us had grown up together—and had her read it. I anticipated that she was going to raise violent objections to my mentioning the fact that my mother had been pregnant before her marriage. And she did object, but not violently. Rationally, she said she thought that was a disgraceful thing to publish about Mother. And I told her pretty much what I've just told you: that I thought honesty would serve my mother best in the long run; it would make her plausible in this book, in which she might live longer than most of us if it worked right. And that anyhow, nowadays, nobody cared. "So be it," said Doris, and we published.

Still, I was very worried about the public reaction. God knows what was going to happen about that. I worried about that more than about anything else in the book. And I remember being deeply moved the day the *Wall Street Journal* ran its review, which was by Michael Gartner. The first sentence began: "Russell Baker's mother, a miraculous woman . . ."

*Q. What were the reactions of your children?*

*A.* I don't know. Although we are very close to our children, there are certain things children don't tell their parents. The children liked the book, surely. And they were proud of it, I think. My daughter, our oldest, said she was grateful for the book because it gave her her grandmother, whom she had only known when she was a baby.

*Q. How much of your book is truthful and how much is good writing?*

*A.* Well, all the incidents are truthful. A book like that has certain things in common with fiction. Anything that is autobiographical is the opposite of biography. The biographer's problem is that he never knows enough. The autobiographer's problem is that he knows much too much. He knows absolutely everything; he knows the whole iceberg, not just the tip. I mean, Henry James knew all the things that have puzzled Leon Edel for years; he knew what that tragic moment was that happened. So when you're writing about yourself, the problem is what to leave out. And I just left out almost everything—there's only about half a percent in that book. You wouldn't want everything; it would be like reading the *Congressional Record*. But the incidents that *are* in the book, of course they happened.

For example, there's a long account of the day of my father's death, which occurred when I was five. People said, "How could you have known that?" I knew that. That was the first thing I knew. That whole day began to happen as if I was sitting in the theater of life and the curtain was going up. It was the start of my life. I can still hear people talking that day. I know what the air smelled like. I know what people's faces looked like. How they were dressed. What they were eating. Don't ask me what I did yesterday—I'd have to look in my diary—but *that* I knew. I didn't do anything in the book that wasn't right.

*Q. How did you decide what to put in and what to leave out?*

*A.* I decided that the story line was the mother and the son: this extremely strong woman and weak male. There are three strong women in the book—the grandmother, the mother and the woman that the son marries at the end—and it's the story of the tension that these various women put on each other and on the male figure. I don't have a lot in the book that doesn't contribute to that point of view of what the story material was.

*Q. I wanted to ask you about another woman in the book that I found unforgettable: your wife. Was she in the first version as she was in the book that I read?*

*A.* She didn't appear in the first version. Because of the business about my mother and my birth, I didn't need Mimi. I didn't want to go that far. But I finally saw that to make the book an integral work I needed her—she was the logical completion of the series of events that started with my birth. I hated to use the material because it was material for another book that I'd often thought of writing. And I threw it away in ten or fifteen thousand words.

Mimi was a good sport, though. When I told her that I thought the book needed this, she was very supportive. I said, "Do you mind if I write about it?" and she said, "No, go ahead." And I interviewed her just the way I did everybody else. She was a terrible interview. She lied like a politician. But I interviewed her and I went up and wrote those concluding chapters. They went very quickly. And I brought it to her finally and said, "Read through it, and if there's anything you want cut, I'll cut it." Well, after reading it she said she thought I had left out certain events that would make it more interesting. I was sort of shocked at some of the things she suggested ought to be added, and I said, "Look, I'm a writer who's used to dealing with sensitive material—let me make the decision." And my decision was not to add a thing.

Well, after several months we got the first copies of the book in the mail, and Mimi immediately grabbed one, took it to the bedroom, closed the door and read all afternoon. When she came out she looked appalled. "Well, what do you think?" I said to her, and she said, "It looks different in print."

"That's what they always say," I told her.

## QUESTIONS

*Looking at Ideas:*

1. Why does Baker feel that coming from a large family helped him develop skills essential for a professional writer?

2. Why did Baker begin writing letters to his children when they became adolescents? These letters later became a part of the memoir he entitled *Growing Up.* How does Baker explain his use of these letters to his adolescent children as well as the relationship between his writing and family life?

3. In the selection Baker explains why he wrote his memoir. What reasons does he give? What were the most difficult challenges that Baker faced as he wrote about his life? Why was Baker's first version of his life story unsuccessful? Why does his second version work?

4. Why was Baker "deeply moved" that the first review from the *Wall Street Journal* began, "Russell Baker's mother, a miraculous woman . . ."?
5. What problems do you think a student writer would have sharing his or her memories?

*Looking at Strategies:*
1. Cite several of Baker's examples that illustrate his main points. Explain why each example helps clarify the main point.
2. What have you learned about the differences between journalism (reporting) and memoir writing (story telling) from reading this selection?
3. What can be learned about the process of revision from what Baker says about how he moved from the first draft of his memoir to his final draft? Can you relate Baker's process of revision to your own?
4. What audiences did Baker rely on in revising his memoirs? In what ways did these audiences help him?

*Looking at Connections:*
1. Baker suggests that the tradition of creating myths and telling stories about family members influenced his decision to become a writer. Which other writers included in this chapter were encouraged by their family's life-style and values to become writers?
2. Compare and contrast Baker's relationship with his mother and Alfred Kazin's relationship with his mother in "In Mother's Kitchen," the next selection in this chapter.

*Suggestions for Writing:*
1. Baker discusses his family's "habit of reminiscent storytelling." If your family followed a similar tradition, narrate a frequently shared family story. Explain how it helped define your family's values and your self-concept.
2. Baker makes a connection between writing and growing up because through both processes he has developed distance or perspective on his experiences and feelings. Like Baker, write about a difficult family situation that you would now like to understand better. After narrating the experience, think about and discuss the insights you have gained from writing about this experience.
3. Compare and contrast your writing and revising process with Baker's. Did learning about Baker's writing process help you understand or develop your own writing process? In what ways?

**JOURNAL ENTRY**

Describe the place where your family came together to eat or to share the
day's experiences when you were a child.

**ALFRED KAZIN: "In Mother's Kitchen"**  Alfred Kazin was born in 1915 and
grew up in Brooklyn, New York. He received his B.S.S. from the City College
of New York (1935) and his M.A. from Columbia University (1938). Kazin has
worked as an editor, a literary critic, and a professor of American literature at
many universities, including Princeton, the University of California at Berkeley,
and the State University of New York at Stony Brook. He is well known for his
autobiography, published in three volumes: *A Walker in the City* (1951), *Starting Out in the Thirties* (1965), and *New York Jew* (1978). "In Mother's Kitchen"
is excerpted from the first volume of his autobiography. As you read Kazin's
portrait of his mother, notice how Kazin describes the ways in which her energy supported and maintained their family.

ALFRED KAZIN

# In Mother's Kitchen

In Brownsville tenements the kitchen is always the largest room and the
center of the household. As a child I felt that we lived in a kitchen to
which four other rooms were annexed. My mother, a "home" dress-
maker, had her workshop in the kitchen. She told me once that she had
begun dressmaking in Poland at thirteen; as far back as I can remember, she was always making dresses for the local women. She had an
innate sense of design, a quick eye for all the subtleties in the latest
fashions, even when she despised them, and great boldness. For three
or four dollars she would study the fashion magazines with a customer,
go with the customer to the remnants store on Belmont Avenue to pick
out the material, argue the owner down—all remnants stores, for some
reason, were supposed to be shady, as if the owners dealt in stolen
goods—and then for days would patiently fit and baste and sew and fit
again. Our apartment was always full of women in their housedresses
sitting around the kitchen table waiting for a fitting. My little bedroom
next to the kitchen was the fitting room. The sewing machine, an old
nut-brown Singer with golden scrolls painted along the black arm and engraved along the two tiers of little drawers massed with needles and
thread on each side of the treadle, stood next to the window and the great
coal-black stove which up to my last year in college was our main source
of heat. By December the two outer bedrooms were closed off, and used
to chill bottles of milk and cream, cold borscht and jellied calves' feet.

The kitchen held our lives together. My mother worked in it all day long, we ate in it almost all meals except the Passover *seder*, I did my homework and first writing at the kitchen table, and in winter I often had a bed made up for me on three kitchen chairs near the stove. On the wall just over the table hung a long horizontal mirror that sloped to a ship's prow at each end and was lined in cherry wood. It took up the whole wall, and drew every object in the kitchen to itself. The walls were a fiercely stippled whitewash, so often rewhitened by my father in slack seasons that the paint looked as if it had been squeezed and cracked into the walls. A large electric bulb hung down the center of the kitchen at the end of a chain that had been hooked into the ceiling; the old gas ring and key still jutted out of the wall like antlers. In the corner next to the toilet was the sink at which we washed, and the square tub in which my mother did our clothes. Above it, tacked to the shelf on which were pleasantly ranged square, blue-bordered white sugar and spice jars, hung calendars from the Public National Bank on Pitkin Avenue and the Minsker Progressive Branch of the Workman's Circle; receipts for the payment of insurance premiums, and household bills on a spindle; two little boxes engraved with Hebrew letters. One of these was for the poor, the other to buy back the Land of Israel. Each spring a bearded little man would suddenly appear in our kitchen, salute us with a hurried Hebrew blessing, empty the boxes (sometimes with a sidelong look of disdain if they were not full), hurriedly bless us again for remembering our less fortunate Jewish brothers and sisters, and so take his departure until the next spring, after vainly trying to persuade my mother to take still another box. We did occasionally remember to drop coins in the boxes, but this was usually only on the dreaded morning of "midterms" and final examinations, because my mother thought it would bring me luck. She was extremely superstitious, but embarrassed about it, and always laughed at herself whenever, on the morning of an examination, she counseled me to leave the house on my right foot. "I know it's silly," her smile seemed to say, "but what harm can it do? It may calm God down."

The kitchen gave a special character to our lives; my mother's character. All my memories of that kitchen are dominated by the nearness of my mother sitting all day long at her sewing machine, by the clacking of the treadle against the linoleum floor, by the patient twist of her right shoulder as she automatically pushed at the wheel with one hand or lifted the foot to free the needle where it had got stuck in a thick piece of material. The kitchen was her life. Year by year, as I began to take in her fantastic capacity for labor and her anxious zeal, I realized it was ourselves she kept stitched together. I can never remember a time when she was not working. She worked because the law of her life was work, work and anxiety; she worked because she would have found life meaningless without work. She read almost no English; she could read the Yiddish paper, but never felt she had time to. We were always talking of a time when I would teach her how to read, but somehow there was never time. When I awoke in the morning she was already at her machine, or in the great morning crowd of housewives at the grocery getting fresh rolls for breakfast. When I returned from school she was at her machine, or conferring over *McCall's* with some neighborhood woman who had come in pointing hopefully to an illustration—"Mrs. Kazin! Mrs. Kazin! Make me a dress like it shows here in the picture!" When my father came home from work she had somehow mysteriously interrupted herself to make supper for us, and the dishes cleared and washed, was back at her machine. When I went to bed at night, often she was still there, pounding away at the treadle, hunched over the wheel, her hands steering a piece of gauze under the needle with a finesse that always contrasted sharply with her swollen hands and broken nails. Her left hand had been pierced through when as a girl she had worked in the infamous Triangle Shirtwaist Factory on the East Side. A needle had gone straight through the palm, severing a large vein. They had sewn it up for her so clumsily that a tuft of flesh always lay folded over the palm.

The kitchen was the great machine that set our lives running; it whirred down a little only on Saturdays and holy days. From my mother's kitchen I gained my first picture of life as a white, overheated, starkly lit workshop redolent with Jewish cooking, crowded with women in housedresses, strewn with fashion magazines, patterns, dress material, spools of thread—and at whose center, so lashed to her machine that bolts of energy seemed to dance out of her hands and feet as she worked, my mother stamped the treadle hard against the floor, hard, hard, and silently, grimly at war, beat out the first rhythm of the world for me.

Every sound from the street roared and trembled at our windows— a mother feeding her child on the doorstep, the screech of the trolley cars on Rockaway Avenue, the eternal smash of a handball against the wall of our house, the clatter of "*der Italyéner*"'s cart packed with watermelons, the sing-song of the old-clothes men walking Chester Street, the cries *"Árbes! Árbes! Kinder! Kinder! Heyse gute árbes!"* All day long people streamed into our apartment as a matter of course—"customers," upstairs neighbors, downstairs neighbors, women who would stop in for a half-hour's talk, salesmen, relatives, insurance agents. Usually they came in without ringing the bell—everyone knew my mother was always at home. I would hear the front door opening, the wind whistling through our front hall, and then some familiar face would appear in our kitchen with the same bland, matter-of-fact inquiring look: no need to stand on ceremony: my mother and her kitchen were available to everyone all day long.

At night the kitchen contracted around the blaze of light on the cloth, the patterns, the ironing board where the iron had burned a black border around the tear in the muslin cover; the finished dresses looked so frilly as they jostled on their wire hangers after all the work my mother had put into them. And then I would get that strangely ominous smell of tension from the dress fabrics and the burn in the cover of the ironing board—as if each piece of cloth and paper crushed with

20

light under the naked bulb might suddenly go up in flames. Whenever I pass some small tailoring shop still lit up at night and see the owner hunched over his steam press, whenever in some poorer neighborhood of the city I see through a window some small crowded kitchen naked under the harsh light glittering in the ceiling, I still smell that fiery breath, that warning of imminent fire. I was always holding my breath. What I must have felt most about ourselves, I see now, was that we ourselves were like kindling—that all the hard-pressed pieces of ourselves and all the hard-used objects in that kitchen were like so many slivers of wood that might go up in flames if we came too near the white-blazing filaments in that naked bulb. Our tension itself was fire, we ourselves were forever burning—to live, to get down the foreboding in our souls, to make good.

Twice a year, on the anniversaries of her parents' deaths, my mother placed on top of the ice-box an ordinary kitchen glass packed with wax, the *yortsayt*, and lit the candle in it. Sitting at the kitchen table over my homework, I would look across the threshold to that mourning-glass, and sense that for my mother the distance from our kitchen to *der heym*, from life to death, was only a flame's length away. Poor as we were, it was not poverty that drove my mother so hard; it was loneliness—some endless bitter brooding over all those left behind, dead or dying or soon to die; a loneliness locked up in her kitchen that dwelt every day on the hazardousness of life and the nearness of death, but still kept struggling in the lock, trying to get us through by endless labor.

With us, life started up again only on the last shore. There seemed to be no middle ground between despair and the fury of our ambition. Whenever my mother spoke of her hopes for us, it was with such unbelievingness that the likes of us would ever come to anything, such abashed hope and readiness for pain, that I finally came to see in the flame burning on top of the ice-box death itself burning away the bones of poor Jews, burning out in us everything but courage, the blind resolution to live. In the light of that mourning-candle, there were ranged around me how many dead and dying—how many eras of pain, of exile, of dispersion, of cringing before the powers of this world!

It was always at dusk that my mother's loneliness came home most to me. Painfully alert to every shift in the light at her window, she would suddenly confess her fatigue by removing her pince-nez, and then wearily pushing aside the great mound of fabrics on her machine, would stare at the street as if to warm herself in the last of the sun. "How sad it is!" I once heard her say. "It grips me! It grips me!" Twilight was the bottommost part of the day, the chillest and loneliest time for her. Always so near to her moods, I knew she was fighting some deep inner dread, struggling against the returning tide of darkness along the streets that invariably assailed her heart with the same foreboding—Where? Where now? Where is the day taking us now?

Yet one good look at the street would revive her. I see her now, perched against the windowsill, with her face against the glass, her eyes

almost asleep in enjoyment, just as she starts up with the guilty cry—
"What foolishness is this in me!"—and goes to the stove to prepare
supper for us: a moment, only a moment, watching the evening crowd
of women gathering at the grocery for fresh bread and milk. But between my mother's pent-up face at the window and the winter sun dying in the fabrics—"Alfred, see how beautiful!"—she has drawn for me
one single line of sentience.

## QUESTIONS

*Looking at Ideas:*

1. What values does Kazin's mother believe in and live by? Refer to several examples in the text to support your response.
2. Why is the kitchen the center of Kazin's life? What do you think it
would be like to grow up in this kitchen?
3. How does Kazin feel about his mother? Refer to specific passages in the
text to support your response.
4. Kazin establishes his mother's devotion to her work: "I can never
remember a time when she was not working. She worked because
the law of her life was work, work and anxiety; she worked because
she would have found life meaningless without work." What com-
pels Kazin's mother to keep struggling? What is she fighting
against?

*Looking at Strategies:*

1. Kazin is a master at using detail; read through the selection to find especially vivid images that help you imagine what life in his mother's
kitchen was like. List several of these passages and explain why you
found them effective.
2. Kazin develops an analogy between his mother's sewing machine and
his mother's kitchen. How does the analogy help you understand what
life in his mother's kitchen was like?
3. How do Kazin's mother's hands symbolize her inner drive to control
her life as well as her struggle to survive?
4. In light of the portrait he has already created of his mother's energy and
moods, explain the meaning of Kazin's final sentence: "But between my
mother's pent-up face at the window and the winter sun dying in the
fabrics— 'Alfred, see how beautiful!'—she has drawn for me one single
line of sentience."

*Looking at Connections:*

1. Which of the mother or grandmother portraits in this chapter best fits
your image and definition of the "traditional" mother figure? Explain
your choice. If none of the portraits included captures your image of the
traditional mother, then describe her image.
2. Kazin connects his memories of his mother to the life they shared in her
kitchen. Which of the other writers in this chapter connects memories
of a parent to a specific place?

*Suggestions for Writing:*

1. Kazin describes the tension in his family and their struggle to survive. Discuss a driving and creative tension that exists within your own family; show how it is both a positive and a negative force and how it has played a central role in shaping your family's values and life-style.

2. Some would argue that Kazin's mother fits the definition of a traditional mother. Do you think she does? Create your own definition of a traditional mother. Refer to examples in history, popular culture, literature, and personal experience to illustrate and develop your definition.

3. Develop your journal entry into an essay, describing and discussing the place where your family came together to share their day's experiences, opinions, and feelings. Why was this place important to you as a child? Is it still important to you, even as an adult? Why?

**SARA LAWRENCE LIGHTFOOT: "Beginnings"**   Sarah Lawrence Lightfoot was born in Nashville, Tennessee, in 1944. Lightfoot is a Professor of Education at Harvard University and the author of *Worlds Apart: Relationships between Families and School* (1978) and *The Good High School* (1983). The five-year stipend that she received for being chosen as the recipient of the MacArthur Prize made it possible for her to take time off from teaching to write *Balm in Gilead: Journey of a Healer* (1988), a biography of her mother, who was one of the first black women to graduate from medical school at Columbia University and become a child psychiatrist. As you read the following selection, which is excerpted from the biography, think about how Lightfoot was affected by her mother's success as a doctor.

SARA LAWRENCE LIGHTFOOT

# *Beginnings*

Even as a young child, I knew both the passion and the reverence my mother brought to her work. At the dinner table, while protecting the privacy and anonymity of her patients, she would reenact the dramas of the clinic, providing enough detail for us to get caught up in the story. I would hear tightness and anger in her voice when children and their families got hopelessly wrapped up in bureaucratic red tape, or when a colleague, out of fear or ignorance, acted unprofessionally. Sometimes I would feel waves of jealousy and abandonment when my mother would go off to help a child in trouble, leaving her three "real" children behind. A Saturday family adventure would be shattered, a cooking project stopped in the middle, the pansies half-planted. I always screamed loudly as she walked out the door, her cape streaming, her gait purposeful. When she returned to us, leaving the clinical emergencies safely out of our view, we would confront her with "how we felt" about her leaving, and she would carefully and candidly explain her devotion to her work *and* her mother-love for us. Didn't we know that the latter was deeper, that it would last "forever"?

From time to time, I remember my mother saying, without sentimentality, "I love my work," a statement I puzzled over as a child. It
made me imagine a day at the office full of pleasure and sunshine.
Since the home scene, with all its love and laughter, had its inevitable
crises and struggles, I occasionally worried whether my mother liked
going to work more than staying home. Many years later, I understood
everything she meant by that brief affirmation. Her work—with its
frustrations and imperfections—offered endless challenges and a few
victories, offered her the chance to use her wisdom and skills, and offered her the "privilege" of healing others. Now that I am middle-aged,
and "loving my work" as well, I know even more clearly how much my
mother gained fulfillment from balancing work and family. And I also
understand some of the high costs of this balance, and of her struggle
with many unyielding institutions to live out these deep, dual commitments.

This realization was just one of the ways in which my feelings and
attitudes toward my mother were transformed as I grew older. For
most of my life, I was regarded as my father's daughter. My likeness to
my father, in appearance, temperament, and style, was always contrasted with my sister, who was seen as my mother's mirror image.
"You're just like your dad," people would say after giving me just one
hard look. "Paula is the spit and image of your mom." For those people
who insisted upon attaching labels to children, Chuck, my brother, was
perceived as the embodiment of both parents. "He is the combination
of Margaret and Charles. . . . You can see his mother's eyes, his father's nose, his mother's quiet, his father's posture. . . ." I remember
feeling that my brother's combined label gave him more room, a more
generous repertoire of ways to be, while staying "in character."

Mostly I enjoyed the parallels people drew between me and my father. I knew they saw him as handsome, vigorous, and intelligent, and I
longed to inherit those fine qualities. But there was a part of me that
yearned to be like my mother. People described her as serene, beautiful,
and wise—like a clear, still pond. I thought that in being outgoing and
energetic like my father, I was missing the mystery, the softness, the
feminine *grace,* of my mother. Over the years, the perceived similarities
were underscored, exaggerated, and I would alternately welcome and
resist them. When, in my mid-twenties, I chose my vocation and my
husband, my father joked: "Now I know Sara is thoroughly identified
with me. She became a sociologist and she married a psychiatrist."

But by then the likeness was largely family myth. Over the years,
without anyone noticing, changes began to take place, until one day I
was met by a total stranger on the streets of New York who recognized
me because of my mother. From way at the other end of a long block,
she watched me striding toward her, *my* cape billowing out behind. As we
came closer, she stopped me with a smile and a look that said, "I know you
from somewhere." She searched her mind while I waited, feeling no familiarity but believing in hers. After a few moments, her brow relaxed.
"You must be Margaret's daughter. You look *just* like her!" . . .

25

By the time I was in my mid-thirties, with two children of my own, the identification with my mother was complete. Now I became a baker of "Maggie Bread," the hearty whole wheat variety, with my own embellishment of raisins. Now I wore colorful shawls like my mother always did, draped for warmth and drama. Now I plaited my daughter's brown braids and could feel the sensations of my mother's soothing hands on my head as I laid mine on my daughter's. Now I tried to put the pieces of my own too-busy life together, racing home to place bright napkins and candles on the dinner table, to create the appearance that I had been there all day. Now I heard my children's harsh complaints or watched their silent resignation when I flew off to distant places to deliver speeches, attend meetings—to do my version of the teaching/healing legacy. Now I could feel so keenly the mothering I was replaying, while being aware that the father in me had not disappeared.

This slow discovery of identification with my mother became intriguing to me. I recognized the ways I incorporated her style and her values, sometimes unknowingly, sometimes on purpose. I began to think of writing her story. If I could learn about her origins, her childhood, her dreams, her fears, I might have greater insight into my own life. If I could move beyond family myths—so static and idealized—to trace the actual events of my mother's life, I might uncover the historical patterns that give shape to my own.

My interest in telling my mother's story, however, was charged by more than my emerging identification with her. I wanted to explore beyond the myth of Margaret Lawrence. All families have elaborate tales that stand as models of courage, wisdom, strength, or loyalty for their members. The tales are told and retold in long embroidered versions or in family shorthand. Everyone is comforted by their familiarity, the promised punch line, but no one would claim that these tales are the whole story. Bigger than life, they have turned into legends, morality plays. For as long as I can remember, my mother had been an idealized figure in our community, put on a pedestal, spoken of with awe and envy. Parents of my friends, neighbors, teachers, shopkeepers in town, would speak about my mother's serenity and quiet intelligence, about the way her very presence seemed to ease their pain. Sometimes their veneration made me wonder.

I remember the day my mother and I went to the Corsette Shop on Main Street to buy my first brassiere. I was twelve and "ample," as my father would say diplomatically. I had been walking around self-consciously for months, enduring my bobbing breasts as a horrible humiliation, and had begged my mother to let me get a bra. She had quietly, but stubbornly, resisted. My mother had never worn a bra, had refused to use the one thrust upon her at age fourteen, and seemed to regard them as nothing but sham and artifice. After weeks of my lobbying, she reluctantly gave in. I think she wanted me to avoid the abuse of my peers, several of whom had sported bras since the fourth grade. The two of us made a special trip to town to search for the most natural, least pointed kind. The Corsette Shop ladies greeted my mother with fanfare, oozing delight out of every pore. "Dr. Lawrence, we are so *thrilled* to see you!" The chatter continued while the ladies passed selections through the green curtains of the dressing room and I fumbled with snaps and straps and "cups." Occasionally one of them would come in unannounced to inspect the fit. During one of those unwelcome intrusions (my mother had gone out briefly to put a nickel in the parking meter), I remember waiting for the inevitable refrain— "Your mother is the loveliest woman I've ever met . . . she's as good as gold." I could be anywhere, even here in this underwear shop, under these embarrassing conditions, and I'd be treated to this familiar litany.

The worshipful praise always seemed genuine, but even as a child I recognized that it came at some cost. People did not always like the image that they had created of Margaret Lawrence. It made them feel inadequate or graceless in contrast. For some, the image of her goodness led to resentment. "How does your mother do it all?" asked the mother of one of my fellow Girl Scouts. "And she always looks so good." Each word of praise bore an edge of cynicism, and I could hear both, having learned early to catch these double-edged inflections.

The world's image of my mother never squared with mine. Yes, I knew she was different, even special, an achiever. I knew of no other mother who seemed to put so many pieces together; whose work seemed to require so much passion, who managed all her competing commitments. But rather than the serenity the world perceived, I saw my mother on the move, beads of sweat above her upper lip, her fingernails filled with paint and clay, brow furrowed, muscles sore and eyelids drooping by day's end. When I bothered to look, I saw a grown-up life that was hard and demanding, that left no time for frivolity. What others saw as peacefulness, I saw as my mother's chief survival strategy—complete concentration. I am sure that the dissonance between the idealized perceptions of Margaret and a daughter's nonheroic view must also have fueled my interest in exploring her life. I mistrusted the legend that seemed in its grandeur to diminish me.

Years later, having written other books that tried to get beyond surface and stereotypes, I felt the impulse to look at my mother's life more deeply, to tell of her grace against odds, of the pain that accompanied achievement, the loss of laughter that came with singleminded pursuits. Not only would the story focus on her triumphs, it would also show how her life was filled with very ordinary twists and turns, with moments of traumatic defeat . . . and slow, purposeful recovery. I wanted to explore the family silences, the breaks in family stories that emerge because people have simply forgotten, because memories have faded with time, because images have had to be repressed in order to move on with life, because people have chosen to hide a piece of the truth for their own peace of mind. In tracing my mother's development, I wanted to undo the caricatures that never wholly fit my view of her. I was particularly fascinated by the way she had transformed hardship into strength, and loneliness into sensitivity and introspection.

27

The project seemed less daunting than it might have because I expected my mother to be able to tell her story well. As an only child with a ruminative temperament, Margaret had watched the family drama and recorded everything within. She turned the images over in her mind, trying to make sense of the mysteries and silences. In her mid-thirties, when Margaret experienced "the couch" for the first time, she was amazed at how her well-developed introspective capacities translated so easily into the psychoanalytic process, how once she decided to "put it out there" it all came so naturally. Free association was much like the uninhibited, wandering fantasies she had enjoyed as a child, like the unspoken questions and observations she silently harbored as an adolescent and young adult. It was not hard for her to dig into her past, to revisit old haunts, and enjoy the fuzzy, refracted quality of early images that she calls "screen memories."

Seventy years later, Margaret can draw a detailed plan of the church and rectory at Widewater, Virginia, a remote, tiny cross-in-the-road that no one can find on a map. She can feel her father's large hand holding hers as they take the slop to the pigs. She has been well practiced in exploring these early experiences, and her belief in their power is deep. As she said in her talk to her fellow analysts, her own childhood stories, their pain and their resonance, are central to her therapeutic work with children and their families. She uses that self-knowledge to gain access to her patients' lives and histories.

For my mother, our collaboration is a psychological and spiritual journey. The journey back through time feels like a tunnel, dark, mysterious, and finally luminous.

## QUESTIONS

*Looking at Ideas:*

1. In this selection Lightfoot traces her growing understanding of her mother's decision to have a career and a family. Why does she come to identify more fully with her mother as she grows older and to appreciate her mother's commitment to both her family and her professional life?

2. Why does Lightfoot decide to write the story of her mother's life? What does she hope to learn? What myths does she hope to understand more fully?

3. As the selection closes, Lightfoot sees herself as a collaborator with her mother. In what sense are they collaborators? Why do they need to take this journey of discovery together?

*Looking at Strategies:*

1. What examples does Lightfoot develop to show the ambivalence she felt about her mother's legendary status in their community? Are these examples effective? Why?

2. How does Lightfoot use the techniques of comparison and contrast to clarify her relationships with her father and mother?

3. Lightfoot concludes this selection, "For my mother, our collaboration is a psychological and spiritual journey. The journey back through time feels like a tunnel, dark, mysterious, and finally luminous." Why do you think Lightfoot concludes with this image?

*Looking at Connections:*
1. Compare and contrast Lightfoot's motivations for writing about her mother's life with Russell Baker's reasons for writing about his mother's life.
2. Contrast Lightfoot's attitudes about the role and limitations of family myths with those of An-mei in Amy Tan's story, "Scar," the next selection in this chapter.

*Suggestions for Writing:*
1. Lightfoot explores her mixed feelings about being compared with her father and contrasted to her mother in her youth. Write an essay in which you explore the types of comparisons and contrasts you were subjected to in your family; then discuss the effects of these comparisons on your personality and values.
2. Lightfoot is implicitly exploring the difficulties of growing up in a family with strong role models. Write an essay in which you identify and give examples of some struggles you had finding an identity of your own within your family with its many expectations of you. What helped you establish an identity of your own?
3. Families often grow from conflict. Write about a struggle you have had with a family member that helped you both to understand one another better and to become closer to one another. Conclude your essay by reflecting on what you learned from writing about this struggle.

**JOURNAL ENTRY**
Discuss a childhood memory that was hard for you to understand.

**AMY TAN: "Scar," from *The Joy Luck Club*** Amy Tan was born in Oakland, California, in 1952, only two and a half years after her parents emigrated from China. She earned her B.A. (1973) and her M.A. (1974) at San Jose State College. Before publishing her best-selling novel, *The Joy Luck Club* (1989), Amy Tan worked as a consultant for disabled children's programs and as a freelance writer. She now writes full-time and has just finished her second novel, *The Kitchen God's Wife* (1991). Tan is also working on a movie script of *The Joy Luck Club* to be directed by Wayne Wang. Amy Tan lives in San Francisco with her husband, Lou DeMattei. As you read the following selection from *The Joy Luck Club*, "Scar," notice how Tan weaves together the memories of her fictional characters to show us how memory needs to be continually reevaluated as we learn more about our pasts.

AMY TAN

# *Scar*

When I was a young girl in China, my grandmother told me my mother was a ghost. This did not mean my mother was dead. In those days, a ghost was anything we were forbidden to talk about. So I knew Popo wanted me to forget my mother on purpose, and this is how I came to remember nothing of her. The life that I knew began in the large house in Ningpo with the cold hallways and tall stairs. This was my uncle and auntie's family house, where I lived with Popo and my little brother.

But I often heard stories of a ghost who tried to take children away, especially strong-willed little girls who were disobedient. Many times Popo said aloud to all who could hear that my brother and I had fallen out of the bowels of a stupid goose, two eggs that nobody wanted, not even good enough to crack over rice porridge. She said this so that the ghosts would not steal us away. So you see, to Popo we were also very precious.

All my life, Popo scared me. I became even more scared when she grew sick. This was in 1923, when I was nine years old. Popo had swollen up like an overripe squash, so full her flesh had gone soft and rotten with a bad smell. She would call me into her room with the terrible stink and tell me stories. "An-mei," she said, calling me by my school name. "Listen carefully." She told me stories I could not understand.

One was about a greedy girl whose belly grew fatter and fatter. This girl poisoned herself after refusing to say whose child she carried. When the monks cut open her body, they found inside a large white winter melon.

"If you are greedy, what is inside you is what makes you always hungry," said Popo.

Another time, Popo told me about a girl who refused to listen to her elders. One day this bad girl shook her head so vigorously to refuse her auntie's simple request that a little white ball fell from her ear and out poured all her brains, as clear as chicken broth.

"Your own thoughts are so busy swimming inside that everything else gets pushed out," Popo told me.

Right before Popo became so sick she could no longer speak, she pulled me close and talked to me about my mother. "Never say her name," she warned. "To say her name is to spit on your father's grave."

The only father I knew was a big painting that hung in the main hall. He was a large, unsmiling man, unhappy to be so still on the wall. His restless eyes followed me around the house. Even from my room at the end of the hall, I could see my father's watching eyes. Popo said he watched me for any signs of disrespect. So sometimes, when I had thrown pebbles at other children at school, or had lost a book through carelessness, I would quickly walk by my father with a know-nothing look and hide in a corner of my room where he could not see my face.

I felt our house was so unhappy, but my little brother did not seem to think so. He rode his bicycle through the courtyard, chasing chickens and other children, laughing over which ones shrieked the loudest. Inside the quiet house, he jumped up and down on Uncle and Auntie's best feather sofas when they were away visiting village friends.

But even my brother's happiness went away. One hot summer day when Popo was already very sick, we stood outside watching a village funeral procession marching by our courtyard. Just as it passed our gate, the heavy framed picture of the dead man toppled from its stand and fell to the dusty ground. An old lady screamed and fainted. My brother laughed and Auntie slapped him.

My auntie, who had a very bad temper with children, told him he had no *shou,* no respect for ancestors or family, just like our mother. Auntie had a tongue like hungry scissors eating silk cloth. So when my brother gave her a sour look, Auntie said our mother was so thoughtless she had fled north in a big hurry, without taking the dowry furniture from her marriage to my father, without bringing her ten pairs of silver chopsticks, without paying respect to my father's grave and those of our ancestors. When my brother accused Auntie of frightening our mother away, Auntie shouted that our mother had married a man named Wu Tsing who already had a wife, two concubines, and other bad children.

And when my brother shouted that Auntie was a talking chicken without a head, she pushed my brother against the gate and spat on his face.

"You throw strong words at me, but you are nothing," Auntie said. "You are the son of a mother who has so little respect she has become *ni,* a traitor to our ancestors. She is so beneath others that even the devil must look down to see her."

That is when I began to understand the stories Popo taught me, the lessons I had to learn for my mother. "When you lose your face, An-mei," Popo often said, "it is like dropping your necklace down a well. The only way you can get it back is to fall in after it."

Now I could imagine my mother, a thoughtless woman who laughed and shook her head, who dipped her chopsticks many times to eat another piece of sweet fruit, happy to be free of Popo, her unhappy husband on the wall, and her two disobedient children. I felt unlucky that she was my mother and unlucky that she had left us. These were the thoughts I had while hiding in the corner of my room where my father could not watch me.

I was sitting at the top of the stairs when she arrived. I knew it was my mother even though I had not seen her in all my memory. She stood just inside the doorway so that her face became a dark shadow. She was much taller than my auntie, almost as tall as my uncle. She looked strange, too, like the missionary ladies at our school who were insolent and bossy in their too-tall shoes, foreign clothes, and short hair.

My auntie quickly looked away and did not call her by name or offer her tea. An old servant hurried away with a displeased look. I tried to keep very still, but my heart felt like crickets scratching to get out of a cage. My mother must have heard, because she looked up. And when she did, I saw my own face looking back at me. Eyes that stayed wide open and saw too much.

In Popo's room my auntie protested, "Too late, too late," as my mother approached the bed. But this did not stop my mother.

"Come back, stay here," murmured my mother to Popo. "*Nuyer* is here. Your daughter is back." Popo's eyes were open, but now her mind ran in many different directions, not staying long enough to see anything. If Popo's mind had been clear she would have raised her two arms and flung my mother out of the room.

I watched my mother, seeing her for the first time, this pretty woman with her white skin and oval face, not too round like Auntie's or sharp like Popo's. I saw that she had a long white neck, just like the goose that had laid me. That she seemed to float back and forth like a ghost, dipping cool cloths to lay on Popo's bloated face. As she peered into Popo's eyes, she clucked soft worried sounds. I watched her carefully, yet it was her voice that confused me, a familiar sound from a forgotten dream.

When I returned to my room later that afternoon, she was there, standing tall. And because I remember Popo told me not to speak her name, I stood there, mute. She took my hand and led me to the settee. And then she also sat down as though we had done this every day.

My mother began to loosen my braids and brush my hair with long sweeping strokes.

"An-mei, you have been a good daughter?" she asked, smiling a secret look.

I looked at her with my know-nothing face, but inside I was trembling. I was the girl whose belly held a colorless winter melon.

"An-mei, you know who I am," she said with a small scold in her voice. This time I did not look for fear my head would burst and my brains would dribble out of my ears.

She stopped brushing. And then I could feel her long smooth fingers rubbing and searching under my chin, finding the spot that was my smooth-neck scar. As she rubbed this spot, I became very still. It was as though she were rubbing the memory back into my skin. And then her hand dropped and she began to cry, wrapping her hands around her own neck. She cried with a wailing voice that was so sad. And then I remembered the dream with my mother's voice.

I was four years old. My chin was just above the dinner table, and I could see my baby brother sitting on Popo's lap, crying with an angry face. I could hear voices praising a steaming dark soup brought to the table, voices murmuring politely, *"Ching! Ching!"*— Please, eat!

And then the talking stopped. My uncle rose from his chair. Everyone turned to look at the door, where a tall woman stood. I was the only one who spoke.

"Ma," I had cried, rushing off my chair, but my auntie slapped my face and pushed me back down. Now everyone was standing up and shouting, and I heard my mother's voice crying, "An-mei! An-mei!" Above this noise, Popo's shrill voice spoke.

"Who is this ghost? Not an honored widow. Just a number-three concubine. If you take your daughter, she will become like you. No face. Never able to lift up her head."

Still my mother shouted for me to come. I remember her voice so clearly now. An-mei! An-mei! I could see my mother's face across the table. Between us stood the soup pot on its heavy chimney-pot stand— rocking slowly, back and forth. And then with one shout this dark boiling soup spilled forward and fell all over my neck. It was as though everyone's anger were pouring all over me.

This was the kind of pain so terrible that a little child should never remember it. But it is still in my skin's memory. I cried out loud only a little, because soon my flesh began to burst inside and out and cut off my breathing air.

I could not speak because of this terrible choking feeling. I could not see because of all the tears that poured out to wash away the pain. But I could hear my mother's crying voice. Popo and Auntie were shouting. And then my mother's voice went away.

Later that night Popo's voice came to me.

"An-mei, listen carefully." Her voice had the same scolding tone she used when I ran up and down the hallway. "An-mei, we have made your dying clothes and shoes for you. They are all white cotton."

I listened, scared.

"An-mei," she murmured, now more gently. "Your dying clothes are very plain. They are not fancy, because you are still a child. If you die, you will have a short life and you will still owe your family a debt. Your funeral will be very small. Our mourning time for you will be very short."

And then Popo said something that was worse than the burning on my neck.

"Even your mother has used up her tears and left. If you do not get well soon, she will forget you."

Popo was very smart. I came hurrying back from the other world to find my mother.

Every night I cried so that both my eyes and my neck burned. Next to my bed sat Popo. She would pour cool water over my neck from the hollowed cup of a large grapefruit. She would pour and pour until my breathing became soft and I could fall asleep. In the morning, Popo would use her sharp fingernails like tweezers and peel off the dead membranes.

In two years' time, my scar became pale and shiny and I had no memory of my mother. That is the way it is with a wound. The wound begins to close in on itself, to protect what is hurting so much. And once it is closed, you no longer see what is underneath, what started the pain.

I worshipped this mother from my dream. But the woman standing by Popo's bed was not the mother of my memory. Yet I came to love this mother as well. Not because she came to me and begged me to forgive her. She did not. She did not need to explain that Popo chased her out of the house when I was dying. This I knew. She did not need to tell me she married Wu Tsing to exchange one unhappiness for another. I knew this as well.

Here is how I came to love my mother. How I saw in her my own true nature. What was beneath my skin. Inside my bones.

It was late at night when I went to Popo's room. My auntie said it was Popo's dying time and I must show respect. I put on a clean dress and stood between my auntie and uncle at the foot of Popo's bed. I cried a little, not too loud.

I saw my mother on the other side of the room. Quiet and sad. She was cooking a soup, pouring herbs and medicines into the steaming pot. And then I saw her pull up her sleeve and pull out a sharp knife. She put this knife on the softest part of her arm. I tried to close my eyes, but could not.

And then my mother cut a piece of meat from her arm. Tears poured from her face and blood spilled to the floor.

My mother took her flesh and put it in the soup. She cooked magic in the ancient tradition to try to cure her mother this one last time. She opened Popo's mouth, already too tight from trying to keep her spirit in. She fed her this soup, but that night Popo flew away with her illness.

Even though I was young, I could see the pain of the flesh and the worth of the pain.

This is how a daughter honors her mother. It is *shou* so deep it is in your bones. The pain of the flesh is nothing. The pain you must forget. Because sometimes that is the only way to remember what is in your bones. You must peel off your skin, and that of your mother, and her mother before her. Until there is nothing. No scar, no skin, no flesh.

## QUESTIONS

*Looking at Ideas:*

1. Why would An-mei's grandmother tell her that her mother is a ghost when An-mei knows that her mother is not dead? How do her grandmother's teachings affect An-mei's behavior toward her elders and her mother?
2. Why doesn't An-mei leave with her mother when she is four years old? What motivates An-mei's struggle to get well after being burned by the boiling soup?
3. How does An-mei's mother help An-mei remember why she had to leave her children behind? Does this selection suggest that the family's rejection of An-mei's mother is just?
4. Explain An-mei's realization at her grandmother's deathbed. What does she see that helps her understand why she loves her mother?
5. Why does the memory of her mother's departure when An-mei was four seem like a part of a forgotten dream? What does the story imply about what one does and does not remember?

*Looking at Strategies:*

1. How does Amy Tan develop the comparison between the forgetting of a painful memory and the healing of a scar? Is her analogy effective and convincing?
2. Why is the story developed in four short segments? How does the sequence of sections help intensify the story's meaning?
3. "Auntie had a tongue like hungry scissors eating silk cloth." Find several other examples of Tan's use of figurative language. How does such use of figurative language contribute to the vividness of her writing?

*Looking at Connections:*

1. Contrast the role of the mother in "Scar" to the role of the mother in Sara Lawrence Lightfoot's essay, "Beginnings."
2. Compare the Asian-American sense of honor toward parents in this selection with the sense of respect shown to parents that is implied in Kazin's "In Mother's Kitchen."

*Suggestions for Writing:*

1. Develop your journal entry into an essay. Write about a complex family experience that was difficult for you to face and understand. Did writing about the experience help you see it in more perspective? Explain.

2. At the end of the story An-mei says, "This is how a daughter honors her mother. It is *shou* so deep it is in your bones. The pain of the flesh is nothing. The pain you must forget. Because sometimes that is the only way to remember what is in your bones. You must peel off your skin, and that of your mother, and her mother before her. Until there is nothing. No scar, no skin, no flesh." Explain what you think this statement means. Then relate An-mei's definition of honor to your own sense of how a daughter honors her mother. Refer to events in your own life to support your definition.

3. Narrate a childhood memory that was influenced by a family myth. Then explain how the myth and your childhood memory helped shape your self-concept.

**JOURNAL ENTRY**

Discuss an activity or sport that you shared with one of your parents. How did sharing this pastime help to build your relationship? Did sharing the pastime have any negative impact on your relationship?

**JOHN CHEEVER: "The National Pastime"** John Cheever (1912–1982) was raised in Massachusetts, where he attended Thayer Academy, a prep school. His expulsion from the academy became the turning point that lead to the beginning of his literary career. Although Cheever wrote TV scripts, he was primarily a writer of short stories and novels. He also taught at many universities, including Barnard College, Boston University, and Harvard, where he was given an honorary doctorate in 1978. Cheever won many national awards during his lifetime. In 1958 he received the National Book Award in fiction for *The Wapshot Chronicle* (1957). *The Wapshot Scandal* (1964) won the *Playboy* Editorial Award, and *The Stories of John Cheever* (1978) was awarded the Pulitzer Prize for fiction. In "The National Pastime," the narrator's memory of his father's rejection of him is linked to a traditional male rite of passage, learning to play baseball. As you read the following story try to understand the narrator's struggle to establish a relationship of mutual respect with his father.

JOHN CHEEVER

# The National Pastime

To be an American and unable to play baseball is comparable to being a Polynesian and unable to swim. It's an impossible situation. This will be apparent to everyone, and it was to me, a country boy brought up on a farm—or, to be precise, in a country house—just outside the village of St. Botolph's, in Massachusetts. The place is called West Farm. My ancestors had lived in that village and in that house since the seventeenth century, and they had distinguished themselves as sailors and athletes. Leander, my father (his brothers were named Orpheus and Hamlet), had played shortstop for the St. Botolph's Hose Company. Although the hose-company games sometimes figured in his recollections, his memories were usually of a different order. He was nearly sixty when I was born, and he could remember the last days of St. Botolph's as a port. My grandfather had been a ship's master, and when I was a boy, our house was partly furnished with things that he had brought back from Ceylon and China. The maritime past that my father glimpsed had been glorious, full of gold and silver, full of Samoan beauties and tests of courage. Then—so he told me—boxwood had grown in our garden, and the paths had been covered once a year with pebbles that were brought from a cove near West Travertine where the stones were as round and white as pearls. In the rear wing of our house, there was a peculiar, clean smell that was supposed to have been left there by my grandfather's Chinese servants. My father liked to recall this period of splendor, but he liked even better to recall his success as a partner in the gold-bead factory that had been built in St. Botolph's when its maritime prosperity was ended. He had gone to work as an office boy, and his rise had been brilliant and swift. He had business acumen, and he was convivial. He took an intense pleasure in having the factory whistle blown. He had it blown for all our birthdays and for his wedding anniversary, and when my mother had guests for lunch, the whistle usually blew as the ladies sat down.

In the twenties, the gold-bead factory was mortgaged and converted to the manufacture of table silver, and presently my father and his partner were ruined. My father felt that he was an old man who had spent all his energy and all his money on things that were unredeemable and vulgar, and he was inconsolable. He went away, and my mother called my two sisters and me to her room and told us that she was afraid he had killed himself. He had left a note hinting at this, and he had taken a pistol with him. I was nine years old then, and my sisters were fourteen and fifteen. Suicide may have been my father's intention, but he returned a few days later and began to support the family by selling the valuables that had come to him from the shipmaster. I had decided to become a professional baseball player. I had bought a Louisville Slugger, a ball, and a first baseman's mitt. I asked my father to play catch with me one Sunday afternoon, but he refused. My mother must have overheard this conversation, because she called him to her room, where they quarreled. In a little while, he came out to the garden and asked me to throw the ball to him. What happened then was ridiculous and ugly. I threw the ball clumsily once or twice and missed the catches he threw to me. Then I turned my head to see something—a boat on the river. He threw the ball, and it got me in the nape of the neck and stretched me out unconscious in my grandfather's ruined garden. When I came to, my nose was bleeding and my mouth was full of blood. I felt that I was being drowned. My father was standing over me. "Don't tell your mother about this," he said. When I sat up and he saw that I was all right, he went down through the garden toward the barn and the river.

My mother called me to her room that night after supper. She had become an invalid and she seldom left her bed. All the furniture in her room was white, and the rugs were white, and there was a picture of "Jesus the Shepherd" on the wall beside her bed. The room was getting dark, I remember, and I felt, from the tone of her voice, that we were approaching a kind of emotional darkness I had noticed before in our family affairs. "You must try to understand your father," she said, putting down her Bible and reaching for my hand. "He is old. He is spoiled." Then, although I don't think he was in the house, she lowered her voice to a whisper, so that we could not be overheard. "You see, some years ago his cousin Lucy Hartshorn left him a great deal of money, in trust. She was a meddlesome old lady. I guess you don't remember her. She was an antivivisectionist, and wanted to abolish the celebration of Christmas. She liked to order your father around, and she felt the family was petering out. We had Grace and Vikery then, and she left your father the money on condition that he not have any more children. He was very upset when he found out that I was *enceinte*. I wouldn't want you to know what went on. He had planned a luxurious old age—he wanted to raise pigeons and have a sailboat— and I think he sometimes sees in you the difference between what he had planned and what he has been reduced to. You'll have to try and understand." Her words made almost no impression on me at the time. I remember counting the larches outside her window while she talked to me, and looking beyond them to the faded lettering on the wall of the barn—"Boston Store: Rock Bottom Prices"—and to some pines ringed with darkness beyond the barn. The little that I knew of our family history was made up of revokable trusts, purloined wills, and dark human secrets, and since I had never seen Lucy Hartshorn, this new secret seemed to have no more to do with me than the others did.

The school I went to was an old frame building in the village, and every morning I walked two miles upriver to get there. Two of the spinster teachers were cousins of mine, and the man who taught manual training and coached athletics was the son of our garbage collector. My parents had helped him through normal school. The New England spring was in force, and one fine morning we left the gymnasium for the ball field. The instructor was carrying some baseball equipment, and as soon as I saw it, the sweet, salty taste of blood came into my mouth. My heart began to pound, my legs felt weak, and while I thought, from these symptoms, that I must be sick, I knew instinctively how to cure myself. On the way to the field, we passed an old field house that stood on some concrete posts, concealed by a scrim of rotten lattice. I began to walk slowly, and when the rest of the class had passed the field house, I got down on my hands and knees and crawled through a broken place in the lattice and underneath the building. There was hardly room for me to lie there between the dirt and the sills that were covered with cobwebs. Someone had stuffed an old sneaker and a rusted watering can under the building, confident that they would never be seen again. I could hear from the field the voices of my friends choosing sides, and I felt the horror of having expelled myself from the light of a fine day, but I also felt, lying in the dirt, that the taste of blood was beginning to leave my mouth, that my heart was beginning to regulate its beating, and that the strength was returning to my legs. I lay in the dirt until the game ended and I could see, through the lattice, the players returning to school.

I felt that the fault was Leander's, and that if I could bring myself to approach him again, when he was in a better humor, he would respond humanely. The feeling that I could not assume my responsibilities as a

39

baseball player without some help from him was deep, as if parental love and baseball were both national pastimes. One afternoon, I got my ball and mitt and went into the library, where he was taking books down from the shelves and tying them up in bundles of ten, to be taken into Boston and sold. He had been a handsome man, I think. I had heard my relations speak of how he had aged, and so I suppose that his looks had begun to deteriorate. He would have been taken for a Yankee anywhere, and he seemed to feel that his alliance to the sea was by blood as well as tradition. When he went into an oyster bar and found people who were patently not American-born eating oysters, he would be stirred. He ate quantities of fish, swam daily in the salt river, and washed himself each morning with a sea sponge, so he always smelled faintly of brine and iodine, as if he had only recently come dripping out of the Atlantic. The brilliant blue of his eyes had not faded, and the boyish character of his face—its lightness and ovalness—was intact. He had not understood the economic fragility of his world, his wife's invalidism seemed to be a manifest rebuke for the confusion of his affairs, and his mind must have been thronged with feelings of being unwanted and also feelings of guilt. The books he was preparing to sell were his father's and his grandfather's; he would rail about this later, feeling that if histrionics would not redeem him, they would at least recapture for a minute his sense of identity and pride. If I had looked closely, I might have seen a face harried with anxiety and the weaknesses of old age, but I expected him, for my sake, to regain his youth and to appear like the paternal images I had seen on calendars and in magazine advertisements.

"Will you please play catch with me, Poppa?" I asked.

"How can you ask me to play baseball when I will be dead in another month!" he said. He sighed and then said, "I won't live through the summer. Your mother has been complaining all morning. She has nothing to say to me unless she has a complaint to make. She's complaining now of pains in her feet. She can't leave her bed because of the pains in her feet. She's trying to make me more unhappy than I already am, but I have some facts to fall back on. Here, let me show you." He took down one of the many volumes in which he had recorded his life, and searched through the pages until he found what he wanted. "Your mother wore custommade shoes from 1904 until 1908, when Mr. Schultz died. He made her six, twelve, fourteen—he made her seventeen pairs of shoes in four years. Then she began buying her shoes at Nettleton's." He wet his finger and turned a page. "She never paid less than twelve dollars a pair there, and in 1908 she bought four pairs of shoes and two pairs of canvas pumps. In 1910, she bought four pairs of shoes at Nettleton's and a pair of evening slippers at Stetson's. She said the slippers pinched her feet, but we couldn't take them back because she'd worn them. In 1911, she bought three pairs of shoes at Stetson's and two at Nettleton's. In 1912, she had Henderson make her a pair of walking shoes. They cost eighteen dollars. She paid twenty-four dollars for a pair of gold pumps at Stetson's. In 1913, she bought another pair

40

of canvas pumps, two pairs of suède shoes, golf shoes, and some beaded shoes." He looked to me for some confirmation of the unreasonableness of my mother's illness, but I hung my head and went out of the library.

The next time the class went out for baseball, I hid in a building closer to the school, where rakes and rollers and other grounds equipment were stored. This place was also dark, but there was room to stand and move and enjoy an illusion of freedom, although the light of day and the voices on the field from which I was hidden seemed like the lights and the sounds of life. I had been there only a few minutes when I heard someone approach and open the door. I had thought it would be the old grounds keeper, but it was a classmate of mine, who recognized, a second after he saw me, what I was doing, and seemed—since he was doing the same thing—delighted to have a conspirator. I disliked him and his friends, but I couldn't have disliked him more than I disliked the symptoms of my own panic, for I didn't leave the building. After this I had to hide not only from the ball game but from my classmate. He continued to hide in the tool shed and I hid near the playing field, in some woods behind the backstop, and chewed pieces of grass until the period ended.

That fall, I went out for football, and I had always liked winter sports, but in the spring, when the garbage man's son took the balls and bats out of the chest near the door of the gymnasium, the taste of blood in my mouth, the beating of my heart, and the weakness in my legs were keener than ever, and I found myself stuffed in the dirt under the track house again, with the old tennis sneaker and the watering can, horrified that I should have chosen or should have been made to lie in this filth when I could be walking freely over a green field. As the season progressed, I began to find new hiding places and to invent new ailments that would excuse me from having to play baseball, and the feeling that Leander had the cure to my cowardice returned, although I could not bring myself to approach him again. He still seemed to preserve, well on the dark side of his mind, some hard feelings about my being responsible for the revocation of Lucy Hartshorn's trust. Several times when I went to a movie or a dance, he locked the house up so tight that I couldn't find any way to get in, and had to sleep in the barn. Once, I returned in the daytime and found the house locked. I heard him moving inside and I rang the bell. He opened the door long enough to say, "Whatever it is you're selling, I don't want any." Then he slammed the door in my face. A minute later, he opened the door again. "I'm sorry, Eben," he said. "I didn't realize it was you."

My mother died when I was in my third year of high school. When I graduated the following year, Leander claimed to be too infirm to come to the ceremony, and when I looked down from the platform into a gathering where there were no near relatives of mine, it occurred to me—without pleasure or guilt—that I had probably not been up to bat more than three times.

My Cousin Juliana put up the money to send me to college, and I

41

entered college feeling that my troubles with Leander and baseball were over. Both my sisters had married by then, and gone to live in the West, and I dutifully spent part of my Christmas holiday at West Farm and planned to spend all my Easter vacation there. On the morning that college closed for the spring recess, I drove with my two roommates over to Mount Holyoke, where we picked up three girls. We were planning to have a picnic somewhere along the river. When we stopped for lunch, one of my roommates went around to the back of the car and got out his camera to take a picture of the girls. Glancing into the luggage compartment, I noticed a baseball and a bat. Everyone was around in front of the car. I couldn't be seen. The ground was loose, and with my hands I dug a hole nearly a foot deep. Then I dropped the baseball into this hole and buried it.

It was late when we got into Boston, and I took the last train to St. Botolph's. I had written Leander that I was coming, in the hope that he would not lock the house up, but when I reached there, after midnight, all the doors and windows were secured. I didn't feel like spending the night in the barn, and I broke a windowpane in the dining room and climbed in. I could hear Leander moving around upstairs, and because I felt irritated, I didn't call out to him. A few seconds later, there was an explosion in the room. Somebody had shot off a pistol and I thought I had been killed. I got to a switch and turned on the lights and saw, with a wild, crazy uprush of joy that I was alive and unharmed. Then I saw Leander standing in the doorway with the pistol in his hand. He dropped it to the floor and, stumbling toward me, laid his head on my shoulder and wept, "Oh, Eben! Eben! Eben!" he sobbed. "I thought it was a prowler! I heard someone trying to get in! I heard the breaking glass. Forgive me, forgive me."

I remember that he was wearing a fez, and some kind of ragged and outrageous robe over his shoulders. He had, up until that year, always dressed with great simplicity and care, feeling that a sensible regard for appearances facilitated human relationships. He had always put on a dark coat for dinner, and he would never consider as acquaintances or as business associates men with grease in their hair, men with curls, men who wore pointed shoes or diamond cuff links or who put pheasant feathers in their colored hats. Age seemed to have revised these principles, and during the Easter holidays he appeared in many brilliant costumes, many of them the robes and surplices of a fraternal order that had been disbanded in the twenties. Once when I stepped into the bathroom, I found him before the full-length mirror in the ostrich-plumed hat, the cross-ribbon heavy with orders, and the ornate sword of a Poor Knight of Christ and the Temple and a Guardian of the Gates of Gaza. He often quoted from Shakespeare.

The first job I got after leaving college was at Chatfield Academy. The school was in New Hampshire—in the mountains—and I went north in the fall. I liked teaching, and the place itself seemed oddly detached and peaceful. Chimes rang at the quarter hour, the buildings were old or copied old forms, the leaves fell past the classroom windows for a month, the nights smelled of smoke, and, leaving my classroom one evening in December, I found the air full of a swift, dry snow. The school was conservative, and at its helm was old Dr. Wareham. Robust on the playing field, tearful in chapel, bull-necked and vigorous in spite of his advanced age, he was that kind of monolithic father image that used to be thought a necessity for the education of youth. After the Easter recess, I signed a contract for the following year and arranged to teach summer school. In April, I got a notice that faculty participation in the annual meeting of the board of trustees was mandatory. I asked a man at supper one night what this meant.

"Well, they come up on Friday," my colleague said, "and Wareham gives them a dinner. Then they have their annual meeting. We have demonstration classes on Saturday and they snoop around, but they're mostly intelligent and they don't make trouble. Then Saturday noon, the old troll barbecues a side of beef and we have lunch with them. After this, there's a ball game between the trustees and the faculty members. The new members are always expected to play, and you'd better be good. The old troll feels that men get to know one another best on the playing field, and he doesn't miss a trick. We had a frail art teacher here a couple of years ago who claimed to have a headache, but Wareham got him out of bed and made him play third base. He made three errors and Wareham fired him. Then, after that, there's a cocktail party at Wareham's house, with good sour-mash bourbon for the brass and sherry for the rest of us. Then they go home."

The old taste of blood came into my mouth. My appetite for the meat and potatoes I had heaped onto my plate was gone. I nevertheless gorged myself, for I seemed to have been put into a position where my only recourse was to overlook my feelings or to conceal them where this was not possible. I knew by then that a thorough inspection of the history of the problem would not alter the facts, and that the best I could bring to the situation was a kind of hollow good cheer. I told myself that the game was inconsequential, and presently I seemed to feel this. There was some gossip the next day about Dr. Wareham's seriousness about the game. The piano teacher—a tall man named Bacon—had refused to play, and somebody said that he would be fired. But I was occupied with my classwork and I nearly forgot about the annual meeting until leaving my classroom on a Friday afternoon, I saw a large car driven by a chauffeur go around the quadrangle and stop at Dr. Wareham's house. The trustees were beginning to arrive.

After supper I corrected papers until about eleven, when I went to bed. Something woke me at three in the morning, and I went to the open window and I looked out at the night for signs of rain before I realized that this was an old habit of childhood. Rain had meant that I would be free, for a day, of hiding under the field house or in the woods behind the backstop. And now, still half asleep, I turned my ear to the window, listening with the purest anxiety, colored by a kind of pleading, for the stir of rain beginning or the heavier sound of a settled

43

storm. A single drop of water would have sounded like music. I knew from which quarter the rain wind might rise; I knew how cumbrously the wind would blow, how it would smell of wetness, how the storm, as it came west through the village, would make a distant roar, how the first drops would sound on the elm trees in the yard and the shrubs against the wall, how the rain would drum in the grass, how it would swell, how it would wet the kindling at the barbecue pit and disintegrate the paper bags that contained the charcoal, how it would confine the trustees to Dr. Wareham's house and prevail on one or two of them to leave before the cocktail party, and how it would first fill in the slight indentation around second base and then spread slowly toward first and third, until the whole field was flooded. . . . But I saw only a starry and a windless night. I got back into bed and, settling for the best I had—a kind of hollow good cheer—fell asleep.

The morning was the best kind of spring weather; even I saw this. The demonstration classes satisfied everyone, and at noon we went over to the barbecue pit to have our lunch with the trustees. The food seemed to stick in my throat, but this may have been the fault of the barbecue itself, because the meat was raw and the cooking arrangements were a disappointment all around. I was still eating my dessert when the Doctor gave the rallying cry, "Into your uniforms, men!" I put down my plate and started for the field house, with the arm of a French instructor thrown warmly over my shoulder and in a cheerful, friendly crowd that seemed blamelessly on their way to recapturing, or at least to reënacting, the secure pleasures of youth. But since the hour they returned to was one that I had never possessed, I felt the falseness of my position. I was handed a uniform—a gesture that seemed unalterably to be one of parting. But it was the too large shoes, wrapped with friction tape, that, when I bent over to lace them, gave me the worst spasm of despair. I picked a glove out of a box near the door and jogged out to the field.

The bleachers were full of students and faculty wives, and Dr. Wareham was walking up and down, leading them in singing to the band. The faculty members were first up, facing a formidable concentration of power and wealth in the field. The first batter got a line drive that was missed by the bank president on first and was good for a double. The second man up struck out, but the third man reached first, and the industrialist who was pitching walked the fourth batter. I gave a yank to my cap and stepped up to the plate, working my mouth and swallowing to clean it, if I could, of the salty taste of blood. I kept my eye on the ball, and when the first pitch seemed to be coming straight over the plate, I chopped at it with all my might. I heard the crack, I felt the vibration up my forearm, and, telling myself that a baseball diamond, like most things, must operate on a clockwise principle, I sprinted for third and knocked down the runner who was coming in to score. I knocked him flat, and bending over to see if he was all right, I heard Dr. Wareham roaring at me, "Get off the field! Get out of my sight!"

I walked back to the field house alone. The soberness of my feeling seemed almost to verge on romantic love—it seemed to make the air I walked through heavy—as if I were sick at heart for some gorgeous raven-haired woman who had been separated from me by a convulsion of nature. I took off my uniform and stood for a long time in the shower. Then I dressed and walked back across the quadrangle, where I could hear, from the open windows of the music building, Bacon playing the Chopin preludes. The music—swept with rains, with ruins, with unrequited and autumnal loves, with here and there a passage of the purest narcissism—seemed to outrage my senses, and I wanted to stop my ears. It took me an hour or so to pack, and when I carried my bags downstairs, I could still hear the cheering from the field. I drove into the village and had the tank filled with gas. At the edge of town, I wondered what direction to take, and then I turned south, for the farm.

It was six or seven when I got to St. Botolph's, and I took the precaution of calling Leander before I drove out to the house. "Hello, hello, hello!" the old man shouted. "You must have the wrong number. Oh, hello, Eben. . . ." When I got to the house, I left my bags in the hall and went upstairs. Leander was in his room. "Welcome home, Eben," he said. "I was reading a little Shakespeare to the cat."

When I sat down, the arm of my chair crashed to the floor, and I let it lie there. On his thick white hair Leander still wore his fez. For clothing, he had drawn from his store of old-fashioned bathing suits one with a striped skirt. It must have been stolen, since there were some numerals stenciled on the back. He had decided some time before that the most comfortable shoes he had were some old riding boots, and he was wearing these. Pictures of lost sailboats, lost cottages, dead friends and dogs gazed down at him from the wall. He had tied a length of string between the four wooden pineapples of his high poster bed and had hung his wash there to dry. The cat and his copy of Shakespeare were on his lap. "What are your plans?" he asked.

"I've been fired," I said. "I thought I'd leave some clothes here. I think I'll go for a swim now."

"Have you any clothes I can wear?"

"You're welcome to anything I have. The bags are downstairs."

"I still swim every day," Leander said. "Every day, that is, until the first of October. Last year I went swimming through the fifteenth—the fifteenth or the sixteenth. If you'll wait a minute, I'll make sure." He got up from his chair, and, stooping a little, so the tassel of his fez hung over his brow, he walked to his journal. After consulting it, he said, "I went swimming on the fifteenth last year. I went swimming on the twenty-fifth the year before that. Of course, that was nothing to what I could do when I was younger. I went swimming on the fourth of December, the eighth of January, the second of March. I went swimming on Christmas Day, New Year's Day, the twelfth of January, and the tenth of February. . . ."

After I left him to go out to the river, he went downstairs to where

45

my bags were. An old pair of riding pants took his eye. He managed to get his legs well into them before he realized they were too small. He tried to remove the pants and couldn't, because his legs had begun to swell. And when he tried to stand, the pants knifed him in the tendons at the back of his knees and brought him to the floor. Halfway out in the river, I could hear him roaring for help, and I swam back to shore and ran up to the house and found him moving slowly and painfully toward the kitchen, where he hoped to find a knife and cut himself free. I cut the riding breeches off him, and we drank some whiskey together, but I left in the morning for New York.

It was a good thing that I did leave, because I got a job the day I reached the city, and sailed three days later for Basra, to work for an oil company. I took the long voyage out on one of the company ships; it was five weeks after leaving New York that we stopped at Aden and another four days before we docked at Basra. It was hot. The flat volcanic ruins trembled in the heat, and the car that took me across the city to the oil-company settlement traveled through a maze of foul-smelling streets. The dormitory where I was to be quartered was like an army barracks, and when I reached it, in midafternoon, there was no one there but some Arabs, who helped me with my bags and told me the other men would be in after four, when the offices closed. When the men I shared the barracks with came in, they seemed pleased to see anyone newly arrived from the States, and they were full of practical information about how to make a life in Basra. "We practice baseball two or three nights a week," one of them said, "and then on Sundays we play Shell or Standard Oil. We only have eleven men on the squad now, so if you could play outfield? We call ourselves the Infidels. . . ."

It was not until long after my return from Basra, long after my marriage, that Leander died, one summer afternoon, sitting in the rose garden, with a copy of "Primitive Sexual Mores" on his lap. The housekeeper found him there, and the local undertaker sent me a wire in New York. I did not feel any grief when I got the news. Alice and I had three children by then, and my life would not in any way be affected by Leander's death. I telephoned my sisters, in Denver, but neither of them felt that they could come East. The next day, I drove to St. Botolph's, and found that the undertaker had made all the arrangements. The services were to be at two. Three old cousins came out from Boston, to my surprise, and we were the only mourners. It was the kind of weather that we used to call haying weather when I lived in the valley. The fields of timothy and sweet grass had been cut, the cemetery smelled of cut hay, and while the minister was praying, I heard the sound of distant thunder and saw the daylight dim, the way the lights dim in a farmhouse during a storm. After the ceremony, I returned to the house, feeling that there would be a lot there to occupy me, but it turned out that there was not much to do. It had begun to rain. I wandered through the rooms to see if there was anything left in them. I found some whiskey. The bird cages, the three-legged tables, and the cracked soup tureens must have been refused by the junkman. I thought that there must be a will, and I went reluctantly—disconsolately, at any rate—up to Leander's room and sat uneasily in his chair. His papers were copious and bizarre, and it took me nearly two hours to find the will. He left the house and the land to my older sister. To my other sister he left the jewelry, but this was immaterial, since all the jewelry had been sold. I was mentioned. "To my changeling son, Eben," he wrote, "the author of all my misfortunes, I leave my copy of Shakespeare, a hacking cough . . ." The list was long and wicked, and although he had written it ten years earlier and although I had buried him that afternoon, I couldn't help feeling, for a minute, that the piece of paper was evidence of my own defeat. It was dark then, and it was still raining. The whiskey bottle was empty and the unshaded electric light was baneful. The old house, which had always seemed to have an extensive life of its own, was creaking and stirring under the slender weight of the storm. The feeling that in burying Leander I had resolved a sad story seemed farcical, and if my reaction to his will was evidence, the old fool had pierced the rites and ceremonies of death. I thought desperately of my family in New York, and of the rooms where my return was waited with anxiety and love, but I had never been able to build any kind of bridge from Leander's world to the worlds where I lived, and I failed now in my efforts to remember New York. I went downstairs to telephone my wife, but the telephone was dead, and for all I knew it might have been disconnected years ago. I packed my bag, turned out the lights, threw the house key into the river, and started home.

In the years that followed, I thought now and then about Leander and the farm, and although I had resolved to break with these memories, they both continued to enjoy the perfect freedom of my dreams; the bare halls of the house, the massive granite stoop, the rain dripping from the wooden gutters, and the mass of weeds in the garden often surrounded me while I slept. My participation in baseball continued to be painful. I drove a ball through my mother-in-law's parlor window— and the rest of the family, who were intimidated, didn't understand why I should feel so happy—but it was not enough to lay Leander's ghost, and I still didn't like old men with white hair to be at the helm of the ships I traveled on. Some years later—my oldest son was nine—I took all five boys uptown to Yankee Stadium to see their first game. It was one of the hottest days of the year. I bought my sons food, eyeshades, pennants, score cards, pencils, and souvenir pins, and I took the youngest two to the bathroom several times. Mantle was up in the sixth, with a count of three and two. He fouled three balls into the netting above the backstop and fouled the fourth straight toward where we were sitting—a little high. It was coming like a shot, but I made the catch—one-handed, barehanded—and although I thought the impact had broken some bones in my hand, the pain was followed swiftly by a sense of perfect joy. The old man and the old house seemed at last to fall from the company and the places of my dreams, and I smelled the timothy and the sweet grass again, and saw a gravedigger hidden behind a marble angel, and the smoky, the grainy light of a thunderstorm, when the clearness of the green world—the emblazoned fields—reminds us briefly of a great freedom of body and mind. Then the boys began to argue for possession of the ball, and I gave it to the oldest one, hoping that I wouldn't have any more use for it. It would have troubled Leander to think that he would be buried in any place as distant from West Farm as Yankee Stadium, but that is where his bones were laid to rest.

## QUESTIONS

*Looking at Ideas:*

1. Why does Leander resent Eben's birth? Describe the negative childhood memory that Eben struggles to overcome throughout the story.

2. Do you think Leander purposely hurt his own son with the baseball?

3. The narrator begins, "To be an American and unable to play baseball is comparable to being a Polynesian and unable to swim. It is an impossible situation." What is the impossible situation in the story? In how many different incidents does the narrator fail to overcome his fear of playing baseball? Why is he finally successful?

4. Although the main conflict in the story is between Leander and Eben, what role does the mother play in their conflict?

5. How did you feel about Leander's treatment of his son? Were you understanding of his rejection of Eben? Is Leander an atypical father?

*Looking at Strategies:*

1. Discuss and analyze one important moment in the narrative where Cheever connects the idea of parental love and "the national pastime"—baseball. How and why does Cheever create this connection?

2. What point is Cheever making about the power of memories and of the unconscious mind to influence the course of one's life? Analyze one representative scene to show how Cheever emphasizes the power of childhood memories and the unconscious mind.

3. Does Cheever's presentation of his story, through the class of his characters, their professions, their birthplace, their interest in baseball, help to make the relationship between Eben and Leander more or less representative and universal? Explain.

4. Discuss several points in the story where Cheever uses dialogue effectively.

5. Discuss the way in which Cheever develops several metaphors, images, or symbols to create a pattern of meaning that engages the reader's imagination in the story.

*Looking at Connections:*

1. Compare and contrast Eben's relationship with his father and Alice Walker's relationship with her father in her essay, "Father" (the next se-

lection in this chapter). What does each learn from his or her relationship?

2. In what ways is Eben's memory of the baseball incident similar to An-mei's scar in Amy Tan's story? In what ways is it different?

*Suggestions for Writing:*

1. Write an essay in which you explore how the sharing of a hobby or sport and parental love are sometimes linked within families. You might decide to focus on your family. In this case, explain why you think the connection was formed, and how it helped you to have a constructive relationship with one of your parents. In addition, you may want to discuss how it made your relationship with your parent more difficult, or painful.

2. Write an essay in which you discuss your own father or yourself as a father in relation to the fathers presented in the selections in this chapter. Of the fathers we have read about in this chapter, which one is most like your own? If you are a father yourself, which of the fathers do you identify with? What have you learned about yourself and your relationship with your father from thinking about the portraits of fathers presented in this chapter? Refer to specific selections and passages in developing your answer.

3. Write an essay in which you discuss what you have learned from the selections in this chapter about the power of childhood memories to shape an individual's self-concept and expectations of family life. Develop examples to support your main points.

**JOURNAL ENTRY**
Write a sketch of a parent or grandparent whose ideas were different from
yours, but who nevertheless influenced you when you were growing up.

**ALICE WALKER: "Father"**   Alice Walker was born in Eatonton, Georgia, in
1944. She attended Spelman College from 1963 to 1965 and completed her
B.A. at Sara Lawrence College (1967). She was active in the civil rights movement during the 1960s and married Melvyn Leventhal, a civil rights lawyer;
they were married until 1976 and have one daughter. Many of Walker's essays, stories, and poems are based on memories of her childhood; she also
writes about the concerns of people in all walks of life who are suffering and
about the concerns of black women in particular. Walker is best known for her
novel *The Color Purple* (1982), which won the Pulitzer Prize and the American Book Award. In 1985 it was adapted for a film directed by Steven Spielberg, which received several Academy Award nominations. Other works by
Walker include *In Love and Trouble: Stories of Black Women* (1973), *Meridian*
(1976), and *The Temple of My Familiar* (1989). As you read the following selection, "Father" (1985), which is taken from her most recent collection of essays, *Living by the Word: Selected Writings (1973–1987),* consider the impact
that Walker's father had on her life.

ALICE WALKER

# Father

Though it is more difficult to write about my father than about my
mother, since I spent less time with him and knew him less well, it is
equally as liberating. Partly this is because writing about people helps
us to understand them, and understanding them helps us to accept
them as part of ourselves. Since I share so many of my father's characteristics, physical and otherwise, coming to terms with what he has
meant to my life is crucial to a full acceptance and love of myself.

I'm positive my father never understood why I wrote. I wonder
sometimes if the appearance, in 1968, of my first book, *Once,* poems
largely about my experiences in the Civil Rights movement and in
other countries, notably African and Eastern European, surprised him.
It is frustrating that, because he is now dead, I will never know.

In fact, what I regret most about my relationship with my father is
that it did not improve until after his death. For a long time I felt so
shut off from him that we were unable to talk. I hadn't the experience,
as a younger woman, to ask the questions I would ask now. These days

I feel we are on good terms, spiritually (my dreams of him are deeply loving and comforting ones), and that we both understand our relationship was a casualty of exhaustion and circumstances. My birth, the eighth child, unplanned, must have elicited more anxiety than joy. It hurts me to think that for both my parents, poor people, my arrival represented many more years of backbreaking and spirit-crushing toil.

I grew up to marry someone very unlike my father, as I knew him— though I feel sure he had these qualities himself as a younger man— someone warm, openly and spontaneously affectionate, who loved to talk to me about everything, including my work. I now share my life with another man who has these qualities. But I would give a lot to be able to talk grownup to grownup with Daddy. I'd like to tell him how hard I am working to understand. And about the humor and solace I occasionally find (while writing *The Color Purple,* for instance, in which some of his early life is imagined) in the work.

> My father
> (back blistered)
> beat me
> because I
> could not
> stop crying.
> He'd had
> enough "fuss"
> he said
> for one damn
> voting day.

In my heart, I have never wanted to be at odds with my father, but I have felt, over the years, especially when I was younger, that he gave me no choice. Perhaps if I could have relaxed and been content to be his favorite, there would have been a chance for closeness, but because a sister whom I loved was clearly not favorite material I did not want to be either. When I look back over my life, I see a pattern in my relationships going back to this, and in my love relationships I have refused men who loved me (at least for a time) if they in turn were loved by another woman but did not love her in return. I am the kind of woman who could positively forbid a married lover to leave his wife.

The poem above is one of my earliest as an adult, written after an abortion of which my father would not have approved, in which I felt that visceral understanding of a situation that for a poet can mean a poem. My father far away in the South, me in college in the North— how far away from each other! Yet in the pain of the moment and the illumination of some of what was wrong between us, how close. If he ever read the poem, I wonder what he thought. We never discussed my work, though I thought he tended to become more like some of my worst characters the older he got. I remember going home once and being told by my mother of some of the curses he was capable of, and hardly believing her, since the most I'd ever heard my father say was

"God damn!" and I could count the number of times on toes and fingers. (In fact, his favorite curse, when a nail refused to go in straight or he dropped the hammer on his sore corn was "God damn the goddam luck to the devil!" which always sounded rather ineffectual and humorous to me, and which, thinking of it, I hear him say and see his perspiring dark face.)

Did he actually beat me on voting day? Probably not. I suppose the illegal abortion caused me to understand what living under other people's politics can force us to do. The only time I remember his beating me was one day after he'd come home tired and hungry from the dairy (where he and my brothers milked a large herd of cows morning and afternoon), and my brother Bobby, three years older than me and a lover of chaos, and I were fighting. He had started it, of course. My mother, sick of our noise, spoke to my father about it, and without asking questions he took off his belt and flailed away, indiscriminately, at the two of us.

Why do certain things stick in the mind? I recall a scene, much earlier, when I was only three or so, in which my father questioned me about a fruit jar I had accidentally broken. I felt he knew I had broken it; at the same time, I couldn't be sure. Apparently breaking it was, in any event, the wrong thing to have done. I could say, Yes, I broke the jar, and risk a whipping for breaking something valuable, or, No, I did not break it, and perhaps bluff my way through.

I've never forgotten my feeling that he really wanted me to tell the truth. And because he seemed to desire it—and the moments during which he waited for my reply seemed quite out of time, so much so I can still feel them, and, as I said, I was only three, if that—I confessed. I broke the jar, I said. I think he hugged me. He probably didn't, but I still feel as if he did, so embraced did I feel by the happy relief I noted on his face and by the fact that he didn't punish me at all, but seemed, instead, pleased with me. I think it was at that moment that I resolved to take my chances with the truth, although as the years rolled on I was to break more serious things in his scheme of things than fruit jars.

It was the unfairness of the beating that keeps it fresh in my mind. (And this was thirty-seven years ago!) And my disappointment at the deterioration of my father's ethics. And yet, since I am never happy in my heart when estranged from my father, any more than I would be happy shut off from sunlight, in writing this particular poem I tried to see my father's behavior in a context larger than our personal relationship.

Actually, my father was two fathers.

To the first four of his children he was one kind of father, to the second set of four he was another kind. Whenever I talk to the elder set I am astonished at the picture they draw, for the man they describe bears little resemblance to the man I knew. For one thing, the man they knew was physically healthy, whereas the man I knew was almost always sick; not sick enough to be in bed, or perhaps he was but with so many children to feed he couldn't afford to lie down, but "dragging-around" sick, in the manner of the very poor. Overweight, high blood pressure, diabetes, or, as it was called, "sugar," rotten teeth. There are certain *facts*, however, that identify our father as the same man; one of which is that, in the 1930s, my father was one of the first black men to vote in Eatonton, Georgia, among a group of men like himself he helped organize, mainly poor sharecroppers with large families, totally at the mercy of the white landlords. He voted for Roosevelt. He was one of the leading supporters of the local one-room black school, and according to everyone who knew him then, including my older brothers and sister, believed in education above all else. Years later, when I knew him, he seemed fearful of both education and politics and disappointed and resentful as well.

And why not? Though he risked his life and livelihood to vote more than once, nothing much changed in his world. Cotton prices continued low. Dairying was hard. White men and women continued to run things, badly. In his whole life my father never had a vacation. (Of course my mother had less of one: she could not even get in the car and drive off to town, as he could.) Education merely seemed to make his children more critical of him. When I went south in the mid-sixties to help register voters, I stopped by our house to say hello but never told either of my parents what I planned to do. I didn't want them to worry about my safety, and it never occurred to me that they cared much about the vote. My father was visibly ill, paranoid, complaining the whole time of my mother's religious activities (she had become a Jehovah's Witness). Then, for no apparent reason, he would come out with one of those startlingly intelligent comments about world affairs or some absolutely clear insight into the deficiencies of national leaders, and I would be reminded of the father I didn't know.

For years I have held on to another early memory of my life between the ages of two and four. Every afternoon a tired but jolly very black man came up to me with arms outstretched. I flew into them to be carried, to be hugged, to be kissed. For years I thought this black man was my father. But no. He was my oldest brother, Fred, whose memories of my father are, surprisingly, as painful as *my* memories of him, because as my father's first child, and a son, he was subjected to my father's very confused notions of what constituted behavior suitable for a male. And of course my father himself didn't really know. He was in his late teens, a child himself, when he married. His mother had been murdered, by a man who claimed to love her, when he was eleven. His father, to put it very politely, drank, and terrorized his children.

My father was so confused that when my sister Ruth appeared in the world and physically resembled his mother, and sounded like his mother, and had similar expressions, he rejected her and missed no opportunity that I ever saw to put her down. I, of course, took the side of my sister, forfeiting my chance to be my father's favorite among the second set of children, as my oldest sister, Mamie, was favorite among the first. In her case the favoritism seemed outwardly caused by her very light color, and of course she was remarkably intelligent as well. In my case, my father seemed partial to me because of my "smartness" and forthrightness, but more obviously because of my hair, which was the longest and "best" in the family.

And yet, my father taught me two things that have been important to me: he taught me not to bother telling lies, because the listener might be delighted with the truth, and he told me never to cut my hair. Though I have tried not to lie, the sister he rejected and I loved became a beautician, and one of the first things she did—partly in defiance of him—was to cut my shoulder-blade-length hair. I did not regret it so much while in high school and college (everyone kept their hair short, it seemed), but years later, after I married, I grew it long again, almost as long as it had been when I was growing up. I'd had it relaxed to feathers. When I walked up to my father, as he was talking to a neighbor, I stooped a little and placed his hand on my head. I thought he'd be pleased. "A woman's hair is her glory," he'd always said. He paid little attention. When the black power movement arrived, with its emphasis on cropped natural hair, I did the job myself, filling the face bowl and bathroom floor with hair and shocking my husband when he arrived home.

Only recently have I come to believe he was right in wanting me to keep my hair. After years of short hair, of cutting my hair back each time it raised its head, so to speak, I have begun to feel each time as if I am mutilating my antennae (which is how Rastafarians, among others, think of hair) and attenuating my power. It seems imperative not to cut my hair anymore.

I didn't listen to my father because I assumed he meant that in the eyes of a *man,* in his eyes, a woman's hair is her glory (unfortunately, he wore his own head absolutely cleanshaven all his life); and that is probably what he did mean. But now I begin to sense something else, that there is power (would an ancient translation of glory *be* power?) in uncut hair itself. The power (and glory) perhaps of the untamed, the undomesticated; in short, the wild. A wildness about the head, as the Rastas have discovered, places us somehow in the loose and spacious freedom of Jah's universe. Hippies, of course, knew this, too.

As I write, my own hair reaches just below my ears. It is at the dangerous stage at which I usually butt my forehead against the mirror and in resignation over not knowing "what to do with it" cut it off. But this time I have thought ahead and have encased it in braids made of someone else's hair. I expect to wear them, braces for the hair, so to speak, until my own hair replaces them. Eventually I will be able, as I was when a child, to tie my hair under my chin. But mostly I would like to set it free.

My father would have loved Jesse Jackson. On the night Jesse addressed the Democratic convention I stayed close to my radio. In my backwoods cabin, linked to the world only by radio, I felt something like my father must have, since he lived most of his life before television and far from towns. He would have appreciated Jesse's oratorical gift, and, unlike some newscasters who seemed to think of it primarily as technique, he would have felt, as I did, the transformation of the spirit of the man implicit in the words he chose to say. He would have felt, as I did, that in asking for forgiveness as well as votes and for patience as well as commitment to the Democratic party, Jackson lost nothing and won almost everything: a cleared conscience and peace of mind.

My father was never able to vote for a black candidate for any national or local political office. By the time black people were running for office and occasionally winning elections, in the late sixties and early seventies, he was too sick to respond with the exhilaration he must have felt. On the night of Jackson's speech, I felt it for him; along with the grief that in neither of our lifetimes is the United States likely to choose the best leadership offered to it. This is the kind of leader, the kind of evergrowing, ever-expanding spirit *you* might have been, Daddy, I thought—and damn it, I love you for what you might have been. And thinking of you now, merging the two fathers that you were, remembering how tightly I hugged you as a small child returning home after two long months at a favorite aunt's, and with what apparent joy you lifted me beside your cheek; knowing now, at forty, what it takes out of body and spirit to go and how much more to stay, and having learned, too, by now, some of the pitiful confusions in behavior caused by ignorance and pain, I love you no less for what you were.

## QUESTIONS

*Looking at Ideas:*
1. Walker states that it is worthwhile to write about her father. What reasons does she present to support her claim? Walker implies that all people can benefit from writing about their families. Do you agree with her?
2. Characterize Walker's "two fathers." What has Walker learned from the two men who make up her father?
3. What does Walker regret most about her relationship with her father? How does she put her disappointment into a positive perspective?
4. Which memories does Walker recount in her essay? According to Walker, why do certain memories "stick in the mind"?
5. How did Walker's relationship with her father affect her choice of a husband and other decisions about forming relationships?

*Looking at Strategies:*
1. What effect does the interruption of the exposition with a poem have? How does the content of the poem reinforce the themes of the essay?
2. If Walker's father didn't actually beat her on voting day, how does Walker explain the inclusion of the claim that he did?
3. Walker implies that memoir writers sometimes manipulate the truth of actual events to convey an emotion true to the memory. Can you understand their position? How do you feel about this strategy?

4. How does Walker develop her hair into a symbol in the essay? What does her hair come to represent for Walker and the reader?

*Looking at Connections:*

1. Compare and contrast Alice Walker's and Russell Baker's reasons for valuing the process of writing about their families and their attitudes about being truthful in recounting their memories.

2. Compare and contrast Walker's process of understanding and accepting her father's character with the narrator's process of understanding and accepting his father's character in "The National Pastime."

*Suggestions for Writing:*

1. As Walker does in "Father," write about a parent with whom you once felt at odds but are now coming to understand and accept.

2. Write an essay in which you discuss the ways in which your relationship with a parent or parent figure has affected your choice of important partners in your adult life.

3. Write an essay in which you explore several reasons why you think it is important to write about the early memories that "stick in the mind." Refer to the ideas of other writers in this chapter to support your point of view, but develop reasons of your own as well, and include discussions of specific memories to support your reasons.

**JOAN DIDION: "On Going Home"**   Joan Didion was born in Sacramento,
California, in 1934. She attended the University of California at Berkeley from
1952 to 1956. Didion has worked as an editor, journalist, essayist, and novelist. With her husband, John Gregory Dunne, she has also collaborated on a
number of screenplays that include *Play It As It Lays* (1972), *A Star Is Born*
(1976), and *True Confessions* (1981). Didion is known for her clear and detailed style. She has published four short novels. Her best-known essay collections include *Slouching Towards Bethlehem* (1967), *The White Album* (1979),
*Salvador* (1983), and *Miami* (1987). "On Going Home" is included in *Slouching Towards Bethlehem.* As you read the essay notice how Didion illustrates
the conflict she feels between her loyalty to her family of origin and to her
husband and young daughter, and how she struggles to find a part of her own
heritage to give to her daughter.

JOAN DIDION

# On Going Home

I am home for my daughter's first birthday. By "home" I do not mean
the house in Los Angeles where my husband and I and the baby live,
but the place where my family is, in the Central Valley of California. It
is a vital although troublesome distinction. My husband likes my family
but is uneasy in their house, because once there I fall into their ways,
which are difficult, oblique, deliberately inarticulate, not my husband's
ways. We live in dusty houses ("D-U-S-T," he once wrote with his finger on surfaces all over the house, but no one noticed it) filled with mementos quite without value to him (what could the Canton dessert
plates mean to him? how could he have known about the assay scales,
why should he care if he did know?), and we appear to talk exclusively
about people we know who have been committed to mental hospitals,
about people we know who have been booked on drunk-driving
charges, and about property, particularly about property, land, price
per acre and C-2 zoning and assessments and freeway access. My
brother does not understand my husband's inability to perceive the ad-

vantage in the rather common real-estate transaction known as "sale-leaseback," and my husband in turn does not understand why so many of the people he hears about in my father's house have recently been committed to mental hospitals or booked on drunk-driving charges. Nor does he understand that when we talk about sale-leasebacks and right-of-way condemnations we are talking in code about the things we like best, the yellow fields and the cottonwoods and the rivers rising and falling and the mountain roads closing when the heavy snow comes in. We miss each other's points, have another drink and regard the fire. My brother refers to my husband, in his presence, as "Joan's husband." Marriage is the classic betrayal.

Or perhaps it is not any more. Sometimes I think that those of us who are now in our thirties were born into the last generation to carry the burden of "home," to find in family life the source of all tension and drama. I had by all objective accounts a "normal" and a "happy" family situation, and yet I was almost thirty years old before I could talk to my family on the telephone without crying after I had hung up. We did not fight. Nothing was wrong. And yet some nameless anxiety colored the emotional charges between me and the place that I came from. The question of whether or not you could go home again was a very real part of the sentimental and largely literary baggage with which we left home in the fifties; I suspect that it is irrelevant to the children born of the fragmentation after World War II. A few weeks ago in a San Francisco bar I saw a pretty young girl on crystal take off her clothes and dance for the cash prize in an "amateur-topless" contest. There was no particular sense of moment about this, none of the effect of romantic degradation, of "dark journey," for which my generation strived so assiduously. What sense could that girl possibly make of, say, *Long Day's Journey into Night?* Who is beside the point?

That I am trapped in this particular irrelevancy is never more apparent to me than when I am home. Paralyzed by the neurotic lassitude engendered by meeting one's past at every turn, around every corner, inside every cupboard, I go aimlessly from room to room. I decide to meet it head-on and clean out a drawer, and I spread the contents on the bed. A bathing suit I wore the summer I was seventeen. A letter of rejection from *The Nation,* an aerial photograph of the site for a shopping center my father did not build in 1954. Three teacups hand-painted with cabbage roses and signed "E.M.," my grandmother's initials. There is no final solution for letters of rejection from *The Nation* and teacups hand-painted in 1900. Nor is there any answer to snapshots of one's grandfather as a young man on skis, surveying around Donner Pass in the year 1910. I smooth out the snapshot and look into his face, and do and do not see my own. I close the drawer, and have another cup of coffee with my mother. We get along very well, veterans of a guerrilla war we never understood.

Days pass. I see no one. I come to dread my husband's evening call, not only because he is full of news of what by now seems to me our remote life in Los Angeles, people he has seen, letters which require attention, but because he asks what I have been doing, suggests uneasily that I get out, drive to San Francisco or Berkeley. Instead I drive across the river to a family graveyard. It has been vandalized since my last visit and the monuments are broken, overturned in the dry grass. Because I once saw a rattlesnake in the grass I stay in the car and listen to a country-and-Western station. Later I drive with my father to a ranch he has in the foothills. The man who runs his cattle on it asks us to the roundup, a week from Sunday, and although I know that I will be in Los Angeles I say, in the oblique way my family talks, that I will come. Once home I mention the broken monuments in the graveyard. My mother shrugs.

I go to visit my great-aunts. A few of them think now that I am my cousin, or their daughter who died young. We recall an anecdote about a relative last seen in 1948, and they ask if I still like living in New York City. I have lived in Los Angeles for three years, but I say that I do. The baby is offered a horehound drop, and I am slipped a dollar bill "to buy a treat." Questions trail off, answers are abandoned, the baby plays with the dust motes in a shaft of afternoon sun.

It is time for the baby's birthday party: a white cake, strawberry-marshmallow ice cream, a bottle of champagne saved from another party. In the evening, after she has gone to sleep, I kneel beside the crib and touch her face, where it is pressed against the slats, with mine. She is an open and trusting child, unprepared for and unaccustomed to the ambushes of family life, and perhaps it is just as well that I can offer her little of that life. I would like to give her more. I would like to promise her that she will grow up with a sense of her cousins and of rivers and of her great-grandmother's teacups, would like to pledge her a picnic on a river with fried chicken and her hair uncombed, would like to give her *home* for her birthday, but we live differently now and I can promise her nothing like that. I give her a xylophone and a sundress from Madeira, and promise to tell her a funny story.

## QUESTIONS

*Looking at Ideas:*

1. Didion concludes her first paragraph, "Marriage is the classic betrayal." Her examples in the first paragraph present the reader with reasons why she comes to this conclusion. Explain Didion's statement and then discuss whether or not you agree with her.

2. Didion says, "Sometimes I think that those of us who are now in our thirties were born into the last generation to carry the burden of 'home,' to find in family life the source of all tension and drama." Do you agree or disagree with Didion? Explain.

3. Why is it difficult for Didion to go home? Is it difficult for you to go home? Explain.

4. As a new mother, Didion is searching through her memories of home, hoping to find a sense of home that she can give her daughter for her

birthday. What does she finally give her daughter for her birthday? Why?

*Looking at Strategies:*

1. Didion develops many images to clarify her concept of home. Discuss several of the details she includes that gave you a clear image about what her home life was like.
2. Describe Didion's writing style. Consider her sentence structure, her use of images and language, the way that she develops ideas. Do you like Didion's style? What is unique or unusual about it?
3. Didion gives her daughter "a xylophone and a sundress from Madeira," and promises "to tell her a funny story." Why do you think she chooses these gifts for her baby daughter? What do they symbolize?

*Looking at Connections:*

1. Contrast Didion's attitude about home with Russell Baker's. Which of these writers' regard for home is closest to your own?
2. Compare Didion's role as a mother to the roles that the mothers in Lightfoot's, Kazin's, and Baker's selections maintain. How do you explain these varieties of mothering styles? Can you say that one of the approaches to mothering is preferable? If you can, which one would you choose and why?

*Suggestions for Writing:*

1. Write about a recent trip home. Did memories of your visit support or clash with your current values and life-style? What is most difficult for you about reconciling the memories of your childhood with the realities of your life now? What is most positive about the family traditions you have brought with you through the memories of your past?
2. After reflecting on a variety of homes which you have lived in or observed, including the one you grew up in, write an essay in which you describe and define the possessions, feelings, ideas, and values that you think make a place a home.
3. Write an essay in which you discuss your expectations of and goals for your next home or for your current home. What have you kept with you from your family of origin? Which of your current values are derived from your original family, and which of your values represent a rebellion against your family?

**AMY MARX: "My Grandfather's Memories"**   Amy Marx grew up in Lexington, Massachusetts. She is majoring in political science and is interested in a career in environmental policy. Along with her academic responsibilities, she is a member of the track team. Writing the following essay, designed as a contrast between her own character and that of her grandfather, was especially difficult for Marx because she had never before attempted to express her thoughts and memories about her grandfather. She was concerned because in writing such a personal memoir and in pointing out conflicting character traits, she did not want to be disrespectful toward a grandparent whom she loves dearly. Writing the paper turned out to be a positive experience for her in that it helped her to clarify her thoughts about the relationship she has with her grandfather and to discover the real basis for the respect she holds for him.

AMY MARX

# My Grandfather's Memories

Shuffling his feet and chewing a toothpick, my grandfather presents himself as a dominant figure of stubbornness and will. A highly opinionated person, he "suggests" with the utmost authority. Whether arguing with restaurant owners or making sarcastic comments about the family inheritance, my grandfather represents the archetype of conservative arrogance. Nevertheless, I view my grandfather with unmatched respect and admiration.

As I stand in the doorway of the store, the familiar rush of anxiety overwhelms me. How can another year have flown by so quickly? Is it possible that it is birthday time, and I am yet again faced with the task of choosing "anything," while my grandfather waits impatiently to pay? My grandfather seems overly materialistic, while I can hardly think of things to ask for on my birthday. He prefers elegant meals, while I am almost always happy with a peanut butter sandwich. My grandfather depends on my grandmother's doing the household chores, while I look forward to marrying a "liberated" man. Only insiders are provided a rare glimpse of the past which has shaped my grandfather's outward personality. Despite his defensiveness, my grandfather's soul abounds with love, compassion, and kindness.

Unlike my grandfather, I have never been totally helpless and completely alone. I cannot imagine the immense pain that he must feel upon seeing a war memorial, reading a mourner's prayer, or viewing the only picture of his family. I will never be able to internalize the void that he feels when the monthly reparation check arrives to compensate for his mother and sister who were slaughtered by the Nazis. How can I say what my personality would be like if I had lived through the night-mare that he still lives?

At the age of eighteen, my grandfather joined the emerging Zionist movement. After leaving Germany to build the state of Israel, he soon discovered that his mother and sister were trapped under the Nazi regime. Already deported, my great-aunt and great-grandmother wrote desperate letters from the concentration camps. My grandfather was helpless; heartbroken, he realized that any effort was futile. His mother and sister inevitably became numbers on the growing list of slaughtered Jews.

My grandfather seldom speaks of his tragic past. What I know of it I have learned from my grandmother's stories, from the letters sent from the concentration camps, and from my grandfather's vague references. The slightest mention of his family's tragic past brings him to tears. I caught a first glimpse at my grandfather's relationship with his memories when we toured Yad Vashem, Israel's largest Holocaust museum.

My grandfather brazenly entered the memorial with me at his side. As he scrutinized each picture, I began to consider his thoughts. I was hit head on with the nightmare that had been my grandfather's reality. I looked at the pictures of emaciated prisoners and wondered if my grandfather recognized his sister. I grimaced at the sight of unmarked bodies, asking myself if my grandfather saw images of his mother. Despite these stirrings of feelings within me, I have never questioned my grandfather on the subject of the Holocaust. I desperately want to know more, but I am equally afraid of bringing up the subject. For no apparent reason, my family has always abided by a tacit agreement never overtly to discuss the subject of the Holocaust. If only I had the courage to cross over these unmarked boundaries.

My grandfather's materialism stems from a fear of losing things. His home, family, and education were once swept from beneath him. As a result, his plate is always cleared out of an unconscious fear that one day there may be no more food. Possessions, bought with hard-earned money, are meticulously maintained. My grandfather built his own life with no parent to send him to college, no sister to chat with on the phone, no house to go home to for Thanksgiving, and no inheritance with which to build a future.

My grandfather is not exactly a philanthropist. From an idealistic point of view, I expect that a persecuted individual would want to turn around and root out all social injustices. After having seen the damage that hate can cause, I would expect him to reach out to all others. My grandfather, on the other hand, has a slightly different view. After all, if he fought the odds and "won," why are the hungry and the poor unable to help themselves?

This is not to say that my grandfather is not kindhearted. Rather, his compassion is reserved. He believes strongly in the ideals of family. He has rebuilt a life and is proud to be the foundation of our tightly knit family. I always feel slightly uneasy in his house, as I enter the rooms full of pictures of myself, my brother, and my sister. Likewise, I feel self-conscious as I meet all his friends who have "heard so much about me," for I know this is by no means a figure of speech.

Although I can never internalize the pain that my grandfather harbors, I can be more understanding toward our differences. I can appreciate his compassionate soul, while coming to terms with our contrasting personalities. In addition, I can recognize my own identity, realizing that I had the privilege to develop under the canopy of a loving and supportive family.

*Questions for Discussion*

1. What are the major contrasts Amy Marx sees between her values and those of her grandfather? What examples does she use to clarify her points?

2. Why do you think that Amy Marx's family never speaks of the Holocaust?

3. Why does Amy Marx's grandfather "believe strongly in the ideals of the family"? What do you know about victims of the Holocaust and its impact on their families?

4. What does the essay suggest about how memories of grandparents affect the lives of their grandchildren? Have any of your grandparents' or relatives' memories had a significant influence on your values?

5. Working individually or in a group, write a peer critique that includes several supportive comments and several suggestions for strengthening the essay by Amy Marx. Comment on the content and writing style.

## Reaching Out: Chapter Activities

1. Try freewriting or invisible writing (dim the computer screen) on the computer. Work in five- or ten-minute periods of time. During each time period focus on a different memory. Then select one memory to develop more fully; freewrite or use invisible writing to develop this memory for ten minutes. Then go on to use the techniques of brainstorming or outlining to develop a tentative plan for a paper focused on the memory you have started to explore through your freewriting or invisible writing. Which technique was most useful?

2. People observe and remember events, places, and people differently; each of us sees and experiences from our own vantage point, our own frame of reference that has been shaped by personal, social, and cultural assumptions. To test this hypothesis, attend an event on campus or in the community with several people in your class. During the following class session, each member of your writing group should try to recount in writing the high points of the event, what seemed most worthwhile or memorable about it. Then get together to write a group report that reflects the different memories/interpretations of the event, some speculation as to why each member of the group experienced the event differently, and what this suggests about how we remember things.

3. Write about an important memory from your childhood. Then ask someone in your family who was part of your memory to recount the same event. Write this person's version, and then try to account for the differences in your memories. What does this say about how we remember? Was the meaning of your memory changed by seeing it from another perspective?

4. Interview a person who has a memory of an important social or political event on your campus or in your community; write up the interview in essay form. Then, if you can, share it with a campus organization that would be interested in the interviewee's memory of the event.

5. See one of the following films, either by yourself or with several of your classmates. Write an individual or collaborative review of the film that takes into account the ways in which the film explores themes of memory and family heritage.

*Avalon.* Dir., Barry Levinson. With Armin Mueller-Stahl, Joan Plowright. 1990.
*I Know Why the Caged Bird Sings.* Dir., Fielder Cook. With Diahann Carroll and Esther Rolle. (Adapted from Maya Angelou's book and screenplay), 1975.
*Mr. and Mrs. Bridge.* Dir., James Ivory. With Paul Newman, Joanne Woodward. 1990.
*Prince of Tides.* Dir., Barbra Streisand. With Nick Nolte, Barbra Streisand. 1991.

*CHAPTER TWO*

# *Relationships*

65

Chapter Two:
Relationships

*Related by blood, we're separated by class, my father and I. Being the white-collar son of a blue-collar man means being the hinge on a door between two ways of life.*
                                        —Alfred Lubrano, "Bricklayer's Boy"

*A girl must brood upon her mother's life. Everything she comes to think about the mother and the act of mothering, everything she knows and senses about the institution of mothering and the particular experience of it her own mother has known bears an immediate and urgent relevance to herself.*
                                        —Kim Chernin, *The Hungry Self*

*I*ntertwined with memories about childhood, family, and home are the relationships among the people who make up the family. A child is born into a family with certain relationships already established; the child's arrival affects family members both within the immediate or "nuclear" family, and in the extended family system. Bonds are established, developed, broken, sometimes renewed, throughout life. The kinds of relationships that develop both result from and contribute to an individual's growth and identity. Inevitably, tensions arise as an individual strives to grow and assert his or her individuality within the family; family ties can foster the development process, while at times they can also make the move into maturity difficult. Nevertheless, the strongest bonds people form in life are often forged in family relationships.

Consciously or unconsciously, the ways in which family members develop their relationships with each other influence the way they form bonds with people outside the family. Parent-child relationships in particular affect a child's lifelong physical and emotional development; the patterns of relating to others formed within the family constellation hold throughout life, sometimes for good, and sometimes for ill—as with cycles of domestic violence, in which children grow up, have children, and then treat their children as they have been treated, perpetuating a chain of abuse. Sibling relationships also contribute significantly to an individual's growth and identity; a child's negotiations, trials, ups and downs with sisters and brothers forecast the ways in which an adult will function within the greater community outside the family.

We present the readings on relationships early in the text because interpersonal family relationships are so integral to understanding how we move from individual identity to membership in a family and ultimately in a community. The readings in this chapter explore a range of concerns while focusing on parent-child and sibling issues. In our first selection, "The Rocking-Horse Winner," D. H. Lawrence writes of a family in which the children, particularly the young son, sense the "whispers" of the house—the family's unspoken fears and needs. Drawing from Lawrence's story, social scientist Susanne Newby Short, in her essay "The Whispering of the Walls," explores the same subject— the damaging, unspoken whispers and "silent facts" in a family. In the memoir "Bricklayer's Boy," Alfred Lubrano contrasts his father's blue-collar world on the "outside" of college and corporate buildings with his own life within them.

Siblings, rather than parents and children, are the focus in the next four readings. The short story "Raymond's Run" by Toni Cade Bambara takes us into the world of a young African-American who experiences a conflict between her dedication to running and her responsibility for her younger brother. Jeremy Seabrook's memoir "A Twin Is Only Half a Person" illustrates some of the difficulties in the twin relationship, while the brothers in "Discarded" by David Sherwood take on different roles in the family because of their different sexual orientations. Sibling relationships often generate tensions and mixed feelings that can stay with us a lifetime. Marie Howe's poem "Letter to My Sister" explores such feelings in the context of later, "singular lives." The chapter concludes with a student essay by Klarice Tsing, "The Violin," that reflects on the ways in which family disagreement over the seemingly minor issue of music lessons can underscore serious differences within a family.

As you read through these selections, reflect on the ways in which relationships with various family members have helped to shape, and continue to shape, who you are and how you relate to others. Consider as well the degree to which members of your extended family may have influenced your passage into adulthood. If we can come to understand our bonds and boundaries, our connections and histories, perhaps we can develop and enrich our relationships in the other communities to which we belong.

**D. H. LAWRENCE: "The Rocking-Horse Winner"**   David Herbert (D. H.) Lawrence (1885–1930), well-known British novelist, essayist, and poet, was born in Nottinghamshire, England. The son of a coal miner and a school-teacher, Lawrence attended University College in Nottingham, taught school from 1908 to 1911, and went on to become a prolific writer of novels, short stories, plays, poetry, letters, and translations. His work dealt with themes of instinct and emotion contrasted with the sterile, dehumanizing rationality and materialism he found in modern society. Lawrence's major novels include *Sons and Lovers* (1913), *The Rainbow* (1915), *Women in Love* (1920), and *Lady Chatterly's Lover* (1928). As you read the following story, "The Rocking-Horse Winner" (1934), notice how Lawrence explores the impact of growing up in a home dominated by economic concerns, as opposed to emotional needs, through showing the gradual deterioration of an emotionally deprived, anxious young boy.

D. H. LAWRENCE

# The Rocking-Horse Winner

*like a fairy tale*

There was a woman who was beautiful, who started with all the advantages, yet she had no luck. She married for love, and the love turned to dust. She had bonny children, yet she felt they had been thrust upon her, and she could not love them. They looked at her coldly, as if they were finding fault with her. And hurriedly she felt she must cover up some fault in herself. Yet what it was that she must cover up she never knew. Nevertheless, when her children were present, she always felt the center of her heart go hard. This troubled her, and in her manner she was all the more gentle and anxious for her children, as if she loved them very much. Only she herself knew that at the center of her heart was a hard little place that could not feel love, no, not for anybody. Everybody else said of her: "She is such a good mother. She adores her children." Only she herself, and her children themselves, knew it was not so. They read it in each other's eyes.

There were a boy and two little girls. They lived in a pleasant house, with a garden, and they had discreet servants, and felt themselves superior to anyone in the neighborhood.

68

Although they lived in style, they felt always an anxiety in the house. There was never enough money. The mother had a small income, and the father had a small income, but not nearly enough for the social position which they had to keep up. The father went into town to some office. But though he had good prospects, these prospects never materialized. There was always the grinding sense of the shortage of money, though the style was always kept up.

At last the mother said: "I will see if *I* can't make something." But she did not know where to begin. She racked her brains, and tried this thing and the other, but could not find anything successful. The failure made deep lines come into her face. Her children were growing up, they would have to go to school. There must be more money, there must be more money. The father, who was always very handsome and expensive in his tastes, seemed as if he never *would* be able to do anything worth doing. And the mother, who had a great belief in herself, did not succeed any better, and her tastes were just as expensive.

And so the house came to be haunted by the unspoken phrase: *There must be more money! There must be more money!* The children could hear it all the time though nobody said it aloud. They heard it at Christmas, when the expensive and splendid toys filled the nursery. Behind the shining modern rocking horse, behind the smart doll's house, a voice would start whispering: "There *must* be more money! There *must* be more money!" And the children would stop playing, to listen for a moment. They would look into each other's eyes, to see if they had all heard. And each one saw in the eyes of the other two that they too had heard. "There *must* be more money! There *must* be more money!"

It came whispering from the springs of the still-swaying rocking horse, and even the horse, bending his wooden, champing head, heard it. The big doll, sitting so pink and smirking in her new pram, could hear it quite plainly, and seemed to be smirking all the more self-consciously because of it. The foolish puppy, too, that took the place of the teddy bear, he was looking so extraordinarily foolish for no other reason but that he heard the secret whisper all over the house: "There *must* be more money!"

Yet nobody ever said it aloud. The whisper was everywhere, and therefore no one spoke it. Just as no one ever says: "We are breathing!" in spite of the fact that breath is coming and going all the time.

"Mother," said the boy Paul one day, "why don't we keep a car of our own? Why do we always use Uncle's, or else a taxi?"

"Because we're the poor members of the family," said the mother.

"But why *are* we, Mother?"

"Well—I suppose," she said slowly and bitterly, "it's because your father has no luck."

The boy was silent for some time.

"Is luck money, Mother?" he asked rather timidly.

"No, Paul. Not quite. It's what causes you to have money."

"Oh!" said Paul vaguely. "I thought when Uncle Oscar said *filthy lucker,* it meant money."

"*Filthy lucre* does mean money," said the mother. "But it's lucre, not luck."

"Oh!" said the boy. "Then what *is* luck, Mother?"

"It's what causes you to have money. If you're lucky you have money. That's why it's better to be born lucky than rich. If you're rich, you may lose your money. But if you're lucky, you will always get more money."

"Oh! Will you? And is Father not lucky?"

"Very unlucky, I should say," she said bitterly.

The boy watched her with unsure eyes.

"Why?" he asked.

"I don't know. Nobody ever knows why one person is lucky and another unlucky."

"Don't they? Nobody at all? Does *nobody* know?"

"Perhaps God. But He never tells."

"He ought to, then. And aren't you lucky either, Mother?"

"I can't be, if I married an unlucky husband."

"But by yourself, aren't you?"

"I used to think I was, before I married. Now I think I am very unlucky indeed."

"Why?"

"Well—never mind! Perhaps I'm not really," she said.

The child looked at her, to see if she meant it. But he saw, by the lines of her mouth, that she was only trying to hide something from him.

"Well, anyhow," he said stoutly, "I'm a lucky person."

"Why?" said his mother, with a sudden laugh.

He stared at her. He didn't even know why he had said it.

"God told me," he asserted, brazening it out.

"I hope He did, dear!" she said, again with a laugh, but rather bitter.

"He did, Mother!"

"Excellent!" said the mother.

The boy saw she did not believe him; or, rather, that she paid no attention to his assertion. This angered him somewhat, and made him want to compel her attention.

He went off by himself, vaguely, in a childish way, seeking for the clue to "luck." Absorbed, taking no heed of other people, he went about with a sort of stealth, seeking inwardly for luck. He wanted luck, he wanted it, he wanted it. When the two girls were playing dolls in the nursery, he would sit on his big rocking horse, charging madly into space, with a frenzy that made the little girls peer at him uneasily. Wildly the horse careered, the waving dark hair of the boy tossed, his eyes had a strange glare in them. The little girls dared not speak to him.

When he had ridden to the end of his mad little journey, he climbed down and stood in front of his rocking horse, staring fixedly into its lowered face. Its red mouth was slightly open, its big eye was wide and glassy-bright.

Now! he would silently command the snorting steed. Now, take me to where there is luck! Now take me!

And he would slash the horse on the neck with the little whip he had asked Uncle Oscar for. He *knew* the horse could take him to where there was luck, if only he forced it. So he would mount again, and start on his furious ride, hoping at last to get there. He knew he could get there.

"You'll break your horse, Paul!" said the nurse.

"He's always riding like that! I wish he'd leave off!" said his elder sister Joan.

But he only glared down on them in silence. Nurse gave him up. She could make nothing of him. Anyhow he was growing beyond her.

One day his mother and his uncle Oscar came in when he was on one of his furious rides. He did not speak to them.

"Hallo, you young jockey! Riding a winner?" said his uncle.

"Aren't you growing too big for a rocking horse? You're not a very little boy any longer, you know," said his mother.

But Paul only gave a blue glare from his big, rather close-set eyes. He would speak to nobody when he was in full tilt. His mother watched him with an anxious expression on her face.

At last he suddenly stopped forcing his horse into the mechanical gallop, and slid down.

"Well, I got there!" he announced fiercely, his blue eyes still flaring, and his sturdy long legs straddling apart.

"Where did you get to?" asked his mother.

"Where I wanted to go," he flared back at her.

"That's right, son!" said Uncle Oscar. "Don't you stop till you get there. What's the horse's name?"

"He doesn't have a name," said the boy.

"Gets on without all right?" asked the uncle.

"Well, he has different names. He was called Sansovino last week."

"Sansovino, eh? Won the Ascot. How did you know his name?"

"He always talks about horse races with Bassett," said Joan.

The uncle was delighted to find that his small nephew was posted with all the racing news. Bassett, the young gardener, who had been wounded in the left foot in the war and had got his present job through Oscar Cresswell, whose batman he had been, was a perfect blade of the "turf." He lived in the racing events, and the small boy lived with him.

Oscar Cresswell got it all from Bassett.

"Master Paul comes and asks me, so I can't do more than tell him, sir," said Bassett, his face terribly serious, as if he were speaking of religious matters.

"And does he ever put anything on a horse he fancies?"

"Well—I don't want to give him away—he's a young sport, a fine sport, sir. Would you mind asking him himself? He sort of takes a pleasure in it, and perhaps he'd feel I was giving him away, sir, if you don't mind."

Bassett was serious as a church.

The uncle went back to his nephew and took him off for a ride in the car.

71

"Say, Paul, old man, do you ever put anything on a horse?" the uncle asked.

The boy watched the handsome man closely.

"Why, do you think I oughtn't to?" he parried.

"Not a bit of it! I thought perhaps you might give me a tip for the Lincoln."

The car sped on into the country, going down to Uncle Oscar's place in Hampshire.

"Honor bright?" said the nephew.

"Honor bright, son!" said the uncle.

"Well, then, Daffodil."

"Daffodil! I doubt it, sonny. What about Mirza?"

"I only know the winner," said the boy. "That's Daffodil."

"Daffodil, eh?"

There was a pause. Daffodil was an obscure horse comparatively.

"Uncle!"

"Yes, son?"

"You won't let it go any further, will you? I promised Bassett."

"Bassett be damned, old man! What's he got to do with it?"

"We're partners. We've been partners from the first. Uncle, he lent me my first five shillings, which I lost. I promised him, honor bright, it was only between me and him; only you gave me that ten-shilling note I started winning with, so I thought you were lucky. You won't let it go any further, will you?"

The boy gazed at his uncle from those big, hot, blue eyes, set rather close together. The uncle stirred and laughed uneasily.

"Right you are, son! I'll keep your tip private. Daffodil, eh? How much are you putting on him?"

"All except twenty pounds," said the boy. "I keep that in reserve."

The uncle thought it a good joke.

"You keep twenty pounds in reserve, do you, you young romancer? What are you betting, then?"

"I'm betting three hundred," said the boy gravely. "But it's between you and me, Uncle Oscar! Honor bright?"

The uncle burst into a roar of laughter.

"It's between you and me all right, you young Nat Gould,"[1] he said, laughing. "But where's your three hundred?"

"Bassett keeps it for me. We're partners."

"You are, are you! And what is Bassett putting on Daffodil?"

"He won't go quite as high as I do, I expect. Perhaps he'll go a hundred and fifty."

"What, pennies?" laughed the uncle.

"Pounds," said the child, with a surprised look at his uncle. "Bassett keeps a bigger reserve than I do."

Between wonder and amusement Uncle Oscar was silent. He pur-

---

[1]Nathaniel Gould (1857-1919), British novelist and sports columnist known for a series of novels about horse racing.

sued the matter no further, but he determined to take his nephew with him to the Lincoln races.

"Now, son," he said, "I'm putting twenty on Mirza, and I'll put five for you on any horse you fancy. What's your pick?"

"Daffodil, Uncle."

"No, not the fiver on Daffodil!"

"I should if it was my own fiver," said the child.

"Good! Good! Right you are! A fiver for me and a fiver for you on Daffodil."

The child had never been to a race meeting before, and his eyes were blue fire. He pursed his mouth tight, and watched. A Frenchman just in front had put his money on Lancelot. Wild with excitement, he flailed his arms up and down, yelling *"Lancelot! Lancelot!"* in his French accent.

Daffodil came in first, Lancelot second, Mirza third. The child, flushed and with eyes blazing, was curiously serene. His uncle brought him four five-pound notes, four to one.

"What am I to do with these?" he cried, waving them before the boy's eyes.

"I suppose we'll talk to Bassett," said the boy. "I expect I have fifteen hundred now; and twenty in reserve; and this twenty."

His uncle studied him for some moments.

"Look here, son!" he said. "You're not serious about Bassett and that fifteen hundred, are you?"

"Yes I am. But it's between you and me, Uncle. Honor bright!"

"Honor bright all right, son! But I must talk to Bassett."

"If you'd like to be a partner, Uncle, with Bassett and me, we could all be partners. Only, you'd have to promise, honor bright, Uncle, not to let it go beyond us three. Bassett and I are lucky, and you must be lucky, because it was your ten shillings I started winning with. . . ."

Uncle Oscar took both Bassett and Paul into Richmond Park for an afternoon, and there they talked.

"It's like this, you see, sir," Bassett said. "Master Paul would get me talking about racing events, spinning yarns, you know, sir. And he was always keen on knowing if I'd made or if I'd lost. It's about a year since, now, that I put five shillings on Blush of Dawn for him—and we lost. The the luck turned, with that ten shillings he had from you, that we put on Singhalese. And since then, it's been pretty steady, all things considering. What do you say, Master Paul?"

"We're all right when we're sure," said Paul. "It's when we're not quite sure that we go down."

"Oh, but we're careful then," said Bassett.

"But when are you *sure*?" Uncle Oscar smiled.

"It's Master Paul, sir," said Bassett, in a secret, religious voice. "It's as if he had it from heaven. Like Daffodil, now, for the Lincoln. That was as sure as eggs."

"Did you put anything on Daffodil?" asked Oscar Cresswell.

"Yes, sir. I made my bit."

"And my nephew?"

Bassett was obstinately silent, looking at Paul.

"I made twelve hundred, didn't I, Bassett? I told Uncle I was putting three hundred on Daffodil."

"That's right," said Bassett, nodding.

"But where's the money?" asked the uncle.

"I keep it safe locked up, sir. Master Paul he can have it any minute he likes to ask for it."

"What, fifteen hundred pounds?"

"And twenty! And *forty*, that is, with the twenty he made on the course."

"It's amazing!" said the uncle.

"If Master Paul offers you to be partners, sir, I would, if I were you; if you'll excuse me," said Bassett.

Oscar Cresswell thought about it.

"I'll see the money," he said.

They drove home again, and sure enough, Bassett came round to the garden house with fifteen hundred pounds in notes. The twenty pounds reserve was left with Joe Glee, in the Turf Commission deposit.

"You see, it's all right, Uncle, when I'm *sure!* Then we go strong, for all we're worth. Don't we, Bassett?"

"We do that, Master Paul."

"And when are you sure?" said the uncle, laughing.

"Oh, well, sometimes I'm *absolutely* sure, like about Daffodil," said the boy; "and sometimes I have an idea; and sometimes I haven't even an idea, have I, Bassett? Then we're careful, because we mostly go down."

"You do, do you! And when you're sure, like about Daffodil, what makes you sure, sonny?"

"Oh, well, I don't know," said the boy uneasily. "I'm sure, you know, Uncle; that's all."

"It's as if he had it from heaven, sir," Bassett reiterated.

"I should say so!" said the uncle.

But he became a partner. And when the Leger was coming on, Paul was "sure" about Lively Spark, which was a quite inconsiderable horse. The boy insisted on putting a thousand on the horse, Bassett went for five hundred, and Oscar Cresswell two hundred. Lively Spark came in first, and the betting had been ten to one against him. Paul had made ten thousand.

"You see," he said, "I was absolutely sure of him."

Even Oscar Cresswell had cleared two thousand.

"Look here, son," he said, "this sort of thing makes me nervous."

"It needn't, Uncle! Perhaps I shan't be sure again for a long time."

"But what are you going to do with your money?" asked the uncle.

"Of course," said the boy, "I started it for Mother. She said she had no luck, because Father is unlucky, so I thought if I was lucky, it might stop whispering."

74

"What might stop whispering?"

"Our house. I _hate_ our house for whispering."

"What does it whisper?"

"Why—why"—the boy fidgeted—"why, I don't know. But it's always short of money, you know, Uncle."

"I know it, son, I know it."

"You know people send Mother writs, don't you, Uncle?"

"I'm afraid I do," said the uncle.

"And then the house whispers, like people laughing at you behind your back. It's awful, that is! I thought if I was lucky. . . ."

"You might stop it," added the uncle.

The boy watched him with big blue eyes, that had an uncanny cold fire in them, and he said never a word.

"Well, then!" said the uncle. "What are we doing?"

"I shouldn't like Mother to know I was lucky," said the boy.

"Why not, son?"

"She'd stop me."

"I don't think she would."

"Oh!"—and the boy writhed in an odd way—"I _don't_ want her to know, Uncle."

"All right, son! We'll manage it without her knowing."

They managed it very easily. Paul, at the other's suggestion, handed over five thousand pounds to his uncle, who deposited it with the family lawyer, who was then to inform Paul's mother that a relative had put five thousand pounds into his hands, which sum was to be paid out a thousand pounds at a time, on the mother's birthday, for the next five years.

"So she'll have a birthday present of a thousand pounds for five successive years," said Uncle Oscar. "I hope it won't make it all the harder for her later."

Paul's mother had her birthday in November. The house had been "whispering" worse than ever lately, and, even in spite of his luck, Paul could not bear up against it. He was very anxious to see the effect of the birthday letter, telling his mother about the thousand pounds.

When there were no visitors, Paul now took his meals with his parents, as he was beyond the nursery control. His mother went into town nearly every day. She had discovered that she had an odd knack of sketching furs and dress materials, so she worked secretly in the studio of a friend who was the chief artist for the leading drapers. She drew the figures of ladies in furs and ladies in silk and sequins for the newspaper advertisements. This young woman artist earned several thousand pounds a year, but Paul's mother only made several hundreds, and she was again dissatisfied. She so wanted to be first in something, and she did not succeed, even in making sketches for drapery advertisements.

She was down to breakfast on the morning of her birthday. Paul watched her face as she read her letters. He knew the lawyer's letter. As

Chapter Two: Relationships

his mother read it, her face hardened and became more expressionless. Then a cold, determined look came on her mouth. She hid the letter under the pile of others, and said not a word about it.

"Didn't you have anything nice in the post for your birthday, Mother?" said Paul.

"Quite moderately nice," she said, her voice cold and absent.

She went away to town without saying more.

But in the afternoon Uncle Oscar appeared. He said Paul's mother had had a long interview with the lawyer, asking if the whole five thousand could not be advanced at once, as she was in debt.

"What do you think, Uncle?" said the boy.

"I leave it to you, son."

"Oh, let her have it, then! We can get some more with the other," said the boy.

"A bird in the hand is worth two in the bush, laddie!" said Uncle Oscar.

"But I'm sure to *know* for the Grand National; or the Lincolnshire; or else the Derby. I'm sure to know for *one* of them," said Paul.

So Uncle Oscar signed the agreement, and Paul's mother touched the whole five thousand. Then something very curious happened. The voices in the house suddenly went mad, like a chorus of frogs on a spring evening. There were certain new furnishings, and Paul had a tutor. He was *really* going to Eton, his father's school, in the following autumn. There were flowers in the winter, and a blossoming of the luxury Paul's mother had been used to. And yet the voices in the house, behind the sprays of mimosa and almond blossom, and from under the piles of iridescent cushions, simply trilled and screamed in a sort of ecstasy: "There *must* be more money! Oh-h-h; there *must* be more money. Oh, now, now-w! Now-w-w—there *must* be more money!—more than ever! More than ever!"

It frightened Paul terribly. He studied away at his Latin and Greek. But his intense hours were spent with Bassett. The Grand National had gone by; he had not "known," and had lost a hundred pounds. Summer was at hand. He was in agony for the Lincoln. But even for the Lincoln he didn't "know," and he lost fifty pounds. He became wild-eyed and strange, as if something were going to explode in him.

"Let it alone, son! Don't you bother about it!" urged Uncle Oscar. But it was as if the boy couldn't really hear what his uncle was saying.

"I've got to know for the Derby! I've got to know for the Derby!" the child reiterated, his big blue eyes blazing with a sort of madness.

His mother noticed how overwrought he was.

"You'd better go to the seaside. Wouldn't you like to go now to the seaside, instead of waiting? I think you'd better," she said, looking down at him anxiously, her heart curiously heavy because of him.

But the child lifted his uncanny blue eyes. "I couldn't possibly go before the Derby, Mother!" he said. "I couldn't possibly!"

"Why not?" she said, her voice becoming heavy when she was opposed. "Why not? You can still go from the seaside to see the Derby with your uncle Oscar, if that's what you wish. No need for you to wait here. Besides, I think you care too much about these races. It's a bad sign. My family has been a gambling family, and you won't know till you grow up how much damage it has done. But it has done damage. I shall have to send Bassett away, and ask Uncle Oscar not to talk racing to you, unless you promise to be reasonable about it; go away to the seaside and forget it. You're all nerves!"

"I'll do what you like, Mother, so long as you don't send me away till after the Derby," the boy said.

"Send you away from where? Just from this house?"

"Yes," he said, gazing at her.

"Why, you curious child, what makes you care about this house so much, suddenly? I never knew you loved it."

He gazed at her without speaking. He had a secret within a secret, something he had not divulged, even to Bassett or to his uncle Oscar.

But his mother, after standing undecided and a little bit sullen for some moments, said:

"Very well, then! Don't go to the seaside till after the Derby, if you don't wish it. But promise me you won't let your nerves go to pieces. Promise you won't think so much about horse racing and *events*, as you call them!"

"Oh, no," said the boy casually. "I won't think much about them, Mother. You needn't worry. I wouldn't worry, Mother, if I were you."

"If you were me and I were you," said his mother, "I wonder what we *should* do!"

"But you know you needn't worry, Mother, don't you?" the boy repeated.

"I should be awfully glad to know it," she said wearily.

"Oh, well you *can*, you know. I mean, you *ought* to know you needn't worry," he insisted.

"Ought I? Then I'll see about it," she said.

Paul's secret of secrets was his wooden horse, that which had no *(Biblical)* name. Since he was emancipated from a nurse and a nursery governess, he had had his rocking horse removed to his own bedroom at the top of the house.

"Surely, you're too big for a rocking horse!" his mother had remonstrated.

"Well, you see, Mother, till I can have a *real* horse, I like to have *some* sort of animal about," had been his quaint answer.

"Do you feel he keeps you company?" She laughed.

"Oh yes! He's very good, he always keeps me company, when I'm there," said Paul.

So the horse, rather shabby, stood in an arrested prance in the boy's bedroom.

The Derby was drawing near, and the boy grew more and more tense. He hardly heard what was spoken to him, he was very frail, and his eyes were really uncanny. His mother had sudden strange seizures of uneasiness about him. Sometimes, for half an hour, she would feel a sudden anxiety about him that was almost anguish. She wanted to rush to him at once, and know he was safe.

Two nights before the Derby, she was at a big party in town, when one of her rushes of anxiety about her boy, her firstborn, gripped her heart till she could hardly speak. She fought with the feeling, might and main, for she believed in common sense. But it was too strong. She had to leave the dance and go downstairs to telephone to the country. The children's nursery governess was terribly surprised and startled at being rung up in the night.

"Are the children all right, Miss Wilmot?"

"Oh, yes, they are quite all right."

"Master Paul? Is he all right?"

"He went to bed as right as a trivet. Shall I run up and look at him?"

"No," said Paul's mother reluctantly. "No! Don't trouble. It's all right. Don't sit up. We shall be home fairly soon." She did not want her son's privacy intruded upon.

"Very good," said the governess.

It was about one o'clock when Paul's mother and father drove up to their house. All was still. Paul's mother went to her room and slipped off her white fur cloak. She had told her maid not to wait up for her. She heard her husband downstairs, mixing a whisky and soda.

And then, because of the strange anxiety at her heart, she stole upstairs to her son's room. Noiselessly she went along the upper corridor. Was there a faint noise? What was it?

She stood, with arrested muscles, outside his door, listening. There was a strange, heavy, and yet not loud noise. Her heart stood still. It was a soundless noise, yet rushing and powerful. Something huge, in violent, hushed motion. What was it? What in God's name was it? She ought to know. She felt that she knew the noise. She knew what it was.

Yet she could not place it. She couldn't say what it was. And on and on it went, like a madness.

Softly, frozen with anxiety and fear, she turned the door handle.

The room was dark. Yet in the space near the window, she heard and saw something plunging to and fro. She gazed in fear and amazement.

Then suddenly she switched on the light, and saw her son, in his green pajamas, madly surging on the rocking horse. The blaze of light suddenly lit him up, as he urged the wooden horse, and lit her up, as she stood, blonde, in her dress of pale green and crystal, in the doorway.

"Paul!" she cried. "Whatever are you doing?"

"It's Malabar!" he screamed, in a powerful, strange voice. "It's Malabar!"

His eyes blazed at her for one strange and senseless second, as he ceased urging his wooden horse. Then he fell with a crash to the ground and she, all her tormented motherhood flooding upon her, rushed to gather him up.

But he was unconscious, and unconscious he remained, with some brain fever. He talked and tossed, and his mother sat stonily by his side.

"Malabar! It's Malabar! Bassett, Bassett, I *know!* It's Malabar!"

So the child cried, trying to get up and urge the rocking horse that gave him his inspiration.

"What does he mean by Malabar?" asked the heart-frozen mother.

"I don't know," said the father stonily.

"What does he mean by Malabar?" she asked her brother Oscar.

"It's one of the horses running for the Derby," was the answer.

And, in spite of himself, Oscar Cresswell spoke to Bassett, and himself put a thousand on Malabar: at fourteen to one.

The third day of the illness was critical: they were waiting for a change. The boy, with his rather long, curly hair, was tossing ceaselessly on the pillow. He never slept nor regained consciousness, and his eyes were like blue stones. His mother sat, feeling her heart had gone, turned actually into a stone.

In the evening, Oscar Cresswell did not come, but Bassett sent a message, saying could he come up for one moment, just one moment? Paul's mother was very angry at the intrusion, but on second thought she agreed. The boy was the same. Perhaps Bassett might bring him to consciousness.

The gardener, a shortish fellow with a little brown mustache, and sharp little brown eyes, tiptoed into the room, touched his imaginary cap to Paul's mother, and stole to the bedside, staring with glittering, smallish eyes at the tossing, dying child.

"Master Paul!" he whispered. "Master Paul! Malabar came in first all right, a clean win. I did as you told me. You've made over seventy thousand pounds, you have; you've got over eighty thousand. Malabar came in all right, Master Paul."

"Malabar! Malabar! Did I say Malabar, Mother? Did I say Malabar? Do you think I'm lucky, Mother? I knew Malabar, didn't I? Over eighty thousand pounds! I call that lucky, don't you, Mother? Over eighty thousand pounds! I knew, didn't I know I knew? Malabar came in all right. If I ride my horse till I'm sure, then I tell you, Bassett, you can go as high as you like. Did you go for all you were worth, Bassett?"

"I went a thousand on it, Master Paul."

"I never told you, Mother, that if I can ride my horse, and *get there,* then I'm absolutely sure—oh, absolutely! Mother, did I ever tell you? I *am* lucky!"

"No, you never did," said the mother.

But the boy died in the night.

And even as he lay dead, his mother heard her brother's voice saying to her: "My God, Hester, you're eighty-odd thousand to the good, and a poor devil of a son to the bad. But, poor devil, poor devil, he's best gone out of a life where he rides his rocking horse to find a winner."

*Looking at Ideas:*

1. What do Paul's mother and father value? How would you characterize their relationship? How do their values influence Paul?

2. How does the whispering change as the story progresses? What is the significance of these changes?

3. In what ways do the adults in the story contribute to the whispering of the house? Why couldn't, or wouldn't, they help Paul confront the whispering?

4. What are the values of the uncle and the gardener? How do their values influence Paul?

5. Examine the theme of luck in the story. Why are luck and gambling emphasized? How do these concepts dominate Paul's family?

*Looking at Strategies:*

1. Examine Lawrence's imagery, particularly of fire, cold, and stone. How do these images underscore Lawrence's themes? What other stylistic devices does the writer use?

2. What writing techniques does Lawrence use to reveal character? Select a character or scene to analyze and discuss.

3. Discuss the symbol of the rocking horse. From what does the rocking horse derive its powers? What are its limits? Why does it ultimately fail Paul?

*Looking at Connections:*

1. Contrast the fictional treatment of the whispering house with Susanne Newby Short's expository essay on the subject, which appears next in this chapter. Consider thematic development, narrative technique, voice, style, and imagery. Which piece of writing is more persuasive about the damage of "whispering walls" to children? Support your answer with examples from the text.

2. Compare the whispering Paul heard in this story with the whispers that Andy might have heard about himself in David Sherwood's memoir "Discarded," also in this chapter.

*Suggestions for Writing:*

1. Write an essay in which you explore the awareness you had as a child of problems within your family. You might consider the economic concerns discussed in your journal entry. What conclusions can you draw from your experiences? Do you think that parents should discuss such problems openly with their children? Or should young people be shielded from the harsher realities of adult life?

2. In what ways do children try either to solve a family problem on their own or to ignore or defuse it? Write an essay in which you develop several examples from your experience or observations to support your points.

3. Write an essay in which you compare and contrast the unspoken messages in the parent-child relationship expressed in this story with those discussed in another chapter reading, such as "A Twin Is Only Half a Person" or "Discarded."

**SUSANNE NEWBY SHORT: "The Whispering of the Walls"** Susanne Newby
Short, an analyst who follows the approach and views of C. G. Jung, originally
published this essay as part of a larger piece in *Psychological Perspectives*
(1989) in an issue of that journal devoted to the child. The essay also appeared
in *Reclaiming the Inner Child,* a volume edited by Jeremiah Abrams and also
published in 1989. As you read the essay, think about whether it would appeal
to a general audience as well as to a specialized audience of social scientists.

SUSANNE NEWBY SHORT

# The Whispering of the Walls

"The whispering of the walls" comes from a story by D. H. Lawrence.
It refers to what is unspoken in the family, particularly what is palpable
but unarticulated in the lives of the parents, and how it affects the
child. Jung felt that "nothing influences children more than the silent
facts in the background" of the home. One of the silent facts was the
"unlived life of the parents," as he called it: the part of life affected by
circumstance that had prevented the parents from pursuing their own
fulfillment, or the part of life they had shirked, either consciously or
unconsciously. Another was the denial of their own needs for love or
power. He especially thought that parents' troubles in love relationships
had a great effect on how children were able to negotiate their own love
lives. And the final silent fact was the parents' quiet expectation that the
child fulfill their narcissistic needs. In other words, in one way or another, the child is forced to live out the shadow side of the parents.

These subtle forms of cruelty often pass for good parenting and
hardly give us a clue to what has gone wrong in the psychic development of the child. Lawrence's short story, "The Rocking-Horse Winner," illustrates this subtle wounding. It is a story analysts might well
hear in their consulting rooms:

And so the house came to be haunted by the unspoken phrase: *There
must be more money! There must be more money!* The children could hear
it all the time, though nobody said it aloud. They heard it at Christmas,
when the expensive and splendid toys filled the nursery. Behind the

shining modern rocking horse, a voice would start whispering: There *must* be more money! There *must* be more money! And the children would stop playing, to listen for a moment. They would look into each other's eyes, to see if they had all heard. . . . There *must* be more money! There *must* be more money! . . .

Yet nobody ever said it aloud. The whisper was everywhere, and therefore no one spoke it.

The story focuses on the boy, Paul, who goes mad trying to make his mother happy so that she will be free to love him. Paul thinks that if he can just get enough money for his mother, she will be happy. (It is not uncommon for children to resort to magical thinking when they cannot understand what is going on in the world around them.) With the help of the family gardener who bets on race horses, Paul begins to win money by knowing which horse will win a race. The gardener tells him the names of the horses in a race; Paul gets on his rocking horse and rides until the right name comes to him—by riding himself into a trance, he eventually gets the name of the horse from the unconscious; the gardener puts a bet on the horse and they both make money. All of this takes place in secret. The boy then gives the money to his uncle to give to his mother anonymously. But no matter how much money Paul gives her, it is never enough. Finally, he exhausts himself riding his horse, becomes ill and dies, but not before winning for his mother the last amount of 80,000 pounds. In one of the final lines in the story, Paul's uncle says to the mother, "You are 80,000 pounds to the good and a poor son to the bad."

Many children sacrifice themselves to their parents' needs. They kill themselves trying to make their parents happy and trying to live up to their parents' and society's expectations of them. As Jung has said, they live the unlived life of the parents rather than their own, and they don't even know they are doing it. In the past few years we have all become aware of the increasing child and adolescent suicide rate in the affluent suburbs of our cities. Suicidal children are typically superachievers. The youngest I have heard of was 10 years old. Many school systems now teach a suicide prevention course. Such young people come to analysis depressed and cut off from their own feelings, without any notion of who they are. Usually the one feeling available to them is a sense of emptiness, or what Jungians would call a "hopeless loss of soul." They feel emotionally abandoned, as if they are nothing more than a product of parents' and society's expectations, as I have said.

In order to understand your own childhood, it is important to know what the house whispered when you were a child, or what it continues to whisper. It can whisper, *There's not enough money.* (In America's imperial cities where money is abundant, this is an often-heard whisper, even among the rich.) The house can whisper, *There's no one in charge here.* Or, *You're not good enough, you're not as pretty as your sister, you're not as smart as your brother, you'll never amount to anything, you must distinguish yourself or have a worthy career.* Or, *It's not perfect enough,*

82

*what you are doing is not good enough for someone as gifted as you are, you really could do better* (a comment which makes any child's giftedness a curse).

One of the natural jobs of childhood is to develop an ego. When you are a child and following this natural path, it is tragic to hear in the silence that something is wrong with you or that something vaguely sensed is expected of you. T. S. Eliot has said: "It is the conversation not overheard, not intended to be heard, with the sidewise looks, that brings death to the heart of a child." "These are the things that hang in the air," Jung wrote, "and are vaguely felt by the child, the oppressive atmosphere of foreboding, that seeps into the child's soul like a poisonous vapor . . . through the thickest walls of silence, through the whitened sepulcher of deceit, complacency, and evasion."

Even though unspoken, the messages are heard in the psyche of the child as clearly as any spoken word. In fact, the more hidden something is, the more powerful it becomes. The unspoken word is insidious and harmful and can drive one to madness, because there is no evidence of what is really happening. (Analysts often hear patients say of their childhoods, "There was absolutely no evidence for what I was experiencing.") The spoken word wounds and angers, causes children either to rebel or capitulate, but it is the whisper of the house that drives them to neurosis because they are never sure where it comes from, who says it, or what exactly it means. Whispered messages come out of the woodwork, so to speak, to eat away at the child's confidence, sense of well-being, and sense of being loved. Instead of being a safe, secure place for the child, the home then becomes a container that does not contain, a container that does not reflect back to the child who he is or what she feels. According to Jung, the child picks up only the unresolved conflicts of the parents.

A child needs to have its mysterious feelings made conscious, to hear someone confirm that the unspoken message is, in fact, true. If someone had said to Paul, "It sounds as if the walls are whispering. . . . What is really happening is that your mother isn't happy because she can never be satisfied with what she has. . . . But your parents don't talk about this, so you feel you have to do something to make her happy and therefore free her to love you"—then Paul would have known what the real suffering was: that his mother could not love him no matter what he did or how he tried. *His* suffering, then, would have been legitimated and it would not have made him sick.

Jung says that neurosis is the avoidance of legitimate suffering. By *suffering* here I mean conscious suffering. It seems odd to be in favor of a child suffering, but, paradoxically, conscious legitimate suffering is what saves a child. When a child is not allowed to experience feelings of sadness, anger, loss, and frustration, his or her real feelings become neurotic and distorted; in adulthood, that child will unconsciously arrange life to repeat these same repressions of feeling. Child psychologist Bruno Bettelheim laments that children are not being allowed legitimate suffering. He states that even the books children read in school show life as nothing but a succession of pleasures. Nobody is really angry, nobody truly suffers, there are no real emotions. Bettelheim is recognizing the same problem Jung has described.

Paul's mother avoided legitimate suffering. If she had been able to talk with someone and say, "I love my children, but when I'm with them my heart goes hard, and I think I should cover up some fault in myself," she would have come to understand the underlying problem. Not only did she need to speak about her experience, she needed to know what her real suffering was. When a child seeks love, attention, or confirmation from an unloving parent, we know that that is what the parent also needs: Paul's mother sought the same thing he did—love and attention—which apparently she had never gotten.

How can we hope to extricate ourselves from this morass? It may seem as if our lives are very determined and restricted by the potency of the family's influence. But does a child's fate lie totally within the boundaries of the family?

Jung's statement in 1928 that "parents should always be conscious of the fact that they themselves are the principal cause of neurosis in their children" is very disquieting. His notion that "the things which have the most powerful effect on children don't necessarily come from the conscious state of the parents but from their unconscious background" is frightening because we can control our conscious lives more or less, but the unconscious is uncontrollable. It is important to recognize that although Jung's view here is true to some extent, it ignores the fact that the *child* has a nature of his or her own, which may or may not include a predisposition to embody the neurosis of the family. There is a fascinating body of psychological research based on the work of Manfred Bleuler, whose 30-year investigation of the *healthy* children of *schizophrenic* parents illustrates this point. The role of the child's own personality in the generation of his or her psychology and fate as the symptom-bearer in the family must not be overlooked. Psychological difficulties are ultimately the result of both family dynamics and the child's unique constitutional variables. We have learned since 1928 that a child is an individual, and that the theory of parent-child fusion can be overdone. In fact, even Jung softened his views over the years.

The child, no matter how young, is a person in his or her own right—not a blank slate, a *tabula rasa,* for adults to "write on," as some philosophers have thought. Certainly, a very small infant is a person in formation, but he or she is nonetheless an individual.

A child brings something special and unique to the context of the relationship with parents. When children are born a part of what they will become is born in them; they have within them the "raw materials" they will need to grow and mature. They will unfold not only physically but psychically as well. The adults' task is not to violate the essence of the child but to trust what is within the child. Gertrude Stein once said that it wasn't what Paris gave you, but what it didn't take away. This holds true for children. The issue is not so much what parents give to them as what they *don't take away*. We can apply this idea to ourselves: we need to understand what we have been allowed to keep, what was not taken away from us, and what was taken away so that we can replace it. Jung said: "If parents because of their own insecurity cannot accept sufficiently the basic nature of the child, then its personality becomes damaged. If it is beyond the normal bruising of life the child becomes estranged from his center of being and feels forced to abandon his natural pattern of unfoldment."

How is this natural pattern of unfoldment facilitated? We know of the importance of mirroring: when there is a significant person in a child's world who is well trusted or well loved and who can interpret to the child what the child is experiencing, then that child will experience his or her reality as a true reality. To prevent the walls from whispering, the adult must speak out the whispers. A child feels what he or she feels, but the language and conceptual equipment to interpret these feelings are not fully developed. Ideally, the job of the responsible adult who is equipped with rational thinking processes and undistorted perception is to observe and reflect what the child is feeling.

Mirroring is self-affirming and reveals to the child who he/she is and what he/she is becoming. It is important to distinguish between *praise* and *mirroring*. Praise tends to be evaluative; it implies judgment, and can create the need for constant reassurance. Mirroring, however, affirms the *self*. For example, if I praise you, I am telling you what I feel or think about you. If I *mirror* you, I am reflecting to you what *you* feel or think about *yourself*. If there is no verification of the child's own reality, the child can feel disoriented. Lack of verification creates the feeling of non-being. Then a child can feel that it is his or her own fault that something bad is happening.

Remember, for instance, the D. H. Lawrence story. What was so tragic was that the whispers were never concretized into speaking, into real communication within the family. They remained the whisperings of the walls. To undo the damage that such murmurings can cause we need to make real whatever is the message of the family.

Children need to have all of their true feelings confirmed and mirrored in order to develop faith in and allegiance to their own experiences. When a child realizes that her parents will never confirm what she senses, she gives up and develops a false persona that covers a very fragile foundation. If she is not allowed to be herself and experience her own feelings, then she will become someone else. This is true for most of us. We have become our mothers or our fathers or the fantasy of what the good little child is or what the bad little child is. Sometimes we hide ourselves so well that eventually even we no longer recognize our own disguises. Wearing these disguises, we stray far from our original connection to the self. Only in the discomfort of our depressions or anxieties are we forced to seek out a reconciliation. It is in the vague feeling of being "homesick even when we are at home" that we begin to search for answers in the dark caves of infancy.

Jung has said: "In the adult there lurks a child—an eternal child, something that is always becoming, is never completed, and that calls for increasing care, attention, and education. This is the part of the human personality that wishes to develop and become whole." Our highly developed ego-consciousness strongly resists this inner child. Such resistance makes the task of discovering the inner child a critical one. What are its qualities? Jung has several responses. The inner child is "something that existed not only in the past but exists now"; that "is not only a picture of certain forgotten things in childhood but a preconscious aspect of the collective psyche. . . . The idea of child is a means to express a psychic fact that cannot be formulated more exactly. . . . It is a system functioning to compensate a one-sidedness of conscious mind . . . consciousness needs compensating through the still existing state of childhood."

The part of our psyches that experiences distress and suffering is the part containing the inner child. Unless we make ourselves aware of this child within, we will sometimes behave unconsciously from that part of ourselves. Many of us have repressed or ignored childhood experiences and our inner child. When we are blinded in this way, we are limiting our consciousness and our ability to experience life. Unless we listen to the child within us, we are like parents who do not hear their own children.

## QUESTIONS

*Looking at Ideas:*

1. Short discusses what can be the devastating effects of "silent facts" on children. What are some of the silent facts described in the passage?
2. In Short's opinion, what are the short-term and long-term effects on a child of "the whispering of the walls"?
3. What is *mirroring* as discussed in the essay? What is the connection between mirroring and establishing a child's sense of reality? Why is this so important for a child's development?

*Looking at Strategies:*

1. Does Short's technique of drawing on literature to discuss psychological issues help to clarify key concepts? How does this approach differ from relying on case histories for examples? Which approach do you prefer, and why?
2. Does the author adequately explain her references to Jung and Bettelheim and to specific psychological terminology? Is the essay more suitable for a general or a specialized audience?
3. Is the term *suffering,* as it is used in the context of this essay, adequately explained? How does Short define the term? How does she support her definition?

*Looking at Connections:*

1. Are there any parallels between "whispering walls" and the conscious or unconscious attempts of parents to shape their children, as discussed

in Jeremy Seabrook's essay "A Twin Is Only Half a Person" later in this chapter?

*Suggestions for Writing:*

1. Write an essay comparing the fictional treatment of the unspoken word in "The Rocking-Horse Winner" with the expository approach in "The Whispering of the Walls." Which approach did you prefer, and why?

2. Do you think the metaphor of the inner child adequately helps explain or clarify how a person's inner world functions? Do you find Short's explanation of this concept convincing? Write an essay in which you explain your response. Use evidence and experiences to support your point of view.

3. Through reading and discussion, explore the concept of the inner child as a focus for psychological study and treatment. Interpret and evaluate your findings in the form of an expository essay.

**JOURNAL ENTRY**

Discuss a difference of opinion you have had with parents or other family members about what you should do with your life. How was the conflict resolved, if at all?

**ALFRED LUBRANO: "Bricklayer's Boy"**  Alfred Lubrano is a reporter for the *New York Newsday* as well as a contributor to *Gentleman's Quarterly*. He often writes on issues of personal relationships and family life. The following essay was first published in *Gentleman's Quarterly* in June, 1989. In his essay, Lubrano writes of his upbringing in a blue-collar household and of the values with which he grew up and by which his father, now a bricklayer foreman, still lives. As you read the essay, think about the contrasts Lubrano develops in terms of home life, values, views on family, on women, on work, on money. Consider, too, the vibrant images that convey Lubrano's feelings about his father and his early family life.

ALFRED LUBRANO

# *Bricklayer's Boy*

My father and I were college buddies back in the mid-1970s. While I was in class at Columbia, struggling with the esoterica du jour, he was on a bricklayer's scaffold not far up the street, working on a campus building.

Sometimes we'd hook up on the subway going home, he with his tools, I with my books. We didn't chat much about what went on during the day. My father wasn't interested in Dante, I wasn't up on arches. We'd share a *New York Post* and talk about the Mets.

My dad has built lots of places in New York City he can't get into: colleges, condos, office towers. He makes his living on the outside. Once the walls are up, a place takes on a different feel for him, as if he's not welcome anymore. It doesn't bother him, though. For my father, earning the dough that paid for my entrée into a fancy, bricked-in institution was satisfaction enough, a vicarious access.

We didn't know it then, but those days were the start of a branching off, a redefining of what it means to be a workingman in our family. Related by blood, we're separated by class, my father and I. Being the white-collar son of a blue-collar man means being the hinge on the door between two ways of life.

It's not so smooth jumping from Italian old-world style to U.S. yuppie in a single generation. Despite the myth of mobility in America, the

true rule, experts say, is rags to rags, riches to riches. According to
Bucknell University economist and author Charles Sackrey, maybe 10
percent climb from the working to the professional class. My father has
had a tough time accepting my decision to become a mere newspaper
reporter, a field that pays just a little more than construction does. He
wonders why I haven't cashed in on that multi-brick education and
taken on some lawyer-lucrative job. After bricklaying for thirty years,
my father promised himself I'd never pile bricks and blocks into walls
for a living. He figured an education—genielike and benevolent—
would somehow rocket me into the consecrated trajectory of the up-
wardly mobile, and load some serious loot into my pockets. What he
didn't count on was his eldest son breaking blue-collar rule No. 1:
Make as much money as you can, to pay for as good a life as you can
get.

He'd tell me about it when I was 19, my collar already fading to
white. I was the college boy who handed him the wrong wrench on
help-around-the-house Saturdays. "You better make a lot of money,"
my blue-collar handy dad wryly warned me as we huddled in front of a
disassembled dishwasher I had neither the inclination nor the aptitude
to fix. "You're gonna need to hire someone to hammer a nail into a wall
for you."

In 1980, after college and graduate school, I was offered my first
job, on a now-dead daily paper in Columbus, Ohio. I broke the news in
the kitchen, where all the family business is discussed. My mother wept
as if it were Vietnam. My father had a few questions: "Ohio? Where the
hell is Ohio?"

I said it's somewhere west of New York City, that it was like Pennsylvania, only more so. I told him I wanted to write, and these were the
only people who'd take me.

"Why can't you get a good job that pays something, like in advertising in the city, and write on the side?"

"Advertising is lying," I said, smug and sanctimonious, ever the
unctuous undergraduate. "I wanna tell the truth."

"The truth?" the old man exploded, his face reddening as it does
when he's up twenty stories in high wind. "What's truth?" I said it's
real life, and writing about it would make me happy. "You're happy
with your family," my father said, spilling blue-collar rule No. 2.
"That's what makes you happy. After that, it all comes down to dollars
and cents. What gives you comfort besides your family? Money, only
money."

During the two weeks before I moved, he reminded me that newspaper journalism is a dying field, and I could do better. Then he
pressed advertising again, though neither of us knew anything about it,
except that you could work in Manhattan, the borough with the water-
beading high gloss, the island polished clean by money. I couldn't explain myself, so I packed, unpopular and confused. No longer was I the
good son who studied hard and fumbled endearingly with tools. I was
hacking people off.

One night, though, my father brought home some heavy tape and that clear, plastic bubble stuff you pack your mother's second-string dishes in. "You probably couldn't do this right," my father said to me before he sealed the boxes and helped me take them to UPS. "This is what he wants," my father told my mother the day I left for Columbus in my grandfather's eleven-year-old gray Cadillac. "What are you gonna do?" After I said my good-byes, my father took me aside and pressed five $100 bills into my hands. "It's okay," he said over my weak protests. "Don't tell your mother."

When I broke the news about what the paper was paying me, my father suggested I get a part-time job to augment the income. "Maybe you could drive a cab." Once, after I was chewed out by the city editor for something trivial, I made the mistake of telling my father during a visit home. "They pay you nothin', and they push you around too much in that business," he told me, the rage building. "Next time, you gotta grab the guy by the throat and tell him he's a big jerk."

"Dad, I can't talk to the boss like that."

"Tell him. You get results that way. Never take any shit." A few years before, a guy didn't like the retaining wall my father and his partner had built. They tore it down and did it again, but the guy still bitched. My father's partner shoved the guy into the freshly laid bricks. "Pay me off," my father said, and he and his partner took the money and walked. Blue-collar guys have no patience for office politics and corporate bile-swallowing. Just pay me off and I'm gone. Eventually, I moved on to a job in Cleveland, on a paper my father has heard of. I think he looks on it as a sign of progress, because he hasn't mentioned advertising for a while.

When he was my age, my father was already dug in with a trade, a wife, two sons and a house in a neighborhood in Brooklyn not far from where he was born. His workaday, family-centered life has been very much in step with his immigrant father's. I sublet what the real-estate people call a junior one-bedroom in a dormlike condo in a Cleveland suburb. Unmarried and unconnected in an insouciant, perpetual-student kind of way, I rent movies during the week and feed single women in restaurants on Saturday nights. My dad asks me about my dates, but he goes crazy over the word "woman." "A girl," he corrects. "You went out with a girl. Don't say 'woman.' It sounds like you're takin' out your grandmother."

I've often believed blue-collaring is the more genuine of lives, in greater proximity to primordial manhood. My father is provider and protector, concerned only with the basics: food and home, love and progeny. He's also a generation closer to the heritage, a warmer spot nearer the fire that forged and defined us. Does heat dissipate and light fade further from the source? I live for my career, and frequently feel lost and code-less, devoid of the blue-collar rules my father grew up with. With no baby-boomer groomer to show me the way, I've been choreographing my own tentative shuffle across the wax-shined dance floor on the edge of the Great Middle Class, a different rhythm in a whole new ballroom.

I'm sure it's tough on my father, too, because I don't know much about bricklaying, either, except that it's hell on the body, a daily sacrifice. I idealized my dad as a kind of dawn-rising priest of labor, engaged in holy ritual. Up at five every day, my father has made a religion of responsibility. My younger brother, a Wall Street white-collar guy with the sense to make a decent salary, says he always felt safe when he heard Dad stir before him, as if Pop were taming the day for us. My father, 55 years old, but expected to put out as if he were three decades stronger, slips on machine-washable vestments of khaki cotton without waking my mother. He goes into the kitchen and turns on the radio to catch the temperature. Bricklayers have an occupational need to know the weather. And because I am my father's son, I can recite the five-day forecast at any given moment.

My father isn't crazy about this life. He wanted to be a singer and actor when he was young, but that was frivolous doodling to his Italian family, who expected money to be coming in, stoking the stove that kept hearth fires ablaze. Dreams simply were not energy-efficient. My dad learned a trade, as he was supposed to, and settled into a life of pre-scripted routing. He says he can't find the black-and-white publicity glossies he once had made.

Although I see my dad infrequently, my brother, who lives at home, is with the old man every day. Chris has a lot more blue-collar in him than I do, despite his management-level career; for a short time, he wanted to be a construction worker, but my parents persuaded him to go to Columbia. Once in a while he'll bag a lunch and, in a nice wool suit, meet my father at a construction site and share sandwiches of egg salad on semolina bread.

It was Chris who helped my dad most when my father tried to change his life several months ago. My dad wanted a civil-service, bricklayer foreman's job that wouldn't be so physically demanding. There was a written test that included essay questions about construction work. My father hadn't done anything like it in forty years. Why the hell they needed bricklayers to write essays I have no idea, but my father sweated it out. Every morning before sunrise, Chris would be ironing a shirt, bleary-eyed, and my father would sit at the kitchen table and read aloud his practice essays on how to wash down a wall, or how to build a tricky corner. Chris would suggest words and approaches.

It was so hard for my dad. He had to take a Stanley Kaplan–like prep course in a junior high school three nights a week after work for six weeks. At class time, the outside men would come in, twenty-five construction workers squeezing themselves into little desks. Tough blue-collar guys armed with No. 2 pencils leaning over and scratching out their practice essays, cement in their hair, tar on their pants, their work boots too big and clumsy to fit under the desks.

"Is this what finals felt like?" my father would ask me on the phone when I pitched in to help long-distance. "Were you always this nervous?" I told him yes, I told him writing's always difficult. He thanked Chris and me for the coaching, for putting him through school this

91

time. My father thinks he did okay, but he's still awaiting the test results. In the meantime, he takes life the blue-collar way, one brick at a time.

When we see each other these days, my father still asks how the money is. Sometimes he reads my stories; usually he likes them, although he recently criticized one piece as being a bit sentimental: "Too schmaltzy," he said. Some psychologists say that the blue-white-collar gap between fathers and sons leads to alienation, but I tend to agree with Dr. Al Baraff, a clinical psychologist and director of the Men-Center in Washington, D.C. "The core of the relationship is based on emotional and hereditary traits," Baraff says. "Class [distinctions] just get added on. If it's a healthful relationship from when you're a kid, there's a respect back and forth that'll continue."

Nice of the doctor to explain, but I suppose I already knew that. Whatever is between my father and me, whatever keeps us talking and keeps us close, has nothing to do with work and economic class.

During one of my visits to Brooklyn not long ago, he and I were in the car, on our way to buy toiletries, one of my father's weekly routines. "You know, you're not as successful as you could be," he began, blue-collar blunt as usual. "You paid your dues in school. You deserve better restaurants, better clothes." Here we go, I thought, the same old stuff. I'm sure every family has five or six similar big issues that are replayed like well-worn videotapes. I wanted to fast-forward this thing when we stopped at a red light.

Just then my father turned to me, solemn and intense. His knees were aching and his back muscles were throbbing in clockable intervals that registered in his eyes. It was the end of a week of lifting fifty-pound blocks. "I envy you," he said quietly. "For a man to do something he likes and get paid for it—that's fantastic." He smiled at me before the light changed, and we drove on. To thank him for the understanding, I sprang for the deodorant and shampoo. For once, my father let me pay.

## QUESTIONS

*Looking at Ideas:*

1. Compare the author's view of the workingman with those of his father and brother. What is the writer's attitude toward his father? Toward his upbringing? Toward his current lifestyle? Identify passages in the text through which you sense these attitudes.

2. What is the "myth of mobility" mentioned in the fifth paragraph?

3. Discuss the different ideas and meanings of *manhood* in the essay as they relate to values and class. Do blue-collar and white-collar men seem to define manhood differently?

4. Why is Alfred's brother more in tune with their father's way of life? How does the author demonstrate this?

*Looking at Strategies:*

1. This memoir contains a number of symbols and metaphors: "the hinge on the door between two ways of life"; "collar . . . fading to white"; "Pop . . . taming the day for us"; "a warmer spot near the fire." Select a metaphor you find particularly effective and discuss how it develops the theme of the essay.

2. How does the author, a trained journalist, use observations and descriptive details to underscore the distinctions between his own middle-class life and the working-class world of his family?

3. How are gender roles described in the memoir? To what extent do they reflect differences in class?

*Looking at Connections:*

1. Do you see any similar family values articulated in Toni Cade Bambara's story, "Raymond's Run," also in this chapter, and "Bricklayer's Boy"? Discuss.

2. Compare the father-son relations discussed in this essay with those explored in David Sherwood's "Discarded," also in this chapter.

*Suggestions for Writing:*

1. Write an essay in which you compare your own values relative to work, money, and family relations with the values of Lubrano and his family.

2. Lubrano's father must ultimately take a written test to advance to foreman. Do you think it an appropriate test for Mr. Lubrano? Write an essay in which you discuss the role of experiential learning versus book learning and argue that one or the other is more appropriate (or that both are important) for a construction supervisor.

3. Develop an essay comparing and contrasting the importance of money in "Bricklayer's Boy" and in "The Rocking-Horse Winner." You might consider both the class differences between the two families and the openness with which family values are communicated in each story.

**JOURNAL ENTRY**

Do you have a younger sibling or cousin to whom you feel particularly close? Discuss how that relationship evolved as you grew to maturity.

**TONI CADE BAMBARA: "Raymond's Run"**   Toni Cade Bambara, writer, civil rights activist, lecturer, and professor, was born in 1939 in New York City. She received her B.A. from Queens College in 1959, attended the University of Florence, and received her M.A. from City College of the City University of New York in 1964. Bambara worked for the State Department of Welfare from 1959 to 1961; she was also an instructor at City College of C.U.N.Y. from 1965 to 1969 and founder/director of Pajola Writers Collective from 1976 to 1985. She received the American Book Award in 1981 for *The Salt Eaters.* Among other subjects, her writing explores the importance of relationships in the African-American family and the problems in black neighborhoods in big cities as well as in small Southern towns. As you read her story, "Raymond's Run," from her book *Gorilla, My Love* (1970), consider especially the evolving, caring relationship between the talented youngster and her brother Raymond.

TONI CADE BAMBARA

# *Raymond's Run*

I don't have much work to do around the house like some girls. My mother does that. And I don't have to earn my pocket money by hustling; George runs errands for the big boys and sells Christmas cards. And anything else that's got to get done, my father does. All I have to do in life is mind my brother Raymond, which is enough.

Sometimes I slip and say my little brother Raymond. But as any fool can see he's much bigger and he's older too. But a lot of people call him my little brother cause he needs looking after cause he's not quite right. And a lot of smart mouths got lots to say about that too, especially when George was minding him. But now, if anybody has anything to say to Raymond, anything to say about his big head, they have to come by me. And I don't play the dozens or believe in standing around with somebody in my face doing a lot of talking. I much rather just knock you down and take my chances even if I am a little girl with skinny arms and a squeaky voice, which is how I got the name Squeaky. And if things get too rough, I run. And as anybody can tell you, I'm the fastest thing on two feet.

There is no track meet that I don't win the first place medal. I use to win the twenty-yard dash when I was a little kid in kindergarten.

Nowadays it's the fifty-yard dash. And tomorrow I'm subject to run the quarter-meter relay all by myself and come in first, second, and third. The big kids call me Mercury cause I'm the swiftest thing in the neighborhood. Everybody knows that—except two people who know better, my father and me.

He can beat me to Amsterdam Avenue with me having a two fire-hydrant headstart and him running with his hands in his pockets and whistling. But that's private information. Cause can you imagine some thirty-five-year-old man stuffing himself into PAL shorts to race little kids? So as far as everyone's concerned, I'm the fastest and that goes for Gretchen, too, who has put out the tale that she is going to win the first place medal this year. Ridiculous. In the second place, she's got short legs. In the third place, she's got freckles. In the first place, no one can beat me and that's all there is to it.

I'm standing on the corner admiring the weather and about to take a stroll down Broadway so I can practice my breathing exercises, and I've got Raymond walking on the inside close to the buildings cause he's subject to fits of fantasy and starts thinking he's a circus performer and that the curb is a tightrope strung high in the air. And sometimes after a rain, he likes to step down off his tightrope right into the gutter and slosh around getting his shoes and cuffs wet. Then I get hit when I get home. Or sometimes if you don't watch him, he'll dash across traffic to the island in the middle of Broadway and give the pigeons a fit. Then I have to go behind him apologizing to all the old people sitting around trying to get some sun and getting all upset with the pigeons fluttering around them, scattering their newspapers and upsetting the waxpaper lunches in their laps. So I keep Raymond on the inside of me, and he plays like he's driving a stage coach which is O.K. by me so long as he doesn't run me over or interrupt my breathing exercises, which I have to do on account of I'm serious about my running and don't care who knows it.

Now some people like to act like things come easy to them, won't let on that they practice. Not me. I'll high prance down 34<sup>th</sup> Street like a rodeo pony to keep my knees strong even if it does get my mother uptight so that she walks ahead like she's not with me, don't know me, is all by herself on a shopping trip, and I am somebody else's crazy child.

Now you take Cynthia Procter for instance. She's just the opposite. If there's a test tomorrow, she'll say something like, "Oh I guess I'll play handball this afternoon and watch television tonight," just to let you know she ain't thinking about the test. Or like last week when she won the spelling bee for the millionth time, "A good thing you got 'receive,' Squeaky, cause I would have got it wrong. I completely forgot about the spelling bee." And she'll clutch the lace on her blouse like it was a narrow escape. Oh, brother.

But of course when I pass her house on my early morning trots around the block, she is practicing the scales on the piano over and over and over and over. Then in music class, she always lets herself get bumped around so she falls accidently on purpose onto the piano stool and is so surprised to find herself sitting there, and so decides just for fun to try out the ole keys and what do you know—Chopin's waltzes just spring out of her fingertips and she's the most surprised thing in the world. A regular prodigy. I could kill people like that.

I stay up all night studying the words for the spelling bee. And you can see me anytime of day practicing running. I never walk if I can trot and shame on Raymond if he can't keep up. But of course he does, cause if he hangs back someone's liable to walk up to him and get smart, or take his allowance from him, or ask him where he got that great big pumpkin head. People are so stupid sometimes.

So I'm strolling down Broadway breathing out and breathing in on counts of seven, which is my lucky number, and here comes Gretchen and her sidekicks—Mary Louise who used to be a friend of mine when she first moved to Harlem from Baltimore and got beat up by everybody till I took up for her on account of her mother and my mother used to sing in the same choir when they were young girls, but people ain't grateful, so now she hangs out with the new girl Gretchen and talks about me like a dog; and Rosie who is as fat as I am skinny and has a big mouth where Raymond is concerned and is too stupid to know that there is not a big deal of difference between herself and Raymond and that she can't afford to throw stones. So they are steady coming up Broadway and I see right away that it's going to be one of those Dodge City scenes cause the street ain't that big and they're close to the building just as we are. First I think I'll step into the candy store and look over the new comics and let them pass. But that's chicken and I've got a reputation to consider. So then I think I'll just walk straight on through them or over them if necessary. But as they get to me, they slow down. I'm ready to fight, cause like I said I don't feature a whole lot of chitchat, I much prefer to just knock you down right from the jump and save everybody a lotta precious time.

"You signing up for the May Day races?" smiles Mary Louise, only it's not a smile at all.

A dumb question like that doesn't deserve an answer. Besides, there's just me and Gretchen standing there really, so no use wasting my breath talking to shadows.

"I don't think you're going to win this time," says Rosie, trying to signify with her hands on her hips all salty, completely forgetting that I have whupped her behind many times for less salt than that.

"I always win cause I'm the best," I say straight at Gretchen who is, as far as I'm concerned, the only one talking in this ventriloquist-dummy routine.

Gretchen smiles but it's not a smile and I'm thinking that girls never really smile at each other because they don't know how and don't want to know how and there's probably no one to teach us how cause grown-up girls don't know either. Then they all look at Raymond who has just brought his mule team to a standstill. And they're about to see what trouble they can get into through him.

"What grade you in now, Raymond?"

"You got anything to say to my brother, you say it to me, Mary Louise Williams of Raggedy Town, Baltimore."

"What are you, his mother?" sasses Rosie.

"That's right, Fatso. And the next word out of anybody and I'll be their mother too." So they just stand there and Gretchen shifts from one leg to the other and so do they. Then Gretchen puts her hands on her hips and is about to say something with her freckle-face self but doesn't. Then she walks around me looking me up and down but keeps walking up Broadway, and her sidekicks follow her. So me and Raymond smile at each other and he says "Gidyap" to his team and I continue with my breathing exercises, strolling down Broadway toward the icey man on 145th with not a care in the world cause I am Miss Quicksilver herself.

I take my time getting to the park on May Day because the track meet is the last thing on the program. The biggest thing on the program is the May Pole dancing which I can do without, thank you, even if my mother thinks it's a shame I don't take part and act like a girl for a change. You'd think my mother'd be grateful not to have to make me a white organdy dress with a big satin sash and buy me new white baby-doll shoes that can't be taken out of the box till the big day. You'd think she'd be glad her daughter ain't out there prancing around a May Pole getting the new clothes all dirty and sweaty and trying to act like a fairy or a flower or whatever you're supposed to be when you should be trying to be yourself, whatever that is, which is, as far as I am concerned, a poor Black girl who really can't afford to buy shoes and a new dress you only wear once a lifetime cause it won't fit next year.

I was once a strawberry in a Hansel and Gretel pageant when I was in nursery school and didn't have no better sense than to dance on tiptoe with my arms in a circle over my head doing umbrella steps and being a perfect fool just so my mother and father could come dressed up and clap. You'd think they'd know better than to encourage that kind of nonsense. I am not a strawberry. I do not dance on my toes. I run. That is what I am all about. So I always come late to the May Day program, just in time to get my number pinned on and lay in the grass till they announce the fifty-yard dash.

I put Raymond in the little swings, which is a tight squeeze this year and will be impossible next year. Then I look around for Mr. Pearson who pins the numbers on. I'm really looking for Gretchen if you want to know the truth, but she's not around. The park is jam-packed. Parents in hats and corsages and breast-pocket handkerchiefs peeking up. Kids in white dresses and light blue suits. The parkees unfolding chairs and chasing the rowdy kids from Lenox as if they had no right to be there. The big guys with their caps on backwards, leaning against the fence swirling the basketballs on the tips of their fingers waiting for all these crazy people to clear out the park so they can play. Most of the kids in my class are carrying bass drums and glockenspiels and flutes. You'd think they'd put in a few bongos or something for real like that.

Then here comes Mr. Pearson with his clipboard and his cards and pencils and whistles and safety pins and fifty million other things he's always dropping all over the place with his clumsy self. He sticks out in a crowd cause he's on stilts. We used to call him Jack and the Beanstalk to get him mad. But I'm the only one that can outrun him and get away, and I'm too grown for that silliness now.

"Well, Squeaky," he says checking my name off the list and handing me number seven and two pins. And I'm thinking he's got no right to call me Squeaky, if I can't call him Beanstalk.

"Hazel Elizabeth Deborah Parker," I correct him and tell him to write it down on his board.

"Well, Hazel Elizabeth Deborah Parker, going to give someone else a break this year?" I squint at him real hard to see if he is seriously thinking I should lose the race on purpose just to give someone else a break.

"Only six girls running this time," he continues, shaking his head sadly like it's my fault all of New York didn't turn out in sneakers. "That new girl should give you a run for your money." He looks around the park for Gretchen like a periscope in a submarine movie. "Wouldn't it be a nice gesture if you were . . . to ahhh . . ."

I give him such a look he couldn't finish putting that idea into words. Grownups got a lot of nerve sometimes. I pin number seven to myself and stomp away—I'm so burnt. And I go straight for the track and stretch out on the grass while the band winds up with "Oh the Monkey Wrapped His Tail Around the Flag Pole," which my teacher calls by some other name. The man on the loudspeaker is calling everyone over to the track and I'm on my back looking at the sky trying to pretend I'm in the country, but I can't, because even grass in the city feels hard as sidewalk and there's just no pretending you are anywhere but in a "concrete jungle" as my grandfather says.

The twenty-yard dash takes all of the two minutes cause most of the little kids don't know no better than to run off the track or run the wrong way or run smack into the fence and fall down and cry. One little kid though has got the good sense to run straight for the white ribbon up ahead so he wins. Then the second graders line up for the thirty-yard dash and I don't even bother to turn my head to watch cause Raphael Perez always wins. He wins before he even begins by psyching the runners, telling them they're going to trip on their shoelaces and fall on their faces or lose their shorts or something, which he doesn't really have to do since he is very fast, almost as fast as I am. After that is the forty-yard dash which I use to run when I was in first grade. Raymond is hollering from the swings cause he knows I'm about to do my thing cause the man on the loudspeaker has just announced the fifty-yard dash, although he might just as well be giving a recipe for Angel Food cake cause you can hardly make out what he's saying for the static. I get up and slip off my sweat pants and then I see Gretchen standing at the starting line kicking her legs out like a pro. Then as I get into place I see that ole Raymond is in line on the other side of the fence, bending down with his fingers on the ground just like he knew what he was doing. I was going to yell at him but then I didn't. It burns up your energy to holler.

Every time, just before I take off in a race, I always feel like I'm in a dream, the kind of dream you have when you're sick with fever and feel all hot and weightless. I dream I'm flying over a sandy beach in the early morning sun, kissing the leaves of the trees as I fly by. And there's always the smell of apples, just like in the country when I was little and use to think I was a choo-choo train, running through the fields of corn and chugging up the hill to the orchard. And all the time I'm dreaming this, I get lighter and lighter until I'm flying over the beach again, getting blown through the sky like a feather that weighs nothing at all. But once I spread my fingers in the dirt and crouch over for the Get on Your Mark, the dream goes and I am solid again and am telling myself, Squeaky you must win, you must win, you are the fastest thing in the world, you can even beat your father up Amsterdam if you really try. And then I feel my weight coming back just behind my knees then down to my feet then into the earth and the pistol shot explodes in my blood and I am off and weightless again, flying past the other runners, my arms pumping up and down and the whole world is quiet except for the crunch as I zoom over the gravel in the track. I glance to my left and there is no one. To the right a blurred Gretchen who's got her chin jutting out as if it would win the race all by itself. And on the other side of the fence is Raymond with his arms down to his side and the palms tucked up behind him, running, in his very own style and the first time I ever saw that and I almost stop to watch my brother Raymond on his first run. But the white ribbon is bouncing toward me and I tear past it racing into the distance till my feet with a mind of their own start digging up footfuls of dirt and brake me short. Then all the kids standing on the side pile on me, banging me on the back and slapping my head with their May Day programs, for I have won again and everybody on 151st Street can walk tall for another year.

"In first place . . ." the man on the loudspeaker is clear as a bell now. But then he pauses and the loudspeaker starts to whine. Then static. And I lean down to catch my breath and here comes Gretchen walking back for she's overshot the finish line too, huffing and puffing with her hands on her hips taking it slow, breathing in steady time like a real pro and I sort of like her a little for the first time. "In first place . . ." and then three or four voices get all mixed up on the loudspeaker and I dig my sneaker into the grass and stare at Gretchen who's staring back, we both wondering just who did win. I can hear old Beanstalk arguing with the man on the loudspeaker and then a few others running their mouths about what the stop watches say.

Then I hear Raymond yanking at the fence to call me and I wave to shush him, but he keeps rattling the fence like a gorilla in a cage like in them gorilla movies, but then like a dancer or something he starts climbing up nice and easy but very fast. And it occurs to me, watching how smoothly he climbs hand over hand and remembering how he

99

looked running with his arms down to his side and with the wind pulling his mouth back and his teeth showing and all, it occurred to me that Raymond would make a very fine runner. Doesn't he always keep up with me on my trots? And he surely knows how to breathe in counts of seven cause he's always doing it at the dinner table, which drives my brother George up the wall. And I'm smiling to beat the band cause if I've lost this race, or if me and Gretchen tied, or even if I've won, I can always retire as a runner and begin a whole new career as a coach with Raymond as my champion. After all, with a little more study I can beat Cynthia and her phony self at the spelling bee. And if I bugged my mother, I could get piano lessons and become a star. And I have a big rep as the baddest thing around. And I've got a roomful of ribbons and medals and awards. But what has Raymond got to call his own?

So I stand there with my new plan, laughing out loud by this time as Raymond jumps down from the fence and runs over with his teeth showing and his arms down to the side which no one before him has quite mastered as a running style. And by the time he comes over I'm jumping up and down so glad to see him—my brother Raymond, a great runner in the family tradition. But of course everyone thinks I'm jumping up and down because the men on the loudspeaker have finally gotten themselves together and compared notes and are announcing "In first place—Miss Hazel Elizabeth Deborah Parker." (Dig that.) "In second place—Miss Gretchen P. Lewis." And I look over at Gretchen wondering what the P stands for. And I smile. Cause she's good, no doubt about it. Maybe she'd like to help me coach Raymond; she obviously is serious about running, as any fool can see. And she nods to congratulate me and then she smiles. And I smile. We stand there with this big smile of respect between us. It's about as real a smile as girls can do for each other, considering we don't practice real smiling every day you know, cause maybe we too busy being flowers or fairies or strawberries instead of something honest and worthy of respect . . . you know . . . like being people.

## QUESTIONS

*Looking at Ideas:*

1. Characterize the narrator: What are her dominant traits? Does she mean it when she says, "don't care who knows it"? How does she characterize those who do seem to care? What is the significance of her insisting on her full, given name for the race, rather than her nickname, "Squeaky"?

2. Characterize the narrator's attitudes toward various members of her family, including Raymond. How are her attitudes revealed? How do the roles and relationships, especially the narrator's role as caretaker for Raymond, evolve through the course of the story?

3. Contrast the narrator's self-perception in paragraphs 20 and 21 with the way other characters seem to perceive her and how you as a reader en-

vision her. Describe the attitudes of other family members toward her. How does her mother's desire for her to dress up contrast with her sense of self?

4. The narrator notes that "girls never really smile at each other." Do you agree with her observation and with her explanation? What does her smile at Gretchen after the race suggest to you?

5. How would you characterize the narrator's code of behavior? How does the author establish a sense of that code throughout the narrative? How does it contrast with Mr. Pearson's suggestion about the race?

6. The narrator alludes to the kind of "real" entertainment or activities that would have been appropriate for May Day. Describe a program of events that Squeaky might find enjoyable. Would such a program satisfy the parents who come to see their children dressed up?

*Looking at Strategies:*

1. Discuss the author's use of diction, imagery, and sentence structure to establish the narrator's voice in the story.

2. Contrast the diction and sentence structure of the "dream" narrative just before the race with Squeaky's voice in the rest of the story. What stylistic differences do you find? What do these differences suggest?

3. Why is the story called "Raymond's Run" rather than "Squeaky's Run"? Relate the title to the story's theme.

*Looking at Connections:*

1. Compare Squeaky's dream for Raymond with the dream Paul experiences in "The Rocking-Horse Winner."

2. Contrast Squeaky and Raymond's relationship with that of the brothers in David Sherwood's "Discarded" and Jeremy Seabrook's "A Twin Is Only Half a Person," later in this chapter.

*Suggestions for Writing:*

1. Discuss the advantages and disadvantages of home care for children such as Raymond. What do the family as a whole and the individual siblings gain or lose? What difficulties may arise that make home care unrealistic? Develop an essay supporting your point of view.

2. Write about a caring relationship you had with a younger sibling or other child who was dependent on you. In what ways was the relationship fulfilling? How was it frustrating? How did the relationship help you grow and mature?

3. Write an essay contrasting the images of "reality" and "dream" that are developed in "Raymond's Run." Cite examples from the text to support your thesis. For instance, you might discuss how the narrator's sense of what is real develops throughout the story, how her sense of reality contrasts with her dream before the race. What point might the author be trying to make by setting up such a contrast? Does the narrator's dream for Raymond's future seem realistic, obtainable?

**JOURNAL ENTRY**

Write about your relationship with a close relative or friend whom you sometimes feel has a similar, complementary personality to your own. Do you sometimes feel this person is like your "twin" or double?

**JEREMY SEABROOK: "A Twin Is Only Half A Person"**  Jeremy Seabrook was born in 1939 in Northhampton, England, and was educated at Cambridge. He attended the London School of Economics and received a diploma in Social Administration in 1967. In addition to working as a journalist, he has worked as a secondary teacher and as a social worker for the Inner London Education Authority. In 1976 he wrote *A Lasting Relationship: Homosexuals and Society.* The following excerpt, "A Twin Is Only Half a Person" (1980), is from his biography, *Mother and Son.* As you read his essay, consider the ways in which his background in social work and teaching may have influenced his reflection on the relationships in his family.

JEREMY SEABROOK

# *A Twin Is Only Half a Person*

Whenever I have told people I've met that I am a twin, there has always come a change of expression in their eyes, a kind of re-focusing, which I came to recognize long before I detected its meaning. I think it is an attempt to discern in me my absent half: everybody knows that a twin is only half a person. There is a distinct withdrawal too, the readjustment people make when they discover someone they have been talking to freely and intimately is married. If you are a twin, people behave as though you are not worth making a relationship with; and they recoil, sensing perhaps that there is no reserve of feeling within you which you could possibly expend on them. They are interested and polite. They say "Oh is he like you?" and you can watch them adjust to the possibility of a replica of the individual they have just met; and your sense of uniqueness is assailed. They ask "Do you feel pain and joy on behalf of each other? If he is suffering, do you feel a pang, can you not bear to be apart?"

It has been nothing like that.

My twin has always been there. This may seem a very banal and obvious thing to say; but he was there as a presence and not as a person. It is only now that we are well into our thirties that we have begun to exist for each other.

Our family made the same assumptions about us that are common in the general response to twinning. The first was that there is a sense of symmetry in nature, and that in a twin situation human characteristics are distributed in compensating opposites: the absence of some feature in one of us was made good by the presence of another, which, in turn, was lacking in the other twin. There was a division of human qualities between us soon after birth, like a fairy-tale christening at which all the members of the family bestowed a gift upon us, or, in some cases, a curse, according to their disposition. And it seems to have occurred to no one that the same features might have been present in both of us. In this way, our natures were built by our relatives, an elaborate and ingenious construct which it has taken half a lifetime to demolish.

It was clear from the beginning that my brother was a good child who didn't cry. All that remained for me was to be bad; but to make up for that, it was decided I would be clever. This implied that Jack would be dull; so it was decreed that he would be practical, skilled with his hands, which he became. This caused me to be clumsy and maladroit; and to make up for this, I was given a loving disposition, which I faithfully set about developing—even though I occasionally sensed guiltily that it wasn't true, and I longed to express my hatred of Aunt Maud and my loathing of bunny rabbits.

Our whole personalities were created rather than allowed to develop, and the pace was forced. When one of us gave any sign of a preference or an ability, there was a rush to seek out its opposite in the other.

This meant over time that we became, each for the other, objects of great mystery; and in this lay the deeper purpose of our contrived complementarity. The other was always endowed with what one didn't have, with what one lacked. My twin was a reproach to me for all the things I would never be. He was the beautiful one; and this meant, not simply that I was plain, or even of tolerably neutral appearance, but that I was ugly. For many years I observed people overcome what I imagined must be their revulsion before they could even bear to talk to me. But if I was bright, this implied that my brother was not merely average, but that he was backward. And we obliged by carrying out these determinants whispered over our cradle by malevolent adults. It was discovered—in early infancy somehow—that my brother would never be able to read or write. Later, when I went to the Grammar School, he was consigned to the C stream of the Secondary Modern in compliance with this melancholy fact. These roles pursued us far into adult life; and it wasn't until he was in the army, in Germany, that my brother realized, with wonder, that he was writing to his girl friend every day, letters he was amazed to find linguistically quite competent and marvellously rich in ideas.

In this way we grew up as strangers to each other; strangers who had nothing in common and therefore no reason to make each other's acquaintance. The qualities which each of us possessed were not seen by the other as complementary. They had evolved to satisfy other people's sense of the rightness of things. We were immured in separate

103

chambers of the body of the family, with our respective myths about ourselves and each other. It wouldn't be true to say that I disliked my brother. I regarded him with distant curiosity, as someone governed by quite different laws and values from myself—the kind of anthropological detachment which is normally brought to the observation of remote outlandish customs and practices. He was inaccessible, because apparently there was nothing we shared—not even our mother. She was a different person with each of us, as became someone with compassion for the monster of ugliness and the subnormal she had brought into the world.

But at the same time, my brother was the embodiment of all the things I could never be. I grew up with my own deficiencies constantly illuminated by the model of the child I understood him to be. The pain of this was made worse by our close relatives. Why can't you be more like Jack, I was asked with despairing insistence. It was a question I didn't have an answer to then. I do now, but it is thirty years too late to be of use to either of us.

If each of us was held up as an example of human perfection to the other, it meant that we both grew up with a deepened sense of our own inadequacy. The relationship with our mother always seemed to take place privately, with only one at a time; and this didn't strike us as odd. Each of us was so dazzled by the vaunted perfection of the other, that he could only expect to wait, humble, patient, excluded from the mystical bond that existed between brother and mother. I often wondered what she said to him, as she washed him at night if I had been put to bed first and was waiting to go to sleep; or why she talked to me all the time about him if he were already washed and in bed. When he and I were together, we were like indifferent stepchildren, sullenly accepting each other's presence, but unable to find any area of common interest. We had no idea then of our mother's resentment of what men had done to her. She must have dreaded above all else that my brother and I might combine against her.

Mealtimes were the worst. I could never understand why other families would spend perhaps an hour at table, when our meals were such functional occasions, concerned with nothing but the assimilation of food. My brother and I would sit in morose silence as we played with the food on our plates, damming the gravy within an embankment of mashed potato and waiting for the rampart to give way, heads lowered, not even looking at each other. We simply eliminated one another from our consciousness; and in order to survive, each had to make light of the qualities the other had, and which were always being set before him as an example. I learned to undervalue practical ability in anything, so that I came to adulthood unable to pay a bill, mend a fuse, change a plug, mow a lawn. And in our competitive struggle I made a virtue of these things, because I was the only person who sought my true good qualities in vain. If I was patient or kind, I failed to observe it, or assumed patience and kindness to be of little worth because they were mine; or perhaps I considered them deeply contaminated by the fact

104

that I was cowardly, ugly, and greedy. So I had to diminish physical beauty. It was after all, I never ceased telling myself, merely a shell; it indicated nothing of the person you really were. I had to despise tractability and the quiet acceptance of the adult timetable for sleep, food or play; I questioned the purpose of these rituals endlessly, disputed them with tears and refusal, until the adults despaired over my causeless grief.

My brother and I both tried to be as worthy as each suspected the other of being of our mother's love; and it was given to us both to understand that each was always on the brink of ousting the preferred other. This meant that neither finally gave up the struggle; neither became totally indifferent or demoralized. A competitive tension persisted. I promised my mother that when I grew up, I would take her away with me to live in Canada, not knowing that my brother had promised to make a life for both of them in Australia.

So we grew, slightly deformed, like trees that have common root but have no room to grow to their full height side by side. We were shadows cast over each other's childhood. I have a photograph of us at the age of about seven. We are holding hands in front of the lilac bush, and we are dressed identically. I have no recollection of the picture having been taken; only I am incredulous that we could ever have held hands. He was always there, with his beautiful violet eyes, silent and reproachful over his model-making, building aeroplanes with strips of frail balsawood, exuding a smell of pear drops from the adhesive he used. Once or twice he did initiate a clumsy attempt to get close to me. When Gran died, he tried to put an arm around me; when he was fourteen, he tried to talk to me about his loneliness. Terrified, I fled. It seemed like being molested by a stranger.

But now that we are grown up and our lives are separate in every way—we sometimes don't meet for a year or more at a time—there remains, curiously, an ache and an absence. There is a sense of emptiness where he should have been and yet never was. When we are together, the old rivalry erupts readily in argument and misunderstanding; but when it doesn't there is a strange unspoken pain, which is present to a lesser degree with other members of the family—the scars of kinship.

At times I feel incomplete. The space he occupied has remained vacant. It seems to me now that much of my adult life has been spent looking for people who resemble, not him but myself: a belated and doomed search for the things I ought to have shared with my twin. I remain with a persistent fear of being alone; and yet with others I feel inadequate, half a person. But it is half a person with no complement.

### QUESTIONS

*Looking at Ideas:*

1. What is the author's attitude toward his twin brother? How is that attitude revealed? Do you think both twins would feel more complete as

adults if they had been closer as children? Do you think Seabrook and his brother had a typical twin relationship?

2. How did the mother's attitude toward men contribute to the way she raised the twins? What passage from the text supports your view?

3. Is the author angry at his brother, his mother, society, or himself for his feelings of sadness and emptiness? Do twins you know share his negative assessment of being a twin? Does he share any positive feelings or experiences about being a twin?

4. The author writes, "Our whole personalities were created rather than allowed to develop, and the pace was forced." What does he mean? Cite examples from the text that support his claim.

*Looking at Strategies:*

1. When two ideas/things/people are being compared, a writer often relies on coordination and compound sentences to convey information concisely and without repetition. Note some examples of coordination in the text, and examine how they echo the notions of "half" and "whole."

2. How effective is the essay's opening paragraph? Is it likely to encourage the audience to read on? Why? How effective are the repeated questions from people who know the author is a twin?

3. The author uses a number of metaphors in this essay, such as "scars of kinship." Discuss the imagery in this selection. Do you see any patterns or repeated images? What do such images and patterns contribute to the overall meaning and mood of the essay?

*Looking at Connection:*

1. Does the relationship Seabrook describes have any parallels to that of the brothers in the next selection, "Discarded"? Do the memoirs have a similar tone? Discuss.

2. Seabrook writes that "our natures were built by our relatives, an elaborate and ingenious construct which has taken half a lifetime to demolish." How might his observation relate to Susanne Short's argument that adults should "mirror" children and reflect what children feel rather than what adults feel about them?

*Suggestions for Writing:*

1. Write an essay in which you explore the ways in which an individual is shaped by his or her relationships with others in the family. You can use examples from your own family or the families of people you know.

2. The author states that "our whole personalities were created, rather than allowed to develop." Can parents fully shape one's personality? Do you believe "nature" (genetic composition) or "nurture" (upbringing) to be the primary force that shapes the individual? Write an essay in which you argue a position on this issue.

3. If you are a twin, or if you have a sibling close to your age, write about what you feel have been the most significant aspects of your relationship with this person. What special insights and sensitivity have you derived from the relationship? Refer to specific examples to support your assertions.

Is there a member of your family, circle of friends, or community who is perceived as "different" from others? When did you first become aware of this difference? How has your attitude about this individual changed over time?

**DAVID SHERWOOD: "Discarded"**   David Sherwood, father of five, first published the following essay in the *New York Times Magazine* in 1986, under the title *"Discarded Son."* As you read, consider the viewpoint the author takes as a grown man and father looking back on the family relationships of his youth and on his brother's sexual orientation.

DAVID SHERWOOD

# *Discarded*

My younger brother, Andy, lives in Paris and I in Hartford. Neither of us ever has any money to speak of, so we hardly get to see each other or even to talk on the phone. We keep in touch by sending letters back and forth across the Atlantic.

Judging by the letters, I think of Andy as a fine, fine writer. But lately, he has been writing a book, and, based on the chapters he's sent me, I'd say that publishers won't be encouraging. Andy's book is about our small family and, most especially, Andy's unhappy childhood some forty years ago. What happens, I think, is that as Andy writes about his childhood, he sort of becomes again the child he once was—a child having a hard time of it. The change he undergoes changes his writing for the worse.

Andy was a boy whose father seemed to show him next to no sign of love or respect. "Next to no" will allow for signals of affection and esteem perhaps apparent at the time, but of which we have no recollection. We had the same father, but he was not the same with the two of us. He was all I could ever have wished for, but he never took a shine to Andy.

Andy liked to try on women's clothes; he would draw picture after picture of plume-hatted hoop-skirted women; his favorite playmates were girls; his gestures were effeminate. It was all beyond endurance for our father, who, aside from being the schoolteacher to whom a Class of 1945 yearbook was dedicated, was a graceful athlete, a dead-pan poker player and a man who had a way with the ladies. His small son's achievements—good comportment, words spelled right—were, so far as one could tell, scant source of pleasure to him. Our father had a wry sense of humor and a quicksilver laugh, but he seemed to lose his light touch in my brother's presence. Altogether then, Andy found little to assure him that he was in any way precious to his father. When we were still kids, our father, barely forty, died.

We'd been raised in Delaware, on a boarding school's campus, among people we'd known forever: teachers, support staff, their wives and children. Nobody there made an issue of Andy. But once our father died, we moved to Wilmington so our mother could find work. And in the Wilmington of 1945, among my new seventh-grade pals, Andy seemed suddenly exotic. What had bothered my father about him now bothered me. So I was glad we were enrolled in separate schools, glad that Andy was away at piano lessons when my friends dropped by, glad not to have to introduce him or even have them see him. I remember once meeting a boy who'd just transferred to my school from Andy's. The name Sherwood registered with him right off. "You got a fairy named Andy for a brother?" he asked.

I kept Andy at more than arm's length for years thereafter. But once I'd become the father of a boy myself, we became brothers again. What happened, I think, was two things. Andy liked being Uncle Andy. It gave him a valued mainstream credential. And I, living a humdrummish life, found myself now pleased to tell friends about this gay brother of mine who lived in New York, as he did then, with an illustrator of medical textbooks and relaxed at restaurants like Max's Kansas City. In those days I wished to seem more interesting than I knew myself to be. Acknowledging Andy and visiting him was a way to do it. More than that, I'd be in his living room watching him amusing my son, and I'd feel shame for having never been an older brother to him. One day, I called up two of his former friends and threatened to rip their place up if they didn't quickly return to Andy some furniture they owed him money for. It was the first favor I'd ever done him.

Andy's adult life, in my eyes, has been one of accomplishment. He tutors private pupils in voice and piano; he once taught harpsichord; he has sung countertenor with chamber groups, and these are not his primary endeavors. Mostly, he teaches English to French adults whose tuitions are paid by their employers. The head of his school, he wrote in 1981, "has told me I'm her best teacher. She's been putting me with new students who've come to test the school out for their companies, so that, if they like it, more will follow. I, then, have to create the most favorable impression, a sort of . . . seduction. . . ."

My brother, in fact, has fashioned for himself a life that leans often on the seducer's art. Apart from his classroom role, he is a photographer whose prints are, once in a while, exhibited and sold in galleries, and he must coax from acquaintances who pose for him a certain moroseness of expression that flavors his photographs and causes the public and an occasional magazine or museum to buy them. Engaged in the 1960s for anonymous bit parts in opera—no singing, no dancing— Andy was reproved sometimes for diverting attention from the principals. "Mr. Rudel at the New York City Opera," he said, "told me everyone was watching me in *The Flaming Angel* instead of the heroine. Mr. Bing at the Met told me the same thing in *Andrea Chenier.*"

"I turn many fewer heads than I used to," he now writes. "A friend and I have a pastime we call 'Existing,' which consists of guessing if a stranger is aware of us, and if so, of which one, or whether we obviously don't 'exist' and are looked through, not at." These strangers, by whom Andy and his friend define their "existence," are boys and men first seen from afar, then from up close as they pass one another on the sidewalk. "When we do get a glance," he adds, "it is usually for Patrice, who is 15 years younger."

Andy can handle the increasing absence of glances from strangers. But he is encumbered by having never seduced an affectionate glance from our father. I want to believe that, had our father lived longer, he'd have made his peace with Andy. Their love of music and language, their storytelling skills, their parallel teaching careers—there is common ground there now. But I also know, as a father of five, how tough it is to look with new eyes upon a child who baffles you, disappoints you.

Andy will live out his years not knowing how things might have worked out between them. Each draft of his book that arrives shows how punishing his recollections are, how infirm they make him, and how hard it is to get out from under the shadow of a father who hasn't loved you.

## QUESTIONS

*Looking at Ideas:*

1. Why is the essay entitled "Discarded"? What tone and meaning are suggested by the title? How was Andy discarded by his father, his brother, and society?

2. Does the author seem to accept his brother's identity? Do you think that the author, as an adult, has come to respect and appreciate his brother for who he is? Why or why not?

3. If the father had not died, do you believe that Andy's relationship with him would have changed? Would Andy's life have turned out differently if he had been closer to his father? What role do social conventions play in how the father and brother perceive Andy?

*Looking at Strategies:*

1. The author uses brief, specific details to convey a picture of a person or a situation. What details best reveal for you his perceptions of Andy as a child, of his father, and of his childhood shame in having a homosexual brother?

2. How sincere does the author's "voice" seem in this essay? Do you believe what he writes about his family and about his own attitudes? Why or why not?

3. How effective is the "frame" for the story—the opening and closing segments about the book Andy is writing?

*Looking at Connections:*

1. How does the relationship between brothers in this essay compare with the one David Seabrook describes in "A Twin Is Only Half a Person"? In which relationship has there been the more conflict?
2. Why do you think Andy is discarded and Raymond, in Toni Cade Bambara's "Raymond's Run," is not?

*Suggestions for Writing:*

1. Write a brief memoir in which you describe a relationship between you and some member of your family that has special meaning for you, but which has changed or evolved over time. How has it changed, and why?
2. Consider a relationship that you now have with a friend or family member. Now visualize how you think your relationship will be in ten years or so. Write a future projection of the relationship. Indicate why you think the relationship will change in certain ways.
3. What is the impact on the family when one member is rejected? How does it affect the rejected one? The rest of the family? To what extent might the family feel guilty? How would they compensate for such rejection of one of their own? Write a reflective essay focusing on the impact of rejection in the family.

**JOURNAL ENTRY**

Write a "letter" to a relative, explaining some qualities in yourself or in
your feelings about him or her that he or she isn't likely to be aware of or
to understand easily.

**MARIE HOWE: "Letter to My Sister"** Educated at Columbia University,
where she received her M.F.A. in 1983, Marie Howe has also been a Bunting
Fellow at Radcliffe College. She has taught at Dartmouth, Tufts University, and
Warren Wilson College. Her first book, *The Good Thief* (1988), appeared in
the National Poetry Series. Howe's poetry has been published in such magazines as *The Atlantic, The American Poetry Review,* and *The Partisan Review.*
Margaret Atwood has described Howe's writing as "poems of obsession that
transcend their own dark roots." In "Letter to My Sister" Howe explores mixed
feelings about a sibling and the tensions of family life that can continue to
haunt us long after we are grown.

MARIE HOWE

## Letter to My Sister

We lived one life on the surface.
How could I have imagined your dark room?

I tell you I slept in the arms of the laddering beech
where even the numbing kitchen light
couldn't reach trembling in.

But this also is fiction.

I slept in fear. Then too
the beast crouched at my door
whimpering,

and it's true, I sometimes
offered you to him.

Forgive me the circumstances of my life.

This no one told us,
there is no such thing as family.

Nevertheless, today your voice reaches me,
deliberate on the wire,

and I, still older,
answer.

Perhaps this is the love we earn.

And if, with our words, the glass house cracks
and tumbles,

thus speaking, we stand clear,
the slivers sifting into our singular lives.

## QUESTIONS

*Looking at Ideas*

1. What do the first two lines of the poem mean to you? What do these lines suggest about the hidden nature of personalities within a family? Do you think that family members often really know one another beyond "the surface"?

2. What do you infer when the narrator says, "But this also is fiction"? Do you think that many of the "confidences" we share with family members are, in fact, "fictions," at least to some degree?

3. The narrator remarks that she sometimes "offered" the sister to the "beast crouched at my door." To what or whom might she be referring? What seems to be her motivation here? Why does she ask the sister to "forgive . . . the circumstances of my life"?

4. When the speaker remarks, "there is no such thing as family," in what sense is she speaking? Do you think Howe expects us to consider this literally or symbolically? What is the definition of family in this poem?

5. How does the love we experienced within the family as children change into "the love we earn" as we grow older?

*Looking at Strategies*

1. What is the significance of the image of the "laddering beech" where the narrator claims that she slept, away from the "numbing kitchen light"?

2. What might the "beast" in the poem represent, to the narrator and to her sister? How does your interpretation of this figure affect your reading of the poem?

3. What does the glass house in the poem, which breaks and "tumbles," leaving only "slivers," represent? Does the breaking up of the glass house seem a negative image, or does it have positive implications as well?

*Looking at Connections*

1. Compare the unspoken tension Howe seems to weave into the poem with the notion of whispering walls discussed in Susanne Short's essay in this chapter.

2. In what ways do Seabrook in "A Twin Is Only Half a Person" and Howe in this poem address issues particular to same-gender siblings? Consider communication, or lack of it, between siblings.

*Suggestions for Writing*

1. Howe's poem seems to treat "family" as a myth or a fiction, not as a

tangible reality that we can hang on to or take comfort from in later life. Do you agree or disagree with this view of the family? Write an essay in which you argue a position on the issue of the family as a myth or a false hope.

2. Write an analysis of a relationship you have had with a sibling or other close relative in which you have felt, as the speaker seems to in this poem, that despite the fact you grew up in the same home and shared many "surface" experiences, there was a barrier to understanding the different inner world of the person, their own "dark room." What was it about the relative you didn't understand while growing up with him or her? Do you understand your relative better now?

3. Write a response to the poem, taking up the point of view of the sister; or write a dialogue between the two sisters, using the poem as a starting point. Then, write a reflective essay discussing why the response or dialogue evolved in the way it did.

**KLARICE TSING: "The Violin"**   Klarice Tsing, a freshman in pre-medical studies when she wrote the following essay, spent half her life on the East Coast before moving to Texas. She currently attends college in the San Francisco Bay Area. Klarice Tsing enjoys drawing, hiking, sailing, and the California outdoors. Her writing process for this essay was quite a lengthy one. Initially she had chosen another topic, a very broad character sketch. In her rewrite, she changed her focus to a narrower concern, the memory of a particular childhood conflict in her relationship with her parents. Tsing comments: "A fundamental question occurred to me during the process of writing the paper: In writing do we create truth, or does truth create writing? I have tried to accurately recapture a sensitive aspect of my life, but I fear that my words will exaggerate, underscore, or connote unintended meanings. After several revisions, I feel that the following fine-tuned essay reflects truth, or at least a part of the truth."

KLARICE   TSING

# *The Violin*

The slightest sound, sight, or mention of stringed instruments can create in me a vague, at times overwhelming sense of discomfort, disappointment, or insecurity. Even the silent, dust-gathering presence of the frail violin entombed in a blue, velvet-lined case beneath my bed is enough to resurrect turbulent scenes from the past. The violin itself, however, does not inflict painful realizations. Rather, the stilled violin strings evoke a relationship connecting the instrument, myself, and my parents that continues to haunt my present.

The relationship started innocently enough. When I was four, my family and I attended a special Suzuki concert in New York. This particular concert demonstrated the Suzuki method of musical learning, using an elite young group of Japanese and American student-musicians. According to my mother, I pointed to the stage filled with rows of these precocious violinists and declared "I want to do that, too." With my parents eagerly capitalizing on my "Me too" enthusiasm, my first lessons with the fake replicas of violins, the standard Suzuki "Twinkle, Twinkle, Little Star," and our group concerts all began to develop this aspect of the parent-child relationship. Conflict, unfortunately, soon entered our lives around the issue of practice time. My practice sessions consisted of perfunctory, rushed renditions of songs, followed by a mad rush to join my violinless comrades outside. My distressed parents, eyeing their investment in lessons and rental fees, would usually ask me to practice some more.

Eventually, I came to refuse with frustrating obstinacy to practice regularly, so that my parents' pleadings eventually evolved into bribes, force, threats, and anger. All of this only resulted in negative feelings on both sides. With my growing resistance, my mother's belief in her parenting ability gradually disintegrated into bribes of clothing, candy, or toys exchanged for practice time. My father's use of the extreme opposite approach—threats and displays of force—drained my faith in fatherly benevolence, as well as adding stress to his hectic life. The scare factor of threats (loss of toys, playtime) also resulted in emotional stress, leading to a sulking despisal of both myself and my parents. Even worse, my mother's channeling of her anger into the silent treatment, punctuated by unexpected outbursts, strained the house with tension. I recall one particularly unpleasant instance of such treatment, in which I crawled hesitantly across the kitchen floor to hide from my mother's accusatory and tight-lipped presence in the dining room. My efforts and aching knees did not go unnoticed—a tirade of words and screams suddenly issued from her mouth, entering my guilty ears.

Out of all of these emotionally charged memories, one relatively peaceful incident serves as the touchstone for my explorations into our family's relationships. When I was in the third grade, the Bakers, old and respected friends of my parents, came over for dinner one summer evening. After a huge American-Chinese feast and a conversation about the old and the new, my parents announced that I would play the violin for the Bakers, who insisted, smiling expectantly over their cups of after-dinner coffee, that they would love a private and impromptu violin concert. The evening thus took an abrupt turn into misery for all of us.

Despite the excitement of having guests to dinner, I adamantly declined to perform and promptly avoided the violin by reading books, watching television, and hiding. I remember my father whispering a few words into my unhappy ear, as well as my mother begging me quietly before appealing in embarrassment to Mrs. Baker for time. I cannot recall whether or not I eventually did give a private concert, but I can recall my ashamed tears and my parents' disappointment.

Viewing this incident from the present, I realize that the underlying current of all these battles was the struggle for power, love, and approval. Strangely enough, my parents and I used (and still use) the violin as the instrument to communicate our expectations of each other. My father, who was raised during a time of bare necessities, translates his deprivation into profuse accommodations on my behalf. His anger arose in this case from the fact that I had a *choice* to refuse the luxury of music. My mother similarly places a heavy meaning upon the violin. Through the violin, she sees the chance to reexperience a life free from the confines of tradition and family that overshadowed her career development. As a result of the times in which she grew up, she was discouraged from selecting her desired career and relegated to attending to the household. My mother believed that the opportunities offered along with the violin would be one path of freedom for both of us. As for me, I interpret our unhappy coexistence with the violin as my struggle for personal identity beyond a parental-shaped destiny. I rebel-

115

liously and legitimately wanted an identity beyond the idealistic one my parents desired. Finally, the violin symbolized a confused contest for affection and self-worth that no one really won. We were all merely contenders groping wildly for the utopia of a child prodigy–parent relationship.

On the other hand, not all of these strings reveal disturbing memories. Some recall shared times of enjoyment such as concerts, orchestra trips, awards, and good friends. My father's most relaxed times involved his self-imposed duty as concert photographer, while in the preconcert rush, my mother lovingly would make last-minute check-ups on my appearance, typing ribbons or adjusting a hem. My mother also emphasized her supporting role by attending almost all of my performances and joining orchestra trips as a chaperone, despite the horrors of the long bus trips. We met wonderful friends through music, providing us with an abundant supply of vivid memories.

Looking into the future, I can only hope that eventually my violin will see happier times. Meanwhile, my parents still ask if I practice. No, I tell them, but every once in a while I steal a look within the case at the instrument that has carried me through life on its many strings. For the time being, I continue to hold a silent instrument, tightening and loosening the pegs that tune my relationship to my parents.

*Questions for Discussion*

1. Does the essay seem to be balanced between the positive and the negative aspects of the experience of the violin? Do you think the student presents a fair picture of her parents and their reasons for involving her in the rigors of violin practice? What has she learned from her experience?

2. Although the student presents a conflict in her relationship with her parents around the subject of the violin, does the conflict seem to be typical of her relations with them? What overall feelings does she seem to have toward her parents?

3. How effectively does the student use the symbol of the violin to organize her essay and to help convey her feelings toward her parents and their ambitions for her? Notice particularly how the image of the violin is used both to introduce and to conclude the essay.

4. One interesting element of this essay is its use of contrast. How does the student contrast her own feelings and life experiences with those of her parents? What other contrasts help to structure the essay and its ideas?

5. What advice would you give the student for revising this essay? For instance, could any of the incidents she describes from her past be developed into fuller, more vivid narratives?

## Reaching Out: Chapter Activities

1. Working in small groups, read out loud and discuss one another's essays. After the workshop, reflect on this peer review experience and write up your findings. How did you establish your working relationships? Do you understand and relate to each other differently now than you did before this activity? Did a group identity seem to evolve? What effects will this workshop and perhaps future workshops have on class discussion? On class interactions in general? On how you view the role of the teacher and peers in your class?

2. Take part in a computer bulletin board or discussion group through networked computers with members of your class. You could take one of the readings in this chapter as a starting point or just open up the discussion on family relationships. Save and study the responses and exchanges that appear on your computer screen. How do people seem to relate to each other through this electronic medium? What sort of tone do the comments have? Do people display humor? Warmth? Anger? Amusement? Do participants argue? Do you think people get to know each other well after a while? What is it like participating in a discussion when you can't see the other "speakers" face to face, but only know them through written words on a computer screen, when you don't have clues about tone of voice, appearance, ethnicity, gender, accent, style of dress? Reflect on your experience and share your impressions with your classmates, either orally or in writing.

3. Are there agencies in your town or area that support families having difficulties in relationships (e.g., a marital-stress hotline, Adult Children of Alcoholics, family therapy services)? Look into what your local community provides. Then interview someone who works in such an agency to determine how the agency tries to help mediate or improve family relationships and write up the results of your interview.

4. Create a picture symbol for a parent; explain what you think the symbol reflects about your relationship. Have your parent reflect on the meaning of the picture symbol and then have a relative reflect on the picture symbol. Why does each person interpret the symbol differently?

5. With your peer review group of several members of your class, see a film focusing on family relationships. Compare your reactions to the film, perhaps in the form of brief film reviews that you share with each other and with class members. You might consider one of the films listed below.

*Hannah and Her Sisters.* Dir., Woody Allen. With Mia Farrow, Barbara Hershey, Michael Caine. 1986.

*In Country.* Dir., Norman Jewison. With Bruce Willis and Emily Lloyd. 1989.

*Parenthood.* Dir., Ron Howard. With Steve Martin. 1989.

*Rain Man.* Dir., Barry Levinson. With Tom Cruise and Dustin Hoffman. 1988.

*Terms of Endearment.* Dir., James Brooks. With Deborah Winger, Shirley Maclaine. 1983.

CHAPTER THREE

# *Myths and Rituals*

*The myth, whatever its nature, is always a precedent and an example.*
—Mircea Eliade, *Patterns in Comparative Religion*

*The great enemy of the truth is very often not the lie—deliberate, contrived and dishonest—but the myth—persistent, persuasive and unrealistic.*
—John F. Kennedy, commencement address, Yale University, 1962

*We should be wise . . . to arrange good special days for our children and also to enjoy these events to the full.*
—Bruno Bettelheim, "Magic Days"

The vivid memories as well as the close relationships you established with your family as a child have helped to shape your identity and view of the world, creating a personal mythology. As Mircea Eliade says in the quotation above, the stories a culture tells and retells in its myths create for the individual and for society both "a precedent and an example," guiding the choices people make in their lives. The myths you have created about the family, as well as what your culture and society tell you about the family—that it is a paradise with wise, benevolent parent figures, or a hell complete with "bad seed" siblings and evil stepmothers—will determine, at least in part, what kind of family you create in the future, what kind of family heritage you pass on to your own children.

Along with the family stories about parents, grandparents, and relatives that you were told as children, your personality and values have been influenced by the folktales and myths that are common to your culture. Traditional tales such as "Cinderella," Dickens's *A Christmas Carol,* or *Little House on the Prairie* have helped many generations of children find a sense of hope and heroism as well as a fundamental pattern or example for their own lives and the lives of their families. In coming to understand and define your belief system through reflecting on values that your family upholds, you may rethink a familiar family myth or story and find new meanings in it. However, as John F. Kennedy suggests in the quotation at the beginning of this chapter, the mythical or idealized images of life that such stories contain may not be borne out in reality, sometimes resulting in disillusion or disappointment in the values the myths were designed to uphold.

Along with the myths, stories, or legends told within the family, ritual observances—holiday celebrations, family games, and vacations—also play important roles in shaping an individual's inner life. These rituals reinforce the myths of the family through repetition, as the Christmas celebration, for instance, tells Christians each December 25 to honor the birth of Jesus through rituals of family togetherness, visits of relatives, and the exchange of gifts among family members.

Each family creates its own family rituals from the repertoire of beliefs and repeated practices handed down within a culture. Celebrating a holiday in a special way, going on family outings or vacations, participating in a sport as a family, even eating together at a regular time and place can bring family members closer and give their shared life a pattern in which to create understanding and value. However, in our rapidly changing world, families may find that members are simply too busy with work, activities with peers, or media consumption to spend time at home in leisurely family meals and other family-oriented, activities.

The readings in this chapter will help you explore the ways in which family myths and rituals have helped shape your self-concept and values. The chapter contains a selection from Charles Dickens's *A Christmas Carol* which presents an old-fashioned English family Christmas; an essay by Bruno Bettelheim, "Magic Days," that argues for the importance of myth-oriented family rituals and celebrations in the life of children; a selection from Laura Ingalls Wilder's *Little House on the Prairie* that illustrates the early American pioneer myth of family life; and, in vivid contrast, an essay by journalist Lance Morrow which points out that many American families will never be able to own their own home.

In "Explanation Myths" sociologist Elizabeth Stone discusses the ways in which family stories help create family values while the next selection, "No Name Woman" from Maxine Hong Kingston's memoir *The Woman Warrior,* provides a haunting example of a Chinese family story. In Alberto Rios's poem "Nani," family traditions and stories are explored. The chapter concludes with an essay by a student, Carlos Perez, who argues that the public myths and rituals practiced in our society can have a negative effect on those whose heritage has been uprooted by the dominant American culture.

Reflecting on the essays, stories, and poetry in this section should help you understand your own family as well as your connections to the legacy of family myths and ideals embedded in your culture. These reading selections may lead you to ask some questions about the continued relevance of myths and traditions from earlier times as well as to contemplate new myths and rituals that may help you plan for your future.

**CHARLES DICKENS: "The Cratchits' Christmas," from *A Christmas Carol***
Charles Dickens (1812–1870), an English novelist, was born into a large, impoverished family. Dickens' first-hand knowledge of debtors' prison and child
labor came to play a major part in his socially critical novels. Dickens turned
to writing early in his life, working first as a newspaper reporter and then de-
voting himself full-time to writing his novels after the success of *The Pickwick
Papers* (1837). Children play a prominent role in many of his novels, such as
*Oliver Twist* (1839) and *David Copperfield* (1850). In the seasonal favorite, *A
Christmas Carol* (1843), from which the following selection is taken, Dickens
again focuses on the struggle by children and families to survive poverty in
mid-nineteenth-century England. However, the novel has a positive outcome,
as the central character, the stingy and alienated Scrooge, rediscovers his humanity and experiences the redemptive power of the family and the "Christmas spirit." As you read the following selection from the novel, notice how
Dickens creates a magical sense of the power of the family holiday celebration
through using strong sensory images to describe the Cratchits' Christmas feast.

CHARLES DICKENS

# *The Cratchits' Christmas*

And perhaps it was the pleasure the good Spirit had in showing off this
power of his, or else it was his own kind, generous, hearty nature, and
his sympathy with all poor men, that led him straight to Scrooge's
clerk's; for there he went, and took Scrooge with him, holding to his
robe; and on the threshold of the door the Spirit smiled, and stopped to
bless Bob Cratchit's dwelling with the sprinkling of his torch. Think of
that! Bob had but fifteen "Bob" a-week himself; he pocketed on Saturdays but fifteen copies of his Christian name; and yet the Ghost of
Christmas Present blessed his four-roomed house!

Then up rose Mrs. Cratchit, Cratchit's wife, dressed out but poorly
in a twice-turned gown, but brave in ribbons, which are cheap and
make a goodly show for sixpence; and she laid the cloth, assisted by
Belinda Cratchit, second of her daughters, also brave in ribbons; while
Master Peter Cratchit plunged a fork into the saucepan of potatoes,
and getting the corners of his monstrous shirtcollar (Bob's private
property, conferred upon his son and heir in honour of the day) into

his mouth, rejoiced to find himself so gallantly attired, and yearned to show his linen in the fashionable Parks. And now two smaller Cratchits, boy and girl, came tearing in, screaming that outside the baker's they had smelt the goose, and known it for their own; and basking in luxurious thoughts of sage and onion, these young Cratchits danced about the table, and exalted Master Peter Cratchit to the skies, while he (not proud, although his collars nearly choked him) blew the fire, until the slow potatoes bubbling up, knocked loudly at the saucepan-lid to be let out and peeled.

"What has ever got your precious father then," said Mrs. Cratchit. "And your brother, Tiny Tim; and Martha warn't as late last Christmas Day by half-an-hour!"

"Here's Martha, mother!" said a girl, appearing as she spoke.

"Here's Martha, mother!" cried the two young Cratchits. "Hurrah! There's *such* a goose, Martha!"

"Why, bless your heart alive, my dear, how late you are!" said Mrs. Cratchit, kissing her a dozen times, and taking off her shawl and bonnet for her, with officious zeal.

"We'd a deal of work to finish up last night," replied the girl, "and had to clear away this morning, mother!"

"Well! Never mind so long as you are come," said Mrs. Cratchit. "Sit ye down before the fire, my dear, and have a warm, Lord bless ye!"

"No no! There's father coming," cried the two young Cratchits, who were everywhere at once. "Hide Martha, hide!"

So Martha hid herself, and in came little Bob, the father, with at least three feet of comforter exclusive of the fringe, hanging down before him; and his thread-bare clothes darned up and brushed, to look seasonable; and Tiny Tim upon his shoulder. Alas for Tiny Tim, he bore a little crutch, and had his limbs supported by an iron frame!

"Why, where's our Martha?" cried Bob Cratchit looking round.

"Not coming," said Mrs. Cratchit.

"Not coming!" said Bob, with a sudden declension in his high spirits; for he had been Tim's blood horse all the way from church, and had come home rampant. "Not coming upon Christmas Day!"

Martha didn't like to see him disappointed, if it were only in joke; so she came out prematurely from behind the closet door, and ran into his arms, while the two young Cratchits hustled Tiny Tim, and bore him off into the wash-house, that he might hear the pudding singing in the copper.

"And how did little Tim behave?" asked Mrs. Cratchit, when she had rallied Bob on his credulity and Bob had hugged his daughter to his heart's content.

"As good as gold," said Bob, "and better. Somehow he gets thoughtful sitting by himself so much, and thinks the strangest things you ever heard. He told me, coming home, that he hoped the people saw him in the church, because he was a cripple, and it might be pleasant to them to remember upon Christmas Day, who made lame beggars walk and blind men see."

Bob's voice was tremulous when he told them this, and trembled more when he said that Tiny Tim was growing strong and hearty.

His active little crutch was heard upon the floor, and back came Tiny Tim before another word was spoken, escorted by his brother and sister to his stool before the fire; and while Bob, turning up his cuffs—as if, poor fellow, they were capable of being made more shabby—compounded some hot mixture in a jug with gin and lemons, and stirred it round and round and put it on the hob to simmer; Master Peter, and the two ubiquitous young Cratchits went to fetch the goose, with which they soon returned in high procession.

Such a bustle ensued that you might have thought a goose the rarest of all birds; a feathered phenomenon, to which a black swan was a matter of course; and in truth it was something very like it in that house. Mrs. Cratchit made the gravy (ready beforehand in a little saucepan) hissing hot; Master Peter mashed the potatoes with incredible vigour; Miss Belinda sweetened up the apple-sauce; Martha dusted the hot plates; Bob took Tiny Tim beside him in a tiny corner at the table; the two young Cratchits set chairs for everybody, not forgetting themselves, and mounting guard upon their posts, crammed spoons into their mouths, lest they should shriek for goose before their turn came to be helped. At last the dishes were set on, and grace was said. It was succeeded by a breathless pause, as Mrs. Cratchit, looking slowly all along the carving-knife, prepared to plunge it in the breast; but when she did, and when the long expected gush of stuffing issued forth, one murmur of delight arose all round the board, and even Tiny Tim, excited by the two young Cratchits, beat on the table with the handle of his knife, and feebly cried Hurrah!

There never was such a goose. Bob said he didn't believe there ever was such a goose cooked. Its tenderness and flavour, size and cheapness, were the themes of universal admiration. Eked out by the apple-sauce and mashed potatoes, it was a sufficient dinner for the whole family; indeed, as Mrs. Cratchit said with great delight (surveying one small atom of a bone upon the dish), they hadn't ate it all at last! Yet every one had had enough, and the youngest Cratchits in particular, were steeped in sage and onion to the eyebrows! But now, the plates being changed by Miss Belinda, Mrs. Cratchit left the room alone—too nervous to bear witnesses—to take the pudding up, and bring it in.

Suppose it should not be done enough! Suppose it should break in turning out! Suppose somebody should have got over the wall of the back-yard, and stolen it, while they were merry with the goose: a supposition at which the two young Cratchits became livid! All sorts of horrors were supposed.

Hallo! A great deal of steam! The pudding was out of the copper. A smell like a washing-day! That was the cloth. A smell like an eating-house, and a pastry cook's next door to each other, with a laundress's next door to that! That was the pudding. In half a minute Mrs. Cratchit entered: flushed, but smiling proudly: with the pudding, like a speckled cannon-ball, so hard and firm, blazing in half of half-a-quartern of ignited brandy, and bedight with Christmas holly stuck into the top.

Oh, a wonderful pudding! Bob Cratchit said, and calmly too, that he regarded it as the greatest success achieved by Mrs. Cratchit since their marriage. Mrs. Cratchit said that now the weight was off her mind, she would confess she had had her doubts about the quantity of flour. Everybody had something to say about it, but nobody said or thought it was at all a small pudding for a large family. It would have been flat heresy to do so. Any Cratchit would have blushed to hint at such a thing.

At last the dinner was all done, the cloth was cleared, the hearth swept, and the fire made up. The compound in the jug being tasted, and considered perfect, apples and oranges were put upon the table, and a shovel-full of chestnuts on the fire. Then all the Cratchit family drew round the hearth, in what Bob Cratchit called a circle, meaning half a one; and at Bob Cratchit's elbow stood the family display of glass; two tumblers, and a custard-cup without a handle.

These held the hot stuff from the jug, however, as well as golden goblets would have done; and Bob served it out with beaming looks, while the chestnuts on the fire sputtered and crackled noisily. Then Bob proposed:

"A Merry Christmas to us all, my dears. God bless us!"

Which all the family re-echoed.

"God bless us every one!" said Tiny Tim, the last of all.

He sat very close to his father's side, upon his little stool. Bob held his withered little hand in his, as if he loved the child, and wished to keep him by his side, and dreaded that he might be taken from him.

"Spirit," said Scrooge, with an interest he had never felt before, "tell me if Tiny Tim will live."

"I see a vacant seat," replied the Ghost, "in the poor chimney corner, and a crutch without an owner, carefully preserved. If these shadows remain unaltered by the Future, the child will die."

"No, no," said Scrooge. "Oh no, kind Spirit! say he will be spared."

"If these shadows remain unaltered by the Future, none other of my race," returned the Ghost, "will find him here. What then? If he be like to die, he had better do it, and decrease the surplus population."

Scrooge hung his head to hear his own words quoted by the Spirit, and was overcome with penitence and grief.

"Man," said the Ghost, "if man you be in heart, not adamant, forbear that wicked cant until you have discovered What the surplus is, and Where it is. Will you decide what men shall live, what men shall die? It may be, that in the sight of Heaven, you are more worthless and less fit to live than millions like this poor man's child. Oh God! to hear the Insect on the leaf pronouncing on the too much life among his hungry brothers in the dust!"

125

*Looking at Ideas:*

1. What is the economic status of Bob Cratchit and his family? What does the story suggest about the role that economic status plays in the traditional power and meaning of Christmas?

2. How effectively does the Cratchit family cooperate in preparing their Christmas feast? What role does each family member play in the celebration?

3. Mrs. Cratchit asks Bob how Tiny Tim behaved in church and Bob replies, "As good as gold." What are the implications of this response, in terms of both the value of material wealth and the nature of Tiny Tim's character and value within the family?

4. What impact does the spectacle of Cratchit's family have upon Scrooge? What is the Ghost's reply to Scrooge's question? Based on what you know of Scrooge's character, does the Ghost seem unnecessarily cruel to Scrooge?

*Looking at Strategies:*

1. How does Dickens's use of descriptive detail appeal to the readers' senses, making us feel like participants at the Cratchits' feast? Refer to passages in the text.

2. How does the presence of the characters of Scrooge and the Ghost help to present the image of the Cratchits' Christmas in a larger social and economic context?

3. What devices does Dickens use to contrast the relative lavishness of the Cratchits' Christmas with their poverty? Which seems more effective at presenting this contrast—Dickens's use of details, or the filmed versions of the story you have seen in the past?

*Looking at Connections:*

1. Compare the view of the importance of family traditions and ritual celebrations presented here with the views of Bettelheim in "Magic Days," the next selection in this chapter. Do the Cratchits' attitudes and behavior seem to support Bettelheim's theories?

2. Compare Dickens's image of the family as a refuge and a bulwark against a threatening world with that presented in the third reading in this chapter, the selection from Wilder's *Little House on the Prairie.* Which selection reflects more confidence in the family's powers to withstand the forces of the outside world?

*Suggestions for Writing:*

1. Develop the journal entry at the beginning of the chapter into an essay on the value of traditional ritual celebrations for your family. Did such celebrations constitute an essential core of your family life? Did they give your family courage to survive the pressures of routine existence? Did they point out for you underlying conflicts and inconsistencies in your family's values and life-style?

2. Write an essay in which you contrast the image portrayed in the Cratchits' nineteenth-century English Christmas with Christmas or some

other holiday ritual as celebrated within your family and community. What differences do you perceive in the content of the ritual, the participation by family members, and the sense of a shared, clear meaning for the celebration as a whole?

3. Poverty is a disturbing theme in Dickens's narrative. Based on your experiences, observations, or research, contrast the way Christmas or some other holiday is celebrated in your community by affluent or middle-class families with the way it is celebrated by poor families or homeless people.

**JOURNAL ENTRY**

Describe how you celebrate Christmas or some other holiday according to
your own beliefs and values. Do you draw upon the rituals and activities
you remember from your childhood holiday observances, or have you
modified older rituals to accommodate your new values or those of your
current family or friendship group?

**BRUNO BETTELHEIM: "Magic Days"**   Born in Vienna, Austria, and educated
in psychology at the University of Vienna, Bruno Bettelheim (1903–1990) became a well-known child psychologist and author. After surviving the concentration camps at Dachau and Buchenwald, Bettelheim emigrated to the United
States in 1939. He settled in Chicago, where he became a professor of psychiatry and worked as head of the Orthogenic School, which provided a therapeutic environment for autistic children. Bettelheim was especially interested
in the child's intellectual and emotional growth through reading and acculturation. He was the author of over 20 books, which include *The Uses of Enchantment: The Meaning and Importance of Fairy Tales* (1976), *On Learning to
Read: The Child's Fascination with Meaning* (1982), and *A Good Enough Parent* (1987), from which the following selection is taken. Notice how Bettelheim draws on his own childhood experiences to persuade his modern readers
of the importance of familiar, traditional games, rituals, and celebrations in
helping children develop emotional stability and an optimistic world view.

BRUNO BETTELHEIM

# *Magic Days*

*Young and old come forth to play*
*On a sunshine holiday.*                    —John Milton, "L'Allegro"

It is very exhilarating to feel that one is the special cause of a celebration, as a child may experience on his birthday. Such personally significant moments are truly to be cherished, for they provide us with great
happiness at the moment and also with a sustaining hope for the future. The more insignificant and insecure we feel about our place in the
world, the more we need the affirmation of our importance—if possible
from the whole universe, but at least from those persons who mean
most to us.

   Children especially need this experience, as we recognize when we
celebrate children's holidays, both individual ones such as birthdays
and others when all children are made to feel very special, such as
Christmas. On these occasions children stand in the center of affection-

ate attention and are made to feel important; the gifts they receive prove to them that they are loved and also that they are worthwhile persons. If such occasions are celebrated in the right spirit, the glow from these days can spread out over the rest of life. The regular repetition of these events is the child's guarantee of his continuing importance; holidays punctuate the child's year and with it his life; they are the highlights of the year for him, which demonstrates that such organization of one's life is best achieved around happy events.

We do not know exactly what the first holidays expressed symbolically, but there is little doubt that they were celebrations of life and of that which sustains it; thus the ample, festive meal is still the centerpiece of any true holiday and often symbolizes the holiday spirit. A distinction must be made here between religious *holy days* such as fast days and days of contrition—which to the believer are important spiritual observances—and the more secular occasions experienced as *holidays* by children and often the whole community, universal festivals when even a deeply religious person like Milton felt it was appropriate for young and old to "come forth to play."

The first organized and regularly observed holidays were ritual evocations meant to assure the fertility and with it the birth and rebirth of plants, animals, and men. Others were rites of passage to secure, solemnize, and glorify stages in the maturing of man, or seasons of the year. In the ancient Judeo-Christian tradition, religious festivals were manifestations of communal joy. In fact, the Hebrew word for holiday or festival, *chag,* is derived from the root word *chug,* which means to dance in a circle, and this is the way the Hasidic Jew still celebrates religious feasts; the Hebrew for Passover means literally "the feast of leaping." Today our greatest holidays, whether religious or patriotic, solemnize and celebrate birth: that of the Christ child; the Resurrection—the rebirth—of the Lord; and the birth of nations, just as the child's birthday celebrates his own birth. (That the Christian church decided to commemorate the unknown date of Christ's birth at the time of the winter solstice indicates the close symbolic connection between the birth of the Savior and the reawakening of nature's yearly life cycle in the Western world.) Passover also celebrates not only gaining freedom from slavery, but also the birth of the Jewish nation. It led to the giving of the Ten Commandments, the basis of Jewish law. The Last Supper, which was the Passover meal, began the sequence of events which led to Redemption and the Resurrection on Easter Sunday with its chance for "a new life."

All these festivals are magical events, for what could be more magical than the birth of a child, or the rebirth of the world? What holds more magic for mankind than the promise of a chance for a new beginning? Originally, the celebration of these holidays included donning of vestments of ritual or magical significance; new Easter finery and the funny hats people put on at birthday or New Year's parties are the last vestiges of this practice. The presents a child receives at Christmas and on his birthday are symbolic of the gifts of the three holy kings; and

129

fireworks are symbols of a new sun which will bring the light and joy of freedom and a new life, a hope that the lighted Christmas tree also symbolizes.

Long before the lighting of the Christmas tree became part of the celebration of this holiday in northern Europe, huge bonfires were started in pagan times on the mountaintops on the day of the winter solstice to symbolically or magically encourage the sun to increase the length of days and again warm the earth. The bringing in and lighting of the yule log is a remnant of this custom, reduced to just one large log. Even more ancient than the lighted Christmas tree is the Jewish custom of lighting candles during the feast of Hanukkah, which celebrates a magic event: namely, that the lamp in the Temple in Jerusalem continued to burn although its oil supply had been exhausted. Thus, as often happens, the magic ritual (in this case consisting of lighting trees and candles) continues, while with the passing of time, different meanings are attached to the ritual. Whatever the meaning of the rituals which have entered our Christmas celebrations may have been in the past, now they symbolize the wondrous birth of a child who created a new era—our own—and gave a new meaning to all of human life.

Children's holidays have one unique feature: distinctions of rank or authority are obliterated or reversed. A child is king on his birthday; he can make demands of adults or even make them fear him on Halloween; and he is allowed to fool them on April Fools' Day. These status reversals and magical connotations are important reasons why holidays are especially meaningful and pleasurable for children. A child is badly deprived if he cannot fully enjoy special holidays or benefit from what these symbolize; such symbolic meanings are built permanently into our unconscious experience of the world. Thus while holidays are here for all of us to enjoy, how they were celebrated when we were children can and does have the most far-reaching consequences over the rest of our lives.

"Holidays are the secret anniversaries of the heart," the poet Longfellow reminds us, speaking as an adult to adults. And when we were young, these yearly recurring days were joyously and eagerly awaited, their festive pleasures anticipated for many weeks, if not for months or even all year long. Holidays most pleasantly punctuated our lives and gave a positive meaning to the ongoing days. As mature adults, we often decide that we no longer ought to give in to such childish views of what makes life worth living, so many of us tend to keep our feelings about holidays secret, not only from others, but also from ourselves. Their meaning to us, however, remains deeply anchored in our unconscious; this is why Longfellow called them secret anniversaries of the heart. Our feelings about these special days thus become internalized as part of our hidden inner life.

## The Symbolic Meaning of Holidays

The way we celebrate many holidays has changed quite a bit. For example, Christmas, from being an essentially religious festivity, with the giving of gifts only to children, had developed during the last century into more and more of a family holiday, in which all members participate equally—now everybody gives presents to everyone else. There is certainly nothing wrong with any sort of family holiday; in fact, it would be most beneficial if families were to celebrate such holidays more often. Older generations can remember when in their childhood almost every Sunday was a family holiday—the occasion for a gathering of the clan; this might mean twenty people or more all together, because families tended to be larger then, and also because kinfolk lived physically, emotionally, and socially much closer to each other. Even when there were occasional arguments, these added excitement to the enjoyment and were soon amicably settled, as everybody had a good time around a plentiful meal. The adults enjoyed each other, the children played together, and family problems could be discussed and resolved.

Among the happiest memories of my childhood are the times when I and the cousins near my age—we were called "the little ones"—played under the huge table around which a dozen or more adult members of the family had gathered, often forgetting that we were literally underfoot. We would play together in the cozy darkness, hidden by the huge tablecloth that hung down nearly to the floor; as we played we listened to the talk and arguments of those we called "the big ones." We and they, each group on its own level, thus had a grand time every Sunday.

The closest many of our children and our families come to this type of experience is at Thanksgiving. To the young child, Thanksgiving means first and foremost the turkey dinner with all its trimmings, and secondly, the family getting together to enjoy a very special occasion. Teachers and parents might explain the history of the holiday, but what stands out in the child's mind—and in adults' minds as well—is the plentiful food and the spirit of good fellowship. On a conscious level, such holidays are meaningful to the child mainly because of the warm feelings evoked in him by all the festivity, and this may later reflect a pleasant glow onto the more abstract ideas connected with the celebration. However, on a subconscious level, some of what the day symbolizes continues to exercise its influence.

Fear of physical and emotional deprivation are the two greatest anxieties of man. Hunger and starvation are the basic forms of the first, desertion—of which death is only the last and ultimate form—of the second. The young child does not understand death and thus does not fear his own, while that of his parents is feared in the form of permanent desertion. Although in our society children do not actually starve, everyone experiences more or less severe pangs of hunger at one time or another; and all children suffer temporary desertion when their parents are not available. These two forms of the first real deprivations most children experience become greatly magnified in the unconscious, where they come to stand for, and are symbols of, all anxiety. (Even fears of dangerous animals, so frequent in the nightmares of children,

131

are experienced by them as special cases of the fear of desertion, because these ferocious animals are dangerous only because of the absence of parents, who otherwise would chase them away and thus fully protect the child.)

Family holidays celebrated around a table set with an ample and festive meal thus combat the child's greatest anxieties, both as real experiences and, what is much more important, also on a symbolic level. The "gathering of the clan" reassures the child that for his security against desertion he need not rely solely on his parents, that there are many other relatives who would be available in a crisis and would protect him against desertion. The ample meal similarly provides security, both on the real and much more important on a symbolic level against starvation anxiety. In this way such family holidays are, both as a conscious experience and on an unconscious level, one of the most reassuring experiences the child can have in regard to his most fervent anxieties. They are among the most constructive experiences we can provide for him to buttress his security.

Thus, with good reason the story of Thanksgiving stresses that a successful harvest saved the Pilgrims from the starvation and privation they had known the winter before. In this way the holiday symbolizes a rescue, and the beginning of a better and more secure life, a symbolic rebirth on a better plane. At base, all our most important celebrations— Christmas, Easter, Fourth of July, birthdays—commemorate births or rebirths. The hope inherent in this symbolic meaning continues to reverberate in us, whether we know it or not.

Throughout the history of man, holiday ceremonies themselves and the happy feelings attached to them have outlasted the specific event or idea which originally sparked the holiday; as noted before, these ideas alter over time. For example, Christmas was at first a pagan ritual celebrating the rebirth of the sun and of nature, long before the idea of the birth of Christ became attached to it. Similarly, the most ancient holiday rituals, those carrying the deepest unconscious and emotional significance, have a way of reappearing in different form, sometimes after a lapse of centuries. So the huge fires lighted on high mountaintops at the winter solstice to encourage the sun to start remaining longer in the sky reappear after centuries, as lights on the Christmas tree. Such celebrations are simply too important to be relinquished, because they serve deep, often unconscious needs. As the way these traditional celebrations have been observed has changed over time, and different ideas have become attached to them, so too do we as individuals alter the way we celebrate holidays over our lifetimes. From our own experience we all know how the ideas we connect with Christmas changed as we matured, from Santa and his reindeers to the spirit of giving, from the enjoyment of receiving presents to that of giving them to others. . . .

The wonderful thing about the positive magic of holiday happiness is that it can provide security all during the year when it is most needed, even under life's worst circumstances. Children know this, and when given the chance, they use the symbolic security which the holiday spirit offers to provide themselves with moral support when they need it most desperately. A story told by the Swedish psychoanalyst Stefi Pedersen may illustrate this:

When the Nazis occupied Norway, Pedersen served as a guide for a group of refugees, including several children, who made their escape by fleeing in deep winter over the high mountains into Sweden. Nobody could take more than he could easily carry on his back, because the climb was difficult and speed was of the essence. For most of the group it was not their first escape from the Nazis, since a few years previously they had fled from Germany or Austria into Norway. Thus these refugees had experience with what it means to have to abandon almost all of one's possessions, taking along only what is most important. The group took its first, desperately needed rest only after reaching safety within the Swedish border. Once they had eaten the small amount of food they had taken along, very little was left in the children's small knapsacks. Pedersen happened to look into one child's bag, and there she found among the pitifully few objects a small silver star, the sort people hang on Christmas trees. She picked it up in surprise, but then she sensed that the child was staring at her in embarrassment, as if she had discovered a most precious secret. Without saying anything, Pedersen put the star carefully back in the child's bag.

Since she would be responsible for the children once they reached their destination in Sweden, and since as a child psychoanalyst she was deeply interested in what might provide psychological safety for them there, Pedersen decided to explore what else the children might have chosen as their most valuable possessions to bring along on their flight from home. So she looked into the bags of the other children, and again and again she found cheap Christmas-tree decorations— stars and bells made out of cardboard, covered with silver glitter. This was what these children—most of them of Jewish origin but raised in assimilated families who celebrated Christmas as a family and mainly a children's holiday, though not as a religious event—had chosen to take with them from Norway in preference to all else. Otherwise, they owned nothing but the clothes they wore. Pedersen concluded that they had taken along these symbols of a happy past because these alone could cast a spell of safety over the anguish they felt as they embarked on a trip into the fearful unknown. On their journey out into nothing, the tinselly little ornaments—symbols of a happiness they had once known in their homes and with their families—assuaged their feeling of loneliness and impotence and held out a promise of hope.

The same evening, when they had reached a Swedish border village, a young Norwegian woman joined them. She had had to make a frantic escape to save her life, without even a half-hour's notice to pack a few essentials. Her flight had entailed several days of travel through the wilderness, so her knapsack could not be heavy. Now for the first time, she had the leisure to unpack her things. Besides a minimum of clothing, all she had carried with her was a heavy brass music box. Her

133

apologetic explanation was: "Well, I had to take something nice with me since I was going to leave forever."

The Danish actor Texiere once reported that the only thing he had managed to take with him on his flight to Sweden was a little snuffbox that had belonged to Hans Christian Andersen. Of little value in itself, the snuffbox was a symbol of the abundant life he had to leave behind. And a woman carried, among a few sturdy sports clothes appropriate to a trek over the mountains, a pair of high-heeled gold shoes. Again and again among the scant belongings that these refugees took along when leaving their homes forever there were things which, viewed objectively, would have seemed peculiar choices, completely inappropriate when considering what a refugee would need most. None of these objects related in any rational way to the situation of these refugees. But they were objects which had come to represent symbolically what had been best in their lives, and as such were both last remnants of a good life and the promise of a continuing life that would have its happy moments.

Anyone who has had experience with people in similar desperate situations could easily duplicate these stories. Most remarkable here is the difference between what adults and children trusted to sustain them in extreme adversity. Adults typically took along some object that symbolized for them experiences of happiness with real people. The heavy music box, it turned out, had been given to the lady by someone who had loved her, and whom she had loved. The woman who took along the golden shoes had worn them on the happiest day of her life, when she had felt particularly beautiful and successful. On the other hand, the children sought and found comfort in something that reminded them of a happy occasion they had shared with their parents, but which at the same time symbolized powers even higher than their parents. Most of all, their tokens stood for a predictably recurring, particularly happy day for children. Desperate as their situation was at the moment, these Christmas decorations seemed to assure the children that in the future, happiness would again be theirs.

This, then, is probably the deepest and most reassuring meaning of Christmas for a child: a memory that sustains him in situations of adversity, as it did the young refugees in their extreme distress. The symbolic promise contained in the little Christmas ornaments spelled hope to these children, when everything seemed utterly hopeless. Children feel this subconsciously; that is why they hold on to the fiction of Santa Claus, who is the carrier of a very special symbolic meaning.

## QUESTIONS

*Looking at Ideas*

1. According to Bettelheim, what do holidays actually celebrate? What support does he provide for his position?

2. How are customary positions of power within the family reversed during children's holidays?

3. According to Bettelheim, how has the way we celebrate major holidays such as Christmas changed in the past century?
4. Why does Bettelheim believe that family holidays help children to combat their greatest anxieties? Do you agree?
5. Why is it important, in Bettelheim's opinion, for children to believe in such figures as Santa Claus and the Easter Bunny? Did you believe in these or other mythical characters as a child?
6. How can holidays help adults make up for past disappointments in childhood?

*Looking at Strategies:*
1. Bettelheim, an experienced child psychiatrist, gives a number of case histories to support his general observations about the function of holidays in family life. Which of his examples were most convincing? Were there any that could have used development?
2. Bettelheim makes the discussion in the essay personal by including some reminiscences of his own childhood. Is this an effective strategy in an essay intended for a general audience?
3. Psychiatrists are trained in the analysis of symbols, many of which occur in dreams as well as in daily life. How does Bettelheim analyze the significance of key symbols, both private and public, attached to holiday observances?

*Looking at Connections:*
1. Compare Bettelheim's view of ritual celebrations with the ritual of the meal in Alberto Rios's poem "Nani" at the end of this chapter. Which writer sees the power of ritual more positively? What different values does each writer emphasize?
2. Contrast Bettelheim's view of ritual with that of P. W. Alexander in Chapter Nine, in her essay about the importance of Christmas as a time for helping others. How do you think Bettelheim would respond to Alexander's thesis?

*Suggestions for Writing:*
1. Write an essay about a holiday observance that helped you get over a feeling of loss or anxiety you had experienced earlier in the year, or a holiday in which the joy of the season was overshadowed by a loss.
2. Write an essay in which you compare your feelings about a recent holiday celebration to your responses to the ritual as a child. How was this holiday different for you as an adult? Did you experience a feeling of loss, of new insight, or of growth and renewal?
3. Argue either the advantages or disadvantages to children of believing in mythical holiday figures such as Santa, the Easter Bunny, or the Tooth Fairy. How might such figures help children learn a meaningful value system or possibly perpetrate unrealistic fantasies?

**JOURNAL ENTRY**

Write about the experience of moving with your family to a new home or apartment, or moving away from your family and into your own apartment or room. What did you discover about your family and yourself through this experience?

**LAURA INGALLS WILDER: "Moving In," from *Little House on the Prairie***
From a family of pioneer farmers, Laura Ingalls Wilder (1867–1957) lived most of her life in the Midwest/Great Plains states of Iowa, Missouri, Kansas, and South Dakota. A graduate of a one-room schoolhouse, Wilder became, at age 15, a teacher in such a school. Wilder began to write her "Little House on the Prairie" stories at her daughter's insistence. The stories, a realistic picture of pioneer life in the Midwest based on her own girlhood, eventually became one of America's most famous series of children's books and formed the basis of a long-running television series. In the following selection, a chapter from *Little House on the Prairie* (1945), Wilder tells how her family built a cabin on the frontier. Notice how Wilder emphasizes the need for cooperation in the pioneer family's efforts to survive in a sometimes threatening environment.

LAURA INGALLS WILDER

# *Moving In*

"The walls are up," Pa was saying to Ma in the morning. "We'd better move in and get along as best we can without a floor or other fixings. I must build the stable as fast as I can, so Pet and Patty can be inside walls, too. Last night I could hear wolves howling from every direction, seemed like, and close, too."

"Well, you have your gun, so I'll not worry," said Ma.

"Yes, and there's Jack. But I'll feel easier in my mind when you and the girls have good solid walls around you."

"Why do you suppose we haven't seen any Indians?" Ma asked.

"Oh, I don't know," Pa replied, carelessly. "I've seen their camping-places among the bluffs. They're away on a hunting-trip now, I guess."

Then Ma called: "Girls! The sun's up!" and Laura and Mary scrambled out of bed and into their clothes.

"Eat your breakfasts quickly," Ma said, putting the last of the rabbit stew on their tin plates. "We're moving into the house today, and all the chips must be out."

So they ate quickly, and hurried to carry all the chips out of the house. They ran back and forth as fast as they could, gathering their skirts full of chips and dumping them in a pile near the fire. But there were still chips on the ground inside the house when Ma began to sweep it with her willow-bough broom.

Ma limped, though her sprained ankle was beginning to get well. But she soon swept the earthen floor, and then Mary and Laura began to help her carry things into the house.

Pa was on top of the walls, stretching the canvas wagon-top over the skeleton roof of saplings. The canvas billowed in the wind, Pa's beard blew wildly and his hair stood up from his head as if it were trying to pull itself out. He held onto the canvas and fought it. Once it jerked so hard that Laura thought he must let go or sail into the air like a bird. But he held tight to the wall with his legs, and tight to the canvas with his hands, and he tied it down.

"There!" he said to it. "Stay where you are, and be—"

"Charles!" Ma said. She stood with her arms full of quilts and looked up at him reprovingly.

"—and be good," Pa said to the canvas. "Why, Caroline, what did you think I was going to say?"

"Oh, Charles!" Ma said. "You scalawag!"

Pa came right down the corner of the house. The ends of the logs stuck out, and he used them for a ladder. He ran his hand through his hair so that it stood up even more wildly, and Ma burst out laughing. Then he hugged her, quilts and all.

Then they looked at the house and Pa said, "How's that for a snug house!"

"I'll be thankful to get into it," said Ma.

There was no door and there were no windows. There was no floor except the ground and no roof except the canvas. But that house had good stout walls, and it would stay where it was. It was not like the wagon, that every morning went on to some other place.

"We're going to do well here, Caroline," Pa said. "This is a great country. This is a country I'll be contented to stay in the rest of my life."

"Even when it's settled up?" Ma asked.

"Even when it's settled up. No matter how thick and close the neighbors get, this country'll never feel crowded. Look at that sky!"

Laura knew what he meant. She liked this place, too. She liked the enormous sky and the winds, and the land that you couldn't see to the end of. Everything was so fresh and clean and big and splendid.

By dinner time the house was in order. The beds were neatly made on the floor. The wagon-seat and two ends of logs were brought in for chairs. Pa's gun lay on its pegs above the doorway. Boxes and bundles were neat against the walls. It was a pleasant house. A soft light came through the canvas roof, wind and sunshine came through the window holes, and every crack in the four walls glowed a little because the sun was overhead.

Only the camp fire stayed where it had been. Pa said he would build a fireplace in the house as soon as he could. He would hew out slabs to

137

make a solid roof, too, before winter came. He would lay a puncheon floor, and make beds and tables and chairs. But all that work must wait until he had helped Mr. Edwards and had built a stable for Pet and Patty.

"When that's all done," said Ma, "I want a clothes-line."

Pa laughed. "Yes, and I want a well."

After dinner he hitched Pet and Patty to the wagon and he hauled a tubful of water from the creek, so that Ma could do the washing. "You could wash clothes in the creek," he told her. "Indian women do."

"If we wanted to live like Indians, you could make a hole in the roof to let the smoke out, and we'd have the fire on the floor inside the house," said Ma. "Indians do."

That afternoon she washed the clothes in the tub and spread them on the grass to dry.

After supper they sat for a while by the camp fire. That night they would sleep in the house; they would never sleep beside a camp fire again. Pa and Ma talked about the folks in Wisconsin, and Ma wished she could send them a letter. But Independence was forty miles away, and no letter could go until Pa made the long trip to the post-office there.

Back in the Big Woods so far away, Grandpa and Grandma and the aunts and uncles and cousins did not know where Pa and Ma and Laura and Mary and Baby Carrie were. And sitting there by the camp fire, no one knew what might have happened in the Big Woods. There was no way to find out.

"Well, it's bedtime," Ma said. Baby Carrie was already asleep. Ma carried her into the house and undressed her, while Mary unbuttoned Laura's dress and petticoat waist down the back, and Pa hung a quilt over the door hole. The quilt would be better than no door. Then Pa went out to bring Pet and Patty close to the house.

He called back, softly, "Come out here, Caroline, and look at the moon."

Mary and Laura lay in their little bed on the ground inside the new house, and watched the sky through the window hole to the east. The edge of the big, bright moon glittered at the bottom of the window space, and Laura sat up. She looked at the great moon, sailing silently higher in the clear sky.

Its light made silvery lines in all the cracks on that side of the house. The light poured through the window hole and made a square of soft radiance on the floor. It was so bright that Laura saw Ma plainly when she lifted the quilt at the door and came in.

Then Laura very quickly lay down, before Ma saw her naughtily sitting up in bed.

She heard Pet and Patty whinnying softly to Pa. Then the faint thuds of their feet came into her ear from the floor. Pet and Patty and Pa were coming toward the house, and Laura heard Pa singing.

> "Sail on, silver moon!
> Shed your radiance o'er the sky—"

His voice was like a part of the night and the moonlight and the stillness of the prairie. He came to the doorway, singing,

"By the pale, silver light of the moon—"

Softly Ma said, "Hush, Charles. You'll wake the children."

So Pa came in without a sound. Jack followed at his heels and lay down across the doorway. Now they were all inside the stout walls of their new home, and they were snug and safe. Drowsily Laura heard a long wolf-howl rising from far away on the prairie, but only a little shiver went up her backbone and she fell asleep.

## QUESTIONS

*Looking at Ideas:*

1. What traditional images of parental responsibility are presented in this selection? What seem to be the strengths and abilities of the father and the mother? How are their roles distinguished?

2. The story explores the early American myth of the "new start." In the early pioneer days of America, it was possible for a family who had suffered financial problems or discrimination to start over again simply by loading their possessions in a wagon and heading West. Does this myth of the new start still persist in the American family today?

3. An important aspect of the family rituals of the past came from family encounters with nature—camping out and together observing the changes in the weather, the scenery, and the wildlife. Has family togetherness in nature continued to be a significant aspect of family rituals in America? Why or why not?

*Looking at Strategies:*

1. How does Wilder's physical description of her parents and their chores help to clarify family relationships in the story? If you have seen the television version of *Little House*, you might comment on the differences between the characters in the TV version and the characters as you imagined them after reading the "Moving In" selection.

2. Wilder describes the family's cabin, only half-finished, in great detail. What does her description reveal about her feelings for the house and her new life on the prairie?

3. What do the singing and joking of the father add to the story? Why does Wilder use a simile to describe his voice: "His voice was like a part of the night and the moonlight and the stillness of the prairie"?

*Looking at Connections:*

1. Contrast the ability of the frontier family in "Moving In" to obtain their dream of home ownership with the obstacles in the path of the modern families profiled in the next selection, Lance Morrow's "Downsizing an American Dream."

2. Contrast the family home in "Moving In" with the futuristic home in Bradbury's "The Veldt" (Chapter Four). What would Bradbury think of

the Wilders' cabin? Would he consider it a satisfactory, humane environment for children to grow up in?

*Suggestions for Writing:*

1. Argue for or against the importance of clearly defined gender roles and home-oriented responsibilities for family members, such as those portrayed in "Moving In."
2. The selection from *Little House on the Prairie* presents an image of home and family as a bulwark of safety against a dangerous and threatening outside world. Contrast this frontier myth of the family with the modern status of home and family. Does the family still play the role of bulwark, or protective shield, for its members?
3. Some communities today offer special classes in building one's own home, while many families, particularly in rural areas, still create, or at least remodel, their own homes. Do some research into the do-it-yourself housing movement today and contrast it with the cooperative image of frontier cabin-building presented in "Moving In."

**LANCE MORROW: "Downsizing an American Dream"**  The son of a speech
writer for Nelson Rockefeller, Lance Morrow was born in 1939 in Lewisburg,
Pennsylvania, and educated at Harvard. Morrow is a journalist and free-lance
writer; currently he is a senior writer and editorialist with *Time* magazine. Morrow has written an autobiographical work, *The Chief: A Memoir of Fathers and
Sons* (1984), and has edited a collection of his own essays, *Fishing in the Tiber*
(1988). Morrow is known for his wit, his broad range of cultural reference, and
his grasp of recent history and political events. The following essay, "Downsizing an American Dream," which originally appeared in *Time,* was included in
*Fishing in the Tiber.* As you read Morrow's essay, notice how he sets out to
accomplish a double goal: to clarify how the dream of ownership of a large
home is no longer an option for many families and to argue for the advantages
of "downsizing" the egoism upon which such dreams are based.

LANCE MORROW

# Downsizing an American Dream

It is not really what we had in mind. It is not the American house we
dreamed of, not even the house we grew up in, the house we remember. Sometimes it stands a little too near the freeway, in a raw mat of
sodden lawn—a poignant dry-green whiffle of grass with a single sap-
ling in it that gives no more shade than a swizzle stick. The house has
the frank, bleak starkness of the cut-rate. Its interiors are minimalist,
and grimly candid about it. No woodwork, no extras, no little frills of
gentility anymore. No front hall. One bathroom, with the cheapest fix-
tures, no bathtub. Closets as shallow as medicine chests. Walls like shirt
cardboards, walls that will not hold the nail when we move in and try to
hang the family pictures.

All of this—the economy model stripped down to an irreducible as-
cetic tackiness—can be ours for more dollars than our fathers used to
earn, total, in ten or fifteen years, for a price that once would have purchased Tara, or at least the six-bedroom Lake Forest spread of a successful cardiologist.

Americans have always cherished an almost ideological longing for a
house of their own. Today, the fantasy of the dream house, the little fortress of home, My Blue Heaven, has jolted up against hard economics.

If inflation has not exactly devoured the dream, it has taken a painful bite out of it. Good, even splendid houses are still built; America is not suddenly being driven out into hovels and Hoovervilles. But the number of Americans who can afford first-class housing is dwindling. The traditional budget formula said that a family should spend no more than one-quarter of gross income on housing. If they obey that rule, less than 10 percent of Americans can afford a median-priced house.

Some older or more nimble Americans (especially those lucky enough to have bought a house in, say, the Eisenhower or Johnson or Nixon years) have done handsomely in the housing bazaar. But a lot of Americans have been left out. Some began to suspect that they were operating under some vast cultural misunderstanding. In a way, they were. Owning a house—a home, "the most lyrical of American symbols," Max Lerner once called it—began generations ago as one of the most basic aspirations. It was merely a hope then, not a sure thing. But some time during the suburban idyll of the postwar years, the idea of owning a house came to harden into a kind of entitlement. The baby-boom children of the broad American middle class were especially seduced by the illusion. Until now, through many headlong cultural confusions, they carried with them a barely conscious expectation, a sort of buried genetic code. When they chose to do so, when the babies started arriving, they could transform themselves into Ozzie and Harriet and find houses like the ones their parents owned—or nicer, maybe—and therein comfortably get on with the American dream. Now they scrunch down in a garden-apartment rental somewhere, with the crib in the living room and wolf frisking in the vestibule, and wonder what went wrong.

Americans feel a little foolish about complaining, or they should. The bungalow on the wrong side of the beltway is still no Mongolian yurt, no tar-paper shack in one of Rio's mountainside *favelas*. It is not Soviet housing, with the five-year waiting list for a room of one's own, and couples sometimes stolidly enduring their marriages because there is no other apartment (no other bed, even) to escape to. It is not like the arrangements in dense Hong Kong, as busily transient as an ant colony, or Tokyo, where much middle-class housing looks like the crew's quarters on a submarine.

The barest ticky-tacky American apartment or tract house gives the occupant on whim: hot water, electric lights, air conditioning pretty often, and far more sheltered space than anyone in the world (except for the most imperial and ostentatious) has ever had the luxury of rattling around in. Neolithic villagers periodically burned down their huts to incinerate their vermin; in the South Bronx people burn out their own apartments to obtain the welfare moving allowance, or landlords torch their buildings for the insurance: life among the ruins. Americans who feel sorry for themselves about their housing, middle-class Americans at least, have not explored the alternatives on the down side of civilization. Anyway, ideals of privacy, cleanliness, spaciousness, and a certain

142

domestic dignity are fairly new to the history of housing. It is not so many generations ago that we stopped keeping pigs in the house. At Tolstoy's estate, Yasnaya Polyana, the serfs curled up anywhere in the house that they felt drowsy and went to sleep like cats.

But Americans always claim their dispensation. A dream house has been a vision at the core of American hopes, a tender blend of expectation and nostalgia. It derives its imagery from the historical spaciousness of the land (God's country, after all, his bounteous land grant, the interminable individualist homestead unfolding toward the horizon) and the simultaneous need for shelter that its harshness imposed. A people so socially and geographically mobile used housing as an instrument to proclaim their wherewithal, their substance, their civic presence. They have sometimes nearly impoverished themselves to anchor their identities in their homes. In a 1920 magazine serial called "More Stately Mansions," a social-climbing wife pouts and wheedles her husband: "Dickie, I've simply *got* to have it. . . . A nice house gives a man self-respect and confidence." A house of one's own is refuge, a tangible, physical thing that implies stability in a democracy all liquid and stormily insecure. American history has sometimes been a wild ride: a house traditionally served as the private fortress in which to recover, in which to repel night prowlers and dangerous social change.

The "nation of immigrants" arrived homeless. From the Pilgrims on, they carved their shelter out of wilderness. Lincoln was born in a frontier hovel. Later generations crowded ten to a squalid room in Lower East Side ghettos. Yet Americans operated on a premise of expansion and progress: the private home—more important, more basic, than the automobile, that bright headlong vehicle of the dream—was the outward artifact by which Americans defined themselves. Perhaps some ancient ghost of feudalism, a deep, fundamental fear of dependence and submission, spooked around the edges of the American's pride of ownership: *this place is mine.* The prototype of Mr. Blandings's dream house was Monticello, that cool Palladian vision built by the American prince of the Enlightenment, Thomas Jefferson.

In a way, the American housing crisis is simply a variation of the American car crisis: in years past, both were overbuilt. Now, in housing as in cars, Americans are suffering the discomforts of what Detroit calls "downsizing." The ultimate result could be both better transportation and better shelter.

Housing has always demanded a sacrifice. Certain chiefs of Pacific Northwest tribes once killed slaves and captives and erected their new houses upon the bodies, for luck. Americans may have come by their housing a little too easily in the past two generations. Starting in the Depression, government agencies like the FHA and later the VA set about turning the United States into a nation of home owners. A young family could start off by paying nothing down and take thirty years to pay off the mortgage. The result was an astonishing national domestication. Today two-thirds of Americans own the places where they live. Home ownership helped to stabilize the United States around a vast and settled middle class; property taxes built the system of public education that gave the United States a good deal of its moral ballast.

But the postwar golden age of American housing (all those folks grinning out at the Eisenhower years from their patios, their barbecues) may have overdone the home comforts. It diverted billions that perhaps should have gone into the nation's industrial plant. The Reagan Administration (for all its warm rhetorical embrace of hearth and family) wants to readjust the nation's tax and credit policies to favor business investment over mortgage investment.

After an initial period of bleakness while the adjustments get made, downsizing and cost cutting may make people think more intelligently about the thing, about the house as an artifact, about what can be done with it. Ultimately, optimistically, the way out of the American housing crisis may not be lower inflation but better design and technology.

Too much American housing, of course, is insipid: mass-stamped suburbs as standardized as boxes on supermarket shelves. It may be fatuous to envision new splendors of design in a nation going to condo and cluster. But interesting, occasionally bizarre ideas are turning up. In the Midwest some builders are digging underground houses with skylights and atriums and a thick dome of earth on top that eliminates abrupt temperature changes from season to season. Friends, even strangers, are getting together to buy a house and share it. Under some arrangements, two couples may buy a condominium with two master bedrooms and two master baths and share the kitchen and living room.

Some construction companies now work at what they call retrofitting, building additions to old houses, opening up interiors, reclaiming the old stock. In central cities, much gentrification is going on: the stylish middle class takes over and polishes up the housing of the poor, leaving the poor to look elsewhere for shelter.

Americans still think of a home of their own as a free-standing one-family house (independence, shelter, family, the Little House on the Prairie still, even when the prairie has turned into Iowa City). One author, Jane Davidson, called one-family suburban houses "an oppressive Utopian idea, a spiritual imperative"—the Levittown version of Ibsen's dollhouse. But economics and demographics intrude on the vision. The size of the average American household has shrunk in twenty years from 3.3 to 2.75, a fragmentation that demands more housing units even at a moment when housing is harder than ever to finance.

With shelter so expensive to build and, once built, to heat and cool, designers are continually trying to redefine what goes into a house. No rearrangement of walls and furniture, however, can endow a building with the sort of soul that houses once possessed. It takes a heap of living, etc. Americans, a nation of transients, seldom linger long enough in a condo to give it ghosts. There was a time when houses—some houses—sheltered whole generations in sequence, witnessed them and thus acquired a numinous life of their own, a moral dimension that was once much sentimentalized. It was real enough all the same. Certain American neighborhoods once possessed a similar palpable soul, the neighborhood being the urban apartment dweller's substitute for an ancestral house and grounds. In a sense, it is the soul that Americans yearn after when they think of houses. After an earthquake or tornado, the news always lists the dead, the missing, and the "homeless," the last being itself a kind of wound, a private desolation. We all drive past the house where we grew up and stare at it oddly, with a strange ache, as if to extract some meaning from it that has been irrecoverably lost.

In 1902 the genteel architect-writer Joy Wheeler Dowd wrote: "Every man or woman hopes one day to realize his or her particular dream of home." It did not have to be a Newport "cottage" or the Baths of Diocletian. It was a small internal grandeur that counted, the sense of refuge and privacy, the Marxist's "bourgeois individualism" tricked out with antimacassars and, in the fullness of time, an island in the kitchen. Americans may have overdone some of that a little.

The turtle comes equipped with a carapace. Is there some naturally ordained allotment for human shelter? In 1920 the Russian "sanitary housing norm" decreed that each citizen was entitled to one hundred square feet of living space, an expansive ideal seldom achieved. Americans occupy at least 140 square feet on average; by most of the world's standards, they live like caliphs. The current constriction of their housing may make some Americans claustrophobic, but cross-cultural comparison might also remind them to be grateful for what they have. It might encourage them, as well, to shift their perspectives outward a little, to conceive of themselves less as isolated units, more as communities. It is not the individual hut that has cultural force and meaning, but the village as a whole, the sum of our larger arrangements as a tribe.

## QUESTIONS

*Looking at Ideas:*

1. Why does Morrow believe the American dream home has had to be downsized? Are there other social and economic factors he could have mentioned to explain the change in housing expectations in recent years?

2. What are the origins of the American dream of owning a one-family home? How does Morrow suggest that the mass media reinforce our desire to own a home? Can you think of examples from real estate advertisements, films, and television shows that feature large single-family homes as symbols of the good life?

3. What is Morrow's position on America's new adjustment to housing limitations? Does he feel that the complaints of Americans are justified? Do you agree with his perspective?

4. Morrow believes that some positive benefits might come from downsizing America's dream of a large, separate home for every family. Why does he feel this way? Does he give enough evidence to support his position?

145

*Looking at Strategies:*

1. Morrow begins his essay with a paragraph of description. What is the purpose of his description? How effective is his use of this technique for an introduction?
2. What examples does Morrow provide to clarify his point that America's current housing crisis has led to lowered expectations? What other examples might he have used?
3. Many of the examples Morrow uses in his essay are designed to provide a sense of contrast between life in middle-class America and life in countries where people have never had the housing expectations we once had. What examples does he provide? How effective are they at supporting his position?

*Looking at Connections:*

1. Compare Morrow's description of the American family dream home with the dream home featured in Ray Bradbury's "The Veldt" in Chapter Four. What would Morrow think of the Hadley's home in "The Veldt"?
2. Compare Morrow's image of the American dream home and the difficulty of obtaining it with the way the pioneer family in Wilder's "Moving In" go about obtaining their dream of a home—through hard work. What would Morrow's response to the Wilders' quest be?

*Suggestions for Writing:*

1. Write an essay about a particular family-oriented film or television show in which a house is the dominant setting or symbol of the family's life-style, social status, and camaraderie. Describe the home of the fictional family and draw some conclusions about what kind of values it reflects for the viewers of the show.
2. Write an essay in which you evaluate Morrow's conclusion about the positive benefits that can come from the current crisis in housing. Use examples from your own experience with securing housing, either in this country or abroad.
3. Write an essay in which you suggest an alternative to the current model of the single-family, separate home. What kind of family housing might be both affordable and supportive of shared facilities and responsibilities among a number of families? You might read Kathryn McCamant and Charles Durrett's essay on cohousing in Chapter Seven for an interesting alternative model of family housing.

**JOURNAL ENTRY**

Think about the stories people in your family tell about themselves and other family members. Write up such a "family story" that you remember from your childhood.

**ELIZABETH STONE: "Explanation Myths"** Elizabeth Stone is an associate professor of media studies and English at Fordham University in New York City. She grew up in a large Italian family listening to the stories about her American and Sicilian relatives. Her own family's stories inspired her to conduct the research that eventually became the book *Black Sheep and Kissing Cousins* (1988), from which the following selection is taken. As you read Stone's essay, notice how she explores the positive as well as the distorting and limiting impact of family legends, myths, and role models.

ELIZABETH STONE

# *Explanation Myths*

My father was one of seven children—three boys and four girls—born to his parents over nearly twenty years. The eldest two had been born in Austria before my grandparents came here, in the first days of this century, to Ludlow Street on the Lower East Side. My father, William, was the first child born here.

My father's parents were very devout Orthodox Jews. My father always told me his father was a rabbi (though a sister of his whom I once asked said it wasn't so) and among their beliefs was a belief in arranged marriages. My father's first marriage had been arranged by his parents in his absence. He had run away to some cousins in Wyoming, and his mother, so the story goes, came and got him so she could bring him back and marry him off. My most benign assessment of this story is that she hoped marriage would settle him down, stop him from running away, as he had, on and off, since he was a youngster.

She did bring him back and the marriage did eventually take place, but it was not a happy one, or even a tolerable one. They divorced two years later. When my father later married my mother, he said his parents, considering him lost to the family, sat *shiva*, a mourning ritual for the dead. His brothers and sisters say this isn't so.

Whatever the case, it is not in dispute that my father's next-to-youngest sister was Naomi, nor is it disputed that when she was in her late teens and of marriageable age, her parents arranged for her to be married to a man a good deal older than herself. Shortly after her marriage, she had a nervous breakdown and had to be institutionalized.

147

Later the family learned that Naomi's husband was impotent and that their marriage was never consummated. They explained her breakdown this way. Whether protracted virginity is enough to induce a nervous breakdown seems questionable, especially in light of what happened to Naomi later on. The second story takes place a few years later. By then, Naomi was married again and had become pregnant. Whether this was an arranged marriage or not, I don't know. At any rate, after Naomi's child was born, she went into a severe postpartum depression. This became yet another explanation for the next trauma that ensued. Naomi was again institutionalized, and this time was given a prefrontal lobotomy. She remains institutionalized to this day.

While it's true that lobotomies were in medical vogue during the 1950s, I find it hard to believe that these two separate events—an impotent husband and a postpartum depression—truly explain so much distress. But the fact remains that although I don't think of myself as psychologically naive, until now I have never challenged—even to myself—the explanations offered by the stories.

And I think I know why. My Aunt Naomi was not the only troubled member of that family. My father was an unstable and unhappy man. During his life, he was tormented by demons I didn't—and really still don't—understand, which made him drink too much liquor and swallow too many pills. Another member of his family, in my generation, also had to be hospitalized for mental illness. What was going on there? Was it the genes? Was it some psychic time bomb long ago planted on Ludlow Street? If it was, then I had to worry, too. I believed in my Aunt Naomi's first impotent husband with the same frightened fervor I believed in the story my mother told me about why my father drank too much. She said his drinking had become a problem while he was in the army during World War II.

Mental illness is a crucial event not only to the afflicted person but to the surrounding family members. It is a preoccupying event, an event to brood over, an event which can bring the emotional life of a family to a tense standstill while its members stare at it, transfixed by the event and worried about their own vulnerabilities.

Family stories, such as the ones about my Aunt Naomi, belong to a special category. They are family myths because, like classical myths, they are meant to explain *why*—why the flood covered the earth, why the desert is parched, why my Aunt Naomi wound up spending half her life locked up with only half a brain in her head, why my father annually tried to drink and drug himself into oblivion. If I challenge the myths now, it is only because—grown, with a family of my own, and still no demons in sight, at least not unmanageable ones—I can afford to. If I couldn't I suppose I wouldn't have noticed them at all.

The term "myth" also suggests that the explanation offered might well be untrue, or at least too limited, which all such explanations very likely are. But at least they offer possible, if not always plausible, explanations for emotional cataclysms within the family and can be an adroit solution to our worries. They offer a simple, one-dimensional cause, and in so doing, they seem to put a fence around the event, releasing us from our preoccupation so we can move on. And even if such myths of explanation don't succeed altogether in reassuring us, they perhaps make our uneasiness more manageable. They obscure our deeper conviction that what is in the blood will out, that shared blood means shared susceptibilities.

Furthermore, family stories, including myths, are well equipped to lull us. We accede to the nature of the genre, and enter into it on its own terms. As part of the oral tradition, family stories do not easily encompass intricate analyses or explanations of the many causes for an event. In fact, they obey the conventions of the oral tradition, reducing complex phenomena to single comprehensible causes. Because they are casually told and even more casually heard, we hear without alerting our more critical faculties. And so we may believe emotionally without truly assenting intellectually.

As Bruno Bettelheim explained in *The Uses of Enchantment,* simple fables speak metaphorically to the unconscious. "Fairy tales," writes Bettelheim, "convey at the same time overt and covert meanings, [they] speak simultaneously to all levels of the human personality, communicating in a manner which reaches the uneducated mind of the child as well as that of the sophisticated adult. Applying the psychoanalytic model of the human personality, fairy tales carry important messages to the conscious, the preconscious, and the unconscious mind, on whatever level each is functioning at the time."

And so it may be with family explanation myths, which, like fairy tales, deal in code with the important human issues of birth, death, sexuality, injury, and what used to be called madness. My Aunt Naomi, like some latter-day Sleeping Beauty permanently imprisoned, never awakened to or acceded to adult sexuality. At least her unconsummated marriage and her postpartum depression, functioning almost as symbols, suggest her deep uneasiness with sexuality.

And certainly there was enough in her childhood to occasion such uneasiness. She grew up in exceedingly cramped quarters on the Lower East Side. Certainly there wasn't a bedroom for every child, and undoubtedly there weren't even enough bedrooms to separate the girls from the boys, or for that matter, the children from their parents. In addition, a stint with an impotent husband did her no good, but it's unlikely that that alone was the direct cause of her turmoil. It's not unlikely, however, that the sexual climate of her childhood, filled with half a dozen adolescent siblings as well as her parents, was distressing, and perhaps distressing enough to account for her later difficulties.

The most metaphoric explanation fable I ever heard came from David Moses, a law student who grew up in a very well-to-do Black family. As in other cases, the myth he repeated was meant to explain the emotional illness that has made an appearance in some family member or other in almost every generation as far back as he can trace.

The risk of such instability's surfacing yet again seems truly to haunt the Moses family. In fact, his father's fear of it dominates even the story of David's own birth. "The story I've gotten is that the first question my father asked my mother when I was born was 'Is he O.K.?' meaning 'Is he disturbed?' They were always wondering, 'When is that madness going to surface again?' "

David turned out to be quite sturdy in both mind and body, though he says that one of his four sisters is "extremely fragile." In his father's generation there is a troubled uncle, though David's own father, a Justice Department attorney, has never had any such problems.

But the facts are quite different in David's father's mother's generation. "My grandmother and her two sisters—all three of them were crazy, though my grandmother probably had more moments of lucidity during her life than her sisters. Her sister Martine, who was a concert pianist, had a coming-out party at the Plaza. It was her debut to colored society in New York, back before World War I. The way my father tells it, Martine went insane at her coming-out party and was put away as a result."

Those are the facts as David Moses knows them. It is in explaining why the family is so susceptible to mental illness that the Moses family explanation myth, and its coded metaphor, come into play. According to what David has heard, such derangement first entered the family through an illustrious white ancestor, a slave owner, and this ancestor had something to do with a curse. "Either a curse was put on him," says David, "or he put it on his own illegitimate Black offspring."

This is all the explanation David has. As for decoding the metaphor—it has certainly been the case historically that Blacks in this country have been cursed and indeed driven crazy by the conditions imposed by powerful white oppressors. This may be even more true for those Blacks, like David's family, who are extremely ambitious and therefore likely to come into the most extended contact with white society. The Moses family explanation myth is unusual in that it offers the family no protection at all against further psychic derailment, and indeed suggests such distress will be the family's perpetual legacy. But the myth does, in code, explain that racism is what has caused so many generations of the family so much distress, and indeed this is exactly how David Moses understands the story.

But families believe in their myths for reasons more compelling than respect for the versatility of metaphor. What the family tells us has a force and power that we never quite leave behind. What they tell us is our first syntax, our first grammar, the foundation onto which we later add our own perceptions and modifications. We are not entirely free to challenge the family's beliefs as we might challenge any other system of belief. And even when we do challenge, we half disbelieve ourselves.

## QUESTIONS

*Looking at Ideas:*

1. What is an "explanation myth"? What does Stone believe is the origin of such myths? What human needs do such myths and stories appeal

to? From what do they release us? How do they deaden our critical faculties?

2. What parallels does Stone draw between explanation myths and fairy tales?

3. Why does Stone believe it is so difficult for us "to challenge the family's beliefs as we might challenge any other system of belief"? Can you think of negative effects of believing in explanation myths? From what might they distract us?

4. Do you think that many educated families today continue to believe in explanation myths, or do we rely more on professional explanations for family problems, such as those provided by physicians and psychologists?

5. Based on the information provided in Stone's essay, what do you believe caused Naomi's insanity and the father's drinking problem? Do Stone's own explanations seem any more perceptive than those provided by the myths?

6. In the case of David Moses's family history of insanity, what causes might have there been other than the "curse" of a white slave owner or Stone's explanation of life in a racist society?

*Looking at Strategies:*
1. Why does the selection begin with a story about Stone's father's rebellion against the custom of arranged marriage? How does this story reinforce the meaning of the essay and emphasize Stone's attitudes toward family customs and myths?

2. Examine the other stories Stone presents in her essay. Are they clearly and concisely narrated? How well do they function as examples of explanation myths?

3. What is the difference between an ordinary metaphor and a *coded metaphor* as Stone uses the term? How effectively does Stone use the concept of a coded metaphor to analyze and decode the explanation myth of David Moses's family?

*Looking at Connections:*
1. Is Maxine Hong Kingston's "No Name Woman," the next selection in this chapter, an explanation myth according to Stone's definition? Why or why not?

*Suggestions for Writing:*
1. Examine the family story you wrote for the journal entry that introduces this selection. Write an essay about the impact this story or myth has had on your beliefs and on your perceptions of your place in your family's history.

2. Using some of the examples that Stone discusses and others from your own experience and reading, write an essay in which you discuss whether or not explanation myths do in fact have the power to control family members' behavior as Stone believes they do.

3. Create an argument for or against the need for family stories and explanation myths to create a sense of the uniqueness of a family history.

151

Chapter Three: Myths and Rituals

**JOURNAL ENTRY**

Write about a member of your family, a relative, or an ancestor about
whom critical or negative stories were told as you were growing up. How
did the stories you heard about this relative influence your ideas of
honorable, as opposed to unacceptable or destructive, behavior?

**MAXINE HONG KINGSTON: "No Name Woman"**  Born in 1940 to a Chi-
nese immigrant family that owned a laundry in Stockton, California, Maxine
Hong Kingston received a B.A. and teaching certificate from the University of
California, Berkeley. She worked as a high school teacher in Hawaii from
1967 to 1977; in 1977 she became an associate professor of English at the
University of Hawaii. She currently resides in Oakland, where she writes and
lectures. Her first book, the autobiographical *Woman Warrior* (1976), won the
National Book Critics Circle Award. She has also written a historical account
of Chinese-American life, *China Men* (1980), as well as a novel, *Tripmaster
Monkey: His Fake Book* (1989). Maxine Hong Kingston's writing, a blend of
history, myth, legend, and autobiography, provides a unique portrait history of
Chinese-American life. The following selection, the first chapter of *The
Woman Warrior*, contrasts the fate of women in a Chinese village with Hong
Kingston's own experiences growing up in California.

MAXINE HONG KINGSTON

# No Name Woman

You must not tell anyone," my mother said, "what I am about to tell
you. In China your father had a sister who killed herself. She jumped
into the family well. We say that your father has all brothers because it
is as if she had never been born.

"In 1924 just a few days after our village celebrated seventeen hur-
ry-up weddings—to make sure that every young man who went 'out on
the road' would responsibly come home—your father and his brothers
and your grandfather and his brothers and your aunt's new husband
sailed for America, the Gold Mountain. It was your grandfather's last
trip. Those lucky enough to get contracts waved good-bye from the
decks. They fed and guarded the stowaways and helped them off in
Cuba, New York, Bali, Hawaii. 'We'll meet in California next year,' they
said. All of them sent money home.

"I remember looking at your aunt one day when she and I were
dressing; I had not noticed before that she had such a protruding
melon of a stomach. But I did not think, 'She's pregnant,' until she be-

gan to look like other pregnant women, her shirt pulling and the white tops of her black pants showing. She could not have been pregnant, you see, because her husband had been gone for years. No one said anything. We did not discuss it. In early summer she was ready to have the child, long after the time when it could have been possible.

"The village had also been counting. On the night the baby was to be born the villagers raided our house. Some were crying. Like a great saw, teeth strung with lights, files of people walked zigzag across our land, tearing the rice. Their lanterns doubled in the disturbed black water, which drained away through the broken bunds. As the villagers closed in, we could see that some of them, probably men and women we knew well, wore white masks. The people with long hair hung it over their faces. Women with short hair made it stand up on end. Some had tied white bands around their foreheads, arms, and legs.

"At first they threw mud and rocks at the house. Then they threw eggs and began slaughtering our stock. We could hear the animals scream their deaths—the roosters, the pigs, a last great roar from the ox. Familiar wild heads flared in our night windows; the villagers encircled us. Some of the faces stopped to peer at us, their eyes rushing like searchlights. The hands flattened against the panes, framed heads, and left red prints.

"The villagers broke in the front and the back doors at the same time, even though we had not locked the doors against them. Their knives dripped with the blood of our animals. They smeared blood on the doors and walls. One woman swung a chicken, whose throat she had slit, splattering blood in red arcs about her. We stood together in the middle of our house, in the family hall with the pictures and tables of the ancestors around us, and looked straight ahead.

"At that time the house had only two wings. When the men came back, we would build two more to enclose our courtyard and a third one to begin a second courtyard. The villagers rushed through both wings, even your grandparents' rooms, to find your aunt's, which was also mine until the men returned. From this room a new wing for one of the younger families would grow. They ripped up her clothes and shoes and broke her combs, grinding them underfoot. They tore her work from the loom. They scattered the cooking fire and rolled the new weaving in it. We could hear them in the kitchen breaking our bowls and banging the pots. They overturned the great waist-high earthenware jugs; duck eggs, pickled fruits, vegetables burst out and mixed in acrid torrents. The old woman from the next field swept a broom through the air and loosed the spirits-of-the-broom over our heads. 'Pig.' 'Ghost.' 'Pig,' they sobbed and scolded while they ruined our house.

"When they left, they took sugar and oranges to bless themselves. They cut pieces from the dead animals. Some of them took bowls that were not broken and clothes that were not torn. Afterward we swept up the rice and sewed it back up into sacks. But the smells from the spilled preserves lasted. Your aunt gave birth in the pigsty that night. The next morning when I went for the water, I found her and the baby plugging up the family well.

"Don't let your father know that I told you. He denies her. Now that you have started to menstruate, what happened to her could happen to you. Don't humiliate us. You wouldn't like to be forgotten as if you had never been born. The villagers are watchful."

Whenever she had to warn us about life, my mother told stories that ran like this one, a story to grow up on. She tested our strength to establish realities. Those in the emigrant generations who could not reassert brute survival died young and far from home. Those of us in the first American generations have had to figure out how the invisible world and the emigrants built around our childhoods fit in solid America.

The emigrants confused the gods by diverting their curses, misleading them with crooked streets and false names. They must try to confuse their offspring as well, who, I suppose, threaten them in similar ways—always trying to get things straight, always trying to name the unspeakable. The Chinese I know hide their names; sojourners take new names when their lives change and guard their real names with silence.

Chinese-Americans, when you try to understand what things in you are Chinese, how do you separate what is peculiar to childhood, to poverty, insanities, one family, your mother who marked your growing with stories from what is Chinese? What is Chinese tradition and what is the movies?

If I want to learn what clothes my aunt wore, whether flashy or ordinary, I would have to begin, "Remember Father's drowned-in-the-well sister?" I cannot ask that. My mother has told me once and for all the useful parts. She will add nothing unless powered by Necessity, a riverbank that guides her life. She plants vegetable gardens rather than lawns; she carries the odd-shaped tomatoes home from the fields and eats food left for the gods.

Whenever we did frivolous things, we used up energy; we flew high kites. We children came up off the ground over the melting cones our parents brought home from work and the American movie on New Year's Day—*Oh, You Beautiful Doll* with Betty Grable one year, and *She Wore a Yellow Ribbon* with John Wayne another year. After the one carnival ride each, we paid in guilt; our tired father counted his change on the dark walk home.

Adultery is extravagance. Could people who hatch their own chicks and eat the embryos and the heads for delicacies and boil the feet in vinegar for party food, leaving only the gravel, eating even the gizzard lining—could such people engender a prodigal aunt? To be a woman, to have a daughter in starvation time was a waste enough. My aunt could not have been the lone romantic who gave up everything for sex. Women in the old China did not choose. Some man had commanded her to lie with him and be his secret evil. I wonder whether he masked himself when he joined the raid on her family.

Perhaps she encountered him in the fields or on the mountain where the daughters-in-law collected fuel. Or perhaps he first noticed her in the marketplace. He was not a stranger because the village housed no strangers. She had to have dealings with him other than sex. Perhaps he worked an adjoining field, or he sold her the cloth for the dress she sewed and wore. His demand must have surprised, then terrified her. She obeyed him; she always did as she was told.

When the family found a young man in the next village to be her husband, she stood tractably beside the best rooster, his proxy, and promised before they met that she would be his forever. She was lucky that he was her age and she would be the first wife, an advantage secure now. The night she first saw him, he had sex with her. Then he left for America. She had almost forgotten what he looked like. When she tried to envision him, she only saw the black and white face in the group photograph the men had had taken before leaving.

The other man was not, after all, much different from her husband. They both gave orders: she followed. "If you tell your family, I'll beat you. I'll kill you. Be here again next week." No one talked sex, ever. And she might have separated the rapes from the rest of living if only she did not have to buy her oil from him or gather wood in the same forest. I want her fear to have lasted just as long as rape lasted so that the fear could have been contained. No drawn-out fear. But women at sex hazarded birth and hence lifetimes. The fear did not stop but permeated everywhere. She told the man, "I think I'm pregnant." He organized the raid against her.

On nights when my mother and father talked about their life back home, sometimes they mentioned an "outcast table" whose business they still seemed to be settling, their voices tight. In a commensal tradition, where food is precious, the powerful older people made wrongdoers eat alone. Instead of letting them start separate new lives like the Japanese, who could become samurais and geishas, the Chinese family, faces averted but eyes glowering sideways, hung on to the offenders and fed them leftovers. My aunt must have lived in the same house as my parents and eaten at an outcast table. My mother spoke about the raid as if she had seen it, when she and my aunt, a daughter-in-law to a different household, should not have been living together at all. Daughters-in-law lived with their husbands' parents, not their own; a synonym for marriage in Chinese is "taking a daughter-in-law." Her husband's parents could have sold her, mortgaged her, stoned her. But they had sent her back to her own mother and father, a mysterious act hinting at disgraces not told me. Perhaps they had thrown her out to deflect the avengers.

She was the only daughter; her four brothers went with her father, husband and uncles "out on the road" and for some years became western men. When the goods were divided among the family, three of the brothers took land, and the youngest, my father, chose an education. After my grandparents gave their daughter away to her husband's family, they had dispensed all the adventure and all the property. They expected her alone to keep the traditional ways, which her brothers, now among the barbarians, could fumble without detection. The heavy, deep-rooted women were to maintain the past against the flood, safe for returning. But the rare urge west had fixed upon our family, and so my aunt crossed boundaries not delineated in space.

The work of preservation demands that the feelings playing about in one's guts not be turned into action. Just watch their passing like cherry blossoms. But perhaps my aunt, my forerunner, caught in a slow life, let dreams grow and fade and after some months or years went toward what persisted. Fear at the enormities of the forbidden kept her desires delicate, wire and bone. She looked at a man because she liked the way the hair was tucked behind his ears, or she liked the question-mark line of a long torso curving at the shoulder and straight at the hip. For warm eyes or a soft voice or a slow walk—that's all—a few hairs, a line, a brightness, a sound, a pace, she gave up family. She offered us up for a charm that vanished with tiredness, a pigtail that didn't toss when the wind died. Why, the wrong lighting could erase the dearest thing about him.

It could very well have been, however, that my aunt did not take subtle enjoyment of her friend, but, a wild woman, kept rollicking company. Imagining her free with sex doesn't fit, though. I don't know any women like that, or men either. Unless I see her life branching into mine, she gives me no ancestral help.

To sustain her being in love, she often worked at herself in the mirror, guessing at the colors and shapes that would interest him, changing them frequently in order to hit on the right combination. She wanted him to look back.

On a farm near the sea, a woman who tended her appearance reaped a reputation for eccentricity. All the married women blunt-cut their hair in flaps about their ears or pulled it back in tight buns. No nonsense. Neither style blew easily into heart-catching tangles. And at their weddings they displayed themselves in their long hair for the last time. "It brushed the backs of my knees," my mother tells me. "It was braided, and even so, it brushed the backs of my knees."

At the mirror my aunt combed individuality into her bob. A bun could have been contrived to escape into black streamers blowing in the wind or in quiet wisps about her face, but only the older women in our picture album wear buns. She brushed her hair back from her forehead, tucking the flaps behind her ears. She looped a piece of thread, knotted into a circle between her index fingers and thumbs, and ran the double strand across her forehead. When she closed her fingers as if she were making a pair of shadow geese bite, the string twisted together catching the little hairs. Then she pulled the thread away from her skin, ripping the hairs out neatly, her eyes watering from the needles of pain. Opening her fingers, she cleaned the thread, then rolled it along her hairline and the tops of her eyebrows. My mother did the same to me and my sisters and herself. I used to believe that the expression "caught by the short hairs" meant a captive held with a depilatory string. It especially hurt at the temples, but my mother said we were lucky we didn't have to have our feet bound when we were seven. Sisters used to sit on their beds and cry together, she said, as their mothers or their slave removed the bandages for a few minutes each night and let the blood gush back into their veins. I hope that the man my aunt loved appreciated a smooth brow, that he wasn't just a tits-and-ass man.

Once my aunt found a freckle on her chin, at a spot that the almanac said predestined her for unhappiness. She dug it out with a hot needle and washed the wound with peroxide.

More attention to her looks than these pullings of hairs and pickings at spots would have caused gossip among the villagers. They owned work clothes and good clothes, and they wore good clothes for feasting the new seasons. But since a woman combing her hair hexes beginnings, my aunt rarely found an occasion to look her best. Women looked like great sea snails—the corded wood, babies, and laundry they carried were the whorls on their backs. The Chinese did not admire a bent back; goddesses and warriors stood straight. Still there must have been a marvelous freeing of beauty when a worker laid down her burden and stretched and arched.

Such commonplace loveliness, however, was not enough for my aunt. She dreamed of a lover for the fifteen days of New Year's, the time for families to exchange visits, money, and food. She plied her secret comb. And sure enough she cursed the year, the family, the village, and herself.

Even as her hair lured her imminent lover, many other men looked at her. Uncles, cousins, nephews, brothers would have looked, too, had they been home between journeys. Perhaps they had already been restraining their curiosity, and they left, fearful that their glances, like a field of nesting birds, might be startled and caught. Poverty hurt, and that was their first reason for leaving. But another, final reason for leaving the crowded house was the never-said.

She may have been unusually beloved, the precious only daughter, spoiled and mirror gazing because of the affection the family lavished on her. When her husband left, they welcomed the chance to take her back from the in-laws; she could live like the little daughter for just a while longer. There are stories that my grandfather was different from other people, "crazy ever since the little Jap bayoneted him in the head." He used to put his naked penis on the dinner table, laughing. And one day he brought home a baby girl, wrapped up inside his brown western-style greatcoat. He had traded one of his sons, probably my father, the youngest, for her. My grandmother made him trade back. When he finally got a daughter of his own, he doted on her. They must have all loved her, except perhaps my father, the only brother who never went back to China, having once been traded for a girl.

Brothers and sisters, newly men and women, had to efface their sexual color and present plain miens. Disturbing hair and eyes, a smile like no other, threatened the ideal of five generations living under one roof. To focus blurs, people shouted face to face and yelled from room to room. The immigrants I know have loud voices, unmodulated to American tones even after years away from the village where they called their friendships out across the fields. I have not been able to stop my mother's screams in public libraries or over telephones. Walking erect (knees straight, toes pointed forward, not pigeon-toed, which is Chinese-feminine) and speaking in an inaudible voice, I have tried to turn myself American-feminine. Chinese communication was loud, public. Only sick people had to whisper. But at the dinner table, where the family members came nearest one another, no one could talk, not the outcasts nor any eaters. Every word that falls from the mouth is a coin lost. Silently they gave and accepted food with both hands. A preoccupied child who took his bowl with one hand got a sideways glare. A complete moment of total attention is due everyone alike. Children and lovers have no singularity here, but my aunt used a secret voice, a separate attentiveness.

She kept the man's name to herself throughout her labor and dying; she did not accuse him that he be punished with her. To save her inseminator's name she gave silent birth.

He may have been somebody in her own household, but intercourse with a man outside the family would have been no less abhorrent. All the village were kinsmen, and the titles shouted in loud country voices never let kinship be forgotten. Any man within visiting distance would have been neutralized as a lover—"brother," "younger brother," "older brother"—one hundred and fifteen relationship titles. Parents researched birth charts probably not so much to assure good fortune as to circumvent incest in a population that has but one hundred surnames. Everybody has eight million relatives. How useless then sexual mannerisms, how dangerous.

As if it came from an atavism deeper than fear, I used to add "brother" silently to boys' names. It hexed the boys, who would or would not ask me to dance, and made them less scary and as familiar and deserving of benevolence as girls.

But, of course, I hexed myself also—no dates. I should have stood up, both arms waving, and shouted out across libraries, "Hey, you! Love me back." I had no idea, though, how to make attraction selective, how to control its direction and magnitude. If I made myself American-pretty so that the five or six Chinese boys in the class fell in love with me, everyone else—the Caucasian, Negro, and Japanese boys—would too. Sisterliness, dignified and honorable, made much more sense.

Attraction eludes control so stubbornly that whole societies designed to organize relationships among people cannot keep order, not even when they bind people to one another from childhood and raise them together. Among the very poor and the wealthy, brothers married their adopted sisters, like doves. Our family allowed some romance, paying adult brides' prices and providing dowries so that their sons and daughters could marry strangers. Marriage promises to turn strangers into friendly relatives—a nation of siblings.

In the village structure, spirits shimmered among the live creatures,

balanced and held in equilibrium by time and land. But one human being flaring up into violence could open up a black hole, a maelstrom
that pulled in the sky. The frightened villagers, who depended on one
another to maintain the real, went to my aunt to show her a personal,
physical representation of the break she had made in the "roundness."
Misallying couples snapped off the future, which was to be embodied
in true offspring. The villagers punished her for acting as if she could
have a private life, secret and apart from them.

If my aunt had betrayed the family at a time of large grain yields
and peace, when many boys were born, the wings were being built on
many houses, perhaps she might have escaped such severe punishment.
But the men—hungry, greedy, tired of planting in dry soil, cuckolded—
had had to leave the village in order to send food-money home. There
were ghost plagues, bandit plagues, wars with the Japanese, floods. My
Chinese brother and sister had died of an unknown sickness. Adultery,
perhaps only a mistake during good times, became a crime when the
village needed food.

The round moon cakes and round doorways, the round tables of
graduated size that fit one roundness inside another, round windows
and rice bowls—these talismans had lost their power to warn this family of the law: a family must be whole, faithfully keeping the descent
line by having sons to feed the old and the dead, who in turn look after
the family. The villagers came to show my aunt and her lover-in-hiding
a broken house. The villagers were speeding up the circling of events
because she was too shortsighted to see that her infidelity had already
harmed the village, that waves of consequences would return unpre-
dictably, sometimes in disguise, as now, to hurt her. This roundness had
to be made coin-sized so that she would see its circumference: punish
her at the birth of her baby. Awaken her to the inexorable. People who
refused fatalism because they could invent small resources insisted on
culpability. Deny accidents and wrest fault from the stars.

After the villagers left, their lanterns now scattering in various directions toward home, the family broke their silence and cursed her.
"Aiaa, we're going to die. Death is coming. Death is coming. Look
what you've done. You've killed us. Ghost! Dead ghost! Ghost! You've
never been born." She ran out into the fields, far enough from the
house so that she could no longer hear their voices, and pressed herself
against the earth, her own land no more. When she felt the birth coming, she thought that she had been hurt. Her body seized together.
"They've hurt me too much," she thought. "This is gall, and it will kill
me." With forehead and knees against the earth, her body convulsed
and then relaxed. She turned on her back, lay on the ground. The black
well of sky and stars went out and out and out forever; her body and
her complexity seemed to disappear, without home, without a companion, in eternal cold and silence. An agoraphobia rose in her, speeding
higher and higher, bigger and bigger; she would not be able to contain
it; there would be no end to fear.

Flayed, unprotected against space, she felt pain return, focusing her

159

body. This pain chilled her—a cold, steady kind of surface pain. Inside, spasmodically, the other pain, the pain of the child, heated her. For hours she lay on the ground, alternately body and space. Sometimes a vision of normal comfort obliterated reality: she saw the family in the evening gambling at the dinner table, the young people massaging their elder's backs. She saw them congratulating one another, high joy on the mornings the rice shoots came up. When these pictures burst, the stars drew yet further apart. Black space opened.

She got to her feet to fight better and remembered that old-fashioned women gave birth in their pigsties to fool the jealous, pain-dealing gods, who do not snatch piglets. Before the next spasms could stop her, she ran to the pigsty, each step a rushing out into emptiness. She climbed over the fence and knelt in the dirt. It was good to have a fence enclosing her, a tribal person alone.

Laboring, this woman who had carried her child as a foreign growth that sickened her every day, expelled it at last. She reached down to touch the hot, wet, moving mass, surely smaller than anything human, and could feel that it was human after all—fingers, toes, nails, nose. She pulled it up on to her belly, and it lay curled there, butt in the air, feet precisely tucked one under the other. She opened her loose shirt and buttoned the child inside. After resting, it squirmed and thrashed and she pushed it up to her breast. It turned its head this way and that until it found her nipple. There, it made little snuffling noises. She clenched her teeth at its preciousness, lovely as a young calf, a pig-let, a little dog.

She may have gone to the pigsty as a last act of responsibility: she would protect this child as she had protected its father. It would look after her soul, leaving supplies on her grave. But how would this tiny child without family find her grave when there would be no marker for her anywhere, neither in the earth nor the family hall? No one would give her a family hall name. She had taken the child with her into the wastes. At its birth the two of them had felt the same raw pain of sep-aration, a wound that only the family pressing tight could close. A child with no descent line would not soften her life but only trail after her, ghost-like, begging her to give it purpose. At dawn the villagers on their way to the fields would stand around the fence and look.

Full of milk, the little ghost slept. When it awoke, she hardened her breasts against the milk that crying loosens. Toward morning she picked up the baby and walked to the well.

Carrying the baby to the well shows loving. Otherwise abandon it. Turn its face into the mud. Mothers who love their children take them along. It was probably a girl; there is some hope of forgiveness for boys.

"Don't tell anyone you had an aunt. Your father does not want to hear her name. She has never been born." I have believed that sex was unspeakable and words so strong and fathers so frail that "aunt" would do my father mysterious harm. I have thought that my family, having settled among immigrants who had also been their neighbors in the ancestral land, needed to clean their name, and a wrong word would incite the kinspeople even here. But there is more to this silence: they want me to participate in her punishment. And I have.

In the twenty years since I heard this story I have not asked for details nor said my aunt's name; I do not know it. People who can comfort the dead can also chase after them to hurt them further—a reverse ancestor worship. The real punishment was not the raid swiftly inflicted by the villagers, but the family's deliberately forgetting her. Her betrayal so maddened them, they saw to it that she would suffer forever, even after death. Always hungry, always needing, she would have to beg food from other ghosts, snatch and steal it from those whose living descendants give them gifts. She would have to fight the ghosts massed at crossroads for the buns a few thoughtful citizens leave to decoy her away from village and home so that the ancestral spirits could feast unharassed. At peace, they could act like gods, not ghosts, their descent lines providing them with paper suits and dresses, spirit money, paper houses, paper automobiles, chicken, meat, and rice into eternity—essences delivered up in smoke and flames, steam and incense rising from each rice bowl. In an attempt to make the Chinese care for people outside the family, Chairman Mao encourages us now to give our paper replicas to the spirits of outstanding soldiers and workers, no matter whose ancestors they may be. My aunt remains forever hungry. Goods are not distributed evenly among the dead.

My aunt haunts me—her ghost drawn to me because now, after fifty years of neglect, I alone devote pages of paper to her, though not origamied into houses and clothes. I do not think she always means me well. I am telling on her, and she was a spite suicide, drowning herself in the drinking water. The Chinese are always very frightened of the drowned one, whose weeping ghost, wet hair hanging and skin bloated, waits silently by the water to pull down a substitute.

## QUESTIONS

*Looking at Ideas:*

1. Why have the identity and crime of the aunt in China been concealed or repressed, "as if she never had been born"?
2. What motivated the villagers to destroy the aunt's home compound after finding out about her pregnancy? Why was the pregnancy threatening to the community?
3. In what ways is this story a warning to young Maxine?
4. For the narrator, what was hard to accept or understand about the aunt's story? What details and events seemed ambiguous, even contradictory to her own experiences of life as a Chinese American?
5. What does the story reveal about the roles and status of women and of men in the Chinese family?

*Looking at Strategies:*

1. Explore some of the Chinese cultural rituals, customs, and observances, such as eating and grooming rituals for women, that Kingston presents

here. What do these descriptions of rituals and customs add to the story's portrait of Chinese culture?

2. Discuss the metaphor of "roundness." What is the importance of roundness in Chinese village life? What symbols of roundness does the narrative include in order to emphasize its significance?

3. An important metaphor/symbol in this narrative and elsewhere in *The Woman Warrior* is the ghost. What role do ghosts play in the narrative? What does the story reveal about the literal and symbolic significance of "ghosts," both in Chinese and in Chinese-American culture and family life?

*Looking at Connections:*

1. Would Kingston be likely to agree with Elizabeth Stone's view of the power and influence of family stories? Is young Maxine influenced by her mother's story of the "ghost" aunt? In what ways?

2. Compare Kingston's account of a family story in a Chinese-American family with "Scar," Amy Tan's account of a family story in Chapter One.

*Suggestions for Writing:*

1. Discuss a custom or ritual in American society that you find objectionable or difficult to understand. Describe the custom, indicate its origins, and discuss whether or not it should be maintained or abandoned. You might consider such customs as religious practices, dating rituals, accepted ways of grooming or dressing, marriage rites, or other customs you consider controversial.

2. Discuss some of the rituals and customs through which the culture of girls and women in the American family is distinguished from the culture of boys and men. Which of these rituals or customs do you find objectionable?

3. Take a family myth or custom that had relevance in your parents' upbringing and contrast their attitude toward this myth or custom with your own. What experiences in your life have shaped the different attitude you hold?

**JOURNAL ENTRY**
Write about a time when you were served a meal in your parents' or
grandparents' home after being away. What did you observe about the
"ritual" quality of the meal and the stories told? Did you feel separate, an
"observer" rather than a participant in once-familiar customs?

**ALBERTO ALVARO RIOS: "Nani"** Born in 1952 in the border town of
Nogales, Arizona, Alberto Alvaro Rios comes from a multicultural family, with
a Mexican-American father and an English mother. Rios studied English, creative writing, and psychology at the University of Arizona, where he earned a
B.A. and an M.F.A. He continued his studies at the University of Arizona in
psychology and law. Currently, Rios teaches English at Arizona State University, Tempe. His books include *Whispering to Fool the Wind* (1982), *The
Iguana Killer: Twelve Stories of the Heart* (1984), and *Five Indiscretions* (1985).
In his poetry and stories Rios looks for the "unheard of" aspects of his heritage,
examining the culturally diverse stories of his family through a kind of "magical realism" that mixes the real and the fantastic in a tradition familiar to readers of Mexican and South American literature. "Nani" is representative of
Rios's poetry in that it begins with an ordinary event in family life and explores
its personal, cultural, and imaginative complexity.

ALBERTO ALVARO RIOS

# *Nani*

Sitting at her table, she serves
the sopa de arroz[1] to me
instinctively, and I watch her,
the absolute mamá, and eat words
I might have had to say more
out of embarrassment. To speak,
now-foreign words I used to speak,
too, dribble down her mouth as she serves
me albóndigas.[2] No more
than a third are easy to me.
By the stove she does something with words
and looks at me only with her
back. I am full. I tell her
I taste the mint, and watch her speak

[1]Rice soup.
[2]Meatballs.

15  smiles at the stove. All my words
    make her smile. Nani never serves
    herself, she only watches me
    with her skin, her hair. I ask for more.

    I watch the mamá warming more
20  tortillas for me. I watch her
    fingers in the flame for me.
    Near her mouth, I see a wrinkle speak
    of a man whose body serves
    the ants like she serves me, then more words
25  from more wrinkles about children, words
    about this and that, flowing more
    easily from these other mouths. Each serves
    as a tremendous string around her,
    holding her together. They speak
30  nani was this and that to me
    and I wonder just how much of me
    will die with her, what were the words
    I could have been, was. Her insides speak
    through a hundred wrinkles, now, more
35  than she can bear, steel around her,
    shouting, then, What is this thing she serves?

    She asks me if I want more.
    I own no words to stop her.
    Even before I speak, she serves.

## QUESTIONS

*Looking at Ideas:*

1. What do you think Rios means by his description of Nani as "the absolute mamá"? In what sense is she "absolute" or mythical in her presence and activities?
2. The narrator in Rios's poem sits silent at the table "out of embarrassment." About what is he embarrassed?
3. The narrator comments that Nani's abundant speech is full of "now-
   foreign words I used to speak." Why might these once-familiar words
   now be "foreign" to him?
4. What does Rios's narrator mean when he wonders, "just how much of
   me / will die with her"? How does this line comment on the way our
   existence is bound up with that of other family members, and with the
   stories and the myths they tell about us?

*Looking at Strategies:*

1. Rios develops his poem with several key images and metaphors. One
   key image is that of Nani's wrinkles. What do they signify in the poem?
   How do they "speak" and what family story do they tell?
2. Nani's serving is a central metaphor in the poem. What does the act of

"serving" signify in the poem? What is meant by the riddle in line 36: "What is this thing she serves?"

3. Rios creates an image to describe Nani's expressive wrinkles. "Each serves / as a tremendous string around her, / holding her together." How does this image communicate both a literal and a figurative vision of Nani?

4. Despite the contemporary setting of "Nani," Rios has used the highly formal, archaic poetic form of the sestina to pattern his poem, repeating a set of six key words (serves, me, her, words, more, speak) at the ends of the lines with variation throughout the stanzas. Why do you think Rios chose such a traditional form? How does it add to the poem's meaning and intensity?

*Looking at Connections:*

1. Compare the image Rios creates of Nani as the serving mother with Tillie Olsen's image of a mother's ritual stance at the ironing board in the story, "I Stand Here Ironing" in Chapter Six. Which image seems more affirmative?

2. Compare "Nani" with Maxine Hong Kingston's "No Name Woman" as narratives about family stories. Does Rios's narrator seem to experience Nani's stories in a way similar to the way Kingston experiences her mother's stories?

*Suggestions for Writing:*

1. Write an essay in which you discuss your changing relationship with an older relative who carried along the family tradition, as Nani does in this selection, through stories and ritual observances. Do you perceive the value of this relative's maintenance of family tradition the same way now as you did when you were younger?

2. Because the interests and life-styles of younger people are quite different from those of their elders, little time is spent today in the ritual sharing of family traditions. What suggestions might you have for ways in which your family could maintain the vitality of its stories, rituals, and traditions?

165

**CARLOS PEREZ: "Once Upon a Time in New England"** Carlos Perez was born and raised in Tijuana, Mexico, and San Diego, California. An engineering major who is also interested in world history, Perez wishes to explore "both the popular and known histories of conquerors and victors as well as the often forgotten and painful past of the defeated." He wrote the following essay for his freshman English class, in response to a question that asked him to "discuss a custom or ritual in American society that you find strange or contradictory in its meaning, perhaps even objectionable." Carlos Perez decided to write about one of the most popular American rituals, that of Thanksgiving, in order provide the reader with a "new perspective from which to examine the effects of a cultural tradition on different groups in society." His essay went through six drafts. Perez showed his paper to and received comments from his English instructor and the teaching assistant. He also read different drafts aloud to friends. With each revision, he felt his satisfaction with the essay gradually increase, as revision after revision "added more clarity and focus to the thesis and the subject."

CARLOS PEREZ

# *Once Upon a Time in New England*

Once upon a time, a group of oppressed people made a perilous voyage across a great ocean to a land where they could be free from persecution and could practice democracy. They landed at a place called Plymouth Rock and settled nearby to build their own town. Due to their determination and bravery, these people were able to survive countless unknown dangers and harsh winters with very meagre supplies. These hardy pioneers were the Pilgrims, the first Americans.

As a young boy in grammar school, I heard the teacher tell this tale every November. Like other kids in my class, I was amazed every time I was told the stories that eventually led up to the first Thanksgiving. I would wear my paper Pilgrim hat proudly and pretend that I had actually been part of the glory of the first Thanksgiving dinner. The images of turkeys, children playing, and men and women laughing together with their Indian friends seemed vividly exciting to me.

These positive thoughts about Thanksgiving changed as I got older. As I advanced in my studies, I began to concentrate more and more on one particular aspect of that first dinner. The image of the Indian, which my teachers had barely mentioned before, suddenly began to take on a greater importance. When I learned the truth concerning the ways of the Pilgrims against the Native Americans in my history and social science classes in junior high school, I could not help but replace rosy images with images of death, destruction, and anger. It became clear to me that behind the first dinner at Plymouth was a disturbing example of injustice towards the Native Americans, and for that reason I felt sensitive to their plight. However, even though the historical facts in my book marred the background of Thanksgiving, I still accepted the holiday's basic premise, the idea of giving thanks for all that one has received. Despite the fact that being thankful is a virtue, in order to create more sensitivity for the cause of the Native American, I believe that all children should experience at a young age the realization of the true events concerning the tradition of Thanksgiving.

In building a successful town, the Pilgrims eradicated the Native American from lands on which the latter had originally settled. As the Indians attempted to defend their land and culture, the Pilgrims carried out vengeful raids against nearby tribes, slaughtering multitudes of Native Americans for every Pilgrim killed. Such actions were only the beginning of the long history of injustice against the Native Americans. While most youngsters are unaware of these facts, these are the painful images that a young Native American child remembers about Thanksgiving. So why shouldn't the other children of America also take part in the pain by learning about the suffering of the Native Americans at the hands of the Pilgrims? Several psychoanalysts have criticized how American children's perception of life is an unrealistic one, a sort of utopia in which Americans are seen as happy and prosperous. In her essay, "The Whispering of the Walls," Susanne Short comments on the consequences of such distorted perceptions:

> Jung says that neurosis is the avoidance of legitimate suffering. . . . When a child is not allowed to experience feelings of sadness, anger, loss, and frustration, his or her real feelings become neurotic and distorted. . . . Child psychologist Bruno Bettelheim laments that children are not being allowed legitimate suffering. He states that even the books children read in school show life as nothing but a succession of pleasures. Nobody is really angry, nobody truly suffers, there are no real emotions.

As Short points out, it is necessary for children to grieve in order to grow and mature as full human beings. For this reason, grammar schools should teach students both the positive and the negative traditions behind Thanksgiving. If they learn about the role of the Native Americans as it relates to Thanksgiving later in their lives, adolescents are likely to give little thought to the issue, to perceive it as simply another injustice in an imperfect world. Thus schools must help children to understand early the mournful plight of the Native American and to realize, because parents who were taught the storybook approach to Thanksgiving will themselves teach their sons and daughters the same distorted version of history, that Thanksgiving is not as full of niceties as it seems. Children's awareness of suffering will by no means devalue their celebration of the holiday. On the contrary, the emotional pain that children may experience as a result of learning about the effect on the Native American of the Pilgrims' arrival will enable youngsters to see how fortunate they truly are. Their giving of thanks at the dinner table will be more significant and sincere.

Human beings celebrate holidays in order to get away from the monotonous routines of everyday life and to pay homage to those events in their history which affect their present lives. Thanksgiving allows these two events to occur because it brings families together to reflect on their good fortunes. However, the problem with Thanksgiving is that a significant number of families in this country find it difficult, with a clear conscience, to take part in the festivities of the holiday. Specifically, Thanksgiving not only excludes Native American families from taking part in the festivities; it also reminds them of their tragic past which began with the arrival of the Pilgrims. By dedicating one day, either directly before or after the holiday, to mourn for those braves who faced the Pilgrims, the celebration of Thanksgiving would be improved. Although Native Americans would still not experience joy on that day, a national recognition of the plight and heroics of the tribes of Plymouth would honor these people, the first Americans.

*Questions for Discussion*

1. Would Bruno Bettelheim be likely to agree with Perez's view of the dangers of unrealistic holiday celebrations? Compare Perez's view of the subject with Bettelheim's in his essay "Magic Days," included in this chapter.

2. Does Perez provide enough evidence to support his view of the Pilgrims' negative interaction with the Native Americans and to sustain his judgment of American children as believers in a utopian image of our society and its history? What additional facts and sources might he have cited to strengthen his position?

3. Perez argues in his essay for revising the current Thanksgiving celebration to include both school instruction and a day of mourning for the Native Americans who suffered and lost their lives at the hands of the Pilgrims. Do you think his solution is appropriate and realistic? Are there other holidays you would like to see similarly revised or modified for greater historical accuracy?

4. Perez rewrote his essay many times, but, he says, it is his belief that "there is no such thing as a final draft." If you were to do another revision of Perez's essay, what would you wish to rearrange, rephrase, add, or omit?

1. Work in a group of four or five students to create a composite myth or story that represents a view of life or a moral "lesson" that is common to all of your family backgrounds and that you can all bring yourselves to accept. After writing the myth down, duplicate it and hand it out to the whole class. Your group can lead a discussion about the compromises that individuals in the group had to make in order to create the story.

2. Working in the computer classroom, compose a version of a family-oriented myth as you recall it from childhood; then write a second draft that presents the values and beliefs you currently hold. Print both versions. Include a written commentary/analysis contrasting the two versions and explaining what caused you to revise your myth and what changed values the revision is designed to embody.

3. Visit an institution in your community (convalescent home, child care center, public school classroom). Use a tape recorder to collect representative myths and rituals. Ask people you meet at the agency to tell their own version of a common myth or ritual: a harvest myth, Passover, the Christmas celebration, or a story indicating the origins of life. Draw some conclusions based on your research and write them up in the form of a paper focusing on what this experience reveals about the diversity, as well as the commonality, of the myths and rituals we live by.

4. Have your group see a film on the following list or another, similar film that relates to family myths and celebrations. Write up either individual or collaborative film reviews, in which you or your group members describe the myth, celebration, or family rituals the film presents as well as the kind of commentary or criticism the film seems to be making about the role such myths or rituals play in family life. Finally, try to draw a conclusion about whether you and/or your group found the film's commentary on family life interesting and thought-provoking.

*Avalon.* Dir., Barry Levinson. With Armin Mueller-Stahl, Joan Plowright. 1990.
*Dim Sum.* Dir., Wayne Wang. With Victor Wong, Ida Foo. 1985.
*Eating.* Dir., Henry Jaglom. 1991.
*The Godfather, Parts I, II, and III.* Dir., Francis Ford Coppola. With Marlon Brando, Al Pacino, Diane Keaton. 1972, 1974, 1991.

CHAPTER FOUR

# The Mass-Produced Family

*It is television's primary damage that it provides ten million children with the same fantasy, ready-made and on a platter.*

—Marya Mannes, *More in Anger*

*It [television] is a medium of entertainment which permits millions of people to listen to the same joke at the same time, and yet remain lonesome.*

—T.S. Eliot, *New York Post* (1963)

*F*amilies today spend more time together viewing television and videos than they do in any other form of common activity; in fact, the average American family may spend as many as thirty to forty hours a week in front of a television set. Because of the power of the images presented by the media and the enormous amount of time spent consuming media programs and related products, families are likely to identify strongly with the images and portrayals they see in the media. Consciously or unconsciously, many Americans perceive the families shown on television as models for behavior. Through these characters, settings, and plot situations, the mass electronic media today serve as powerful forces in molding values and life-styles.

Children, who generally spend two to three more hours each day watching television than do adults, are likely to be influenced strongly by the media because their educational background and life experiences are as yet too limited to serve as a counterbalance to media role models. As a result, children are especially susceptible to the influences of television and other media, and may tend to imitate the roles and story lines provided them by television programs and advertisements. Children sometimes feel disappointed if their homes lack the excitement, affluence, or freedom from parental control of their TV heroes and heroines.

Films and television also help mold the political outlook of families, providing images of "good" or "bad" families to emulate or reject, sometimes concealing or distorting the problems that families face as well as the underlying causes of family conflict and tensions. Television commercials for political candidates and issues provide images of the ideal American family—either that of the candidate or of fictional families—with whom to identify. Often these "all-American" families are nuclear families, with two or three healthy, well-groomed children and a loyal spouse—a type of family quite different from the families of average viewers, who may nevertheless be motivated to vote for a candidate or party because of a feeling that *this* party or politician can restore the essence of a vanishing family wholeness and security.

The readings in this chapter explore the impact of the mass media on family values and self-image. We have included an essay by Marie Winn, "Television and Family Rituals," on the impact of television on family rituals; an essay by Ella Taylor, "Prime-Time Families," on the changing image of television families in recent years; and "The Wretched of the Hearth," a review by Barbara Ehrenreich of Roseanne

Barr's autobiography and Roseanne's feisty political stance in her television situation comedy. We have also included two selections—an essay by Stephen Kline, "Television and Children's Play," and a story, "The Veldt," by Ray Bradbury—commenting on the relationship between the media and patterns of children's play. An essay by Robert Coles and a poem by Stephen Dunn examine the ways in which Americans' political views and outlook on reality are molded by their exposure to television news. We conclude the chapter with a student essay that demonstrates how the science fiction film *Terminator 2* reflects on the breakdown of the modern family in a world of encroaching technology.

Social critics do not agree on the exact influence of the media on the family; after all, television is only one factor molding our values and ways of communicating. Ultimately it is up to you, as reader, media watcher, and family member, to evaluate the viewpoints expressed in this chapter. By comparing the responses of these writers to your own experiences of the media's influences on you, your family, and the families of your friends, you can develop arguments and examples that either support or contradict the conclusions drawn by the authors included here.

**JOURNAL ENTRY**

Discuss a period in your life when your family did without television.
How did the pattern of communication between family members change?
How did you spend the time freed from television viewing?

**MARIE WINN: "Television and Family Rituals"** Marie Winn was born in 1936 in Prague, Czechoslovakia, and came to the United States in 1939. Educated in psychology at Radcliffe College and Columbia University, she has worked primarily as a free-lance writer specializing in the area of child development. Winn is particularly concerned with the impact of television on the mental outlook of the child and on the structure of family life. Her books include *The Baby Reader* (1973), *Children without Childhood* (1983), and *The Plug-In Drug: Television, Children and the Family* (1977, revised 1985), from which the following selection on family rituals and television is taken. As you read "Television and Family Rituals," consider how Winn is able to draw on a broad range of authorities and case histories to clarify her viewpoint on the impact of television.

MARIE WINN

# Television and Family Rituals

Less than forty years after the introduction of television into American society, a period that has seen the medium become so deeply ingrained in American life that in at least one state the television set has attained the rank of a legal necessity, safe from repossession in case of debt along with clothes, cooking utensils, and the like, television viewing has become an inevitable and ordinary part of daily life. Only in the early years of television did writers and commentators have sufficient perspective to separate the activity of watching television from the actual content it offers the viewer. In those early days writers frequently discussed the effects of television on family life. However, a curious myopia afflicted those early observers: almost without exception they regarded television as a favorable, beneficial, indeed, wondrous influence upon the family.

"Television is going to be a real asset in every home where there are children," predicts a writer in 1949.

"Television will take over your way of living and change your children's habits, but this change can be a wonderful improvement," claims another commentator.

"No survey's needed, of course, to establish that television has brought the family together in one room," writes *The New York Times'* television critic in 1949.

Each of the early articles about television is invariably accompanied by a photograph or illustration showing a family cozily sitting together before the television set, Sis on Mom's lap, Buddy perched on the arm of Dad's chair, Dad with his arm around Mom's shoulder. Who could have guessed that twenty or so years later Mom would be watching a drama in the kitchen, the kids would be looking at cartoons in their room, while Dad would be taking in the ball game in the living room?

Of course television sets were enormously expensive in those early days. The idea that by 1982 more than half of all American families would own two or more sets seemed preposterous. The splintering of the multiple-set family was something the early writers could not foresee. Nor did anyone imagine the number of hours children would eventually devote to television, the changes television would effect upon child-rearing methods, the increasing domination of family schedules by children's viewing requirements—in short, the *power* of television to dominate family life.

After the first years, as children's consumption of the new medium increased, together with parental concern about the possible effects of so much television viewing, a steady refrain helped to soothe and reassure anxious parents. "Television always enters a pattern of influences that already exist: the home, the peer group, the school, the church and culture generally," wrote the authors of an early and influential study of television's effects on children. In other words, if the child's home life is all right, parents need not worry about the effects of all that television watching.

But television did not merely influence the child; it deeply influenced that "pattern of influences" everyone hoped would ameliorate the new medium's effects. Home and family life have changed in important ways since the advent of television. The peer group has become television-oriented, and much of the time children spend together is occupied by television viewing. Culture generally has been transformed by television. Therefore it is improper to assign to television the subsidiary role its many apologists (too often members of the television industry) insist it plays. Television is not merely one of a number of important influences upon today's child. Through the changes it has made in family life, television emerges as *the* important influence in children's lives today.

## The Quality of Family Life

Television's contribution to family life has been an equivocal one. For while it has, indeed, kept the members of the family from dispersing, it has not served to bring them *together*. By its domination of the time families spend together, it destroys the special quality that distinguishes one family from another, a quality that depends to a great extent on what a family *does*, what special rituals, games, recurrent jokes, familiar songs, and shared activities it accumulates.

"Like the sorcerer of old," writes Urie Bronfenbrenner, "the television set casts its magic spell, freezing speech and action, turning the living into silent statues so long as the enchantment lasts. The primary danger of the television screen lies not so much in the behavior it produces—although there is danger there—as in the behavior it prevents: the talks, the games, the family festivities and arguments through which much of the child's learning takes place and through which his character is formed. Turning on the television set can turn off the process that transforms children into people."

Yet parents have accepted a television-dominated family life so completely that they cannot see how the medium is involved in whatever problems they might be having. A first-grade teacher reports:

"I have one child in the group who's an only child. I wanted to find out more about her family life because this little girl was quite isolated from the group, didn't make friends, so I talked to her mother. Well, they don't have time to do anything in the evening, the mother said. The parents come home after picking up the child at the baby-sitter's. Then the mother fixes dinner while the child watches TV. Then they have dinner and the child goes to bed. I said to this mother, 'Well, couldn't she help you fix dinner? That would be a nice time for the two of you to talk,' and the mother said, 'Oh, but I'd hate to have her miss "Zoom." It's such a good program!' "

Even when families make efforts to control television, too often its very presence counterbalances the positive features of family life. A writer and mother of two boys aged 3 and 7 described her family's television schedule in an article in *The New York Times:*

> We were in the midst of a full-scale War. Every day was a new battle and every program was a major skirmish. We agreed it was a bad scene all around and were ready to enter diplomatic negotiations. . . . In principle we have agreed on 2½ hours of TV a day, "Sesame Street," "Electric Company" (with dinner gobbled up in between) and two half-hour shows between 7 and 8:30 which enables the grown-ups to eat in peace and prevents the two boys from destroying one another. Their pre-bedtime choice is dreadful, because, as Josh recently admitted, "There's nothing much on I really like." So . . . it's "What's My Line" or "To Tell the Truth." . . . Clearly there is a need for first-rate children's shows at this time. . . .

Consider the "family life" described here: Presumably the father comes home from work during the "Sesame Street"–"Electric Company" stint. The children are either watching television, gobbling their dinner, or both. While the parents eat their dinner in peaceful privacy, the children watch another hour of television. Then there is only a half-hour left before bedtime, just enough time for baths, getting pajamas on, brushing teeth, and so on. The children's evening is regimented with an almost military precision. They watch their favorite programs, and when there is "nothing much on I really like," they watch whatever else is on—because *watching* is the important thing. Their mother does not see anything amiss with watching programs just for the sake of watching; she only wishes there were some first-rate children's shows on at those times.

Without conjuring up memories of the Victorian era with family games and long, leisurely meals, and large families, the question arises: isn't there a better family life available than this dismal, mechanized arrangement of children watching television for however long is allowed them, evening after evening?

Of course, families today still do *special* things together at times: go camping in the summer, go to the zoo on a nice Sunday, take various trips and expeditions. But their *ordinary* daily life together is diminished—that sitting around at the dinner table, that spontaneous taking up of an activity, those little games invented by children on the spur of the moment when there is nothing else to do, the scribbling, the chatting, and even the quarreling, all the things that form the fabric of a family, that define a childhood. Instead, the children have their regular schedule of television programs and bedtime, and the parents have their peaceful dinner together.

The author of the article in the *Times* notes that "keeping a family sane means mediating between the needs of both children and adults." But surely the needs of the adults are being better met than the needs of the children, who are effectively shunted away and rendered untroublesome, while their parents enjoy a life as undemanding as that of any childless couple. In reality, it is those very demands that young children make upon a family that lead to growth, and it is the way parents accede to those demands that builds the relationships upon which the future of the family depends. If the family does not accumulate its backlog of shared experiences, shared *everyday* experiences that occur and recur and change and develop, then it is not likely to survive as anything other than a caretaking institution.

## Family Rituals

Ritual is defined by sociologists as "that part of family life that the family likes about itself, is proud of and wants formally to continue." Another text notes that "the development of a ritual by a family is an index of the common interest of its members in the family as a group."

What has happened to family rituals, those regular, dependable, recurrent happenings that gave members of a family a feeling of *belonging* to a home rather than living in it merely for the sake of convenience, those experiences that act as the adhesive of family unity far more than any material advantages?

Mealtime rituals, going-to-bed rituals, illness rituals, holiday rituals—how many of these have survived the inroads of the television set?

A young woman who grew up near Chicago reminisces about her childhood and gives an idea of the effects of television upon family rituals:

"As a child I had millions of relatives around—my parents both come from relatively large families. My father had nine brothers and sisters. And so every holiday there was this great swoop-down of aunts, uncles, and millions of cousins. I just remember how wonderful it used to be. These thousands of cousins would come and everyone would play and ultimately, after dinner, all the women would be in the front of the house, drinking coffee and talking, all the men would be in the back of the house, drinking and smoking, and all the kids would be all over the place, playing hide and seek. Christmas time was particularly nice because everyone always brought all their toys and games. Our house had a couple of rooms with go-through closets, so there were always kids running in a great circle route. I remember it was just wonderful.

"And then all of a sudden one year I remember becoming suddenly aware of how different everything had become. The kids were no longer playing Monopoly or Clue or the other games we used to play together. It was because we had a television set which had been turned on for a football game. All of that socializing that had gone on previously had ended. Now everyone was sitting in front of the television set, on a holiday, at a family party! I remember being stunned by how awful that was. Somehow the television had become more attractive."

As families have come to spend more and more of their time together engaged in the single activity of television watching, those rituals and pastimes that once gave family life its special quality have become more and more uncommon. Not since prehistoric times, when cave families hunted, gathered, ate, and slept, with little time remaining to accumulate a culture of any significance, have families been reduced to such a sameness.

## Real People

It is not only the activities that a family might engage in together that are diminished by the powerful presence of television in the home. The relationships of the family members to each other are also affected, in both obvious and subtle ways. The hours that children spend in a one-way relationship with television people, an involvement that allows for no communication or interaction, surely affect their relationships with real-life people.

Studies show the importance of eye-to-eye contact, for instance, in real-life relationships, and indicate that the nature of one's eye-contact patterns, whether one looks another squarely in the eye or looks to the side or shifts one's gaze from side to side, may play a significant role in one's success or failure in human relationships. But no eye contact is possible in the child-television relationship, although in certain children's programs people purport to speak directly to the child and the camera fosters this illusion by focusing directly upon the person being filmed. (Mister Rogers is an example, telling the child, "I like you, you're special," etc.). How might such a distortion of real-life relationships affect a child's development of trust, of openness, of an ability to relate well to other *real* people?

Bruno Bettelheim writes:

Children who have been taught, or conditioned, to listen passively most of the day to the warm verbal communications coming from the TV screen, to the deep emotional appeal of the so-called TV personality, are often unable to respond to real persons because they arouse so much less feeling than the skilled actor. Worse, they lose the ability to learn from reality because life experiences are much more complicated than the ones they see on the screen. . . .

A teacher makes a similar observation about her personal viewing experiences:

"I have trouble mobilizing myself and dealing with real people after watching a few hours of television. It's just hard to make that transition from watching television to a real relationship. I suppose it's because there was no effort necessary while I was watching, and dealing with real people always requires a bit of effort. Imagine, then, how much harder it might be to do the same thing for a small child, particularly one who watches a lot of television every day."

But more obviously damaging to family relationships is the elimination of opportunities to talk, and perhaps more important, to argue, to air grievances, between parents and children and brothers and sisters. Families frequently use television to avoid confronting their problems, problems that will not go away if they are ignored but will only fester and become less easily resolvable as time goes on.

A mother reports:

"I find myself, with three children, wanting to turn on the TV set when they're fighting. I really have to struggle not to do it because I feel that's telling them this is the solution to the quarrel—but it's so tempting that I often do it."

A family therapist discusses the use of television as an avoidance mechanism:

"In a family I know the father comes home from work and turns on the television set. The children come and watch with him and the wife serves them their meal in front of the set. He then goes and takes a shower, or works on the car or something. She then goes and has her own dinner in front of the television set. It's a symptom of a deeper-rooted problem, sure. But it would help them all to get rid of the set. It would be far easier to work on what the symptom really means without the television. The television simply encourages a double avoidance of each other. They'd find out more quickly what was going on if they weren't able to hide behind the TV. Things wouldn't necessarily be better, of course, but they wouldn't be anesthetized."

The decreased opportunities for simple conversation between parents and children in the television-centered home may help explain an observation made by an emergency room nurse at a Boston hospital. She reports that parents just seem to sit there these days when they come in with a sick or seriously injured child, although talking to the child would distract and comfort him. "They don't seem to know *how*

179

to talk to their own children at any length," the nurse observes. Similarly, a television critic writes in *The New York Times*: "I had just a day ago taken my son to the emergency ward of a hospital for stitches above his left eye, and the occasion seemed no more real to me than Maalot or 54th Street, south-central Los Angeles. There was distance and numbness and an inability to turn off the total institution. I didn't behave at all; I just watched. . . ."

A number of research studies substantiate the assumption that television interferes with family activities and the formation of family relationships. One survey shows that 78 percent of the respondents indicate no conversation taking place during viewing except at specified times such as commercials. The study notes: "The television atmosphere in most households is one of quiet absorption on the part of family members who are present. The nature of the family social life during a program could be described as 'parallel' rather than interactive, and the set does seem to dominate family life when it is on." Thirty-six percent of the respondents in another study indicated that television viewing was the only family activity participated in during the week.

In a summary of research findings on television's effect on family interactions James Garbarino states: "The early findings suggest that television had a disruptive effect upon interaction and thus presumably human development. . . . It is not unreasonable to ask: 'Is the fact that the average American family during the 1950's came to include two parents, two children and a television set somehow related to the psychosocial characteristics of the young adults of the 1970's?' "

## Undermining the Family

In its effect on family relationships, in its facilitation of parental withdrawal from an active role in the socialization of their children, and in its replacement of family rituals and special events, television has played an important role in the disintegration of the American family. But of course it has not been the only contributing factor, perhaps not even the most important one. The steadily rising divorce rate, the increase in the number of working mothers, the decline of the extended family, the breakdown of neighborhoods and communities, the growing isolation of the nuclear family—all have seriously affected the family.

As Urie Bronfenbrenner suggests, the sources of family breakdown do not come from the family itself, but from the circumstances in which the family finds itself and the way of life imposed upon it by those circumstances. "When those circumstances and the way of life they generate undermine relationships of trust and emotional security between family members, when they make it difficult for parents to care for, educate and enjoy their children, when there is no support or recognition from the outside world for one's role as a parent and when time spent with one's family means frustration of career, personal fulfillment and peace of mind, then the development of the child is adversely affected," he writes.

But while the roots of alienation go deep into the fabric of American social history, television's presence in the home fertilizes them, encourages their wild and unchecked growth. Perhaps it is true that America's commitment to the television experience masks a spiritual vacuum, an empty and barren way of life, a desert of materialism. But it is television's dominant role in the family that anesthetizes the family into accepting its unhappy state and prevents it from struggling to better its condition, to improve its relationships, and to regain some of the richness it once possessed.

Others have noted the role of mass media in perpetuating an unsatisfactory *status quo*. Leisure-time activity, writes Irving Howe, "must provide relief from work monotony without making the return to work too unbearable; it must provide amusement without insight and pleasure without disturbance—as distinct from art which gives pleasure through disturbance. Mass culture is thus oriented towards a central aspect of industrial society: the depersonalization of the individual." Similarly, Jacques Ellul rejects the idea that television is a legitimate means of educating the citizen: "Education . . . takes place only incidentally. The clouding of his consciousness is paramount. . . ."

And so the American family muddles on, dimly aware that something is amiss but distracted from an understanding of its plight by an endless stream of television images. As family ties grow weaker and vaguer, as children's lives become more separate from their parents', as parents' educational role in their children's lives is taken over by television and schools, family life becomes increasingly more unsatisfying for both parents and children. All that seems to be left is love, an abstraction that family members *know* is necessary but find great difficulty giving each other because the traditional opportunities for expressing love within the family have been reduced or destroyed.

For contemporary parents, love toward each other has increasingly come to mean successful sexual relations, as witnessed by the proliferation of sex manuals and sex therapists. The opportunities for manifesting other forms of love through mutual support, understanding, nurturing, even, to use an unpopular word, *serving* each other, are less and less available as mothers and fathers seek their independent destinies outside the family.

As for love of children, this love is increasingly expressed through supplying material comforts, amusements, and educational opportunities. Parents show their love for their children by sending them to good schools and camps, by providing them with good food and good doctors, by buying them toys, books, games, and a television set of their very own. Parents will even go further and express their love by attending PTA meetings to improve their children's schools, or by joining groups that are acting to improve the quality of their children's television programs.

But this is love at a remove, and is rarely understood by children.

181

The more direct forms of parental love require time and patience, steady, dependable, ungrudgingly given time actually spent *with* children, reading to them, comforting them, playing, joking, and working with them. But even if parents were eager and willing to demonstrate that sort of direct love to their children today, the opportunities are diminished. What with school and Little League and piano lessons and, of course, the inevitable television programs, a day seems to offer just enough time for a good-night kiss.

## QUESTIONS

*Looking at Ideas:*

1. How were early predictions of the impact of television mistaken? According to Winn, has television resulted in an overall improvement or a deterioration in the quality of family life?

2. In the first part of her essay, Winn paints a picture of typical American families coming home to a world of total television immersion with little or no time left over for family interaction. Does this seem like a typical picture of family life to you, or is she presenting an extreme situation?

3. How has television eroded family rituals and created a sameness in American families? Do you agree with Winn?

4. Why does Winn believe that television makes it difficult for family members to sustain meaningful relationships, to confront emotional problems, and to feel empathy for one another's suffering? Are her arguments persuasive?

5. How do the mass media perpetuate "an unsatisfactory *status quo*" in our society? Are the mass entertainment media different from other art forms in this respect?

*Looking at Strategies:*

1. What examples does Winn use in her essay to substantiate her views about the impact of television on family life? Find instances of several types of example: case histories, personal testimony, and expert observation. Is her use of example convincing and persuasive?

2. How does Winn use research studies to make her essay more convincing?

3. Give examples of Winn's quoting of authorities to supply a context for her more specific observations about the impact of media on our awareness and sense of ourselves as family members. Do these authorities help make her arguments more convincing?

*Looking at Connections:*

1. Compare Winn's view of the influence of television on family life to that provided by Bradbury later in this chapter in "The Veldt." Which author seems to be most disturbed about television's effects? On what points would the two authors be likely to agree? On what points would they disagree?

*Suggestions for Writing:*

1. Interview a person who grew up without television and write up your results in the form of an essay. What kind of games and family rituals does this person remember from his or her childhood that have generally been abandoned or forgotten in our society? Would you attribute the abandonment of such rituals to television or to other social influences?

2. Observe a family that watches little or no television; then write an essay comparing the way its members communicate with one another with the way another family you know whose members watch a good deal of television interacts. Do your observations of the impact of television on family interactions coincide with Marie Winn's views?

3. How could families that watch too much television manage to cut back on their excessive reliance on the medium? Imagine that you are writing an essay or letter to such a family. What kind of activities would you suggest to help the family limit their television viewing as the central focus of their home life?

**ELLA TAYLOR: "Prime-Time Families"**   Born in Israel in 1948, Ella Taylor spent most of her early years in England. She was educated at the London School of Economics and at Brandeis University, where she received a Ph.D. in sociology in 1985. Currently she is an instructor of popular culture at the University of Washington. Taylor has written extensively on film and television in such periodicals as the *New York Times* and the *Village Voice*. The following selection is from her book *Prime-Time Families* (1990), a profile of the American family as portrayed in television programs over four decades. As you read the selection, notice how Taylor criticizes a very popular 1980s family program, *The Cosby Show,* according to her belief that television should show us realistic depictions of family life.

ELLA TAYLOR

# Prime-Time Families

Although family remains the significant frame of both comedy and drama, whether about home or workplace, its meaning changes. The inevitability of nuclear-family life is increasingly called into question, and understandings of family relativized, in a variety of representations of domesticity.

Yet in many series this potential for creating alternative meanings is undercut or diluted by the level of generality, the cheery politics of social adjustment, with which family change is endorsed even in shows that experiment self-consciously with gender and family roles. With few exceptions the family comedies of the 1980s are less genuinely adversarial than those of the early 1970s. "Do I have to be a relative to be family?" a confused little boy asks his mother in *Who's the Boss?*, a role-reversal comedy about two single parents (she the breadwinner, he the housekeeper) living together. "Not necessarily," his mother smiles down at him, "a family means people who share each other's lives and care about each other." This may be an unexceptionable definition, given the variety of domestic living arrangements revealed by census data, but it is also virtually meaningless. With the sting of divorce, family poverty, and other problems removed, single parenthood and step-parenting turn into a romp, a permanent pajama party. Even *Kate and*

*Allie,* which began as a witty comedy of divorce manners and a chronicle of the single life encountered the second time around, slipped into the mold of didactic "parenting psychology," focusing more traditionally on children's and teenagers' rites of passage than on adults reinventing normative life. Here the television narrative hedges its bets by nodding in the direction of radical changes in family form and structure without taking them seriously. . . .

The vigorous airing of women's concerns observed in the primetime feminism of the 1970s has been attenuated or transformed. The few attempts to create comedies revolving around single women (including *Mary,* a new vehicle for Mary Tyler Moore) in the first half of the 1980s were quickly cut short when they failed to become immediate ratings successes. In the dramatic series working women abound, but with few exceptions they have become career women, with all the ambivalence that surrounds that trend. In *Cagney and Lacey* both the ambitious Christine Cagney and her partner, the harried working mother Marybeth Lacey, are constantly confronting the conflicts between their police careers and their private lives. In *Thirtysomething* Hope returns to the job she thinks she misses after having a baby—but subsequent episodes virtually ignore her dilemma. Her friend Ellen, a high-powered executive, agonizes frequently about not having the correct maternal or emotional instincts. *The Cosby Show's* Clair Huxtable, a lawyer, is superwoman incarnate; she embodies a feminine mystique for the 1980s and is rarely seen working or even discussing her work. *Day by Day* plays off its central character, a lawyer who abandons her career to run a day-care center at home with her husband, against a child-hating, narcissistic female stockbroker. The theme of the disillusioned career woman returning home to her suburban family has been featured in more than one late-1980s made-for-TV movie. Thus the celebration of the opening up of women's roles in the 1970s shows becomes, in the 1980s, at best a rehearsal of the costs of careerism for women, at worst an outright reproof for women who seek challenging work. In this way the genuine difficulties women face in reconciling home and work are often casually translated into a backlash against feminism itself. . . .

If popular shows are those that most nearly approximate dominant ideas, then it is to *The Cosby Show,* whose phenomenal success set a trend for a new wave of comedies with intact nuclear families, that one must turn to read those ideas. Like *All in the Family* a decade earlier, *The Cosby Show* has attracted an enormous amount of attention (most of it favorable) from critics and public interest groups as well as a vast and devoted audience; but there the similarity ends. The robustly working-class Bunker household was never a model of consumer vitality, nor did it aspire to be. If Archie was dragged by the scruff of his reluctant neck into the 1970s, the Huxtable family embraces modernity with enthusiasm. Surrounded by the material evidence of their success, the Huxtables radiate wealth, health, energy, and up-to-the-minute style. Indeed *The Cosby Show* offers the same pleasures as a television commercial—a parade of gleaming commodities and expensive designer clothing unabashedly enjoyed by successful professional families. Cosby himself is a gifted salesman of the goods and services, from Jell-O Pops to E. F. Hutton, that finance his series.

This conspicuous consumption is a far cry from the relaxed, unostentatious assumption of material comfort in *Ozzie and Harriet* or *Father Knows Best.* Some critics have concluded that *The Cosby Show* and its imitators signify a return to 1950s-style consensual domestic comedy. Week after week, the show supplies the same rewards as those offered by family comedy in the 1950s and 1960s—the continuity of orderly lives lived without major trauma or disturbance, stretching back into an identical past and reaching forward into an identical future. But whereas the television families of the 1950s casually took harmony and order for granted, indeed took *the institution of the stable family* for granted, the Huxtables work strenuously and self-consciously at persuading viewers how well they get along. Given the troubled condition of many families in the 1980s, *The Cosby Show* must be palpably compensatory or redemptive for many of its devotees, responding to family distress by articulating the shrill (but reassuringly unambiguous) fundamentalist rhetoric to be found in many areas of private and public life today.

Nothing, in the classical dramatic sense, ever really happens on *The Cosby Show,* which is a virtually plotless chronicle of the small, quotidian details of family life, at whose heart lies a moral etiquette of parenting and a developmental psychology of growing up. Narrative resolution, far tighter than in most domestic comedies since the early 1970s, comes in the form of a learning experience, a lesson in social adjustment for the children. The relentlessly cute Rudy learns to stop bossing her friends around. Theo learns not to embark on expensive projects he has no intention of completing. Sandra and her boyfriend learn to arbitrate their own quarrels over the division of labor. Even Cliff and Clair, despite high-powered careers as physician and lawyer respectively, have all the leisure in the world to spend "quality time" with their offspring, teaching one another parenting by discussion as well as by example. Yet the learning is abstract; in contrast to the families in the character comedies of the 1970s, not one of the Huxtables ever develops. Didacticism is nothing new in network television, but in *The Cosby Show* moral and psychological instruction become monolithic and indisputable. Unlike the Bunkers, for whom every problem became the occasion for an all-out war of ideas, the Huxtables never scream or lose control. True, beneath their beguiling mildness there lurks a casual hostility in which everyone, Mom and Dad included, trades insults and mocks everyone else. But there is no dissent, no real difference of opinion or belief, only vaguely malicious banter that quickly dissolves into sweet agreement—all part of the busy daily manufacture of consensus.

Undercutting the warm color and light and the joking bonhomie is a persistent authoritarianism. The tone is set by Cosby himself, whose prodigious charm overlays a subtle menace: Father knows best, or else.

The cuddly, overgrown schoolboy becomes the amused onlooker and then the oracle; he is master of both the strategic silence and the innocent question that lets his children know they have said or done something dumb or gives his wife to understand that her independence is slipping into bossiness. Indeed the impeccable but perfunctory salutes to feminism serve to gloss over the enormous difficulty a woman like Clair might have in juggling her many roles. Behind the democratic gloss of family meetings and the insistence on "communication," Cliff practices a thoroughly contemporary politics of strong leadership, managing conflict with all the skill of a well-trained corporate executive. So too does his lawyer wife, who in one episode during the 1987–1988 season stages a kangaroo court at home for her teenage son Theo, whose crime is not merely arriving home fifteen minutes late but, worse, refusing to tell his parents why. By the end of the show Theo sees the error of his ways.

There is none of the generational warfare that rocked the Bunker household, and this family scarcely needs the openly repressive "tough love" therapy that has cropped up with some regularity in 1980s made-for-TV movies because parental authority has already been internalized. The children put up token displays of playful resistance, then surrender happily to the divine right of parents whose facile knowledge of the difference between right and wrong irons out the inconvenient ambiguities of contemporary life. Since the Huxtables are a supremely intact nuclear family, these ambiguities rarely come up; when they do, though, they occur outside the charmed family circle and remain there. A teenage pregnancy, a drug problem, a worker laid off—occasionally one of the problems that bedevil most families casts a brief shadow on the bright domestic scene and then slinks away, intimidated by the fortress of Huxtable togetherness.

Unlike the sitcoms of the 1950s, whose vision of the social terrain outside the family was as benign as that inside it, and those of the 1970s, which conducted a useful if testy dialogue with public institutions, the world outside *The Cosby Show* appears both diffuse and downright perilous, to the degree that it exists at all. The Huxtables have friends who drift in and out of their lives but no discernible community, indeed no public life to speak of aside from their jobs, which seem to run on automatic pilot. Like Norman Lear's "ethnic comedies" in the 1970s, *The Cosby Show* inhabits a visibly black world, but here its blackness is scarcely alluded to. All social and moral choice is subsumed within the category of the domestic, suggesting not only that family integrity transcends politics but also that collective affiliation is reducible to being nice to other people—especially relatives. Even *Family Ties*, its white obverse, whose premise of ex-hippie parents with a precorporate, neoconservative son promises some energizing friction, smoothes genuine argument into the cozy warmth of domestic affection. The mild-mannered Keaton father Stephen is persuaded by an old friend from the campus left to restart a radical magazine. A difference of opinion results in Stephen being accused of copping out, but his wife Elyse assures him that "you're making a statement by the way you live your life and raise your children."

Bill Cosby, whose diploma in education is always prominently featured in his show's credits, takes his responsibilities as an educator very seriously. *Newsweek* reported in 1984 that Cosby had commissioned black psychiatrist Alvin Poussaint to review every *Cosby Show* script for "authenticity." The actor told the *Los Angeles Times* in 1985 that viewers loved the series because it showed that "the people in this house respect the parents and the parents respect the children and that there is a l-o-v-e generated in this house." Norman Lear, in his time, felt convinced that viewers liked *All in the Family* not only because it was funny or endearing but because it exposed bigotry and addressed topical issues. There is always a potential asymmetry between producers' intentions and viewers' readings. . . . Bunker fans may just as plausibly have identified with the diffuse rage that imprinted itself on almost every episode of *All in the Family* as with its liberal political stance.

Similarly, the Huxtable brand of patriarchal dominance may strike as resonant a chord as the l-o-v-e Cosby cited—to which the success of his book *Fatherhood,* which topped the bestseller list in 1986, may testify. And if Cosby's childlike charm also works, this dualism in him and in *The Cosby Show* narrative may cater to what is most childlike in his viewers—namely, the yearning (all the more powerful because for many Americans it seems to go unfulfilled) for a perfectly synchronized family or community that provides for the needs of all its members and regulates itself through a benevolent dictatorship. The show's endless rehearsal and efficient mopping up of mild domestic disorder stakes a claim for a perfect family that works, but its closure of all open endings, relative viewpoints, and ethical ambiguities and its energetic repression of the sources of suffering that afflict many families (especially black families) suggest a political retrenchment born of cultural exhaustion, a fearful inability to confront current reality and imagine new forms of community or new ways of living. Both form and meaning work in *The Cosby Show* to obliterate the indeterminacies that emerged in family comedy in the 1970s and to supersede the diversity of family forms in other contemporary series, at the same time binding the interpretive imagination of the viewer. . . .

Since the early 1970s a dualism has developed in the thinking and practice of those who make and sell television. On the one hand, industry rhetoric stresses the importance of "demographics," the effort to make and schedule "quality" programs for target audiences whose purchasing power and life-style will be attractive to advertisers even though they comprise a smaller audience. On the other hand, the mass audience remains a pertinent category for network programmers, who must still demonstrate (through ratings) to sponsors that their shows draw vast numbers of viewers. Indeed that need grows more urgent as the challenge from pay and cable television, syndicated programming, and home video technology grows stronger since the networks must prove their worth on the basis of crude numbers, in contrast with the more specialized appeal of their competitors. But the dualism . . . also has a broader social base; the mass audience exists largely as a construct in the minds of those who make and sell television. The heterogeneity of viewers must be simultaneously catered to with pluralistic images and glossed over with a more universal language in order to *create* a mass audience. In the 1970s . . . "relevance" was acceptable because it was framed in a universal institution, the family. The "family pluralism" suggested by the episodic series in the 1980s is weak and tentative, acknowledging more the *variety* of family forms than the *struggle* over meanings of family at the level of gender, race, class, and generation and at the intersection of family with the public world of work. Moreover, family pluralism exists in tension with, and may be contained by, the more monolithic forms and meanings of the top-rated family shows, which insist on a rigidly revisionist interpretation of family life.

In each successive television era a particular congruence of marketing exigencies and cultural trends has produced different portraits of American social life. In network television genre is always about 80 percent commerce. But in the 1970s commercial imperatives made room for lively, innovative programming that interrupted the hitherto bland conventions of the television family, giving us programming that above all did not condescend to its audiences. The Bunkers were never a restful or reassuring family, but their battles, however strident, raised the possibility that there might be—might *have* to be—more ways than one to conduct family life, that blood ties are not the only bonds of community, that divorce is a feature of modern life to be confronted, and that men and women must find new ways of living together and raising children.

In the 1980s too the plurality of form and meaning and the relativistic sensibility of the "dramadies" offer the alarming but challenging proposition that for many Americans in the 1980s, the damaged boundaries of family, love, and work have rendered the texture of modern life so fluid that it becomes not merely uncontrollable but incomprehensible. This proposition has to be confronted, and it is the kind of critical commentary that good storytelling can always provide. The television series did, for a while, provide it, and still does here and there. At its best, television sets up a public argument about volatile matters that resonate deeply with audiences and even threaten to divide them. At its worst, the medium cranks out a pedestrian supply of toothless sermonizing.

In the late 1980s the generous space that was opened up in the 1970s for public discussion is once again being narrowed. With their eyes firmly fixed on the new mass audience (especially its children), *The Cosby Show* and its imitators threaten to quash the quarrelsome liveliness of the shows of the 1970s and the healthy diversity of 1980s television families by burying their heads in the nostalgic sands of "traditional values" that never were. Many family-oriented public interest groups are pleased with the domestic harmony they see in some current entertainment programming, but the obsession with engineering a spurious consensus returns us to the flattest kind of television with its twin besetting sins, sentimentality and a profound horror of argument. For the most part the way the industry works sets limits on the articulation of ambiguity, uncertainty, and the dissident voice. As long as television producers continue to be rewarded for seeing their viewers as markets, they will continue to crank out sentimentally idealized families or "human-condition" shows about "relevant" problems the viewers can weep over, and move on. Over and over, the narratives of television tell us that we are all brothers and sisters under the skin. But it is the social divisions outside the skin that need the public ventilation that television could be giving them but only occasionally does.

## QUESTIONS

*Looking at Ideas*

1. How have the family shows of the 1980s reflected the increasing diversity of the American family? How do they distort such trends? How and why do they avoid tension?

2. How did family shows of the 1980s demonstrate "the theme of the disillusioned career woman returning home"? Can you think of more recent shows that demonstrate this trend? Do you believe that today's television shows reflect this issue in a realistic way?

3. How do the material consumption, parental authority, conflict and resolution, and character development portrayed in *The Cosby Show* differ from earlier television shows' portrayals of family life? Do you agree with Taylor's critique of this show?

4. According to Taylor, how does the need to create a mass audience for commercial purposes influence the images of the family available to viewers of network television? Do you agree with her perspective?

*Looking at Strategies*

1. Taylor's primary organizing strategy is comparison/contrast. What points of comparison does she make, and how does she support them?

2. Comment on Taylor's use of examples from shows of the 1980s. How effective are her references to particular shows? Does she include enough details from the shows to back up her conclusions? Do you think the shows she mentions are typical ones of the period?

3. Examine Taylor's extended analysis of *The Cosby Show*. How effectively does she use strategies of analysis and argumentation in her critique of this show? Do you find her arguments convincing?

*Looking at Connections*

1. Compare Taylor's comments on the conservatively oriented *Cosby Show* with Barbara Ehrenreich's view of the more controversial *Roseanne* show as described in "The Wretched of the Hearth." Do you think Taylor would be supportive of this show and its heroine, or would she object to it? Why or why not?

2. Compare what Marie Winn says about the erosion of traditional family rituals with the images of the family as seen in the kind of contemporary family shows described in Taylor's essay. What kind of family rituals do television families practice? Are there contemporary shows that feature families watching television together or that are critical of excessive television watching?

*Suggestions for Writing:*

1. Compare a family-oriented or "workplace-family" television program currently in reruns, or one that you remember from your childhood, with a typical show of today. What major distinctions do you notice? What elements of the earlier type of program seem to persist?

2. Develop a story idea for a family-oriented television drama or comedy that would accurately reflect a quality of American family life seldom seen on television. Why do you think such a show has not yet been produced?

3. What do you think family situation comedies on television will be like four or five years from now? Give the plot of such a show of the future and explain why is is likely to be popular.

**JOURNAL ENTRY**

How are mothers typically portrayed on television? Write about your image of the TV stereotype of the mother. Does she work? Is she patient with her family? Devoted? Nurturing? Funny? Angry? Capable? Self-reliant? How do you respond to the image?

**BARBARA EHRENREICH: "The Wretched of the Hearth"**   Born in 1941, Barbara Ehrenreich holds a Ph.D. from Rockefeller University. She is a fellow of the Institute for Policy Studies in Washington, D.C., and is concerned in her writing with social justice and a reevaluation of the relation between the sexes and traditional gender roles. Ehrenreich has been a regular columnist for magazines such as *New Republic, Ms.,* and *Mother Jones.* Her recent books include *Flight from Commitment* (1983), *Fear of Falling: The Inner Life of the Middle Class* (1989), and *The Worst Years of Our Lives: Irreverent Notes from a Decade of Greed* (1990). The positive view of the iconoclastic Roseanne Barr (now Roseanne Arnold) in the following selection, "The Wretched of the Hearth," is consistent with the critique of traditional values that underlies much of Ehrenreich's writing. As you read the selection, notice how Ehrenreich uses her own type of humor to create a sympathetic portrait of Roseanne.

BARBARA EHRENREICH

# The Wretched of the Hearth

In the second half of the eighties, when American conservatism had reached its masochistic zenith with the re-election of Ronald Reagan, when women's liberation had been replaced by the more delicate sensibility known as post-feminism, when everyone was a yuppie and the heartiest word of endorsement in our vocabulary was "appropriate," there was yet this one paradox: our favorite TV personages were a liberal black man and a left-wing white feminist. Cosby could be explained as a representative of America's officially pro-family mood, but Roseanne is a trickier case. Her idea of humor is to look down on her sleeping family in the eponymous sitcom and muse, "Mmmm, I wonder where we could find an all-night taxidermist."

If zeitgeist were destiny, Roseanne would never have happened. Only a few years ago, we learn from her autobiography, Roseanne Barr was just your run-of-the-mill radical feminist mother-of-three, writing poems involving the Great Goddess, denouncing all known feminist leaders as sellout trash, and praying for the sixties to be born again in a female body. Since the entertainment media do not normally cast about for fat, loud-mouthed feminists to promote to superstardom, we must assume that Roseanne has something to say that many millions of people have been waiting to hear. Like this, upon being told of a woman who stabbed her husband thirty-seven times: "I admire her restraint."

Roseanne is the neglected underside of the eighties, bringing together its great themes of poverty, obesity, and defiance. The overside is handled well enough by Candice Bergen *(Murphy Brown)* and Madonna, who exist to remind us that talented women who work out are bound to become fabulously successful. Roseanne works a whole different beat, both in her sitcom and in the movie *She-Devil,* portraying the hopeless underclass of the female sex: polyester-clad, overweight occupants of the slow track; fast-food waitresses, factory workers, housewives, members of the invisible pink-collar army; the despised, the jilted, the underpaid.

But Barr—and this may be her most appealing feature—is never a victim. In the sitcom, she is an overworked mother who is tormented by her bosses at such locales as Wellman Plastics (where she works the assembly line) and Chicken Divine (a fast-food spot). But Roseanne Connor, her sitcom character, has, as we say in the blue-collar suburbs, a mouth on her. When the cute but obnoxious boss at Wellman calls the workers together and announces, "I have something to tell you," Roseanne yells out, "What? That you feel you're a woman trapped in a man's body?" In *She-Devil,* where Barr is unfortunately shorn of her trademark deadpan snarl, revenge must take more concrete forms: she organizes an army of the wretched of the earth—nursing home patients and clerical workers—to destroy her errant husband and drive the slender, beautiful, rich-and-famous Other Woman dotty.

At some point, the women's studies profession is bound to look up from its deconstructions and "re-thinkings" and notice Roseanne. They will then observe, in article and lecture form, that Barr's radicalism is distributed over the two axes of gender and class. This is probably as good an approach as any. Barr's identity is first of all female—her autobiography is titled *My Life As a Woman*—but her female struggles are located in the least telegenic and most frequently overlooked of social strata—the white, blue-collar working class. In anticipation of Roseannology, let us begin with Barr's contribution to the sociology of social class, and then take up her impressive achievements in the area of what could be called feminist theory.

*Roseanne* the sitcom, which was inspired by Barr the stand-up comic, is a radical departure simply for featuring blue-collar Americans—and for depicting them as something other than half-witted greasers and low-life louts. The working class does not usually get much of a role in the American entertainment spectacle. In the seventies mumbling, muscular blue-collar males *(Rocky, The Deer Hunter, Saturday Night Fever)* enjoyed a brief modishness on the screen, while Archie Bunker, the consummate blue-collar bigot, raved away on the tube. But even these grossly stereotyped images vanished in the eighties, as the spectacle narrowed in on the brie-and-chardonnay class. Other than *Roseanne,* I can find only one sitcom that deals consistently with the sub-yuppie condition: "Married . . . with children," a relentlessly nasty portrayal of a shoe salesman and his cognitively disabled family members. There may even be others, but sociological zeal has not sufficed to get me past the opening sequences of *Major Dad, Full House,* or *Doogie Howser.*

Not that *Roseanne* is free of class stereotyping. The Connors must bear part of the psychic burden imposed on all working-class people by their economic and occupational betters: they inhabit a zone of glad-handed gemeinschaft, evocative, now and then, of the stock wedding scene *(The Godfather, The Deer Hunter, Working Girl)* that routinely signifies lost old-world values. They indulge in a manic physicality that would be unthinkable among the more controlled and genteel Huxtables. They maintain a traditional, low-fiber diet of white bread and macaroni. They are not above a fart joke.

Still, in *Roseanne* I am willing to forgive the stereotypes as markers designed to remind us of where we are: in the home of a construction worker and his minimum-wage wife. Without the reminders, we might not be aware of how thoroughly the deeper prejudices of the professional class are being challenged. Roseanne's fictional husband Dan (played by the irresistibly cuddly John Goodman) drinks domestic beer and dedicates Sundays to football; but far from being a Bunkeresque boor, he looks to this feminist like the fabled "sensitive man" we have all been pining for. He treats his rotund wife like a sex goddess. He picks up on small cues signaling emotional distress. He helps with homework. And when Roseanne works overtime, he cooks, cleans, and rides herd on the kids without any of the piteous whining we have come to expect from upscale males in their rare, and lavishly documented, encounters with soiled Pampers.

Roseanne Connor has her own way of defying the stereotypes. Variously employed as a fast-food operative, a factory worker, a bartender, and a telephone salesperson, her real dream is to be a writer. When her twelve-year-old daughter Darlene (brilliantly played by Sara Gilbert) balks at a poetry-writing assignment, Roseanne gives her a little talking-to involving Sylvia Plath: "She inspired quite a few women, including *moi.*" In another episode, a middle-aged friend thanks Roseanne for inspiring her to dump her chauvinist husband and go to college. We have come a long way from the dithering, cowering Edith Bunker.

Most of the time the Connors do the usual sitcom things. They have the little domestic misunderstandings that can be patched up in twenty-four minutes with wisecracks and a round of hugs. But *Roseanne* carries working-class verisimilitude into a new and previously taboo dimension—the workplace. In the world of employment, Roseanne knows exactly where she stands: "All the good power jobs are taken. Vanna turns the letters. Leona's got hotels. Margaret's running England . . . 'Course she's not doing a very good job. . . ."

And in the workplace as well as the kitchen, Roseanne knows how to dish it out. A friend of mine, herself a denizen of the low-wage end of the work force, claims to have seen an episode in which Roseanne led an occupational health and safety battle at Wellman Plastics. I missed that one, but I have seen her, on more than one occasion, reduce the boss's ego to rubble. At Chicken Divine, for example, she is ordered to work weekends—an impossibility for a working mother—by an officious teenage boss who confides that he doesn't like working weekends either. In a sequence that could have been crafted by Michael Moore, Roseanne responds: "Well, that's real good 'cause you never do. You sit in your office like a little Napoleon, making up schedules and screwing up people's lives." To which he says, "That's what they pay me for. And you are paid to follow my orders." Blah blah blah. To which she says, staring at him for a long time and then observing with an evil smile: "You know, you got a little prize hanging out of your nose there."

The class conflict continues on other fronts. In one episode, Roseanne arrives late for an appointment with Darlene's history teacher, because she has been forced to work overtime at Wellman. The teacher, who is leaning against her desk stretching her quadriceps when Roseanne arrives, wants to postpone the appointment because she has a date to play squash. When Roseanne insists, the teacher tells her that Darlene has been barking in class, "like a dog." This she follows with some psychobabble—on emotional problems and dysfunctional families—that would leave most mothers, whatever their social class, clutched with guilt. Not Roseanne, who calmly informs the yuppie snit that, in the Connor household, everybody barks like dogs.

Now this is the kind of class-militant populism that the Democrats, most of them anyway, never seem to get right: up with the little gal; down with the snotty, the pretentious, and the overly paid. At least part of the appeal of *Roseanne* is that it ratifies the resentments of the underdog majority. But this being a sitcom, and Barr being a pacifist, the class-anger never gets too nasty. Even the most loathsome bosses turn out to be human, and in some cases pathetically needy. Rather than hating the bad guys, we end up feeling better about ourselves, which is the function of all good and humanistic humor anyway.

According to high conservative theory, the leftish cast to a show like *Roseanne* must reflect the media manipulations of the alleged "liberal elite." But the politics of *Roseanne* —including its feminist side, which we will get to in a minute—reflects nothing so much as the decidedly un-elite politics of Barr herself. On the Larry King show a few weeks ago, Barr said that she prefers the term "working class" to "blue collar" because (and I paraphrase) it reminds us of the existence of class, a reality that Americans are all too disposed to forget. In her autobiography, right up front in the preface, she tells us that it is a "book about the women's movement . . . a book about the left."

*Roseanne: My Life As a Woman* traces her journey from alienation to political commitment. It must stand as another one of Barr's commanding oddities. Where you would expect a standard rags-to-riches story, you find a sort of rags-to-revolution tale: more an intellectual and spiritual memoir than the usual chronicle of fearsome obstacles and lucky breaks. She was born the paradigmatic outsider, a Jew in Mormon Utah, and a low-income Jew at that. Within the Mormon culture, she was the "Other" (her own term), the "designated Heathen" in school Christmas pageants, always being reminded that "had we been in a Communist country, I would never have been allowed to express my religion, because 'dissent' is not tolerated there." At home she was loved and encouraged, but the emotional density of the Holocaust-haunted Barr family eventually proved too much for her. After a breakdown and several months of hospitalization, she ran away, at nineteen, to find the sixties, or what was left of them in 1971.

Her hippie phase left Barr with some proto-politics of the peace-and-love variety, three children, and an erratic wage-earner for a husband. It was in this condition that she wandered into the Woman to Woman bookstore on Colfax Avenue in Denver, where she discovered the Movement. Barr seems to have required very little in the way of consciousness-raising. With one gigantic "click," she jumped right in, joined the collective, and was soon occupied giving "seminars on racism, classism, anti-Semitism, pornography, and taking power." If this seems like a rather sudden leap to political leadership, I can attest from my own experience with venues like Woman to Woman that it happens every day.

But even within the ecumenical embrace of feminism, Barr remained the Outsider. "We did not agree anymore," she tells us of her collective, "with Betty Friedan, Gloria Steinem, or party politics within the women's movement," which she believes has turned into "a professional, careerist women's thing." When she found her "voice," it spoke in a new tone of working-class existentialism: "I began to speak as a working-class woman who is a mother, a woman who no longer believed in change, progress, growth, or hope." It was this special brand of proletarian feminism that inspired her stand-up comic routine. "I am talking about organizing working-class women and mothers," she tells us, and her comic persona was her way of going about it.

Middle-class feminism has long admitted the possibility of a working-class variant, but the general expectation has been that it would be a diluted version of the "real," or middle-class, thing. According to the conventional wisdom, working-class women would have no truck with the more anti-male aspects of feminism, and would be repelled by the least insult to the nuclear family. They would be comfortable only with the bread-and-butter issues of pay equity, child care, and parental leave. They would be culturally conservative, sensible, dull.

But we had not met Barr. Her stand-up routine was at first almost too vulgar and castrating for Denver's Comedy Works. In her autobiography, Barr offers an example. Heckled by a drunk for not being "feminine," she turned around, stared at her assailant, and said, "Suck my dick." I wish *Roseanne: My Life As a Woman* gave more examples of her early, Denver-era, stand-up style, but the recently released videotape *Roseanne* (made later in a Los Angeles club) may be a fair representation. On it she promotes a product called "Fem-Rage," designed to overcome female conditioning during that "one day of the month when you're free to be yourself," and leaves her female fans with the memorable question: "Ever put those maxi-pads on adhesive side up?"

In *Roseanne,* the sitcom, however, Barr has been considerably tamed. No longer standing bravely, and one must admit massively, alone with the microphone, she comes to us now embedded in the family: overwhelmed by domestic detail, surrounded by children too young for R-rated language, padding back and forth between stove, refrigerator, and kitchen table. Some of the edge is off here. There are no four-letter words, no menstruation jokes; and Roseanne's male-baiting barbs just bounce off her lovable Dan. Still, what better place for the feminist comic than in a family sitcom? Feminist theory, after all, cut its teeth on the critique of the family. Barr continues the process—leaving huge gaping holes where there was sweetness and piety.

All family sitcoms, of course, teach us that wisecracks and swift put-downs are the preferred modes of affectionate discourse. But Roseanne takes the genre a step further—over the edge, some may say. In the era of big weddings and sudden man shortages, she describes marriage as "a life sentence, without parole." And in the era of the biological time clock and the petted yuppie midlife baby, she can tell Darlene to get a fork out of the drawer and "stick it through your tongue." Or she can say, when Dan asks "Are we missing an offspring?" at breakfast, "Yeah. Where do you think I got the bacon?"

It is Barr's narrow-eyed cynicism about the family, even more than her class consciousness, that gives *Roseanne* its special frisson. Archie Bunker got our attention by telling us that we (blacks, Jews, "ethnics," WASPS, etc.) don't really like each other. Barr's message is that even within the family we don't much like each other. We love each other (who else do we have?); but The Family, with its impacted emotions, its lopsided division of labor, and its ancient system of age-graded humiliations, just doesn't work. Or rather, it doesn't work unless the contradictions are smoothed out with irony and the hostilities are periodically blown off as humor. Coming from mom, rather than from a jaded teenager or a bystander dad, this is scary news indeed.

So Barr's theoretical outlook is, in the best left-feminist tradition, dialectical. On the one hand, she presents the family as a zone of intimacy and support, well worth defending against the forces of capitalism, which drive both mothers and fathers out of the home, scratching around for paychecks. On the other hand, the family is hardly a haven, especially for its grown-up females. It is marred from within by—among other things—the patriarchal division of leisure, which makes dad and the kids the "consumers" of mom's cooking, cleaning, nurturing, and (increasingly) her earnings. Mom's job is to keep the whole thing together—to see that the mortgage payments are made, to fend off the viperish teenagers, to find the missing green sock—but mom is no longer interested in being a human sacrifice on the altar of "pro-family values." She's been down to the feminist bookstore; she's been reading Sylvia Plath.

This is a bleak and radical vision. Not given to didacticism, Barr offers no programmatic ways out. Surely, we are led to conclude, pay equity would help, along with child care, and so on. But Barr leaves us hankering for a quality of change that goes beyond mere reform: for a world in which even the lowliest among us—the hash-slinger, the sock-finder, the factory hand—will be recognized as the poet she truly is.

Maybe this is just too radical. The tabloids have taken to stalking Barr as if she were an unsightly blot on the electronic landscape of our collective dreams. *The New York Times* just devoted a quarter of a page to some upscale writer's prissy musings on Roseanne. "Was I just being squeamish" for disliking Barr, she asks herself: "a goody-two-shoes suburban feminist who was used to her icons being chic and sugar-coated instead of this gum-chewing, male-bashing . . . working-class mama with a big mouth?" No, apparently she is not squeamish. Barr is just too, well, unfeminine.

We know what Barr would say to that, and exactly how she would say it. Yeah, she's crude, but so are the realities of pain and exploitation she seeks to remind us of. If middle-class feminism can't claim Roseanne, maybe it's gotten a little too dainty for its own good. We have a long tradition of tough-talking females behind us, after all, including that other great working-class spokesperson, Mary "Mother" Jones, who once advised the troops, "Whatever you do, *don't* be ladylike."

## QUESTIONS

*Looking at Ideas:*

1. What is the paradox of the late 1980s that Ehrenreich discusses in her first paragraph?

2. How does Ehrenreich explain the success of the *Roseanne* situation comedy? Do you agree with the explanation?

3. Ehrenreich says that Roseanne is "never a victim." Do you agree, based on episodes of the show you have seen?

4. Do you agree that Roseanne exhibits "radical" ideas about gender and class? What is radical and what is traditional about her TV show? How do Roseanne Arnold's ideas differ from those of more middle-class feminists?

5. Ehrenreich states that she is "willing to forgive" some of the class stereotyping that occurs on the *Roseanne* show. Why? Do you agree that the show contains some such stereotyping? Are you willing to forgive or to justify it?

*Looking at Strategies:*

1. This article appeared originally as a review of Roseanne Barr's autobiography. How does Ehrenreich use references to the book *Roseanne: My Life As a Woman* to support her interpretation of Roseanne's vision and political stance? Is the essay effective as a book review?

2. How are examples drawn from particular episodes on the *Roseanne* show used to back up and clarify Ehrenreich's view of the significance

of Roseanne and her ideas? Would other examples or references from more recent episodes have provided a different perspective?

3. Ehrenreich makes some attempts to place *Roseanne* within the tradition of other television sitcoms and family shows, such as *Major Dad* and *The Cosby Show,* and films like *Working Girl.* How effectively does she present these examples as parallels and contrasts to what Roseanne is attempting to do? Are there other films or shows she could have mentioned as examples?

4. Ehrenreich's tone is ironic, at times sarcastic. Point out examples of ironic or sarcastic language used in the article. Does Ehrenreich's use of such language contribute to or detract from the effectiveness of her argument?

*Looking at Connections:*
1. Compare Ehrenreich's view of the impact of television on the family with Marie Winn's. Who is more optimistic about television's power to influence family life?
2. Contrast the *Roseanne* show's response to the conditions of working-class life with those of the earlier family programs explored in Ella Taylor's essay. What factors have made it possible for an image like Roseanne's to be acceptable in today's commercialized mass media?

*Suggestions for Writing:*
1. Write an essay in which you compare *Roseanne* with an earlier program or programs that profiled working-class family life, such as *All in the Family* or *The Honeymooners.* Do you feel *Roseanne* provides more realistic, less stereotypical views of life than other working-class–oriented shows?
2. Television situation comedies typically show a family confronting a problem together, working through it, and resolving it, at least temporarily. Write an essay discussing an episode of Barr's show in which a problem is confronted and (possibly) resolved. What is the problem or source of conflict? Who seems to be in charge? Who helps resolve the problem? What conclusions would you draw about the way the fictional family on this show handles problem solving?
3. Some critics have argued that *Roseanne* and other recent family shows, such as *The Simpsons* and *Married with Children,* are actually potentially damaging to family life, presenting viewers with negative role models of dysfunctional families with lazy, out-of-shape parents and low-achieving youngsters. Write an essay in which you respond either positively or negatively to such criticisms of the newer family shows.

**JOURNAL ENTRY**

Write about particular toys or sets of toys you played with as a child that were strongly promoted as "tie-ins" with other media, such as films and cartoon shows. What impact do you think these toys had on your imagination?

**STEPHEN KLINE: "Limits to the Imagination: Marketing and Children's Culture"** Stephen Kline is a professor at York University in Toronto. He is the co-author of *Social Communication in Advertising* and of the forthcoming *Technicians of the Imagination.* Kline's writings explore the ways in which media and advertising influence values, cultural sensibilities, and the imagination. The following selection, from the collection *Cultural Politics in America* (1990), grew out of Kline's research for *Technicians of the Imagination.* As you read Kline's essay, notice how he draws on data from a variety of disciplines, including sociology, economics, business, and psychology, to support his arguments about the influence of advertising and commercial children's programs on the imaginations of today's youth.

STEPHEN KLINE

# *Limits to the Imagination: Marketing and Children's Culture*

*The dynamic principle of fantasy is play, and as such it seems inconsistent with serious work. But, without play with fantasy, no creative work has ever come to birth. The debt that we owe to the play of the imagination is incalculable.*
                                                                                    —Carl Jung

*Psychic structure must always be passed from generation to generation through the narrow funnel of childhood; society's child-rearing practices are not just one item in a list of cultural traits. They are the very condition for the transmission and development of all other cultural elements, and place definite limits on what can be achieved in all other spheres of history.*
                                                                                    —Lloyd deMause

## *The Patterns of Child-Rearing*

This essay argues that a transition is taking place in the "funnel" of contemporary American socialization. Children's obsessions with toys and their apparent "capture" by television fictions are the surface indications of a deeper process. Children's imaginative play has become the target of marketing strategy, allowing marketing to define the limits of children's imaginations.

In *The Evolution of Childhood*, Lloyd deMause has argued that the notion of "socialization" is historical. Socialization, he writes, is a fairly recent way of thinking about and rearing children which arises in the late Victorian period and persists as a dominant feature of American society. "Childhood is a nightmare from which we have only recently begun to awaken."

Earlier approaches to child-rearing, deMause notes, ranged from the "infanticidal" attitudes in Rome to the purposefully harsh and intrusive approaches of eighteenth-century England which reflected a propertarian orientation to children. The contemporary "socialization" phase is characterized by new attitudes which are less concerned with conquering the child and dominating its will than with "guiding it into proper paths, teaching it to conform." In industrial society, learning, especially the acquisition of skills (including social skills) and moral codes of conduct, becomes the most important modality of childhood.

DeMause writes optimistically of an emerging postwar American child-rearing practice he terms "helping," in which the parent believes the "child knows better than the parent what it needs at each stage of its life" and parents struggle to "empathize with and expand its particular needs." The aim of such a practice is the liberation of the child, producing a generation which, parents hope, will be "gentle, sincere, never depressed, never imitative or group orientated, strong willed and unintimidated by authority." While helping children play their way into adulthood is not the predominant mode in contemporary child-rearing, it is one deMause identifies as likely to increase.

## Child-Rearing in the Culture of Consumption

Writing as he did in the early 1970s, deMause may be forgiven for his mistaken optimism about emerging approaches to childhood. David Reisman and W. Rosenborough, in their outlook at postwar child-rearing, observe a similar growing emphasis on meeting autonomous needs through play and imagination; but they interpret this pattern as pertaining to the problems of socialization in a consumerist "other-oriented" society. As they note, the new consumption ethic is embracing the new child-rearing practice. American socialization processes are being transformed as the exigencies of life in fluid and socially complex consumer culture are destabilizing many of the moral and social dispositions of an earlier work-oriented society.

As William Leiss, Sut Jhally, and I have also argued, market society is a distinctive phase of industrialization which privileges the discourse "through and about goods." In market society, the desire for, and relationships between, persons and products is transformed—as are the social relations and identities which people establish in their everyday life. In contemporary America, the perception of needs and the ability to achieve satisfaction are subsumed by a "magical rationality" of self-transformation through possession and use. This privileged discourse helps to locate satisfaction within the regions of immediate gratification—particularly leisure and entertainment—and accentuates social interactions which engage social judgment and identity. It is not surprising therefore that new patterns of child-rearing reflect these changes, positioning entertainment and play as the crucial activities of childhood. For modern childhood learning about identities and roles has become more important than acquiring skills and moral codes of conduct.

More recent trends only extend these observations. By the time of high school graduation, the average American child spends 17,000 hours being entertained by television while only 11,000 in schooled learning. Before age 12, children average over four hours of television viewing per day (up from about 1.2 hours spent with media in 1955). This implies that they have seen about 20,000 advertisements in a given year or 350,000 before they leave high school. Television advertising for children rose from a very limited $25 million in 1956 (mostly cereal) to over half a billion by 1986. About 55 percent of this current advertising budget, or $350 million, is for toys.

Parents report rarely watching television with their kids, and have limited ability to play with them on a regular, daily basis. When not in front of the TV or at the movies, the modern child is generally encouraged to play—by which is meant to interact with toys and games either alone or among peers. The toy and games market, which is now a $12.3 billion business, has grown enormously since 1955. Statistics like this might lead one to wonder whether modern "child-oriented" practices constitute "liberation"—or the abdication of child-rearing itself. . . .

## Children's Influence on Parents

Spending by children is only a fraction of the spending going on in the children's market. In 1988, parental spending on children under age 12 could total up to $50 billion in the United States. S. Ward and D. Wackman long ago remarked that children's personal consumption is only one of their points of contact in the market and only one of the reasons for marketing through children. A marketing director recently echoed their observation: "The trend is for children to get more decision making authority and exercise that authority at a younger and younger age."

Children influence their parents', friends', and relatives'—especially grandparents'—choices in spending money on them. Children do this in several ways, including direct requests in stores and at home, and through "passive dictation" of daily dialogue with parents wanting to avoid conflict and who know what "children want." Much of the purchasing of kids' things is done by others, although giving presents of money to children is, in the late 1980s, increasingly popular. Christmas has always played an important part in children's lives. In 1955, 80% of the toy sales used to be in the three months leading up to this holiday. This is now closer to 60 percent, in part reflecting kids' own purchase of play things but also the relative expansion of toy gifts for birthdays or even their importance as everyday expressions of parental "caring."

Children shop with parents frequently and many make requests for specific products like cereal and candy. And family life entails a heavy dose of children informing parents, and being consulted about their preferences. A marketing executive from Kenner states "Kids are the determining factor for toy purchases 90 percent of the time." The changing patterns in the relation between kids and parents and the role of the dialogue about consumption is a crucial element in marketing toys. It means advertising must get kids to want a particular toy and to be able to communicate that want to a parent, friend, or relative. Although children are clearly influencing more of the spending decisions there are also clear limitations as to what marketing to children can achieve. As one executive observes, the ability to motivate pressure on others has limits: "This has to stop some place. There's a point where children simply do not communicate well enough to select favorite brands."

The above limitations help to put changes in the attitudes of parents and kids, and the interactions between them, properly in the context of changes in marketing, because this relationship is a crucial problem for the expansion of the children's market. If special marketing methods are to be developed for the children's market they have first to attract children, provide them with the means of forming and retaining branded preferences, and then enable them to communicate these preferences clearly and directly to those who are purchasing for them.

## Marketing to Children

Children are back in style. With their increasing numbers, their own purchasing power, the billions spent on them by their families and their influence on family purchasing decisions, the children's market is strong and will be getting stronger in the years ahead.

As this document for marketers trumpets, kids marketing has arrived in the 1980s. The current changes in the children's market do not merely reflect a shift in parental attitudes, but arise from the concentrated attention of manufacturers and marketers.

More importantly, the 1980s have seen the development of a new strategy for marketing to children. Tom Englehart has termed this the "Strawberry Shortcake" strategy in recognition of the fact that everything that marketers had learned about children's marketing was crystalized as an intentional plan in the marketing of this new line. Brought out in 1980, Strawberry Shortcake wasn't just another doll promoted by mass market advertising. She was a sellable image conceived of by Those Characters from Cleveland, the licensing branch of American

Greetings Cards Ltd., to provide instant strong public identification. The image was worth several hundred million dollars in sales of a wide variety of licensed goods ranging from the Kenner produced doll and accessories to stickers, cut-out books, clothing, cups, jewelry, shoes, and food. Moreover, Strawberry Shortcake was not only a decorative motif, but an identifiable character carefully crafted and conveyed through advertising and her very own series of TV specials—the 30 minute animated commercial provided as cheap programming to syndicated private TV stations. These combined licenses provided the total exposure and momentum the new comprehensive strategy demanded.

This combination of television and playthings in a comprehensive and integrated market gambit reversed the time-honored marketing approaches of spin-offs and changed the way kids' cultural products are developed. As Cy Schneider put it these "programming properties are now being designed more for their merchandising potential than for their pure entertainment value." The new barrier to entry into this market is the $20 million or so development costs to be raised by the licensing agent or toy manufacturer for the product-featuring animation program.

Mattel had tried to launch a program featuring its Hot Wheels toys in 1969, but the FTC had frowned on this approach. But in the new climate of the 1980s the FTC and FCC did not seem to object. Licensed character tie-ins have become the new standard. He-Man, Thundercats, Transformers, and Care Bears all quickly followed this new pattern, extending the television special to a full 65-episode, animated serial, providing even higher definition to what had now become the hordes of character toys. The toy market boomed as licenses proliferated and new animation programs flooded the screens. There are currently over 45 different product-tied animation programs showcased on kids-time TV or about 65 percent of children's programming. Character toys have become the biggest sellers, not only in the traditional girls' doll markets but also with boys who used to play predominantly with vehicles. Whereas in 1976, licensed toys represented 20 percent of the toy market, they now account for almost 70 percent of toy sales.

*The License*

Although this strategy is new, in the sense that it has now become the predominant approach for marketing to kids, its roots are deep. Many of the elements of the strategy have been developed in kids marketing over the last 80 years. Product licensing, a crucial aspect of this approach, dates from Teddy Roosevelt's licensing of his name for the "Teddy" Bear (he gave the money to nature conservation). The success of Walt Disney's 1920s Mickey Mouse cartoons soon proved that fictional characters could provide the basis for effective licenses. Disney called his animation "imagineering"—the engineering of imagination; Herman Kamen, an advertising executive, quickly showed him that kids imagining happened while playing, eating, and dressing too. By

1933, over 10 million dollars of Disney licensed merchandise was sold. The subsequent licensing of Disney cartoon characters and later the Disney fantasy world—Disneyland and Disneyworld—is reputed to be making 2 billion dollars a year worldwide for Disney enterprises.

Licensing has become a 54.3-billion-dollar-a-year business with a 15.5 percent share located in the toy market. Both well-known stars (i.e., Mr. T and Michael Jackson) as well as fictional characters (Care Bears, Transformers, etc.) provide the models for these toys while many other lines (clothes, food) reveal a children's character imprint. One of the biggest boosts to licensing in the toy industry were the *Star Wars*/Lucas Films sequels, which have spawned over 2 billion dollars in licensed goods and created an avalanche of character licenses. Licensed toys grossed 8.2 billion dollars in 1986, proving that popular characters could spawn profitable playthings.

### Spin-Offs

A second element in the strategy was the spin-off. Popular media events could also replicate themselves in other venues. Wrestlemania characters, Farrah Fawcett, A-Team, and Superman have all parlayed their exposure in one venue and market into spin-offs for kids, each with a toy tie-in. The crucial feature of the spin-off is that it cashes in on the already established character and media exposure which helps to increase the personality's definition and recognizability inexpensively.

The most important spin-off in the development of the kids market was probably the Mickey Mouse Club television program created in 1955. Before that time, total children's market advertising only amounted to about one million dollars and the product array for children was rather narrow. Toy manufacturers were on record as believing that they would thrive without mass market advertising on television. Television advertising on kids' TV (especially before the development of video tape) was very limited, consisting of sponsorship announcements and product demonstrations. The problem of funding children's production reflected the lack of interest of advertisers in this market. Kids, they believed, didn't have much money to spend and kids' programming was not sufficiently enticing to draw big audiences.

By transposing Mickey's established film reputation into another venue, the Mickey Mouse Club almost single-handedly established the mass market for kids' cultural products by proving these assumptions misguided. Kids it turned out, even with their limited disposable incomes could still influence consumption. And programming could be devised that provided a full 90 percent exposure in the marketplace and a sizeable and loyal market share. The unheard-of sum of $10 million in advertising revenues was necessary to launch it, but daring marketers, like Mattel with its burp gun promotion, quickly learned of the benefits of mass advertising to kids.

### The Character

The third and most important element in tie-in marketing is the personality toy. Although Mickey Mouse showed that animal cartoons could be popular with the very young, it was Barbie—the bestselling character of all time—who during the late 1950s and 1960s provided the object lesson in character marketing. "The people at Mattel and the agency . . . began thinking of toys in an entirely new way. We began to see toys as concepts that could be depicted or demonstrated in television commercials" argued one the originators of this approach. Barbie was carefully and consciously designed and marketed not just as another doll, but as a personality. "We didn't depict Barbie as a doll, we treated her as a real-life teenage fashion model." And so Barbie was provided with a Barbie story—a narrative that established Barbie's personality profile within an imaginary but familiar universe.

Barbie's attraction as a doll lay in the way children identified with her character rather than her role. Hence the way they played with her changed. "Somehow Barbie filled a very special need for little girls' imaginations. She was the fulfillment of every little girl's dream of glamour, fame, wealth and stardom." Young girls identified with Barbie and became deeply involved with her. They didn't rehearse motherhood as they did with other dolls but spent hours dressing and undressing her, or just staring and admiring her in her various outfits. The Barbie-story worked and Barbie sold in the millions.

Although character toys came to dominate the girls' market of the 1970s, action toys, especially vehicles for boys, were still dominant attractions. Darth Vadar, the first technomorphic character toy tie-in, showed that the action character doll could sell brilliantly to boys as well. Pretty soon, science fiction became the parable of the toy and character toys were freed from the identity constraints of the familiar and the personal. Transformers—half vehicle and half being—parlayed this into a multi-million-dollar iconography. The invention of character toys for the boys' market is probably one of the most significant breakthroughs resulting from the tie-in strategy.

*Comprehensive Strategy*

The final element in the total approach to tie-ins is concept marketing, which uses a comprehensive strategic communication plan. It is comprehensive in that it orchestrates all available channels of communication, achieving a kind of synergy amongst them. This synergy is contained by the unified thematic framework (including the imagery, narratives, characters, and music) which establishes the concept. This concept gives shape to all executions in the strategy, including in-store display, interpersonal communication, advertising, and television programing. Total marketing positions the character toy and its fantasy world as the overarching concept for a whole range of licensed products to be marketed through saturation of all media. The animated series featuring the character toy as its hero is the flagship of this flotilla because of the importance of TV exposure.

Herein we see the deeper problem, as children's cultural-product design becomes completely subsumed within the tie-in strategy. He-Man, like so many other children's heros, is not just scripted for a child's amusement and moral education. Children must want him, to own and to play with him, to recreate the He-Man Universe within their bedroom. To quote even an outspoken supporter of marketing to children, "What was once the sole province of children's authors, comic strip artists and film artists . . . has now become a creative outlet for toy and greeting card manufacturers." In contemporary television, marketing, rather than entertainment, considerations dominate the design of children's characters, the fictions in which they appear, and hence the way children play. Play, the most important modality of childhood learning, is thus colonized by marketing objectives, making the imagination the organ of corporate desire. The consumption ethos has become the vortex of children's culture.

## Barbie's Problem—The Limits of Imagination

All products have a limited lifetime, toys more so than most. Kids lose interest in particular toys, quickly moving on to other things. After all, emotional and cognitive maturation implies that new psychological needs and states are being expressed and worked out in the child's imaginative play. And besides, kids are extremely peer-oriented. They are subject to the collective whims of their immediate cultural environment, which is constantly changing shape and focus. Barbie's miraculous longevity is testimony to the perspicacity of her creators. In part this can be explained by the constant updating of her image achieved through advertising and accessory design. But Barbie represented an old strategy. She was not a tie-in with a show of her own. She was a stand-alone character toy. Barbie relied on children's active imaginations.

Barbie's current rival in the market—Gem—was launched by Hasbro in 1984 with her own Japanese-produced animation series and is outselling Barbie. Gem is the embodiment of a comprehensive market strategy—she is a total package. Gem's character is clearly defined and punkishly modern. But most importantly Gem's personality, friends, and exploits are vividly portrayed in a animated television series with a narrative that kids can identify with and follow regularly. Gem achieves this weekly exposure in most young girls' households.

Barbie has a problem. The solution is for Barbie to go modern. She needs a TV show and a rock band and she will be getting both before the 1987 season is out. Barbie's problem is that of the whole toy industry which is changing in the face of the new tie-in strategy. Animate or perish. Barbie's creators believed that Barbie's personality should not be too specific because this might limit the imaginations of the girls who play with dolls. "Each little girl has her own dreams about who Barbie is. . . . If you give her a specific personality it could mean that little girls will lose their ability to project whatever personalities they want onto Barbie." Gem proves that the fiction and fantasy provided by programing serve the purposes of marketing more effectively than little girls' imaginations.

Bruno Bettelheim has pointed out what every parent knows: children's fiction serves an important part in socializing children, in forming their imaginations, and in creating the framework for learning about their social world. What is at stake is the shape and structure of children's popular culture—children's mythology, heros, and view of the world. As marketing criteria begin to dominate the conjunction of television and toys, so too they underwrite children's imaginative activities through narrative and play.

The 30-minute commercial disguised as a program starts with the distinct advantage that young children don't really conceptually differentiate the toy, the commercial, and the program. Older ones who are more cynical about advertising's persuasiveness than the under-7-year-olds also do not see the same intent-to-sell hidden in these "programs." In both cases what matters to the child is the fictional universe which envelops product, program, and advertisement. Children are disarmed by their absorption in the story.

More to the point, the marketing orientation fundamentally changes the nature of the television programs themselves, and hence their broader impact as children's myth and folklore. Programing designed to move products has features unique to those purposes. The fiction in the tie-in strategy must also be cheaply produced while still holding the audience's attention. Moreover it must involve the child with the toy's personality and provide the child with a simple means of communicating with parents their preference for this product. This must be done within the child's limitations of understanding, retention, and communication. These programs reflect everything that marketers have learned about selling to children.

First and foremost, in the 1980s children's fictions are more specifically targeted for children's audiences than previous kids' programing. This represents clear market segmentation. Unlike Bill Cosby or Disney's nature programs these animations are not intended as family viewing, or even for mixed age groups of children. These programs are designed for afternoon or Saturday morning "ghetto" viewing, with only young children watching. By implication the stories they present preoccupy the child's imagination and fantasy life, but remain almost unknown to the parent. This is a radical departure from folklore traditions where the shared narrative provides a means for parents to convey complex and subtle moral and ethical ideas to their children.

The new programing is animated not only because of the ease and swiftness of production but because, as Disney long ago showed, animation is the superior form of imaginative fiction. Disney discovered that animation brings to life in the visual media themes and characters long extant in old folk and fairy tales. The vividness and attractiveness of anthropomorphic beings represents an acute balance between the familiarity necessary for recognition and the distance necessary for allegory. (Bugs Bunny, for instance, is a classic trickster.) Animation has the added feature that it is never constrained to real objects and their physical properties of movement, transformability, and potential. Animation codifies the break with reality. It is the genre of fantasy par excellence.

Action, especially battle sequences, is easily executed in animation. The sequences appear little more than a continuity of poses reminiscent of actors' movements in Kabuki drama. The cartoon creature who acts, thinks, and feels just like humans, but is simplified in form and personality provides a perfect vehicle for children's characterization. The drawings appear infantalized. Characters' features and expressions are reduced to the simplest and most easily recognized by the young. Animators emphasize those features and expressions that children most quickly and easily identify with. Indeed, the characters rarely learn anything in these programs—their nature is inherent and fixed by their species-specific and immutable characteristics. Children can remember these characters well enough to ask their parents for Liono or Starburst She-ra without ever knowing the Mattel name or label. Character serves this function better than brand names.

The narratives are similarly simplified along with the characters. Repetition and predictability are important because younger kids can only remember sequences as isolated bits; only older kids get a sense of the program as a whole. Older cartoon shows, such as ones featuring Bugs Bunny or Donald Duck, have folktale characteristics combined with common quotidian domestic conflicts. Newer cartoon programs are more mytho-heroic in nature. The moral struggles are basic bouts between good and evil, the social contexts less quotidian and realistic, and the resolutions more predictable. Good and evil are clearly differentiated and rarely ambiguous. The forces of evil are always anti-democratic in their social organization.

Newer cartoon stories have a strange quality of simplified abstraction. For example, in the Care Bears there are no integrated personalities. Each bear represents a single emotional dimension. Similarly, the forces of good and evil are often deployed in teams. This not only arrays the action around specifically skilled personalities (i.e., in the Thundercats each character has a special ability like speed, technical intelligence, strength) but also means that children have to buy multiple characters to reproduce the whole concept in their play.

These narratives are highly gendered. Market research taught the designers that boys and girls respond to different things and become engaged in TV through different forms of imaginative engagement. Action is necessary for boys and caring and social relations for girls. Boys like to engage in conflict and solve problems in play; girls like to touch, cuddle, stroke, dress, and care for their toys. Whereas Bugs Bunny and the Flintstones have been appreciated by both audiences, the current programing reflects a stronger gender bias—with action-oriented science fiction and cute animal fantasies defining the divide.

In fact, the overall momentum of these new animated narratives is towards the fantastic. Each story creates an alternative fictional world in which imagination is (presumably) given free reign. This is the seemingly creative and exciting feature of these programs which have made fantastic fiction and sci-fi the idiom of childhood. Were these fictions unconstrained by the marketing concept one might be in a better position to celebrate this new dimension of children's culture. It is clear, however, this shift to the fantastic is dictated by the marketing problem. As one toy marketer aptly puts this point, "We also realized something more important that persists to this day. The play situation in which you place a toy becomes a fantasy for the child. The fantasy presented becomes as important as the Product." The problem is to engage children's imagination so that the whole of their creative impulse is directed to absorbing the desired orientation to the toy product.

## Playing with Imagination

By fusing television and toys within a singular fantasy world, the tie-in strategy must have its most serious consequences on children's play. It is no longer the case that children's television programing functions as a spectacle, drawing children to the medium like the modern Pied Piper. The programing is there to provide a fictional world in which the attraction to and characteristics of the toy are defined and situated. When the television is off, the fantasy world lives on in the child's imagination, and is recreated regularly in their play. The child therefore, is still "working for" the toy manufacturer long after the program has ended for as long as the fictional world generated in programing still defines the play of the child.

The consequence then is the overdetermination of the structure of play—and the social interaction which surrounds it—by marketing considerations. Observations of children playing with these toys or conversations with them about what they are doing quickly indicates that the emphasis on multiple characters and accessories and on conflict, the bifurcation of good and evil, the simplification of character and narrative, the episodic fragmentation, and the mythological social framework are all internalized and reenacted in play. Play in fact has become highly ritualized—less an exploration and solidification of personal experiences and developing conceptual schema than a rearticulation of the fantasy world provided by market designers. Imaginative play has shifted one degree closer to mere imitation and assimilation.

The consequences, however, go beyond these limitations on creative exploration. In the first place, because play entails the recreation of a "total fantasy world," multiple character toys, their accessories, and special bases, etc., are necessary for appropriate play. The expense of toys and the numbers of them one must buy to engage in appropriate fantasy play have increased. In addition the child-orientation itself and the segmentation of audiences by gender implicit within the marketing strategy have a most noticeable effect. First, parents are further excluded from play with their children simply because parents do not know the fantasy world well enough to engage their children in imaginative play with these toys. Most parents report hating playing with

these character toys (they find it boring and pointless), and most children report that their parents don't know what to do with them. What
neither understands is that playing together assumes a shared fantasy—a condition which no longer exists.

The same exclusion by imagination is at the root of a growing divide between boys and girls at play. Since the marketing targets and
features different emotional and narrative elements (action/conflict vs.
emotional attachment and maintenance) boys and girls also experience
difficulty in playing together with these toys. The advertisements, which
most precisely represent marketing's conception of how children play
with toys, reveal single-sex groupings in 95 percent of ads.

No parent can deny that toys and television are attractive, some
would say obsessive, mainstays of contemporary child-rearing. Yet
watching children play, absorbed in their packaged fantasy life, many
have begun to wonder whether ritualized imaginative production isn't
limiting children's creativity while isolating the child from parents and
children of the other sex. Yet these are the direct consequences of letting the increasingly sophisticated marketing orientation dominate the
most important modalities of socialization—children's imaginations.
More worrisome still is the possibility that the marketing approach developed in the children's market will become the adult marketing of the
future: Coming soon—the Miami Vice Strategy.

## QUESTIONS

*Looking at Ideas:*
1. How does Kline demonstrate that child-rearing practices have changed
   in the "culture of consumption"?
2. How do children influence their parents' spending patterns and purchases?
3. What new television marketing strategies emerged in the 1980s to sell
   more children's products?
4. How do the new toy and media marketing strategies isolate children
   from their parents and have a negative impact on their imaginations?
   Contrast the socialization and creativity of children raised on mass-produced toys and media tie-ins to the imaginative worlds of children
   raised on traditional children's literature and games.

*Looking at Strategies:*
1. What impact do the quotations from Carl Jung and Lloyd deMause that
   begin the essay have on your understanding of Kline's thesis?
2. How does Kline use market research and statistics on children's viewing
   and spending habits to support his arguments?
3. How does Kline analyze marketing strategies such as Strawberry Shortcake, Barbie and Gem? What conclusions does he draw from their successes?
4. How does Kline make use of the strategy of comparison to support his
   ideas? Provide examples of the comparisons he draws between chil-

dren's toys, children's fiction, children's programs, and child-oriented advertising campaigns.

*Looking at Connections:*

1. Apply Kline's ideas about the impact of children's games and programs on the imagination to the fantasy world described in Ray Bradbury's "The Veldt." What differences do you perceive in the two authors' views about the impact of media and marketing on children and family life?

2. Klein presents a picture of today's children as being imaginatively limited, even stunted, by the product-oriented TV programs that fuel their fantasy lives. Compare Klein's portrait of these children with the portrait of a child obsessed with money and gambling in D. H. Lawrence's "The Rocking Horse Winner" in Chapter Two.

*Suggestions for Writing:*

1. Write a response to Kline's essay from the perspective of a toy manufacturer, an advertiser, or a producer of children's television programs. What defense of your profession and its influences on children and family life could you make?

2. Do your own analysis of a particular tie-in phenomenon you have observed, such as Mutant Ninja Turtles or the Nintendo games and TV characters. Write an essay in which you discuss the different aspects of the tie-in sequence. Do you agree with Kline that such tie-ins operate to produce greater sales and more obsessive involvement on the part of children?

3. Use your personal experience with a media figure featured in tie-ins, such as Barbie or Superman, and compare its impact on your imagination and creativity with that resulting from the more traditional children's books you read in early childhood. Which experience do you feel had the most positive impact on your creativity and imagination? Why?

**RAY BRADBURY: "The Veldt"**   Born in 1920, Ray Bradbury attended public
schools in Illinois and Los Angeles before beginning to work full-time as a
writer of fantasy and science fiction in 1943. Bradbury has written plays and
screenplays as well as hundreds of stories and many novels. His works include
*Fahrenheit 451,* and *The Martian Chronicles,* which has been made into a play
and a TV series. His recent works include *Death Is a Lonely Business* (1985)
and *A Graveyard for Lunatics* (1990). His fiction explores the impact of scien-
tific development and technology on ordinary human lives. Bradbury is particularly concerned about the dangers of becoming too dependent on science at
the expense of moral considerations. Notice how the theme of an out-of-con-
trol technology forms the basis for his fantasy of children lost in the high-tech
play environment portrayed in "The Veldt."

RAY BRADBURY

# *The Veldt*

"George, I wish you'd look at the nursery."

"What's wrong with it?"

"I don't know."

"Well, then."

"I just want you to look at it, is all, or call a psychologist in to look
at it."

"What would a psychologist want with a nursery?"

"You know very well what he'd want." His wife paused in the middle of the kitchen and watched the stove busy humming to itself, making supper for four.

"It's just that the nursery is different now than it was."

"All right, let's have a look."

They walked down the hall of their soundproofed Happy-life
Home, which had cost them thirty thousand dollars installed, this
house which clothed and fed and rocked them to sleep and played and
sang and was good to them. Their approach sensitized a switch somewhere and the nursery light flicked on when they came within ten feet
of it. Similarly, behind them, in the halls, lights went on and off as they
left them behind, with a soft automaticity.

"Well," said George Hadley.

They stood on the thatched floor of the nursery. It was forty feet across by forty feet long and thirty feet high; it had cost half again as much as the rest of the house. "But nothing's too good for our children," George had said.

The nursery was silent. It was empty as a jungle glade at hot high noon. The walls were blank and two-dimensional. Now, as George and Lydia Hadley stood in the center of the room, the walls began to purr and recede into crystalline distance, it seemed, and presently an African veldt appeared, in three dimensions; on all sides, in colors reproduced to the final pebble and bit of straw. The ceiling above them became a deep sky with a hot yellow sun.

George Hadley felt the perspiration start on his brow.

"Let's get out of the sun," he said. "This is a little too real. But I don't see anything wrong."

"Wait a moment, you'll see," said his wife.

Now the hidden odorophonics were beginning to blow a wind of odor at the two people in the middle of the baked veldtland. The hot straw smell of lion grass, the cool green smell of the hidden water hole, the great rusty smell of animals, the smell of dust like a red paprika in the hot air. And now the sounds: the thump of distant antelope feet on grassy sod, the papery rustling of vultures. A shadow passed through the sky. The shadow flickered on George Hadley's upturned, sweating face.

"Filthy creatures," he heard his wife say.

"The vultures."

"You see, there are the lions, far over, that way. Now they're on their way to the water hole. They've just been eating," said Lydia. "I don't know what."

"Some animal." George Hadley put his hand up to shield off the burning light from his squinted eyes. "A zebra or a baby giraffe, maybe."

"Are you sure?" His wife sounded peculiarly tense.

"No, it's a little late to be *sure,*" he said, amused. "Nothing over there I can see but cleaned bone, and the vultures dropping for what's left."

"Did you hear that scream?" she asked.

"No."

"About a minute ago?"

"Sorry, no."

The lions were coming. And again George Hadley was filled with admiration for the mechanical genius who had conceived this room. A miracle of efficiency selling for an absurdly low price. Every home should have one. Oh, occasionally they frightened you with their clinical accuracy, they startled you, gave you a twinge, but most of the time what fun for everyone, not only your own son and daughter, but for yourself when you felt like a quick jaunt to a foreign land, a quick change of scenery. Well, here it was!

And here were the lions now, fifteen feet away, so real, so feverishly and startlingly real that you could feel the prickling fur on your hand, and your mouth was stuffed with the dusty upholstery smell of their heated pelts, and the yellow of them was in your eyes like the yellow of an exquisite French tapestry, the yellows of lions and summer grass, and the sound of matted lion lungs exhaling on the silent noontide, and the smell of meat from the panting, dripping mouths.

The lions stood looking at George and Lydia Hadley with terrible green-yellow eyes.

"Watch out!" screamed Lydia.

The lions came running at them.

Lydia bolted and ran. Instinctively, George sprang after her. Outside, in the hall, with the door slammed, he was laughing and she was crying and they both stood appalled at the other's reaction.

"George!"

"Lydia! Oh, my dear poor sweet Lydia!"

"They almost got us!"

"Walls, Lydia, remember; crystal walls, that's all they are. Oh, they look real, I must admit—Africa in your parlor—but it's all dimensional superactionary, supersensitive color film and mental tape film behind glass screens. It's all odorophonics and sonics, Lydia. Here's my handkerchief."

"I'm afraid." She came to him and put her body against him and cried steadily. "Did you see? Did you *feel?* It's too real."

"Now, Lydia . . ."

"You've got to tell Wendy and Peter not to read any more on Africa."

"Of course—of course." He patted her.

"Promise?"

"Sure."

"And lock the nursery for a few days until I get my nerves settled."

"You know how difficult Peter is about that. When I punished him a month ago by locking the nursery for even a few hours—the tantrum he threw! And Wendy too. They *live* for the nursery."

"It's got to be locked, that's all there is to it."

"All right." Reluctantly he locked the huge door. "You've been working too hard. You need a rest."

"I don't know—I don't know," she said, blowing her nose, sitting down in a chair that immediately began to rock and comfort her. "Maybe I don't have enough to do. Maybe I have time to think too much. Why don't we shut the whole house off for a few days and take a vacation?"

"You mean you want to fry my eggs for me?"

"Yes." She nodded.

"And darn my socks?"

"Yes." A frantic, watery-eyed nodding.

"And sweep the house?"

"Yes, yes—oh, yes!"

215

"But I thought that's why we bought this house, so we wouldn't have to do anything?"

"That's just it. I feel like I don't belong here. The house is wife and mother now and nursemaid. Can I compete with an African veldt? Can I give a bath and scrub the children as efficiently or quickly as the automatic scrub bath can? I cannot. And it isn't just me. It's you. You've been awfully nervous lately."

"I suppose I have been smoking too much."

"You look as if you don't know what to do with yourself in this house, either. You smoke a little more every morning and drink a little more every afternoon and need a little more sedative every night. You're beginning to feel unnecessary too."

"Am I?" He paused and tried to feel into himself to see what was really there.

"Oh, George!" She looked beyond him, at the nursery door. "Those lions can't get out of there, can they?"

He looked at the door and saw it tremble as if something had jumped against it from the other side.

"Of course not," he said.

At dinner they ate alone, for Wendy and Peter were at a special plastic carnival across town and had televised home to say they'd be late, to go ahead eating. So George Hadley, bemused, sat watching the dining-room table produce warm dishes of food from its mechanical interior.

"We forgot the ketchup," he said.

"Sorry," said a small voice within the table, and ketchup appeared.

As for the nursery, thought George Hadley, it won't hurt for the children to be locked out of it awhile. Too much of anything isn't good for anyone. And it was clearly indicated that the children had been spending a little too much time on Africa. That *sun*. He could feel it on his neck, still, like a hot paw. And the *lions*. And the smell of blood. Remarkable how the nursery caught the telepathic emanations of the children's minds and created life to fill their every desire. The children thought lions, and there were lions. The children thought zebras, and there were zebras. Sun—sun. Giraffes—giraffes. Death and death.

That *last*. He chewed tastelessly on the meat that the table had cut for him. Death thoughts. They were awfully young, Wendy and Peter, for death thoughts.

But you were never too young, really. Long before you knew what death was you were wishing it on someone else. When you were two years old you were shooting people with cap pistols.

But this—the long, hot African veldt—the awful death in the jaws of a lion. And repeated again and again.

"Where are you going?"

He didn't answer Lydia. Preoccupied, he let the lights glow softly on ahead of him, extinguish behind him as he padded to the nursery door. He listened against it. Far away, a lion roared.

He unlocked the door and opened it. Just before he stepped inside, he heard a faraway scream. And then another roar from the lions, which subsided quickly.

He stepped into Africa. How many times in the last year had he opened this door and found Wonderland, Alice, the Mock Turtle, or Aladdin and his Magical Lamp, or Jack Pumpkinhead of Oz, or Dr. Doolittle, or the cow jumping over a very real-appearing moon—all the delightful contraptions of a make-believe world. How often had he seen Pegasus flying in the sky ceiling, or seen fountains of red fireworks, or heard angel voices singing. But now, this yellow hot Africa, this bake oven with murder in the heat. Perhaps Lydia was right. Perhaps they needed a little vacation from the fantasy which was growing a bit too real for ten-year-old children. It was all right to exercise one's mind with gymnastic fantasies, but when the lively child mind settled on *one* pattern . . .? It seemed that, at a distance, for the past month, he had heard lions roaring, and smelled their strong odor seeping as far away as his study door. But, being busy, he had paid it no attention.

George Hadley stood on the African grassland alone. The lions looked up from their feeding, watching him. The only flaw to the illusion was the open door through which he could see his wife, far down the dark hall, like a framed picture, eating her dinner abstractedly.

"Go away," he said to the lions.

They did not go.

He knew the principle of the room exactly. You sent out your thoughts. Whatever you thought would appear.

"Let's have Aladdin and his lamp," he snapped.

The veldtland remained; the lions remained.

"Come on, room! I demand Aladdin!" he said.

Nothing happened. The lions mumbled in their baked pelts.

"Aladdin!"

He went back to dinner. "The fool room's out of order," he said. "It won't respond."

"Or—"

"Or what?"

"Or it *can't* respond," said Lydia, "because the children have thought about Africa and lions and killing so many days that the room's in a rut."

"Could be."

"Or Peter's set it to remain that way."

"*Set* it?"

"He may have got into the machinery and fixed something."

"Peter doesn't know machinery."

"He's a wise one for ten. That I.Q. of his—"

"Nevertheless—"

"Hello, Mom. Hello, Dad."

The Hadleys turned. Wendy and Peter were coming in the front door, cheeks like peppermint candy, eyes like bright blue agate marbles, a smell of ozone on their jumpers from their trip in the helicopter.

"You're just in time for supper," said both parents.

217

"We're full of strawberry ice cream and hot dogs," said the children, holding hands. "But we'll sit and watch."

"Yes, come tell us about the nursery," said George Hadley.

The brother and sister blinked at him and then at each other. "Nursery?"

"All about Africa and everything," said the father with false joviality.

"I don't understand," said Peter.

"Your mother and I were just traveling through Africa with rod and reel; Tom Swift and his Electric Lion," said George Hadley.

"There's no Africa in the nursery," said Peter simply.

"Oh, come now, Peter. We know better."

"I don't remember any Africa," said Peter to Wendy. "Do you?"

"No."

"Run see and come tell."

She obeyed.

"Wendy, come back here!" said George Hadley, but she was gone. The house lights followed her like a flock of fireflies. Too late, he realized he had forgotten to lock the nursery door after his last inspection.

"Wendy'll look and come tell us," said Peter.

"She doesn't have to tell *me*. I've seen it."

"I'm sure you're mistaken, Father."

"I'm not, Peter. Come along now."

But Wendy was back. "It's not Africa," she said breathlessly.

"We'll see about this," said George Hadley, and they all walked down the hall together and opened the nursery door.

There was a green, lovely forest, a lovely river, a purple mountain, high voices singing, and Rima, lovely and mysterious, lurking in the trees with colorful flights of butterflies, like animated bouquets, lingering in her long hair. The African veldtland was gone. The lions were gone. Only Rima was here now, singing a song so beautiful that it brought tears to your eyes.

George Hadley looked in at the changed scene. "Go to bed," he said to the children.

They opened their mouths.

"You heard me," he said.

They went off to the air closet, where a wind sucked them like brown leaves up the flue to their slumber rooms.

George Hadley walked through the singing glade and picked up something that lay in the corner near where the lions had been. He walked slowly back to his wife.

"What is that?" she asked.

"An old wallet of mine," he said.

He showed it to her. The smell of hot grass was on it and the smell of a lion. There were drops of saliva on it, it had been chewed, and there were blood smears on both sides.

He closed the nursery door and locked it, tight.

In the middle of the night he was still awake and he knew his wife

was awake. "Do you think Wendy changed it?" she said at last, in the
dark room.

"Of course."

"Made it from a veldt into a forest and put Rima there instead of
lions?"

"Yes."

"Why?"

"I don't know. But it's staying locked until I find out."

"How did your wallet get there?"

"I don't know anything," he said, "except that I'm beginning to be
sorry we bought that room for the children. If children are neurotic at
all, a room like that—"

"It's supposed to help them work off their neuroses in a healthful
way."

"I'm starting to wonder." He stared at the ceiling.

"We've given the children everything they ever wanted. Is this our
reward—secrecy, disobedience?"

"Who was it said, 'Children are carpets, they should be stepped on
occasionally'! We've never lifted a hand. They're insufferable—let's admit it. They come and go when they like; they treat us as if *we* were
offspring. They're spoiled and we're spoiled."

"They've been acting funny ever since you forbade them to take the
rocket to New York a few months ago."

"They're not old enough to do that alone, I explained."

"Nevertheless, I've noticed they've been decidedly cool toward us
since."

"I think I'll have David McClean come tomorrow morning to have
a look at Africa."

"But it's not Africa now, it's Green Mansions country and Rima."

"I have a feeling it'll be Africa again before then."

A moment later they heard the screams.

Two screams. Two people screaming from downstairs. And then a
roar of lions.

"Wendy and Peter aren't in their rooms," said his wife.

He lay in his bed with his beating heart. "No," he said. "They've
broken into the nursery."

"Those screams—they sound familiar."

"Do they?"

"Yes, awfully."

And although their beds tried very hard, the two adults couldn't be
rocked to sleep for another hour. A smell of cats was in the night air.

"Father?" said Peter.

"Yes."

Peter looked at his shoes. He never looked at his father any more,
nor at his mother. "You aren't going to lock up the nursery for good,
are you?"

"That all depends."

219

"On what?" snapped Peter.

"On you and your sister. If you intersperse this Africa with a little variety—oh, Sweden perhaps, or Denmark or China—"

"I thought we were free to play as we wished."

"You are, within reasonable bounds."

"What's wrong with Africa, Father?"

"Oh, so now you admit you have been conjuring up Africa, do you?"

"I wouldn't want the nursery locked up," said Peter coldly. "Ever."

"Matter of fact, we're thinking of turning the whole house off for about a month. Live sort of a carefree one-for-all existence."

"That sounds dreadful! Would I have to tie my own shoes instead of letting the shoe tier do it? And brush my own teeth and comb my hair and give myself a bath?"

"It would be fun for a change, don't you think?"

"No, it would be horrid. I didn't like it when you took out the picture painter last month."

"That's because I wanted you to learn to paint all by yourself, Son."

"I don't want to do anything but look and listen and smell; what else *is* there to do?"

"All right, go play in Africa."

"Will you shut off the house sometime soon?"

"We're considering it."

"I don't think you'd better consider it any more, Father."

"I won't have any threats from my son!"

"Very well." And Peter strolled off to the nursery.

"Am I on time?" said David McClean.

"Breakfast?" asked George Hadley.

"Thanks, had some. What's the trouble?"

"David, you're a psychologist."

"I should hope so."

"Well, then, have a look at our nursery. You saw it a year ago when you dropped by; did you notice anything peculiar about it then?"

"Can't say I did; the usual violences, a tendency toward a slight paranoia here or there, usual in children because they feel persecuted by parents constantly, but, oh, really nothing."

They walked down the hall. "I locked the nursery up," explained the father, "and the children broke back into it during the night. I let them stay so they could form the patterns for you to see."

There was a terrible screaming from the nursery.

"There it is," said George Hadley. "See what you make of it."

They walked in on the children without rapping.

The screams had faded. The lions were feeding.

"Run outside a moment, children," said George Hadley. "No, don't change the mental combination. Leave the walls as they are. Get!"

With the children gone, the two men stood studying the lions clustered at a distance, eating with great relish whatever it was they had caught.

220

"I wish I knew what it was," said George Hadley. "Sometimes I can almost see. Do you think if I brought high-powered binoculars here and—"

David McClean laughed dryly. "Hardly." He turned to study all four walls. "How long has this been going on?"

"A little over a month."

"It certainly doesn't *feel* good."

"I want facts, not feelings."

"My dear George, a psychologist never saw a fact in his life. He only hears about feelings; vague things. This doesn't feel good, I tell you. Trust my hunches and my instincts. I have a nose for something bad. This is very bad. My advice to you is to have the whole damn room torn down and your children brought to me every day during the next year for treatment."

"Is it that bad?"

"I'm afraid so. One of the original uses of these nurseries was so that we could study the patterns left on the walls by the child's mind, study at our leisure, and help the child. In this case, however, the room has become a channel toward—destructive thoughts, instead of a release away from them."

"Didn't you sense this before?"

"I sensed only that you had spoiled your children more than most. And now you're letting them down in some way. What way?"

"I wouldn't let them go to New York."

"What else?"

"I've taken a few machines from the house and threatened them, a month ago, with closing up the nursery unless they did their homework. I did close it for a few days to show I meant business."

"Ah, ha!"

"Does that mean anything?"

"Everything. Where before they had a Santa Claus now they have a Scrooge. Children prefer Santas. You've let this room and this house replace you and your wife in your children's affections. This room is their mother and father, far more important in their lives than their real parents. And now you come along and want to shut it off. No wonder there's hatred here. You can feel it coming out of the sky. Feel that sun. George, you'll have to change your life. Like too many others, you've built it around creature comforts. Why, you'd starve tomorrow if something went wrong in your kitchen. You wouldn't know how to tap an egg. Nevertheless, turn everything off. Start new. It'll take time. But we'll make good children out of bad in a year, wait and see."

"But won't the shock be too much for the children, shutting the room up abruptly, for good?"

"I don't want them going any deeper into this, that's all."

The lions were finished with their red feast.

The lions were standing on the edge of the clearing watching the two men.

221

"Now *I'm* feeling persecuted," said McClean. "Let's get out of here. I never have cared for these damned rooms. Make me nervous."

"The lions look real, don't they?" said George Hadley. "I don't suppose there's any way—"

"What?"

"—that they could *become* real?"

"Not that I know."

"Some flaw in the machinery, a tampering or something?"

"No."

They went to the door.

"I don't imagine the room will like being turned off," said the father.

"Nothing ever likes to die—even a room."

"I wonder if it hates me for wanting to switch it off?"

"Paranoia is thick around here today," said David McClean. "You can follow it like a spoor. Hello." He bent and picked up a bloody scarf. "This yours?"

"No." George Hadley's face was rigid. "It belongs to Lydia."

They went to the fuse box together and threw the switch that killed the nursery.

The two children were in hysterics. They screamed and pranced and threw things. They yelled and sobbed and swore and jumped at the furniture.

"You can't do that to the nursery, you can't!"

"Now, children."

The children flung themselves onto a couch, weeping.

"George," said Lydia Hadley, "turn on the nursery, just for a few moments. You can't be so abrupt."

"No."

"You can't be so cruel."

"Lydia, it's off, and it stays off. And the whole damn house dies as of here and now. The more I see of the mess we've put ourselves in, the more it sickens me. We've been contemplating our mechanical, electronic navels for too long. My God, how we need a breath of honest air!"

And he marched about the house turning off the voice clocks, the stoves, the heaters, the shoe shiners, the shoe lacers, the body scrubbers and swabbers and massagers, and every other machine he could put his hand to.

The house was full of dead bodies, it seemed. It felt like a mechanical cemetery. So silent. None of the humming hidden energy of machines waiting to function at the tap of a button.

"Don't let them do it!" wailed Peter at the ceiling, as if he was talking to the house, the nursery. "Don't let Father kill everything." He turned to his father, "Oh, I hate you!"

"Insults won't get you anywhere."

"I wish you were dead!"

"We were, for a long while. Now we're going to really start living. Instead of being handled and massaged, we're going to *live*."

222

Wendy was still crying and Peter joined her again. "Just a moment, just one moment, just another moment of nursery," they wailed.

"Oh, George," said the wife, "it can't hurt."

"All right—all right, if they'll only just shut up. One minute, mind you, and then off forever."

"Daddy, Daddy, Daddy!" sang the children, smiling with wet faces.

"And then we're going on a vacation. David McClean is coming back in half an hour to help us move out and get to the airport. I'm going to dress. You turn the nursery on for a minute, Lydia, just a minute, mind you."

And the three of them went babbling off while he let himself be vacuumed upstairs through the air flue and set about dressing himself. A minute later Lydia appeared.

"I'll be glad when we get away," she sighed.

"Did you leave them in the nursery?"

"I wanted to dress too. Oh, that horrid Africa. What can they see in it?"

"Well, in five minutes we'll be on our way to Iowa. Lord, how did we ever get in this house? What prompted us to buy a nightmare?"

"Pride, money, foolishness."

"I think we'd better get downstairs before those kids get engrossed with those damned beasts again."

Just then they heard the children calling, "Daddy, Mommy, come quick—quick!"

They went downstairs in the air flue and ran down the hall. The children were nowhere in sight. "Wendy? Peter!"

They ran into the nursery. The veldtland was empty save for the lions waiting, looking at them. "Peter, Wendy?"

The door slammed.

"Wendy, Peter!"

George Hadley and his wife whirled and ran back to the door.

"Open the door!" cried George Hadley, trying the knob. "Why, they've locked it from the outside! Peter!" He beat at the door. "Open up!"

He heard Peter's voice outside, against the door.

"Don't let them switch off the nursery and the house," he was saying.

Mr. and Mrs. George Hadley beat at the door. "Now, don't be ridiculous, children. It's time to go. Mr. McClean'll be here in a minute and . . ."

And then they heard the sounds.

The lions on three sides of them, in the yellow veldt grass, padding through the dry straw, rumbling and roaring in their throats.

The lions.

Mr. Hadley looked at his wife and they turned and looked back at the beasts edging slowly forward, crouching, tails stiff.

Mr. and Mrs. Hadley screamed.

And suddenly they realized why those other screams had sounded familiar.

"Well, here I am," said David McClean in the nursery doorway. "Oh, hello." He stared at the two children seated in the center of the open glade eating a little picnic lunch. Beyond them was the water hole and the yellow veldtland; above was the hot sun. He began to perspire. "Where are your father and mother?"

The children looked up and smiled. "Oh, they'll be here directly."

"Good, we must get going." At a distance Mr. McClean saw the lions fighting and clawing and then quieting down to feed in silence under the shady trees.

He squinted at the lions with his hand up to his eyes.

Now the lions were done feeding. They moved to the water hole to drink.

A shadow flickered over Mr. McClean's hot face. Many shadows flickered. The vultures were dropping down the blazing sky.

"A cup of tea?" asked Wendy in the silence.

## QUESTIONS

*Looking at Ideas:*

1. What criticism does this story make about the "high-tech" home? Do you agree with Bradbury about the negative impact of a reliance on technology as a substitute for family communication?

2. Why has the nursery malfunctioned despite its positive purpose? What suggestion does this make about technological solutions to psychological and interpersonal problems?

3. What kind of advice does the psychologist give the Hadleys about the nursery? Does he seem to understand what the real problem is? Why do the Hadleys have difficulty carrying out his advice?

*Looking at Strategies:*

1. What is the symbolism of the children's fascination with Africa as a setting for their nursery fantasy world? Why is the veldt setting so compelling for them?

2. In "The Veldt" the modern house is developed as a symbol of the modern consumer society. How is the Hadleys' home described? What can it do that might have seemed amazing in the 1950s when the story was written, but which now is possible?

3. Bradbury uses the device of allusion by naming the Hadley children Wendy and Peter, after Wendy and Peter Pan in the famous children's book, also set in a nursery and in a children's fantasy land. What ironic contrast does the story make with *Peter Pan*?

*Looking at Connections:*

1. Compare Bradbury's view of the modern home with Lance Morrow's in "Downsizing an American Dream" in Chapter Three. Would Morrow

be likely to agree with Bradbury's implicit criticism of the modern home and family?

2. How do both Bradbury and D. H. Lawrence in "The Rocking-Horse Winner" (in Chapter Two) criticize materialism in the family and its impact on the emotional and imaginative life of children?

3. Compare the relationships between the parents and children in Bradbury's story with the relationships and attitudes discussed in Marie Winn's "Television and Family Rituals." How does each selection comment on technology and materialism's impact on parent-child relationships?

*Suggestions for Writing:*

1. Write an essay in which you describe and discuss some modern technological inventions that you have read about recently, perhaps some aspect of computer or video technology (such as "virtual reality") that could create an environment for children something like the nursery in this story. Could there be negative effects on children who become obsessed with such powerful playthings, or would the results be no worse, say, than the current influence of television and video games? What positive influences might such environments have on children's knowledge and imaginations?

2. Write a fantasy in which you demonstrate the impact of technology on the life of a fictional family. Set your fantasy in the present or in the near future. Do you think family members would tend to become isolated from one another in the "high-tech" home, with each member playing with specialized technological toys, or could technology have a positive impact on family life?

3. Observe and interview children about the influence of interactive technology, such as video games, on their play. Do the children seem to become obsessed by violent play with toys like the Nintendo games to the extent that they seem to lose track of normal human interactions and communications? Write up your conclusions in the form of an essay in which you present the major positive and/or negative effects of playing with video games.

**JOURNAL ENTRY**

Make a brainstorming list of your political values and beliefs. For instance, do you believe that politicians are honest? Do you consider it important to vote? After making your list of beliefs, ask yourself which of your beliefs have been molded by or influenced by television, which of them you have arrived at on your own, and which have come from your parents.

**ROBERT COLES: "What TV Teaches Children about Politics"** Born in 1929, a native of Boston, and a graduate of Harvard and Columbia University Medical School, Robert Coles is a child psychiatrist, a researcher, a scholar, and a professor of psychiatry at Harvard. Coles is a leading authority on the issues of poverty and racial discrimination, especially insofar as these issues affect children and their self-esteem. Coles is a prolific writer who has traveled to all parts of the country and all over the world studying children's feelings and values. Coles received the Pulitzer Prize in 1973 for his ambitious multivolume work, *Children in Crisis.* The following selection, originally written as an article for *TV Guide* in 1988, was developed from Coles's extensive world travel and international study of the mental world of children. As you read the article, notice how it reveals Coles's positive estimation of children and their potential for individual thought and judgment.

ROBERT COLES

# *What TV Teaches Children about Politics*

For many years now I have been trying to learn how children in this country and abroad get their political ideas and opinions. Rather obviously, parents can help shape the way their sons and daughters think about the world, including how one or another nation should be ruled. Children who grow up in a home where strong political views are upheld constantly learn to pay attention to such matters and often (even at six or seven) can be heard echoing what they have heard in the kitchen or the living room. On the other hand, children whose parents have little or no interest in politics tend themselves to be quite indifferent to the subject.

But these days the home is not only a place occupied by parents and children. Every day, all over the world, children see and hear others in their homes and pay them close heed, indeed—the people who appear on television. Many of us have come to realize how significantly television comes to bear on the lives of children. We rightfully worry about what our children ought to see—the impact of violence or all-too-explicit sexuality upon their moral and psychological development. We worry, too, that wonderful educational opportunities are lost—the prevalence of a host of foolish and sometimes loony cartoons when the alternative might be first-rate stories that both capture the interest of the young and help them to think about all sorts of important moral and social issues.

Yet children are often not as "passive" before those television screens as they may appear to be, a conclusion to which I've especially come in the course of studying the political attitudes of various boys and girls. In this country, for instance, I am constantly struck by the amused and somewhat cynical interest many young people show toward the mayors, governors, representatives, senators, and yes, Presidents they get to see in the course of their childhood.

I will never forget the remark I heard from a nine-year-old Massachusetts boy, the son of an automobile factory worker, after he'd heard a couple of senators make some comments about an upcoming political matter. "They're both 'going through the motions' [a comment his teacher used in order to criticize those who were not fully absorbed in their schoolwork]. They say one thing, then they cover their bases with something else they say." Some veteran journalists, skilled observers of the American scene, might not have a better analysis of the statements that some of our politicians make.

I have also noted how commonly many children in this country remark upon the personal qualities of the various political leaders they see on television. Again and again a child will ignore the content of a politician's statement but tell me that so-and-so is "pleasant" or "nice" or "sneaky-looking" or a "phony" or a "plastic fake."

When I ask American children what kind of political leader they would like, the most frequent adjective response is someone who is "honest." When I ask them whether they, in fact, know any "honest" politicians, they rather often will say no. When I ask them to spell out what they mean by "honest," I get interesting replies, such as this one, by an eleven-year-old Georgia girl. "If you're honest, you work hard, and you don't just talk a lot on television, and you don't take money to do people a lot of favors." It does not take a child psychiatrist like me, I fear, to figure out the assumptions that child had that prompted her commentary.

All in all, I have found a skepticism, if not a cynicism, in American children toward politics that easily matches (and no doubt reflects) what many adults feel. When many of those children have been shown the Congress in action on television (at school, or usually by accident when switching channels at home) their reaction is frequently one of boredom: let's see something else quick!

The contrast with children in certain other countries is quite remarkable. In Poland I have been astonished to hear vigorous criticism directed not only at the government but at the television it owns and runs. Whereas American children mock politicians but declare their love for their government as a whole and their vast interest in television as a presence in their lives, Polish children heap scorn on the entire government that rules them and vent a particular disgust for those who run the television programs: "They are liars; they are trying to turn us into their slaves. They won't win." So a ten-year-old Warsaw boy once remarked to me, waving aside a historical drama being shown one day.

We are constantly told how powerfully television influences those who view it, surely the case for many of us, young and old alike, the world over. Yet, for some forty years the Polish government has tried hard to politically indoctrinate its people (and especially its children, who are, after all, its future) and has failed to do so. Communism is scorned by children all the time, no matter what the television programs have urged them to believe.

The moral of the story? When parents themselves have their own strong religious and political convictions—as do the great majority of Poland's adults—their children will take notice, will follow suit, and will tend to be resistant, indeed, to the blandishments of television if they contradict what the child has learned at home. The children who are most inclined to go along with television, to lap up its messages uncritically, are those who have received little in the way of guidance at home, hence their susceptibility to whatever the big tube sends their way.

Polish homes, strongly Catholic, strongly connected, still, to family traditions and a fierce nationalism that resists Soviet ideological power, have been quite able to nourish in several generations of Polish children a profound and unyielding antagonism to totalitarianism.

In other countries one is reminded, yet again, that television most certainly has a power all its own but will only persuade those who are ready for it.

For instance, in Northern Ireland, when the BBC offers various celebrations of the Royal Family, Protestant children take eager notice and can be heard later on repeating what they have heard on the "telly." Not so for Catholic children, who are quick to turn off the set or seek other channels or, if the program is kept on the tube, mock what appears, strenuously and vocally.

A ruddy-faced boy of twelve in the Ardoyne district of Belfast, heavily Catholic, with no small number of IRA sympathizers if not members, made the following analysis for me of "the television the Brits send" to his native Northern Ireland is an unforgettable political statement and an example of how a child can do his own kind of cultural and political analysis, not to mention television commentary.

The Brits have their Queen, and they use her to put on a show for people. We're supposed to forget all the trouble here, to swoon over her. I'll not do it, none of us here will. When they show us her and her palace, we turn the telly off. My sister likes that young one [Princess Diana], but I tell her to watch out—she'll get tricked by a pretty face. We don't have to let that crowd [the Royal Family] into our house. We can give them the exit—just turn that knob there. Why don't the British people come and talk with my sister? She's as smart as that princess. She's as pretty, too. The telly shows off the rich, and the poor are supposed to feel better for what we see.

Such words are a reminder, one among many I've received in the course of working with boys and girls in various countries, that children are not always uncritically docile with respect to the so-called power of television programming—even as they can also be far more shrewdly political than some of us "experts" in child development give them credit for being. Yes, television can sway minds, imprint images on them, win them over to various social or political points of view— sometimes. But the influence television has on children, I keep realizing, whether with respect to its psychological or political effect, usually correlates with the nature of the child's family life. A young person brought up in a strong and attentive family, with its own explicitly acknowledged social, moral, and political values, is by no means a setup for the world's growing number of television scriptwriters and cameramen.

## QUESTIONS

*Looking at Ideas:*

1. What influence does Coles believe parents have on children's political outlook? How does television influence this legacy of values?

2. What do the children Coles has observed in the United States typically notice about politicians? Do they have a positive attitude toward politicians? How are they influenced by the "look" of political figures as they appear on the media? What does this suggest to you about the nature of televised political information and reporting?

3. How do the political views of children in Poland differ from the political attitudes of American children? Which group is more critical of its government? To what does Coles attribute the typical attitude of Polish children toward their government and toward state-run TV?

4. What attitude do the Catholic children of Northern Ireland have toward television programs about the life of the British royal family? To what does Coles attribute this attitude? How does Coles relate this point back to the thesis of his essay?

5. What conclusions does Coles draw from his research into children's political attitudes and the impact of TV on these attitudes? Do you agree with his conclusions?

*Looking at Strategies:*

1. How effectively does Coles use examples and quotations derived from his research and observation of children in the United States and elsewhere in the world? Do his examples support his thesis about television and political awareness on the part of parents and children? Does he cite enough examples to be convincing?

2. Has Coles been entirely objective in his gathering of evidence, or

do you suspect that he had strong preconceptions on the issue under discussion before he began his research? Explain your response.

3. Coles originally wrote this essay for *TV Guide.* Define one other audience for whom he might have written on this topic and then discuss how he would have changed his writing style, content, and documentation for this second audience.

*Looking at Connections:*

1. Compare Coles's position on the impact of television on children's values with Marie Winn's. What similar perspectives do they have? On what points would they differ? Who seems more concerned about the role of television in the home?

*Suggestions for Writing:*

1. Develop the journal entry for this selection into an essay about your own political beliefs. Begin with a brief statement of your beliefs. For each belief, provide an example of a major influence on your belief: either a family member, a political figure you admire, or something you saw on television that you feel had an impact on your values.

2. Study the political attitudes of your friends. Interview several of them and ask them about their political beliefs and where they originated. Write an essay in which you draw conclusions of your own about the impact of television and/or family values on the political beliefs of young people.

3. If you believe that American children today derive too many of their political opinions from television, write an essay in which you suggest some ways that the impact of TV on young people's political thinking could be decreased. What do you believe are better alternative sources of political information?

---

**JOURNAL ENTRY**

To what extent does the picture of the world brought to you by television
and other news media have an impact on your private dreams and
fantasies, your inner life? Do you ever dream about issues and figures
from the news? If so, narrate such a dream.

---

**STEPHEN DUNN: "Middle Class Poem"**   Born in New York City in 1939 and
educated at the New School for Social Research and Syracuse University,
Stephen Dunn has been a professional basketball player, an advertising copy-
writer, an editor, and a professor of creative writing. He is currently poet in
residence at Stockton State College in New Jersey. His books of poetry include
*A Circus of Needs* (1978), *Work and Love* (1981), and *Not Dancing* (1984).
Dunn writes about his family, his past, and the world around him. In the following selection, "Middle Class Poem" (1984), notice how Dunn explores the
way people's awareness of the world is conditioned by memory, family relationships, and the experiences brought to us by the mass media.

STEPHEN DUNN

# *Middle Class Poem*

In dreams, the news of the world
comes back, gets mixed up
with our parents and the moon.
We can't help but thrash.
Those with whom we sleep, never equally,
roll away from us and sigh.

When we wake
the news of the world embraces us,
pulls back. Who let go first?—
a lover's question, the lover
who's most alone.
We purchase a little forgetfulness
at the mall. We block the entrance
to our hearts.

Come evening, the news of the world
is roaming the streets
while we bathe our children,
while we eat what's plentiful
and scarce. We know what we need
to keep out, what's always there—
painful to look at, bottomless.

# QUESTIONS

*Looking at Ideas*

1. What causes the "we" in the poem to "thrash"? Why do the sleeping partners never sleep "equally"? What two meanings does the word *equally* have in the context of the poem?

2. Why does the "news of the world" first embrace us and then "pull back"? How do the news media contribute to our sense of being alone?

3. How does going to the shopping mall help the "we" in the poem buy "forgetfulness"? What point is the poem making here about the function of nonessential consuming, particularly with the line, "We block the entrance / to our hearts"?

4. At the end of the poem, the middle-class "we" of the poem "know what we need / to keep out." What exactly does "know" refer to? What is the "painful . . . bottomless" thing we are trying so hard to keep out?

*Looking at Strategies*

1. Why does the poem use the second person pronoun *we?* Try rewriting the poem using "I" or "they" in place of "we." How does the impact of the poem shift?

2. The author uses the device of personification (that is, making abstract ideas and objects into human entities) throughout the poem. Give examples of the way the personification in the poem helps develop the central idea of the poem about the impact of the news on people's emotional lives.

*Looking at Connections*

1. Compare Dunn's view of family life in the information age with Robert Coles's essay on the impact of news and political broadcasting on the family. Whose view seems more optimistic? Which is closest to your own?

*Suggestions for Writing*

1. Write an essay based on your journal entry about the impact of the news media on your family and on American families in general. Do you believe that news events have a strong impact on fears and family tensions? Develop examples that support your ideas.

2. One reason why news programming may have the disturbing effect it does on many families is that it seems to focus on violence and disaster. Watch several hours of news programming over the course of a week. Do you feel you are getting a distorted view of reality from the events selected as newsworthy?

3. Write an essay on any excessive shopping or overconsuming you have noticed in your family or among your friends; refer to specific episodes or shopping sprees you have witnessed or participated in. What motivates people to buy compulsively and to spend large amounts of time in shopping malls? Do you believe that compulsive shopping undermines the stability of family life? How?

**JAVIER RUIZ:** *"Terminator 2: A Machine That Loves"*   Javier Ruiz, from Pacifica, California, is currently considering a career in mechanical engineering. In the little free time he has as a full-time student, Javier enjoys cycling and drawing pictures of Spiderman, his cartoon idol. Javier Ruiz wrote the following essay on *Terminator 2* for his English composition class in response to the Reaching Out Activity in Chapter Four that asks students to write about a film that reflects issues explored in the chapter.

JAVIER RUIZ

# Terminator 2: A Machine That Loves

The summer of 1991's most-awaited movie was *Terminator 2: Judgment Day*, a film that made many millions of dollars in theaters and in promotional ventures such as toys, clothes, and video games. A sequel of the first Terminator film, starring Arnold Schwarzenegger and Linda Hamilton as Sarah Connor, *Terminator 2* continues Sarah's obsession to keep her son, a future military leader, alive. In the film, an advanced model Terminator machine is sent from the future by a living, destructive computer, SKYNET, to kill the ten-year-old John Connor. An earlier model Terminator machine, played by Arnold Schwarzenegger, is programmed and sent back in time also to protect the young Connor by the future John Connor, the leader of the human resistance against SKYNET.

While the action, violence, and special effects may prevent some viewers from seriously analyzing the movie, several relevant social issues can be seen after close observation. The most obvious theme presented concerns our growing dependency on mass media, computers, and other high-tech machines. In a technological, rapidly changing world, family structures often break down and are inadequate to provide children with the nurturance and intimate interaction they crave. Intimate family rituals and relationships are frequently replaced by relationships with objects of electronic technology. As Marie Winn puts it in her essay, "Television and Family Rituals," the modern family is often anesthetized by television and other media into "accepting its unhappy state and prevent[ed] from struggling to better its condition, to improve its relationships, and to regain some of the richness it once possessed." Despite the decline of the modern family, children continue to dream of and to be needy of a good home, positive role models, and loving parent figures who will help them and listen to their problems. In *Terminator 2*, the characters Sarah Connor, young John Connor, and the Terminator-cyborg portrayed by Arnold Schwarzenegger form a small futuristic family. By the end of the movie, John Connor attains the frustrated dream of many modern, alienated children, as he comes to perceive and relate to his Terminator machine-man as a loving father figure.

At the start of the film, because his mother is in an insane asylum and his father is dead, John Connor lives in a foster home. The foster parents provide John with food and shelter but neglect his most important need, love. The foster father spends most of his time in front of the television, and the foster mother seems to spend most of her time trying to maintain a clean house. One of the first things that the foster mother says about John is, "I'm fed up with that damn kid. . . ."

This scene shows us how the foster parenting system (as well as parenting in general) often fails in our society. The foster parents do not provide John with the love or role models that he needs. As a result, he rebels and resorts to cursing his foster parents, stealing money from ATM's, and hanging out in video arcades. His only real companion is a picture of his "lunatic" real mother. As a critique of the modern family, the scene with John and his foster family suggests that many children today are being raised by strangers: teachers, foster parents, TV sets, and video games, rather than by true parents who care about them.

Both the "Arnold" Terminator and the assassin Terminator reach John at the same time. The Arnold Terminator is able to save John and both begin to run from the assassin Terminator. John tells Arnold that he hates his mother "for all the stuff" that she put him through, such as gun running and tactics training. As he exposes his feelings for the first time, John Connor realizes that at last he has found someone that will listen to him. Ironically, a machine has the patience to listen, more so than the "real" people in John's life.

After his conversation with the Arnold Terminator, John chooses to liberate his mother from the insane asylum. The assassin Terminator has found out where Sarah Connor is and travels to the institution to murder her. After several extremely close calls with the assassin Terminator, John and Arnold are able to escape from the hospital with Sarah. After the trio has succeeded in fighting off the assassin Terminator, John's mother becomes extremely angry with her son for rescuing her:

"That was stupid of you, John. You shouldn't have gone for me . . ."

"I had to get you out . . . I was only trying to help. I'm sorry."

"Sorry is not good enough . . . I don't need your help. I can take care of myself."

John begins to cry silently in the back seat of their getaway vehicle, and the Terminator asks him, "What's wrong with your eyes?"

This confrontation scene shows how much John wants to have a family and how cold and unloving humans can be at times. He rescues his mother from jail and hopes that their reunion will be happy, not expecting a cold stare and the cutting words. Sarah is so caught up with her obsession to keep John alive so that he will be able to fight SKY-NET in the future, that she does not realize the pain that she causes her son. She does not provide him with any "motherly" love as he hoped that she would. Ironically, the Terminator shows more concern for John than his mother does. This scene emphasizes the film's commentary on the way that driven, obsessive parents fail to listen to their children's deepest needs.

The three characters are able to escape to Mexico where John bonds closely to the Arnold Terminator. In a scene that might remind viewers of the new generation of "user-friendly," customizable, talking computers and their users, John teaches Arnold how to act more human. He teaches the Terminator how to give him a "high five" and educates him on how to say catchy, slangy phrases such as "Hasta la vista, baby!" In this sequence John also reveals some personal experiences to the Terminator, including all the relationships that his mother has had with men: "She always screwed [the relationships] up. She would talk about Judgment Day and how I would be some great military leader." When the Terminator asks him, "Why do you cry?" John answers "Because it hurts." The Terminator tries to find the reasons for John's pain and then attempts to comfort him. No person has ever showed as much concern toward the child as the machine reveals here. The Terminator has become more than a protector; he has become John's best friend.

Sarah watches the interaction between the Terminator and John. In this scene, she realizes how the Terminator is being converted into John's father:

> It all became so clear. . . . It would never leave him, get drunk, or beat him. . . . He would never be too busy and would always be there for him and it would die to protect him. Of all the would-be fathers that came and went over the years, this thing, this machine was the only one who measured up. In an insane world, it was the sanest choice.

Sarah realizes that John has been in need of a father or someone who can pay attention to him and love him. The Terminator has changed from a deadly assassin to a father figure.

After this scene, Sarah has a dream about the end of the world, destroyed by a nuclear bomb in a war started by SKYNET. Consequently, she decides to hunt down Miles Dison—the inventor of SKYNET—to destroy a computer chip that will lead in the future to the creation of the powerful computer. In the process of their quest, the three heroes (Sarah, John, and Arnold, now working together as closely as a family unit) encounter the assassin Terminator again. After a lengthy and violent chase, the family and the assassin Terminator end up in a steel-melting plant. The Terminator machines battle, and after many melees, the assassin Terminator is destroyed. The trio has succeeded in capturing the chip that leads to the construction of SKYNET. However, all SKYNET chips have to be eradicated including the microchips in the Arnold Terminator's head. As the Terminator makes his decision to lower himself into the burning vat that will destroy him, John begins to cry and pleads with Arnold not to go:

"I order you not go . . . I order you not go . . . I can't let you . . ."

"I know now why you cry," the Terminator responds.

The Terminator hugs the crying boy and bids farewell to Sarah. As he is being burned up in the molten steel, the Terminator gives John a final thumbs up and a smile. Through an act which reveals that he has learned the value of human life, the Terminator sacrifices himself to save John and his fellow humans from their miserable future.

By the end of the film, John has grown extremely close to the Terminator machine. He finds inside the maze of circuits and wires something that he never was able to find in humans: someone that will love. The Terminator protects him and listens to him at all times. One of the ironies in the film is that John found a "father" in something that was not human; the Terminator loves him more than his foster parents or even his own mother. At first, the Terminator was a metaphor for destruction and absence of feeling, yet it learns how to love John more than any other man or woman ever did. *Terminator 2* makes us wonder if humans will be able to exist without being able to love one another. It shows us disturbing problems that society faces today, including inadequate foster parents and the lack of love and stability in families, while at the same time implying that children not given love from their parents will turn, like the children in Ray Bradbury's science fiction story, "The Veldt," to seemingly responsive machines: to television, user-friendly computers, videogames, and virtual reality environments.

Although one vision of the future implicit in *Terminator 2* is that of a high-tech nightmare world dominated by machines that love (or seem to), I believe that we human beings can learn to peacefully exist with each other and make better lives for ourselves and for unfortunate children like John Connor. Sarah Connor states it best at the end of the movie when she says, "If a Terminator can learn the value of a human life, maybe we can too."

### QUESTIONS FOR DISCUSSION

1. According to Ruiz, what are the two main, related themes of *Terminator 2?* Do you agree with his interpretation of the film?

2. How effective are Ruiz's background references, including his allusions to television, to video games, and to selections included in Chapter Four of this book, such as Winn's essay and Bradbury's story, "The Veldt"? How do these allusions and parallels help to deepen his analysis of the film? What other stories, essays, programs, and media might he have alluded to?

3. How well does Ruiz bring in and analyze particular scenes from the film in order to demonstrate his interpretation? How reasonable and appropriate do the conclusions he draws from these scenes seem to be? Does he ever seem to be just retelling the story?

4. Although he does provide a bleak possible view of the future of the family and technology, Ruiz ends his essay on a positive, hopeful note. Do you agree with his conclusion? Did you feel this was an effective way to end the essay?

## Reaching Out: Chapter Activities

1. A group of students should examine together several advertisements, either from magazines or television, that attempt to sell products to family members and that provide images of the family, both in photographs and in language. The group should characterize the images and stereotypes of families that emerge in these advertisements and should share their findings with the class, in the form of a group presentation (with accompanying slides or overhead projections) or a written, illustrated report.

2. Work as a group to develop a proposal for a television show that you think will portray a type of American family you believe has not yet been accurately represented in that medium. Indicate what type of viewers the show would appeal to, what sort of typical settings, characters, and interactions the show would portray, and what types of problems the underrepresented family would have to face and handle. Groups might divide up the work, with one member making suggestions for settings, others proposing major characters, others providing key plot line elements and dialogue.

3. Prepare a multimedia presentation (using video, tape recordings, and/or slide projections) to preview a coming attraction or to convince the class to subscribe to certain family-oriented beliefs or values. If possible, "broadcast" your presentation to your class via a video monitor or audio tape and slides. In your presentation try to persuade the class of a certain view of the family or of contemporary politics.

4. If there is a television, newspaper, or radio station in your community that provides special programming or features about family life, go to the station or office and interview some of the people who work on these features or who have been in the studio audience. Draw up a series of questions to ask them about the purpose and intended impact of these features on family life in your community. Conclude by writing a paper in which you evaluate the benefits or weaknesses of the features you have studied.

5. View a film on video from the list below. Working either individually or with your group, prepare a discussion of the values relating to family life and the impact of the mass media on the family that the film seems to embody.

*Being There.* Dir., Hal Ashby. With Peter Sellers, Shirley MacLaine, and Melvyn Douglas. 1979.

*Broadcast News.* Dir., James Brooks. With William Hurt, Holly Hunter. 1987.

*Network.* Dir., Sidney Lumet. With Faye Dunaway, Peter Finch, and William Holden. 1976.

CHAPTER FIVE

# The Family in a Multicultural Society

*To forget one's ancestors is to be a brook without a source, a tree without a root.* —Chinese proverb

*There are only two lasting gifts we can give our children. One of these is roots, the other wings.* —Hebraic proverb

*I have a dream my four little children will one day live in a nation where they will not be judged by the color of their skin but by the content of their character.* —Martin Luther King, Jr., "I Have a Dream"

*I*n tribal cultures and in rural villages, in communities where people share similar values and customs, each person claims a heritage that can be traced back through many generations. Children and adolescents growing up in such traditional societies naturally assume that the family values that helped shape their self-concepts will be understood and respected by the other families in their community. Although growing up within a homogeneous community can have limitations, such an upbringing can also give young people the security that comes from knowing that they share a common language, values, and history with their neighbors.

In contrast to life in a single-culture community, many of today's children and adolescents, especially those living in urban areas, are growing up in neighborhoods with people from a variety of cultures. These young people will inevitably realize that their family's values, traditions, and culture are not necessarily shared and respected by the majority of people in their community. Even within a particular family in a culturally diverse community, values and customs may differ among grandparents, parents, and relatives. Family members may believe to varying degrees in the importance of their traditional or ethnic culture; some may have different interpretations of the customs they have brought with them from another country. In addition, through intermarriage or friendship networks, some family members may feel allegiances to more than one family structure and/or ethnic tradition.

How do children of immigrant and minority families respond and adjust to mainstream American culture? If a mother and father have different attitudes toward assimilation, how do their children decide which parent's values to follow? On the other hand, what happens if children from an immigrant or minority family decide to reject their family's traditions and values, believing that they need to conform to majority American values in order to succeed, to participate fully in the American dream? For members of immigrant and minority families, these are complex questions for which there are no easy answers. For many such families the paradoxes they experience become the haunting and compelling forces that drive their lives. Furthermore, many mainstream American families are also changing in dramatic ways as the adjustment to and understanding of diverse cultural norms becomes increasingly complex.

Each of the writers selected for this chapter has a particular set of experiences to explore that present issues about the dilemmas facing the family in a multicultural society. These issues range from concerns about learning a new language, to struggles about which parent's attitude toward assimilation to adopt, to projections about the social and political future of the black family. A consensus on how to react to the demands of a multicultural community does not exist. Thinking about the selections in this chapter can help you develop a better understanding of the rich and complex cultural world in which you live. Learning about the different cultures, struggles, and values of families and individuals can help you become more informed and more empathetic. Learning about other cultures and life-styles can be fascinating. We can strengthen our community as we work to acknowledge and utilize the cultural and spiritual diversity of its members.

In this chapter's first selections, "A Slow Walk of Trees" by Toni Morrison and "Being Black and Feeling Blue," excerpted from Shelby Steele's *The Content of Our Character,* two prominent African-American writers reflect on their families and the way in which handed-down family attitudes about social oppression can either be a source of strength or a handicap. The writers of the next two selections provide different perspectives on the effects of having to learn English as a second language in elementary school. Richard Rodriguez explains why he came to separate his private family language and private sense of self, while in "The Language We Know" Simon Ortiz reveals how he has continued to find inspiration for his writing and speaking in both English and his Native American language.

The next two selections, "Silent Dancing," by Judith Ortiz Cofer, and Amy Tan's "Four Directions" (from her novel *The Joy Luck Club*), present family rituals that bring out conflicts related to issues of assimilation. In a narrative poem, "Indian Movie, New Jersey," Chitra Divakaruni explores the comforting escape to the past that East Indian movie heroes and heroines provide for immigrant Indian moviegoers. In the final selection, Josephine Ramos, a student writer, discusses the rewards she discovers as she integrates two different family traditions.

The selections that follow will challenge your mind and imagination as you come to realize more fully how complex the struggles of immigrant and minority families can be. We hope you will come to think more critically and to uncover the underlying assumptions you have made about your own family and the cultures of other families in your community. Through thinking about these assumptions, you can begin to appreciate more fully what is unique about your family and gain a greater empathy for families and cultures quite different from your own.

**JOURNAL ENTRY**

Write about a conflict that two of your relatives had about a social or political issue. How did the conflict affect your perception, understanding, and position on the issue?

**TONI MORRISON: "A Slow Walk of Trees"**   In 1931 Toni Morrison was born Chloe Anthony Wofford. She grew up in Lorrain, Ohio, completing her B.A. at Howard University in 1953 and her M.A. at Cornell University in 1955. In 1964 she began working as an editor at Random House and was instrumental in publishing the works of such black writers as Angela Davis and Toni Cade Bambara. Morrison has taught at many universities, including Howard, Princeton, and the University of California at Berkeley. All Morrison's novels have received national acclaim, particularly *Sula* (1973), *Song of Solomon* (1977), and *Beloved,* which was awarded the Pulitzer Prize in 1987. In "A Slow Walk of Trees," which first appeared in the *New York Times Magazine* (July 4, 1976), Morrison shows how her grandparents' and parents' conflicting views of the history and future of the black family and race shaped her values and her vision.

TONI MORRISON

# *A Slow Walk of Trees*

His name was John Solomon Willis, and when at age 5 he heard from the old folks that "the Emancipation Proclamation was coming," he crawled under the bed. It was his earliest recollection of what was to be his habitual response to the promise of white people: horror and an instinctive yearning for safety. He was my grandfather, a musician who managed to hold on to his violin but not his land. He lost all 88 acres of his Indian mother's inheritance to legal predators who built their fortunes on the likes of him. He was an unreconstructed black pessimist who, in spite of or because of emancipation, was convinced for 85 years that there was no hope whatever for black people in this country. His rancor was legitimate, for he, John Solomon, was not only an artist but a first-rate carpenter and farmer, reduced to sending home to his family money he made playing the violin because he was not able to find work. And this during the years when almost half the black male population were skilled craftsmen who lost their jobs to white ex-convicts and immigrant farmers.

His wife, however, was of a quite different frame of mind and believed that all things could be improved by faith in Jesus and an effort

242

of the will. So it was she, Ardelia Willis, who sneaked her seven children out of the back window into the darkness, rather than permit the patron of their sharecropper's existence to become their executioner as well, and headed north in 1912, when 99.2 percent of all black people in the U.S. were native-born and only 60 percent of white Americans were. And it was Ardelia who told her husband that they could not stay in the Kentucky town they ended up in because the teacher didn't know long division.

They have been dead now for 30 years and more and I still don't know which of them came closer to the truth about the possibilities of life for black people in this country. One of their grandchildren is a tenured professor at Princeton. Another, who suffered from what the Peruvian poet called "anger that breaks a man into children," was picked up just as he entered his teens and emotionally lobotomized by the reformatories and mental institutions specifically designed to serve him. Neither John Solomon nor Ardelia lived long enough to despair over one or swell with pride over the other. But if they were alive today each would have selected and collected enough evidence to support the accuracy of the other's original point of view. And it would be difficult to convince either one that the other was right.

Some of the monstrous events that took place in John Solomon's America have been duplicated in alarming detail in my own America. There was the public murder of a President in a theater in 1865 and the public murder of another President on television in 1963. The Civil War of 1861 had its encore as the civil-rights movement of 1960. The torture and mutilation of a black West Point Cadet (Cadet Johnson Whittaker) in 1880 had its rerun with the 1970's murders of students at Jackson State College, Texas Southern and Southern University in Baton Rouge. And in 1976 we watch for what must be the thousandth time a pitched battle between the children of slaves and the children of immigrants—only this time, it is not the New York draft riots of 1863, but the busing turmoil in Paul Revere's home town, Boston.

Hopeless, he'd said. Hopeless. For he was certain that white people of every political, religious, geographical and economic background would band together against black people everywhere when they felt the threat of our progress. And a hundred years after he sought safety from the white man's "promise," somebody put a bullet in Martin Luther King's brain. And not long before that some excellent samples of the master race demonstrated their courage and virility by dynamiting some little black girls to death. If he were here now, my grandfather, he would shake his head, close his eyes and pull out his violin—too polite to say, "I told you so." And his wife would pay attention to the music but not to the sadness in her husband's eyes, for she would see what she expected to see—not the occasional historical repetition, but, *like the slow walk of certain species of trees from the flatlands up into the mountains,* she would see the signs of irrevocable and permanent change. She, who pulled her girls out of an inadequate school in the Cumberland Mountains, knew all along that the gentlemen from Alabama who had killed the little girls would be rounded up. And it wouldn't surprise her in the least to know that the number of black college graduates jumped 12 percent in the last three years: 47 percent in 20 years. That there are 140 black mayors in this country; 14 black judges in the District Circuit, 4 in the Courts of Appeals and one on the Supreme Court. That there are 17 blacks in Congress, one in the Senate; 276 in state legislatures—223 in state houses, 53 in state senates. That there are 112 elected black police chiefs and sheriffs, 1 Pulitzer Prize winner; 1 winner of the Prix de Rome; a dozen or so winners of the Guggenheim; 4 deans of predominantly white colleges. . . . Oh, her list would go on and on. But so would John Solomon's sweet sad music.

While my grandparents held opposite views on whether the fortunes of black people were improving, my own parents struck similarly opposed postures, but from another slant. They differed about whether the moral fiber of white people would ever improve. Quite a different argument. The old folks argued about how and if black people could improve themselves, who could be counted on to help us, who would hinder us and so on. My parents took issue over the question of whether it was possible for white people to improve. They assumed that black people were the humans of the globe, but had serious doubts about the quality and existence of white humanity. Thus my father, distrusting every word and every gesture of every white man on earth, assumed that the white man who crept up the stairs one afternoon had come to molest his daughters and threw him down the stairs and then our tricycle after him. (I think my father was wrong, but considering what I have seen since, it may have been very healthy for me to have witnessed that as my first black-white encounter.) My mother, however, *believed* in them—their possibilities. So when the meal we got on relief was bug-ridden, she wrote a long letter to Franklin Delano Roosevelt. And when white bill collectors came to our door, it was she who received them civilly and explained in a sweet voice that we were people of honor and that the debt would be taken care of. Her message to Roosevelt got through—our meal improved. Her message to the bill collectors did not always get through and there was occasional violence when my father (self-exiled to the bedroom for fear he could not hold his temper) would hear that her reasonableness had failed. My mother was always wounded by these scenes, for she thought the bill collector knew that she loved good credit more than life and that being in arrears on a payment horrified her probably more than it did him. So she thought he was rude because he was white. For years she walked to utility companies and department stores to pay bills in person and even now she does not seem convinced that checks are legal tender. My father loved excellence, worked hard (he held three jobs at once for 17 years) and was so outraged by the suggestion of personal slackness that he could explain it to himself only in terms of racism. He was a fastidious worker who was frightened of one thing: unemployment. I can remember now the doomsday-cum-graveyard sound of "laid off" and how the minute school was out he asked us, "Where you workin'?"

Both my parents believed that all succor and aid came from themselves and their neighborhood, since "they"—white people in charge and those not in charge but in obstructionist positions—were in some way fundamentally, genetically corrupt.

So I grew up in a basically racist household with more than a child's share of contempt for white people. And for each white friend I acquired who made a small crack in that contempt, there was another who repaired it. For each one who related to me as a person, there was one who in my presence at least, became actively "white." And like most black people of my generation, I suffer from racial vertigo that can be cured only by taking what one needs from one's ancestors. John Solomon's cynicism and his deployment of his art as both weapon and solace, Ardelia's faith in the magic that can be wrought by sheer effort of the will; my mother's open-mindedness in each new encounter and her habit of trying reasonableness first; my father's temper, his impatience and his efforts to keep "them" (throw them) out of his life. And it is out of these learned and selected attitudes that I look at the quality of life for my people in this country now. These widely disparate and sometimes conflicting views, I suspect, were held not only by me, but by most black people. Some I know are clearer in their positions, have not sullied their anger with optimism or dirtied their hope with despair. But most of us are plagued by a sense of being worn shell-thin by constant repression and hostility as well as the impression of being buoyed by visible testimony of tremendous strides. There *is* repetition of the grotesque in our history. And there *is* the miraculous walk of trees. The question is whether our walk is progress or merely movement. O.J. Simpson leaning on a Hertz car *is* better than the Gold Dust Twins on the back of a soap box. But is "Good Times" better than Stepin Fetchit? Has the first order of business been taken care of? Does the law of the land work for us?

Are white people who murder black people punished with at least the same dispatch that sends black teen-age truants to Coxsackie? Can we relax now and discuss "The Jeffersons" instead of genocide? Or is the difference between the two only the difference between a greedy pointless white life-style and a messy pointless black death? Now that Mr. Poitier and Mr. Belafonte have shot up all the racists in "Buck and the Preacher," have they all gone away? Can we really move into better neighborhoods and not be set on fire? Is there anybody who will lay me a $5 bet on it?

The past decade is a fairly good index of the odds at which you lay your money down.

Ten years ago in Queens, as black people like me moved into a neighborhood 20 minutes away from the Triborough Bridge, "for sale" signs shot up in front of white folks' houses like dandelions after a hot spring rain. And the black people smiled. "Goody, goody," said my neighbor. "Maybe we can push them on out to sea. You think?"

Now I live in another neighborhood, 20 minutes away from the George Washington Bridge, and again the "for sale" signs are pushing

245

up out of the ground. Fewer, perhaps, and for different reasons, perhaps. Still the Haitian lady and I smile at each other. "My, my," she says "they goin' on up to the hills? Seem like they just come from there." "The woods," I say. "They like to live in the woods." She nods with infinite understanding, then shrugs. The Haitians have already arranged for one mass in the church to be said in French, already have their own newspaper, stores, community center. That's not movement. That's progress.

But the decade has other revelations. Ten years ago, young, bright, energetic blacks were sought out, pursued and hired into major corporations, major networks, and onto the staffs of newspapers and national magazines. *Many survived that courtship, some even with their souls intact.* Newscasters, corporate lawyers, marketing specialists, journalists, production managers, plant foremen, college deans. But many more spend a lot of time on the telephone these days, or at the typewriter preparing résumés, which they send out (mostly to friends now) with little notes attached: "Is there anything you know of?" Or they think there is a good book in the story of what happened to them, the great hoax that was played on them. They are right, of course, about the hoax, for many of them were given elegant executive jobs with the work drained out. Work minus power. Work minus decision-making. Work minus dominion. Affirmative Action Make Believe that a lot of black people *did* believe because they also believed that the white people in those nice offices were not like the ones in the general store or in the plumbers' union—that they were fundamentally kind, or fair, or something. Anything but the desperate prisoners of economics they turned out to be, holding on to their dominion with a tenacity and sang-froid that can only be described as Nixonian. So the bright and the black (architects, reporters, vice-presidents in charge of public relations) walk the streets right along with that astounding 38 percent of the black teen-aged female work force that does not have and never has had a job. So the black female college graduate earns two-thirds of what a white male high-school dropout earns. So the black people who put everything into community-action programs supported by Government funds have found themselves bereft of action, bereft of funds and all but bereft of community.

This decade has been rife with disappointment in practically every place where we thought we saw permanent change: Hostos, CUNY, and the black-studies departments that erupted like mini-volcanoes on campuses all over the nation; easy integrations of public-school systems; acceleration of promotion in factories and businesses. But now when we describe what has happened we cannot do it without using the verbs of upheaval and destruction: Open admission *closes;* minority-student quotas *fall* or *discontinue;* salary gaps between blacks and whites *widen;* black-studies departments *merge.* And the only growth black people can count on is in the prison population and the unemployment line. Even busing, which used to be a plain, if emotional, term at best, has now taken on an adjective normally reserved for rape and burglary—it is now called "forced" busing.

All of that counts, but I'm not sure that in the long haul it matters. Maybe Ardelia Willis had the best idea. One sees signs of her vision and the fruits of her prophecy in spite of the dread-lock statistics. The trees *are* walking, albeit slowly and quietly and without the fanfare of a cross-country run. It seems that at last black people have abandoned our foolish dependency on the Government to do the work that we once thought all of its citizenry would be delighted to do. Our love affair with the Federal Government is over. We misjudged the ardor of its attention. We thought its majority constituency would *prefer* having their children grow up among happy, progressive, industrious, contented black children rather than among angry, disenchanted and dangerous ones. That the profit motive of industry alone would keep us employed and therefore spending, and that our poverty was bad for business. We thought landlords wanted us to have a share in our neighborhoods and therefore love and care for them. That city governments wanted us to control our schools and therefore preserve them.

We were wrong. And now, having been eliminated from the lists of urgent national priorities, from TV documentaries and the platitudes of editorials, black people have chosen, or been forced to seek safety from the white man's promise, but happily not under a bed. More and more, there is the return to Ardelia's ways: the exercise of the will, the recognition of obstacles as only that—obstacles, not fixed stars. Black judges are fixing appropriate rather than punitive bail for black "offenders" and letting the rest of the community of jurisprudence scream. Young black women are leaving plush Northern jobs to sit in their living rooms and teach black children, work among factory women and spend months finding money to finance the college education of young blacks. Groups of blacks are buying huge tracts of land in the South and cutting off entirely the dependency of whole communities on grocery chains. For the first time, significant numbers of black people are returning or migrating to the South to focus on the acquisition of land, the transferral of crafts and skills, and the sharing of resources, the rebuilding of neighborhoods.

In the shambles of closing admissions, falling quotas, widening salary gaps and merging black-studies departments, builders and healers are working quietly among us. They are not like the heroes of old, the leaders we followed blindly and upon whom we depended for everything, or the blacks who had accumulated wealth for its own sake, fame, medals or some public acknowledgment of success. These are the people whose work is real and pointed and clear in its application to the race. Some are old and have been at work for a long time in and out of the public eye. Some are new and just finding out what their work is. But they are unmistakably the natural aristocrats of the race. The ones who refuse to imitate, to compromise, and who are indifferent to public accolade. Whose work is free or priceless. They take huge risks economically and personally. They are not always popular, even among black people, but they are the ones whose work black people respect. They are the healers. Some are nowhere near the public eye: Ben Chavis, preacher and political activist languishing now in North Carolina prisons; Robert Moses, a pioneering activist; Sterling Brown, poet and teacher; Father Al McKnight, land reformer; Rudy Lombard, urban sociologist; Lerone Bennett, historian; C.L.R. James, scholar; Alyce Gullattee, psychologist and organizer. Others are public legends: Judge Crockett, Judge Bruce Wright, Stevie Wonder, Ishmael Reed, Miles Davis, Richard Pryor, Muhammad Ali, Fannie Lou Hamer, Eubie Blake, Angela Davis, Bill Russell. . . .

But a complete roll-call is neither fitting nor necessary. They know who they are and so do we. They clarify our past, make livable our present and are certain to shape our future. And since the future is where our immortality as a race lies, no overview of the state of black people at this time can ignore some speculation on the only ones certain to live it—the children.

They are both exhilarating and frightening, those black children, and a source of wonderment to me. Although statistics about black teen-age crime and the "failure" of the courts to cut them are regularly printed and regularly received with outrage and fear, the children I know and see, those born after 1960, do not make such great copy. They are those who have grown up with nothing to prove to white people, whose perceptions of themselves are so new, so different, so focused they appear to me to be either magnificent hybrids or throwbacks to the time when our ancestors were called "royal." They are the baby sisters of the sit-in generation, the sons of the neighborhood blockbusters, the nephews of jailed revolutionaries, and a huge number who have had college graduates in their families for three and four generations. I thought we had left them nothing to love and nothing to want to know. I thought that those who exhibited some excitement about their future had long ago looked into the eyes of their teachers and were either saddened or outraged by the death of possibility they found there. I thought that those who were interested in the past had looked into the faces of their parents and seen betrayal. I thought the state had deprived them of a land and the landlords and banks had deprived them of a turf. So how is it that, with nothing to love, nothing they need to know, landless, turfless, minus a future and a past, these black children look us dead in the eye? They seem not to know how to apologize. And even when they are wrong they do not ask for forgiveness. It is as though they are waiting for us to apologize to them, to beg their pardon, to seek their approval. What species of black is this that not only does not choose to grovel, but doesn't know how? How will they keep jobs? How will they live? Won't they be killed before they reproduce? But they are unafraid. Is it because they refuse to see the world as we did? Is it because they have rejected both land and turf to seek instead a world? Maybe they finally got the message that we had been shouting into their faces; that they *live* here, *belong* here on this planet earth and that it is *theirs*. So they watch us with the eyes of poets and carpenters and musicians and scholars and other people who know who they are because they have invented themselves and know where they are going because they have envisioned it. All of which would please Ardelia—and John Solomon, too, I think. After all, he did hold on to his violin.

## QUESTIONS

*Looking at Ideas:*

1. Characterize Morrison's grandfather and grandmother; contrast their values and attitudes toward the white race.
2. Contrast Morrison's parents' values and attitudes toward whites.
3. Morrison states, "I grew up in a basically racist household with more than a child's share of contempt for white people." How does Morrison learn to tolerate the racial situation in America?
4. What conclusions does Morrison come to about the future of the black race in America? How do her grandparents' and parents' values and visions help her arrive at her position?
5. Why does Morrison see the future of blacks in their children? Why does she have faith in these children? How are they different from her generation?

*Looking at Strategies:*

1. Morrison sees contrasts between the values of her grandmother and grandfather and between the values of her mother and father. How does her presentation of these conflicts affect the reader's interpretation of her essay?
2. List several of the comparative strategies Morrison uses to organize her essay.
3. Discuss several of Morrison's effective details, patterns of imagery, and/or examples.
4. How does Morrison develop the symbolism of her title, "A Slow Walk of Trees"? What meanings does the symbol create?

*Looking at Connections:*

1. Compare and contrast Morrison's attitudes toward affirmative action and the future of social equality with those of Shelby Steele in "Being Black and Feeling Blue," also included in this chapter.
2. Compare and contrast Morrison's approach to understanding and reconciling the value conflicts between her parents with that of Judith Cofer in her memoir, "Silent Dancing," later in this chapter.

*Suggestions for Writing:*

1. Explain how a conflict of values experienced by your parents or other relatives influenced you in making an important decision or in formulating a position on a social or political issue.
2. Write an essay in which you predict the future of your ethnic group and/or gender in our rapidly changing multicultural society.

*3.* Select an issue that reflects a racial conflict within our society. Then write a hypothetical dialogue about the issue between Toni Morrison and Shelby Steele (or between Morrison and one of the other writers included in this chapter). Use their dialogue to explore the issue, basing their positions on your reading of their essays. After you complete the dialogue explain your own position on the issue.

**JOURNAL ENTRY**

Steele develops the concept of a "disbelieving anti-self" in his selection. Before reading the following selection, think about what you think the term means and whether you have ever felt that you had such an anti-self. Develop an example to illustrate the power of your negative self.

**SHELBY STEELE: "Being Black and Feeling Blue"**  Shelby Steele was born in Chicago in 1946 and raised by parents who were deeply involved in the 1960s civil rights movement. Steele's early life influenced his development as a writer. Like his parents, he continues to analyze the relationships between whites and blacks and to advocate solutions to the racial injustices in our society. Steele received his B.A. from Coe College in Iowa, his M.A. in sociology at Southern Illinois University, and his Ph.D. in English from the University of Utah (1974). Steele has taught literature and writing at San Jose State University in Northern California since 1974. His essays have appeared in *The American Scholar*, the *Washington Post*, the *New Republic*, and *Harper's*. In the following selection, "Being Black and Feeling Blue," which is excerpted from *The Content of Our Character* (1990), Steele asks blacks to look within themselves for the strength to overcome our society's prejudices.

SHELBY STEELE

# Being Black and Feeling Blue

In the early seventies when I was in graduate school, I went out for a beer late one afternoon with another black graduate student whom I'd only known casually before. This student was older than I—a stint in the army had interrupted his education—and he had the reputation of being bright and savvy, of having applied street smarts to the business of getting through graduate school. I suppose I was hoping for what would be called today a little mentoring. But it is probably not wise to drink with someone when you are enamored of his reputation, and it was not long before we stumbled into a moment that seemed to transform him before my very eyes. I asked him what he planned to do when he finished his Ph.D., fully expecting to hear of high aspirations matched with shrewd perceptions on how to reach them. But before he could think, he said with a kind of exhausted sincerity, "Man, I just want to hold on, get a job that doesn't work me too hard, and do a lot of fishing." Was he joking, I asked. "Hell, no," he said with exaggerated umbrage. "I'm not into it like the white boys. I don't need what they need."

I will call this man Henry and report that, until five or six years ago when I lost track of him, he was doing exactly as he said he would do. With much guile and little ambition he had moved through a succession of low-level administrative and teaching jobs, mainly in black studies programs. Of course, it is no crime to just "hold on," and it is hardly a practice limited to blacks. Still, in Henry's case there was truly a troubling discrepancy between his ambition and a fine intelligence recognized by all who knew him. But in an odd way this intelligence was more lateral than vertical, and I would say that it was rechanneled by a certain unseen fear into the business of merely holding on. It would be easy to say that Henry had simply decided on life in a slower lane than he was capable of traveling in, or that he was that rare person who had achieved ambitionless contentment. But if this was so, Henry would have had wisdom rather than savvy, and he would not have felt the need to carry himself with more self-importance than his station justified. I don't think Henry was uninterested in ambition; I think he was afraid of it.

It is certainly true that there is a little of Henry in most people. My own compulsion to understand him informs me that I must have seen many elements of myself in him. And though I'm sure he stands for a universal human blockage, I also believe that there is something in the condition of being black in America that makes the kind of hesitancy he represents one of black America's most serious and debilitating problems. As Henry reached the very brink of expanded opportunity, with Ph.D. in hand, he diminished his ambition almost as though his degree delivered him to a kind of semiretirement. I don't think blacks in general have any illusions about semiretirement, but I do think that, as a group, we have hesitated on the brink of new opportunities that we made enormous sacrifices to win for ourselves. The evidence of this lies in one of the most tragic social ironies of late twentieth-century American life: as black Americans have gained in equality and opportunity, we have also declined in relation to whites, so that by many socioeconomic measures we are further behind whites today than before the great victories of the civil rights movement. By one report, even the black middle class, which had made great gains in the seventies, began to lose ground to its white counterpart in the eighties. Most distressing of all, the black underclass continues to expand rather than shrink.

Of course, I don't suggest that Henry's peculiar inertia singularly explains social phenomena so complex and tragic. I do believe, however, that blacks in general are susceptible to the same web of attitudes and fears that kept Henry beneath his potential, and that our ineffectiveness in taking better advantage of our greater opportunity has much to do with this. I think there is a specific form of racial anxiety that all blacks are vulnerable to that can, in situations where we must engage the mainstream society, increase our self-doubt and undermine our confidence so that we often back away from the challenges that, if taken, would advance us. I believe this hidden racial anxiety may well now be the strongest barrier to our full participation in the American mainstream; that it is as strong or stronger even than the discrimination we still face. To examine this racial anxiety, allow me first to look at how the Henry was born in me.

Until the sixth grade, I attended a segregated school in a small working-class black suburb of Chicago. The school was a dumping ground for teachers with too little competence or mental stability to teach in the white school in our district. In 1956, when I entered the sixth grade, I encountered a new addition to the menagerie of misfits that was our faculty—an ex-Marine whose cruelty was suggested during our first lunch hour when he bit the cap off his Coke bottle and spit it into the wastebasket. Looking back I can see that there was no interesting depth to the cruelty he began to show us almost immediately—no consumptive hatred, no intelligent malevolence. Although we were all black and he was white, I don't think he was even particularly racist. He had obviously needed us to like him though he had no faith that we would. He ran the class like a gang leader, picking favorites one day and banishing them the next. And then there was a permanent pool of outsiders, myself among them, who were made to carry the specific sins that he must have feared most in himself.

The sin I was made to carry was the sin of stupidity. I misread a sentence on the first day of school, and my fate was sealed. He made my stupidity a part of the classroom lore, and very quickly I in fact became stupid. I all but lost the ability to read and found the simplest math beyond me. His punishments for my errors rose in meanness until one day he ordered me to pick up all of the broken glass on the playground with my bare hands. Of course, this would have to be the age of the pop bottle, and there were sections of this playground that glared like a mirror in sunlight. After half an hour's labor I sat down on strike, more out of despair than rebellion.

Again, cruelty was no more than a vibration in this man, and so without even a show of anger he commandeered a bicycle, handed it to an eighth-grader—one of his lieutenants—and told the boy to run me around the school grounds "until he passes out." The boy was also given a baseball bat to "use on him when he slows down." I ran two laps, about a mile, and then pretended to pass out. The eighth-grader knew I was playing possum but could not bring himself to hit me and finally rode off. I exited the school yard through an adjoining cornfield and never returned.

I mention this experience as an example of how one's innate capacity for insecurity is expanded and deepened, of how a disbelieving part of the self is brought to life and forever joined to the believing self. As children we are all wounded in some way and to some degree by the wild world we encounter. From these wounds a disbelieving *anti-self* is born, an internal antagonist and saboteur that embraces the world's negative view of us, that believes our wounds are justified by our own unworthiness, and that entrenches itself as a lifelong voice of doubt. This anti-self is a hidden aggressive force that scours the world for fresh evidence of our unworthiness. When the believing self announces

253

its aspirations, the anti-self always argues against them, but never on their merits (this is a healthy function of the believing self). It argues instead against our worthiness to pursue these aspirations and, by its lights, we are never worthy of even our smallest dreams. The mission of the anti-self is to deflate the believing self and, thus, draw it down into inertia, passivity, and faithlessness.

The anti-self is the unseen agent of low self-esteem; it is a catalytic energy that tries to induce low self-esteem in the believing self as though it were the complete truth of the personality. The anti-self can only be contained by the strength of the believing self, and this is where one's early environment becomes crucial. If the childhood environment is stable and positive, the family whole and loving, the schools good, the community safe, then the believing self will be reinforced and made strong. If the family is shattered, the schools indifferent, the neighborhood a mine field of dangers, the anti-self will find evidence everywhere with which to deflate the believing self.

This does not mean that a bad childhood cannot be overcome. But it does mean—as I have experienced and observed—that one's *capacity* for self-doubt and self-belief are roughly the same from childhood on, so that years later when the believing self may have strengthened enough to control the anti-self, one will still have the same capacity for doubt whether or not one has the *actual* doubt. I think it is this struggle between our capacities for doubt and belief that gives our personalities one of their peculiar tensions and, in this way, marks our character.

My own anti-self was given new scope and power by this teacher's persecution, and it was so successful in deflating my believing self that I secretly vowed never to tell my parents what was happening to me. The anti-self had all but sold my believing self on the idea that I was stupid, and I did not want to feel that shame before my parents. It was my brother who finally told them, and his disclosure led to a boycott that closed the school and eventually won the dismissal of my teacher and several others. But my anti-self transformed even this act of rescue into a cause of shame—if there wasn't something wrong with me, why did I have to be rescued? The anti-self follows only the logic of self-condemnation.

But there was another dimension to this experience that my anti-self was only too happy to seize upon. It was my race that landed me in this segregated school and, as many adults made clear to me, my persecution followed a timeless pattern of racial persecution. The implications of this were rich food for the anti-self—my race was so despised that it had to be segregated; as a black my education was so unimportant that even unbalanced teachers without college degrees were adequate; ignorance and cruelty that would be intolerable in a classroom of whites was perfectly all right in a classroom of blacks. The anti-self saw no injustice in any of this, but instead took it all as confirmation of a racial inferiority that it could now add to the well of personal doubt I already had. When the adults thought they were consoling me—*"Don't worry. They treat all blacks this way"*—they were also deepening the wound and expanding my capacity for doubt.

And this is the point. The condition of being black in America means that one will likely endure more wounds to one's self-esteem than others and that the capacity for self-doubt born of these wounds will be compounded and expanded by the black race's reputation of inferiority. The anti-self will most likely have more ammunition with which to deflate the believing self and its aspirations. And the universal human struggle to have belief win out over doubt will be more difficult.

More than difficult, it is also made inescapable by the fact of skin color, which, in America, works as a visual invocation of the problem. Black skin has more dehumanizing stereotypes associated with it than any other skin color in America, if not the world. When a black presents himself in an integrated situation, he knows that his skin alone may bring these stereotypes to life in the minds of those he meets and that he, as an individual, may be diminished by his race before he has a chance to reveal a single aspect of his personality. By the symbology of color that operates in our culture, black skin accuses him of inferiority. Under the weight of this accusation, a black will almost certainly doubt himself on some level and to some degree. The ever-vigilant anti-self will grab this racial doubt and mix it into the pool of personal doubt, so that when a black walks into an integrated situation—a largely white college campus, an employment office, a business lunch—he will be vulnerable to the entire realm of his self-doubt before a single word is spoken.

This constitutes an intense and lifelong racial vulnerability and anxiety for blacks. Even though a white American may have been wounded more than a given black, and therefore have a larger realm of inner doubt, his white skin, with its connotations of privilege and superiority, will actually help protect him from that doubt and from the undermining power of his anti-self, at least in relations with blacks. In fact, the larger the realm of doubt, the more he may be tempted to rely on his white skin for protection from it. Certainly in every self-avowed white racist, whether businessman or member of the Klan, there is a huge realm of self-contempt and doubt that hides behind the mythology of white skin. The mere need to pursue self-esteem through skin color suggests there is no faith that it can be pursued any other way. But if skin color offers whites a certain false esteem and impunity, it offers blacks vulnerability.

This vulnerability begins for blacks with the recognition that we belong, quite simply, to the most despised race in the human community of races. To be a member of such a group in a society where all others gain an impunity by merely standing in relation to us is to live with a relentless openness to diminishment and shame. By the devious logic of the anti-self, one cannot be open to such diminishment without in fact being inferior and therefore deserving of diminishment. For the anti-self, the charge verifies the crime, so that racial vulnerability itself is evidence of inferiority. In this sense, the anti-self is an internalized

255

racist, our own subconscious bigot, that conspires with society to diminish us.

So when blacks enter the mainstream, they are not only vulnerable to society's racism but also to the racist within. This internal racist is not restricted by law, morality, or social decorum. It cares nothing about civil rights and equal opportunity. It is the self-doubt born of the original wound of racial oppression, and its mission is to establish the justice of that wound and shackle us with doubt.

Of course, the common response to racial vulnerability, as to most vulnerabilities, is denial—the mind's mechanism for ridding itself of intolerable possibilities. For blacks to acknowledge a vulnerability to inferiority anxiety, in the midst of a society that has endlessly accused us of being inferior, feels nothing less than intolerable—as if we were agreeing with the indictment against us. But denial is not the same as eradication, since it only gives unconscious life to what is intolerable to our consciousness. Denial reassigns rather than vanquishes the terror of racial vulnerability. This reassignment only makes the terror stronger by making it unknown. When we deny, we always create a dangerous area of self-ignorance, an entire territory of the self that we cannot afford to know. Without realizing it, we begin to circumscribe our lives by avoiding those people and situations that might breach our denial and force us to see consciously what we fear. Though the denial of racial vulnerability is a human enough response, I think it also makes our public discourse on race circumspect and unproductive, since we cannot talk meaningfully about problems we are afraid to name.

Denial is a refusal of painful self-knowledge. When someone or something threatens to breach this refusal, we receive an unconscious shock of the very vulnerability we have denied—a shock that often makes us retreat and more often makes us intensify our denial. When blacks move into integrated situations or face challenges that are new for blacks, the myth of black inferiority is always present as a *condition* of the situation, and as such it always threatens to breach our denial of racial vulnerability. It also threatens to make us realize consciously what is intolerable to us—that we have some anxiety about inferiority. We feel this threat unconsciously as a shock of racial doubt delivered by the racist anti-self (always the inner voice of the myth of black inferiority). Consciously, we feel this shock as a sharp discomfort or a desire to retreat from the situation. Almost always we will want to intensify our denial.

I will call this *integration shock,* since it occurs most powerfully when blacks leave their familiar world and enter the mainstream. Integration shock and denial are mutual intensifiers. The stab of racial doubt that integration shock delivers is a pressure to intensify denial, and a more rigid denial means the next stab of doubt will be more threatening and therefore more intense. The symbiosis of these two forces is, I believe, one of the reasons black Americans have become preoccupied with racial pride, almost to the point of obsession over the past twenty-five or so years. With more exposure to the mainstream, we have endured more integration shock, more jolts of inferiority anxiety. And, I think, we have often responded with rather hyperbolic claims of black pride by which we deny that anxiety. In this sense, our self-consciousness around pride, our need to make a point of it, is, to a degree, a form of denial. Pride becomes denial when it ceases to reflect self-esteem quietly and begins to compensate loudly for unacknowledged inner doubt. Here it also becomes dangerous since it prevents us from confronting and overcoming that doubt.

I think the most recent example of black-pride-as-denial is the campaign (which seems to have been launched by a committee) to add yet another name to the litany of names that blacks have given themselves over the past century. Now we are to be African-Americans instead of, or in conjunction with, being black Americans. This self-conscious reaching for pride through nomenclature suggests nothing so much as a despair over the possibility of gaining the less conspicuous pride that follows real advancement. In its invocation of the glories of a remote African past and its wistful suggestion of homeland, this name denies the doubt black Americans have about their contemporary situation in America. There is no element of self-confrontation in it, no facing of real racial vulnerabilities, as there was with the name "black." I think "black" easily became the name of preference in the sixties, precisely because it was not a denial but a confrontation of inferiority anxiety, with the shame associated with the color black. There was honest self-acceptance in this name, and I think it diffused much of our vulnerability to the shame of color. Even between blacks, "black" is hardly the drop-dead fighting word it was when I was a child. Possibly we are ready now for a new name, but I think "black" has been our most powerful name yet because it so frankly called out our shame and doubt and helped us (and others) to accept ourselves. In the name "African-American" there is too much false neutralization of doubt, too much looking away from the caldron of our own experience. It is a euphemistic name that hides us even from ourselves.

I think blacks have been more preoccupied with pride over the past twenty-five years because we have been more exposed to integration shock since the 1964 Civil Rights Act made equal opportunity the law of the land (if not quite the full reality of the land). Ironically, it was the inequality of opportunity and all the other repressions of legal segregation that buffered us from our racial vulnerability. In a segregated society we did not have the same accountability to the charge of racial inferiority since we were given little opportunity to disprove the charge. It was the opening up of opportunity—anti-discrimination laws, the social programs of the Great Society, equal opportunity guidelines and mandates, fair housing laws, affirmative action, and so on—that made us individually and collectively more accountable to the myth of black inferiority and therefore more racially vulnerable.

This vulnerability has increased in the same proportion that our freedom and opportunity have increased. The exhilaration of new freedom is always followed by a shock of accountability. Whatever unresolved doubt follows the oppressed into greater freedom will be inflamed since freedom always carries a burden of proof, always throws us back on ourselves. And freedom, even imperfect freedom, makes blacks a brutal proposition: if you're not inferior, prove it. This is the proposition that shocks us and makes us vulnerable to our underworld of doubt. The whispers of the racist anti-self are far louder in the harsh accountability of freedom than in subjugation, where the oppressor is so entirely to blame.

The bitter irony of all this is that our doubt and the hesitancy it breeds now help limit our progress in America almost as systematically as segregation once did. Integration shock gives the old boundaries of legal segregation a regenerative power. To avoid the shocks of doubt that come from entering the mainstream, or plunging more deeply into it, we often pull back at precisely those junctures where segregation once pushed us back. In this way we duplicate the conditions of our oppression and reenact our role as victims even in the midst of far greater freedom and far less victimization. Certainly there is still racial discrimination in America, but I believe that the unconscious replaying of our oppression is now the greatest barrier to our full equality.

## QUESTIONS

*Looking at Ideas:*

1. Does Steele's concept of the "disbelieving anti-self" make sense to you? Give some examples to illustrate your understanding of the anti-self. How does Steele show that his teacher contributed to the creation of his anti-self?

2. Implicit in Steele's analysis is the idea that we often see the negative aspects of our personalities in the people around us and that we want to reject these people, not wanting to admit to our own weaknesses. Do you agree with Steele's analysis? Give examples from your own experiences to support or refute his position.

3. Why does Steele argue that blacks have more capacity for self-doubt than other groups, making "the universal human struggle to have belief win out over doubt . . . more difficult"? Do you agree or disagree with Steele on this point? Develop examples to support your position.

4. Explain Steele's claim that "the anti-self is an internalized racist, our own subconscious bigot, that conspires with society to diminish us." Do you agree or disagree with Steele? Develop examples to support your point of view.

5. How does Steele relate "integration shock" and denial of the fear of racial inferiority to the current preoccupation with racial pride? Steele further argues that "there is still racial discrimination in America, but I believe that the unconscious replaying of our oppression is now the greatest barrier to our full equality." Do you agree with Steele's analysis? Why or why not?

*Looking at Strategies:*

1. Identify Steele's thesis statement and explain its strategic positioning in the essay.
2. Explain why Steele begins with an example of his friend Henry's decision not to choose the path to success that is open to him and then follows this example with a story about his own persecution in the sixth grade. How are the two examples related? Are they effective?
3. How does Steele define the anti-self? What rhetorical strategies does he use?
4. Identify several of Steele's argumentative strategies. What makes his point of view convincing?

*Looking at Connections:*

1. Do you think that Richard Rodriguez, the author of the next selection in this chapter, would agree or disagree with Steele's analysis of the paralysis of African Americans today? Would Rodriguez be likely to see parallels between the consciousness of Mexican Americans and that of African Americans?
2. Based on your reading of the selection from "Notes of a Native Son" (included in Chapter Eight), do you think that James Baldwin would agree with Steele's analysis of the destructive power of internalized prejudice and self-hatred? Why or why not?

*Suggestions for Writing:*

1. Develop an essay in which you discuss and define your understanding of the concept of an anti-self. Include examples to illustrate how your anti-self functions and then analyze its impact on your personality. Conclude by discussing what you have learned from sharing, reflecting upon, and evaluating your anti-self.
2. Write an essay in which you support or refute Steele's explanation of the lack of progress by African Americans in our society. Be sure to include examples from your own experiences, observations, and/or readings to support your point of view.
3. Steele's argument is primarily a psychological one. Do you find his analysis convincing? Do you think that psychological explanations for ethnic conflicts are likely to be adequate or convincing? Write an essay in which you explain your position on the kind of psychological arguments Steele uses in his essay.

**JOURNAL ENTRY**

How would you describe your family's attitudes toward language and literacy? How did their attitudes influence your language development?

**RICHARD RODRIGUEZ: "Public and Private Language"**   Richard Rodriguez was born in 1944 to immigrant parents and raised in Sacramento, California. He earned his B.A. at Stanford (1967), his M.A. at Columbia (1969), and his Ph.D. at the University of California at Berkeley (1972). An essayist and memoirist, Rodriguez is best known for his autobiography, *The Hunger of Memory: The Education of Richard Rodriguez* (1982). *Mexico's Children* (1990) is his latest work. Rodriguez is well known for his analysis of his experiences as a bilingual student in which he shows how the conflicts of language and culture shaped his identity as a writer and at times separated him from his family. As you read "Public and Private Language," which is excerpted from *The Hunger of Memory,* trace Rodriguez's argument against bilingual education and think about how the experiences he had growing up influenced his point of view.

RICHARD RODRIGUEZ

# *Public and Private Language*

I remember, to start with, that day in Sacramento, in a California now nearly thirty years past, when I first entered a classroom—able to understand about fifty stray English words. The third of four children, I had been preceded by my older brother and sister to a neighborhood Roman Catholic school. But neither of them had revealed very much about their classroom experiences. They left each morning and returned each afternoon, always together, speaking Spanish as they climbed the five steps to the porch. And their mysterious books, wrapped in brown shopping-bag paper, remained on the table next to the door, closed firmly behind them.

An accident of geography sent me to a school where all my classmates were white, and many were the children of doctors and lawyers and business executives. On that first day of school, my classmates must certainly have been uneasy to find themselves apart from their families, in the first institution of their lives. But I was astonished. I was fated to be the "problem student" in class.

The nun said, in a friendly but oddly impersonal voice: "Boys and girls, this is Richard Rodriguez." (I heard her sound it out: *Rich-heard Road-ree-guess.*) It was the first time I had heard anyone say my name in English. "Richard," the nun repeated more slowly, writing my name down in her book. Quickly I turned to see my mother's face dissolve in a watery blur behind the pebbled-glass door.

Now, many years later, I hear of something called "bilingual education"—a scheme proposed in the late 1960s by Hispanic-American social activists, later endorsed by a congressional vote. It is a program that seeks to permit non-English-speaking children (many from lower-class homes) to use their "family language" as the language of school. Such, at least, is the aim its supporters announce. I hear them and am forced to say no: It is not possible for a child, any child, ever to use his family's language in school. Not to understand this is to misunderstand the public uses of schooling and to trivialize the nature of intimate life.

Memory teaches me what I know of these matters. The boy reminds the adult. I was a bilingual child, but of a certain kind: "socially disadvantaged," the son of working-class parents, both Mexican immigrants.

In the early years of my boyhood, my parents coped very well in America. My father had steady work. My mother managed at home. They were nobody's victims. When we moved to a house many blocks from the Mexican-American section of town, they were not intimidated by those two or three neighbors who initially tried to make us unwelcome. ("Keep your brats away from my sidewalk!") But despite all they achieved, or perhaps because they had so much to achieve, they lacked any deep feeling of ease, of belonging in public. They regarded the people at work or in crowds as being very distant from us. Those were the others, *los gringos*. That term was interchangeable in their speech with another, even more telling: *los americanos*.

I grew up in a house where the only regular guests were my relations. On a certain day, enormous families of relatives would visit us, and there would be so many people that the noise and the bodies would spill out to the back yard and onto the front porch. Then for weeks no one would come. (If the doorbell rang, it was usually a salesman.) Our house stood apart—gaudy yellow in a row of white bungalows. We were the people with the noisy dog, the people who raised chickens. We were the foreigners on the block. A few neighbors would smile and wave at us. We waved back. But until I was seven years old, I did not know the name of the old couple living next door or the names of the kids living across the street.

In public, my father and mother spoke a hesitant, accented, and not always grammatical English. And then they would have to strain, their bodies tense, to catch the sense of what was rapidly said by *los gringos*. At home, they returned to Spanish. The language of their Mexican past sounded in counterpoint to the English spoken in public. The words would come quickly, with ease. Conveyed through those sounds was the pleasing, soothing, consoling reminder that one was at home.

During those years when I was first learning to speak, my mother and father addressed me only in Spanish; in Spanish I learned to reply. By contrast, English *(inglés)* was the language I came to associate with gringos, rarely heard in the house. I learned my first words of English

261

overhearing my parents speaking to strangers. At six years of age, I knew just enough words for my mother to trust me on errands to stores one block away—but no more.

I was then a listening child, careful to hear the very different sounds of Spanish and English. Wide-eyed with hearing, I'd listen to sounds more than to words. First, there were English (gringo) sounds. So many words still were unknown to me that when the butcher or the lady at the drugstore said something, exotic polysyllabic sounds would bloom in the midst of their sentences. Often the speech of people in public seemed to me very loud, booming with confidence. The man behind the counter would literally ask, "What can I do for you?" But by being so firm and clear, the sound of his voice said that he was a gringo; he belonged in public society. There were also the high nasal notes of middle-class American speech—which I rarely am conscious of hearing today because I hear them so often, but could not stop hearing when I was a boy. Crowds at Safeway or at bus stops were noisy with the birdlike sounds of *los gringos*. I'd move away from them all— all the chirping chatter above me.

But then there was Spanish: *español*, the language rarely heard away from the house; *español*, the language that seemed to me, therefore, a private language, my family's language. To hear its sounds was to feel myself specially recognized as one of the family, apart from *los otros*. A simple remark, an inconsequential comment could convey that assurance. My parents would say something to me, and I would feel embraced by the sounds of their words. Those sounds said: *I am speaking with ease in Spanish. I am addressing you in words I never use with* los gringos. *I recognize you as someone special, close, like no one outside. You belong with us. In the family, Ricardo.*

At the age of six, well past the time when most middle-class children no longer notice the difference between sounds uttered at home and words spoken in public, I had a different experience. I lived in a world compounded of sounds. I was a child longer than most. I lived in a magical world, surrounded by sounds both pleasing and fearful. I shared with my family a language enchantingly private—different from that used in the city around us.

Supporters of bilingual education imply today that students like me miss a great deal by not being taught in their family's language. What they seem not to recognize is that, as a socially disadvantaged child, I regarded Spanish as a private language. It was a ghetto language that deepened and strengthened my feeling of public separateness. What I needed to learn in school was that I had the right, and the obligation, to speak the public language. The odd truth is that my first-grade classmates could become bilingual, in the conventional sense of the word, more easily than I. Had they been taught early (as upper-middle-class children often are taught) a "second language" like Spanish or French, they could have regarded it simply as another public language. In my case, such bilingualism could not have been so quickly achieved. What I did not believe was that I could speak a single public language.

Without question, it would have pleased me to have heard my teachers address me in Spanish when I entered the classroom. I would have felt much less afraid. I would have imagined that my instructors were somehow "related" to me; I would indeed have heard their Spanish as my family's language. I would have trusted them and responded with ease. But I would have delayed—postponed for how long?—having to learn the language of public society. I would have evaded—and for how long?—learning the great lesson of school: that I had a public identity.

Fortunately, my teachers were unsentimental about their responsibility. What they understood was that I needed to speak public English. So their voices would search me out, asking me questions. Each time I heard them I'd look up in surprise to see a nun's face frowning at me. I'd mumble, not really meaning to answer. The nun would persist. "Richard, stand up. Don't look at the floor. Speak up. Speak to the entire class, not just to me!" But I couldn't believe English could be my language to use. (In part, I did not want to believe it.) I continued to mumble. I resisted the teacher's demands. (Did I somehow suspect that once I learned this public language my family life would be changed?) Silent, waiting for the bell to sound, I remained dazed, diffident, afraid.

Three months passed. Five. A half year. Unsmiling, ever watchful, my teachers noted my silence. They began to connect my behavior with the slow progress my brother and sisters were making. Until, one Saturday morning, three nuns arrived at the house to talk to our parents. Stiffly they sat on the blue living-room sofa. From the doorway of another room, spying on the visitors, I noted the incongruity, the clash of two worlds, the faces and voices of school intruding upon the familiar setting of home. I overheard one voice gently wondering, "Do your children speak only Spanish at home, Mrs. Rodriguez?" While another voice added, "That Richard especially seems so timid and shy."

*That Rich-heard!*

With great tact, the visitors continued. "Is it possible for you and your husband to encourage your children to practice their English when they are home?" Of course my parents complied. What would they not do for their children's well-being? And how could they question the church's authority, which those women represented? In an instant they agreed to give up the language (the sounds) that had revealed and accentuated our family's closeness. The moment after the visitors left, the change was observed. "*Ahora,* speak to us only *en inglés,*" my father and mother told us.

At first, it seemed a kind of game. After dinner each night, the family gathered together to practice "our" English. It was still then *inglés,* a language foreign to us, so we felt drawn to it as strangers. Laughing, we would try to define words we could not pronounce. We played with strange English sounds, often overanglicizing our pronunciations. And we filled the smiling gaps of our sentences with familiar Spanish sounds. But that was cheating, somebody shouted, and everyone laughed.

In school, meanwhile, like my brother and sisters, I was required to attend a daily tutoring session. I needed a full year of this special work. I also needed my teachers to keep my attention from straying in class by calling out, *"Richheard!"*—their English voices slowly loosening the ties to my other name, with its three notes, *Ri-car-do*. Most of all, I needed to hear my mother and father speak to me in a moment of seriousness in "broken"—suddenly heartbreaking—English. This scene was inevitable. One Saturday morning I entered the kitchen where my parents were talking, but I did not realize that they were talking Spanish until, the moment they saw me, their voices changed and they began speaking English. The gringo sounds they uttered startled me. Pushed me away. In that moment of trivial misunderstanding and profound insight, I felt my throat twisted by unsounded grief. I simply turned and left the room. But I had no place to escape to where I could grieve in Spanish. My brother and sisters were speaking English in another part of the house.

Again and again in the days following, as I grew increasingly angry, I was obliged to hear my mother and father encouraging me: "Speak to us *en inglés*." Only then did I determine to learn classroom English. Thus, sometime afterward it happened: One day in school, I raised my hand to volunteer an answer to a question. I spoke out in a loud voice, and I did not think it remarkable when the entire class understood. That day I moved very far from being the disadvantaged child I had been only days earlier. Taken hold at last was the belief, the calming assurance, that I *belonged* in public.

Shortly after, I stopped hearing the high, troubling sounds of *los gringos*. A more and more confident speaker of English, I didn't listen to how strangers sounded when they talked to me. With so many English-speaking people around me, I no longer heard American accents. Conversations quickened. Listening to persons whose voices sounded eccentrically pitched, I might note their sounds for a few seconds, but then I'd concentrate on what they were saying. Now when I heard someone's tone of voice—angry or questioning or sarcastic or happy or sad—I didn't distinguish it from the words it expressed. Sound and word were thus tightly wedded. At the end of each day, I was often bemused, and always relieved, to realize how "soundless," though crowded with words, my day in public had been. An eight-year-old boy, I finally came to accept what had been technically true since my birth: I was an American citizen.

But diminished by then was the special feeling of closeness at home. Gone was the desperate, urgent, intense feeling of being at home among those with whom I felt intimate. Our family remained a loving family, but one greatly changed. We were no longer so close, no longer bound tightly together by the knowledge of our separateness from *los gringos*. Neither my older brother nor my sisters rushed home after school any more. Nor did I. When I arrived home, often there would be neighborhood kids in the house. Or the house would be empty of sounds.

Following the dramatic Americanization of their children, even my parents grew more publicly confident—especially my mother. First she learned the names of all the people on the block. Then she decided we needed to have a telephone in our house. My father, for his part, continued to use the word gringo, but it was no longer charged with bitterness or distrust. Stripped of any emotional content, the word simply became a name for those Americans not of Hispanic descent. Hearing him, sometimes, I wasn't sure if he was pronouncing the Spanish word *gringo,* or saying gringo in English.

There was a new silence at home. As we children learned more and more English, we shared fewer and fewer words with our parents. Sentences needed to be spoken slowly when one of us addressed our mother or father. Often the parent wouldn't understand. The child would need to repeat himself. Still the parent misunderstood. The young voice, frustrated, would end up saying, "Never mind"—the subject was closed. Dinners would be noisy with the clinking of knives and forks against dishes. My mother would smile softly between her remarks; my father, at the other end of the table, would chew and chew his food while he stared over the heads of his children.

My mother! My father! After English became my primary language, I no longer knew what words to use in addressing my parents. The old Spanish words (those tender accents of sound) I had earlier used— *mamá* and *papá*—I couldn't use any more. They would have been all-too-painful reminders of how much had changed in my life. On the other hand, the words I heard neighborhood kids call their parents seemed unsatisfactory. "Mother" and "father," "ma," "papa," "pa," "dad," "pop" (how I hated the all-American sound of that last word)— all these I felt were unsuitable terms of address for *my* parents. As a result, I never used them at home. Whenever I'd speak to my parents, I would try to get their attention by looking at them. In public conversations, I'd refer to them as my "parents" or my "mother" and "father."

My mother and father, for their part, responded differently as their children spoke to them less. My mother grew restless, seemed troubled and anxious at the scarceness of words exchanged in the house. She would question me about my day when I came home from school. She smiled at my small talk. She pried at the edges of my sentences to get me to say something more. ("What . . .?") She'd join conversations she overheard, but her intrusions often stopped her children's talking. By contrast, my father seemed to grow reconciled to the new quiet. Though his English somewhat improved, he tended more and more to retire into silence. At dinner he spoke very little. One night his children and even his wife helplessly giggled at his garbled English pronunciation of the Catholic "Grace Before Meals." Thereafter he made his wife recite the prayer at the start of each meal, even on formal occasions when there were guests in the house.

Hers became the public voice of the family. On official business it was she, not my father, who would usually talk to strangers on the phone or in stores. We children grew so accustomed to his silence that years later we would routinely refer to his "shyness." (My mother often tried to explain: both of his parents died when he was eight. He was raised by an uncle who treated him as little more than a menial servant. He was never encouraged to speak. He grew up alone—a man of few words.) But I realized my father was not shy whenever I'd watch him speaking Spanish with relatives. Using Spanish, he was quickly effusive. Especially when talking with other men, his voice would spark, flicker, flare alive with varied sounds. In Spanish he expressed ideas and feelings he rarely revealed when speaking English. With firm Spanish sounds he conveyed a confidence and authority that English would never allow him.

The silence at home, however, was not simply the result of fewer words passing between parents and children. More profound for me was the silence created by my inattention to sounds. At about the time I no longer bothered to listen with care to the sounds of English in public, I grew careless about listening to the sounds made by the family when they spoke. Most of the time I would hear someone speaking at home and didn't distinguish his sounds from the words people uttered in public. I didn't even pay much attention to my parents' accented and ungrammatical speech—at least not at home. Only when I was with them in public would I become alert to their accents. But even then, their sounds caused me less and less concern. For I was growing increasingly confident of my own public identity.

I would have been happier about my public success had I not recalled, sometimes, what it had been like earlier, when my family conveyed its intimacy through a set of conveniently private sounds. Sometimes in public, hearing a stranger, I'd hark back to my lost past. A Mexican farm worker approached me one day downtown. He wanted directions to some place. *"Hijito, . . ."* he said. And his voice stirred old longings. Another time I was standing beside my mother in the visiting room of a Carmelite convent, before the dense screen that rendered the nuns shadowy figures. I heard several of them speaking Spanish in their busy, singsong, overlapping voices, assuring my mother that, yes, yes, we were remembered, all our family were remembered in their prayers. Those voices echoed faraway family sounds. Another day, a dark-faced old woman touched my shoulder lightly to steady herself as she boarded a bus. She murmured something to me I couldn't quite comprehend. Her Spanish voice came near, like the face of a never-before-seen relative in the instant before I was kissed. That voice, like so many of the Spanish voices I'd hear in public, recalled the golden age of my childhood.

Bilingual educators say today that children lose a degree of "individuality" by becoming assimilated into public society. (Bilingual schooling is a program popularized in the seventies, that decade when middle-class "ethnics" began to resist the process of assimilation—the

"American melting pot.") But the bilingualists oversimplify when they scorn the value and necessity of assimilation. They do not seem to realize that a person is individualized in two ways. So they do not realize that, while one suffers a diminished sense of *private* individuality by being assimilated into public society, such assimilation makes possible the achievement of *public* individuality.

Simplistically again, the bilingualists insist that a student should be reminded of his difference from others in mass society, of his "heritage." But they equate mere separateness with individuality. The fact is that only in private—with intimates—is separateness from the crowd a prerequisite for individuality; an intimate "tells" me that I am unique, unlike all others, apart from the crowd. In public, by contrast, full individuality is achieved, paradoxically, by those who are able to consider themselves members of the crowd. Thus it happened for me. Only when I was able to think of myself as an American, no longer an alien in gringo society, could I seek the rights and opportunities necessary for full public individuality. The social and political advantages I enjoy as a man began on the day I came to believe that my name is indeed *Rich-heard Road-ree-guess*. It is true that my public society today is often impersonal; in fact, my public society is usually mass society. But despite the anonymity of the crowd, and despite the fact that the individuality I achieve in public is often tenuous—because it depends on my being one in a crowd—I celebrate the day I acquired my new name. Those middle-class ethnics who scorn assimilation seem to me filled with decadent self-pity, obsessed by the burden of public life. Dangerously, they romanticize public separateness and trivialize the dilemma of those who are truly socially disadvantaged.

I grew up the victim of a disconcerting confusion. As I became fluent in English, I could no longer speak Spanish with confidence. I continued to understand spoken Spanish, and in high school I learned how to read and write Spanish. But for many years I could not pronounce it. A powerful guilt blocked my spoken words; an essential glue was missing whenever I would try to connect words to form sentences. I would be unable to break a barrier of sound, to speak freely. I would speak, or try to speak, Spanish, and I would manage to utter halting, hiccupping sounds that betrayed my unease. (Even today, I speak Spanish very slowly, at best.)

When relatives and Spanish-speaking friends of my parents came to the house, my brother and sisters would usually manage to say a few words before being excused. I never managed so gracefully. Each time I'd hear myself addressed in Spanish, I couldn't respond with any success. I'd know the words I wanted to say, but I couldn't say them. I would try to speak, but everything I said seemed to me horribly anglicized. My mouth wouldn't form the sounds right. My jaw would tremble. After a phrase or two, I'd stutter, cough up a warm, silvery sound, and stop.

My listeners were surprised to hear me. They'd lower their heads to grasp better what I was trying to say. They would repeat their questions in gentle, affectionate voices. But then I would answer in English. No, no, they would say, we want you to speak to us in Spanish *("en español")*. But I couldn't do it. Then they would call me *Pocho*. Sometimes playfully, teasing, using the tender diminutive—*mi pochito*. Sometimes not so playfully but mockingly, *pocho*. (A Spanish dictionary defines that word as an adjective meaning "colorless" or "bland." But I heard it as a noun, naming the Mexican-American who, in becoming an American, forgets his native society.) *"¡Pocho!"* my mother's best friend muttered, shaking her head. And my mother laughed, somewhere behind me. She said that her children didn't want to practice "our Spanish" after they started going to school. My mother's smiling voice made me suspect that the lady who faced me was not really angry at me. But searching her face, I couldn't find the hint of a smile.

Yet, even during those years of guilt, I was coming to grasp certain consoling truths about language and intimacy—truths that I learned gradually. Once, I remember playing with a friend in the back yard when my grandmother appeared at the window. Her face was stern with suspicion when she saw the boy (the *gringo* boy) I was with. She called out to me in Spanish, sounding the whistle of her ancient breath. My companion looked up and watched her intently as she lowered the window and moved (still visible) behind the light curtain, watching us both. He wanted to know what she had said. I started to tell him, to translate her Spanish words into English. The problem was, however, that though I knew how to translate exactly what she had told me, I realized that any translation would distort the deepest meaning of her message: it had been directed only to me. This message of intimacy could never be translated because it did not lie in the actual words she had used but passed through them. So any translation would have seemed wrong; the words would have been stripped of an essential meaning. Finally, I decided not to tell my friend anything—just that I didn't hear all she had said.

This insight was unfolded in time. As I made more and more friends outside my house, I began to recognize intimate messages spoken in English in a close friend's confidential tone or secretive whisper. Even more remarkable were those instances when, apparently for no special reason, I'd become conscious of the fact that my companion was speaking *only to me*. I'd marvel then, just hearing his voice. It was a stunning event to be able to break through the barrier of public silence, to be able to hear the voice of the other, to realize that it was directed just to me. After such moments of intimacy outside the house, I began to trust what I heard intimately conveyed through my family's English. Voices at home at last punctured sad confusion. I'd hear myself addressed as an intimate—in English. Such moments were never as raucous with sound as in past times, when we had used our "private" Spanish. (Our English-sounding house was never to be as noisy as our Spanish-sounding house had been.) Intimate moments were usually moments of soft sound. My mother would be ironing in the dining room while I did my homework nearby. She would look over

268

at me, smile, and her voice sounded to tell me that I was her son. *Richard*.

Intimacy thus continued at home; intimacy was not stilled by English. Though there were fewer occasions for it—a change in my life that I would never forget—there were also times when I sensed the deep truth about language and intimacy: *Intimacy is not created by a particular language; it is created by intimates.* Thus the great change in my life was not linguistic but social. If, after becoming a successful student, I no longer heard intimate voices as often as I had earlier, it was not because I spoke English instead of Spanish. It was because I spoke a public language for most of my day. I moved easily at last, a citizen in a crowded city of words.

As a man I spend most of my day in public, in a world largely devoid of speech sounds. So I am quickly attracted by the glamorous quality of certain alien voices. I still am gripped with excitement when someone passes me on the street speaking in Spanish. I have not moved beyond the range of the nostalgic pull of those sounds. And there is something very compelling about the sounds of lower-class blacks. Of all the accented versions of English that I hear in public, I hear theirs most intently. The Japanese tourist stops me downtown to ask me a question, and I inch my way past his accent to concentrate on what he is saying. The Eastern European immigrant in the neighborhood delicatessen speaks to me, and, again, I do not pay much attention to his sounds, nor to the Texas accent of one of my neighbors or the Chicago accent of the woman who lives in the apartment below me. But when the ghetto black teenagers get on the city bus, I hear them. Their sounds in my society are the sounds of the outsider. Their voices annoy me for being so loud—so self-sufficient and unconcerned by my presence, but for the same reason they are glamorous: a romantic gesture against public acceptance. And as I listen to their shouted laughter, I realize my own quietness. I feel envious of them—envious of their brazen intimacy.

I warn myself away from such envy, however. Overhearing those teenagers, I think of the black political activists who lately have argued in favor of using black English in public schools—an argument that varies only slightly from that of foreign-language bilingualists. I have heard "radical" linguists make the point that black English is a complex and intricate version of English. And I do not doubt it. But neither do I think that black English should be a language of public instruction. What makes it inappropriate in classrooms is not something in the language itself but, rather, what lower-class speakers make of it. Just as Spanish would have been a dangerous language for me to have used at the start of my education, so black English would be a dangerous language to use in the schooling of teenagers for whom it reinforces feelings of public separateness.

This seems to me an obvious point to make, and yet it must be said. In recent years, there have been many attempts to make the language

of the alien a public language. "Bilingual education, two ways to understand . . ." television and radio commercials glibly announce. Propo-
nents of bilingual education are careful to say that above all they want
every student to acquire a good education. Their argument goes something like this: Children permitted to use their family language will not
be so alienated and will be better able to match the progress of English-
speaking students in the crucial first months of schooling. Increasingly
confident of their ability, such children will be more inclined to apply
themselves to their studies in the future. But then the bilingualists also
claim another very different goal. They say that children who use their
family language in school will retain a sense of their ethnic heritage and
their family ties. Thus the supporters of bilingual education want it
both ways. They propose bilingual schooling as a way of helping students acquire the classroom skills crucial for public success. But they
likewise insist that bilingual instruction will give students a sense of
their identity apart from the English-speaking public.

Behind this scheme gleams a bright promise for the alien child: One
can become a public person while still remaining a private person. Who
would not want to believe such an appealing idea? Who can be surprised that the scheme has the support of so many middle-class ethnic
Americans? If the barrio or ghetto child can retain his separateness
even while being publicly educated, then it is almost possible to believe
that no private cost need be paid for public success. This is the consolation offered by any of the number of current bilingual programs.
Consider, for example, the bilingual voter's ballot. In some American
cities, one can cast a ballot printed in several languages. Such a document implies that it is possible for one to exercise that most public of
rights—the right to vote—while still keeping oneself apart, unassimi-
lated in public life.

It is not enough to say that such schemes are foolish and certainly
doomed. Middle-class supporters of public bilingualism toy with the
confusion of those Americans who cannot speak standard English as
well as they do. Moreover, bilingual enthusiasts sin against intimacy. A
Hispanic-American tells me, "I will never give up my family language,"
and he clutches a group of words as though they were the source of his
family ties. He credits to language what he should credit to family
members. This is a convenient mistake, for as long as he holds on to
certain familiar words, he can ignore how much else has actually
changed in his life.

It has happened before. In earlier decades, persons ambitious for
social mobility, and newly successful, similarly seized upon certain
"family words." Workingmen attempting to gain political power, for example, took to calling one another "brother." The word as they used it,
however, could never resemble the word (the sound) "brother" exchanged by two people in intimate greeting. The context of its public
delivery made it at best a metaphor; with repetition it was only a vague
echo of the intimate sound. Context forced the change. Context could
not be overruled. Context will always protect the realm of the intimate

from public misuse. Today middle-class white Americans continue to prove the importance of context as they try to ignore it. They seize upon idioms of the black ghetto, but their attempt to appropriate such expressions invariably changes the meaning. As it becomes a public expression, the ghetto idiom loses its sound, its message of public separateness and strident intimacy. With public repetition it becomes a series of words, increasingly lifeless.

The mystery of intimate utterance remains. The communication of intimacy passes through the word and enlivens its sound, but it cannot be held by the word. It cannot be retained or ever quoted because it is too fluid. It depends not on words but on persons.

My grandmother! She stood among my other relations mocking me when I no longer spoke Spanish. *Pocho,* she said. But then it made no difference. She'd laugh, and our relationship continued because language was never its source. She was a woman in her eighties during the first decade of my life—a mysterious woman to me, my only living grandparent, a woman of Mexico in a long black dress that reached down to her shoes. She was the one relative of mine who spoke no word of English. She had no interest in gringo society and remained completely aloof from the public. She was protected by her daughters, protected even by me when we went to Safeway together and I needed to act as her translator. An eccentric woman. Hard. Soft.

When my family visited my aunt's house in San Francisco, my grandmother would search for me among my many cousins. When she found me, she'd chase them away. Pinching her granddaughters, she would warn them away from me. Then she'd take me to her room, where she had prepared for my coming. There would be a chair next to the bed, a dusty jellied candy nearby, and a copy of *Life en Español* for me to examine. "There," she'd say. And I'd sit content, a boy of eight. *Pocho,* her favorite. I'd sift through the pictures of earthquake-destroyed Latin-American cities and blonde-wigged Mexican movie stars. And all the while I'd listen to the sound of my grandmother's voice. She'd pace around the room, telling me stories of her life, her past. They were stories so familiar that I couldn't remember when I'd heard them for the first time. I'd look up sometimes to listen. Other times she'd look over at me, but she never expected a response. Sometimes I'd smile or nod. (I understood exactly what she was saying.) But it never seemed to matter to her one way or the other. It was enough that I was there. The words she spoke were almost irrelevant to that fact. We were content. And the great mystery remained: intimate utterance.

The child reminds the adult: to seek intimate sounds is to seek the company of intimates. I do not expect to hear those sounds in public. I would dishonor those I have loved, and those I love now, to claim anything else. I would dishonor our intimacy by holding on to a particular language and calling it my family language. Intimacy cannot be trapped within words; it passes through words. It passes. Intimates leave the room. Doors close. Faces move away from the window. Time passes,

271

and voices recede into the dark. Death finally quiets the voice. There is no way to deny it, no way to stand in the crowd claiming to utter one's family language.

The last time I saw my grandmother I was nine years old. I can tell you some of the things she said to me as I stood by her bed, but I cannot quote the message of intimacy she conveyed with her voice. She laughed, holding my hand. Her voice illumined disjointed memories as it passed them again. She remembered her husband—his green eyes, his magic name of Narcissio, his early death. She remembered the farm in Mexico, the eucalyptus trees nearby (their scent, she remembered, like incense). She remembered the family cow, the bell around its neck heard miles away. A dog. She remembered working as a seamstress, how she'd leave her daughters and son for long hours to go into Guadalajara to work. And how my mother would come running toward her in the sun—in her bright yellow dress—on her return. "MMMMAAAAMMMMÁÁÁÁ," the old lady mimicked her daughter (my mother) to her daughter's son. She laughed. There was the snap of a cough. An aunt came into the room and told me it was time I should leave. "You can see her tomorrow," she promised. So I kissed my grandmother's cracked face. And the last thing I saw was her thin, oddly youthful thigh, as my aunt rearranged the sheet on the bed.

At the funeral parlor a few days after, I remember kneeling with my relatives during the rosary. Among their voices I traced, then lost, the sounds of individual aunts in the surge of the common prayer. And I heard at that moment what since I have heard very often—the sound the women in my family make when they are praying in sadness. When I went up to look at my grandmother, I saw her through the haze of a veil draped over the open lid of the casket. Her face looked calm—but distant and unyielding to love. It was not the face I remembered seeing most often. It was the face she made in public when the clerk at Safeway asked her some question and I would need to respond. It was her public face that the mortician had designed with his dubious art.

## QUESTIONS

*Looking at Ideas:*

1. Rodriguez writes from his own experiences of learning a second language in the early 1950s in order to establish a public identity at school. Would his experience have been different were he attending elementary school in the early 1990s? Why or why not?

2. Why does Rodriguez finally decide that he will learn how to speak English fluently? How does his perception of the English language and his self-concept change? What does he lose and what does he gain?

3. Why does Rodriguez emphasize the difference between the way his family and the Catholic nuns pronounced his name? How does their pronunciation begin to separate him from his family and their shared, comforting intimacy? When does he learn to accept the nuns' pronun-

ciation of his name? Like Rodriguez, have you ever had a nickname that signified a particular intimacy and that you did not use in public situations?

4. Rodriguez argues that public and family language must be separated in order not to trivialize the intimacy of family language. Do you agree with him? Do you think that Rodriguez succeeds in demonstrating the value and importance of a private family language?

*Looking at Strategies:*

1. List several examples of Rodriguez's use of details to create an understanding of the isolation that he and his family felt in their neighborhood in Sacramento. How effective are his examples?

2. Why does Rodriguez distinguish between Spanish and English (gringo) sounds? How does he deepen the meaning and importance of language through his comparison? How and why does Rodriguez link his acceptance of English with a growing "silence" at home?

3. What audience do you think Rodriguez had in mind when he wrote his essay? Would the essay be interpreted differently by bilingual educators, Latino college students, and nonminority students? Why?

*Looking at Connections:*

1. Contrast the ways that Rodriguez and Judith Ortiz Cofer, author of "Silent Dancing" (included in this chapter) value their native languages as aspects of their self-concepts, both as children and as adults.

2. Do you think Shelby Steele would agree with Rodriguez's position on bilingual education? Explain your response.

*Suggestions for Writing:*

1. Write an essay in which you agree or disagree with Rodriguez's position on bilingual education. Try doing library research on the issue and/or interviewing friends who are not native speakers of English to develop evidence for your position.

2. Write an essay in which you examine the relationship between language and culture. Refer to some of the selections in this chapter and to your own experiences and observations.

3. Write an essay in which you show how your early experiences with language helped shape your self-concept and identity as a literate adult.

**SIMON J. ORTIZ: "The Language We Know"** Simon Ortiz was born in Acoma Pueblo, New Mexico, and was raised in his tribe until he began elementary school at the Bureau of Indian Affairs, where he was forced to speak only English. Ortiz believes that he learned English easily because of his love of language. In his writing Ortiz integrates his concern for the political and social rights of Native Americans with his respect for the traditions of his Acoma heritage. Twelve of Ortiz's books of poetry have been published; he also writes for popular magazines and scholarly journals. Currently Ortiz is director of the creative writing program at Sinte Gleska College in Mission, South Dakota. As you read "The Language We Know," which appeared in *I Tell You Now: Autobiographical Essays by Native American Writers* (1984), contrast the ways in which Ortiz and Rodriguez have come to integrate their family's culture and language into their identities as writers.

SIMON J. ORTIZ

# The Language We Know

I don't remember a world without language. From the time of my earliest childhood, there was language. Always language, and imagination, speculation, utters of sound. Words, beginnings of words. What would I be without language? My existence has been determined by language, not only the spoken but the unspoken, the language of speech and the language of motion. I can't remember a world without memory. Memory, immediate and far away in the past, something in the sinew, blood, ageless cell. Although I don't recall the exact moment I spoke or tried to speak, I know the feeling of something tugging at the core of the mind, something unutterable uttered into existence. It is language that brings us into being in order to know life.

My childhood was the oral tradition of the Acoma Pueblo people—Aaquumeh hano—which included my immediate family of three older sisters, two younger sisters, two younger brothers, and my mother and father. My world was our world of the Aaquumeh in McCartys, one of the two villages descended from the ageless mother pueblo of Acoma. My world was our Eagle clan-people among other clans. I grew up in Deetziyamah, which is the Aaquumeh name for McCartys, which is posted at the exit off the present interstate highway in western New Mexico. I grew up within a people who farmed small garden plots and fields, who were mostly poor and not well schooled in the American system's education. The language I spoke was that of a struggling people who held ferociously to a heritage, culture, language, and land despite the odds posed them by the forces surrounding them since 1540 A.D., the advent of Euro-American colonization. When I began school in 1948 at the BIA (Bureau of Indian Affairs) day school in our village, I was armed with the basic ABC's and the phrases "Good morning, Miss Oleman" and "May I please be excused to go to the bathroom," but it was an older language that was my fundamental strength.

In my childhood, the language we all spoke was Acoma, and it was a struggle to maintain it against the outright threats of corporal punishment, ostracism, and the invocation that it would impede our progress towards Americanization. Children in school were punished and looked upon with disdain if they did not speak and learn English quickly and smoothly, and so I learned it. It has occurred to me that I learned English simply because I was forced to, as so many other Indian children were. But I know, also, there was another reason, and this was that I loved language, the sound, meaning, and magic of language. Language opened up vistas of the world around me, and it allowed me to discover knowledge that would not be possible for me to know without the use of language. Later, when I began to experiment with and explore language in poetry and fiction, I allowed that a portion of that impetus was because I had come to know English through forceful acculturation. Nevertheless, the underlying force was the beauty and poetic power of language in its many forms that instilled in me the desire to become a user of language as a writer, singer, and storyteller. Significantly, it was the Acoma language, which I don't use enough of today, that inspired me to become a writer. The concepts, values, and philosophy contained in my original language and the struggle it has faced have determined my life and vision as a writer.

In Deetziyamah, I discovered the world of the Acoma land and people firsthand through my parents, sisters and brothers, and my own perceptions, voiced through all that encompasses the oral tradition, which is ageless for any culture. It is a small village, even smaller years ago, and like other Indian communities it is wealthy with its knowledge of daily event, history, and social system, all that make up a people who have a many-dimensioned heritage. Our family lived in a two-room home (built by my grandfather some years after he and my grandmother moved with their daughters from Old Acoma), which my father added rooms to later. I remember my father's work at enlarging our home for our growing family. He was a skilled stoneworker, like many other men of an older Pueblo generation who worked with standstone and mud mortar to build their homes and pueblos. It takes time, persistence, patience, and the belief that the walls that come to stand will do so for a long, long time, perhaps even forever. I like to think that by helping to mix mud and carry stone for my father and other elders I managed to bring that influence into my consciousness as a writer.

Both my mother and my father were good storytellers and singers (as my mother is to this day—my father died in 1978), and for their generation, which was born soon after the turn of the century, they were relatively educated in the American system. Catholic missionaries had taken both of them as children to a parochial boarding school far from Acoma, and they imparted their discipline for study and quest for education to us children when we started school. But it was their indigenous sense of gaining knowledge that was most meaningful to me. Acquiring knowledge about life was above all the most important item; it was a value that one had to have in order to be fulfilled personally and on behalf of his community. And this they insisted upon imparting through the oral tradition as they told their children about our native history and our community and culture and our "stories." These stories were common knowledge of act, event, and behavior in a close-knit pueblo. It was knowledge about how one was to make a living through work that benefited his family and everyone else.

Because we were a subsistence farming people, or at least tried to be, I learned to plant, hoe weeds, irrigate, and cultivate corn, chili, pumpkins, beans. Through counsel and advice I came to know that the rain which provided water was a blessing, gift, and symbol and that it was the land which provided for our lives. It was the stories and songs which provided the knowledge that I was woven into the intricate web that was my Acoma life. In our garden and our cornfields I learned about the seasons, growth cycles of cultivated plants, what one had to think and feel about the land; and at home I became aware of how we must care for each other: all of this was encompassed in an intricate relationship which had to be maintained in order that life continue. After supper on many occasions my father would bring out his drum and sing as we, the children, danced to themes about the rain, hunting, land, and people. It was all that is contained within the language of oral tradition that made me explicitly aware of a yet unarticulated urge to write, to tell what I had learned and was learning and what it all meant to me.

My grandfather was old already when I came to know him. I was only one of his many grandchildren, but I would go with him to get wood for our households, to the garden to chop weeds, and to his sheep camp to help care for his sheep. I don't remember his exact words, but I know they were about how we must sacredly concern ourselves with the people and the holy earth. I know his words were about how we must regard ourselves and others with compassion and love; I know that his knowledge was vast, as a medicine man and an elder of his kiva, and I listened as a boy should. My grandfather represented for me a link to the past that is important for me to hold in my memory because it is not only memory but knowledge that substantiates my present existence. He and the grandmothers and grandfathers before him thought about us as they lived, confirmed in their belief of a continuing life, and they brought our present beings into existence by the beliefs they held. The consciousness of that belief is what informs my present concerns with language, poetry, and fiction.

My first poem was for Mother's Day when I was in the fifth grade, and it was the first poem that was ever published, too, in the Skull Valley School newsletter. Of course I don't remember how the juvenile poem went, but it must have been certain in its expression of love and reverence for the woman who was the most important person in my young life. The poem didn't signal any prophecy of my future as a poet, but it must have come from the forming idea that there were things one could do with language and writing. My mother, years later, remembers how I was a child who always told stories—that is, tall tales—who always had explanations for things probably better left unspoken, and she says that I also liked to perform in school plays. In remembering, I do know that I was coming to that age when the emotions and thoughts in me began to moil to the surface. There was much to experience and express in that age when youth has a precociousness that is broken easily or made to flourish. We were a poor family, always on the verge of financial disaster, though our parents always managed to feed us and keep us in clothing. We had the problems, unfortunately ordinary, of many Indian families who face poverty on a daily basis, never enough of anything, the feeling of a denigrating self-consciousness, alcoholism in the family and community, the feeling that something was falling apart though we tried desperately to hold it all together.

My father worked for the railroad for many years as a laborer and later as a welder. We moved to Skull Valley, Arizona, for one year in the early 1950s, and it was then that I first came in touch with a non-Indian, non-Acoma world. Skull Valley was a farming and ranching community, and my younger brothers and sisters and I went to a one-room school. I had never really had much contact with white people except from a careful and suspicious distance, but now here I was, totally surrounded by them, and there was nothing to do but bear the experience and learn from it. Although I perceived there was not much difference between *them* and *us* in certain respects, there was a distinct feeling that we were not the same either. This thought had been inculcated in me, especially by an Acoma expression—*Gaimuu Mericano*—that spoke of the "fortune" of being an American. In later years as a social activist and committed writer, I would try to offer a strong positive view of our collective Indianness through my writing. Nevertheless, my father was an inadequately paid laborer, and we were far from our home land for economic-social reasons, and my feelings and thoughts about that experience during that time would become a part of how I became a writer.

Soon after, I went away from my home and family to go to boarding school, first in Santa Fe and then in Albuquerque. This was in the 1950s, and this had been the case for the past half-century for Indians:

we had to leave home in order to become truly American by joining the mainstream, which was deemed to be the proper course of our lives. On top of this was termination, a U.S. government policy which dictated that Indians sever their relationship to the federal government and remove themselves from their lands and go to American cities for jobs and education. It was an era which bespoke the intent of U.S. public policy that Indians were no longer to be Indians. Naturally, I did not perceive this in any analytical or purposeful sense; rather, I felt an unspoken anxiety and resentment against unseen forces that determined our destiny to be un-Indian, embarrassed and uncomfortable with our grandparents' customs and strictly held values. We were to set our goals as American working men and women, singlemindedly industrious, patriotic, and unquestioning, building for a future which ensured that the U.S. was the greatest nation in the world. I felt fearfully uneasy with this, for by then I felt the loneliness, alienation, and isolation imposed upon me by the separation from my family, home, and community.

Something was happening; I could see that in my years at Catholic school and the U.S. Indian school. I remembered my grandparents' and parents' words: educate yourself in order to help your people. In that era and the generation who had the same experience I had, there was an unspoken vow: we were caught in a system inexorably, and we had to learn that system well in order to fight back. Without the motive of a fight-back we would not be able to survive as the people our heritage had lovingly bequeathed us. My diaries and notebooks began then, and though none have survived to the present, I know they contained the varied moods of a youth filled with loneliness, anger, and discomfort that seemed to have unknown causes. Yet at the same time, I realize now, I was coming to know myself clearly in a way that I would later articulate in writing. My love of language, which allowed me to deal with the world, to delve into it, to experiment and discover, held for me a vision of awe and wonder, and by then grammar teachers had noticed I was a good speller, used verbs and tenses correctly, and wrote complete sentences. Although I imagine that they might have surmised this as unusual for an Indian student whose original language was not English, I am grateful for their perception and attention.

During the latter part of that era in the 1950s of Indian termination and the Cold War, a portion of which still exists today, there were the beginnings of a bolder and more vocalized resistance against the current U.S. public policies of repression, racism, and cultural ethnocide. It seemed to be inspired by the civil rights movement led by black people in the U.S. and by decolonization and liberation struggles worldwide. Indian people were being relocated from their rural homelands at an astonishingly devastating rate, yet at the same time they resisted the U.S. effort by maintaining determined ties with their heritage, returning often to their native communities and establishing Indian centers in the cities they were removed to. Indian rural communities, such as Acoma Pueblo, insisted on their land claims and began to initiate legal battles in the areas of natural and social, political and economic human rights. By the retention and the inspiration of our native heritage, values, philosophies, and language, we would know ourselves as a strong and enduring people. Having a modest and latent consciousness of this as a teenager, I began to write about the experience of being Indian in America. Although I had only a romanticized image of what a writer was, which came from the pulp rendered by American popular literature, and I really didn't know anything about writing, I sincerely felt a need to say things, to speak, to release the energy of the impulse to help my people.

My writing in my late teens and early adulthood was fashioned after the American short stories and poetry taught in the high schools of the 1940s and 1950s, but by the 1960s, after I had gone to college and dropped out and served in the military, I began to develop topics and themes from my Indian background. The experience in my village of Deetziyamah and Acoma Pueblo was readily accessible. I had grown up within the oral tradition of speech, social and religious ritual, elders' counsel and advice, countless and endless stories, everyday event, and the visual art that was symbolically representative of life all around. My mother was a potter of the well-known Acoma clayware, a traditional art form that had been passed to her from her mother and the generations of mothers before. My father carved figures from wood and did beadwork. This was not unusual, as Indian people know; there was always some kind of artistic endeavor that people set themselves to, although they did not necessarily articulate it as "Art" in the sense of Western civilization. One lived and expressed an artful life, whether it was in ceremonial singing and dancing, architecture, painting, speaking, or in the way one's social-cultural life was structured. When I turned my attention to my own heritage, I did so because this was my identity, the substance of who I was, and I wanted to write about what that meant. My desire was to write about the integrity and dignity of an Indian identity, and at the same time I wanted to look at what this was within the context of an America that had too often denied its Indian heritage.

To a great extent my writing has a natural political-cultural bent simply because I was nurtured intellectually and emotionally within an atmosphere of Indian resistance. Aacquu did not die in 1598 when it was burned and razed by European conquerors, nor did the people become hopeless when their children were taken away to U.S. schools far from home and new ways were imposed upon them. The *Aaquumeh hano*, despite losing much of their land and surrounded by a foreign civilization, have not lost sight of their native heritage. This is the factual case with most other Indian peoples, and the clear explanation for this has been the fight-back we have found it necessary to wage. At times, in the past, it was outright armed struggle, like that of present-day Indians in Central and South America with whom we must identify; currently, it is often in the legal arena, and it is in the field of literature. In 1981, when I was invited to the White House for an event cel-

279

ebrating American poets and poetry, I did not immediately accept the invitation. I questioned myself about the possibility that I was merely being exploited as an Indian, and I hedged against accepting. But then I recalled the elders going among our people in the poor days of the 1950s, asking for donations—a dollar here and there, a sheep, perhaps a piece of pottery—in order to finance a trip to the nation's capital. They were to make another countless appeal on behalf of our people, to demand justice, to reclaim lost land even though there was only spare hope they would be successful. I went to the White House realizing that I was to do no less than they and those who had fought in the Pueblo Revolt of 1680, and I read my poems and sang songs that were later described as "guttural" by a Washington, D.C., newspaper. I suppose it is more or less understandable why such a view of Indian literature is held by many, and it is also clear why there should be a political stand taken in my writing and those of my sister and brother Indian writers.

The 1960s and afterward have been an invigorating and liberating period for Indian people. It has been only a little more than twenty years since Indian writers began to write and publish extensively, but we are writing and publishing more and more; we can only go forward. We come from an ageless, continuing oral tradition that informs us of our values, concepts, and notions as native people, and it is amazing how much of this tradition is ingrained so deeply in our contemporary writing, considering the brutal efforts of cultural repression that was not long ago outright U.S. policy. We were not to speak our languages, practice our spiritual beliefs, or accept the values of our past generations; and we were discouraged from pressing for our natural rights as Indian human beings. In spite of the fact that there is to some extent the same repression today, we persist and insist in living, believing, hoping, loving, speaking, and writing as Indians. This is embodied in the language we know and share in our writing. We have always had this language, and it is the language, spoken and unspoken, that determines our existence, that brought our grandmothers and grandfathers and ourselves into being in order that there be a continuing life.

## QUESTIONS

*Looking at Ideas:*

1. What two reasons does Ortiz give to explain why he learned English? Which language inspired him to become a writer?

2. Why were the stories that Ortiz's family told him important to the development of his self-concept and his identity as a writer?

3. In what ways does Ortiz integrate the experiences of his early life as an American and a Native American? Why and how does Ortiz learn to fight back?

4. What conflicting feelings does Ortiz have about accepting the invitation to the event celebrating American poets and poetry at the White House

in 1981? Why does he finally decide to attend? Do you think he made the right decision?

*Looking at Strategies:*

1. Ortiz explains why he wrote a childhood poem, notebooks, and adolescent stories. What was his purpose in writing this essay?
2. Discuss several of Ortiz's examples that give you a good sense of his heritage.
3. What is the tone of this essay? Identify a passage that exemplifies Ortiz's voice and indicates his assessment of his political position as a Native American.

*Looking at Connections:*

1. Compare and contrast Rodriguez's and Ortiz's attitudes about the importance and role of a writer's first language, family, and heritage.
2. Contrast Steele's perspective on the changing role of blacks in American society to Ortiz's on the changing role of Native Americans in American society. How do you think Ortiz would respond to Steele's concept of the disbelieving anti-self?

*Suggestions for Writing:*

1. Write an essay in which you define and argue either for or against the need for bilingualism.
2. Write an essay in which you define the concept of "tribe"; then discuss whether a tribal identity is still possible in a mass society like that of the United States.
3. The existence of a multicultural society creates many tensions, including negative feelings and stereotypes which often arise from ignorance of the traditions and beliefs of cultures that differ from the majority culture. Write an essay in which you discuss one or two of the tensions created within a multicultural society and offer some ways to reduce them.

**JOURNAL ENTRY**

Write about a photograph or a home movie that evokes memories of your childhood.

**JUDITH ORTIZ COFER: "Silent Dancing"**  Judith Ortiz Cofer was born in Puerto Rico in 1952. When she was four, she emigrated with her family to the United States, where they settled in New Jersey. Cofer earned her B.A. from Augusta College and her M.A. from Florida Atlantic University. She has taught Spanish and English at several universities, including the University of Miami and the University of Georgia. Her publications include four books of poetry, one play, and two autobiographical works. In the following selection, "Silent Dancing," which is excerpted from *Silent Dancing: A Partial Remembrance of a Puerto Rican Childhood* (1990), Cofer frames the memories of her early childhood in New Jersey through her interpretation of a home video of a typical family party.

JUDITH ORTIZ COFER

# Silent Dancing

*We have a home movie of this party. Several times my mother and I have watched it together, and I have asked questions about the silent revellers coming in and out of focus. It is grainy and of short duration but a great visual aid to my first memory of life in Paterson at that time. And it is in color—the only complete scene in color I can recall from those years.*

We lived in Puerto Rico until my brother was born in 1954. Soon after, because of economic pressures on our growing family, my father joined the United States Navy. He was assigned to duty on a ship in Brooklyn Yard, New York City—a place of cement and steel that was to be his home base in the States until his retirement more than twenty years later. He left the Island first, tracking down his uncle who lived with his family across the Hudson River, in Paterson, New Jersey. There he found a tiny apartment in a huge apartment building that had once housed Jewish families and was just being transformed into a tenement by Puerto Ricans overflowing from New York City. In 1955 he sent for us. My mother was only twenty years old, I was not quite three, and my brother was a toddler when we arrived at *El Building,* as the place had been christened by its new residents.

My memories of life in Paterson during those first few years are in shades of gray. Maybe I was too young to absorb vivid colors and details, or to discriminate between the slate blue of the winter sky and the darker hues of the snowbearing clouds, but the single color washes over the whole period. The building we lived in was gray, the streets were gray with slush the first few months of my life there, the coat my father had bought for me was dark in color and too big. It sat heavily on my thin frame.

I do remember the way the heater pipes banged and rattled, startling all of us out of sleep until we got so used to the sound that we automatically either shut it out or raised our voices above the racket. The hiss from the valve punctuated my sleep, which has always been fitful, like an nonhuman presence in the room—the dragon sleeping at the entrance of my childhood. But the pipes were a connection to all the other lives being lived around us. Having come from a house made for a single family back in Puerto Rico—my mother's extended-family home—it was curious to know that strangers lived under our floor and above our heads, and that the heater pipe went through everyone's apartments. (My first spanking in Paterson came as a result of playing tunes on the pipes in my room to see if there would be an answer.) My mother was as new to this concept of beehive life as I was, but had been given strict orders by my father to keep the doors locked, the noise down, ourselves to ourselves.

It seems that Father had learned some painful lessons about prejudice while searching for an apartment in Paterson. Not until years later did I hear how much resistance he had encountered with landlords who were panicking at the influx of Latinos into a neighborhood that had been Jewish for a couple of generations. But it was the American phenomenon of ethnic turnover that was changing the urban core of Paterson, and the human flood could not be held back with an accusing finger.

"You Cuban?" the man had asked my father, pointing a finger at his name tag on the Navy uniform—even though my father had the fair skin and light brown hair of his northern Spanish family background and our name is as common in Puerto Rico as Johnson is in the U.S.

"No," my father had answered looking past the finger into his adversary's angry eyes, "I'm Puerto Rican."

"Same shit." And the door closed. My father could have passed as European, but we couldn't. My brother and I both have our mother's black hair and olive skin, and so we lived in El Building and visited our great-uncle and his fair children on the next block. It was their private joke that they were the German branch of the family. Not many years later that area too would be mainly Puerto Rican. It was as if the heart of the city map were being gradually colored in brown—*café-con-leche* brown. Our color.

*The movie opens with a sweep of the living room. It is "typical" immigrant Puerto Rican decor for the time: the sofa and chairs are square and hard-looking, upholstered in bright colors (blue and yellow in this instance) and covered in the transparent plastic that furniture salesmen then were adept at making women buy. The linoleum on the floor is light blue, and if it was subjected to spike heels as it was in most places, there were dime-sized indentations all over it that cannot be seen in this movie. The room is full of people dressed in mainly two colors: dark suits for the men, red dresses for the women. I have asked my mother why most of the women are in red that night, and she shrugs, "I don't remember. Just a coincidence." She doesn't have my obsession for assigning symbolism to everything.*

*The three women in red sitting on the couch are my mother, my eighteen-year-old cousin, and her brother's girlfriend. The "novia" is just up from the Island, which is apparent in her body language. She sits up formally, and her dress is carefully pulled over her knees. She is a pretty girl but her posture makes her look insecure, lost in her full-skirted red dress which she has carefully tucked around her to make room for my gorgeous cousin, her future sister-in-law. My cousin has grown up in Paterson and is in her last year of high school. She doesn't have a trace of what Puerto Ricans call "la mancha" (literally, the stain: the mark of the new immigrant—something about the posture, the voice, or the humble demeanor making it obvious to everyone that that person has just arrived on the mainland; has not yet acquired the polished look of the city dweller). My cousin is wearing a tight red-sequined cocktail dress. Her brown hair has been lightened with peroxide around the bangs, and she is holding a cigarette very expertly between her fingers, bringing it up to her mouth in a sensuous arc of her arm to her mouth as she talks animatedly with my mother, who has come up to sit between the two women, both only a few years younger than herself. My mother is somewhere halfway between the poles they represent in our culture.*

It became my father's obsession to get out of the barrio, and thus we were never permitted to form bonds with the place or with the people who lived there. Yet the building was a comfort to my mother, who never got over yearning for *la isla*. She felt surrounded by her language: the walls were thin, and voices speaking and arguing in Spanish could be heard all day. *Salsas* blasted out of radios turned on early in the morning and left on for company. Women seemed to cook rice and beans perpetually—the strong aroma of red kidney beans boiling permeated the hallways.

Though Father preferred that we do our grocery shopping at the supermarket when he came home on weekend leaves, my mother insisted that she could cook only with products whose labels she could read, and so, during the week, I accompanied her and my little brother to *La Bodega*—a hole-in-the-wall grocery store across the street from El Building. There we squeezed down three narrow aisles jammed with various products. Goya and Libby's—those were the trademarks trusted by her Mamá, and so my mother bought cans of Goya beans, soups and condiments. She bought little cans of Libby's fruit juices for us. And she bought Colgate toothpaste and Palmolive soap. (The final *e* is pronounced in both those products in Spanish, and for many years I believed that they were manufactured on the Island. I remember my surprise at first hearing a commercial on television for the toothpaste in which Colgate rhymed with "ate.") We would linger at La Bodega, for it was there that mother breathed best, taking in the familiar aromas of the foods she knew from Mamá's kitchen, and it was also there that she got to speak to the other women of El Building without violating out-right Father's dictates against fraternizing with our neighbors.

But he did his best to make our "assimilation" painless. I can still see him carrying a Christmas tree up several flights of stairs to our apartment, leaving a trail of aromatic pine. He carried it formally, as if it were a flag in a parade. We were the only ones in El Building that I knew of who got presents on both Christmas Day and on *Día de Reyes,* the day when the Three Kings brought gifts to Christ and to Hispanic children.

Our greatest luxury in El Building was having our own television set. It must have been a result of Father's guilty feelings over the isolation he had imposed on us, but we were one of the first families in the barrio to have one. My brother quickly became an avid watcher of Captain Kangaroo and Jungle Jim. I loved all the family series, and by the time I started first grade in school, I could have drawn a map of Middle America as exemplified by the lives of characters in "Father Knows Best," "The Donna Reed Show," "Leave It to Beaver," "My Three Sons," and (my favorite) "Bachelor Father," where John For-sythe treated his adopted teenage daughter like a princess because he was rich and had a Chinese houseboy to do everything for him. Com-pared to our neighbors in El Building, we were rich. My father's Navy check provided us with financial security and a standard of life that the factory workers envied. The only thing his money could not buy us was a place to live away from the barrio—his greatest wish and Mother's greatest fear.

*In the home movie the men are shown next, sitting around a card table set up in one corner of the living room, playing dominoes. The clack of the ivory pieces is a familiar sound. I heard it in many houses on the Island and in many apartments in Paterson. In "Leave It to Beaver," the Cleavers played bridge in every other episode; in my childhood, the men started every social occasion with a hotly debated round of dominoes: the women would sit around and watch, but they never participated in the games.*

*Here and there you can see a small child. Children were always brought to parties and, whenever they got sleepy, put to bed in the host's bedrooms. Babysitting was a concept unrecognized by the Puerto Rican women I knew: a responsible mother did not leave her children with any stranger. And in a culture where children are not considered intrusive, there is no need to leave the children at home. We went where our mother went.*

Of my pre-school years I have only impressions: the sharp bite of the wind in December as we walked with our parents towards the brightly lit stores downtown; how I felt like a stuffed doll in my heavy coat, boots and mittens; how good it was to walk into the five-and-dime and sit at the counter drinking hot chocolate.

On Saturdays our whole family would walk downtown to shop at the big department stores on Broadway. Mother bought all our clothes at Penney's and Sears, and she liked to buy her dresses at the women's specialty shops like Lerner's and Diana's. At some point we would go into Woolworth's and sit at the soda fountain to eat.

We never ran into other Latinos at these stores or eating out, and it became clear to me only years later that the women from El Building shopped mainly at other places—stores owned either by other Puerto Ricans, or by Jewish merchants who had philosophically accepted our presence in the city and decided to make us their good customers, if not neighbors and friends. These establishments were located not downtown, but in the blocks around our street, and they were referred to generically as *La Tienda, El Bazar, La Bodega, La Botánica.* Everyone knew what was meant. These were the stores where your face did not turn a clerk to stone, where your money was as green as anyone else's.

On New Year's Eve we were dressed up like child models in the Sears catalogue—my brother in a miniature man's suit and bow tie, and I in black patent leather shoes and a frilly dress with several layers of crinolines underneath. My mother wore a bright red dress that night, I remember, and spike heels; her long black hair hung to her waist. Father, who usually wore his Navy uniform during his short visits home, had put on a dark civilian suit for the occasion: we had been invited to his uncle's house for a big celebration. Everyone was excited because my mother's brother, Hernan—a bachelor who could indulge himself in such luxuries—had bought a movie camera which he would be trying out that night.

Even the home movie cannot fill in the sensory details such a gathering left imprinted in a child's brain. The thick sweetness of women's perfume mixing with the ever-present smells of food cooking in the kitchen: meat and plantain *pasteles,* the ubiquitous rice dish made special with pigeon peas—*gandules*—and seasoned with the precious *sofrito* sent up from the island by somebody's mother or smuggled in by a recent traveler. *Sofrito* was one of the items that women hoarded, since it was hardly ever in stock at La Bodega. It was the flavor of Puerto Rico.

The men drank Palo Viejo rum and some of the younger ones got weepy. The first time I saw a grown man cry was at a New Year's Eve party. He had been reminded of his mother by the smells in the kitchen. But what I remember most were the boiled *pasteles*—boiled plantain or yucca rectangles stuffed with corned beef or other meats, olives, and many other savory ingredients, all wrapped in banana leaves. Everyone had to fish one out with a fork. There was always a "trick" pastel—one without stuffing—and whoever got that one was the "New Year's Fool."

There was also the music. Long-playing albums were treated like precious china in these homes. Mexican recordings were popular, but the songs that brought tears to my mother's eyes were sung by the melancholic Daniel Santos, whose life as a drug addict was the stuff of legend. Felipe Rodríguez was a particular favorite of couples. He sang about faithless women and broken-hearted men. There is a snatch of a lyric that has stuck in my mind like a needle on a worn groove: *"De piedra ha de ser mi cama, de piedra la cabecera . . . la mujer que a mi me quiera . . . ha de quererme de veras. Ay, Ay, corazón, ¿por qué no amas . . . ?"* I must have heard it a thousand times since the idea of a bed made of stone, and its connection to love, first troubled me with its disturbing images.

The five-minute home movie ends with people dancing in a circle. The creative filmmaker must have asked them to do that so that they could file past him. It is both comical and sad to watch silent dancing. Since there is no justification for the absurd movements that music provides for some of us, people appear frantic, their faces embarrassingly intense. It's as if you were watching sex. Yet for years, I've had dreams in the form of this home movie. In a recurring scene, familiar faces push themselves forward into my mind's eye, plastering their features into distorted close-ups. And I'm asking them: "Who is she? Who is the woman I don't recognize? Is she an aunt? Somebody's wife? Tell me who she is. Tell me who these people are."

"No, see the beauty mark on her cheek as big as a hill on the lunar landscape of her face—well, that runs in the family. The women on your father's side of the family wrinkle early; it's the price they pay for that fair skin. The young girl with the green stain on her wedding dress is *La Novia*—just up from the Island. See, she lowers her eyes as she approaches the camera like she's supposed to. Decent girls never look you directly in the face. *Humilde,* humble, a girl should express humility in all her actions. She will make a good wife for your cousin. He should consider himself lucky to have met her only weeks after she arrived here. If he marries her quickly, she will make him a good Puerto Rican-style wife; but if he waits too long, she will be corrupted by the city, just like your cousin there."

"She means me. I do what I want. This is not some primitive island I live on. Do they expect me to wear a black *mantilla* on my head and go to mass every day? Not me. I'm an American woman and I will do as I please. I can type faster than anyone in my senior class at Central High, and I'm going to be a secretary to a lawyer when I graduate. I can pass for an American girl anywhere—I've tried it—at least for Italian, anyway. I never speak Spanish in public. I hate these parties, but I wanted the dress. I look better than any of these *humildes* here. My life is going to be different. I have an American boyfriend. He is older and has a car. My parents don't know it, but I sneak out of the house late at night sometimes to be with him. If I marry him, even my name will be American. I hate rice and beans. It's what makes these women fat."

"Your *prima* is pregnant by that man she's been sneaking around with. Would I lie to you? I'm your great-uncle's common-law wife—the one he abandoned on the Island to marry your cousin's mother. I was not invited to this party, but I came anyway. I came to tell you that story about your cousin that you've always wanted to hear. Remember that comment your mother made to a neighbor that has always haunted you? The only thing you heard was your cousin's name and then you saw your mother pick up your doll from the couch and say: 'It was as big as this doll when they flushed it down the toilet.' This image has bothered you for years, hasn't it? You had nightmares about babies be-

287

ing flushed down the toilet, and you wondered why anyone would do such a horrible thing. You didn't dare ask your mother about it. She would only tell you that you had not heard her right and yell at you for listening to adult conversations. But later, when you were old enough to know about abortions, you suspected. I am here to tell you that you were right. Your cousin was growing an *Americanito* in her belly when this movie was made. Soon after she put something long and pointy into her pretty self, thinking maybe she could get rid of the problem before breakfast and still make it to her first class at the high school. Well, *Niña*, her screams could be heard downtown. Your aunt, her Mamá, who had been a midwife on the Island, managed to pull the little thing out. Yes, they probably flushed it down the toilet, what else could they do with it—give it a Christian burial in a little white casket with blue bows and ribbons? Nobody wanted that baby—least of all the father, a teacher at her school with a house in West Paterson that he was filling with real children, and a wife who was a natural blond.

Girl, the scandal sent your uncle back to the bottle. And guess where your cousin ended up? Irony of ironies. She was sent to a village in Puerto Rico to live with a relative on her mother's side: a place so far away from civilization that you have to ride a mule to reach it. A real change in scenery. She found a man there. Women like that cannot live without male company. But believe me, the men in Puerto Rico know how to put a saddle on a woman like her. *La Gringa,* they call her. Ha, ha, ha. *La Gringa* is what she always wanted to be. . . ."

The old woman's mouth becomes a cavernous black hole I fall into. And as I fall, I can feel the reverberations of her laughter. I hear the echoes of her last mocking words: *La Gringa, La Gringa!* And the conga line keeps moving silently past me. There is no music in my dream for the dancers.

When Odysseus visits Hades asking to see the spirit of his mother, he makes an offering of sacrificial blood, but since all of the souls crave an audience with the living, he has to listen to many of them before he can ask questions. I, too, have to hear the dead and the forgotten speak in my dream. Those who are still part of my life remain silent, going around and around in their dance. The others keep pressing their faces forward to say things about the past.

My father's uncle is last in line. He is dying of alcoholism, shrunken and shriveled like a monkey, his face is a mass of wrinkles and broken arteries. As he comes closer I realize that in his features I can see my whole family. If you were to stretch that rubbery flesh, you could find my father's face, and deep within *that* face—mine. I don't want to look into those eyes ringed in purple. In a few years he will retreat into silence, and take a long, long time to die. *Move back, Tío,* I tell him. *I don't want to hear what you have to say. Give the dancers room to move, soon it will be midnight. Who is the New Year's Fool this time?*

# QUESTIONS

*Chapter Five:*
*The Family in*
*a Multicultural*
*Society*

*Looking at Ideas:*

1. After her life in Puerto Rico, of what contrasts in life-style is Cofer most conscious when she first arrives in Paterson, New Jersey? What kind of prejudice does Cofer's father encounter when he tries to find a place for his family to live? Did your family or other families you know ever have to face similar types of prejudice in relocating?

2. What do Cofer and her brother learn about mainstream American family life from watching television? How does the knowledge she acquires from watching these programs affect her assimilation into American life and her evaluation of her own family's life-style?

3. Why does Cofer's father forbid his family to shop or socialize in the neighborhood? Why does Cofer's mother feel more comfortable at the neighborhood markets? Why does she violate her husband's "dictates"? With whose point of view do you feel most sympathetic? Which parent's point of view does Cofer adopt as she matures into womanhood?

4. Why is Cofer haunted by the dream-story her great-aunt tells about *La Gringa?* In what ways is *La Gringa's* story a symbol of traditional Puerto Rican values by which Cofer does not want to be limited?

5. Explain the meaning of the recurring dream that Cofer has when she remembers the silent dancing at the end of the home movie.

*Looking at Strategies:*

1. Cofer says she has an "obsession for assigning symbolism to everything." Discuss three symbols that she develops in her memoir. How do these symbols help you understand her experience of growing up in a Puerto Rican neighborhood? Why are her symbols effective?

2. Why does Cofer use italics when she writes about the memories associated with the home movie of her life in Paterson? Is this strategy effective? Why?

3. "Even the home movie cannot fill in the sensory details such a gathering left imprinted in a child's brain." How does Cofer's use of language help her to realize the sensory dimension of her childhood? Give several examples of Cofer's images and details that are especially effective.

4. Why is the selection entitled "Silent Dancing"? What meaning does Cofer read into the silent dancing that she watches at the end of the home movie? What meaning do you read into the image?

*Looking at Connections:*

1. Compare and contrast Cofer's and Rodriguez's process of assimilating into the American way of life. Do they have similar reasons for rejecting the values of their original culture? Do they find comfort and/or are they fearful when contemplating the life-styles of their relatives?

2. Compare and contrast Cofer's and Steele's perspectives on why acceptance into American culture can be frustrating, difficult, and sometimes destructive. Do they both feel that inner conflicts are more inhibiting than the culture of middle America and the American dream in which

289

there is an implicit prejudice against immigrants and outsiders? Explain your response.

*Suggestions for Writing:*

1. Write an essay in which you define what the term *assimilation* means to you through discussing your own family's degree of assimilation into mainstream American life. Like Cofer, you might want to start with an especially vivid memory of childhood that embodies the conflicts you felt about your family's ability to adopt the American way of life and to fit into the mythical mainstream of traditional American values.

2. How do you think the different family cultures within a multi-ethnic society should interact? Do you think families should be more concerned with maintaining their own separateness and traditional heritage or with blending into the mainstream? How can the different cultures in America develop respect for one another's individuality? Write an essay focusing on several particular experiences and issues while arguing in favor of your position.

3. Write an essay in which you compare two versions of the same folktale from different cultures. (If you don't have a selection of folktales at home, you can visit your neighborhood library, where you will find collections of tales from different countries in the adult section and various versions of individual tales in the children's section.) Explore and contrast the ways in which the culture-bound definitions of self, family, and community are expressed by each tale. Does each tale value the family for different reasons?

**AMY TAN: "Four Directions"**  For biographical information about Amy Tan,
see the introduction to her story, "The Scar," in Chapter One. As you read the
following selection from *The Joy Luck Club,* notice the humorous and ironic
ways in which Tan explores the possibilities for miscommunication when families and potential families from different cultures share a meal together.

AMY TAN

# Four Directions

After much thought, I came up with a brilliant plan. I concocted a way
for Rich to meet my mother and win her over. In fact, I arranged it so
my mother would want to cook a meal especially for him. I had some
help from Auntie Suyuan. Auntie Su was my mother's friend from way
back. They were very close, which meant they were ceaselessly tormenting each other with boasts and secrets. And I gave Auntie Su a
secret to boast about.

After walking through North Beach one Sunday, I suggested to
Rich that we stop by for a surprise visit to my Auntie Su and Uncle
Canning. They lived on Leavenworth, just a few blocks west of my
mother's apartment. It was late afternoon, just in time to catch Auntie
Su preparing Sunday dinner.

"Stay! Stay!" she had insisted.

"No, no. It's just that we were walking by," I said.

"Already cooked enough for you. See? One soup, four dishes. You
don't eat it, only have to throw it away. Wasted!"

How could we refuse? Three days later, Auntie Suyuan had a
thank-you letter from Rich and me. "Rich said it was the best Chinese
food he has ever tasted," I wrote.

And the next day, my mother called me, to invite me to a belated
birthday dinner for my father. My brother Vincent was bringing his
girlfriend, Lisa Lum. I could bring a friend, too.

I knew she would do this, because cooking was how my mother expressed her love, her pride, her power, her proof that she knew more

291

than Auntie Su. "Just be sure to tell her later that her cooking was the best you ever tasted, that it was far better than Auntie Su's," I told Rich. "Believe me."

The night of the dinner, I sat in the kitchen watching her cook, waiting for the right moment to tell her about our marriage plans, that we had decided to get married next July, about seven months away. She was chopping eggplant into wedges, chattering at the same time about Auntie Suyuan: "She can only cook looking at a recipe. My instructions are in my fingers. I know what secret ingredients to put in just by using my nose!" And she was slicing with such a ferocity, seemingly inattentive to her sharp cleaver, that I was afraid her fingertips would become one of the ingredients of the red-cooked eggplant and shredded pork dish.

I was hoping she would say something first about Rich. I had seen her expression when she opened the door, her forced smile as she scrutinized him from head to toe, checking her appraisal of him against that already given to her by Auntie Suyuan. I tried to anticipate what criticisms she would have.

Rich was not only *not* Chinese, he was a few years younger than I was. And unfortunately, he looked much younger with his curly red hair, smooth pale skin, and the splash of orange freckles across his nose. He was a bit on the short side, compactly built. In his dark business suits, he looked nice but easily forgettable, like somebody's nephew at a funeral. Which was why I didn't notice him the first year we worked together at the firm. But my mother noticed everything.

"So what do you think of Rich?" I finally asked, holding my breath.

She tossed the eggplant in the hot oil and it made a loud, angry hissing sound. "So many spots on his face," she said.

I could feel the pinpricks on my back. "They're freckles. Freckles are good luck, you know," I said a bit too heatedly in trying to raise my voice above the din of the kitchen.

"Oh?" she said innocently.

"Yes, the more spots the better. Everybody knows that."

She considered this a moment and then smiled and spoke in Chinese: "Maybe this is true. When you were young, you got the chicken pox. So many spots, you had to stay home for ten days. So lucky, you thought."

I couldn't save Rich in the kitchen. And I couldn't save him later at the dinner table.

He had brought a bottle of French wine, something he did not know my parents could not appreciate. My parents did not even own wineglasses. And then he also made the mistake of drinking not one but two frosted glasses full, while everybody else had a half-inch "just for taste."

When I offered Rich a fork, he insisted on using the slippery ivory chopsticks. He held them splayed like the knock-kneed legs of an ostrich while picking up a large chunk of sauce-coated eggplant. Halfway between his plate and his open mouth, the chunk fell on his crisp white shirt and then slid into his crotch. It took several minutes to get Shoshana to stop shrieking with laughter.

And then he had helped himself to big portions of the shrimp and snow peas, not realizing he should have taken only a polite spoonful, until everybody had had a morsel.

He had declined the sautéed new greens, the tender and expensive leaves of bean plants plucked before the sprouts turn into beans. And Shoshana refused to eat them also, pointing to Rich: "He didn't eat them! He didn't eat them!"

He thought he was being polite by refusing seconds, when he should have followed my father's example, who made a big show of taking small portions of seconds, thirds, and even fourths, always saying he could not resist another bite of something or other, and then groaning that he was so full he thought he would burst.

But the worst was when Rich criticized my mother's cooking, and he didn't even know what he had done. As is the Chinese cook's custom, my mother always made disparaging remarks about her own cooking. That night she chose to direct it toward her famous steamed pork and preserved vegetable dish, which she always served with special pride.

"Ai! This dish not salty enough, no flavor," she complained, after tasting a small bite. "It is too bad to eat."

This was our family's cue to eat some and proclaim it the best she had ever made. But before we could do so, Rich said, "You know, all it needs is a little soy sauce." And he proceeded to pour a riverful of the salty black stuff on the platter, right before my mother's horrified eyes.

And even though I was hoping throughout the dinner that my mother would somehow see Rich's kindness, his sense of humor and boyish charm, I knew he had failed miserably in her eyes.

Rich obviously had had a different opinion on how the evening had gone. When we got home that night, after we put Shoshana to bed, he said modestly, "Well. I think we hit it off *A-o-kay.*" He had the look of a dalmation, panting, loyal, waiting to be petted.

"Uh-hmm," I said. I was putting on an old nightgown, a hint that I was not feeling amorous. I was still shuddering, remembering how Rich had firmly shaken both my parents' hands with that same easy familiarity he used with nervous new clients. "Linda, Tim," he said, "we'll see you again soon, I'm sure." My parents' names are Lindo and Tin Jong, and nobody, except a few older family friends, ever calls them by their first names.

"So what did she say when you told her?" And I knew he was referring to our getting married. I had told Rich earlier that I would tell my mother first and let her break the news to my father.

"I never had a chance," I said, which was true. How could I have told my mother I was getting married, when at every possible moment we were alone, she seemed to remark on how much expensive wine Rich liked to drink, or how pale and ill he looked, or how sad Shoshana seemed to be.

293

Rich was smiling. "How long does it take to say, Mom, Dad, I'm getting married?"

"You don't understand. You don't understand my mother."

Rich shook his head. "Whew! You can say that again. Her English was *so* bad. You know, when she was talking about that dead guy showing up on *Dynasty,* I thought she was talking about something that happened in China a long time ago."

## QUESTIONS

*Looking at Ideas:*

1. How does the narrator manage to get her mother to invite her boyfriend over for dinner? Why doesn't she simply ask her mother to invite Rich? What does the narrator want to accomplish at the meal? Why does her "brilliant plan" fail?

2. Why is the mother critical of Rich? Refer to specific passages in the text to support your answer. How do the mother's criticisms affect the narrator? Why is she influenced by her mother's judgments?

3. Why does Rich fail to see that he has actually offended the narrator's mother? Do you think Rich is simply insensitive or is his misreading of the conversation during the meal a consequence of his lack of understanding of Chinese values in general and of the narrator's family in particular?

4. After reading this scene, what do you think the narrator should and will do? Will she go ahead and marry Rich? Will she pay more careful attention to her mother's point of view?

*Looking at Strategies:*

1. How does Tan use dialogue to develop the humorous and ironic tone and meaning of this scene? Refer specifically to the text to support your response.

2. Examine several humorous images that Tan develops in this scene to make the miscommunication between the narrator's family and the boyfriend more dramatic.

3. Point to several moments when Rich interprets the narrator's and her mother's comments in a strictly literal sense although their intentions are not simply literal. Why are these exchanges humorous? How do they point to the different values held by the two respective cultures?

*Looking at Connections:*

1. Contrast Tan's and Cofer's attitudes about the importance of native language and culture.

2. How is Tan's approach to exploring the conflicts within a multicultural family different from the approach of other writers included in this section? Which writer's approach and style do you prefer and why?

*Suggestions for Writing:*

1. Describe a humorous and/or ironic scene in your family, or in a family you know well, that reflects the differing cultural values held by the

family members. After describing the scene, analyze the reasons for the miscommunication and discuss whether or not you believe the differing points of view can be resolved.

2. Do you think intimate relationships become more difficult when the partners come from different ethnic or religious backgrounds? If you believe such relationships can succeed, how can the difficulties be reconciled or overcome? Refer to specific examples to support your response.

3. Write an essay in which you compare attributes of family life as revealed in two of the selections in this chapter. How do the families portrayed in these selections represent unique cultures within American mainstream culture? What did you learn about the nature of the family from developing your comparison?

---

**JOURNAL ENTRY**

Write about a place that feels safe to you and that helps you to affirm your sense of ethnic or cultural identity.

---

**CHITRA DIVAKARUNI: "Indian Movie, New Jersey"**  Chitra Divakaruni was born in Calcutta, India. She completed her B.A. at the University of Calcutta (1976) and her Ph.D. in English Literature at the University of California at Berkeley (1985). Chitra Divakaruni lives in the San Francisco Bay area with her husband and teaches composition, creative writing, and literature at Foothill College, where she is a codirector of the annual national creative writing conference. Her poems, short stories, and translations have appeared in numerous magazines and anthologies in India and the United States. She has published three books of poetry: *Dark Like the River* (1987), *The Reason for Nasturtiums* (1990), and *The Black Candle* (1991). As you read "Indian Movie: New Jersey," which first appeared in the *Indiana Review* (1991), think about the ways in which Divakaruni contrasts the hopes and expectations of the Indian immigrants with the realities of their daily lives.

CHITRA DIVAKARUNI

# *Indian Movie, New Jersey*

Not like the white filmstars, all rib
and gaunt cheekbone, the Indian sex-goddess
smiles plumply from behind a flowery
branch. Below her brief red skirt, her thighs
are satisfying-solid, redeeming
as tree trunks. She swings her hips
and the men-viewers whistle. The lover-hero
dances in to a song, his lip-sync
a little off, but no matter, we
know the words already and sing along.
It is safe here, the day
golden and cool so no one sweats,
roses on every bush and the Dal Lake
clean again.
                    The sex-goddess switches
to thickened English to emphasize
a joke. We laugh and clap. Here
we need not be embarrassed by words
dropping like lead pellets into foreign ears.

The flickering movie-light
wipes from our faces years of America, sons
who want mohawks and refuse to run
the family store, daughters who date
on the sly.
   When at the end the hero
dies for his friend who also
loves the sex-goddess and now can marry her,
we weep, understanding. Even the men
clear their throats to say, "What *qurbani!*[1]
What *dosti!*"[2] After, we mill around
unwilling to leave, exchange greetings
and good news: a new gold chain, a trip
to India. We do not speak
of motel raids, cancelled permits, stones
thrown through glass windows, daughters and sons
raped by Dotbusters.[3]
   In this dim foyer
we can pull around us the faint, comforting smell
of incense and *pakoras,*[4] can arrange
our children's marriages with hometown boys and girls,
open a franchise, win a million
in the mail. We can retire
in India, a yellow two-storeyed house
with wrought-iron gates, our own
Ambassador car. Or at least
move to a rich white suburb, Summerfield
or Fort Lee, with neighbors that will
talk to us. Here while the film-songs still echo
in the corridors and restrooms, we can trust
in movie truths: sacrifice, success, love and luck,
the America that was supposed to be.

## QUESTIONS

*Looking at Ideas:*

1. The poem implies that there is a generation gap between the Indian immigrants who are watching the film and the children of these immigrants. Refer to lines that establish this sense of generation gap. What
reasons does the poet offer to account for the generation gap? What
reasons can you add?

2. The narrator realizes that while viewing the film she and her Indian
friends are only escaping from the troubling and disappointing realities

[1] *qurbani:* sacrifice
[2] *dosti:* friendship
[3] *Dotbusters:* growing anti-Indian gangs in New Jersey
[4] *pakoras:* fried appetizers

of their lives in America. Why do they attend? According to the poem, what benefits are there in this form of escapism?

3. What is the relationship between the films the Indian immigrants go to see and their dreams of "success, love and luck" that they expected to realize in America?

4. What differences between American and Indian values are implied in the poem? Refer to the text to support your response.

5. How does the speaker of the poem define the dreams of the Indian immigrants?

*Looking at Strategies:*

1. Why does Divakaruni begin by contrasting the white film stars to the Indian film heroine? What is the effect of this contrast?

2. Why does the poet use Indian words? What is the effect of this technique? The poet also uses American slang. What is the effect of the juxtaposition of the slang and the native Indian words?

3. Like many immigrants, the Indians in this poem feel embarrassed by their use of language. What specific images does the poet create to clarify and emphasize this idea? Why does the narrator share their embarrassment?

*Looking at Connections:*

1. Compare and contrast Chitra Divakaruni's, Amy Tan's, and Judith Ortiz Cofer's view of the generation gap as it is reflected in their respective cultures.

2. In what different ways do Chitra Divakaruni and Richard Rodriquez value their cultural legacy? Compare their views on the value of cultural assimilation.

*Suggestions for Writing:*

1. Based on your own experiences, observations, and exposure to the media and readings, write an essay in which you explain why you think immigrant families face generation-gap conflicts. Discuss several typical issues that focus the conflicts, and use examples to support your explanations and analysis.

2. Write an essay in which you explore your own feelings of prejudice against individuals from another cultural background in your community. Contrast your expectations of family life with their culture's expectations of family life. Have thinking and writing about your prejudice helped you become more tolerant?

3. Write about a film that tries to define the immigrant experience through exploring the conflicts of an immigrant family in its process of assimilating into the American way of life. Was the film insightful? What conflicts did it define? How did it resolve these conflicts? Did you agree or disagree with the film's perspective and evaluation of the family's process of assimilation?

**JOSEPHINE RAMOS: "Growing Up Bilingual"**   Josephine Ramos grew up in Pasadena, California, in a lower-middle-class Mexican-American family. The first of her generation to attend college, she met students from many new cultures at college, which made her more aware of the uniqueness of her own culture, its importance, and the way it was being subtly reinterpreted through her new experiences. Josephine Ramos was especially interested in writing about her experiences as a bilingual citizen because she has met so many students in situations similar to hers. In the following essay, Ramos compares and contrasts her experiences as a bilingual student with Richard Rodriguez's, which are presented in his essay in this chapter.

*Chapter Five:*
*The Family in*
*a Multicultural*
*Society*

JOSEPHINE RAMOS

# *Growing Up Bilingual*

While reading "Public and Private Language," by Richard Rodriguez, I found a number of strong similarities to my own experiences of growing up in a bilingual Mexican-American family. Unlike Rodriguez, however, I have come to believe that learning to speak both languages has not alienated me from society nor my family, but rather has strengthened the connections I feel with my heritage. For me, learning Spanish was vital since it was the first step towards understanding the Mexican culture I was born into as well as the power base from which all of my family's interactions and traditions were built.

Unlike Rodriguez, learning English was not difficult for me since I learned both languages at home, speaking only in English to my father and only in Spanish to my mother. I suppose this is a special case, for, as with Richard Rodriguez, one language is usually learned first, at home. Later on, in a school setting, a second, "public" language may be studied. I still find it strange to think that I have always known two words for everything. However, when growing up I shared Rodriguez's sense that Spanish was a private language and that English was to be used when I wanted to make myself understood by the outside world. Spanish was, and still is, synonymous with the word *home,* for it was at home that the language became a reality in the traditions and cultural customs of my family. For example, I was expected to refer to my mother by the formal pronoun of "usted" instead of the familiar term, "tu"; this subtlety was not readily understood by anyone outside of our immediate family. In this sense, the language was immediately made private by the fact that while this particular custom would have been interpreted as a sign of distance to most, in my family we understood it to be a sign of great respect and love. A private language has positive connotations for me, while Rodriguez constructs a negative image of it, stating, "Nervously, I'd arrive at the grocery store to hear the sounds of the gringo—foreign to me—reminding me that the world was so big and I was a foreigner."

Instead of feeling alienated from either my family or the rest of society as Rodriguez did, I felt comfortable in both cultures. While I was exposed to a different way of life at school, I was naturally attached to my Mexican heritage through the language if nothing else. I frequently found myself actually thinking in Spanish after having spoken it all day. I remember dreaming in Spanish as well, and it was always when I was having a conversation with a person in my family. Despite these signs of fluency, I think that my assimilation into the American life-style was made easier by my father, who had lived in California most of his life. This is a major factor in my belief that this private language has been a positive influence in my life, for while I had someone on the "inside" to teach me English as well as American customs, Rodriguez's parents were both immigrants so that he had no source on which to draw for knowledge of English. Assimilation for my mother, however, was relatively unsuccessful, for she still clings to her Mexican traditions and has learned just enough English to get through simple, everyday situations.

Because I spoke both languages equally well, I did not have the difficulties in school that Rodriguez did. Speaking two languages gave me a sense of both the public and private individuality that Rodriguez describes. My private individuality came from the fact that I could communicate completely with my family. Unlike Rodriguez, who in his early years lacked a public individuality, my identity as a public person was achieved because I could facilitate communication between my mother and the outside world. This privilege made me very aware of the unique position I held. Rodriguez, on the other hand, came to resent the fact that Spanish was *his* private language because, "What I needed to learn in school was that I had the right—and the obligation— to speak the public language of *los gringos*." Thus, while I adopted a public and a private individuality simultaneously and with ease, Rodriguez had to learn and suffer to reach his own public individuality.

The only negative aspect of my public individuality that I was able to share with Rodriguez was his shock or dislike of listening to his parents speak in English to other people. Like Rodriguez, ". . . it was unsettling to hear my parents [my mother] struggle with English . . . hearing them I'd grow nervous, my clutching trust in their protection and power weakened." I, too, quickly learned to distinguish between the lower, guttural sound of English and the softer, rhythmic sounds of Spanish. While my father spoke both languages without an accent, my mother's English was very broken. I remember wishing that she would learn to either speak English perfectly or not have to speak it at all. When she talked to strangers, her first question was always, "Do you speak Spanish?" As a result of countless negative answers, I found myself doing a fair bit of translating. While this saved my mother (and me) from the immediate embarrassment of her speaking, it also prevented her from learning the language. On the positive side, translating gave me the opportunity to acquire a mastery of both languages.

Unfortunately, as was the case with Richard Rodriguez, my proficiency in Spanish has greatly diminished with time. After I began to spend a large part of my time at school, I discovered that I could not fully relate important events in Spanish as well as I could in English. For example, I found myself at a loss when I attempted to explain the purpose of writing a research paper to my mother. In spite of the relatively short amount of time I've been away from home at college, I realize that I have forgotten many Spanish words and expressions. However, instead of weakening my ties with my mother and the Spanish language in general, I feel that my connection with my culture has been strengthened. I am now able to explain the subtle differences in my culture as well as in the language to those who are curious to know the reason why I refer to my mother formally in Spanish. I find that now I relish the sounds of the words slipping from my mouth when I speak to my mother on the phone. I feel naturally drawn to a room were several students are unknowingly speaking in the rhythmic sounds of home. Spanish is now truly my private language. Its absence in my daily life has made it all that more special to me.

## QUESTIONS FOR DISCUSSION:

1. Why does Josephine Ramos disagree with Richard Rodriguez? On what issue does she agree with him?
2. How does the essay encourage you to think about the differences between your family's language and public language?
3. Josephine Ramos presents a variety of examples to illustrate how her knowledge of two languages was a positive force in her life. Which of her examples is most convincing? Why?
4. From your point of view what would be the advantages and disadvantages of growing up as a bilingual child? For you, would the advantages or disadvantages be stronger?
5. Working individually or in a group, write a peer critique that includes several supportive comments and several suggestions for strengthening the essay. Comment on the content and writing style.

*Reaching Out: Chapter Activities*

1. Working as a class, select a question or writing assignment from one of the readings in this chapter. Using the school's computer lab, participate in a networked, on-line discussion of the issue with several other students. Then discuss the issue with your classmates face to face. How did the two types of discussion differ? Did cultural and gender assumptions and stereotypes play a more important role in the face-to-face class discussion? What did you learn from comparing these two ways of communicating?

2. In a peer group, decide on an issue related to the family in a multicultural society that you would like to understand better. Have each student in your group of three to five people find an article in a newspaper or magazine that presents a perspective on the issue and summarize the content of the article and its position on the issue. Working as a group, make a summary of the different points of view. The group can present its findings to the class as a whole orally or in the form of a collaborative essay.

3. Have everyone in your group select a multicultural event in your community to attend. Decide on different aspects of the event and have each member report on one aspect. After writing up reports separately, have the group make a presentation to the class that discusses the event from several different perspectives.

4. Working as a group, decide on a culture within your community that you would like to understand better. Have each member find a poem, play, short story, folktale, or essay that explores a traditional aspect of the culture and clarifies values relating to family life within the culture. As a group, write an introduction to the materials you have found. If possible, produce a book, using desktop publishing, to share with your class.

5. See one of the following films, either by yourself or with several of your classmates. Write an individual or collaborative review of the film that takes into account the way that the film explores issues related to the multicultural family.

*Crossing Delancey.* Dir., Joan Micklin Silver. With Amy Irving, Peter Riegert. 1989.

*The Color Purple.* Dir., Stephen Spielberg. With Whoopi Goldberg, Danny Glover. 1986.

*Eat a Bowl of Tea.* Dir., Wayne Wang. With Victor Wong. 1989.

*El Norte.* Dir., Gregory Nava. With Zaide Gutierrez, David Villal Pando. 1983.

*Jungle Fever.* Dir., Spike Lee. With Spike Lee, Wesley Snipes. 1991.

*La Bamba.* Dir., Luis Valdez. With Lou Diamond Phillips. 1987.

*Mississippi Masala.* Dir., Mira Nair. With Denzel Washington. 1991.

# CHAPTER SIX

# *Tensions*

*The Family! Home of all social evils, a charitable institution for indolent women, a prison workshop for slaving breadwinners, and a hell for children.*
—August Strindberg, *The Son of a Servant*

*As we begin to forgive our parents, we begin to forgive ourselves. And we begin to forgive the world for not being perfect either.*
—Dwight Lee Wolter, *Forgiving our Parents*

Seen in the nineteenth century as a bulwark against social pressures, the family today is an arena where many of the tensions in our daily lives are played out, often with destructive results. In fact, the average duration of a modern marriage is less than seven years—a testimony in part to the negative impact of the stress of life in our times. In Chapters Four and Five of this book we examined two of the major sources of family tension: the dislocations of cultural identity experienced by immigrant and minority-ethnic families and the intrusion of the mass media, which undermine traditional familial myths and values. The selections in this chapter explore other tensions that affect the family and examine the effects of these tensions on the inner lives of individual family members.

Within the family, a number of sources of stress converge and interact. Economic problems play a significant role, as many of today's families, particularly minority families, large families, and single-parent families, live on incomes that are well below the poverty line. Economic stress is linked with psychological stress: in order to escape their economic limits, one or both parents often have to work long hours away from home. The pressures of work can weaken family ties, as children can no longer rely exclusively on their parents for attention and emotional nurturing. While children grow increasingly estranged from their families, overworked parents in turn may feel impatient with the demands children make on them at the end of a long day's work. The quarrels that break out in families under pressure may result in physical violence or divorce.

Often family members seek an outlet from the pressures of modern life through the use of drugs or alcohol. Excessive reliance on alcohol and drugs makes parents less able to meet the needs of their children and increases the likelihood of spousal and child abuse. Tensions can also be generated by the institutions within our society that are designed to help families in need, such as agencies designed to assist with education, employment, housing, food stamps, and aid to dependent children. Such institutions can contribute to feelings of guilt, powerlessness, and entrapment, since overworked governmental bureaucracies often view individual families according to statistical norms rather than in terms of individual needs.

In this chapter we have included readings that reflect on the causes and long-term impact of some of the tensions mentioned above. Three selections examine the influence of alcohol and abusive homes on the development of children and their adult self-images: "My Papa's

Waltz," a poem by Theodore Roethke; "Step by Step," an essay by Lily Collett; and "Adult Children: Tied to the Past," in which Melinda Blau argues that followers of the Adult Children movement often blame their parents for problems grown-ups should take responsibility for and try to solve on their own. The fourth selection, David Elkind's "The Child Inside," discusses the pressures ambitious families place on children by pushing their youngsters too soon toward adult responsibility, while an essay by sociologist Arlie Hochschild, "Stepping into Old Biographies or Making History Happen?" explores the tensions that build up in dual-career families. Judith Wallerstein's "On the Brow of the Hill" examines the effects of marital breakdown and divorce on the children involved.

The final selections in this chapter explore the issues of class and economic deprivation as sources of tension in a family. Dan Zegart's "Solomon's Choice" examines the sometimes negative impact of well-meaning but biased social workers, while Tillie Olsen's classic story, "I Stand Here Ironing," makes a similar point from the perspective of a mother who is questioned by a school counselor. Our student essay for the chapter, "Sharing the Blame," describes the way the stress of holding a large, immigrant family together helped lead a student's mother into alcoholism.

Other kinds of tensions affect the family in addition to the ones we have described here. As you read these selections, consider your own experience of family life and your own reading and research. What tensions troubled your parents as you were growing up? What concerns do you have about the future as you move into adulthood and plan a family of your own? What do you perceive to be the major causes of tension within the modern family, and what do you think might be done to reduce such tensions or to help people come to terms with the stress that is inevitable in today's society?

*Chapter Six:*
*Tensions*

**JOURNAL ENTRY**

Write about a time in your childhood when a parent or other adult frightened and/or excited you with boisterous, roughhousing behavior.

**THEODORE ROETHKE: "My Papa's Waltz"**   A deeply emotional poet with an intense love of nature, Theodore Roethke (1908–1963) was born in Saginaw, Michigan, to a family that kept greenhouses. Educated at the University of Michigan and Harvard, Roethke taught at a number of colleges and settled in Washington state, where he was a professor of creative writing for a number of years at the University of Washington. Roethke's poetry celebrates his students, about whom he cared greatly, the natural world, and spiritual transcendence. Roethke's *Collected Poems* were published after his death in 1966. His other books include *On the Poet and His Craft: Selected Prose* (1966) and *Straw for the Fire: From the Notebooks of Theodore Roethke, 1943–1966* (ed. David Wagoner, 1972). Notice how the following poem, "My Papa's Waltz," contrasts mixed family emotions of joy and intimacy, fear and pain.

THEODORE ROETHKE

# My Papa's Waltz

The whiskey on your breath
Could make a small boy dizzy;
But I hung on like death:
Such waltzing was not easy.

We romped until the pans
Slid from the kitchen shelf;
My mother's countenance
Could not unfrown itself.

The hand that held my wrist
Was battered on one knuckle;
At every step you missed
My right ear scraped a buckle.

You beat time on my head
With a palm caked hard by dirt,
Then waltzed me off to bed
Still clinging to your shirt.

*Looking at Ideas*

1. What is the waltz that the narrator and his father are performing in the poem? Does the narrator seem to enjoy this activity? Why or why not?
2. What is the mother's attitude toward the dancing? Does her attitude seem justified?
3. What has the father done just prior to the activity described in the poem? How does the father's earlier behavior affect your judgment of him?

*Looking at Strategies*

1. What physical details and images are used to describe the waltzing in the poem? Which of these details create a positive impression? Which could be interpreted negatively?
2. What physical details are used to describe the father, the mother, and the boy in the poem? How do these descriptive details help define the poem's characters and feelings?
3. Read the poem aloud, noticing the overall form, line lengths, and rhythms. (Note: the poem uses a ballad stanza). What role do the form, rhythm, and sound of the poem play in helping you evaluate the significance of the activities portrayed? Do the form and overall rhythm of the poem give you a happy and carefree impression of the events described, or a negative and critical one?

*Looking at Connections*

1. Compare Roethke's portrait of a drinking father who is physically rough with his son to Lily Collett's view of an abusive, alcoholic father in "Step by Step," included in this chapter. Which portrait seems more critical of the parent?
2. Compare Roethke's portrait of abuse and family tensions with the case histories examined by Dan Zegart in his essay in this chapter, "Solomon's Choice." Would social workers be critical of the family described in the poem?

*Suggestions for Writing*

1. Using examples from experience and reading, write an essay in which you contrast family interactions that could be described as abusive with behavior that could more accurately be considered merely boisterous, ill-mannered, or unsophisticated. Include clear definitions and criteria for classifying behavior as "abusive."
2. Many personal and social factors could lead to the type of rough behavior explored in Roethke's poem. Write an essay in which you explore several possible causes for a father treating his son the way the father does in the poem.
3. Write about an experience from your childhood in which you experienced tension or disagreement between your parents over some aspect of child rearing. How do you understand the nature and origins of the conflict differently now than you did as a child?

**JOURNAL ENTRY**

Write about an incident from your childhood in which you were around adults who seemed to you to be intoxicated or otherwise not in control of their behavior. How did this make you feel? How did you try to deal with your feelings about this?

**LILY COLLETT: "Step by Step"** Lily Collett is the pseudonym for a well-known journalist who has written for publications such as the *Village Voice,* the *Washington Post,* and the *New Yorker.* The following article originally appeared in *Mother Jones* (1988). In "Step by Step" Collett traces her long-term depression and confusion as an adult who grew up as the child of an abusive, alcoholic father, as well as her rehabilitation as a follower of the Adult Children of Alcoholics movement. As you read Collett's essay, notice how, as a trained journalist, she systematically records her emotions and behavior patterns both prior to and after her contact with the Adult Children's movement.

LILY COLLETT

# Step by Step

My father was no cartoon drunk. He never passed out on the couch or lost his job or went to jail. He sang me nursery rhymes and taught me to read when I was small, and when people came to dinner, he wore a nice tweed jacket and held the women's coats for them. I loved him so much I thought they ought to make him a movie star.

The year I turned ten, he began getting off the train in the evenings, saying, "I need a drink. I deserve a drink." He stared at the TV, bourbon in hand, saying, "This is my anesthetic." One night, at dinner, in the candlelight my mother hoped would teach us better manners, I made a child's pronouncement on a subject now long forgotten.

"No," said my father, and there was a bulge in his thickening jaw. I argued. "Don't contradict me," he shouted. It was the end of friendly dinner-table talks and the beginning of a father who dug his teeth into disagreements like a ferret, shaking and tearing at my words until my dinner ended night after night with slaps and tears and being sent from the table.

My mother sat in the candlelight with a pained expression on her face, but did nothing. It was as though a huge black dog that we all worked hard not to see had moved into the living room. My mother tried to limit my father to tomato juice and caught him secretly adding vodka. Their tension spilled over onto us children.

My father shouted at me to improve my schoolwork. "You drive me to drink," he yelled. "You're lazy, and you're sick in the head." My mother said to me, "You're selfish, you're clumsy, you've got no visual sense, no sense of time." Both of them hit me so frequently that I still flinch at sudden movements. I learned in my bones that alcoholics don't have relationships; they take hostages.

For the first couple of years, no matter how bad the drunken dinnertime scene, I floated up out of sleep each morning with the sense that it was a new day. But when I was 12 I began to wake up feeling as bad as I had the night before. I spent that summer reading in my room, gaining 15 pounds from eating chocolates stolen from supermarkets. I got into fancy schools and got thrown out of them, skipped grades, and then was held back. I blamed myself for my father's pain, for our relationship breaking down, for my failure to shine in school, for being an inexplicably bad girl. In high school, I wrote poetry, edited the literary magazine, played the lead in school plays, was a National Merit Scholar, stayed out all night, and nearly slit my wrists.

I escaped from home in the late 1960s like someone who'd done hard prison time, and plunged with delight into a new world. I tried psychedelics, took part in union and student organizing, moved to the mountains, and wrote for an alternative newspaper. When the political community that had sustained me evaporated, I moved, seemingly effortlessly, to a big city paper. In my spare time, I practiced Zen meditation.

My life looked good from the outside, but it didn't feel easy from the inside. By the time I was 35, I had white-knuckled my way to everything I thought stood between me and happiness—a house, a job, and a husband—and it had all turned to ashes in my mouth. I didn't think of myself as a "child of an alcoholic," yet I was living on blues power, depressed and unable to trust. I was a workaholic flake: late everywhere, speeding the freeways, my car perpetually running on empty. I was in a car crash that knocked me from my psychic moorings. My husband withdrew, and I spent my weekends crying and screaming at him. The world looked flat, and my heart felt enclosed in a Plexiglas box.

Three years ago, when I was 36 and the numbness had become unbearable, I walked into a church basement for a meeting of adult children of alcoholics, clutching a list of meeting places obtained from the local alcoholism council. I thought I was embarking on a last-ditch attempt at personal healing; I later discovered I had joined a cultural movement that incorporates much of the spiritual exploration, group energy, folk wisdom, and effective anarchy that I had loved about the '60s. But that came later: on first impression, it seemed corny, passive, and pious.

I sat in the back. A volunteer read aloud, "We welcome you to the Monday Night Adult Children Al-Anon Family Group, and hope that you may find in it the help and friendship we have been privileged to enjoy." We were asked to introduce ourselves by our first names, and I blushed when the crowd replied, "Hi Lily," the secretary said, "Welcome," and everyone clapped. The crowd wasn't straight-looking—many were gay, some wore leather jackets over their T-shirts and jeans, and only a few wore business suits—but they acted as though they were at a midwestern summer camp. Or was it a revival meeting?

On a bulletin board, I saw a cloth banner listing the "Twelve Steps" for spiritual progress, adopted from Alcoholics Anonymous: "1. We admitted we were powerless over alcohol—that our lives had become unmanageable. 2. Came to believe that a Power greater than ourselves could restore us to sanity." I stopped there: it didn't apply to me. I'm a Buddhist, a feminist, and a big-time reporter, I thought. I'm not powerless, I don't believe in any Power, and my life's not unmanageable. But I stayed; a friend from work who had recently joined Alcoholics Anonymous advised me to forget the religion and go for the group support.

A speaker—a businesswoman in a purple wool dress—briefly told us how her alcoholic father had pulled her out of bed in the middle of the night and beat her when she was a child. "When I first came here," she said, "I had 500 self-help books and no self." When she finished, we clapped for her, and then she called on raised hands.

People spoke in monologues, part group therapy and part Quaker meeting, of their own lives and what they called "serenity"—something that had never been a value in my life. Some rambled, full of pain; others spoke in aphorisms. Nobody gave advice, criticism, or help. One woman said, "In adult life, there are no victims, only volunteers." Another, who fit what I would later learn is a pattern of children of alcoholics, gravitating toward people with drug or alcohol problems, described herself as a "co-alcoholic"—part of that army of busybodies who marry alcoholics and then pour the bourbon down the sink, or show up at the jail at midnight with bail money. She described the side effects of her bootless attempts to control others: rage, exhaustion, denial, blame, a bitchy superiority, and a sense of personal failure.

We clapped again. Another volunteer then suggested that newcomers find themselves sponsors: "A sponsor is someone with more time in the program than you, who helps you work the steps." Another volunteer read aloud, "Changed attitudes can aid recovery. . . . You may not like all of us, but in time you will come to love us in a very special way, the same way we already love you." We held hands and recited something that ended with a rah-rah "Keep coming back! It works!" Mystified, I asked someone, "What am I supposed to do now?" She said, "It works by osmosis."

Corny and weird as it was, I went back every week. I was desperate, and there was something intoxicating about listening to a whole roomful of people telling the truth.

Around the time I was awarded a plastic poker chip (more clapping, more hugs) for having attended meetings for six months, I noticed that some of my other friends were approaching 40 and hitting a wall. The newspapers were running crack stories, and the country seemed to be undergoing a spiritual fracturing to which neither the Left nor the Right had an adequate response. Nancy Reagan Just Said No, while her husband allowed the number of drug treatment beds to decline; the Left protested urine testing as an invasion of privacy and defended our right to do what we wish with our bodies. It all seemed to miss the point.

A rancher friend from the Great Plains, who also wrote songs for one of the best-loved surviving rock bands from the '60s, drank and tripped so much that one year he didn't stack his hay until after the first snow. A writer I knew disappeared up-country, smoking seven or eight sinsemilla joints a day. I dropped in one night on a friend, an elegant and beautiful magazine editor, and found her drunk and alone with her three-year-old son. Novels went unfinished, promises were broken, faces grew puffy. I was losing my faith in the '60s belief that the road of excess necessarily leads to the palace of wisdom.

A few months later, my rancher friend hit town with a button on his denim jacket saying "Clean, Sober, and Bored Shitless." His Christmas letter announced that he had joined Alcoholics Anonymous and had taken what he called The Big Cure. "Those meetings are what church would be if churches let you come as you are, swear when you felt like it, and believe in whatever vision of The Other Party suited your spirit," he wrote. "On the morning of February 10, I had an exquisitely clear moment in which I surrendered to the fact that I not only can't drink, I also can't handle the uppers, downers, and all-around-towners which have skewed my life since the Sixties. The means (drugs) gradually superseded the ends (decency, community, peace, love). The party was over," the Christmas letter continued, "but we didn't leave. It's time for me to take it the way the Lord made it. Turns out that isn't half bad."

I congratulated and hugged him, but in my adult children of alcoholics meetings, I still sat in the back and clung to my own sense of personal superiority. Then one night, after a year of meetings, I heard myself tell the group, "I've been depressed for years and there's no reason for it." After so many years of denying my suffering—and making it so much worse—I had told the truth. I blushed and then cried; I felt sure I would be ostracized for revealing how numb and exhausted I felt. Without knowing it, I had taken the first step: I had admitted my life was unmanageable. It was a radical and empowering moment.

I had become part of a mushrooming national movement. There are an estimated 23 million adult children of alcoholics in the United States, but in 1981, there were only 14 adult children of alcoholics groups registered with the headquarters of Al-Anon, an organization founded in the 1950s by wives of alcoholics. In 1988, there are more than 1,100 such groups, which typically hold meetings once a week. The size of those meetings has grown rapidly: the one I sometimes attended in the Catholic school gymnasium down the street from my

311

house grew so huge that the speaker, sitting in a folding chair under the basketball hoops and the statues of Our Lady, needed to use a microphone.

In a parallel trend among alcoholics, AA membership in 1988 reached 750,000, up from 550,000 in 1983. In the last two decades, the movement of Twelve Step groups has grown beyond alcoholics and their relatives. Dozens of groups now apply the principles of Alcoholics Anonymous to other human problems—groups like Debtors Anonymous, Overeaters Anonymous, Sex and Love Addicts Anonymous, Cocaine Anonymous, Smokers Anonymous, Incest Survivors Anonymous, Narcotics Anonymous, even Unsafe Drivers Anonymous and, for procrastinating artists, Arts Anonymous.

All of the groups use the Twelve Step program for spiritual growth that was originally adapted from a Christian conversion process by a failed New York stockbroker and hopeless drunk named Bill Wilson, who founded AA in 1935. The steps may seem arcane, but in essence they boil down to this: with group help, abstain from your compulsion—alcohol, sex, or chronic credit-card debt. Admit you can't do it alone. Straighten out your relationships with your fellow humans by admitting your faults. Accept help from your Higher Power, defining him or her any way you want to. Do these things, help others, and your compulsions will lift as if by magic.

I began consciously working the steps shortly after I confessed my depression to my Al-Anon group. One evening I asked Carl, a bouncy drama student of 24 with streaked blond hair, to be my sponsor. In a coffee shop after a meeting, I told him, "I want to stop being so unhappy," and I started to cry. He put his hand on my arm.

"Buy a spiral notebook," he said. "Write down all the ways that you're powerless over other people's drinking, and over people, places, and things. Write how your life is unmanageable. Go to an Alcoholics Anonymous meeting and buy the book called *Alcoholics Anonymous*—the Big Book. Start reading it."

When things were going badly, I cried my way through two or three meetings in a single week, feeling something like the pain of thawing frostbite. I realized I had spent my life blaming myself for my father's pain, and had called myself crazy for feeling pain of my own. Meanwhile, I systematically filled my spiral notebook with thoughts on how each of the Twelve Steps applied to my own life, talking them over with Carl in our weekly sessions at the coffee shop. This went well until I hit step three: "Made a decision to turn our will and our lives over to the care of God as we understood Him."

I told Carl I couldn't do it. The AA Big Book said God didn't have to be Christian—it could be anything bigger than my small self, like nature, my Al-Anon group, or a spirit underlying things. Yet the language of the Big Book was archaic, Christian, and patriarchal: God (and the book's assumed reader) was male.

Prayer had repelled me since childhood, and so did Christianity, in both its lukewarm, liberal form and its coercive, fundamentalist form. A personal god, I thought, was like an alcoholic father who would pretend to be loving and then demand things I couldn't deliver without destroying my soul. But because I was so unhappy, I rewrote the Big Book's suggested prayer ("God, I offer myself to Thee to build with me and to do with me as Thou wilt") into a Buddhist form I could live with. Kneeling on my bedroom floor for the first time since childhood, I prayed, "Force of rhythm and meaning moving through all things including me, harmony understood by the Buddha and other enlightened human beings, I offer myself to you. . . . Please relieve me of investment in the illusion of the separate self." It felt foreign; I felt humiliated and embarrassed. I went to sleep.

Surrender, like most religious acts, is a paradox. For years I had felt as though my heart was enclosed in a Plexiglas box. The next day, I went to work with a warmth in my chest, as though someone was home there. Nagging internal voices accusing me of failure—what Twelve Step groups call "the shitty committee"—were temporarily silent. Had I unlocked self-love? Come in tune with The Great Way, or Tao? Been heard by a personal god out there somewhere?

After that, the other steps came easier. I brought more lists to the coffee shop in my spiral-bound notebook (four: "Made a searching and fearless moral inventory of ourselves"; five: "Admitted to God, to ourselves and to another human being the exact nature of our wrongs"; six: "Were entirely ready to have God remove all these defects of character"; seven: "Humbly asked Him to remove our shortcomings").

Another night, I read Carl step eight: "Made a list of all persons we had harmed, and became willing to make amends to them all." Then I took steps nine and ten: "Made direct amends to such people wherever possible, except when to do so would injure them or others"; and "continued to take personal inventory, and when we were wrong promptly admitted it." I paid off a man whose fender I had dented ten years ago, apologized to my brother and my husband for treating them as if they weren't smart enough to run their own lives, and wrote a letter to an old friend, admitting I'd betrayed her. My old friend still wouldn't speak to me afterward, but I felt unburdened, because nobody held anything over me anymore.

My life changed in many small ways. I dropped my self-appointed role as chief therapist and manipulator within my marriage. I left the job I had worked at for a decade out of fear—of displeasing my father, of not being famous, of being poor. I whined less about President Reagan and made amends politically by tithing to the Jackson campaign and to anticontra groups, and by writing letters to Congress on issues in which I feel complicit as an American. When it came time to take the eleventh step ("Sought through prayer and meditation to improve our conscious contact with God as we understood Him . . ."), I began taking long, silent walks in the hills.

All this occurred without anybody telling me what to do or what to believe; every meeting closed with, "Take what you like, and leave the rest." But slowly, as I read Al-Anon pamphlets and heard members talk

313

about their lives, serenity became a value of mine, by, you might say, osmosis. One night after a meeting, when I was feeling particularly happy, a woman—who turned out to be a nurse, six years older than me—nervously asked me to be her sponsor. "Buy a spiral notebook," I told her at the coffee shop. "Go to an AA meeting and get hold of a copy of the Big Book." And so I took the twelfth step: "Having had a spiritual awakening as a result of these steps, we tried to carry this message to others and to practice these principles in all our affairs."

Somehow, the Twelve Step groups have fashioned an anarchy that works. Each meeting is autonomous and self-supporting—we pass the basket and pay about a dollar each to cover room rentals and administrative costs. Leadership jobs are simple—running the meeting, volunteering as a speaker, making coffee—and rotate every six months. People from all races and walks of life communicate freely because we do not discuss professions or specific religious beliefs. Donations from outsiders—even million-dollar bequests—are refused. The groups own no real estate and take no positions on political issues. So there's very little money, power, or fame to fight over, and the work of healing goes on, almost unnoticed by the public world.

I know some people, especially on the Left, who think Twelve Step groups encourage conformity and passivity. Perhaps that's inevitable, given our generation's cultural history: rebellion, sex, drugs, and rock and roll broke over our lives in one big wave that looked like liberation. But I know my friend Walter, the alternative journalist, didn't experience liberation when he smoked so much sinsemilla that he couldn't go to the garage without forgetting what he'd gone for. In true '60s style, he first thought he had a premature case of Alzheimer's, contracted from using aluminum cookware. Then a friend in AA suggested he lay off dope for a while, and he found that he couldn't do it alone.

I ran into Walter recently on the street. He was back in town; he had joined AA and was working again. Over a Chinese lunch, he said, "I can still remember the day with SNCC [Student Nonviolent Coordinating Committee] organizers in Jackson, Mississippi, that I first smoked dope. A woman friend there, an organizer, had just spent the night with a guy not her husband, and it just all seemed far out and all intertwined. I have to go back over my memories now, and separate out the drug aspect, the sensual aspect, and the civil rights aspect."

I nodded. And yet—and yet. I won't abandon drugs entirely; I know intoxicants can be sacramental. Last New Year's Eve I sat with 11 close friends in silence, by candlelight, drinking champagne and eating a grape for each month of the coming year. It was the peak of an evening in which one friend had read her translations of Japanese erotic court poetry and we all had said things we would not have said sober. My husband and I still sometimes walk the hills and take Ecstasy, speaking to each other in a language deeper than the vulgate of the marketplace and the mortgage payment.

I like being where parts of the self, usually drowned out by conventional life, are heard. I still honor the impulses that lead me to use drugs to get to those parts. But I have to rein in my own romanticism, and remember that a little intoxication goes a long way. For some people I know, drinking and drug use have not been gates to a spiritual life, but substitutes for it. Intoxicants have come to symbolize the freedom they crave in their off-work hours. They may not like what they have to do on the job, but within their homes, their families, and their bodies—the last unconquered spheres—they express what remains of their freedom: freedom to be left alone, freedom to buy—and freedom to party.

The resulting national epidemic of drug use and alcoholism is the product, I think, of a culture that offers so few sustainable, nondrug opportunities for interconnection, self-expression, and spiritual meaning. Religions have traditionally provided such opportunities, and my involvement with adult children of alcoholics gives them to me in a nondogmatic way. I have been able to rethink Buddhism and make it mine, and since I began going to meetings, I no longer have to be high to lie alone on a grassy hillside, listening to the sound of a hawk's wings riffling the air.

For years, I had lived my life on the assumption that if I could just figure out how to force other people to behave, I could be happy. Now, my life is not perfect, but Al-Anon helps me give meaning to that part of my suffering that is unavoidable. Talking and listening at meetings helps me accept the given world, and helps me see the limits of my power to create my own reality. We have a prayer in Al-Anon: "God, grant me the serenity to accept the things I cannot change, the courage to change the things I can, and the wisdom to know the difference."

I keep coming back; it works. After years of trying to stare down my problems, I go at them obliquely, and they melt. After years of locked combat, my relationship with my father eases. I no longer listen on the phone for slurred words like a little detective; I no longer send him furious letters listing every broken promise, every mean remark, every drunken embarrassment, and every blow. I no longer triumph when he stops drinking or get crushed when he begins again.

Instead, we talk about writing. I stand up for myself, but with a sense of humor. When he's emotionally absent, I get off the phone instead of trying to suck juice from a stone. I try to face my own life—this mysterious life that I influence, but do not control—instead of trying to live my father's. In the process, I spontaneously recall moments of childhood grace.

The year I turned ten, I spent the day before Christmas with my best friend Janet. Janet's mother's alcoholism was well advanced—she sometimes passed out on the couch—and Janet was a little adult who ironed her own clothes and made her own meals. There were lots of grown-ups there that day, drinking and smoking in the kitchen. Janet cooked us a lunch of SpaghettiOs. In the early afternoon it began to snow, and by nightfall, the highway between Janet's house and my own was closed.

315

At first, I thought I would spend Christmas Eve with Janet and nobody would much care. But my father called to say he would walk halfway to meet me. It was a long, cold way to go alone, but as I walked through the falling snow, from street lamp to street lamp along the soft, silent highway, I was not afraid. It was a beautiful night, and the snow, caught in the street lamps, sparkled as it whirled and fell. The memory is precious to me, a talisman that reminds me how much my father loved me. He was there to meet me halfway, and sober, and together we walked home.

## QUESTIONS

*Looking at Ideas:*

1. What does Collett mean by the comment, "alcoholics don't have relationships; they take hostages"? Do you agree with this view of the alcoholic personality?

2. Despite her depression and negative home life, Collett was successful in school and a high achiever, particularly in extracurricular activities. To what would you attribute her high achievement?

3. What particular events led Collett to begin attending Al-Anon's Adult Children of Alcoholics meetings? What other types of spiritual quest had she tried earlier? How did her past experiments prepare her for the Adult Child movement? What prevented her at first from feeling comfortable at the meetings? Why did she return?

4. What advice did Carl, her sponsor in the movement, have for Lily? Why did she have trouble following his advice? How did she overcome her reservations?

5. Collett says that she continues to take intoxicants, despite the AA prohibitions against this kind of behavior. What is your response to her drug and alcohol use? Does she seem able to control her use of these substances?

6. How has Collett's relationship to her father changed since she joined the movement? How is she now able to use her positive memory of her childhood walk with him as "a talisman"?

*Looking at Strategies*

1. Read over the incidents Collett narrates from her early life, both at the beginning and the end of the essay. How does the contrast between these incidents and the tone in which they are told help emphasize the personal growth Collett has achieved through Al-Anon?

2. Collett brings the eye of a trained journalist to her portrait of an Adult Children of Alcoholics meeting and the encounters she has with participants. Give examples of effective details she uses in her portrait of the Twelve Step process.

3. What stories does Collett tell to justify her rejection of excessive drinking and drug use? Are the portraits she provides of "1960s types" convincing? Do Collett's examples and portraits of excess make you more inclined to accept the principles of the Twelve Step programs, or do her examples seem sensationalist?

4. Collett uses cause-and-effect reasoning in her essay to demonstrate that the Twelve Step programs are an effective way for alcoholics, drug users, children of alcoholic families, and people with other types of social addictions to overcome their problems. Is her reasoning convincing, or could other programs work equally well?

*Looking at Connections:*

1. This narrative stands in strong contrast to Melinda Blau's essay, which is the next selection in this chapter. To what do you attribute Collett's strongly positive view of the Adult Children's movement, as opposed to Blau's negative opinion of it? Which view seems more accurate to you? For instance, in Collett's firsthand account of Adult Children of Alcoholics groups and practices, does she say they encouraged her to blame and condemn her parents for her problems, as Blau implies such groups do?

2. Compare Collett's home life with that of the children profiled in David Elkind's "The Child Inside," also included in this chapter. What elements in Collett's home and in those described by Elkind might lead a child into self-destructive behavior?

*Suggestions for Writing:*

1. Write about an experience in your family life in which you felt unfairly criticized by your parents because they were having trouble controlling their own lives or feelings. What advice would you have for people who might feel bad about themselves because of being unfairly treated by their parents?

2. After doing some further research, write either a supportive or a critical view of the Twelve Step process as a recovery method for children of alcoholics and others whose early life has left them with feelings of rejection, dependence, and inadequacy. Does Adult Children of Alcoholics seem a viable way to handle such problems?

3. Write an essay in which you argue for either the advantages or the disadvantages of relying on a "spiritual power" for strength to resist the temptation of drugs and alcohol.

**JOURNAL ENTRY**

Write about a conflict you had with your parents that caused long-term resentment. Has the conflict been resolved or does it continue to influence your feelings about your parents and the world around you?

**MELINDA BLAU: "Adult Children: Tied to the Past"** A journalist who has written frequently on mental health issues, Melinda Blau prepared the following essay for *American Health* (1990). Blau interviewed a number of health care workers and psychologists on the impact of the Adult Children of Alcoholics movement. This movement originated with the philosophy of Alcoholics Anonymous but attempts to extend that philosophy to "co-dependents" and "adult children" who have trouble functioning as mature adults because they have been raised within families in which there is a pattern of alcoholism, drug abuse, physical abuse, or psychological abuse. Notice how Blau presents statements from psychologists as well as case histories to make her point that the consequence of the Adult Child movement has been to shift the blame for personal problems to parents rather than to helping people to stand on their own.

MELINDA BLAU

# *Adult Children: Tied to the Past*

Barbara and her mother are trying to work out their conflicts in a family therapy session. Recovering from the most recent of many love affairs gone sour, Barbara is convinced her shattered romances reflect an abusive childhood. Her anger is palpable.

"How do you have a good relationship?" she asks the therapist, her eyes narrowing as she leans forward in her chair. "If you grew up in a house where relationships were good, you learned that. I'm 44 years old and I'm reading books like *Toxic Parents* to learn what healthy is about!"

The "toxic parent," 75-year-old Evelyn, seems willing to make peace with her daughter. But Barbara has another agenda: "Without some resolution of the past, I can't go forward," Barbara asserts. "Part of this has to do with my mother . . . obviously. Whether she will take any level of responsibility and make it easier for me is questionable."

Barbara sees herself as the victim. "It's very painful. The way I feel has to do with things done *to me*—not because of who I am as a person. I'm dealing with it on several levels. I'm going to a therapist. I'm also starting to go to ACOA."

318

The mother looks confused. Her daughter is speaking a foreign language. "AC-what?" she asks.

"Adult Children of Alcoholics and other dysfunctional families," Barbara explains authoritatively. She makes it clear that there was "absolutely no alcohol" in her house—but her childhood was nonetheless "dysfunctional."

The mother inhales deeply and sighs. She asks innocently, "I'd like to know—how many *functional* families are there?"

These two generations are worlds apart. The mother, a child of the Depression, was taught to put others' needs first, to repress her feelings and silently endure life's hard knocks. In contrast, Barbara flaunts her distress; she is low on compassion. A grown woman, she laments, "There is a little girl inside of me who never got the mothering she wanted—and she still wants it."

But that's not all she wants. The therapist, who had warned her client "mother bashing" would not be permitted, says, "Barbara wanted someone to hold her mother still, so she could beat her up."

Blaming parents for what they did or didn't do has become a national obsession—and big business. Like Barbara, increasing numbers of people are now referring to themselves as "Adult Children," a curious metaphor. With selfhelp groups and a spate of books such as the best-selling and pointedly titled *Toxic Parents* to guide them, plus magazines and TV talk shows eager to air their dirty laundry, Adult Children are definitely front and center on the American scene.

The movement began about 10 years ago with survivors of extreme abuse: children of alcoholics and drug abusers or victims of incest and physical or mental violence, who very early in life learned the unwritten credo—don't feel, don't think, and don't trust. What once was survival for the child became a way of life for the adult. "I lived in constant terror," recalls a 34-year-old incest survivor whose parents were alcoholics. "One time, on the way home from a restaurant, my father was speeding recklessly, shouting, 'I've met my Maker, and I don't care who I take with me!' "

But the scope of the movement has grown enormously. It now includes a cadre of parent-bashing Adult Children eager to tell their parents, It's your fault we love too much or not at all and *never* the right person; that we don't trust ourselves or anyone else; that we are "afflicted and addicted," as a recent *Newsweek* cover story declared; that we are divorced, drunk, desperate and—pardon the jargon—"dysfunctional." These Adult Children are looking for the Answer—and many think their parents are *it*.

If you believe some experts, 90 percent of us are suffering from the ravages of childhood. And salvation, say the gurus who lead these flocks of Adult Children, lies in the embrace of the recovery movement. You must face the reality of your chaotic childhood and reclaim your life by looking at the pain you've never been allowed to talk about, much less feel.

But therapists are concerned. "The whole new 'wounded child' mythology has given people a language for talking about pain, grieving over it," notes family therapist Jo-Ann Krestan, coauthor of *Too Good for Her Own Good.* "But there's really no such thing as an 'Adult Child.' That's a description of where you came from, not a diagnosis of who you are today."

Certainly, the Adult Child movement will help many people exorcise childhood demons of shame and isolation. It will also help them understand that what happened to them as children wasn't their fault and that as adults they need no longer be victims. They don't have to stay stuck in the problem—they can *do* something.

But as the media and the fluorescent self-help movement continue to encourage Adult Children to stand up and be counted, many experts now ask: Will those same people get stuck in the solution? In therapy, Barbara dumps her sorrows on her mother; other Adult Children assemble to flesh out forgotten images from painful childhoods. But there may be little talk of forgiveness, much about blame, and, sometimes, fantasies of revenge. Will chronic angst simply be transmuted to chronic anger? And if parent bashing *is* the prescription, what are the long-term effects of that "medicine" on succeeding generations? How will the children of these Adult Children view *their* parents?

## *Why Now?*

Parent bashing isn't new. Freud sparked the idea around the turn of the century. Convinced that adult problems were reflections of childhood conflicts, Freud unwittingly laid the groundwork upon which modern-day pop-psychology empires have been built, explains psychologist Ronald Taffel, director of family and couples treatment at the Institute for Contemporary Psychotherapy in New York City. In many of the therapies popularized since the '50s—analysis, the child guidance movement, encounter groups—"parents have always been deemed at fault, especially mothers," says Taffel.

Many therapists agree that parent bashing is often a euphemism for mother bashing. Most post-Freudian therapists—reflecting society in general—promoted the basic assumption that mothers, as the family "gatekeepers," were somehow responsible for how children turned out. If the kids had problems, Mother was either too involved or not enough; if Dad was depressed, it was because Mom was emasculating him. If fathers have been blamed for anything, it's that they haven't been there. Even in cases of incest, the mother has often been held responsible—for not stopping it.

In her recent book, *Don't Blame Mother,* psychologist Paula Caplan reports that on reviewing 125 articles published between 1970 and 1982, mothers were blamed for 72 different kinds of problems in their offspring, ranging from bed-wetting and learning problems to schizophrenia.

No segment of our population has been more affected by the prevailing winds of psychotherapy than the children raised by these mothers—the 76 million baby boomers, now 26 to 44 years old. "Children of Dr. Spock," they grew up in a permissive, child-oriented era when it was okay to be rebellious, even to tell parents what was wrong with them. Not only was it no longer a stigma to be "in therapy," the implication was that somehow they could perfect themselves.

To be sure, the boomers have tried just about everything: est and self-actualization, aerobics and health foods, Eastern philosophies and Western materialism, therapy and more therapy—but nothing has "worked." As Taffel observes, "Many of them have been through it all. And guess what? The problems are still there. They can't make their marriages work, their kids are troubled and their own personalities haven't changed that much."

The mere fact that adults are labeling themselves "children" implies that there's some resistance to actually growing up and facing adult responsibilities. Landon Jones, the journalist whose *Great Expectations* tracked these whiz kids through 1980, also suspects it's in keeping with the baby boom mentality. "All of their life stages have been prolonged—their childhood and adolescence—and they stayed in college and were single longer," says Jones. "Now they're approaching middle age, when one of the tasks is to come to terms with your parents. But they're not ready to accept who they really are."

In the '80s, disco glitter began to lose its charm; midlife caught up with the boomers and suddenly they found themselves running out of time and bottoming out on sex and substances, the magical elixirs that had once worked so well. Escalating divorce rates, child abuse, wife battering, drug overdoses and the specter of AIDS have cast a pall upon the boomers' adolescent dreams—that promise of infinite happiness and eternal prosperity.

The boomers' parents had lived through the Depression, witnessed the devastation of World War II and learned to live with it all. In contrast, the children of the Me Generation had the time and money to indulge themselves in the pursuit of perfection. When their dreams began to shatter, say the experts, the boomers began to point a finger at their parents. After all, it must be *someone's* fault.

"When you look at the 'recovery movement,' you see a mass audience turning childhood into an illness you recover from," says Taffel. "They even have networks and support systems to keep it going. These obviously serve a useful purpose—but only if parent bashing doesn't become an end in itself."

## Trapped in Childhood

If the fitness movement belonged to the '80s, then "recovery" may well be the hallmark of the '90s. An influx of alcoholic and addicted boomers caused Alcoholics Anonymous to double its membership between 1977 and 1987. Al-Anon, AA's companion program, now has over 19,000 groups nationwide; and scores of me-too groups, like Cocaine Anonymous and Shopaholics, have been created to accommodate boomers who didn't drink but found other ways to soothe inner discontent. But none responded to the grassroots call for self-help in greater numbers than the unhappy adults who called themselves Adult Children.

Although ACOA's original focus was on alcohol, the Adult Child movement now reaches out to all kinds of suffering adults. ACOA's growth has been staggering—at last count, from 14 Al-Anon-affiliated ACOA groups in 1981 to over 4,000 meetings nationwide, many of them independent of Al-Anon.

Predictably, big business, always monitoring the pulse of the baby boom generation, has also jumped on—and propelled—the Adult Child bandwagon. Between 1978 and 1984, the number of private residential treatment centers in the country increased 350 percent, and case loads quadrupled. Thanks to the marketing genius of the recovery industry, these rehabs, with their promises of "renewal" and "hope," are becoming the spas of the '90s.

And there's no shortage of reading material. A plethora of self-help books describes various "types" of Adult Children and offers a laundry list of characteristics, which are also read aloud at many meetings. But individuals are not so easily quantified.

"I had a man call me and say, 'I'm an Adult Child, and Dr. So-and-So said I'm one of the worst cases he's ever seen.' I cracked up," recalls Marianne Walters, director of The Family Therapy Practice Center in Washington, D.C. "I told him I'd see him, but as an Adult Person. I'm concerned about these typologies—not that they don't resonate with some truth. But if you're so self-absorbed and only understand yourself this way, you don't take as much responsibility for your own behavior, for others, or for the world you live in."

What's more, Adult Children expect others to understand "where they're coming from." Howard, a recovering alcoholic familiar with many 12-step recovery programs, observes, "It used to be people took time getting to know one another. Nowadays, you go out on a date and within the first few minutes she tells you her father is an alcoholic, her mother committed suicide, a cousin abused her sexually, and she's bulimic—so you'd better watch her boundaries. Everyone talks in terms of 'fear of intimacy.' Meanwhile, the real message comes through: 'I'm damaged goods—so hands off.' "

## Stuck in Blame

Many therapists encourage clients to attend programs like AA and Al-Anon as an important adjunct to treatment and a safe place to share feelings. After all, the 12-step structure calls for admitting you're powerless over the problem—whether due to your own behavior or someone else's—and then, with group support, looking honestly at *your own* contribution.

But some Adult Child meetings, which tend to be "younger" than the more established 12-step programs, may encourage just the opposite: blame. There isn't as much guidance from seasoned veterans who've worked through their anger, observes New York City therapist Nancy Napier, author of *Recreating Your Self*. "So you've got a bunch of people in pain, and the pain just builds up."

Also, AA and Al-Anon have always urged members to keep the focus on themselves. But at ACOA meetings, parents and other caregivers are fair game.

"I went to ACOA meetings for about a year—but week after week people just dumped." Karen, whose mother was alcoholic, is referring to the litany of complaints common to many of these meetings. One of her resentments was that her parents had refused to send her to college: "I carried that around for years." Her brothers were sent to college, her parents went to Europe, but "poor" Karen had to go to a local junior college. "I'd share it at meetings, but I'd leave feeling worse," she says.

Some meetings were also downright frightening, says Karen. She recalls the time an angry woman screamed about her father and threw a chair across the room. "It scared the s—t out of me. I couldn't take it anymore."

"In ACOA groups, people definitely have to get through the anger and denial," says Michael Elkin, a family therapist at a school for disturbed adolescents in Stockbridge, MA. "But that's only the first step in the process—it's where people have to start. Hopefully, they'll move past the blame. However, some people get stuck—they misuse the program."

Family therapist Jo-Ann Krestan also sees some people using "recovery" in much the same way they used drugs or other substances—to avoid their real feelings. "They think if they could only do recovery 'right,' they won't have to feel uncomfortable," she points out. "But if you really begin to look at your own choices, at who you are, it's going to be uncomfortable."

Karen decided to go through the pain. A counselor at an ACOA rehab she attended encouraged her to write letters to each of her parents, telling them everything she was angry about. "When I had to read them aloud and talk about my part, I realized I always blamed *them* when I failed."

Karen, a recovering alcoholic, now takes full responsibility for her choices as an adult. "Sure, there was a lot of anger over my mother's drinking, and for years I blamed my own drinking on her. It made it easier for me. She did inappropriate things to me as a child, such as making me her confidante and telling me about her sex life, but I was never physically abused. There is no fault, no blame. Millions of people grow up in the same kind of household I did, and they don't all drink. It was easier to blame than to take responsibility for my own lifestyle."

Equally important, Karen now also understands the context of her own mother's life. "This was the early '50s; my father traveled, my mother was young and knew nothing about having a child. She was lonely. There were no support groups then."

323

## Confronting "Toxic Parents"

Had Karen read California therapist Susan Forward's *Toxic Parents,* she might have gained no such insight. Nor would she have been interested in hearing a basic truth about many supposedly "abusive" parents: Most never intended to hurt their children.

Even Dr. Alice Miller, the Swiss psychoanalyst who unwittingly inspired much of the popular focus on the "inner child," stressed that the issue is not culpability. In *Prisoners of Childhood* (later changed to *The Drama of the Gifted Child*), Miller wrote: "Many parents, even with the best intentions, cannot always understand their child, since they, too, have been stamped by their experience with their own parents and have grown up in a different generation."

Therapist Marilyn R. Frankfurt, of the Ackerman Institute for Family Therapy in New York City, agrees that parental attitudes of the earlier child-centered *Not-Me* Generation are totally foreign to today's Me Generation. "Those earlier mothers," she says, "were told they had to shape their children and make them conform to cultural expectations. But often they had no emotional attention from their own parents. Despite this, they didn't complain. Now they're being held responsible for how their children feel.

"We're imposing ideas on the past generation that don't apply," says Frankfurt. "These Adult Children act as if their parents knew all of this and chose not to act."

But Dr. Forward offers no such compassion in *Toxic Parents.* Relentlessly presenting case after case of manipulative, selfish parents, she tells readers it's not their fault. That's fine, but as Frankfurt points out, "Forward also implies, 'Someone's got to be responsible.' The author even goes so far as to warn readers not to be fooled by comments like 'We did the best we could' or 'You'll never understand what I was going through.' She says that's the parents' problem."

Forward declined several requests to be interviewed for this article, but it's clear she has tapped into a ripe market. Although drawing its examples from the extremes—people who were terribly abused—the book *Toxic Parents* seems to appeal to anyone along the continuum of an "unhappy childhood."

Though Krestan doesn't support the idea of blaming parents, she does agree with Forward on one point: "Adult Children need to acknowledge what's theirs and what belongs to their parents—and get through the grieving process. Forward's book will certainly help validate those negative shameful experiences that people have had." Krestan adds, however, "You have to get good and God-damned angry, but that doesn't constitute healing. It's not helpful to confront and cut off."

Janet Woititz, author of the landmark work *Adult Children of Alcoholics* (Health Communications, 1983) and an unofficial "grandmother" of the Adult Child movement, points out that an understanding of our childhood "gives us insight into who we are and what gets in the way of our achieving healthy relationships in adulthood—but that's all. If we get stuck in blame, it develops a smoke screen so that we don't have to make changes ourselves.

"Books can just offer awareness," she stresses. "Looking at our parents is step one. Then we have to look at ourselves and what we're doing to the next generation."

Without doubt, there are abusive parents who will fully brutalize their children, but most are themselves victims. As Michael Elkin puts it, "Toxic parents have toxic kids who become toxic parents and so on. In the end, forgiveness is the only place peace comes from. That doesn't mean overlooking the pain and harm—it means understanding that you have emerged from it."

Psychologist Augustus Napier, director of the Family Workshop in Atlanta and author of *The Fragile Bond* (Harper & Row, 1988), which discusses intimacy in marriage, is also opposed to "making parents the villains."

People have a right to their anger, he says, but in some cases there's a kind of excuse-making going on for the purpose of gaining sympathy. "I help patients express their feelings about the past without having them actually take it out on the parent. My work honors both generations."

"Life is basically unfair," says Betty Carter, director of the Family Institute of Westchester, New York. "Our families are dealt to us like a deck of cards. So it's to your advantage to come to terms with the hand you were given. It's understandable that the person is furious about whatever happened—and I empathize and try to get him or her to ventilate the feelings. But anger and blame poison them." Forgiveness is important, adds Carter. "I don't mean an intellectual gloss-over; I mean a forgiveness of the heart that comes out of a very long journey."

"If you continue to blame your parents, you'll feel all right for a while, but it's no way to live. You then use blame to resolve other problems," Taffel observes. When his clients get into relationships, he says, many try to solve problems by blaming or disengaging altogether. "We need to try to see what our parents were up against," he suggests. His reason is simple: "Until you can see your parents as human beings you can't see yourself as a human being."

The baby boomers are now referred to as the Sandwich Generation—caught between the needs of their children and the needs of their aging parents. Baby boom chronicler Landon Jones suggests parent bashing may be just an evolutionary step toward the Me Generation's finally accepting the burden of middle age. Indeed, there are signs the Adult Child movement is in transition.

The recent publication—and instant popularity—of Dwight Lee Wolter's newest book, *Forgiving Our Parents* (CompCare Publishers, 1989), mirrors a hopeful trend. Wolter, 39, in recovery as an Adult Child for the past five years, says he couldn't have written the book earlier. "But I finally walked around angry at my parents long enough.

"I'm not talking about the fact that my daddy wouldn't let me go to

Harvard. Mine is an open-and-shut case of child abuse," says Wolter, referring to an anecdote in his first book: One day when he forgot to walk his dog, to teach young Dwight a lesson, his father shot the dog. "The question no longer is: 'Who is to blame?' or 'How could they do such things?' " Wolter writes. "The question is: 'Who has been hurt and how can we get [him or her] back on track?' "

59    And as Adult Children mature, moving from anger and blame toward forgiveness and acceptance, they might also teach society a valuable lesson about being human. In Wolter's words, "As we begin to forgive our parents, we begin to forgive ourselves. And we begin to forgive the world for not being perfect either."

## QUESTIONS

*Looking at Ideas:*

1. In the conflict between 44-year-old Barbara and her mother, Evelyn, what is the source of the tension and misunderstanding between mother and daughter? Does the daughter's attendance at ACOA meetings help or hinder their understanding?

2. How has the Adult Child movement changed over the past ten years? What new type of adult seems to be interested in the movement? Do the complaints of these individuals against their "dysfunctional families" seem justified?

3. What is typical of the "baby boom mentality" in the Adult Child movement? Do you agree with this critique of baby boomers?

4. According to therapists Michael Elkin and Jo-Ann Krestan, how do people sometimes misuse the ACOA program?

*Looking at Strategies:*

1. How effectively does this selection use the testimony of actual members of the Adult Child movement? Do these testimonials seem representative of people involved in the movement?

2. How well does the essay use the authoritative testimony of therapists? Do you think that these therapists are objective in their comments about the Adult Child movement, or might some of them have a bias or special interest in criticizing the movement?

3. How does Blau use causal reasoning here? For instance, does she provide evidence to demonstrate why the baby boom generation is drawn to the Adult Child movement or why this movement can have negative effects on its followers and their families? Does she draw appropriate cause-and-effect conclusions from the evidence she presents?

*Looking at Connections:*

1. Contrast this account of the negative side of the Adult Child movement with Lily Collett's "Step by Step." Does Collett blame her parents for her problems as do the groups and individuals portrayed in this essay?

2. Compare the way this article examines the long-term effects of an unhappy childhood with the view of the long-term aftermath of divorce as

viewed by Judith Wallerstein in "On the Brow of the Hill," also included in this chapter. Which writer is more optimistic about the possibility of surviving such early catastrophes without serious psychological damage? Which account seems more realistic to you?

*Suggestions for Writing:*

1. Write an essay in which you explore what you believe to be the most serious long-term effects of growing up in an abusive family. You might begin with your own definition and examples of abusive family behavior.

2. Argue for or against the Adult Children movement as a way of understanding and coming to terms with the effects of growing up in a dysfunctional or abusive family.

3. Write a review of a film or TV movie that presents an image of an abusive or dysfunctional family. Did the fictionalized family seem to be portrayed stereotypically or in an accurate and insightful way? What did you learn about dysfunctional families from watching this show?

**DAVID ELKIND: "The Child Inside"**   A professor of child psychology at Tufts University, David Elkind has devoted his career to exploring the ways in which social pressures affect children's development. Elkind was born in Detroit in 1931 and is the father of three children. He has taught at UCLA and the University of Rochester, New York, and has published a number of books in the area of child development, including *The Child's Reality* (1978), *The Child and Society* (1979), *The Hurried Child* (1981), and *Mis-Education: Preschoolers at Risk* (1987). As you read the following selection from *The Hurried Child,* notice how Elkind explores the destructive impact of parents' efforts to push children to be high achievers at an early age.

DAVID ELKIND

# The Child Inside

Some of the more negative consequences of hurrying usually become evident in adolescence, when the pressures to grow up fast collide with institutional prohibitions. Children pushed to grow up fast suddenly find that many adult prerogatives—which they assumed would be their prerogative—such as smoking, drinking, driving, and so on, are denied them until they reach a certain age. Many adolescents feel betrayed by a society that tells them to grow up fast but also to remain a child. Not surprisingly, the stresses of growing up fast often result in troubled and troublesome behavior during adolescence.

In a recent article, Patricia O'Brien gave some examples of what she called "the shrinking of childhood." Her examples reflect a rush to experiment that is certainly one consequence of growing up fast:

> Martin L (not his real name) confronted his teenager who had stayed out very late the night before. The son replied, "Look, Dad, I've done it all—drugs, sex, and booze, there is nothing left I don't know about." This young man is twelve years old!

> In Washington, D.C. area schools administrators estimate that many thousands of teenagers are alcoholics, with an estimated 30,000 such young people in Northern Virginia alone.

The rush to experiment is perhaps most noticeable in teenage sexual behavior. Although survey data are not always as reliable as one might wish, the available information suggests that there has been a dramatic increase in the number of sexually active teenage girls in the last decade. Melvin Zelnick and John F. Kanther, professors of public health at Johns Hopkins University in Baltimore, conclude that nearly 50 percent of the total population of teenage girls between the ages of fifteen and nineteen (about 10.3 million females) have had premarital sex. The percentage has nearly doubled since the investigators first undertook their study in 1971. "Things that supported remaining a virgin in the past—the fear of getting pregnant, being labelled the 'town pump,' or whatever have disappeared," observes Zelnick.

Young people themselves are very much aware of this trend. "I'd say half the girls in my graduating class are virgins," says an eighteen-year-old high school senior from New Iberia, Louisiana. "But you wouldn't believe those freshmen and sophomores. By the time they graduate there aren't going to be any virgins left."

There are a number of disturbing consequences of this sexual liberation. The number of teenage pregnancies is growing at a startling rate. About 10 percent of all teenage girls, one million in all, get pregnant each year and the number keeps increasing. About 600,000 teenagers give birth each year, and the sharpest increase in such births is for girls under fourteen! In addition, venereal disease is a growing problem among teenagers, who account for 25 percent of the one million or so cases of gonorrhea each year.

The causes of this enhanced sexual activity among young people today are many and varied. The age of first menstruation, for example, has dropped from age seventeen about a century ago to age twelve and a half today. Fortunately this seems to be the lower limit made possible by good health care and nutrition. However, this age of first menstruation has remained stable over the past decade, so it cannot account for the increased sexual activity of young women during this period. Other contributing factors include rapid changes in social values, women's liberation, the exploding divorce rate, the decline of parental and institutional authority, and the fatalistic sense, not often verbalized, that we are all going to die in a nuclear holocaust anyway, so "what the hell, have a good time."

Although the media are quick to pick up these sexual trends and exploit them for commercial purposes (for example, the cosmetics for girls four to nine years old currently being marketed by toy manufacturers), the immediate adult model is perhaps the most powerful and the most pervasive. Married couples are generally discreet about their sexuality in front of their offspring—in part because of a natural tendency to avoid exposing children to what they might not understand, but also because by the time the children are born, much of the romantic phase of the relationship for many couples is in the past.

But single parents who are dating provide a very different model for children. Quite aside from confrontations such as that in *Kramer vs. Kramer* wherein the son encounters the father's naked girlfriend, single parents are likely to be much more overtly sexual than married couples.

With single parents, children may witness the romantic phase of court-ship—the hand-holding, the eye-gazing, the constant touching and fon-dling. This overt sexuality, with all the positive affection it demon-strates, may encourage young people to look for something similar.

It is also true, as Professor Mavis Hetherington of the University of Virginia has found in her research, that daughters of divorced women tend to be more sexually oriented, more flirtatious with men than daughters of widowed mothers or daughters from two-parent homes. Because there are more teenage daughters from single-parent homes today than ever before, this too could contribute to enhanced sexual activity of contemporary teenage girls.

While it is true that some young people in every past generation have engaged in sex at an early age, have become pregnant, contracted venereal disease, and so on, they were always a small proportion of the population. What is new today are the numbers, which indicate that pressures to grow up fast are social and general rather than familial and specific (reflecting parental biases and needs). The proportion of young people who are abusing drugs, are sexually active, and are be-coming pregnant is so great that we must look to the society as a whole for a full explanation, not to just the parents who mirror it.

Paralleling the increased sexuality of young people is an increase in children of what in adults are known as stress diseases. Pediatricians re-port a greater incidence of such ailments as headaches, stomachaches, allergic reactions, and so on in today's youngsters than in previous gen-erations. Type A behavior (high-strung, competitive, demanding) has been identified in children and associated with heightened cholesterol levels. It has also been associated with parental pressure for achieve-ment.

Another negative reflection of the pressure to grow up fast is teen-age (and younger) crime. During 1980, for example, New York police arrested 12,762 children aged sixteen and under on felony charges. In Chicago the figure for the same period was 18,754 charges. Having worked for juvenile courts, I am sure that these figures are underesti-mated. Many children who have committed felonies are released with-out a formal complaint so that they will not have a police record. The children who are "booked" have usually had several previous encoun-ters with the law.

The following examples, recent cases from the New York Police De-partment, illustrate the sort of activities for which children get arrested:

- On 27 February 1981, a boy who had to stand on tiptoes to speak to the bank teller made off with $118 that he had secured at gunpoint. He was nine years old, the youngest felon ever sought by the F.B.I.
- A ten-year-old Brooklyn girl was apprehended in December after she snatched a wallet from a woman's purse. Police said it was the girl's nineteenth arrest.
- One of four suspects captured in the murder of a policeman in Queens on 12 January 1981 was a fifteen-year-old youth.

- A thirteen-year-old Bronx boy was arrested in March 1981 on charges that he killed two elderly women during attempted purse snatchings.
- Another thirteen-year-old boy had a record of thirty-two arrests when seized last year on a charge of attempted murder. He later confessed to an incredible 200-plus felonies.

Such crimes are not being committed just by poor disadvantaged youth who are acting out against a society prejudiced against them. Much teenage crime is committed by middle-class youngsters. However, it tends to be concealed because police and parents try to protect the children; but sometimes this is not possible. One case involved a thirteen-year-old Long Island boy who was killed by three teenagers who stomped on him and strangled him by stuffing stones down his throat. He was attacked because he accidentally discovered that the other boys had stolen an old dirt bike worth only a couple of dollars. It was one of the most brutal and gruesome murders to be committed on Long Island.

. . . There are many . . . solutions to [the] pressure to achieve early. One such solution is to join a cult, such as the "Moonies." What characterizes such cults is that they accept young people unconditionally, regardless of academic success or failure. The cults, in effect, provide an accepting family that does not demand achievement in return for love, although cults do demand obedience and adherence to a certain moral ethic. Even rebellious young people find it easy to adhere to these rules in the atmosphere of acceptance and lack of pressure and competition offered by the cult group. Cult membership is [a] form of negative identity in which young people adopt a group identity rather than an individual one.

A case in point is the Christ Commune (a pseudonym), a branch of the best-organized and most rapidly growing sect of what has been called the Jesus movement. The Commune is a summer camp where members come from their homes for a few months each year. The population (about one hundred) consists of young adults between the ages of fifteen and thirty (average age twenty-one) who are white and come from large (four to eight children), middle-class families. Most have completed high school and some have done college work. One gets the impression they are young people who have not distinguished themselves socially, academically, or athletically and who have held boring, low-paying jobs.

The group offers a strict moral code, a rigid behavioral program, and a sense of mission, of being chosen by and working for God through the mediation of Christ. The members work hard—they get up at 4:30 A.M. and go to sleep at 11:00 P.M. They seem happy with simple food (little meat, water to drink, peanut butter sandwiches for lunch) and strenuous work six days a week. Entertainment and recreation are limited to sitting in a common room, talking, singing spirituals, and engaging in spontaneous prayer.

Such communes, the Jesus movement, and other religious groups are attractive to young people whose personal styles are at variance with those of the larger society. Such groups offer recognition and status to young people who tend to be noncompetitive, anti-intellectual, and spiritual in orientation. Thus the groups provide a needed haven from the pressure to grow up fast, to achieve early, and to make a distinctive mark in life.

The last phenomenon in relation to hurrying to be discussed here is teenage suicide. Currently, suicide is the third leading cause of death during the teen years—preceded only by death via accidents and homicide. An American Academy of Pediatrics report on teenage suicide indicates a large increase in the number of suicides by adolescents in the last decade—the number is now about 5000 per year. For young people between the ages of fifteen to nineteen, the number of suicides per year doubled during the period from 1968 to 1976. The data for young adolescents of ages ten to fourteen are even more distressing: The number of suicides was 116 in 1968 and rose to 158 by 1976.

For every suicide completed, some 50 to 200 are attempted but not successful. Adolescents from all walks of life, all races, religions, and ethnic groups commit or attempt to commit suicide. Boys are generally more successful than girls because they use more lethal methods—boys tend to shoot or hang themselves whereas girls are more likely to overdose on pills or to cut their wrists. "For most adolescents," the pediatric report concludes, "suicide represents an attempt to resolve a difficult conflict, escape an intolerable living arrangement, or punish important individuals in their lives."

To illustrate how hurrying can contribute to teenage suicide, consider the data from the most affluent suburbs of Chicago, a ten-mile stretch of communities along Chicago's northside lakefront that is one of the richest areas in the country. It is the locale chosen by director Robert Redford for the movie *Ordinary People*. The median income per family is about $60,000. Children in these areas attend excellent schools, travel about the world on vacations, are admitted to the best and most prestigious private colleges, and often drive their own cars (which can sometimes be a Mercedes). These are children of affluence who would seem to have it made.

And yet, this cluster of suburbs has the highest number of teenage suicides per year in the state, and almost in the nation. There has been a 250 percent increase in suicides per year over the past decade. These figures are dismaying not only in and of themselves but because the community has made serious efforts at suicide prevention, including the training of teachers in suicide detection and the provision of a twenty-four-hour hot line. One hot line, provided by Chicago psychoanalyst Joseph Pribyl, receives some 150 calls per month. But the suicides continue.

A nineteen-year-old from Glencoe, Illinois, says, "We have an outrageous number of suicides for a community our size." One of this teenager's friends cut her wrist and two others drove their cars into trees. "Growing up here you are handed everything on a platter, but something else is missing. The one thing parents don't give is love, understanding, and acceptance of you as a person." And Isadora Sherman, of Highland Park's Jewish Family and Community Service says, "People give their kids a lot materially, but expect a lot in return. No one sees his kids as average, and those who don't perform are made to feel like failures."

Chicago psychiatrist Harold Visotsky succinctly states how pressure to achieve at an early age, to grow up and be successful fast can contribute to teenage suicide: "People on the lower end of the social scale expect less than these people. Whatever anger the poor experience is acted out in antisocial ways—vandalism, homicide, riots—and the sense of shared misery in the lower income groups prevents people from feeling so isolated. With well-to-do kids, *the rattle goes in the mouth and the foot goes on the social ladder.* The competition ethic takes over, making a child feel even more alone. He's more likely to take it out on himself than society."

Adolescents are very audience conscious. Failure is a public event, and the adolescent senses the audience's disapproval. It is the sense that "everyone knows" that is so painful and that can lead to attempted and successful suicides in adolescents who are otherwise so disposed. Hurrying our children has, I believe, contributed to the extraordinary rise in suicide rates among young people over the past decade.

## All Grown Up and No Place to Go

Sigmund Freud was once asked to describe the characteristics of maturity, and he replied: *lieben und arbeiten* ("loving and working"). The mature adult is one who can love and allow himself or herself to be loved and who can work productively, meaningfully, and with satisfaction. Yet most adolescents, and certainly all children, are really not able to work or to love in the mature way that Freud had in mind. Children love their parents in a far different way from how they will love a real or potential mate. And many, probably most, young people will not find their life work until they are well into young adulthood.

When children are expected to dress, act, and think as adults, they are really being asked to playact, because all of the trappings of adulthood do not in any way make them adults in the true sense of *lieben und arbeiten.* It is ironic that the very parents who won't allow their children to believe in Santa Claus or the Easter Bunny (because they are fantasy and therefore dishonest) allow their children to dress and behave as adults without any sense of the tremendous dishonesty involved in allowing children to present themselves in this grown-up way.

It is even more ironic that practices once considered the province of lower-class citizens now have the allure of middle-class chic. Divorce, single parenting, dual-career couples, and unmarried couples living together were common among the lower class decades ago. Such arrangements were prompted more often than not by economic need, and the children of low-income families were thus pressured to grow up fast out of necessity. They were pitied and looked down upon by upper- and middle-class parents, who helped provide shelters like the Home for Little Wanderers in Boston.

Today the middle class has made divorce its status symbol. And single parenting and living together without being married are increasingly commonplace. Yet middle-class children have not kept pace with the adjustments these adult changes require. In years past a child in a low-income family could appreciate the need to take on adult responsibilities early; families needed the income a child's farm or factory labor would bring, and chores and child-rearing tasks had to be allocated to even younger members of the family. But for the middle-income child today, it is hard to see the necessity of being relegated to a baby sitter or sent to a nursery school or a day care center when he or she has a perfectly nice playroom and yard at home. It isn't the fact of parents' being divorced that is so distressing to middle-class children, but rather that often it seems so unnecessary, so clearly a reflection of parent and not child need. . . . It is the feeling of being used, of being exploited by parents, of losing the identity and uniqueness of childhood without just cause that constitutes the major stress of hurrying and accounts for so much unhappiness among affluent young people today.

It is certainly true that the trend toward obscuring the divisions between children and adults is part of a broad egalitarian movement in this country that seeks to overcome the barriers separating the sexes, ethnic and racial groups, and the handicapped. We see these trends in unisex clothing and hairstyles, in the call for equal pay for equal work, in the demands for affirmative action, and in the appeals and legislation that provide the handicapped with equal opportunities for education and meaningful jobs.

From this perspective, the contemporary pressure for children to grow up fast is only one symptom of a much larger social phenomenon in this country—a movement toward true equality, toward the ideal expressed in our Declaration of Independence. While one can only applaud this movement with respect to the sexes, ethnic and racial groups, and the handicapped, its unthinking extension to children is unfortunate.

Children need time to grow, to learn, and to develop. To treat them differently from adults is not to discriminate against them but rather to recognize their special estate. Similarly, when we provide bilingual programs for Hispanic children, we are not discriminating against them but are responding to the special needs they have, which, if not attended to, would prevent them from attaining a successful education and true equality. In the same way, building ramps for handicapped students is a means to their attaining equal opportunity. Recognizing special needs is not discriminatory; on the contrary, it is the only way that true equality can be attained.

All children have, vis-à-vis adults, special needs—intellectual, social, and emotional. Children do not learn, think, or feel in the same way as adults. To ignore these differences, to treat children as adults, is really not democratic or egalitarian. If we ignore the special needs of children, we are behaving just as if we denied Hispanic or Indian children bilingual programs, or denied the handicapped their ramps and guideposts. In truth, the recognition of a group's special needs and accommodation to those needs are the only true ways to insure equality and true equal opportunity.

## QUESTIONS

*Looking at Ideas:*

1. What pressures lead modern parents to hurry their children to grow up? Do you agree with Elkind about these pressures and their impact?

2. What double messages do modern adolescents receive about acting grown-up? What impact can the pressure to grow up early have on teenage drug, alcohol, and sexual experimentation? Do you think that Elkind establishes clear causal relationships?

3. What impact does Elkind believe that single parents have on their children's early sexual experiences? Do you think Elkind is accurate in his assessment of the effect of the behavior of single parents?

4. Why does Elkind believe that many teenagers today join cult groups? How do these groups represent a reaction against the pressures that modern life places on young people?

5. How have the pressures on young people today led to a rise in the rate of teen suicide, particularly among upper-middle-class youth? Do you agree with Elkind's analysis? Could there be other causal factors?

*Looking at Strategies:*

1. How effectively does Elkind integrate statistics on teenage behavior to demonstrate the trends he analyzes in his essay? Are there any points in the essay that could have been made more effectively with other types of statistical support?

2. Elkind uses a number of briefly narrated case histories to illustrate and support his thesis about teenage grown-up behavior. What examples are particularly effective? Do any seem misleading, sensationalized, or atypical?

3. Elkind uses testimony by both teenagers and adult experts and authorities to clarify and support his conclusions. How effective is his use of quotations from such sources? Do the sources he cites seem credible, or could he have found more impressive ones?

*Looking at Connections:*

1. Contrast the portrait of unhappy teenagers presented in Elkind's essay with the images of children from divorced homes in Wallerstein's "On the Brow of the Hill," also included in this chapter. Which would be more likely to cause the teenage alcohol abuse, crime, suicide, and cult activity that Elkind discusses—divorced families, or families that put too many demands for excellence on their children?

2. Compare Elkind's analysis of the problems of children forced to grow up too quickly with the problems of the "adult children" explored in Melinda Blau's essay. How would Blau respond to Elkind's critique of parents as the most significant cause of their children's problems?

*Suggestions for Writing:*

1. Write a response to Elkind's essay in which you argue for other causes than the ones he explores for one of the problems and tensions he discusses: youth crime, early sexual experimentation, drug abuse, or teen suicide.

2. Write an essay in which you discuss some of your own experiences as a child or adolescent being pushed to grow up quickly. Who or what pushed you, and what impact did this "pushing" have on your personality and development?

3. Select one of the issues raised in Elkind's essay and develop a solution for it based on your reading and your own experiences.

**ARLIE HOCHSCHILD: "Stepping into Old Biographies or Making History Happen?"**   Born in Boston, Massachusetts, in 1940, Arlie Hochschild was educated at Swarthmore College and the University of California at Berkeley. She has been a professor of sociology at the University of California at Santa Cruz and currently teaches at the University of California at Berkeley. She is the author of a number of books on women and the family, including *The Unexpected Community* (1973), *The Managed Heart* (1983), and *The Second Shift* (1989), from which the following section is taken. As you read "Stepping into Old Biographies or Making History Happen?," notice how Hochschild draws from interviews she has conducted a series of disturbing conclusions about the relationships that working women have with their husbands and families.

ARLIE HOCHSCHILD

# Stepping into Old Biographies or Making History Happen?

The woman with the flying hair offers a picture of what it should be like to work and raise a family; busy, active, fun. But the female mannequin in the apron, wide-eyed and still, arms folded, peering outside my neighbor's bay window, a picture of the falsely present mother, is often a more real picture of life at home when two-job couples "cut back" at home and diminish their idea about what a child, a marriage, a home really needs. She is my neighbor's joke but she also symbolizes a certain emotional reality when men don't share the second shift.

The woman with the flying hair and the mannequin are reminders of two sides of this major ongoing revolution in the role of women. As women have been catapulted into the economy, their pocketbooks, their self-respect, their notion of womanhood, and their daily lives have been transformed. The "motor" of this revolution is the changing economy—the decline in the purchasing power of the male wage, the decline in "male" blue-collar jobs, and the rise in "female" jobs in the growing service sector. A new gender ideology has become a powerful prod, as well, by creating an egalitarian code of honor and identity for men and women that fits the evolving circumstances.

But the revolution has influenced women faster than it has influenced men. The unevenness of this revolution has thus driven a wedge between such husbands and wives as Evan and Nancy Holt, Nina and Peter Tanagawa, Ray and Anita Judson. Home is far from a "haven in a heartless world," as Christopher Lasch has noted; home has become the shock absorber of contradictory pressures from the world outside it.

The gender revolution is primarily *caused* by changes in the economy, but people *feel* it in marriage. In a parallel way, economic shifts have been the "motor" of changing relations between blacks and whites. As the number of unskilled jobs declines, as capital moves out of the central cities to suburbs or to cheap labor in Third World countries, blacks and whites are left to compete for the remaining jobs. It is in the back rooms of investment banks, personnel offices, and union halls that the strain between the races might be said to *originate*. But it is in the school yard, in the prison, on the street that racial tension is actually *felt*. Just as American blacks have "absorbed" a higher unemployment rate "for whites," in the same sense, the growing number of working women have absorbed the contradictory demands of family and work "for men," by working the extra month a year. If blacks have lowered the unemployment rate for whites, women have reduced the family-work conflict for men. But unlike most blacks and whites, men and women *live* together; the female absorption of a male problem becomes part of marriage, and strains it.

Although most working mothers I talked with did most of the work of the home, they felt more permission to complain about it than did working women fifty years ago. Many of them wanted to share or wanted to believe they already did. A hundred years ago, American women lacked social permission to ask for a man's help in "women's work." As Gwendolyn Hughes pointed out in 1925, in her book *Mothers in Industry*, earlier in the century supermoming wasn't a "strategy," it was a normal way of life. Today women feel they are allowed to ask for help at home; but on the other hand, they still have to ask. A hundred years from now men may presume it's their role to share. We're in the middle of a social revolution.

The women I studied usually pursued several strategies over time; first a woman would be a supermom, then cut back her hours at home which would set off a crisis and lead her either to cut back her hours at work or further limit her work at home. At the time of my first interview, 18 percent of the wives were married to men who shared the second shift. Most of the rest—52 percent—were not trying to change the division of labor. They were either supermoming, cutting back their hours at work, or cutting back at home. They complained, they joked, they sighed fatalistically; they collected a certain moral credit for doing "so much," but they didn't press their husbands to change. Some of these women didn't want their husbands to share because they didn't believe it was right (they were traditionalists, like Carmen Delacorte) or because they were making up for having surpassed a certain appropriate "power mark." By doing more at home, those women, like Nina Tanagawa, were "balancing." Other women in the study wanted their husbands to share (about half were egalitarian in ideology)—but they didn't press for it.

Many women cut back what had to be done at home by redefining what the house, the marriage and, sometimes, what the child needs. One woman described a fairly common pattern: "I do my half. I do half of his half, and the rest doesn't get done." Others cut back their hours or commitment at work, or sought help from relatives or friends, or older children. These women don't press their husbands to help more either. Most would have loved more help, but getting help was second on their "wish list" after "want fewer marital tensions." And other women had other motives for not persuading their husbands to do more. Ann Myerson didn't want to ask for more help—she wanted to put her husband's job first, because she thought he was smarter and had more to contribute to the world. After a period of disenchantment with her marriage, Jessica Stein didn't want to ask for help because that would bring her closer to Seth, and would force them to face the estrangement they were tacitly agreeing to ignore.

Some women who didn't urge their husbands to share at home also didn't "make room" for his hand at home; they played expert with the baby, the dinner, the social schedule. Something in their tone of voice said, "This is my domain." They edged their husbands out, and then collected credit for "doing it all."

At the time of my first interview, about a third of women were in the course of pressing their husbands to do more. But another *third* of the women I talked to *had* at some point already pushed their husbands to share, and didn't get very far. Some, like Adrienne Sherman and Nancy Holt, tried active renegotiation—holding long discussions, making lists and schedules, saying they can't go on like this. Or they tried passive renegotiation—they played dumb, got sick, or indirectly induced their husbands to do more at home.

For their part, 20 percent of the men felt they should share the responsibility and work at home (egalitarian ideology), and 80 percent did not (traditional or transitional ideology). Men whose wives pressed them to do more often resisted by a strategy of "needs reduction"; they claimed they didn't need the bed made, didn't need a cooked meal, or didn't need a vacation planned. Indeed, some men seemed to covertly compete with their wives over who could care the least about how the house looked, how the meal tasted, what the guests would think. Other men denied the fact they didn't share by not acknowledging the extra kinds of work their wives did. Some men made alternative offerings to the home. Peter Tanagawa offered his wife great emotional support for her career instead of more help at home. Seth Stein offered his wife the money and status of his career instead of help at home. Others made furniture, or built additions on the house their wives could have done without. These were strategies of substitution.

Some men covertly referred their wives to "all the sacrifices" to their manhood they had already suffered—compared to other men, present and past. They made their wives feel "luckier than other women." Unconsciously, they made a gift out of not being as patriarchal as they *could* be. And men obscured their strategies by explaining that they were not "brought up" to do the work at home.

If there is one truth that emerges from all the others, it is that the most important injury to women who work the double day is not the fact they work too long or get too tired. That is only the obvious and tangible cost. The deeper problem such women face is that they can not afford the luxury of unambivalent love for their husbands. Like Nancy Holt, many women carry into their marriage the distasteful and unwieldy burden of resenting their husbands.

Like some hazardous waste produced by a harmful system, this powerful resentment is hard to dispose of.

When women repress their resentment, many, like Nancy Holt, also pay a certain cost in self-knowledge. The mental tricks that kept Nancy Holt from blowing up at Evan or sinking into depression were also the mental tricks that prevented her from admitting her real feelings and understanding the ultimate causes for them. Her psychological "maintenance program"—a program that kept her comparing herself to other women and not to Evan, readjusting correlations she made between love and respect, respect and actions, and reminding herself that she was "lucky" and "equal anyway"—all these habits of thought smoothed the way for a grand rationalization. They softened both sides of a strong contradiction—between her ardent desire for an equal marriage and all that prevented her from having it. They blinded her to what she really felt about her life.

Some women didn't want their husbands to share the second shift and didn't resent their not sharing. But they seemed to pay another emotional price—a devaluation of themselves or their daughters as females. Ann Myerson managed the home because she wanted to protect her husband's time so that he could make his "greater contribution" at work. She felt hers was the "less important" work. Despite herself, she also regretted having daughters, because they too would grow up managing the house in order to protect the greater work contributions of their husbands. However driven, however brilliant, Ann felt, girls could never enjoy the privilege of smooth, unambivalent devotion to work which in our society is the work that is most highly rewarded. Instead of seeing a problem in the system of rewards or the arrangement between the sexes, Ann felt it was too bad she didn't have boys who could "cash in" on it. In this Ann articulated a contradiction I believe every woman faces: women end up doing the second shift when the second shift is secondary. The more important cost to women is not that they work the extra month a year; it is that society devalues the work of the home and sees women as inferior because they do devalued work.

Devalued as the work of rearing children is, it is probably one of the most humanly rewarding occupations. In appreciating the toll of living in a stalled revolution, then, we should count as part of that cost the missing connections between Seth Stein, Evan Holt, and their children. Resentful of Seth's long absences, his older son sullenly withdrew and at bedtime the younger one dashed around frantically. Drawing the one out and calming the other down became one more hassle at the end of Seth's long day. He is missing the feelings his children would feel toward him if they didn't resent his absence; Seth is missing the tangles and the arguments that ultimately remind a parent that they matter to a child. But he is also missing the cuddles, the talks about what holds the clouds up, and why people get sad.

Although fathers pay most of this particular emotional cost, in a different way many mothers do too. As the main managers of the second shift, women become the "heavies," the "time and motion" persons of the family-and-work speed-up. They hurry children through their daily rounds—"Hurry up and eat. . . ." "Hurry and get into your pajamas. . . ."—and thus often become the targets of children's aggression.

## QUESTIONS

*Looking at Ideas:*

1. How has the "revolution" of women working outside the home transformed women and family life? Why has this revolution generally had less influence on men than on women?

2. Why is the home no longer "a haven in a heartless world"? Into what has it been transformed?

3. What male problem have working women "absorbed"? Why do women today feel more able to complain about the stress of their lives and housework pressures than women of previous generations?

4. Although Hochschild points out that more working women today feel free to complain about the unequal male-female division of housework, only a small percentage seem to actually insist on a fair division. Why?

5. How did the husbands in the study avoid equal sharing of household chores and responsibility for their children? What psychological impact does this evasion have on their wives and the attitudes of working wives towards their husbands, themselves, and their work in the home?

*Looking at Strategies:*

1. What is the impact of the two opposed images at the beginning of the selection: the woman with the flying hair and the mannequin? How do these images help Hochschild to make her points about the conflict that working wives feel about their opposed roles?

2. How effectively does Hochschild use her study of working wives to support the conclusions she draws in this selection? What particular examples and cases does she draw upon?

3. Hochschild uses an analogy between women and blacks to clarify her

comments about the function of women in the American workplace. Is this a valid parallel? How does Hochschild also *contrast* the relations between black workers and white workers? Is her contrast effective?

*Looking at Connections:*

1. Compare the image of tensions brought on in families where women work as presented here with the portrait of life growing up with a medical doctor as mother as seen in Sarah Lightfoot's essay "Beginnings" in Chapter 1.

2. Compare Hochschild's portrait of stressful life in the modern dual-career family with the picture of married life in the 1950s portrayed in Tillie Olsen's "I Stand Here Ironing" (included in this chapter). Does Olsen's narrator have enough time to attend to the needs of her family? Does her husband seem to help out?

*Suggestions for Writing:*

1. Write an essay in which you discuss what you feel are the most significant consequences and tensions of women assuming the burden of a "second shift."

2. From a male perspective, how accurate is Hochschild's portrayal of the second shift? What would a working, married male with a working wife say in response to the essay?

3. Write an essay in which you discuss ways in which working women and men could design an arrangement for a more equal sharing of responsibilities for housework and family-related chores than was seen in the families Hochschild studied.

**JUDITH WALLERSTEIN AND SANDRA BLAKESLEE: "On the Brow of the Hill"** An authority on the subject of divorce, Judith Wallerstein, Ph.D., directs the Center for the Family in Transition, a nationally renowned counseling service for divorcing families. She is a fellow with the Center for Advanced Study in the Behavioral Sciences at Stanford as well as a senior lecturer at the School of Social Welfare at the University of California at Berkeley. She is coauthor (with Joan Kelley) of *Surviving the Breakup: How Children and Parents Cope with Divorce* and, with Sandra Blakeslee, a free-lance science and medical writer, of *Second Chances: Men, Women, and Children a Decade after Divorce* (1989). The following selection, "On the Brow of the Hill" is from *Second Chances* (1990). In this final chapter from the book, notice how Wallerstein concludes her long-term study on the children of divorced families, emphasizing the difficulties that such children have in overcoming the emotional turmoil involved in divorce.

JUDITH WALLERSTEIN AND SANDRA BLAKESLEE

# On the Brow of the Hill

Nearly twenty years have passed since my daughter's friend Karen started me thinking about divorce and its consequences for men, women, and children. Indeed, I have spent almost two decades of my life interviewing families in transition—separating families, divorcing families, and remarried families, all kinds of families with children. It has been a full-time commitment, often running seven days a week.

Since 1980, when I founded the Center for the Family in Transition, and in addition to my regular work, I get at least two, sometimes three, telephone calls on an average day from people asking for help in the midst of divorce. Mostly these are strangers who have read my name in a newspaper or heard of my work from a friend. Many of the calls are from parents. Just the other day a man called from Pennsylvania and said, "I'm a teacher. My wife is suing me for divorce." His voice was strained. "I understand you have written about the importance of fathers, how much their children need to still see them. Can you direct me? Can you send me something to help?"

On the same day I got a call from a woman in southern California who told me that the court had ordered her to send her nursing infant to spend every other weekend with the child's father, who lives several hundred miles away. The woman, who must express and freeze extra breast milk to send along with the baby, told me that she was never married to the baby's father, only lived with him briefly, and has no idea what kind of parent he is. She asked, "What should I do?"

Shocked by her story—reflecting an intrusion into the most intimate of human relationships, that between a nursing mother and her child—I could say only that there is no psychological research anywhere to support the court's decision but that I knew of no immediate way that I could help. We are staying in touch.

Every now and then I get a call from one of the children or parents in our study, usually to announce an important change in his or her life. During this same week, Kedric called to say that he has been accepted into a graduate program in aeronautical engineering—a lifelong dream that he is finally pursuing. And not long ago Denise called from Denmark to say that she is getting married, adding, "You know, I still think about my parents' divorce every day." I made a mental note that she said "every day."

The third telephone call on an average day is from a lawyer, usually asking if I will be an expert witness in a custody dispute. Although the practice could be lucrative, I have never accepted any of these invitations because I do not want to compromise my impartiality. My credibility as a researcher might diminish if I became identified with any particular point of view in the courts.

My daily correspondence also reflects how deeply I have become involved in the issues surrounding divorce and how widespread the divorce phenomenon has become in our country and throughout the world. Last week, I was invited to speak at the University of Rome for two days, to help shape a study of divorce in Italy. I was also asked to attend a conference on child custody in Wisconsin that will attempt to develop national guidelines on these issues. My primary task for the week was to write the keynote address for a family law conference in Los Angeles involving judges, mediators, and attorneys from all over the United States and Canada.

All of these activities—combined with my ongoing long-term research, the work on joint custody, and my close supervision of the various counseling programs at the center—have given me a ringside seat at the drama of changing relationships between the men and women, and the parents and children, in our society. I feel that I have been privileged to observe at first hand, close up, what is undoubtedly one of the most important revolutions of modern times. In looking at divorce, we are looking at the flip side of marriage; and we are gaining new insights into basic family values—what people believe is right and how people behave toward one another. We are a society in the process of fundamental change in a direction that is entirely new and uncharted.

In thinking about these changes, I am reminded of a conversation I had with anthropologist Margaret Mead in 1972. Upset over my early findings at how troubled children are after divorce, I arranged to meet her at the San Francisco airport at midnight. She was on her way to what was to be her last trip to New Guinea, and we had several hours together before she had to leave. She, too, was disturbed by the findings and at one point said, "Judy, there is no society in the world where people have stayed married without enormous community pressure to do so. And I don't think anybody can predict what you will find."

Her words continue to impress on me how little we really know about the world we have created in the last twenty years—*a world in which marriage is freely terminable at any time, for the first time in our history.* Perhaps as a clinician and a psychologist I should confess that when we began to look at family changes caused by divorce, we began at ground zero. We lacked, and continue to lack, the psychological theory that we need to understand and to predict the consequences. This is because psychoanalysis, family systems theory, and child development theory have all developed within the context of the two-parent, intact family. Now we are in the awkward position of inventing the theory we need as we discover new facts. So if we've been sashaying back and forth as new findings come to light, it's because that is the state of our knowledge. Only painfully and slowly, essentially since the mid-seventies, have we begun to build a consensus and theory on which we can agree.

From the stories of these children and their parents and all the other people I have spoken with over the years, however, several lessons do emerge. They have taught all of us a great deal that we did not know, that we had no way of knowing:

• Divorce is a wrenching experience for many adults and almost all children. It is almost always more devastating for children than for their parents.

• Divorce is not an event that stands alone in children's or adults' experience. It is a continuum that begins in the unhappy marriage and extends through the separation, the divorce, and any remarriages and second divorces. Divorce is not the culprit; it may be no more than one of the many experiences that occur in this broad continuum.

• The effects of divorce are often long-lasting. Children are especially affected because divorce occurs during their formative years. What they see and experience becomes a part of their inner world, their view of themselves, and their view of society. The early experiences in a failing marriage are not erased by divorce. Children who witnessed violence between their parents often found these early images dominating their own relationships ten and fifteen years later. Therefore, while divorce can rescue a parent from an intolerable situation, it can fail to rescue the children.

• Almost all children of divorce regard their childhood and adolescence as having taken place in the shadow of divorce. Although many agree by adulthood that their parents were wise to part company, they nevertheless feel that they suffered from their parents' mistakes. In many instances, the conditions in the postdivorce family were more

345

stressful and less supportive to the child than the conditions in the failing marriage.

· Children of divorce come to adulthood eager for enduring love and marriage. They do not take divorce lightly.

· For the children in our study, the postdivorce years brought the following:

Half saw their mother or father get a second divorce in the ten-year period after the first divorce.

Half grew up in families where parents stayed angry at each other.

One in four experienced a severe and enduring drop in their standard of living and went on to observe a major, lasting discrepancy between economic conditions in their mothers' and fathers' homes. They grew up with their noses pressed against the glass, looking at a way of life that by all rights should have been theirs.

Three in five felt rejected by at least one of the parents, sensing that they were a piece of psychological or economic baggage left over from a regretted journey.

Very few were helped financially with college educations, even though they continued to visit their fathers regularly. But because their fathers were relatively well-off, they were ineligible for scholarships.

· Many of the children emerged in young adulthood as compassionate, courageous, and competent people. Those who did well were helped along the way by a combination of their own inner resources and supportive relationships with one or both parents, grandparents, stepparents, siblings, or mentors. Some later experienced nurturing love affairs and good marriages of their own making. Some of those who did well were very much helped by the example of parents who had been able to successfully rebuild their lives after divorce. Others did well because they were deliberately able to turn away from the examples set by their parents. A smaller number benefited from the continued relationship with two good parents who—despite their anger and disappointment with each other—were able to cooperate in the tasks of childrearing.

· In this study, however, almost half of the children entered adulthood as worried, underachieving, self-deprecating, and sometimes angry young men and women. Some felt used in a battle that was never their own. Others felt deprived of the parenting and family protection that they always wanted and never got. Those who were troubled at young adulthood were more depleted by early experiences before and after their parents' divorces, had fewer resources, and often had very little help from their parents or from anybody else. Some children literally brought themselves up, while others were responsible for the welfare of a troubled parent as well.

· Although boys had a harder time over the years than girls, suffering a wide range of difficulties in school achievements, peer relationships, and the handling of aggression, this disparity in overall adjustment eventually dissipated. As the young women stood at the developmental threshold of young adulthood, when it was time to seek commitment with a young man, many found themselves struggling with anxiety and guilt. This sudden shock, which I describe as a sleeper effect, led to many maladaptive pathways, including multiple relationships and impulsive marriages that ended in early divorce.

· Adolescence is a period of grave risk for children in divorced families; those who entered adolescence in the immediate wake of their parents' divorces had a particularly hard time. The young people told us time and again how much they needed a family structure, how much they wanted to be protected, and how much they yearned for clear guidelines for moral behavior. They told us they needed more encouragement from parents in the complicated process of growing up and that, failing to get it, they were seduced by the voices of the street. Feeling abandoned at this critical time in their lives, they were haunted by inner doubts and uncertainties about the future. An alarming number of teenagers felt abandoned, physically and emotionally.

· Finally, and perhaps most important for society, the cumulative effect of the failing marriage and divorce rose to a crescendo as each child entered young adulthood. It was here, as these young men and women faced the developmental task of establishing love and intimacy, that they most felt the lack of a template for a loving, enduring, and moral relationship between a man and a woman. It was here that anxiety carried over from divorced family relationships threatened to bar the young people's ability to create new, enduring families of their own. As these anxieties peak in the children of divorce throughout our society, the full legacy of the past twenty years begins to hit home. The new families that are formed appear vulnerable to the effects of divorce. Although many young people in the study eventually were able to move forward and to establish good relationships and good marriages, this is a critical passage for all.

For adults, divorce more often brings an end to an unhappy chapter in their lives. Many of the individuals in our study succeeded in creating a much happier, better way of life for themselves, often but not necessarily within a happy second marriage.

More, however, experienced divorce as essentially the beginning of a long-lasting discrepancy between themselves and their former spouses. As the years went by, one person was able to create a better quality of life while the other felt left behind—economically, psychologically, and socially. These are the winners and losers in this book, the ex-husbands and ex-wives who—relative to one another—made better or worse use of their second chances in the decade after divorce.

In watching adults take up or fail to take up their second chances, we have learned the following:

347

· Many of the second marriages are in fact happier. These adults learn from their earlier experiences and avoid making the same mistakes.

· Many adults, especially women, show striking growth in competence and self-esteem.

· Recovery is not a given in adult life. The assumption that all people recover psychologically is not based on evidence. On what basis do we make the assumption that after twenty or twenty-five years of marriage people can inevitably pick themselves back up and start over again?

· Feelings, especially angry feelings and feelings of hurt and humiliation, can remain in full force for many years after divorce.

· Some adults are at greater risk than others. Women with young children, especially if they are driven into poverty by divorce, face a Herculean struggle to survive emotionally and physically. The stress of being a single parent with small children, working day shift and night shift without medical insurance or other backup, is unimaginable to people who have not experienced it. No wonder some women told us that they feel dead inside.

· Many older men and women coming out of long-term marriages are alone and unhappy, facing older age with rising anxiety. They lean on their children, with mixed feelings, for support and companionship ten and fifteen years after divorce. Opportunities for work, play, sex, and marriage decline rapidly with age, especially for women.

· Younger men are often adrift. Divorce seems to block them from expanding into their adult roles as husbands and fathers.

· Finally, for adults, the high failure rate of second marriages is serious and, as we discovered, often devastating because it reinforces the first failure many times over.

Many of our more baffling findings have to do with changes in parent-child relationships that occur at the time of divorce and in the years that follow. Because children long remain dependent on parents for economic and emotional support, these changes can have serious consequences. Evidently the relationship between parents and children grows best in the rich soil of a happy, intact family. But without this nurturing growth medium, parent-child relationships can become very fragile and are easily broken. What does this mean for families? What have we learned?

· As in the intact family, the child's continued relationship with good parents who cooperate with each other remains vital to his or her proper development. However, good, cooperative parenting is many times more difficult in the postdivorce family.

· When a marriage breaks down, most men and women experience a diminished capacity to parent. They give less time, provide less discipline, and are less sensitive to their children, being caught up themselves in the personal maelstrom of divorce and its aftermath. Many parents are temporarily unable to separate their children's needs from their own. In many families parenting is restored within a year or two after divorce. But in a surprising number of families, the diminished parenting continues, permanently disrupting the child-rearing functions of the family.

· Since most children live with their mothers after divorce, the single most important protective factor in a child's psychological development and well-being over the years is the mother's mental health and the quality of her parenting.

· We have seen how difficult it is for fathers who have moved out of the house to sustain a close and loving relationship with their children, especially if one or both parents remarry. Yet we have also seen how poignantly the children hold on to an internal image, sometimes a fantasy image, of the absent or even the visiting father and how both fathers and children create phantom relationships with each other.

· We have seen that the children's need for their father continues and that it rises with new intensity at adolescence, especially when it is time for the children to leave home. The nature of the father-child relationship, and not the frequency of visiting, is what most influences the child's psychological development.

· Many a father seems to have lost the sense that his children are part of his own generational continuity, his defense against mortality. This blunting of the father's relationship to his children is a stunning surprise.

· New, unfamiliar parent-child relationships have developed in some families, in which the child is overburdened by responsibility for a parent's psychological welfare or by serving as an instrument of parental rage.

· We have learned that good stepparent-child relationships are not assured. They need to be properly nurtured to take root in the minds and hearts of the children. Many children feel excluded from the remarried family.

· At the same time, we have seen some mothers and fathers, and even some stepparents, undertake heroic measures of loyalty, selflessness, and devotion to their children.

I have asked myself many times if these children and adults who experienced divorce in the early 1970s are different from those who are experiencing divorce today. At the Center for the Family in Transition, we are counseling about thirty new families every month, more than any other agency in the country. Although the divorce rate rose steeply in the 1970s, it reached a plateau in the 1980s, at a level where one in two recent marriages can be expected to end in divorce. Children born in the mid-1980s stand a 38 percent chance of experiencing their parents' divorce before they reach age eighteen.

I see surprisingly little change in how adults or children react emotionally to divorce. Parents still have trouble telling the children. Despite the tremendous proliferation of media attention to divorce, nearly 50 percent of the families that we counsel waited until the day of the separation or afterward to tell their children that their familiar world is coming apart.

The causes of divorce have not changed, nor have men's and women's feelings changed. The amount of suffering is no less. People like to think that because there are so many divorced families, adults and children will find divorce easier or even easy. But neither parents nor children find comfort in numbers. Divorce is not a more "normal" experience simply because so many people have been touched by it. Our findings reveal that all children suffer from divorce, no matter how many of their friends have gone through it. And although the stigma of divorce has been enormously reduced in recent years, the pain that each child feels is not assuaged. Each and every child cries out, "Why me?"

One very worrisome difference between the 1970s and 1980s, based on reports from mental health clinics, is an increase in severe reactions in today's families—more violence, more parental dependence on children, and many more troubled, even suicidal children. I am very worried about the acute depression in many adolescents who functioned well before the divorce. There has been a rise in reports of child abuse and sexual molestation. Although it is sometimes difficult to separate real from fabricated abuse, especially when these are at issue in child custody battles, the problem is alarming. Worse yet, the system set up to deal with the problem is woefully inadequate.

We have seen a major shift in the attitudes of fathers, more of whom are trying to maintain an active parenting role in their children's lives. There is also a greater willingness among women to allow this involvement and a wider expectation that it will occur whatever the custody arrangement. On the other hand, we see a small but significant increase in the number of women who are leaving their children, choosing to place them temporarily or entirely in their ex-husbands' care. There are many motives involved in this decision, including the fact that it has become a more acceptable option in our society.

Economically, the impact of divorce on women and children continues to be a serious problem. As a result of national legislation passed in 1984, states have more tools to enforce child support payment, but it is too soon to tell how much their efforts are helping children. There continues to be little general support for equalizing the standard of living between the fathers' and mothers' homes in the years after divorce. As a result, children continue to be primarily dependent on their mothers' earning power, which is usually less than their fathers'. Despite the women's movement, few mothers in the 1980s are prepared to enter the marketplace with skills that will maintain them and their children at a comparable or a reasonably good standard of living.

One major difference between the 1970s and 1980s has been the rise in joint custody, which can be helpful in families where it has been chosen voluntarily by both parents and is suitable for the child. But there is no evidence to support the notion that "one size fits all" or even most. There is, in fact, a lot of evidence for the idea that different custody models are suitable for different families. The policy job ahead is to find the best match for each family.

Sadly, when joint custody is imposed by the court on families fighting over custody of children, the major consequences of the fighting are shifted onto the least able members of the family—the hapless and helpless children. The children can suffer serious psychological injury when this happens. I am in favor of joint custody in many cases, where parents and children can handle it, but it is no panacea. We still have a great deal to learn.

Another question I have asked myself: Does the experience in California speak for the rest of the nation? It speaks primarily, in my view, to middle-class America and perhaps to middle-class families in other parts of the postindustrial world. We know much less about the divorce experience of families in other social classes and among other ethnic groups. As for middle-class America, however, my findings have held up well in the light of studies conducted in other parts of the country. When I speak at conferences around the country, in Europe, Latin America, and elsewhere abroad, professionals and parents confirm that the reactions they have observed in children and adults are remarkably in accord with my observations.

Although our overall findings are troubling and serious, we should not point the finger of blame at divorce per se. Indeed, divorce is often the only rational solution to a bad marriage. When people ask whether they should stay married for the sake of the children, I have to say, "Of course not." All our evidence shows that children turn out less well adjusted when exposed to open conflict, where parents terrorize or strike one another, than do children from divorced families. And while we lack systematic studies comparing unhappily married families and divorced families, I do know that it is not useful to provide children with a model of adult behavior that avoids problem solving and that stresses martyrdom, violence, or apathy. A divorce undertaken thoughtfully and realistically can teach children how to confront serious life problems with compassion, wisdom, and appropriate action.

Our findings do not support those who would turn back the clock. As family issues are flung to the center of our political arena, nostalgic voices from the right argue for a return to a time when divorce was difficult to obtain. But they do not offer solutions to the serious problems that have contributed to the rising divorce rate in the first place. From the left we hear counterarguments that relationships have become more honest and more equal between men and women and that the changes we face simply represent "the new family form." But to say that all family forms are equivalent is to semantically camouflage the truth: All families are *not* alike in the protection they extend to children. Moreover, the voices of our children are not represented in the political arena. Although men and women talk *about* children, it is hard for me to believe that they are necessarily talking *for* children.

Like it or not, we are witnessing family changes which are an integral part of the wider changes in our society. We are on a wholly new course, one that gives us unprecedented opportunities for creating better relationships and stronger families—but one that has also brought unprecedented dangers for society, especially for our children.

We have reached the brow of the hill at the end of the 1980s. As I survey the landscape, I am encouraged by signs of change for the better:

· Society is beginning to pay attention to the economic plight of its women and children, to the so-called feminization of poverty. We are less tolerant of the economic injustice promoted by divorce.
· There are strong voices raised in the legislatures and the courts that reflect concern about the unmet needs of all children and families in our society.
· There seems to be growing community awareness about the impact of divorce on families and children. Teachers, psychotherapists, clergy, physicians, judges, family lawyers, and parents are more attuned to the special needs of divorcing families.
· There has been an increase in divorce services, including mediation in the courts and more psychological counseling services in the community.

But these encouraging signs still do not measure up to the magnitude of the problem. Legal, mediation, and mental health services focus almost exclusively on the here and now of the divorce crisis. Child support payment is set in accord with the present and not the changing future needs of the children. Even visiting schedules for the children are established on the basis of current need and age. All of these services assume that if only we can help people settle property, custody, and visitation, all else will follow. This is clearly not the case.

If the goal of the legal system is—and I fully believe that it should be—to minimize the impact of divorce on children and to preserve for children as much as possible of the social, economic, and emotional security that existed while their parents' marriage was intact, then we still have very far to go.

At a minimum, the variety of supports and services for divorcing families needs to be expanded in scope and over time. These families need education at the time of the divorce about the special problems created by their decision. They need help in making decisions about living arrangements, visiting schedules, and sole or joint custody. And they need help in implementing these decisions over many years—and in modifying them as the children grow and the family changes. Divorcing families need universally available mediation services. They also need specialized counseling over the long haul in those cases where the children are at clear risk, where the parents are still locked in bitter disputes, and where there has been family violence. Divorcing men and women must make realistic provision for the economic support of their children, backed up by the government when necessary. These provisions should include health care and college education, where it is appropriate.

Beyond all this, we need to learn much more about divorce. We need to learn how and why things worked out so badly between divorced men and women who have had children together, most of whom tell us that they married for love. We need to learn how to reduce the unhappiness, anger, and disappointment that is so widespread in the relationships between men and women. And we need to learn more about courtship, marriage, and remarriage and about what makes good marriages work.

As a society we have always been quick to respond to individual needs; it was easy and natural for us to rivet our collective attention on the little girl who was recently trapped in an abandoned well. But it is harder for us to face up to the problems affecting our collective selves—and for a very good reason. To echo the immortal words of "Pogo" cartoonist Walt Kelly, "We have met the enemy and he is us." Divorce is not an issue of "we" versus "them." Profound changes have shaken the American family. It is not that we are less virtuous or less concerned for our children and their future, but we have been slow to recognize the magnitude of the needs of children of divorce and their parents. And we have been reluctant to take collective responsibility.

A society that allows divorce on demand inevitably takes on certain responsibilities. It is up to us to protect one another, especially our children, to the extent possible against the psychological and economic suffering that divorce can bring. All children in today's world feel less protected. They sense that the institution of the family is weaker than it has ever been before. Children of divorce grow up with the notion that love can be transient and commitment temporary, but all children—even those raised in happy, intact families—worry that their families may come undone as well. Therefore, the task for society in its true and proper perspective is to support and strengthen the family—all families.

As I bring this book to a close, a biblical phrase I have not thought of for many years keeps running through my head: "Watchman, what of the night?" We are not, I'm afraid, doing very well on our watch—at least not for our children—and, consequently, not for the future of our society. By avoiding our task, we have unintentionally placed the primary burden of coping with family change onto the children. To state it plainly, we are allowing our children to bear the psychological, economic, and moral brunt of divorce.

And from what the children are telling us, they recognize the burdens that have been put on their slender shoulders. When six-year-old John came to our center shortly after his parents' divorce, he would only mumble, "I don't know." He would not answer questions; he played games instead. First John hunted all over the playroom for the baby dolls. When he found a good number of them, he stood the baby dolls firmly on their feet and placed the miniature tables, chairs, beds, and eventually all the playhouse furniture on their heads. John looked at me, satisfied. The babies were supporting a great deal on their heads. Then, wordlessly, he placed all the mother dolls and father dolls in pre-

353

carious positions on the steep roof of the dollhouse. As a father doll slid off the roof, John caught him and, looking up at me, said, "He might die." Soon all the mother and father dolls began sliding off the roof. John caught them gently, one by one, saving each from falling to the ground.

"Are the babies the strongest?" I asked.

"Yes," John shouted excitedly. "The babies are holding up the world."

## QUESTIONS

*Looking at Ideas:*

1. Why does Wallerstein believe that divorce signifies "one of the most important revolutions of modern times"? Do you agree?

2. What does Wallerstein mean when she refers to divorce as a "continuum" rather than an "event"?

3. What long-lasting effects of divorce on children does Wallerstein discuss? How do these effects differ for children of different ages and genders?

4. How are the effects of divorce on children different from those on parents? Which types of parents have the hardest time surviving a divorce?

5. What positive and negative changes has Wallerstein observed in the impact of divorce on family members? What has remained constant? What remains to be done in society to improve the circumstances of divorcing families?

*Looking at Strategies:*

1. What common thread is to be found in the series of telephone calls Wallerstein presents at the beginning of the essay? What might we infer from them about the impact of divorce both on parents and children, and on society at large?

2. The conclusions and general statements made in this selection come from a lengthy study on a number of divorced families conducted by Wallerstein. How effectively does she use this study to support her conclusions?

3. The ending of the essay describes a young boy, John, playing with baby dolls and toy furniture in a doll's house. Is the description of John's play and the dialogue he has with Wallerstein an effective ending and commentary on the emotional impact of divorce? Why or why not?

*Looking at Connections:*

1. Compare Wallerstein's view of the impact of divorce and remarriage on modern children with Tillie Olsen's account of a 1950s divorced and remarried family in "I Stand Here Ironing" at the end of this chapter. Is Wallerstein's view any more optimistic than Olsen's? Does the position of the children of divorce seem to have improved or worsened in the last forty years?

2. Compare Wallerstein's account of the family tensions after a divorce

with the tensions described in Arlie Hochschild's "Stepping into Old Biographies or Making History Happen?"

*Suggestions for Writing:*

1. Write an essay in which you discuss whether it is desirable for parents to prolong a troubled marriage in order to protect young children from the kind of confusion relating to divorce that the children in Wallerstein's study have experienced. Use examples from successful or unsuccessful marriages you have observed or read about.

2. What do you think would be a helpful program for lessening some of the ill effects and tensions of a family experiencing a divorce? Write an essay in which you propose some ideas of your own for helping such families.

3. Interview friends of yours from divorced families, asking them to respond to some of the concerns reflected in Wallerstein's essay about the effects of divorce on children. Do your interviewees' experiences parallel those of the children studied in Wallerstein's research? In what ways do their responses differ from those of her subjects? Write up your conclusions in the form of an essay.

**DAN ZEGART: "Solomon's Choice"** Free-lance writer Dan Zegart worked
with photographer Laura Pedrick in preparing the article "Solomon's Choice"
(1989), which appeared in *Ms.* magazine in 1989. The essay is an account of
difficulties social caseworkers encounter in their attempts to interpret the
sometimes ambiguous laws relating to child abuse and to make accurate observations and decisions relative to reported or suspected cases of abuse. As
you read the essay, notice how Zegart narrates case histories of families that
have been damaged by well-intentioned social workers who don't completely
grasp the dynamics of family interactions among the poor or the consequences
of separating children from their families of origin.

DAN ZEGART

# *Solomon's Choice*

Jenny Kracht stood in the living room of her sister-in-law's house in
Newburgh, New York, dialing frantically, trying to reach a lawyer. A
nervous woman, she had always had trouble keeping her head in emergencies. Now she struggled for control as a tense little group of relatives consoled her five terrified kids. Outside the house a small army of
state and local police blocked off any escape.

It was late afternoon on September 26, 1986. Jenny Kracht had just
been accused of child abuse.

A few hours earlier, as she drove to Meadow Hill Elementary
School to pick up three of her children, she had been anticipating a big
Friday night dinner and the season premiere of *Dallas*. But some time
before she arrived, seven-year-old Michael Kracht had told school authorities that a bruise on his back was the result of a beating. Michael
had warned his father, Paul, on several occasions that if he made him
go to school, he'd be sorry. But that afternoon, watching his mother on
the phone, Michael was scared—this wasn't at all what he expected to
happen.

Based solely on a few bruises and Michael's explanation of where
they came from, all five of the Kracht children—Michael, his brother
Matthew, 10, Jessica, five, Ashley, four, and Justin, seven months—were

356

split up that evening and placed in foster homes. It took five weeks and
thousands of dollars in lawyers' and therapists' fees to get them back
home and a year and a half to regain full legal custody. The child protection unit of the Orange County Department of Social Services,
which acted so promptly to rescue the children from their mother, was
agonizingly slow to respond when Michael and Matthew told their
caseworker they were being physically abused in foster care. The long
separation was more puzzling to the family given the fact that Michael
recanted his story soon after reaching the foster home.

"Social services tore this family apart," said Jenny Kracht, sitting in
the kitchen of her two-story home with Paul, who recently retired as a
prison guard. "I used to tell the kids, you've got nothing to ever worry
about, nobody can ever hurt you, don't worry about the bogeyman,
you're safe here with Mom and Dad. You can't tell them that now."

That fall, the Krachts became one of thousands of American families devastated by a false accusation of child abuse. Tragedies such as
the death of Lisa Steinberg in New York City have focused attention on
the vulnerability of children, and the National Committee for Prevention of Child Abuse reports a continuing rise in child abuse fatalities.
But the Krachts also were victims of a child welfare system where overburdened caseworkers face often impossible choices.

Under the watchwords "the best interests of the child," 150,000
kids are taken from their parents each year by a system geared to act
first and ask questions later. However, two thirds of the 2.2 million reports of child maltreatment in 1986 turned out to be unfounded. And
of the substantiated reports, only 15 percent involved any serious risk
to the child's safety, according to Douglas Besharov, a resident scholar
at the American Enterprise Institute and first director of the National
Center on Child Abuse and Neglect. It's this 15 percent, he concluded,
that need the kind of intervention the Krachts received but Lisa Steinberg didn't—immediate removal from the home. An atmosphere of
well-justified concern for maltreated children has bred a monster that
can traumatize both parents and kids, trampling their rights to a parent-child relationship.

It can happen most easily to families that are poor, out of the media's spotlight, and afraid to speak out when faced with the authority of
the social service agencies. In Newburgh's East End, which is across
town from Jenny and Paul Kracht, I spent time with families who had
none of the resources of the middle-class Krachts. Within a two-week
period two years ago, five of these families lost their children for various periods of time. The federal Adoption Assistance and Child Welfare
Act of 1980 requires that "reasonable efforts" be made to keep families
together and that only children in real danger of maltreatment be
placed in foster care. But there is a considerable gap between theory
and practice, according to Mary Lee Allen, director of child welfare
and mental health for the Children's Defense Fund (CDF) in Washington, D.C. Citing antifamily bias in the child welfare system, she expressed concern that children are placed inappropriately when preven-

tive services should be offered instead to poor parents having difficulty caring for their kids.

Fifteen miles southwest of Newburgh in Monroe, New York, Tony Hynson invited intervention from the Department of Social Services when he sought help for his family before the birth of his son Nicholas. Deborah Mangin, the mother of Nicholas and his brother, Joshua, said she and Tony were trying to find work and a better apartment. "They could have offered day-care services," she said. "If we had that at least three times a week, we would have been all right." Instead they were offered parenting classes and a homemaker who, according to Tony, "did nothing but shoot the breeze and smoke cigarettes." In the fall of 1986, a child neglect petition was filed against them, charging that their bungalow was "in an extremely unsanitary condition." Nicholas and Joshua were removed, and they didn't return home for more than a year.

Deborah Mangin feels that she and Tony were punished for asking for help. Friends say that although the couple weren't model homemakers, they never saw garbage strewn over the floor or other horrors detailed in the court papers.

According to Allen of the CDF, the idea behind the 1980 act "is to move away from the 'dirty house cases.' I don't want there to be any mistake about this," said Allen, referring to cases like Debby Mangin's. "Children absolutely should not be removed simply because of poverty." But few if any states are in compliance with the law, according to Marcia Lowry, director of the Children's Rights Project for the American Civil Liberties Union. New York State budgets some $120 million for services to keep families together, but in Orange County, only 14 employees or contract workers are assigned to preventive work, while at least 40 child protection workers have jobs that involve removing kids from families. "For some reason," Allen observed, "the dollars flow more easily to foster care than to pay a 24-hour homemaker or rent for a couple of months." She pointed out that a family living on food stamps may need food at the end of the month more than psychological help, or a new refrigerator to avoid being charged with neglect for giving spoiled milk to their kids. Douglas Besharov, noting that families reported for maltreatment are four times more likely than other families to be on public assistance and almost twice as likely to be black, contends that the "courts and social agencies are overreacting to cases of social deprivation among poor children."

Mary Lou Maisonet, who worked as a homemaker in Newburgh, said social workers, many of them middle-class and college-educated, too often impose their own values on their client families and fail to understand the basic realities of the lives of welfare mothers. Many social workers "come from a culture where you only have the number of children you can afford," she said. "But the system is so badly designed that these women that we're seeing as clients, they need those children economically. If they take those children away from her, she can no longer afford the rent on her apartment because they cut back her grant."

Of the five Newburgh families whose children were removed by social services, two said deception was used to get the kids out of their apartments—a practice both county and state social service officials said is not allowed. Another, Charlotte Tripp, a mother trying to raise eight children by herself on welfare, protested when three social service workers walked into her kitchen on May 15, 1987, and told her they were taking four of her children. But she said they did not explain the charges, which alleged, among other specifications, that the two youngest children had "severe diaper rash" and that the apartment was dirty.

Tripp walked into her living room and stood in front of her kids. At some point, a city detective came in and wrestled her onto the couch. Meanwhile, child protection workers dragged the wailing kids down the stairs into two cars and drove away.

"I mean, they're coming in to take my babies away. Why? They didn't tell me anything. They wouldn't even let me kiss my babies good-bye," said Tripp, who reports that her arm, fractured in the struggle, has never healed properly. She is now suing the detective, Orange County DSS, and the social workers for $3 million. DSS will not comment on the case.

Charlotte Tripp isn't the only mother who says she was not told why her children were being taken away until the kids were gone. The legal system that underlies the machinery of removal is quite unlike that which applies to criminal cases.

Child protective investigations often start with an anonymous phone call to a hotline number, and the parents will probably never learn who turned them in. Alice Williams, another Newburgh mother, said she has been investigated by child protective services on and off for three years because of two of these calls, both, she suspects, made by acquaintances with an ax to grind. No evidence of abuse or neglect has ever been found.

Many states have legal definitions of maltreatment that are vague enough to leave a lot to the discretion of the protective worker. Family and juvenile courts, which provide the legal authority for removing children, operate under flexible rules of evidence that would be unacceptable in criminal cases. Some hearsay evidence is admissible. Parents questioned by social workers are not advised beforehand of any rights they might have. Police can seize evidence without a warrant when a child is considered at immediate risk. The system of charging the parents is also strangely flexible, giving the agency the ability to remove the child and determine the precise reasons later. A child originally removed because of abuse can remain in foster care on a charge of neglect—for up to 18 months in New York State on either charge—if that is what the agency is able to prove in court. Of course, the child has already been taken from home by the time the parents get to tell their story in court. The New York law requires a hearing within 72 hours, but adjournments for weeks and months are common.

Poor families, who are generally assigned overworked legal aid lawyers, face an especially tough battle in family court. "The agencies have

359

all the means to demonstrate that a poor family is wrong," said Leroy Schultz, a professor at the West Virginia University School of Social Work. A Brooklyn legal services attorney, Florence Roberts, who frequently represents parents accused of maltreatment, called it "a less than objective proceeding. Because the assumption almost always is that the parent is guilty. And the judge frequently looks upon them in that way."

The Krachts found the odds heavily stacked against them. Before any evidence had been presented, Jenny and Paul Kracht had been forced to begin counseling, at a cost of $185 per week, as a condition for having Jessica, Ashley, and Justin returned to them and to win weekly visits with Matthew and Michael. Even the children's court-appointed law guardian Michael Schwartz, agreed that the case against them was extremely flimsy. "It was always my position, as the Court is well aware . . . that I thought perhaps the County acted presumptuously in removing the children from this home," he told Judge Victor Ludmerer.

Nevertheless, the Krachts, like many other parents interviewed, say they were advised that the surest way to get the kids back was to confess to something. At a hearing on October 31, 1986, they put themselves on record as having engaged in excessive corporal punishment by admitting that they had "with an open hand, physically disciplined the child Michael Kracht," unintentionally causing bruises. Neighbors and friends of the Krachts say the couple have never been abusive. "If anything," said Jenny's sister-in-law, "she's too good to those kids."

The family was ordered to continue counseling and was placed under an unlimited order of supervision, giving the department continued access to their home. Michael and Matthew returned home the day of the hearing, but the legal custody that had passed over to DSS was only restored to the Krachts in the spring of 1988.

The two boys came home traumatized by their experience in foster care, a nightmare they had been telling their helpless parents about during phone calls and weekly home visits. The Krachts had learned another dismal failure of the child welfare system: Besharov and others say significantly more children are maltreated in foster care or in institutional settings than in their natural homes.

The boys had been placed with a couple whom we will call Madge and Johnny. Matthew remembers his introduction to Madge very well.

"The lady said, 'Sit your dead ass down right now.' So I sat down. And I started crying and stuff," he recalled.

For some reason, Matthew was singled out for the worst punishment. Once, he said, he was forced to strip naked in front of the entire family, accused of stealing some baseball cards from the couple's grandson. On another occasion he was locked in a dark bathroom for an entire night and was slapped at regular intervals to keep him awake. Later in the month, he said, Madge spanked both of them with a wooden paddle for crying when they returned from a visit with their parents, then clouted Matthew on the back of the head, knocking him to the floor.

In Orange County, a foster family receives anywhere from $324 to $450 per month for each child. Foster care money helps "a lot of home-owners pay their mortgages," said a lawyer familiar with the foster care system. "It sounds cynical but it happens to be the truth." However much Madge and Johnny were paid, Matthew and Michael were not getting the benefit of the dollars. Both children say they were subsisting largely on soup and were hungry much of the time. Madge denied all the allegations made against her and her husband. "It didn't work out," she said, adding that Matthew "didn't like us."

Child welfare administrators say they have quite enough work to do without manufacturing cases. But Matthew and Michael described considerable prodding when they were initially questioned by a social service worker and then by state police. And none of the children confirmed Michael's story.

Matthew remembers being asked about Michael's bruise. "They said, 'Did your dad hit him there? Because Michael said that he did.' And I said no, he just spanks him. He doesn't pound him on the back or anything like that." Matthew said he was never asked if he knew how his brother had been hurt. Had anyone asked he could have told them the bruise was inflicted by Matthew himself while the boys were rough-housing in the yard.

According to Leroy Schultz of West Virginia University, the problem often with child protective investigations is that social service workers are bad detectives. "We are rehabilitators, basically," said Schultz. "So we are being thrust into a situation that we are not prepared for."

In sex abuse cases, especially when the charge is fondling, the only basis for the removal may be the word of the child. It's not hard to imagine how a social worker, who by training and inclination may focus on making a client feel comfortable enough to talk about painful stories, might cross the line between questioning and coaxing a young witness.

Sara, now 12 years old, says she was interrogated several times a day about fondling after she told her teacher at the Mark Twain Elementary School in Colorado Springs in February 1986 that her stepfather, Clark, had tickled her. On the basis of statements made by Sara to social service workers, Clark Gabriel was charged with what he now jokingly refers to as "felony tickling." The charge was fondling—sexual assault on a child—and had he not been acquitted, Gabriel could have gone to prison for 16 years.

Susan Gabriel, Sara's mother and a technical writer with TRW Corp., said she was mystified when she first learned from DSS that Sara had been taken from her school and placed in foster care: "They said she specifically said it [the tickling] wasn't between the legs, wasn't on the breast area or anything. And then they said, this is molesting. At that point I really felt like I had been dropped onto an alien planet."

Unlike many parents in similar situations, the outraged Gabriels refused to admit to any wrongdoing and insisted on a trial. The judge told them to get a second opinion from his former law partner, J. Gregory Walta. In a letter to their attorney, Walta wrote that the case fit a "disturbing pattern in which child protection workers induce the child to make allegations not originally made, then resist the child's efforts to recant, and ignore reports by qualified experts questioning the truth of the child's allegations."

As a result of her experience, Susan Gabriel founded southern Colorado VOCAL, Victims of Child Abuse Laws, which has more than 70 chapters nationwide and a membership of roughly 5,000, according to Margaret Gran, who helped establish the group in 1984. Child protectors do most of their work among the poor, but VOCAL's membership, according to Gran, is almost entirely middle class. The American Enterprise Institute's Besharov suggests a major reason for this is a tenfold growth in reports—not necessarily occurrences—of sexual abuse since 1970. And while neglect charges tend to be leveled against poor parents, sexual abuse has proven to be an equal opportunity accusation.

Reports of all types of child maltreatment are more than 14 times what they were in 1963, but neither child abuse nor child removal is a new phenomenon. In *Heroes of Their Own Lives,* a history of family violence from 1880 until 1960, Linda Gordon, a professor of American history at the University of Wisconsin, wrote that concern over maltreated children has risen and fallen many times over the past 100 years, but there is "no evidence the problem is actually increasing." Gordon's book focuses on the Massachusetts Society for Prevention of Cruelty to Children. Before government entered the picture, a relatively recent involvement, it was up to private agencies like the MSPCC to protect children, and their clientele was almost exclusively poor. Most of the legal tools used to remove children today originated with the MSPCC and its sister organizations. And in the nineteenth century, as now, "hostile neighbors and relatives often turned in false accusations," Gordon wrote, adding that from 1890 until 1960, the proportion of false complaints never fell below 65 percent.

Since 1974, as a result of federal mandate, states require almost all professionals who deal with children—from child-care workers and teachers to doctors, psychiatrists, and social workers—to report suspected abuse. These professionals are liable to criminal and civil penalty if they fail to report but are shielded if they do.

Parent advocates complain that because of this, the therapeutic and helping professions are being turned into spies, violating the confidentiality of people who come for help. Robert VanCleave, director of the El Paso County Department of Social Services, said "children rarely fabricate stories," but, he added, "it would be an unusual kid who was not intimidated by a group of authority figures" asking questions.

Connie Antona, senior case supervisor for the Orange County Department of Social Services' children's services division, agrees with VanCleave that investigations are fair. "The department would not be removing children unless it felt there were serious issues." Antona noted that state privacy regulations forbid her to comment on the specifics of cases, but when informed of the details of the Krachts' situation, she said some effort should be made to evaluate the credibility of a person making an accusation of child maltreatment. In the case of a child, an examination by a psychologist might be the optimum method, she said. Whatever the accuser's credibility, the odds are that key decisions about whether a child will be taken from a home will rest with overburdened, underpaid, and inexperienced caseworkers. In New York City, the turnover rate for caseworkers was almost 70 percent in 1987, and each of those workers was carrying an average of 40 cases at one time. No social worker wants to be responsible for the next Lisa Steinberg. Agency workers in general feel if they are going to err, they will err on the side of protecting the child.

But the effects of such an error can be damaging and long-lasting for both children and families. More than two years after the fact, it is still extremely painful for the Kracht children to discuss what happened to them. Until recently, Matthew had frequent nightmares about his experiences at the hands of Madge and Johnny. And the three older children all told me they are afraid it could happen again.

Child psychology experts say the experience of being taken from the family is so devastating, removals should be performed only in the most extreme cases of abuse or gross neglect. "It will be very, very, terrifying," said Lorraine Siegel, a Pleasantville, New York, social worker who deals with children who have been placed in foster care. "They will lose their confidence. They will lose their sense of trust in others."

A number of parents reported serious behavior problems in their children that resulted from being placed in foster care. Jenny Kracht said her children have learned there is an authority above herself and Paul: "Our kids were never this hard to handle before they were taken." Historian Linda Gordon said, "We have not, as a whole society, ever devised any decent alternative for kids other than their families."

As an alternative to the historic inadequacies of the social welfare system, CDF's Mary Lee Allen points to the Homebuilders program, which provides intensive intervention to keep kids with their families. A Homebuilder will spend three to four hours a day, several days a week with the family for a month, an approach that "allows you to really know a lot about the family," said Peter Forsythe, whose Edna McConnell Clark Foundation brought Homebuilders to the Bronx in New York City from the state of Washington where it originated. Workers try to find out "what the adults think the problem is, rather than assuming that what child protective services says is true," he explained. A year after being served by Homebuilders, the children in 88 percent of client families remain out of foster care. And the program is cheap. The cost for foster care nationwide is roughly $10,000 per year per child, and the average length of stay is about three years. Depending on the location of the program, Homebuilders will spend anywhere from $2,000 to $4,000 per child.

The prototypes for the future exist, said Allen. Now it is a matter of getting them funded and giving them a chance to work. But the system needs to be reformed in other ways, including more specific definitions of child abuse, better screening of reports of maltreatment—Congress only recently passed a law requiring the states to keep statistics on false allegations—and some requirement for agencies to demonstrate "probable cause" before taking a child.

"I think the important thing is that we get the rhetoric toned down," said Besharov. "No one will blame you if you take a kid without evidence. But the media will string you up if you leave a child in the home and anything happens."

Many parents compare the experience of being falsely charged with child abuse—the lack of legal safeguards, the terrible stigma of the accusation—to a witchhunt. In the real witch trials of seventeenth century Salem, the little girls making accusations were finally silenced when they began to ensnare prominent citizens of the Massachusetts Bay colony, including Lady Phips, wife of the governor. In *The Devil in Massachusetts,* Marion Starkey wrote that in the final stages of witch-hunt fever, "no degree of eminence ensured one against accusation."

Similarly, the child welfare system may defy reform as long as only the poor suffer. It may well be that the entanglement of increasing numbers of the more visible and vocal middle class in the web of the system will finally bring change.

## QUESTIONS

*Looking at Ideas:*

1. How has the natural concern for the abused or mistreated child bred a "monster" of intervention in family life by government agencies? Why does this monster tend to be most aggressive and damaging in response to poor families?
2. What does Mary Lee Allen of the Children's Defense Fund believe should be the alternative to the tendency of the child welfare system to prematurely place children from homes suspected of abuse in foster care? Do you agree with her proposal?
3. According to Mary Lou Maisonet, what cultural differences make it difficult for social workers to understand the "basic realities in the lives of welfare mothers"? Do you agree with Maisonet that such workers find it difficult to understand their clients' needs?
4. How are workers in social service "bad detectives"? How is "coaxing the witness" an example of such clumsy detective work? Why is it difficult for such workers to play the detective role in response to family crises? Should this be part of their responsibilities?
5. How might the Homebuilder's program provide a valuable alternative to current failings in social welfare family interventions? What process is followed by Homebuilders, and how does it differ from that of the current system?

*Looking at Strategies:*

1. The article uses comparisons and figurative language, including the title, "Solomon's Choice" and expressions like "bad detectives," "create a monster," and "witch hunt" to describe the activities of the current social welfare system. Do you think these comparisons are effective?
2. The article relies on case histories of misjudgment and errors in response to family crises by social welfare agencies and workers. Do you consider these examples effective and appropriately emotional, or do some of them seem atypical and perhaps exaggerated?
3. One of the problems experienced by case workers is defining key terms in the law. How does the article examine such ambiguous legal terms as "maltreatment" and "fondling"? How might such concepts be more clearly defined under law? Why are they so difficult to define?
4. This article presents a number of causes and effects relative to the issue of families menaced by a system designed to protect them. List the major causes and effects presented by the author. How clearly are they presented here? Are there any causes or effects you would have liked to see further developed in the essay?

*Looking at Connections:*

1. How would the social welfare workers portrayed in this article have responded to the family conflict experienced in "My Papa's Waltz"?
2. Compare the handling of family problems portrayed in this article with the way family tensions were handled in Lilly Collett's middle-class home in "Step by Step." Is it less likely that government agencies would follow up accusations of abuse within a middle- or upper-middle-class home as readily as they would follow up similar allegations about abuse within a poor family?

*Suggestions for Writing:*

1. Write an essay in which you explore the social stereotypes that the general public and professionals often have about economically deprived or welfare families. What are the origins of these stereotypes?
2. Write about a perception or preconception that you hold about the economically deprived and their families. What experiences led to the formation of your view? Has reading "Solomon's Choice" changed your ideas or viewpoint in any way? Why or why not?
3. Write an essay in which you suggest a solution for one of the problems explored in this essay. For instance, what could be done to make social workers more sensitive and effective in their interventions with economically deprived families? You might also explore ways that workers evaluating claims of child abuse can find more objective criteria for determining if such abuse exists and how it can be controlled.

*Chapter Six: Tensions*

**JOURNAL ENTRY**

Write about a time when you felt distanced, alienated from, or
self-conscious about your family and their life-style.

**TILLIE OLSEN: "I Stand Here Ironing"** Olsen was born in 1913 in Omaha,
Nebraska. She married a printer, Jack Olsen, with whom she had four children.
Olsen worked in industry and as a typist-transcriber while raising her family.
She began to receive recognition for her writing in 1961 with the publication
of "Tell Me a Riddle," which won the O. Henry award for best American short
story in that year and was later made into a film. She has since published and
edited works of fiction and nonfiction, including a collection of her stories,
*Tell Me a Riddle,* and a book of social and literary criticism, *Silences* (1978).
She has been a lecturer and visiting professor at many universities, including
Stanford, MIT, and the University of California at Berkeley. Olsen often writes
about people who have been denied the opportunity to express and develop
themselves because of their sex, class, or race. As you read this first-person
narrative, consider how effectively the narrator defends herself against charges
of being a less-than-adequate parent.

TILLIE OLSEN

# I Stand Here Ironing

I stand here ironing, and what you asked me moves tormented back
and forth with the iron.

"I wish you would manage the time to come in and talk with me
about your daughter. I'm sure you can help me understand her. She's a
youngster who needs help and whom I'm deeply interested in helping."

"Who needs help." Even if I came, what good would it do? You
think because I am her mother I have a key, or that in some way you
could use me as a key? She has lived for nineteen years. There is all that
life that has happened outside of me, beyond me.

And when is there time to remember, to sift, to weigh, to estimate,
to total? I will start and there will be an interruption and I will have to
gather it all together again. Or I will become engulfed with all I did or
did not do, with what should have been and what cannot be helped.

She was a beautiful baby. The first and only one of our five that was
beautiful at birth. You do not guess how new and uneasy her tenancy in
her now-loveliness. You did not know her all those years she was
thought homely, or see her poring over her baby pictures, making me

366

tell her over and over how beautiful she had been—and would be, I would tell her—and was now, to the seeing eye. But the seeing eyes were few or non-existent. Including mine.

I nursed her. They feel that's important nowadays. I nursed all the children, but with her, with all the fierce rigidity of first motherhood, I did like the books then said. Though her cries battered me to trembling and my breasts ached with swollenness, I waited till the clock decreed.

Why do I put that first? I do not even know if it matters, or if it explains anything.

She was a beautiful baby. She blew shining bubbles of sound. She loved motion, loved light, loved color and music and textures. She would lie on the floor in her blue overalls patting the surface so hard in ecstasy her hands and feet would blur. She was a miracle to me, but when she was eight months old I had to leave her daytimes with the woman downstairs to whom she was no miracle at all, for I worked or looked for work and for Emily's father, who "could no longer endure" (he wrote in his good-bye note) "sharing want with us."

I was nineteen. It was the pre-relief, pre-WPA world of the depression. I would start running as soon as I got off the streetcar, running up the stairs, the place smelling sour, and awake or asleep to startle awake, when she saw me she would break into a clogged weeping that could not be comforted, a weeping I can hear yet.

After a while I found a job hashing at night so I could be with her days, and it was better. But it came to where I had to bring her to his family and leave her.

It took a long time to raise the money for her fare back. Then she got chicken pox and I had to wait longer. When she finally came, I hardly knew her, walking quick and nervous like her father, looking like her father, thin, and dressed in a shoddy red that yellowed her skin and glared at the pockmarks. All the baby loveliness gone.

She was two. Old enough for nursery school they said, and I did not know then what I know now—the fatigue of the long day, and the lacerations of group life in the nurseries that are only parking places for children.

Except that it would have made no difference if I had known. It was the only place there was. It was the only way we could be together, the only way I could hold a job.

And even without knowing, I knew. I knew the teacher that was evil because all these years it has curdled into my memory, the little boy hunched in the corner, her rasp, "why aren't you outside, because Alvin hits you? that's no reason, go out, scaredy." I knew Emily hated it even if she did not clutch and implore "don't go Mommy" like the other children, mornings.

She always had a reason why she should stay home. Momma, you look sick, Momma. I feel sick. Momma, the teachers aren't there today, they're sick. Momma, we can't go, there was a fire there last night. Momma, it's a holiday today, no school, they told me.

But never a direct protest, never rebellion. I think of our others in

their three-, four-year-oldness—the explosions, the tempers, the de-
nunciations, the demands—and I feel suddenly ill. I put the iron down.
What in me demanded that goodness in her? And what was the cost,
the cost to her of such goodness?

The old man living in the back once said in his gentle way: "You
should smile at Emily more when you look at her." What *was* in my
face when I looked at her? I loved her. There were all the acts of love.

It was only with the others I remembered what he said, and it was
the face of joy, and not of care or tightness or worry I turned to them—
too late for Emily. She does not smile easily, let alone almost always as
her brothers and sisters do. Her face is closed and sombre, but when
she wants, how fluid. You must have seen it in her pantomimes, you
spoke of her rare gift for comedy on the stage that rouses a laughter
out of the audience so dear they applaud and applaud and do not want
to let her go.

Where does it come from, that comedy? There was none of it in her
when she came back to me that second time, after I had had to send
her away again. She had a new daddy now to learn to love, and I think
perhaps it was a better time.

Except when we left her alone nights, telling ourselves she was old
enough.

"Can't you go some other time, Mommy, like tomorrow?" she
would ask. "Will it be just a little while you'll be gone? Do you promise?"

The time we came back, the front door open, the clock on the floor
in the hall. She rigid awake. "It wasn't just a little while. I didn't cry.
Three times I called you, just three times, and then I ran downstairs to
open the door so you could come faster. The clock talked loud. I threw
it away, it scared me what it talked."

She said the clock talked loud again that night I went to the hospital
to have Susan. She was delirious with the fever that comes before red
measles, but she was fully conscious all the week I was gone and the
week after we were home when she could not come near the new baby
or me.

She did not get well. She stayed skeleton thin, not wanting to eat,
and night after night she had nightmares. She would call for me, and I
would rouse from exhaustion to sleepily call back: "You're all right,
darling, go to sleep, it's just a dream," and if she still called, in a sterner
voice, "now go to sleep, Emily, there's nothing to hurt you." Twice, only
twice, when I had to get up for Susan anyhow, I went in to sit with her.

Now when it is too late (as if she would let me hold and comfort
her like I do the others) I get up and go to her at once at her moan or
restless stirring. "Are you awake, Emily? Can I get you something?"
And the answer is always the same: "No, I'm all right, go back to sleep,
Mother."

They persuaded me at the clinic to send her away to a convalescent
home in the country where "she can have the kind of food and care
you can't manage for her, and you'll be free to concentrate on the new

baby." They still send children to that place. I see pictures on the society page of sleek young women planning affairs to raise money for it, or dancing at the affairs, or decorating Easter eggs or filling Christmas stockings for the children.

They never have a picture of the children so I do not know if the girls still wear those gigantic red bows and the ravaged looks on the every other Sunday when parents can come to visit "unless otherwise notified"—as we were notified the first six weeks.

Oh it is a handsome place, green lawns and tall trees and fluted flower beds. High up on the balconies of each cottage the children stand, the girls in their red bows and white dresses, the boys in white suits and giant red ties. The parents stand below shrieking up to be heard and the children shriek down to be heard, and between them the invisible wall "Not To Be Contaminated by Parental Germs or Physical Affection."

There was a tiny girl who always stood hand in hand with Emily. Her parents never came. One visit she was gone. "They moved her to Rose College," Emily shouted in explanation. "They don't like you to love anybody here."

She wrote once a week, the labored writing of a seven-year-old. "I am fine. How is the baby. If I write my letter nicely I will have a star. Love." There never was a star. We wrote every other day, letters she could never hold or keep but only hear read—once. "We simply do not have room for children to keep any personal possessions," they patiently explained when we pieced one Sunday's shrieking together to plead how much it would mean to Emily, who loved so to keep things, to be allowed to keep her letters and cards.

Each visit she looked frailer. "She isn't eating," they told us.

(They had runny eggs for breakfast or mush with lumps, Emily said later, I'd hold it in my mouth and not swallow. Nothing ever tasted good, just when they had chicken.)

It took us eight months to get her released home, and only the fact that she gained back so little of her seven lost pounds convinced the social worker.

I used to try to hold and love her after she came back, but her body would stay stiff, and after a while she'd push away. She ate little. Food sickened her, and I think much of life too. Oh she had physical lightness and brightness, twinkling by on skates, bouncing like a ball up and down up and down over the jump rope, skimming over the hill; but these were momentary.

She fretted about her appearance, thin and dark and foreign-looking at a time when every little girl was supposed to look or thought she should look a chubby blonde replica of Shirley Temple. The doorbell sometimes rang for her, but no one seemed to come and play in the house or be a best friend. Maybe because we moved so much.

There was a boy she loved painfully through two school semesters. Months later she told me how she had taken pennies from my purse to buy him candy. "Licorice was his favorite and I brought him some every day, but he still liked Jennifer better'n me. Why, Mommy?" The kind of question for which there is no answer.

School was a worry to her. She was not glib or quick in a world where glibness and quickness were easily confused with ability to learn. To her overworked and exasperated teachers she was an overconscientious "slow learner" who kept trying to catch up and was absent entirely too often.

I let her be absent, though sometimes the illness was imaginary. How different from my now-strictness about attendance with the others. I wasn't working. We had a new baby, I was home anyhow. Sometimes, after Susan grew old enough, I would keep her home from school, too, to have them all together.

Mostly Emily had asthma, and her breathing, harsh and labored, would fill the house with a curiously tranquil sound. I would bring the two old dresser mirrors and her boxes of collections to her bed. She would select beads and single earrings, bottle tops and shells, dried flowers and pebbles, old postcards and scraps, all sorts of oddments; then she and Susan would play Kingdom, setting up landscapes and furniture, peopling them with action.

Those were the only times of peaceful companionship between her and Susan. I have edged away from it, that poisonous feeling between them, that terrible balancing of hurts and needs I had to do between the two, and did so badly, those earlier years.

Oh there are conflicts between the others too, each one human, needing, demanding, hurting, taking—but only between Emily and Susan, no, Emily toward Susan that corroding resentment. It seems so obvious on the surface, yet it is not obvious. Susan, the second child, Susan, golden- and curly-haired and chubby, quick and articulate and assured, everything in appearance and manner Emily was not; Susan, not able to resist Emily's precious things, losing or sometimes clumsily breaking them; Susan telling jokes and riddles to company for applause while Emily sat silent (to say to me later: that was *my* riddle, Mother, I told it to Susan); Susan, who for all the five years' difference in age was just a year behind Emily in developing physically.

I am glad for that slow physical development that widened the difference between her and her contemporaries, though she suffered over it. She was too vulnerable for that terrible world of youthful competition, of preening and parading, of constant measuring of yourself against every other, of envy, "If I had that copper hair," "If I had that skin. . . ." She tormented herself enough about not looking like the others, there was enough of the unsureness, the having to be conscious of words before you speak, the constant caring—what are they thinking of me? without having it all magnified by the merciless physical drives.

Ronnie is calling. He is wet and I change him. It is rare there is such a cry now. That time of motherhood is almost behind me when the ear is not one's own but must always be racked and listening for the child cry, the child call. We sit for a while and I hold him, looking out over the city spread in charcoal with its soft aisles of light. *"Shoogily,"* he breathes and curls closer. I carry him back to bed, asleep. *Shoogily.* A funny word, a family word, inherited from Emily, invented by her to say: *comfort.*

In this and other ways she leaves her seal, I say aloud. And startle at my saying it. What do I mean? What did I start to gather together, to try and make coherent? I was at the terrible, growing years. War years. I do not remember them well. I was working, there were four smaller ones now, there was not time for her. She had to help be a mother, and housekeeper, and shopper. She had to set her seal. Mornings of crisis and near hysteria trying to get lunches packed, hair combed, coats and shoes found, everyone to school or Child Care on time, the baby ready for transportation. And always the paper scribbled on by a smaller one, the book looked at by Susan then mislaid, the homework not done. Running out to that huge school where she was one, she was lost, she was a drop; suffering over the unpreparedness, stammering and unsure in her classes.

There was so little time left at night after the kids were bedded down. She would struggle over books, always eating (it was in those years she developed her enormous appetite that is legendary in our family) and I would be ironing, or preparing food for the next day, or writing V-mail to Bill, or tending the baby. Sometimes, to make me laugh, or out of her despair, she would imitate happenings or types at school.

I think I said once: "Why don't you do something like this in the school amateur show?" One morning she phoned me at work, hardly understandable through the weeping: "Mother, I did it. I won, I won; they gave me first prize; they clapped and clapped and wouldn't let me go."

Now suddenly she was Somebody, and as imprisoned in her difference as she had been in anonymity.

She began to be asked to perform at other high schools, even in colleges, then at city and statewide affairs. The first one we went to, I only recognized her that first moment when thin, shy, she almost drowned herself into the curtains. Then: Was this Emily? The control, the command, the convulsing and deadly clowning, the spell, then the roaring, stamping audience, unwilling to let this rare and precious laughter out of their lives.

Afterwards: You ought to do something about her with a gift like that—but without money or knowing how, what does one do? We have left it all to her, and the gift has as often eddied inside, clogged and clotted, as been used and growing.

She is coming. She runs up the stairs two at a time with her light graceful step, and I know she is happy tonight. Whatever it was that occasioned your call did not happen today.

"Aren't you ever going to finish the ironing, Mother? Whistler painted his mother in a rocker. I'd have to paint mine standing over an ironing board." This is one of her communicative nights and she tells me everything and nothing as she fixes herself a plate of food out of the icebox.

371

She is so lovely. Why did you want me to come in at all? Why were you concerned? She will find her way.

She starts up the stairs to bed. "Don't get me up with the rest in the morning." "But I thought you were having midterms." "Oh, those," she comes back in, kisses me, and says quite lightly, "in a couple of years when we'll all be atom-dead they won't matter a bit."

She has said it before. She *believes* it. But because I have been dredging the past, and all that compounds a human being is so heavy and meaningful in me, I cannot endure it tonight.

I will never total it all. I will never come in to say: She was a child seldom smiled at. Her father left me before she was a year old. I had to work her first six years when there was work, or I sent her home and to his relatives. There were years she had care she hated. She was dark and thin and foreign-looking in a world where the prestige went to blondeness and curly hair and dimples, she was slow where glibness was prized. She was a child of anxious, not proud, love. We were poor and could not afford for her the soil of easy growth. I was a young mother, I was a distracted mother. There were the other children pushing up, demanding. Her younger sister seemed all that she was not. There were years she did not want me to touch her. She kept too much in herself, her life was such she had to keep too much in herself. My wisdom came too late. She has much to her and probably nothing will come of it. She is a child of her age, of depression, of war, of fear.

Let her be. So all that is in her will not bloom—but in how many does it? There is still enough left to live by. Only help her to know—help make it so there is cause for her to know—that she is more than this dress on the ironing board, helpless before the iron.

## QUESTIONS

*Looking at Ideas:*

1. Characterize the narrator. What is tormenting her at the beginning of the story?

2. What circumstances in the narrator's family and economic life influenced Emily's early childhood? What social, economic, and physical factors made it necessary for Emily's mother to give her up temporarily?

3. The story provides images of a number of social institutions designed to help parents who lack the economic means and time to be with their children full-time—child-care centers, a convalescent home, large public schools. Have these institutions helped Emily and her family? Why is the narrator in the story critical of these institutions? Does her criticism seem justified?

4. The mother asks the question, "Where does it come from, that comedy?" What factors in Emily's life might have helped make her a talented comedian?

5. Contrast Emily with Susan, the narrator's second child. What is the source of the rivalry between them?

372

6. Does the narrator's attitude toward Emily and her problems seem to be that of a responsible, realistic parent, or is she trying to evade responsibility and rationalize her failures?

*Looking at Strategies:*

1. Who is the "you" to whom the narrator's remarks are in part directed? How would you characterize this individual in terms of occupation and social class, attitude toward children and their parents? What other audiences would be interested in this story?

2. How do the narrator's successive physical descriptions of Emily as she grows older help to underscore the impact of social institutions on Emily's spirit and her mother's concerned attitude?

3. How does the narrator's physical description of the convalescent home reveal the way that social institutions can alienate children from their families? What descriptive details make this point most powerfully?

4. What do the title and the narrator's final words about not wishing her child to be "helpless before the iron" contribute to the story and its meaning?

*Looking at Connections:*

1. Compare Olsen's view of the way social workers and other "helping" institutions of the 1950s tended to undermine the families they tried to help with the view presented in Dan Zegert's more recent essay, "Solomon's Choice."

2. Imagine Emily as an adult. Would she be likely to have as critical an attitude toward her mother and her "dysfunctional" family as that taken by some members of the Adult Child movement profiled by Melinda Blau? What would be Emily's mother's response to the criticisms some members of this movement make of their parents?

*Suggestions for Writing:*

1. Discuss a social institution you have observed that is designed to supplement the child-rearing efforts of the home: a particular school, a child-care center, a social services department. How effectively does the institution supplement parental efforts? How does the institution tend to distance children from their families? Give particular examples from your reading and observations of how this institution functions.

2. Present some ideas and examples drawn from your own observations of ways that institutions serving children and their families could do so more productively and harmoniously, rather than contributing to family conflict and alienation.

3. Retell the events described in "I Stand Here Ironing," either from the perspective of the daughter, Emily, or that of the counselor who has written a note to the mother at the beginning of the story. How might they view the mother and her parenting skills differently from the way she views the situation?

**ANGEL C. FABIAN: "Sharing the Blame"**   At the age of ten, Angel C. Fabian, the youngest of five children, immigrated to the United States from Mexico City. In grammar school and high school, he participated in and was greatly helped by bilingual migrant education programs. Angel Fabian is the second in his family to attend a university. He is currently seeking a degree in biology and hopes to go to medical school and become a family practitioner or a pediatrician. The following essay was written in response to a question which asked students to write an essay about "the effects of alcohol or drug abuse in the home on family tensions and on your attitudes toward your family and yourself." In writing this essay, Fabian was faced with difficulties both in revealing painful family secrets and in verbalizing his emotions about his mother's problems with alcohol.

ANGEL C. FABIAN

# *Sharing the Blame*

The essay by Melinda Blau on Adult Children of Alcoholics struck a resemblance to my life. I, too, had begun to consider myself an adult child of an alcoholic. Like many of the adults in Blau's essay, I had begun to blame my mother for my emotional problems. This I did without realizing that the constant reproaches did nothing to alleviate her struggle with alcohol. My mother had to go through added pain and suffering before I learned that it was true that, as Dwight Lee Wolter puts it, "As we begin to forgive our parents we begin to forgive ourselves." Although this process of forgiveness has been gradual, my mother and I are slowly beginning to understand each other's pain and are working out our problems. Our relationship now rests on mutual faith and hope for a better future.

When I came to the United States from Mexico City, I did not fully know who my mother was. When I was seven years old, she emigrated to the United States by herself in order to escape poverty and an abusive marriage. For three long years, the only knowledge I had of my mother was what was told to me by my older brothers and the hazy recollections I had of her from my early childhood. I could picture a plump, lively, and affectionate woman, but I really knew very little about her. When she returned to Mexico and brought my brother, my sister, and me to the United States, my relationship with her had to be reestablished. Initially, I was uneasy being around her since there were some unanswered, painful questions about her departure. Eventually, we learned about each other's likes and dislikes. She realized how hard-headed I was, and I learned how stubborn she was. I also found out about her problem with alcohol—a side of her I never could have imagined.

I remember one afternoon when I came home from school and found my mother inebriated. As usual, I came up to her and gave her a hug and a kiss. To my surprise, she turned away from me, tried to avoid my stare, and hugged me with indifference. I knew there was a problem. When I asked her to tell me what had happened, she just said "Nothing is wrong. Is something the matter with you?" As soon as I saw her face, I knew what had occurred. I saw in my mother's face what I had seen in my father and other people who had been drinking. She was very agitated as if she had been doing a lot of work and had a tired look in her eyes as if from lack of sleep or too much crying. I asked her why she had been drinking, but she just told me that I was imagining things. I did not know what to do or how to react. Her actions that night foreshadowed what was to become a habit.

The events the day she drank and the day after were to become a routine. Her character would fluctuate from being overly affectionate, to very depressed, and finally to abusive. Most nights, though, she would become melancholic. She would tell us how hard her life had been, that she had been practically an orphan since she was very young, that she often had to scrounge around and even steal food, and that she had been beaten because of her stealing. She would mention her son, who had been taken away from her when he was three years old, whom she had not seen for the past twenty-five years. She damned her fate since even the desperate economic situation that she had hoped to escape by coming to the United States had not really changed. When we tried to convince her to go to sleep, she would become hostile. She would start screaming, yelling, and hitting anyone who tried to confront her. This ordeal would go on into the night until she passed out. The following day I would reproach my mother. I would not speak to her for the greater part of the day, but when I did, it was to reprimand her for her actions. I would blame her for keeping me awake at night and tried to draw pity from her by telling her how much I had cried and how frightened I had become by her crazed behavior. She would react to my accusations with indifference, shrugging her shoulders, shaking her head, and saying that she did not know or did not remember what had happened the night before. She would further defend herself by saying that I had no right to criticize her since she was my mother and I was her son, not the other way around.

After a few months, the confrontations my brothers and I had with her after she had been drinking became vicious. We could not satisfy ourselves until we had my mother in tears. In our opinion there was, as Blau puts it, "little talk of forgiveness, much about blame and sometimes, fantasies of revenge." We would tell her that she was acting like a fool and would accuse her of being a negligent mother who thought only about herself and not about the effects that her drinking had on the family. We always reminded her of the irony of her life: She had escaped an alcoholic husband only to become an alcoholic herself. By drinking she was saying to us, "Do as I say, not as I do." She had always frowned on my father's alcoholism and had blamed alcohol for family problems. As we were growing up, she would warn us that if we did not want to end up like my father—alone and wretched—then we should avoid having any contact with alcohol. Consequently, when we saw her drinking, we would accuse her of being a hypocrite. In actuality, our constant reproaches only made my mother more depressed, and thus she would drink even more. It was a no-win situation. We sought comfort in yelling at her while she retaliated by drinking more, thus trying to show her control over the situation.

My mother's drinking became an emotional and physical hardship, or so I forced myself to believe. I feared coming home to find her drunk because I knew I had to deal with a nuisance for the rest of the night. Listening to her lamentations for hours became a burden for me. After a few months, I became indifferent to her problem, and thus would go off to sleep and let my family deal with her. When I did stay up all night and was asked in school why I looked so tired, I would break into tears as I explained how wretched my life was because of my mother's drinking. Even when the source of my problems was not because of her alcoholism, I always found a way to blame her. As Karen, a recovering alcoholic, reveals in Blau's essay, "I always blamed [her] when I failed."

I am beginning to understand that my reaction toward my mother's drinking worsened her problem with alcohol. It became too easy to blame her for my emotional distress. As a result, I failed to ask, as Dwight Wolter puts it, "Who has been hurt and how can we get [him or her] back on track?" The thought of getting help for my mother had crossed my mind, but I was too busy seeking help for myself. I attended Al-Anon meetings but did not persist in getting my mother the help she needed. It had taken great courage for her to have come to the United States by herself, let alone having to go back to Mexico to bring my brothers and me with her. Like Barbara's mother in Blau's essay, my mother "was taught to put other's needs first, to repress her feelings and silently endure life's hard knocks." This fact was not enough though, for the pity I had for myself overpowered the respect I had for her. I did not try to understand that many factors (i.e. poverty, my father's alcoholism, and the conflicts she had to confront each day) had contributed to her drinking. It was too easy for me to blame her for my suffering without taking into consideration the ways she was introduced to alcohol and that at times the problems she faced were too strong for her to handle. I had forgotten that she was human and was bound to make mistakes.

My mother's drinking problem is getting better as she begins to realize the effects of alcohol on herself and on her family. Now that she is alone, she is finding the courage to go on with her daily life without drinking. We are slowly learning to forgive each other for the pain that we inflicted upon one another. There is new hope in our relationship. Like Lily Collett's experience with her alcoholic father one Christmas Eve, "He was there to meet me halfway, and sober, and together we walked home," so are my mother and I trying to walk back to recovery together. We are moving on.

# QUESTIONS

1. How does Angel Fabian use details from his mother's early life and from her descent into alcoholism to reveal the nature and causes of her problem with drinking? Is his use of details effective, or could he have used more of them?

2. What blaming behavior did Fabian indulge in as an adolescent as a consequence of his mother's drinking? Do you think he was justified in this behavior?

3. What is Angel Fabian's final realization about his mother's alcoholism and his relationship with her? How have his views on blaming changed? Do you agree with his conclusion?

4. How effectively does Fabian use quotations from readings to create parallels with his own experiences and put his family problems in a larger context?

## Reaching Out: Chapter Activities

1. A group of students who have worked together on a fairly regular basis should discuss the tensions in the group and propose ways for reducing some of the conflicts in order to promote a better working relationship. The group could write up their conclusions in the form of a formal proposal for tension resolution or simply as a brief list of recommendations.

2. Explore an agency, organization, or service in your community dedicated either to reducing tensions in families and relationships or to coping with the results of those tensions. You might examine services for abused and abusing spouses, or resources to support children and elderly victims of abuse. Interview agency workers and read any pamphlets or other materials pertaining to these organizations. Describe one of these agencies in an essay that explains how the agency functions and what impact it may have on helping reduce one or more family tensions.

3. Develop a brochure or directory of local services for families who might need to reduce or better cope with some of the tensions explored in this chapter. Using the desktop publishing facilities available in your school journalism program or computer classroom, produce the brochure or directory and share it with your class or within your community.

4. Either alone or with a group of students from your class, view one of the films on the list below or another film that deals with sources of tension and/or the impact of social forces on family life. Write either an individual or a collaborative critique of the film, in which you indicate what you learned from viewing it about the sources and the effects of tension on the family. Finally, evaluate the film as an image of family life: did it seem illuminating and powerful, or distorted and sensationalist in its portrayal of family life?

*Death of a Salesman.* Dir., Volker Schlondorff. With Dustin Hoffmann, John Malkovitch. 1986.

*Good Mother, The.* Dir., Leonard Nimoy. With Diane Keaton, Jason Robards. 1988.

*Long Day's Journey Into Night.* Dir., Sidney Lumet. With Jason Robards, Jr. 1962.

*Ordinary People.* Dir., Robert Redford. With Mary Tyler Moore, Tim Hutton. 1980.

CHAPTER SEVEN

# Breaking the Mold

*Perhaps our own frustrations were indicative of a larger problem: a diverse population attempting to fit into housing that is simply no longer appropriate for them.* —Kathryn McCamant and Charles Durrett, "Cohousing and the American Dream"

*When does a household become, in lawyer's jargon, "the functional equivalent of a family"? And should the law treat the equivalent the same as the real item? The rise of alternative families makes it essential to find answers.* —Keenan Peck, "When 'Family' Is Not a Household Word"

*I*n previous chapters you have read about the ways in which home and family are recalled in memoirs; developed through relationships; celebrated in rituals; influenced by culture, by mass media, and by the stresses of modern life. Though many of us still think of the stereotypical "married-with-children" as representing the majority of families, in fact only 30 percent of American families fit the husband-wife-children traditional mold. What seems to be emerging, whether out of demographic, economic, or personal and social needs, is an extended kinship system based at least in part on the high divorce-remarriage rate in our society. A new family diversity is emerging in America, leading to new kinds of family relationships established on more democratic and egalitarian grounds than previous models of the family.

With so few Americans apparently living in the traditional family household, any discussion of family and home must include the multitude of alternative arrangements making up the majority of U.S. households. Such arrangements often include people who live together before or without marriage, two or more unmarried people who share a household, and gay and lesbian households—any of which may include children of one or both partners. At the same time, many social scientists, as well as members of such alternative families, see resistance and a lack of tolerance for nontraditional arrangements. Such opposition seems to assume that stability—in homes, in neighborhoods, in communities, in society—comes from households that match the stereotype of married parents with one main breadwinner and two or more children. Despite opposition to new definitions of "family," and although we may feel nostalgic for the mythical stability of the traditional nuclear family, it is unrealistic to demand that society return to family structures that are no longer attuned to the rapidly changing social and economic realities of the world in which we live.

The writers whose works we include in this chapter reflect on the ways in which our old concept of "family" has altered in recent years. In her poem "Love Should Grow Up Like a Wild Iris in the Fields," Susan Griffin contrasts the ordinary, domestic setting where love is most commonly found with the more spontaneous, less-controlled lifestyles that exist in our fantasies as well as in nature. Judith Stacey, in "The Postmodern Family, for Better and Worse," suggests that while we may long for the old days, most people welcome the opportunity to realign family relationships in more democratic and diverse patterns.

The question of how family is defined has extensive legal ramifications, and the next two readings discuss related legal issues. Attorney Keenan Peck argues that modern equivalents of "traditional families" should also have legal rights. Peck argues that the law should focus on society's interest: "long-term, supporting relationships"—with or without marriage certificates. The two readings on gay marriage, Bruce Fein's "No: Reserve Marriage for Heterosexuals" and Thomas Stoddard's "Yes: Marriage Is a Fundamental Right," discuss the pros and cons of same-gender marriage. A same-gender relationship is also the subject of the short story, "The Two," by Gloria Naylor. This story explores community reactions to a lesbian couple who move into an apartment complex. A type of community housing that does reflect changing needs is described in the essay "Cohousing and the American Dream," by architects Kathryn McCamant and Charles Durrett. Finally, student writer Amera Chowhan develops an argument on one of the most controversial economic issues involved in the discussion of alternative families: benefits for domestic partners.

Sociologist Judith Stacey cites a Yale study in which respondents identify family as "a group of people who love and care about each other." As you read through this chapter, consider your own beliefs. What do you consider to be a "family"? Would you argue that only parent-child or heterosexual-marriage relationships form the basis of family and home? Or would you argue for extending the definition of family as members of our society expand the range of relationships that make up that community within the home? Do you find it difficult to accept alternative families? Do you think there are certain rights that should only be granted to traditional families? Is American society ready to move toward a different concept of family? The answers to such questions will affect how government, institutions, and local communities, of which you are a part, meet the needs of contemporary and future families.

**JOURNAL ENTRY**

What pictures do you see when you think of the word *love?*
Brainstorm a series of images to represent love, using colors, sounds,
textures, symbols, metaphors, and similes. Do your images seem
commonplace, exotic, or both?

**SUSAN GRIFFIN: "Love Should Grow Up Like a Wild Iris in the Fields"**   Susan Griffin was born in 1943 in Los Angeles, California. She attended the University of California at Berkeley, and received her B.A. and M.A. from San Francisco State University. In addition to writing poetry, Griffin served as assistant editor of *Ramparts* magazine from 1966 to 1968 and has taught in high schools, at San Francisco State University, and at the University of California at Berkeley. A feminist whose observations have been viewed as controversial, Griffin explores a number of women's issues. She received a National Endowment for the Humanities grant in 1976, an Emmy Award in 1975 for *Voices,* and the Ina Coolbrith Prize for poetry in 1963. Her works include *Like the Iris of an Eye* (1976), *Pornography and Silence* (1981), *An Anthology of Writings* (1983), *Rope* (1986), and *Unremembered Country* (1987). A work in progress is *The First and Last: A Woman Thinks about War.* As you read the poem, notice how Griffin uses a combination of conversational, everyday language and natural imagery to express a complex set of conflicts that many modern people feel between romantic love and ordinary domestic relationships.

SUSAN GRIFFIN

# Love Should Grow Up Like a Wild Iris in the Fields

Love should grow up like a wild iris in the fields,
unexpected, after a terrible storm, opening a purple
mouth to the rain, with not a thought to the future,
ignorant of the grass and the graveyard of leaves
around, forgetting its own beginning. Love should
grow like a wild iris
but does not.
Love more often is to be found in kitchens at the dinner hour,
tired out and hungry, lingers over tables in houses where
the walls record movements; while the cook is probably angry,
and the ingredients of the meal are budgeted, while
a child cries feed me now and her mother not quite
hysterical says over and over, wait just a bit, just a bit,
love should grow up in the fields like a wild iris

382

but never does      *ambiguity of line break*

really startle anyone, was to be expected, was to be
predicted, is almost absurd, goes on from day to day, not quite
blindly, gets taken to the cleaners every fall, sings old
songs over and over, and falls on the same piece of rug that
never gets tacked down, gives up, wants to hide, is not
brave, knows too much, is not like an
iris growing wild but more like
staring into space
in the street
not quite sure
which door it was, annoyed about the sidewalk being
slippery, trying all the doors, thinking
if love wished the world to be well, it would be well.
Love should
grow up like a wild iris, but doesn't, it comes from
the midst of everything else, sees like the iris
of an eye, when the light is right,
feels in blindness and when there is nothing else is
tender, blinks, and opens
face up to the skies.

*Chapter Seven: Breaking the Mold*

*poems & sent*

# QUESTIONS

*Looking at Ideas:*

1. What is a key theme of the poem? Why does the poet contrast the images of love "growing wild" with love being tame and domestic?
2. Is the poem's speaker suggesting that love should "grow up wild"? What seems to be her attitude toward love found "at the dinner hour"?
3. What myths about love are explored in the poem?
4. The narrator suggests that love should grow up "with not a thought to the future" and "forgetting its own beginning." Why should love do so? Do you agree?
5. Why does the narrator say that love "sees like the iris/of an eye"? What comparison is she making? How does love "see"? How is it sensitive? Why must "the light [be] right"?

*Looking at Strategies:*

1. Read the poem aloud, listening to the pauses mid-line and end-of-line. How do these breaks guide your reading of the poem and your understanding of its meaning?
2. Why does the poet develop the long string of clauses and phrases in the second stanza *(sentence)*? What effect does the structure have on your understanding of the poem? Does the succession of phrases and images develop any particular aspect of the poem?
3. The poem begins with the iris "opening a purple mouth to the rain" and ends with "opens/face up to the skies." How effective is this image? How does it support a point the poet is making about love?

4. What images in the poem do you find most vivid? Which images, those associated with wildness, or those linked with domesticity, seem most developed and persuasive?

*Looking at Connections*

1. Compare the images of wildness in this poem with the image of a father's rowdy dancing with his son in Roethke's "My Papa's Waltz" (in Chapter Six). Would that type of behavior meet with the approval of the narrator in Griffin's poem?

2. Contrast the attitude toward wildness and spontaneity versus domesticity and control presented by the narrator of this poem with the attitudes and observations of the narrator in the story "I Stand Here Ironing" (in Chapter Six). What generational differences might account for the different attitudes expressed in these two works?

*Suggestions for Writing:*

1. Drawing on your journal brainstorming about images of love, write up a definition of what you believe love is or should be. Develop an overall point of view or dominant theme and support it with imagery and examples.

2. Write an essay in which you discuss the poem's diction, imagery, syntax, and rhythm. How do they contribute to the poem's meaning and persuasiveness? (Review terms in the Glossary.)

3. Write a response to Griffin's poem expressing your own point of view about what love should be. Consider particularly the issue of whether a strong, deep love can exist within a routine domestic environment.

**JOURNAL ENTRY**

Write about a typical American family of the next generation. How will
this future family differ from today's family?

**JUDITH STACEY: "The Postmodern Family, for Better and Worse"** Judith
Stacey lives in Oakland, California, and is a professor of sociology at the University of California at Davis. Stacey, who has received a Ford Foundation fellowship and a Rockefeller Foundation grant, has, among other projects, studied
working-class families in Santa Clara County in Northern California. She is the
author of *Patriarchy and the Sociologist Revolution in China* (1983) and of *And
Jill Came Tumbling After* (1988). With Susie Girard, Stacey wrote an article on
postfeminist evangelism; some of the article's material was developed in the
book *Brave New Families: Studies of Domestic Upheaval in Late-Twentieth-Cen-
tury America* (1990), from which the following selection was excerpted. One feature of Stacey's essay is the abundance of in-depth notes included with the main
body of text. After you read the text, notice how Stacey's extensive endnotes
provide new perspectives on the issue and indicate the breadth of her research.

JUDITH STACEY

# *The Postmodern Family,*
# *for Better and Worse*

Ironically, while women are becoming the new proletariat and some
men are increasing their participation in housework and childwork, the
postmodern family, even more than the modern family it is replacing, is
proving to be a woman-tended domain. There is some empirical basis
for the enlightened father imagery celebrated by films like *Kramer versus Kramer*. Indeed my fieldwork corroborates evidence that the determined efforts by many working women and feminists to reintegrate
men into family life have had some success. There are data, for example, indicating that increasing numbers of men would sacrifice occupational gains in order to have more time with their families, just as there
are data documenting actual increases in male involvement in child
care.[1] The excessive media attention which the faintest signs of new
paternity enjoy, however, may be symptomatic of a deeper, far less
comforting reality it so effectively obscures. We are experiencing, as demographer Andrew Cherlin aptly puts it, "the feminization of kinship."[2] Demographers report a drastic decline in the average numbers
of years that men live in households with young children.[3] Few of the
women who assume responsibility for their children in 90 percent of

divorce cases in the United States today had to wage a custody battle for this privilege.[4] We hear few proposals for a "daddy track." And few of the adults providing care to sick and elderly relatives are male.[5] Yet ironically, most of the alarmist, nostalgic literature about contemporary family decline impugns women's abandonment of domesticity, the flip-side of our tardy entry into modernity. Rarely do the anxious out-cries over the destructive effects on families of working mothers, high divorce rates, institutionalized child care, or sexual liberalization scrutinize the family behaviors of men. Anguished voices, emanating from all bands on the political spectrum, lament state and market inter-ventions that are weakening "the family."[6] But whose family bonds are fraying? Women have amply demonstrated our continuing commitment to sustaining kin ties. If there is a family crisis, it is a male family crisis.

The crisis cannot be resolved by reviving the modern family sys-tem. While nostalgia for an idealized world of *Ozzie and Harriet* and *Archie Bunker* families abounds, little evidence suggests that most Americans genuinely wish to return to the gender order these symbol-ize. On the contrary, the vast majority, like the people in this book, are actively remaking family life. Indeed a 1989 survey conducted by the *New York Times* found more than two-thirds of women, including a sub-stantial majority of even those living in "traditional"—that is to say, "modern"—households, as well as a majority of men agreeing that "the United States continues to need a strong women's movement to push for changes that benefit women."[7] Yet many seem reluctant to own their family preferences. Like Shirley Moskowitz, they cling to images of themselves as "back from the old days," while venturing ambiv-alently but courageously into the new.[8]

Responding to new economic and social insecurities as well as to feminism, higher percentages of families in almost all income groups have adopted a multiple-earner strategy.[9] Thus, the household form that has come closer than any other to replacing the modern family with a new cultural and statistical norm consists of a two-earner, het-erosexual married couple with children.[10] It is not likely, however, that any single household type will soon achieve the measure of normalcy that the modern family long enjoyed. Indeed, the postmodern success of the voluntary principle of the modern family system precludes this. The routinization of divorce and remarriage generates a diversity of family patterns even greater than was characteristic of the premodern period when death prevented family stability or household homogene-ity. Even cautious demographers judge the new family diversity to be "an intrinsic feature . . . rather than a temporary aberration" of con-temporary family life.[11]

"The family" is *not* "here to stay." Nor should we wish it were. On the contrary, I believe that all democratic people, whatever their kinship preferences, should work to hasten its demise. An ideological concept that imposes mythical homogeneity on the diverse means by which people organize their intimate relationships, "the family" distorts and devalues this rich variety of kinship stories. And, along with the class, racial, and heterosexual prejudices it promulgates, this sentimental fictional plot authorizes gender hierarchy. Because the postmodern family crisis ruptures this seamless modern family script, it provides a democratic opportunity. Efforts to expand and redefine the definition of family by feminists and gay liberation activists and by many minority rights organizations are responses to this opportunity, seeking to extend social legitimacy and institutional support to the diverse patterns of intimacy that Americans have already forged.

If feminist identity threatens many and seems out of fashion, struggles to reconstitute gender and kinship on a just and democratic basis are more popular than ever.[12] If only a minority of citizens are willing to grant family legitimacy to gay domestic partners, an overwhelming majority subscribe to the postmodern definition of a family by which the New York Supreme Court validated a gay man's right to retain his deceased lover's apartment. "By a ratio of 3-to-1" people surveyed in a Yale University study defined the family as "a group of people who love and care for each other." And while a majority of those surveyed gave negative ratings to the quality of American family life in general, 71 percent declared themselves "at least very satisfied" with their own family lives.[13]

There is bad faith in the popular lament over family decline. Family nostalgia deflects social criticism from the social sources of most "personal troubles." Supply-side economics, governmental deregulation, and the right-wing assault on social welfare programs have intensified the destabilizing effects of recent occupational upheavals on flagging modern families and emergent postmodern ones alike. This book is not the first to expose the bitter irony of right-wing politicians manipulating nostalgia for eroding working-class families while instituting policies that deepened their distress. Indeed, the ability to provide financial security was the chief family concern of most surveyed in the Yale study. If the postmodern family crisis represents a democratic opportunity, contemporary economic and political conditions enable only a minority to realize its tantalizing potential.

The bad faith revealed in the discrepant data reported in the Yale study indicates how reluctant most Americans are to fully own the genuine ambivalence we feel about family and social change. Yet ambivalence, as sociologist Alan Wolfe suggests, is an underappreciated but responsible moral stance, and one well suited for democratic citizenship: "Given the paradoxes of modernity, there is little wrong, and perhaps a great deal right, with being ambivalent—especially when there is so much to be ambivalent about."[14]

Certainly, as most of the stories in this ethnography indicate, there are good grounds for ambivalence about postmodern family conditions. Even were a feminist family revolution to succeed, it could never eliminate all family distress. At best, it would foster a social order that could invert Tolstoy's aphorism by granting happy families the freedom

387

to differ, and even to suffer. Truly postfeminist families, however, would suffer only the "common unhappiness" endemic to intimate human relationships; they would be liberated from the "hysterical misery" generated by social injustice.[15] No nostalgic movement to restore the modern family can offer as much. For better and/or worse, the postmodern family revolution is here to stay.

*Notes*

1. The controversial *Time* cover story on the future of feminism, for example, reports a 1989 survey by Robert Half International in which 56 percent of men polled said they would forfeit one-fourth of their salaries "to have more family or personal time," and 45 percent "said they would probably refuse a promotion that involved sacrificing hours with their family." See also the Gallup poll data cited in note 39. And see Zavella, "Sun Belt Hispanics on the Line," for a discussion of the active participation in child care and housework by Hispanic husbands of women who are "mainstay providers" for their households.
2. Cherlin, "Marriage, Divorce, Remarriage," p. 17.
3. Between 1960 and 1980, a 43-percent decline among men between the ages of twenty and forty-nine. Research by Eggebeen and Uhlenberg reported in Furstenberg, "Good Dads—Bad Dads: Two Faces of Fatherhood," p. 201.
4. The 90 percent datum is reported in Cherlin, "Changing American Family and Public Policy," p. 8. See Polikoff, "Gender and Child-Custody Determinations: Exploding the Myths," for a careful refutation of the widespread view that women retain an unfair advantage over men in child custody decisions by divorce courts.
5. Abel, "Adult Daughters and Care for the Elderly."
6. See literature cited in chapter 1, note 4. Recently, Alan Wolfe has attempted to formulate a centrist position in the debate over contemporary family change that would resist nostalgia for patriarchal family forms, while recognizing the destructive effects of state and market intrusions on "the family." *Whose Keeper?* He too worries about women's increasing involvement in the market and fails to question men's inadequate involvement in domesticity.
7. Belkin, "Bars to Equality of Sexes Seen as Eroding, Slowly." Likewise the 1990 Gallup poll reports that 57 percent of adults prefer a marriage in which both spouses work and share child care and housework. Destafano and Colestano, "Most Believe U.S. Men Have Better Life," p. B5.
8. Zavella, "Sunbelt Hispanics on the Line," finds a similar discrepancy between "traditionalist" ideology and reformist practice among Chicanas who serve as primary wage-earners in their households.
9. According to Joan Smith, low-income African-Americans provide the sole exception to this generalization because the majority contain only one possible wage-earner. "Marginalized Labor Forces," p. 1. For additional data, see Strober, "Two-Earner Families."
10. According to Myra Strober, in 1985, 42 percent of households were of this type. "Two-Earner Families," p. 161. However, Census Bureau data for 1988 report that only 27 percent of all households included two parents living with children. Quoted in Gutis, "What Makes a Family? Traditional Limits Are Challenged."
11. Bumpass and Castro, "Recent Trends and Differentials in Marital Disruption," p. 28.
12. As one of the journalists reporting the results of the *New York Times* survey reported above concluded, "Despite much talk about the decline of feminism and the women's movement, American women very much want a movement working on their behalf as they try to win equal treatment in the workplace and to balance the demands of work and family." Dionne, "Struggle for Work and Family Fueling Women's Movement." See also the *Time/CNN* survey that found 77 percent claiming the women's movement made life better for American women and 82 percent claiming it

was still improving women's lives. Wallis, "Onward, Women!" p. 82. The Gallup data, however, reports smaller majorities with such views. See Destafano and Colesanto, "Most Believe U.S. Men Have Better Life," p. B5.

13. Study by Albert Solnit quoted in "Most Regard Family Highly," *New York Times* (10 October 1989), p. A18. Andrew Cherlin also reports increasing marital satisfaction rates despite popular concerns over family decline. "Economic Interdependence and Family Ties."

14. Wolfe, *Whose Keeper?* p. 211.

15. Freud's famous goal for psychoanalysis was to convert "hysterical misery into common unhappiness." Freud with Breuer, *Studies in Hysteria*.

## QUESTIONS

*Looking at Ideas:*

1. How does Stacey define the postmodern family? Is the definition explicit or implicit? Summarize her definition in your own words.

2. What crisis is the author writing about? Why is it particularly a "male family crisis"? Do you agree that women have done their share of maintaining kinship? What is the "feminization of kinship"?

3. What kinds of alternative families does Stacey discuss?

4. When the author states, " 'The family' is *not* 'here to stay' " what does she mean? Do you agree with her conclusions? Why does she restate this assertion differently at the end of this selection?

5. Why, according to the author, are many people ambivalent about changes in family structure in this "postmodern" period? How does her conclusion underscore this ambivalence?

*Looking at Strategies:*

1. What is the level of diction in this selection? For what kind of audience is Stacey writing? Can you infer the meaning of most of the difficult words from the context, or do you need explicit definitions?

2. What is the author's tone? What words, phrases, and expressions in the text convey this tone?

3. How do the endnotes for Stacey's text support and amplify what is being said in the body of the text?

4. What kinds of evidence does Stacey include? What kind of research techniques has she used? How does she use evidence to support her assertions? Is the evidence convincing?

*Looking at Connections:*

1. How might Bruce Fein, who argues against gay marriages in a selection later in this chapter, respond to this essay?

*Suggestions for Writing:*

1. Write an essay in which you argue for or against the notion that any contemporary crisis of the family is fueled by, and must be resolved by, men rather than women. Consider the arguments the author puts forth before framing your essay.

2. Write a summary of this reading in your own words and for a general

audience. Do you agree or disagree with the author's thesis? Why or why not? Write a critique of Stacey's argument.

3. Write your own definition of the postmodern family. Draw on your experience, observations, readings, and perhaps interviews. You may also want to consider representations of postmodern families in popular culture—in books, films, television programs, and songs.

**KEENEN PECK: "When 'Family' Is Not a Household Word"** Keenen Peck
(1960–1990) was an attorney and activist who was deeply involved in the
struggle for human rights and civil liberties. Peck received his bachelor's degree and law degree from the University of Wisconsin. He worked for *The Progressive* before law school and later served on its editorial advisory board. In
Washington, D.C., he served as counsel to Senator Herb Kohl (D-Wisconsin)
and was also chairperson of his local American Civil Liberties Union. Peck's
article, "The Take-Charge Gang," which was published in *The Progressive* in
1985, was an exposé of the Federal Emergency Management Agency. Peck
died of an aneurysm at the age of 29. As you read the following article (originally published in *The Progressive*), consider whether you agree with his arguments in favor of changes in the legal system to accommodate changing definitions of "family."

KEENAN PECK

# When "Family" Is Not a Household Word

If my friends had been married, the three of us could have lived in
peace. Instead, the authorities ordered us to vacate our home. In my
neighborhood, it turned out, three unrelated people could not live together legally. Never mind that we were good, quiet neighbors. Never
mind that we enjoyed the area. No marriage license, no occupancy.
There might as well have been a sign at the end of our street: ALTERNA-
TIVE FAMILIES, KEEP OUT.

I was sharing a three-bedroom house in Madison, Wisconsin, with
an unmarried couple—a man and a woman who intended to make a
life together but didn't want to get married just yet. Our arrangement
was illegal because Madison, like many other cities, prohibits occupancy by more than two unrelated persons in neighborhoods designated for families. It's called "single-family zoning," and it's a pernicious form of discrimination against those in loving but unorthodox relationships.

When Madison told us to move, we sued the city. We argued that

391

the ordinance violated our right to associate with one another. We pointed out that it in no way advanced the admirable goals of residential stability and tranquility. A person's marital status has nothing to do with his or her compatibility with the neighbors, we said. Consanguinity and lawn mowing are not connected. The city should regulate the *use* of dwellings, not the users.

We lost in the trial court (the case is now on appeal), but the experience offered a lesson in civil rights. We discovered that we were part of a growing legal debate over the definition of "family." Increasingly, Americans who live in groupings they regard as families but who are not related by blood, marriage, or adoption are pressing courts, legislatures, and employers for the same rights claimed by traditional families. Although the media have concentrated on the steamy (or contagious) aspects of the sexual revolution, that revolution has also led to a struggle over such mundane but important matters as insurance, housing, and inheritance.

In our case, my roommates and I asserted the simple right to live where and with whom we wanted. But in 1974, the U.S. Supreme Court had held that the Constitution does not stop municipalities from restricting households composed of unrelated persons. The strength of one's rights in these situations turns on the interpretation of each state's constitution by its own judiciary. The high courts of New Jersey, California, New York, and Michigan have used their states' constitutions to protect alternative families; courts in Missouri, New Hampshire, and Hawaii have ruled against nontraditional living arrangements.

To reach their decisions, all of the courts grappled with the same essential questions: When does a household become, in lawyer's jargon, the "functional equivalent" of a family? And should the law treat the functional equivalent the same as the real item? The rise of the alternative family makes it essential to find answers.

The term "alternative family" refers to several kinds of living situations, the most common of which is the unmarried heterosexual couple. In 1980, the year of the last census, some 1.8 million Americans were living as cohabiting couples, a 300 per cent increase from the number in 1970. The Census Bureau called them POSSLQs—Persons of Opposite Sex Sharing Living Quarters. According to two University of Wisconsin sociologists, Larry Bumpass and James Sweet, the proportion of persons cohabiting before their first marriage has quadrupled (to 44 per cent) over the past two decades.

"Cohabitation has not simply become increasingly common," they said upon the release of their $4.5 million study. "If recent trends continue, it will soon be the majority experience."

"Alternative family" also encompasses gay and lesbian couples and the dependents of all unmarried couples. In all, there are about ten million people in the United States who can be classified as belonging to alternative families, reports Steven Ruggles, a demographer at the University of Minnesota. Looked at from the other side of the numbers, fewer than 30 per cent of us live in a traditional nuclear family, defined as a married couple with children.

The law has lagged behind changes in our lifestyle. Twenty states have repealed laws against adultery, but cohabitators in some states still live under the threat of prosecution. Only one state, Wisconsin, prohibits discrimination on the basis of sexual orientation, and no state permits persons of the same sex to marry. Thus, gay and lesbian couples are denied the legal benefits of marriage, such as the automatic passing of property to the surviving partner when the other one dies without a will. To make matters worse, the U.S. Supreme Court ruled in 1986 that Georgia could enforce a law against "homosexual sodomy." (Actually, the law prohibited anal intercourse between men and women as well, but the homophobic majority ignored that fact.)

Like state governments, employers and insurance companies often refuse to treat unmarried or unadopted loved ones as family for the purposes of various benefits. A union contract can help, but only if the union is enlightened enough to deal with the problem in the first place.

Law professor Barbara Cox, writing in the *Wisconsin Women's Law Journal,* has catalogued the entitlements that are extended to nuclear families but withheld from alternative families: "They include the opportunity to live in neighborhoods zoned for single families; receive employment-based health insurance, bereavement and sick leave, pensions, moving expenses, library and recreational privileges, and low-cost day care and travel packages; sue for loss of consortium, worker's compensation or unemployment compensation; visit family members in hospitals and authorize their emergency medical treatment; and receive low-cost family rates from organizations such as health clubs, museums, and art centers."

What is the motive for perpetuating such discrimination? In the field of housing, opposition to alternative families is often really bias against college students who, local governments fear, will wreak havoc in communes. This was the unspoken justification for Madison's ordinance, and it figures in much of the litigation over zoning (including the 1974 U.S. Supreme Court case).

College students, to be sure, can put strain on a family-oriented neighborhood. Still, in the words of a recent New Jersey court opinion, students should not be "required to govern their lifestyle to meet the dictates of those who disapprove of their ways." The same judge hinted at another reason behind hostility toward alternative families: the generation gap. People who set rules and policies are likely to hark back to an era when sexual taboos limited alternative living arrangements. And homophobia afflicts politicians and employers, too. Employers and insurance companies, moreover, don't want to spend the money to cover children and lovers who are deemed family in expanded benefits plans.

But there seems to be a more fundamental concern behind the opposition to alternative families—the feeling that the *nuclear* family forms society's bedrock. New types of loving relationships are perceived as a threat to the very order of things. The problem with this

393

objection is that it ignores the negative attributes of nuclear families and the positive characteristics of alternative families. Something in the nuclear family is wrong if almost half of new marriages end in divorce; and what is wrong with an alternative relationship that's lasting and loving?

Steven Ruggles, the Minnesota demographer, found no significant differences between married and unmarried couples "in terms of satisfaction, commitment, sexual satisfaction, communication, or psychological adjustment." What's more, half of the cohabitants in the University of Wisconsin study married within three years, suggesting that an alternative status is frequently temporary.

A happy or sad, healthy or abusive relationship will not be made less or more so with a marriage certificate. The law should focus on the societal interest, which is in long-term, supportive relationships. Although blood relation, marriage, and adoption have served as useful shorthands for "family," the legal establishment must now find categories that can accommodate new living arrangements without losing all definition.

Two cities have attempted to do so. In Santa Cruz, California, city workers and their loved ones may sign an "Affidavit of Domestic Partnership" to qualify the partners for health benefits. Under penalty of perjury, the two affirm, "We are each other's sole domestic partner and intend to remain so indefinitely and are responsible for our common welfare." The Santa Cruz personnel department indicates that 2 per cent of the municipal work force has signed on the dotted line.

In West Hollywood, California, domestic partners can swear out a form indicating that they "share the common necessities of life," "are each other's sole domestic partner," and "agree to be responsible for each other's welfare." In addition to providing benefits for partners of municipal workers, the ordinance also requires hospitals and jails to permit visitation by partners. About 15 per cent of the work force has signed up in West Hollywood, which has a large gay population.

Following the example of the California cities, a member of the Madison Common Council proposed a similar plan. Partners would be allowed to file an affidavit with the city stating that they are in a relationship of "mutual support, caring, and commitment." The form would make partners and dependents eligible for the benefits given to nuclear families. Despite the support of the Madison Equal Opportunities Commission, however, the proposal encountered resistance in the usually liberal town. As of this writing, the plan has not been adopted.

When I try to fathom why the Madison plan fell flat—and, for that matter, why the city tried to oust three people from their home—one word comes to mind: fright. The powers that be are frightened by the prospect of yet another unfamiliar constituency demanding legal recognition. In Madison and elsewhere, officials are whispering, "Enough is enough." To them, alternative families don't need to live in family-oriented neighborhoods; gay couples don't need to marry; partners don't need benefits that accrue to their lovers.

By the same token, though, blacks didn't need to ride in the front of the bus; women didn't need membership in formerly all-male clubs; poor people didn't need the vote. But in each of those instances, the aggrieved segment of the population persuaded the rest of us that "equal rights" means what it says. In the coming years, many Americans will be asking for equal rights for the ten million members of alternative families.

In the meantime, I'll be asking for nothing more than the right to live with unmarried friends in a house of my choosing.

## QUESTIONS

*Looking at Ideas:*

1. What kinds of alternative families does the author discuss? Do they all fit your understanding of the term *alternative*?

2. In your view, when does a household become the "functional equivalent of a family"? Do you tend to define family in terms of blood and marriage relationships, or do you see new ways to define family?

3. Do you agree with the author's assertion that society in general views the nuclear family as "society's bedrock"? Is it accurate to say, as the author does, that most people believe that "new types of loving relationships" are a threat to "the very order of things"? Does people's resistance to change indeed come down to "fright"?

4. Does Peck argue convincingly that it is in society's interest to foster long-term, stable relationships regardless of marital status? Which are his most specific arguments?

*Looking at Strategies:*

1. How well does the introduction engage your attention? Is it effective? Does it accurately predict the stance and approach of the argument that follows?

2. Examine the ways in which the author weaves personal experience and legal and statistical evidence into the text. Do both kinds of evidence support the thesis equally well? Cite examples.

3. Is the author's analogy in the conclusion—blacks having to ride in the back of the bus, women denied organizational memberships—appropriate and convincing for developing his thesis? Do you agree that we will come to view the "alternative family" struggle in the same light as other civil rights struggles?

*Looking at Connections:*

1. Compare Peck's arguments for recognition of alternative families with Stoddard's arguments in favor of legal gay marriages in his essay (next in this chapter). What similar points do both writers make? Which argument seems most convincing?

2. What common themes run through this essay and the poem, "Love Should Grow Up Like a Wild Iris in the Fields"? Is the poetic or the prose treatment more compelling?

*Suggestions for Writing:*

1. Learn about the zoning laws for group or alternative housing in your neighborhood or the community surrounding your college. Do they support traditional neighborhoods at the expense of alternative living arrangements? Are such regulations enforced? If so, for a general community audience, argue either that the laws should remain in force or that they should change to accommodate changing family patterns.

2. Do you believe that certain rights—of property, of inheritance, of insurance, and of employment benefits—ought to belong only to married heterosexual couples? Develop an argument for or against this notion; support your answer with experience, evidence, expert testimony.

3. Do you agree that single-family zoning is "a pernicious form of discrimination" on the same order as racial and gender discrimination? Write an essay to develop and support your view.

**THOMAS STODDARD: "Yes: Marriage Is a Fundamental Right"**    Thomas
Stoddard, born in 1948, is an attorney and serves as executive director of the
Lambda Legal Defense and Education Fund, a gay rights organization. He is
the author of *The Rights of Gay People* (1983). The following essay by Stoddard first appeared in the *New York Times* and was reprinted in the *ABA Journal* in 1990.

**BRUCE FEIN: "No: Reserve Marriage for Heterosexuals"**    Bruce Fein is a
Washington, D.C., attorney. He is the author of *Significant Decisions of the Supreme Court, 1979–1980;* he has also written articles for the *American Legion
Magazine* and *National Review.* Fein's article was published in the *ABA
Journal* in 1990. After thinking about your own preconceptions on the issue of
gay marriages, try to remain open to the arguments presented by both Stoddard and Fein.

# Gay Marriage:

## Should Homosexual Marriages Be Recognized Legally?

THOMAS STODDARD

### Yes: Marriage Is a Fundamental Right

"In sickness and in health, 'til death do us part." With those words, millions of people each year are married, a public affirmation of a private
bond that both society and the newlyweds hope will endure. Yet for
nearly four years, Karen Thompson was denied the company of the
one person to whom she had pledged life-long devotion.

Her partner is a woman, Sharon Kowalski, and their home state of
Minnesota, like every other in the United States, refuses to permit
same-sex marriages.

Karen Thompson and Sharon Kowalski are spouses in every respect except the legal. They exchanged vows and rings. They lived together until Nov. 13, 1983—when Kowalski, as the result of an automobile accident, was rendered unable to walk and barely able to speak.

Thompson sought a ruling granting her guardianship over her partner, but Kowalski's parents opposed the petition and obtained sole guardianship. They then moved Kowalski to a nursing home 300 miles away from Thompson and forbade all visits between the two women.

In February 1989, in the wake of a reevaluation of Kowalski's mental competence, Thompson was permitted to visit her partner again. But the prolonged injustice and anguish inflicted on both women hold a moral for everyone.

Marriage, the Supreme Court declared in 1967 in *Loving v. Virginia,* is "one of the basic civil rights of man" (and, presumably, of woman as well). The freedom to marry, said the Court, is "essential to the orderly pursuit of happiness."

Marriage is far more than a symbolic state. It can be the key to survival—emotional and financial. Marriage triggers a universe of rights, privileges and presumptions. In every jurisdiction in this country, a married person can share in a spouse's estate even when there is no will. She typically has access to the group insurance and pension programs offered by the spouse's employer, and she enjoys tax advantages.

## Individual Decision

The decision whether or not to marry belongs properly to individuals, not to the government. While marriage historically has required a male and a female partner, history alone cannot sanctify injustice.

If tradition were the only measure, most states still would limit matrimony to partners of the same race. As recently as 1967, before the Supreme Court declared in *Loving* that miscegenation statutes are unconstitutional, 16 states still prohibited marriages between a white person and a black person. When all the excuses were stripped away, it was clear that the only purpose of those laws was to maintain white supremacy.

Those who argue against reforming the marriage statutes because they believe that same-sex marriage would be "anti-family" overlook the obvious: Marriage creates families and promotes social stability. In an increasingly loveless world, those who wish to commit themselves to a relationship founded upon devotion should be encouraged, not scorned. Government has no legitimate interest in how that love is expressed.

And it can no longer be argued—if it ever could—that marriage is fundamentally a procreative unit. Otherwise, states would forbid marriage between those who, by reason of age or infertility, cannot have children, as well as those who elect not to.

The case of Sharon Kowalski and Karen Thompson demonstrates that sanctimonious illusions can lead directly to the suffering of others. Denied the right to marry, these women were left to the whims and prejudices of others, and of the law.

It is time for the marriage statutes to incorporate fully the concept of equal protection of the law by extending to the many millions of gay Americans the right to marry.

BRUCE FEIN

## No: Reserve Marriage for Heterosexuals

Authorizing the marriage of homosexuals, like sanctioning polygamy, would be unenlightened social policy. The law should reserve the celebration of marriage vows for monogamous male-female attachments to further the goal of psychologically, emotionally and educationally balanced offspring.

As Justice Oliver Wendell Holmes noted, the life of the law has not been logic, it has been experience. Experience confirms that child development is skewed, scarred or retarded when either a father or mother is absent in the household.

In the area of adoption, married couples are favored over singles. The recent preferences for joint child-custody decrees in divorce proceedings tacitly acknowledges the desirability of child intimacies with both a mother and father.

As Supreme Court Justice Byron White recognized in *Taylor v. Louisiana* (1975): "[T]he two sexes are not fungible; a community made up exclusively of one is different from a community of both; the subtle interplay of influence one on the other is among the imponderables" (quoting from *Ballard v. United States*).

A child receives incalculable benefits in the maturing process by the joint instruction, consolation, oversight and love of a father and mother—benefits that are unavailable in homosexual households. The child enjoys the opportunity to understand and respect both sexes in a uniquely intimate climate. The likelihood of gender prejudice is thus reduced, an exceptionally worthy social objective.

### Protect Children

The law should encourage male-female marriage vows over homosexual attachments in the interests of physically, mentally, and psychologically healthy children, the nation's most valuable asset.

Crowning homosexual relationships with the solemnity of legal marriage would wrongly send social cues that male-female marriages are not preferable. And there is no constitutional right to homosexual marriage since homosexual sodomy can be criminalized. See *Bowers v. Hardwick* (1986).

The fact that some traditional marriages end in fractious divorce, yield no offspring, or result in families with mistreated children does not discredit limiting marriage to monogamous female-male relationships. Anti-polygamy laws are instructive. They seek to discourage female docility, male autocracy, and intra-family rancor and jealousies

399

that are promoted by polygamous marriages. That some might not exhibit such deplorable characteristics is no reason for their repeal or a finding of constitutional infirmity.

To deny the right of homosexual marriage is not an argument for limiting other rights to gays, because of community animosity or vengeance. These are unacceptable policy motivations if law is to be civilized.

Several states and localities protect homosexuals against discrimination in employment or housing. In New York, a state law confers on a homosexual the rent-control benefits of a deceased partner. Other jurisdictions have eschewed special legal rights for homosexuals, and the military excludes them. Experience will adjudge which of the varied legal approaches to homosexual rights has been the most enlightened.

Sober debate over homosexual rights is in short supply. The subject challenges deep-rooted and passionately held images of manhood, womanhood and parenthood, and evokes sublimated fears of community ostracism or degradation.

Each legal issue regarding homosexuality should be examined discretely with the recognition that time has upset many fighting faiths and with the goal of balancing individual liberty against community interests. With regard to homosexual marriage, that balance is negative.

## QUESTIONS

*Looking at Ideas:*

1. Paraphrase the main argument and supporting ideas of each essay. On what major points do the authors disagree? Is there anything they *do* agree on?

2. Fein's essay highlights the role of children, while Stoddard's stresses personal autonomy. Which primary need or concern do you find most significant?

3. Do the two writers adequately and convincingly refute arguments commonly raised on the issue, or do they mainly argue their own points? If they do attempt refutation, is their refutation convincing?

*Looking at Strategies:*

1. Analyze the first paragraph of each essay and compare the writers' tactics. Why might each author have selected the kind of introduction he used? Why is delaying the thesis statement sometimes advisable in persuasive writing?

2. Both writers cite legal precedent, but Fein cites far more cases than does Stoddard. On what kinds of evidence does Stoddard rely? Which kind of evidence do you find more convincing? Why did Stoddard use an example of two women rather than two men?

3. What tone does each writer develop? Does one or the other seem more reasonable? Do the writers seem personally engaged in the matter or does one (or do both) seem to be writing "for the sake of argument"?

4. Is Stoddard's reference to other types of discrimination, such as the mis-

cegenation laws prohibiting interracial marriages, a convincing analogy to support his argument?

*Looking at Connections:*

1. Consider the family described in "Discarded" in Chapter Two. How might the prospect of a legal marriage or domestic partnership have changed Andy's life?

*Suggestions for Writing:*

1. Draft a letter of response to either Fein or Stoddard, arguing against his point of view. Refute or concede his arguments in your response as well as proposing your own thesis on the issue.
2. After discussing the same-gender marriage issue with students in your class, use your notes and your sense of the issue from reading Fein and Stoddard to write a dialogue between two imaginary people debating the issue.
3. Do more research on the issue of gay marriage. Look into the points raised by both authors: child development, property and inheritance rights, health benefits, and other issues. Develop a researched argumentative paper that supports your own point of view on the subject.

*Chapter Seven:*
*Breaking the*
*Mold*

**JOURNAL ENTRY**

Think about a time when a new individual, a new family, or a new couple
moved into your neighborhood or building who seemed "different" from
the other people there. What initial impressions did you form of the
newcomers?

**GLORIA NAYLOR: "The Two"**   Born in 1950, Gloria Naylor received an
M.A. from Yale University in African-American Studies. She is an essayist, novelist, and lecturer who has taught at a number of universities, including Princeton, New York University, and the University of Pennsylvania. Naylor's essays
have appeared in many periodicals, and her novels include *Linden Hills*
(1985), *Mama Day* (1988), and *The Women of Brewster Place* (1982), from
which the following selection is taken. As you read this story about a lesbian
couple who must cope with the disapproval of their neighbors in a densely
populated housing complex, consider the ways in which emotions and attitudes of the community and the two women are revealed and how such revelations underscore the author's theme.

GLORIA NAYLOR

# The Two

At first they seemed like such nice girls. No one could remember exactly when they had moved into Brewster. It was earlier in the year before Ben[1] was killed—of course, it had to be before Ben's death. But no
one remembered if it was in the winter or spring of that year that the
two had come. People often came and went on Brewster Place like a
restless night's dream, moving in and out in the dark to avoid eviction
notices or neighborhood bulletins about the dilapidated condition of
their furnishings. So it wasn't until the two were clocked leaving in the
mornings and returning in the evenings at regular intervals that it was
quietly absorbed that they now claimed Brewster as home. And Brewster waited, cautiously prepared to claim them, because you never knew
about young women, and obviously single at that. But when no wild
music or drunken friends careened out of the corner building on weekends, and especially, when no slightly eager husbands were encouraged
to linger around that first-floor apartment and run errands for them, a
suspended sigh of relief floated around the two when they dumped
their garbage, did their shopping, and headed for the morning bus.

The women of Brewster had readily accepted the lighter, skinny

---

[1]*Ben:* a caretaker & handyman at Brewster Place.

one. There wasn't much threat in her timid mincing walk and the slightly protruding teeth she seemed so eager to show everyone in her bell-like good mornings and evenings. Breaths were held a little longer in the direction of the short dark one—too pretty, and too much behind. And she insisted on wearing those thin Qiana dresses that the summer breeze molded against the maddening rhythm of the twenty pounds of rounded flesh that she swung steadily down the street. Through slitted eyes, the women watched their men watching her pass, knowing the bastards were praying for a wind. But since she seemed oblivious to whether these supplications went answered, their sighs settled around her shoulders too. Nice girls.

And so no one even cared to remember exactly when they had moved into Brewster Place, until the rumor started. It had first spread through the block like a sour odor that's only faintly perceptible and easily ignored until it starts growing in strength from the dozen mouths it had been lying in, among clammy gums and scum-coated teeth. And then it was everywhere—lining the mouths and whitening the lips of everyone as they wrinkled up their noses at its pervading smell, unable to pinpoint the source or time of its initial arrival. Sophie could—she had been there.

It wasn't that the rumor had actually begun with Sophie. A rumor needs no true parent. It only needs a willing carrier, and it found one in Sophie. She had been there—on one of those August evenings when the sun's absence is a mockery because the heat leaves the air so heavy it presses the naked skin down on your body, to the point that a sheet becomes unbearable and sleep impossible. So most of Brewster was outside that night when the two had come in together, probably from one of those air-conditioned movies downtown, and had greeted the ones who were loitering around their building. And they had started up the steps when the skinny one tripped over a child's ball and the darker one had grabbed her by the arm and around the waist to break her fall. "Careful, don't wanna lose you now." And the two of them had laughed into each other's eyes and went into the building.

The smell had begun there. It outlined the image of the stumbling woman and the one who had broken her fall. Sophie and a few other women sniffed at the spot and then, perplexed, silently looked at each other. Where had they seen that before? They had often laughed and touched each other—held each other in joy or its dark twin—but where had they seen *that* before? It came to them as the scent drifted down the steps and entered their nostrils on the way to their inner mouths. They had seen that—done that—with their men. That shared moment of invisible communion reserved for two and hidden from the rest of the world behind laughter or tears or a touch. In the days before babies, miscarriages, and other broken dreams, after stolen caresses in barn stalls and cotton houses, after intimate walks from church and secret kisses with boys who were now long forgotten or permanently fixed in their lives—that was where. They could almost feel the odor moving about in their mouths, and they slowly knitted themselves together and

403

let it out into the air like a yellow mist that began to cling to the bricks on Brewster.

So it got around that the two in 312 were *that* way. And they had seemed like such nice girls. Their regular exits and entrances to the block were viewed with a jaundiced eye. The quiet that rested around their door on the weekends hinted of all sorts of secret rituals, and their friendly indifference to the men on the street was an insult to the women as a brazen flaunting of unnatural ways.

Since Sophie's apartment windows faced theirs from across the air shaft, she became the official watchman for the block, and her opinions were deferred to whenever the two came up in conversation. Sophie took her position seriously and was constantly alert for any telltale signs that might creep out around their drawn shades, across from which she kept a religious vigil. An entire week of drawn shades was evidence enough to send her flying around with reports that as soon as it got dark they pulled their shades down and put on the lights. Heads nodded in knowing unison—a definite sign. If doubt was voiced with a "But I pull my shades down at night too," a whispered "Yeah, but you're not *that* way" was argument enough to win them over.

Sophie watched the lighter one dumping their garbage, and she went outside and opened the lid. Her eyes darted over the crushed tin cans, vegetable peelings, and empty chocolate chip cookie boxes. What do they do with all them chocolate chip cookies? It was surely a sign, but it would take some time to figure that one out. She saw Ben go into their apartment, and she waited and blocked his path as he came out, carrying his toolbox.

"What ya see?" She grabbed his arm and whispered wetly in his face.

Ben stared at her squinted eyes and drooping lips and shook his head slowly. "Uh, uh, uh, it was terrible."

"Yeah?" She moved in a little closer.

"Worst busted faucet I seen in my whole life." He shook her hand off his arm and left her standing in the middle of the block.

"You old sop bucket," she muttered, as she went back up on her stoop. A broken faucet, huh? Why did they need to use so much water?

Sophie had plenty to report that day. Ben had said it was terrible in there. No, she didn't know exactly what he had seen, but you can imagine—and they did. Confronted with the difference that had been thrust into their predictable world, they reached into their imaginations and, using an ancient pattern, weaved themselves a reason for its existence. Out of necessity they stitched all of their secret fears and lingering childhood nightmares into this existence, because even though it was deceptive enough to try and look as they looked, talk as they talked, and do as they did, it had to have some hidden stain to invalidate it—it was impossible for them both to be right. So they leaned back, supported by the sheer weight of their numbers and comforted by the woven barrier that kept them protected from the yellow mist that enshrouded the two as they came and went on Brewster Place.

Lorraine was the first to notice the change in the people on Brewster Place. She was a shy but naturally friendly woman who got up early, and had read the morning paper and done fifty sit-ups before it was time to leave for work. She came out of her apartment eager to start her day by greeting any of her neighbors who were outside. But she noticed that some of the people who had spoken to her before made a point of having something else to do with their eyes when she passed, although she could almost feel them staring at her back as she moved on. The ones who still spoke only did so after an uncomfortable pause, in which they seemed to be peering through her before they begrudged her a good morning or evening. She wondered if it was all in her mind and she thought about mentioning it to Theresa, but she didn't want to be accused of being too sensitive again. And how would Tee even notice anything like that anyway? She had a lousy attitude and hardly ever spoke to people. She stayed in that bed until the last moment and rushed out of the house fogged-up and grumpy, and she was used to being stared at—by men at least—because of her body.

Lorraine thought about these things as she came up the block from work, carrying a large paper bag. The group of women on her stoop parted silently and let her pass.

"Good evening," she said, as she climbed the steps.

Sophie was standing on the top step and tried to peek into the bag. "You been shopping, huh? What ya buy?" It was almost an accusation.

"Groceries." Lorraine shielded the top of the bag from view and squeezed past her with a confused frown. She saw Sophie throw a knowing glance to the others at the bottom of the stoop. What was wrong with this old woman? Was she crazy or something?

Lorraine went into her apartment. Theresa was sitting by the window, reading a copy of *Mademoiselle*. She glanced up from her magazine. "Did you get my chocolate chip cookies?"

"Why good evening to you, too, Tee. And how was my day? Just wonderful." She sat the bag down on the couch. "The little Baxter boy brought in a puppy for show-and-tell, and the damn thing pissed all over the floor and then proceeded to chew the heel off my shoe, but, yes, I managed to hobble to the store and bring you your chocolate chip cookies."

Oh, Jesus, Theresa thought, she's got a bug up her ass tonight.

"Well, you should speak to Mrs. Baxter. She ought to train her kid better than that." She didn't wait for Lorraine to stop laughing before she tried to stretch her good mood. "Here, I'll put those things away. Want me to make dinner so you can rest? I only worked half a day, and the most tragic thing that went down was a broken fingernail and that got caught in my typewriter."

Lorraine followed Theresa into the kitchen. "No, I'm not really tired, and fair's fair, you cooked last night. I didn't mean to tick off like that; it's just that . . . well, Tee, have you noticed that people aren't as nice as they used to be?"

405

Theresa stiffened. Oh, God, here she goes again. "What people, Lorraine? Nice in what way?"

"Well, the people in this building and on the street. No one hardly speaks anymore. I mean, I'll come in and say good evening—and just silence. It wasn't like that when we first moved in. I don't know, it just makes you wonder; that's all. What are they thinking?"

"I personally don't give a shit what they're thinking. And their good evenings don't put any bread on my table."

"Yeah, but you didn't see the way that woman looked at me out there. They must feel something or know something. They probably—"

"They, they, they!" Theresa exploded. "You know, I'm not starting up with this again, Lorraine. Who in the hell are they? And where in the hell are we? Living in some dump of a building in this God-for-saken part of town around a bunch of ignorant niggers with the cotton still under their fingernails because of you and your theys. They knew something in Linden Hills, so I gave up an apartment for you that I'd been in for the last four years. And then they knew in Park Heights, and you made me so miserable there we had to leave. Now these mysterious theys are on Brewster Place. Well, look out that window, kid. There's a big wall down that block, and this is the end of the line for me. I'm not moving anymore, so if that's what you're working yourself up to—save it!"

When Theresa became angry she was like a lump of smoldering coal, and her fierce bursts of temper always unsettled Lorraine.

"You see, that's why I didn't want to mention it." Lorraine began to pull at her fingers nervously. "You're always flying up and jumping to conclusions—no one said anything about moving. And I didn't know your life has been so miserable since you met me. I'm sorry about that," she finished tearfully.

Theresa looked at Lorraine, standing in the kitchen door like a wilted leaf, and she wanted to throw something at her. Why didn't she ever fight back? The very softness that had first attracted her to Lorraine was now a frequent cause for irritation. Smoked honey. That's what Lorraine had reminded her of, sitting in her office clutching that application. Dry autumn days in Georgia woods, thick bloated smoke under a beehive, and the first glimpse of amber honey just faintly darkened about the edges by the burning twigs. She had flowed just that heavily into Theresa's mind and had stuck there with a persistent sweetness.

But Theresa hadn't known then that this softness filled Lorraine up to the very middle and that she would bend at the slightest pressure, would be constantly seeking to surround herself with the comfort of everyone's goodwill, and would shrivel up at the least touch of disapproval. It was becoming a drain to be continually called upon for this nurturing and support that she just didn't understand. She had supplied it at first out of love for Lorraine, hoping that she would harden eventually, even as honey does when exposed to the cold. Theresa was growing tired of being clung to—of being the one who was leaned on.

She didn't want a child—she wanted someone who could stand toe to toe with her and be willing to slug it out at times. If they practiced that way with each other, then they could turn back to back and beat the hell out of the world for trying to invade their territory. But she had found no such sparring partner in Lorraine, and the strain of fighting alone was beginning to show on her.

"Well, if it was that miserable, I would have been gone a long time ago," she said, watching her words refresh Lorraine like a gentle shower.

"I guess you think I'm some sort of a sick paranoid, but I can't afford to have people calling my job or writing letters to my principal. You know I've already lost a position like that in Detroit. And teaching is my whole life, Tee."

"I know," she sighed, not really knowing at all. There was no danger of that ever happening on Brewster Place. Lorraine taught too far from this neighborhood for anyone here to recognize her in that school. No, it wasn't her job she feared losing this time, but their approval. She wanted to stand out there and chat and trade makeup secrets and cake recipes. She wanted to be secretary of their block association and be asked to mind their kids while they ran to the store. And none of that was going to happen if they couldn't even bring themselves to accept her good evenings.

Theresa silently finished unpacking the groceries. "Why did you buy cottage cheese? Who eats that stuff?"

"Well, I thought we should go on a diet."

"If *we* go on a diet, then you'll disappear. You've got nothing to lose but your hair."

"Oh, I don't know. I thought that we might want to try and reduce our hips or something." Lorraine shrugged playfully.

"No, thank you. We are very happy with our hips the way they are," Theresa said, as she shoved the cottage cheese to the back of the refrigerator. "And even when I lose weight, it never comes off there. My chest and arms just get smaller, and I start looking like a bottle of salad dressing."

The two women laughed, and Theresa sat down to watch Lorraine fix dinner. "You know, this behind has always been my downfall. When I was coming up in Georgia with my grandmother, the boys used to promise me penny candy if I would let them pat my behind. And I used to love those jawbreakers—you know, the kind that lasted all day and kept changing colors in your mouth. So I was glad to oblige them, because in one afternoon I could collect a whole week's worth of jawbreakers."

"Really. That's funny to you? Having some boy feeling all over you."

Theresa sucked her teeth. "We were only kids, Lorraine. You know, you remind me of my grandmother. That was one straight-laced old lady. She had a fit when my brother told her what I was doing. She called me into the smokehouse and told me in this real scary whisper that I could get pregnant from letting little boys pat my butt and that I'd end up like my cousin Willa. But Willa and I had been thick as fleas, and she had already given me a step-by-step summary of how she'd gotten into her predicament. But I sneaked around to her house that night just to double-check her story, since that old lady had seemed so earnest. 'Willa, are you sure?' I whispered through her bedroom window. 'I'm tellin' ya, Tee,' she said. 'Just keep both feet on the ground and you home free.' Much later I learned that advice wasn't too biologically sound, but it worked in Georgia because those country boys didn't have much imagination."

Theresa's laughter bounced off of Lorraine's silent, rigid back and died in her throat. She angrily tore open a pack of the chocolate chip cookies. "Yeah," she said, staring at Lorraine's back and biting down hard into the cookie, "it wasn't until I came up north to college that I found out there's a whole lot of things that a dude with a little imagination can do to you even with both feet on the ground. You see, Willa forgot to tell me not to bend over or squat or—"

"Must you!" Lorraine turned around from the stove with her teeth clenched tightly together.

"Must I what, Lorraine? Must I talk about things that are as much a part of life as eating or breathing or growing old? Why are you always so uptight about sex or men?"

"I'm not uptight about anything. I just think its disgusting when you go on and on about—"

"There's nothing disgusting about it, Lorraine. You've never been with a man, but I've been with quite a few—some better than others. There were a couple who I still hope to this day will die a slow, painful death, but then there were some who were good to me—in and out of bed."

"If they were so great, then why are you with me?" Lorraine's lips were trembling.

"Because—" Theresa looked steadily into her eyes and then down at the cookie she was twirling on the table. "Because," she continued slowly, "you can take a chocolate chip cookie and put holes in it and attach it to your ears and call it an earring, or hang it around your neck on a silver chain and pretend it's a necklace—but it's still a cookie. See—you can toss it in the air and call it a Frisbee or even a flying saucer, if the mood hits you, and it's still just a cookie. Send it spinning on a table—like this—until it's a wonderful blur of amber and brown light that you can imagine to be a topaz or rusted gold or old crystal, but the law of gravity has got to come into play, sometime, and it's got to come to rest—sometime. Then all the spinning and pretending and hoopla is over with. And you know what you got?"

"A chocolate chip cookie," Lorraine said.

"Uh-huh." Theresa put the cookie in her mouth and winked. "A lesbian." She got up from the table. "Call me when dinner's ready, I'm going back to read." She stopped at the kitchen door. "Now, why are you putting gravy on that chicken, Lorraine? You know it's fattening."

# QUESTIONS

*Looking at Ideas*

1. Characterize the residents of Brewster Place. What seem to be their attitudes toward family and community? What are their initial attitudes toward the two newcomers, and why does their initial impression change?

2. What is Sophie's role in the story? How might she represent common attitudes of people who are watchful for signs of sexual "deviance" in their friends and neighbors?

3. Contrast the attitudes of Lorraine and Theresa toward the neighbors. How might their different attitudes underscore deeper differences in their personalities and within the relationship?

4. How is the disagreement between Lorraine and Theresa in the story similar to and different from the kind of arguments that take place within a heterosexual family? How is the disagreement between the two resolved in the story? Do you think the resolution will be a lasting one?

*Looking at Strategies*

1. How does the sentence, "They seemed like such nice girls," set the tone and direction of the story? How are key words from the sentence repeated ironically in the story?

2. Naylor uses numerous metaphors and similes to develop scenes and atmosphere. Select several images and discuss how they work.

3. What is the connection between the story's theme and the shift in point of view midway through the story? Why would the author delay giving the perspective and names of the two women?

4. How does the chocolate chip cookie symbolize and clarify Theresa's point about her sexual orientation? Does Lorraine come to perceive the cookie the same way Theresa does?

*Looking at Connections*

1. Consider the attitudes of the Brewster Place residents in view of Keenan Peck's arguments about alternative families. To what degree can legal measures protect people in nontraditional living arrangements?

2. Examine the arguments exchanged in Stoddard and Fein's debate on gay marriage. What relevance might these arguments have to Naylor's story? How would either Stoddard or Fein react to the relationship portrayed here?

*Suggestions for Writing*

1. Review your journal writing for this selection. Using the experience you wrote about as a starting point, develop a specific scene of a social interaction between old and new neighbors. Use dialogue and sensory details that suggest, rather than explicitly tell, the attitudes of your characters.

2. Making references to this story and to your own observations, write an essay explaining some ways in which heterosexual families might feel threatened by gay couples. Consider how such feelings might be dealt

with more effectively. You might consider the obligation of both the gay and the heterosexual communities to counter homophobic attitudes.

3. Critics have commented that the media tend to foster homophobic stereotypes and attitudes. However, popular novels like *The Women of Brewster Place,* which was made into a successful television series, can do a great deal to correct stereotypical attitudes toward gays and their families. Write an essay in which you examine some recent media portrayals, positive or negative, of gay couples and try to draw some conclusions about recent trends in media representations of gays.

> **JOURNAL ENTRY**
>
> Imagine what it would be like if you lived in a multifamily, multigenerational communal housing environment. What would be the advantages? The disadvantages?

**KATHRYN McCAMANT AND CHARLES DURRETT, "Cohousing and the American Dream"** Kathryn McCamant earned a B.A. in architecture from the University of California at Berkeley in 1983. Her background is primarily in nonprofit housing development, specifically working with groups of residents on participatory design projects and supervising resident-built construction. Charles Durrett received his B.A. in Architecture from California Polytechnic University in San Luis Obispo in 1982. He worked with the San Francisco Mayor's Office of Community Development, supervising the design and construction of child-care facilities. Durrett and McCamant formed the Co-Housing Company and are the authors of *Cohousing,* from which this essay is excerpted, based on years of research in Scandinavia and the Netherlands on cohousing projects. As you read this selection, consider whether the cohousing concept would work as well in America as it does in Europe.

KATHRYN MCCAMANT AND CHARLES DURRETT

# Cohousing and the American Dream

Traditional housing no longer addresses the needs of many people. Dramatic demographic and economic changes are taking place in our society, and most of us feel the effects of these trends in our lives. Things that people once took for granted—family, community, a sense of belonging—must now be actively sought out. Many people are mishoused, ill-housed, or unhoused because of the lack of appropriate options. This article introduces a new housing model that addresses such changes. Pioneered primarily in Denmark and now being adapted in other countries, the cohousing concept reestablishes many of the advantages of traditional villages within the context of late twentieth-century life.

Several years ago, as a young married couple, we began to think about where we were going to raise our children. What kind of setting would allow us to best combine our professional careers with child rearing? Already our lives were hectic. Often we would come home from work exhausted and hungry, only to find the refrigerator empty. Between our jobs and housekeeping, when would we find the time to spend with our kids? Relatives lived in distant cities, and even our

411

friends lived across town. Just to get together for coffee we had to make arrangements two weeks in advance. Most young parents we knew seemed to spend most of their time shuttling their children to and from day care and playmates' homes, leaving little opportunity for anything else.

So many people we knew seemed to be living in places that did not accommodate their most basic needs; they always had to drive somewhere to do anything sociable. We dreamed of a better solution: an affordable neighborhood where children would have playmates and we would have friends nearby; a place with people of all ages, young and old, where neighbors knew and helped each other.

As architects, we had both designed different types of housing. We had been amazed at the conservatism of most architects and housing professionals, and at the lack of consideration given to people's changing personal needs. Single-family houses, apartments, and condominiums might change in price and occasionally in style, but otherwise they were designed to function pretty much as they had for the last 40 years. Perhaps our own frustrations were indicative of a larger problem: a diverse population attempting to fit into housing that is simply no longer appropriate for them.

Contemporary post-industrial societies such as the United States and Western Europe are undergoing a multitude of changes that affect our housing needs. The modern single-family detached home, which makes up 67 percent of American housing, was designed for a nuclear family consisting of a breadwinning father, a homemaking mother, and two to four children. Today, less than one-quarter of the United States population lives in such households. Rather, the family with two working parents predominates, while the single-parent household is the fastest growing family type. Almost one-quarter of the population lives alone, and this proportion is predicted to grow as the number of Americans over the age of 60 increases. At the same time, the surge in housing costs and the increasing mobility of the population combine to break down traditional community ties and place more demands on individual households. These factors call for a thorough reexamination of household and community needs, and the way we house ourselves.

As we searched for more desirable living situations, we kept thinking about the housing developments we had visited while studying architecture in Denmark several years earlier.

In Denmark, people frustrated by the available housing options developed a new kind of housing that redefines the concept of neighborhood to fit contemporary life-styles. Tired of the isolation and impracticalities of single-family houses and apartment units, they built or developed out of existing neighborhoods new housing that combines the autonomy of private dwellings with the advantages of community living. Each household has a private residence, but also shares extensive common facilities with the larger group, such as a kitchen and dining hall, children's playrooms, workshops, guest rooms,

412

and a laundry. Although individual dwellings are designed to function independently and each has its own kitchen, the common facilities, and particularly common dinners, are an important aspect of community life.

As of last year, 67 of these communities had been built in Denmark, and another 38 were planned. They range in size from six to 80 households, with the majority between 15 and 33 residences. These communities are called *bofoellesskaber* in Danish ("living communities"), for which we have coined the term "cohousing." First built in the early 1970s, cohousing developments have quadrupled in number in the last five years. The Netherlands now features 30 cohousing communities and similar projects are being built in Sweden, France, Norway, and Germany.

Imagine . . . It's five o'clock in the evening, and Anne is glad the workday is over. As she pulls into her driveway, she begins to unwind at last. Some neighborhood kids dart through the trees, playing a mysterious game at the edge of the gravel parking lot. Her daughter yells, "Hi Mom!" as she runs by with three other children.

Instead of frantically trying to put together a nutritious dinner, Anne can relax now, spend some time with her children, and then eat with her family in the common house. Walking through the common house on her way home, she stops to chat with the evening's cooks, two of her neighbors, who are busy preparing dinner—broiled chicken with mushroom sauce—in the kitchen. Several children are setting the tables. Outside on the patio, some neighbors share a pot of tea in the late afternoon sun. Anne waves hello and continues down the lane to her own house.

After dropping off her things at home, Anne walks through the birch trees behind the houses to the child-care center where she picks up her four-year-old son, Peter. She will have some time to read Peter a story before dinner, she thinks to herself.

Anne and her husband, Eric, live with their two children in a housing development they helped design. Not that either of them is an architect or builder: Anne works at the county administration office, and Eric is an engineer. Six years ago they joined a group of families who were looking for a realistic housing alternative. At that time, they owned their own home, had a three-year-old daughter, and were contemplating having another child—partly so that their daughter would have a playmate in their predominantly adult neighborhood.

Responding to a newspaper ad, Anne and Eric discovered a group of people who expressed similar frustrations about their existing housing situations. The group's goal was to build a housing development with a lively and positive social environment.

In the months that followed, the group further defined its goals and began the long, difficult process of turning its dream into reality. Some people dropped out, and others joined. Two and a half years later, Anne and Eric moved into their new home—a community of clustered houses that share a large common house. By working together, these

413

people had created the kind of neighborhood they wanted to live in—a cohousing community.

Today Tina, Anne and Eric's eight-year-old daughter, never lacks for playmates. She walks home from school with the other kids in the community. Her mother is usually at work, so Tina goes up to the common house, where one of the adults makes tea and toast for the kids and any adults who are around. Tina liked her family's old house, but this place is much more interesting. There's so much to do; she can play outside all day, and, as long as she doesn't leave the community, her mother doesn't worry about her.

John and Karen moved into the same community a few years after it was built. Their kids were grown and had left home. Now they enjoy the peacefulness of having a house to themselves; they have time to take classes in the evenings, visit art museums, and attend an occasional play in town. John teaches children with learning disabilities and plans to retire in a few years. Karen administers a senior citizens' housing complex and nursing home. They lead full and active lives, but worry about getting older. How long will their health hold out? Will one die, leaving the other alone? Such considerations, combined with the desire to be part of an active community while maintaining their independence, led John and Karen to buy a one-bedroom home in this community. Here they feel secure knowing their neighbors care about them. If John gets sick, people will be there to help Karen with the groceries or join her at the theater. Common dinners relieve them of preparing a meal every night, and their children and grandchildren can stay in the community's guest rooms when they visit. John and Karen enjoy a house with no children, but it's still refreshing to see kids playing outside.

Cohousing is a grass-roots movement that grew directly out of people's dissatisfaction with existing housing choices. Its initiators draw inspiration from the increasing popularity of shared households, in which several unrelated people share a house, and from the cooperative movement in general. Yet cohousing is distinctive in that each family or household has a separate dwelling and chooses how much they want to participate in community activities.

Cohousing also differs from most of the communes and intentional communities we know in the United States, which are often organized around strong ideological beliefs and may depend on a charismatic leader to establish the direction of the community and hold the group together. Based on democratic principles, cohousing developments espouse no ideology other than the desire for a more practical and social home environment. Cohousing communities are organized, planned, and managed by their residents. The great variety in community size, ownership structure, and design illustrates the many diverse applications of the concept.

In many respects, cohousing is not a new idea. In the past, most people lived in villages or tightly knit urban neighborhoods. Even today, people in less industrialized regions typically live in small communities.

Members of such communities know one another for many years; they are familiar with one another's families and histories, talents and weaknesses. This kind of relationship demands accountability, but in return provides security and a sense of belonging.

In previous centuries, households were made up of at least six people. In addition to having many children, families often shared their homes with farmhands, servants, boarders, and relatives. A typical household might include a family with four children, a grandmother or an uncle, and one or more boarders who might also work in the family business. Relatives usually lived nearby. These large households provided both children and adults with a diverse intergenerational network of relationships in the home environment. The idea that the nuclear family should live on its own without the support and assistance of the extended family or surrounding community is relatively new, even in the United States.

To expect that today's small households, as likely to be single parents or single adults as nuclear families, should be self-sufficient and without community support is not only unrealistic but absurd. Each household is expected to prepare its own meals, do its own shopping, and so far as finances permit, own a vacuum cleaner, washing machine, clothes dryer, and other household implements, regardless of whether the household consists of two people or six, and whether there is a full-time homemaker or not.

People need community at least as much as they need privacy. We must reestablish ways compatible with contemporary American lifestyles to accommodate this need. Cohousing offers a new model for recreating a sense of place and neighborhood, while responding to today's needs for a less constraining environment.

## QUESTIONS

*Looking at Ideas:*

1. What changes in contemporary American families indicate the need for a housing option like cohousing?
2. How does cohousing, as defined in this article, parallel village life and earlier kinds of communities? What are the chief advantages? Does the article adequately address disadvantages? For example, we see the advantages for Anne, but we don't hear about the work she contributes. How might various residents contribute to the co-op?
3. The authors cite a lack of options as the main reason why many are "mis-housed, ill-housed, or unhoused." Does the cohousing model discussed by the authors seem an appropriate way to deal with demographic and economic changes?
4. The authors state that people "redefined the concept of neighborhood to fit contemporary life-styles." What are those life-styles, and how has *neighborhood* been redefined?
5. What are the "democratic principles" that direct the ways in which co-

415

housing works? How is cohousing based on these principles essentially different from cohousing that stems from religious beliefs or other organizational connections?

6. Do you agree with the authors that "people need community as much as they need privacy"? Do you agree that cohousing is a good way to meet these dual needs?

*Looking at Strategies:*

1. The writers rely on three kinds of evidence: personal experience, authority, and case history/narrative. How effectively do they use these types of evidence? Which is the most convincing for you?

2. Review the placement of the thesis and the order in which supporting information is presented. Are supporting points presented in the most effective order?

3. How do the authors create a historical context for the argument they are putting forth? Are the references to historical precedents for cohousing convincing?

*Looking at Connections:*

1. Does cohousing seem a feasible solution to the housing problems discussed in Peck's "When 'Family' Is Not a Household Word" earlier in this chapter? Would your community accept such developments?

*Suggestions for Writing:*

1. Write a letter to the editor of a local newspaper, to local housing authorities, or to the city council/board of supervisors urging them to investigate the possibility of cohousing in your community.

2. Investigate alternative forms of housing that presently exist in your community. Summarize your findings in a report to your class or to a local housing agency.

3. Are you convinced that cohousing is a good idea? If not, write an argument in opposition to cohousing addressed to the authors of this article in the form of a letter. Be sure to state your own arguments as well as refuting (or conceding) arguments put forth by the authors.

AMERA CHOWHAN: "Considering Domestic Partnerships" A native resident of Sunnyvale, California, Amera Chowhan enjoys oil painting and has a background in journalism. She is considering ancient history and English as possible majors. She wrote the following essay as a response to a question that asked her to "present some of the major arguments for and against allowing domestic partnership benefits for nonmarried couples, in institutions, businesses, or college housing." When writing this paper Chowhan's most trying problem was being objective and removing preconceptions about this sensitive, controversial issue while working to develop a logical and practical stand. As you read her essay, notice how she objectively sets forth both sides of the argument on domestic partnership arrangements before moving into her refutation and presentation of her own viewpoint on the issue.

Chapter Seven: Breaking the Mold

AMERA CHOWHAN

# Considering Domestic Partnerships

The question of the legal status of gay and lesbian couples, as well as that of heterosexual couples who live together but choose not to marry, has become an issue of some contention over the last two decades. A new word, "domestic partnership," has come into the public vocabulary to describe a long-term living-together arrangement in which a gay or lesbian or unmarried heterosexual couple is both emotionally and economically dependent upon one another. Some believe that people involved in a "domestic partnership" are entitled to the benefits of married couples. These benefits include hospital visitation rights, bereavement leave, coverage under their partners' health and pension plans, rights of inheritance and community property, joint tax returns, and claims to each other's rent-controlled apartments. Yet opponents of domestic partnerships argue that allowing unmarried partners the benefits of marriage undermines the traditional family and will lead to a disintegration of societal values.

The chief objection to domestic partnerships comes on moral grounds. It is not surprising that religious leaders are often at the forefront of fights against new legislation that seems to relax traditional moral standards. An editorial writer in *Christianity Today* argued that measures in support of domestic partnerships give implicit endorsement for such living arrangements, "sending a clear message to impressionable young people that same- or opposite-sex live-in relationships are acceptable" (Jones 14).

Jean Fogassy, an anti–domestic partnership activist in Seattle, says that unmarried heterosexual couples have "freely chosen to reject the benefits that come with marriage." She goes on to ask, "Why should it

417

be called fair for those who don't make that public decision [to marry] to benefit? To pretend that they are the same as married, legally or socially, is dishonest" (qtd. in Gurwitt 28). Fogassy's arguments may be valid for heterosexual couples. For instance, Gail Randall and her live-in boyfriend were involved in a discrimination suit against a landlady who would not allow them to rent an apartment based on religious objections to their living arrangements. The couple's reasons for not marrying are not based on any outside circumstances. "We don't see any reason to get married. We're happy with the way things are now," Randall said (qtd. in Brower 114). Heterosexual couples who actually chose a nonmarital status do not seem particularly deserving of any special benefits. They do, after all, always have the option of getting married.

Homosexual couples, however, do not have such an option. But while it may seem more fair to allow them the benefits of domestic partnership legislation over heterosexual couples who can get married, moral objections exist to giving homosexual couples a seemingly official sanction. Religious objections against homosexuality play a large role in this debate, while objections to both sorts of domestic partnerships also revolve around the idea of the sanctity of the traditional family. John R. Quinn, the Archbishop of San Francisco, called the idea of granting municipal workers certain privileges of domestic partners, "a serious blow to our society's historic commitment to supporting marriage and family life" (qtd. in Isaacson 102).

Whether or not society has historically supported the family is a question open for debate, but the idea that the traditional family will be destroyed by granting domestic partner privileges to couples cannot be supported. The traditional family is already a rarity in American society. Only 27 percent of U.S. households consist of two parents with children (Isaacson 101). From this statistic it might appear that the goal of encouraging the traditional family is already obsolete. Some argue that, with the growing number of alternative life-styles, it is necessary for society to support domestic stability wherever possible. One such area of stability might be created by allowing gays the benefits of marriage and recognition of commitment. As Andrew Sullivan wrote, "Given the fact that we already allow legal gay relationships, what possible social goal is advanced by framing the law to encourage those relationships to [be] unfaithful, undeveloped, and insecure?" (qtd. in Isaacson 102)

It cannot be denied that there is a real need for domestic partner legislation. The issue goes beyond a simple symbolic stand. With the spread of AIDS, gays (as well as some heterosexual couples) have felt a special concern about the need for medical coverage, bereavement-leave policies, pension rules, hospital visitation rights, and laws giving family members the authority to make medical decisions and funeral arrangements. These issues, unlike more symbolic issues of recognition and convenience, are issues of basic need.

One such need is insurance. A practical problem facing the

domestic partner movements is that major U.S. insurance companies have thus far refused to offer group plans that include coverage for unmarried partners, believing the practice too risky. Insurers are not as yet even sure of how to define a domestic partnership. "Will we be able to come up with an equitable way to define eligibility, so people won't be encouraged to become domestic partners simply to cover a heart transplant?" asks Eric Rohlman, a vice president of Blue Cross (qtd. in Gurwitt 28). But Berkeley, along with two other California cities, West Hollywood and Santa Cruz, has offered insurance for employees' domestic partners since the mid-eighties, and has not found any difference between dealing with domestic partners and more traditional, married couples. "Our experience has been unbelievably good," said Steve Replogle, Berkeley's risk manager (qtd. in Gurwitt 28). Although there is no question that misuses of domestic partnership privileges are possible, none of the cities has reported significant instances of people taking unfair advantage of the system. Yet despite the positive experiences of the cities, insurance companies, as yet, remain reluctant to take the risk of trying out domestic partner insurance.

Health plans, pension programs, and inheritance laws are designed to accommodate the traditional family, but with only 27 percent of households fitting into that category, these laws seem to have become obsolete. Activists against domestic partnerships argue that domestic partner legislation will cause further breakdown of society. Yet if religious considerations are placed aside for a moment, it would seem as though forming households of increased stability would be in society's best interest. After all, religion and morality are not matters that should be dictated by the state, but by the individual. The government, however, does have an interest in protecting the stability of society, and it would appear that allowing some domestic partnership legislation would aid that interest.

This legislation should not be in the nature of providing symbols of government sanction. The government has no business either sanctioning or disapproving of private lives. Denying domestic partners visitation rights or bereavement leave seems petty, even if religious beliefs had a place in dictating legislation. Offering insurance, so far successful, will probably eventually be picked up by major insurance companies. Other privileges, such as shared pensions, will no doubt follow. Although, as yet, there are still many practical problems with offering domestic partner privileges, such problems can be worked out over time as various communities and institutions try to implement programs.

In conclusion, domestic partnership benefits do not seem to be an appropriate place for institutions to "draw the line" or to make a moral stand. Such a stand is now useless and antiquated, since nontraditional relationships are so widespread and generally accepted. The question that now remains is whether social institutions and businesses can respond to the practical needs that arise because of such relationships.

*Works Cited*

Brower, Montgomery. "Living in Sin? Not in her Apartments, Vows Christian Landlady Evelyn Smith." *People,* 11 Dec. 1989: 113–114.

Gurwitt, Rob. "Domestic Partners: How Much Recognition?" *Governing,* Oct. 1990: 27–28.

Isaacson, Walter. "Should Gays Have Marriage Rights?" *Time,* 20 Nov. 1989: 101–102.

Jones, Timothy K. "Sort of Married." *Christianity Today,* 8 Sep. 1989: 14.

## QUESTIONS FOR DISCUSSION

1. What are Chowhan's major reasons for supporting domestic partnership arrangements? Does she have any criticisms of such arrangements? Do her reasons seem convincing to you?

2. What arguments does Chowhan examine by the opponents of domestic partnership benefits? Do these reasons seem convincing? How effectively and fairly does Chowhan attempt to refute them?

3. Could Chowhan have found other reasons to support her position, or other convincing objections to it?

4. Chowhan struggled to maintain objectivity in writing about a controversial issue. Does she project enough of her own voice and stance as a writer and as an individual into the essay to maintain reader interest and involvement? Does she seem genuinely concerned about the issue?

5. How effectively does this student writer integrate the voices of authorities, both for and against domestic partner agreements, into her text? Has she selected authorities that seem to you representative of the positions typically taken on the issue?

6. Did you find the conclusion of the essay adequate, or could the student have offered a more concrete, detailed solution for the problems related to the providing of domestic partnership benefits?

## Reaching Out: Chapter Activities

1. Working with a peer or study group from your class, examine an insti- tution—a workplace, a social club, a religious congregation, or an agency. In what ways is the group functioning like a family? In working on this activity, group members must consider and explore the question of how to define "family." Perhaps group members could draft working definitions of family, research an institution, revise their drafts, and then convene to share changing definitions of family based on their observa- tions and reflection.

2. Research alternative families in your community. Search for alternative housing or community-sponsored housing; research religious communi- ties and special interest groups. Determine whether your community meets the needs of nontraditional families, whether extended fam- ilies, single working parents who may need housing subsidies, the working poor, the homeless, and other people who may not feel wel- come in some existing single-family neighborhoods. Working alone or with class members, determine if the city, town, county, or state needs to consider alternatives like the proposals put forth in this chapter's readings.

3. Working with a classmate, debate one of the issues raised in this chap- ter's readings. If you have access to a personal computer, use it to cre- ate an ongoing dialogue on the screen. Each student could take a turn at making a point or rebutting one other's arguments. Keep the list of arguments going on the screen; then save the dialogue and review it. Examine the kinds of appeals and evidence each of you has included to argue the point.

4. Either alone or with a group of students in your class, view a film that portrays alternative family arrangements and write an evaluation of it: How realistically and perceptively does the film portray alternative fam- ilies? The following films present images of alternative families:

*Immediate Family.* Dir., Jonathan Kaplan. With James Woods, Glenn Close. 1990.

*Kramer vs. Kramer.* Dir., Robert Benton. With Meryl Streep, Dustin Hoffman. 1979.

*Longtime Companion.* Dir., Norman Rene. With Brian Cousins. 1990.

*Torch Song Trilogy.* Dir., Paul Bogart. With Anne Bancroft, Harvey Fierstein. 1988.

*World According to Garp, The.* Dir., George Roy Hill. With Robin Williams, Glenn Close. 1982.

CHAPTER EIGHT

# *Growing Away*

*Chapter Eight:*
*Growing Away*

*Congratulations!*
*Today is your day.*
*You're off to Great Places!*
*You're off and away! . . .*
*You're on your own. And you know what you know.*
*And YOU are the guy who'll decide where to go.*
> —Dr. Seuss, "Oh, the Places You'll Go"

> *It was the Lord who knew of the impossibility every parent in that room*
> *faced: how to prepare the child for the day when the child would be despised*
> *and how to create in the child—by what means?—a stronger antidote to this*
> *poison than one had found for oneself.*
> —James Baldwin, *Notes of a Native Son*

*P*receding chapters have focused on how family members establish and develop flexible, lasting relationships and survival strategies to work through the many issues, from personal and practical to social, political, cultural, and spiritual, that families must often face together. While we may think of a family's primary purpose as being one of creating connections and support, separating or growing away is also an important—and inevitable—stage. Children and parents encounter a new set of issues and feelings to understand and adjust to when a family member reaches adolescence, a period when parents' and children's expectations of and needs for one another change dramatically. New bonds can be created to sustain the family's unity through the changes that occur as the family matures, but not without reflection and struggle.

As the quotations that begin the chapter suggest, parents and adolescents experience the process of growing away quite differently. These differences in perception are inevitable; frequently they are at the root of the struggles that occur during this period of transition. To mirror and clarify the process of growing away, the selections we have included present the experiences and issues of maturing and separating from the point of view of both adolescents and parents. Because the class, culture, wealth, political values, education level, and health of family members all play a significant part in the process of growing away, the readings chosen for this chapter represent a range of family backgrounds, including a small-town middle-class home, a Native American adoptive family, and a lower-middle-class family in Harlem. The selections illustrate a variety of ways in which social, economic, and psychological factors influence the way adolescents separate from their families.

Although the anxiety, confusion, and anger connected with growing away from the family of origin may be most intense during adolescence, the struggle for autonomy and separation begins at birth and lasts a lifetime. As with the transitional period of adolescence, parents and children can try to prepare themselves for the death of a family member, yet the feelings of loss and loneliness occasioned by the death of a close family member cannot easily be resolved.

The first two selections in the chapter present typical struggles that young people must work through: social rituals in Susan Toth's "Boyfriends," and the intense, self-conscious, and deeply personal feelings of adolescence in Annie Dillard's "Adolescence." In the third selection, "For Jane at Thirteen," poet Maxine Kumin presents a parent's perspective on her adolescent daughter's growing independence.

The next selection examines conflicts that young men in their early twenties often experience. In his short story, "My Son the Murderer," Bernard Malamud allows the reader to observe a son's fears about entering the world of adult challenges and responsibilities. In the next selection, "Moving Out," from *The Broken Cord,* Michael Dorris writes about the conflicts he feels as a father when his son, a victim of Fetal Alcohol Syndrome with minimal survival skills, is old enough to move away from home.

The next two selections explore the pain as well as the revelations that accompany a permanent separation resulting from the death of a family member. The first of these is a section from James Baldwin's famous essay, "Notes of a Native Son." The second is "The Patient's Family," in which Elizabeth Kubler-Ross, a psychiatrist who has worked for many years with the dying, writes of the impact of death on a patient's loved ones. In this chapter's final essay, "Teamwork," student J. B. Taylor discusses the positive influence his relationships with his volleyball teammates and coach have had on his concept and understanding of an ideal family.

We think that the essays, stories, and poem that follow will help you understand how even when you are stepping out, growing away from your family relationships and your childhood world, you are also redefining and renewing your connection to your personal past. Reflection on this journey through writing can help bring these vital and sometimes tumultuous periods of your life into focus.

**JOURNAL ENTRY**

Write about your first experiences dating or at a social ritual with the
opposite sex. How do you feel about these experiences
now that you are older?

**SUSAN ALLEN TOTH: "Boyfriends"**   Susan Allen Toth was born in Ames,
Iowa, in 1940. She earned her B.A. at Smith College (1961), her M.A. at the
University of California at Berkeley (1963), and her Ph.D. at the University of
Minnesota (1969). Toth was married in 1963 and divorced in 1974; she has
one daughter. After teaching at San Francisco State College from 1963 to 1964,
she went on to become a professor of English at Macalester College in St. Paul,
Minnesota. Toth writes for popular magazines such as *Redbook, Ms., McCall's,*
and *Harper's,* as well as for professional journals. Her latest book, *How to Prepare for Your High School Reunion: And Other Midlife Musings,* was a best-
seller in 1988. As you read "Boyfriends," which was excerpted from *Blooming:
A Small-Town Girlhood* (1981), consider the ways in which your growing-up
experiences have been similar to Toth's.

SUSAN ALLEN TOTH

# *Boyfriends*

Just when I was approaching sixteen, I found Peter Stone. Or did he
find me? Perhaps I magicked him into existence out of sheer need. I
was spooked by the boys who teased us nice girls about being sweet-
sixteen-and-never-been-kissed. I felt that next to being an old maid forever, it probably was most demeaning to reach sixteen and not to have
experienced the kind of ardent embrace Gordon MacRae periodically
bestowed on Kathryn Grayson between choruses of "Desert Song." I
was afraid I would never have a real boyfriend, never go parking, never
know true love. So when Peter Stone asked his friend Ted to ask Ted's
girlfriend Emily who asked me if I would ever neck with anyone, I held
my breath until Emily told me she had said to Ted to tell Peter that
maybe I would.

Not that Peter Stone had ever necked with anyone either. But I
didn't realize that for a long time. High-school courtship usually was
meticulously slow, progressing through inquiry, phone calls, planned
encounters in public places, double or triple dates, single dates, hand-
holding, and finally a good-night kiss. I assumed it probably stopped
there, but I didn't know. I had never gotten that far. I had lots of time to
learn about Peter Stone. What I knew at the beginning already attracted

me: he was a year ahead of me, vice-president of Hi-Y, a shot-putter who had just managed to earn a letter sweater. An older man, *and* an athlete. Tall, heavy, and broad-shouldered, Peter had a sweet slow smile. Even at a distance there was something endearing about the way he would blink nearsightedly through his glasses and light up with pleased recognition when he saw me coming toward him down the hall.

For a long while I didn't come too close. Whenever I saw Peter he was in the midst of his gang, a group of five boys as close and as self-protective as any clique we girls had. They were an odd mixture: Jim, an introspective son of a lawyer; Brad, a sullen hot-rodder; Ted, an unambitious and gentle boy from a poor family; Andy, a chubby comedian; and Peter. I was a little afraid of all of them, and they scrutinized me carefully before opening their circle to admit me, tentatively, as I held tight to Peter's hand. The lawyer's son had a steady girl, a fast number who was only in eighth grade but looked eighteen; the hot-rodder was reputed to have "gone all the way" with his adoring girl, a coarse brunette with plucked eyebrows; gentle Ted pursued my friend Emily with hangdog tenacity; but Peter had never shown real interest in a girlfriend before.

Although I had decided to go after Peter, I was hesitant about how to plot my way into the interior of his world. It was a thicket of strange shrubs and tangled branches. Perhaps I see it that way because I remember the day Peter took me to a wild ravine to shoot his gun. Girls who went with one of "the guys" commiserated with each other that their boyfriends all preferred two other things to them: their cars and their guns. Although Peter didn't hunt and seldom went to practice at the target range, still he valued his gun. Without permits, "the guys" drove outside of town to fire their guns illegally. I had read enough in my *Seventeen* about how to attract boys to know I needed to show enthusiasm about Peter's hobbies, so I asked him if some day he would take me someplace and teach me how to shoot.

One sunny fall afternoon he did. I remember rattling over gravel roads into a rambling countryside that had surprising valleys and woods around cultivated farmland. Eventually we stopped before a barred gate that led to an abandoned bridge, once a railroad trestle, now a splintering wreck. We had to push our way through knee-high weeds to get past the gate. I was afraid of snakes. Peter took my hand; it was the first time he had ever held it, and my knees weakened a little. I was also scared of walking onto the bridge, which had broken boards and sudden gaps that let you look some fifty feet down into the golden and rust-colored brush below. But I didn't mind being a little scared as long as Peter was there to take care of me.

I don't think I had ever held a gun until Peter handed me his pistol, a heavy metal weapon that looked something like the ones movie sheriffs carried in their holsters. I was impressed by its weight and power. Peter fired it twice to show me how and then stood close to me, watching carefully, while I aimed at an empty beer can he tossed into the air. I didn't hit it. The noise of the gun going off was terrifying. I hoped nobody was walking in the woods where I had aimed. Peter said no-body was, nobody ever came here. When I put the gun down, he put his arm around me, very carefully. He had never done that before, ei-ther. We both just stood there, looking off into the distance, staring at the glowing maples and elms, dark red patches of sumac, brown heaps of leaves. The late afternoon sun beat down on us. It was hot, and after a few minutes Peter shifted uncomfortably. I moved away, laughing nervously, and we walked back to the car, watching the gaping boards at our feet.

What Peter and I did with our time together is a mystery. I try to picture us at movies or parties or somebody's house, but all I can see is the two of us in Peter's car. "Going for a drive!" I'd fling at my mother as I rushed out of the house; "rinking" was our high-school term for it, drawn from someone's contempt for the greasy "hoods" who hung out around the roller-skating rink and skidded around corners on two wheels of their souped-up cars. Peter's car barely made it around a cor-ner on all four wheels. Though he had learned something about how to keep his huge square Ford running, he wasn't much of a mechanic. He could make jokes about the Ford, but he didn't like anyone else, includ-ing me, to say it looked like an old black hearse or remind him it could scarcely do forty miles an hour on an open stretch of highway. High-ways were not where we drove, anyway, nor was speed a necessity un-less you were trying to catch up with someone who hadn't seen you. "Rinking" meant cruising aimlessly around town, looking for friends in *their* cars, stopping for conversations shouted out of windows, maybe parking somewhere for a while, ending up at the A&W Root Beer Stand or the pizza parlor or the Rainbow Cafe.

Our parents were often puzzled about why we didn't spend time in each other's homes. "Why don't you invite Peter in?" my mother would ask a little wistfully, as I grabbed my billfold and cardigan and headed toward the door. Sometimes Peter would just pause in front of the house and honk; if I didn't come out quickly, he assumed I wasn't home and drove away. Mother finally made me tell him at least to come to the door and knock. I couldn't explain to her why we didn't want to sit in the living room, or go down to the pine-paneled basement at the Harbingers', or swing on the Harrises' front porch. We might not have been bothered at any of those places, but we really wouldn't have been alone. Cars were our private space, a rolling parlor, the only place we could relax and be ourselves. We could talk, fiddle with the radio if we didn't have much to say, look out the window, watch for friends passing by. Driving gave us a feeling of freedom.

Most of my memories of important moments with Peter center in that old black Ford. One balmy summer evening I remember particu-larly because my friend Emily said I would. Emily and Ted were out cruising in his rusty two-tone Chevy, the lawyer's son Jim and his girl had his father's shiny Buick, and Peter and I were out driving in the Ford. As we rumbled slowly down the Main Street, quiet and dark at night, Peter saw Ted's car approaching. We stopped in the middle of the street so the boys could exchange a few laconic grunts while Emily and I smiled confidentially at each other. We were all in a holiday mood, lazy and happy in the warm breezes that swept through the open windows. One of us suggested that we all meet later at Camp Canwita, a wooded park a few miles north of town. Whoever saw Jim would tell him to join us too. We weren't sure what we would do there, but it sounded like an adventure. An hour or so later, Peter and I bumped over the potholes in the road that twisted through the woods to the parking lot. We were the first ones there. When Peter turned off the motor, we could hear grasshoppers thrumming on all sides of us and leaves rustling in the dark. It was so quiet, so remote, I was a little frightened, remembering one of my mother's unnerving warnings about the dangerous men who sometimes preyed upon couples who parked in secluded places. We didn't have long to wait, though, before Ted's car coughed and sputtered down the drive. Soon Jim arrived too, and then we all pulled our cars close together in a kind of circle so we could talk easily out the windows. Someone's radio was turned on, and Frank Sinatra's mournful voice began to sing softly of passing days and lost love. Someone suggested that we get out of the cars and dance. It wouldn't have been Peter, who was seldom romantic. Ted opened his door so the overhead light cast a dim glow over the tiny area between the cars. Solemnly, a little self-consciously, we began the shuffling steps that were all we knew of what we called "slow dancing." Peter was not a good dancer, nor was I, though I liked putting my head on his bulky shoulder. But he moved me around the small lighted area as best he could, trying not to bump into Ted and Emily or Jim and his girl. I tried not to step on his toes. While Sinatra, Patti Page, and the Four Freshmen sang to us about moments to remember and Cape Cod, we all danced, one-two back, one-two back. Finally Emily, who was passing by my elbow, looked significantly at me and said, "This is something we'll be able to tell our grandchildren." Yes, I nodded, but I wasn't so sure. The mosquitoes were biting my legs and arms, my toes hurt, and I was getting a little bored. I think the others were too, because before long we all got into our cars and drove away.

Not all the time we spent in Peter's car was in motion. After several months, we did begin parking on deserted country roads, side streets, even sometimes my driveway, if my mother had heeded my fierce instructions to leave the light turned off. For a while we simply sat and talked with Peter's arm draped casually on the back of the seat. Gradually I moved a little closer. Soon he had his arm around me, but even then it was a long time before he managed to kiss me good-night. Boys must have been as scared as we girls were, though we always thought of them as having much more experience. We all compared notes, shyly, about how far our boyfriends had gone; was he holding your hand yet, or taking you parking, or . . . ? When a girl finally got kissed, telephone lines burned with the news next day. I was getting a little embarrassed about how long it was taking Peter to get around to it. My sixteenth birthday was only a few weeks away, and so far I had nothing

Growing Away

substantial to report. I was increasingly nervous too because I still didn't know quite how I was going to behave. We girls joked about wondering where your teeth went and did glasses get in the way, but no one could give a convincing description. For many years I never told anyone about what *did* happen to me that first time. I was too ashamed. Peter and I were parked down the street from my house, talking, snuggling, listening to the radio. During a silence I turned my face toward him, and then he kissed me, tentatively and quickly. I was exhilarated but frightened. I wanted to respond in an adequate way, but my instincts did not entirely cooperate. I leaned towards Peter, but at the last moment I panicked. Instead of kissing him, I gave him a sudden lick on the cheek. He didn't know what to say. Neither did I.

Next morning I was relieved that it was all over. I dutifully reported my news to a few key girlfriends who could pass it on to others. I left out the part about the lick. That was my last bulletin. After a first kiss, we girls also respected each other's privacy. What more was there to know? We assumed that couples sat in their cars and necked, but nice girls, we also assumed, went no farther. We knew the girls who did. Their names got around. We marveled at them, uncomprehending as much as disapproving. Usually they talked about getting married to their boyfriends, and eventually some of them did. A lot of "nice" girls suffered under this distinction. One of them told me years later how she and her steady boyfriend had yearned and held back, stopped just short, petted and clutched and gritted their teeth. "When we went together to see the movie *Splendor in the Grass,* we had to leave the theatre," she said ruefully. "The part about how Natalie Wood and Warren Beatty wanted to make love so desperately and couldn't. . . . Well, that was just how we felt."

My mother worried about what was going on in the car during those long evenings when Peter and I went "out driving." She needn't have. Amazing as it seems now, when courting has speeded up to a freeway pace, when I wonder if a man who doesn't try to get me to bed immediately might possibly be gay, Peter and I gave each other hours of affection without ever crossing the invisible line. We sat in his car and necked, a word that was anatomically correct. We hugged and kissed, nuzzling ears and noses and hairlines. But Peter never put a hand on my breast, and I wouldn't have known whether Peter had an erection if it had risen up and thwapped me in the face. I never got that close. Although we probably should have perished from frustration, in fact I reveled in all that holding and touching. Peter seemed pleased too, and he never demanded more. Later, I suppose, he learned quickly with someone else about what he had been missing. But I remember with gratitude Peter's awkward tenderness and the absolute faith I had in his inability to hurt me.

After Peter graduated and entered the university, our relationship changed. Few high-school girls I knew went out with college men; it was considered risky, like dating someone not quite in your social set or from another town. You were cut off. At the few fraternity functions Peter took me to, I didn't know anyone there. I had no idea what to talk about or how to act. So I refused to go, and I stopped asking Peter to come with me to parties or dances at the high school. I thought he didn't fit in there either. When I was honest with myself, I admitted that romance had gone. Already planning to go away to college, I could sense new vistas opening before me, glowing horizons whose light completely eclipsed a boyfriend like Peter. When I got on the Chicago & Northwestern train to go east to Smith, I felt with relief that the train trip was erasing one problem for me. I simply rode away from Peter.

On my sixteenth birthday, Peter gave me a small cross on a chain. All the guys had decided that year to give their girlfriends crosses on chains, even though none of them was especially religious. It was a perfect gift, they thought, intimate without being soppy. Everyone's cross cost ten dollars, a lot of money, because it was real sterling silver. Long after Peter and I stopped seeing each other, I kept my cross around my neck, not taking it off even when I was in the bathtub. Like my two wooden dolls from years before, I clung to that cross as a superstitious token. It meant that someone I had once cared for had cared for me in return. Once I had had a boyfriend.

## QUESTIONS

*Looking at Ideas:*
1. What role does Peter Stone play in Susan Toth's social life, her romantic fantasies, her process of maturing and "growing away"?
2. Compare and contrast the high school courtship rituals at Susan Toth's and your own high school. What changes in dating rituals were you aware of while reading about Toth's experiences? In what ways were her experiences similar to yours?
3. Explain why Toth felt that "cars were our private space, a rolling parlor, the only place we could relax and be ourselves. . . . Driving gave us a feeling of freedom." When you were an adolescent did you participate in similar types of group rituals? What were they?
4. Why was the evening spent at Camp Canwita with Peter and his friends an especially memorable one? Do you remember similar experiences during your adolescence? Which ones? Why?
5. How and why does the author's relationship to Peter change when he leaves for college? Why is she relieved when she leaves for college?

*Looking at Strategies:*
1. Details and examples are central to Toth's technique of reconstructing her adolescent memories. Refer to several passages in which her use of details is especially effective, and explain what these details add to the meaning and feeling of the narrative.
2. While having a boyfriend like Peter Stone was a social necessity, it also involved an "interior" conquest. How does Toth narrate and focus the symbolic moment that establishes the couple's intimacy? What does the

gun symbolize? Where else does Toth use symbols effectively in the memoir?

3. What techniques does the author use to develop her definition of "rinking"? Did your high school friends participate in a similar kind of activity? What word came to define the activity? Do you remember any other words that were particular to your adolescent years? What were they? To what did they refer?

4. Why did Susan Toth give her essay the generic title, "Boyfriends," rather than a specific title, "Peter Stone"?

*Looking at Connections:*

1. How does Toth's explanation of her need for a boyfriend amplify or support Annie Dillard's discussion of adolescent behavior in "Adolescence" (the next selection)?

*Suggestions for Writing:*

1. Why is dating important to high school students? Is a "romantic" relationship in high school desired more for social acceptance or for the intimacy that it brings, or for both reasons? Develop your point of view in an essay based on your own experiences and observations in high school.

2. Write an essay in which you discuss the several most important reasons why peer approval is so important to adolescents. Then discuss the positive and negative effects of peer pressure. Refer to specific experiences that you had with peer groups in junior high and/or high school.

3. Write about an experience in your adolescence when you had a significant realization or discovery about yourself and your world. Then reflect on how it helped you establish your own independence, understand yourself better, and/or develop a significant relationship outside of your family.

---

| JOURNAL ENTRY |
| --- |
| Write about your first memories of becoming an adolescent. |

**ANNIE DILLARD: "Adolescence"**   Annie Dillard was born in Pittsburgh, Pennsylvania, in 1945. She earned her B.A. (1967) and M.A. (1968) from Hollins College in Virginia. Dillard has worked as an editor and teaches at Wesleyan. In 1974 Annie Dillard was awarded the Pulitzer Prize in nonfiction for *Pilgrim at Tinker Creek*. She is best known for her interest in the natural world and for her ability to capture its details and mysteries. Dillard has written one book of poetry, *Holy the Firm* (1978), and several more collections of essays about nature and her craft as a writer: *Teaching a Stone to Talk* (1982), *Living by Fiction* (1982), and *The Writing Life* (1989). The following selection is excerpted from *An American Childhood* (1987), her autobiographical memoir. As you read "Adolescence," compare and contrast the intensity of Dillard's adolescent struggles as she begins to leave her childhood behind and establish a sense of her own identity with your own adolescent transformations.

ANNIE DILLARD

# Adolescence

When I was fifteen, I felt it coming; now I was sixteen, and it hit.

My feet had imperceptibly been set on a new path, a fast path into a long tunnel like those many turnpike tunnels near Pittsburgh, turnpike tunnels whose entrances bear on brass plaques a roll call of those men who died blasting them. I wandered witlessly forward and found myself going down, and saw the light dimming; I adjusted to the slant and dimness, traveled further down, adjusted to greater dimness, and so on. There wasn't a whole lot I could do about it, or about anything. I was going to hell on a handcart, that was all, and I knew it and everyone around me knew it, and there it was.

I was growing and thinning, as if pulled. I was getting angry, as if pushed. I morally disapproved most things in North America, and blamed my innocent parents for them. My feelings deepened and lingered. The swift moods of early childhood—each formed by and suited to its occasion—vanished. Now feelings lasted so long they left stains. They arose from nowhere, like winds or waves, and battered at me or engulfed me.

When I was angry, I felt myself coiled and longing to kill someone or bomb something big. Trying to appease myself, during one winter I

433

whipped my bed every afternoon with my uniform belt. I despised the spectacle I made in my own eyes—whipping the bed with a belt, like a creature demented!—and I often began halfheartedly, but I did it daily after school as a desperate discipline, trying to rid myself and the innocent world of my wildness. It was like trying to beat back the ocean.

Sometimes in class I couldn't stop laughing; things were too funny to be borne. It began then, my surprise that no one else saw what was so funny.

I read some few books with such reverence I didn't close them at the finish, but only moved the pile of pages back to the start, without breathing, and began again. I read one such book, an enormous novel, six times that way—closing the binding between sessions, but not between readings.

On the piano in the basement I played the maniacal "Poet and Peasant Overture" so loudly, for so many hours, night after night, I damaged the piano's keys and strings. When I wasn't playing this crashing overture, I played boogie-woogie, or something else, anything else, in octaves—otherwise, it wasn't loud enough. My fingers were so strong I could do push-ups with them. I played one piece with my fists. I banged on a steel-stringed guitar till I bled, and once on a particularly piercing rock-and-roll downbeat I broke straight through one of Father's snare drums.

I loved my boyfriend so tenderly, I thought I must transmogrify into vapor. It would take spectroscopic analysis to locate my molecules in thin air. No possible way of holding him was close enough. Nothing could cure this bad case of gentleness except, perhaps, violence: maybe if he swung me by the legs and split my skull on a tree? Would that ease this insane wish to kiss too much his eyelids' outer corners and his temples, as if I could love up his brain?

I envied people in books who swooned. For two years I felt myself continuously swooning and continuously unable to swoon; the blood drained from my face and eyes and flooded my heart; my hands emptied, my knees unstrung, I bit at the air for something worth breathing—but I failed to fall, and I couldn't find the way to black out. I had to live on the lip of a waterfall, exhausted.

When I was bored I was first hungry, then nauseated, then furious and weak. "Calm yourself," people had been saying to me all my life. Since early childhood I had tried one thing and then another to calm myself, on those few occasions when I truly wanted to. Eating helped; singing helped. Now sometimes I truly wanted to calm myself. I couldn't lower my shoulders; they seemed to wrap around my ears. I couldn't lower my voice although I could see the people around me flinch. I waved my arm in class till the very teachers wanted to kill me.

I was what they called a live wire. I was shooting out sparks that were digging a pit around me, and I was sinking into that pit. Laughing with Ellin at school recess, or driving around after school with Judy in her jeep, exultant, or dancing with my boyfriend to Louis Armstrong across a polished dining-room floor, I got so excited I looked around wildly for aid; I didn't know where I should go or what I should do with myself. People in books split wood.

When rage or boredom reappeared, each seemed never to have left. Each so filled me with so many years' intolerable accumulation it jammed the space behind my eyes, so I couldn't see. There was no room left even on my surface to live. My rib cage was so taut I couldn't breathe. Every cubic centimeter of atmosphere above my shoulders and head was heaped with last straws. Black hatred clogged my very blood. I couldn't peep, I couldn't wiggle or blink; my blood was too mad to flow.

For as long as I could remember, I had been transparent to myself, unselfconscious, learning, doing, most of every day. Now I was in my own way; I myself was a dark object I could not ignore. I couldn't remember how to forget myself. I didn't want to think about myself, to reckon myself in, to deal with myself every livelong minute on top of everything else—but swerve as I might, I couldn't avoid it. I was a boulder blocking my own path. I was a dog barking between my own ears, a barking dog who wouldn't hush.

So this was adolescence. Is this how the people around me had died on their feet—inevitably, helplessly? Perhaps their own selves eclipsed the sun for so many years the world shriveled around them, and when at last their inescapable orbits had passed through these dark egoistic years it was too late, they had adjusted.

Must I then lose the world forever, that I had so loved? Was it all, the whole bright and various planet, where I had been so ardent about finding myself alive, only a passion peculiar to children, that I would outgrow even against my will?

## QUESTIONS

*Looking at Ideas:*

1. In what ways do Dillard's appearance, emotions, values, and self concept change during her adolescence?

2. Dillard refers to books she read and re-read, songs she listened to again and again, friends and boyfriends to whom she felt intensely connected. How do these experiences serve to profile her adolescent years?

3. How does Dillard feel about relinquishing her childhood? Did she like being an adolescent? Does she feel in control of herself as an adolescent? Refer to specific passages in the selection to support your response.

*Looking at Strategies:*

1. Discuss several examples that Dillard develops to illustrate the intensity of her feelings during adolescence. Are her examples effective? Why?

2. Dillard frequently develops similes and metaphors to describe her be-

havior and feelings as an adolescent: "I had to live on the lip of a waterfall, exhausted." List three of her images that you find especially powerful; then discuss how each expresses its point.

3. Reflect on your own experiences as you interpret Dillard's image of her adolescent self "eclipsing the sun." Is this an effective image? Why?

*Looking at Connections:*

1. Contrast Annie Dillard's and Susan Toth's discussions of adolescence as a rite of passage.

*Suggestions for Writing:*

1. Narrate an experience that you had in adolescence that you remember very well, perhaps because it stands out in your mind as representative of your interests, feelings, and concerns. After narrating the experience, analyze what you learned about yourself from thinking and writing about it. Finally discuss what you think makes adolescence such a special and difficult stage in a young person's life.

2. Write about a book, a song, a friend, or a particular activity that was crucial to you during your adolescence. Explain the role and the meaning that this person or activity played in your life. Have you kept up with this person or activity? Has it influenced your life in a lasting way? Why and how?

3. Adolescence is a time when a child becomes more independent and grows away from his or her family. Often an adolescent separates from his or her family by finding fault in their values and life style as Dillard did. Discuss your process of growing away from your family during your adolescence. In what ways did you establish your uniqueness from your family's values, interests, rituals, and goals? Looking back, how do you feel about the identity you created for yourself during your adolescence? How do feel about the way you related to your family as an adolescent?

**MAXINE KUMIN: "For Jane at Thirteen"**   Maxine Kumin was born in Philadelphia in 1925. From 1942 to 1948 she attended Radcliffe College, where she earned both a B.A. and a M.A. Maxine Kumin is married and has raised three children. She has taught at many universities, including Princeton, Columbia, and the University of Massachusetts. While Kumin is best known for her poetry, she has also written four novels and numerous books for children. As you read "For Jane at Thirteen," think about what kind of voyage the speaker's daughter is about to embark on and whether you took a similar type of journey when you were an adolescent. If you are a parent, reflect on your fears for your child entering adolescence.

MAXINE KUMIN

## For Jane at Thirteen

Papers in order; your face
accurate and on guard in the cardboard house
and the difficult patois you will speak
half-mastered in your jaw;
the funny make-up in your funny pocketbook—
pale lipstick, half a dozen lotions
to save your cloudless skin
in that uncertain sea
where no one charts the laws—
of course you do not belong to me
nor I to you
and everything is only true in mirrors.

I help to lock your baggage:
history book, lace collar and pink pearls
from the five-and-ten,
an expurgated text
of how the gods behaved on Mount Olympus,

and pennies in your shoes.
You lean as bland as sunshine on the rails.
Whatever's next—
the old oncoming uses

of your new troughs and swells—
is coin for trading among girls
in gym suits and geometry classes.

How can you know I traveled here,
stunned, like you, by my reflection
in forest pools;
hunted among the laurel
and whispered to by swans
in accents of my own invention?

It is a dangerous time.
The water rocks away the timber
and here is your visa stamped in red.
You lean down your confident head.
We exchange kisses; I call your name
and wave you off as the bridge goes under.

## QUESTIONS

*Looking at Ideas:*

1. What kind of journey is the daughter about to embark on?

2. Why would the mother say, "of course you do not belong to me/nor I to you/ and everything is only true in mirrors"? What kind of "truth" is reflected in mirrors? Why would a thirteen-year-old be susceptible to seeing the truth in mirrors?

3. Describe Jane's character based on the information the speaker has given us about her daughter. Does she seem like a "typical" adolescent? Why or why not? Explain.

4. Why does the mother feel that she will not be able to protect or help her daughter during her journey: "We exchange kisses; I call your name/and wave you off as the bridge goes under"? Does the poem imply that the daughter will return? Do you think the daughter will return? Explain your response.

*Looking at Strategies:*

1. Contrast the literal and symbolic meanings of the visa stamped in red. Identify other lines or images in the poem that suggest that the daughter is going on a literal and at the same time a "universal" journey.

2. The mother claims, "It is a dangerous time." What lines in the poem suggest that the daughter is leaving on a dangerous journey? How and why?

3. What role does myth play in creating the poem's meaning? What does the mother refer to when she says, "an expurgated text/of how the gods behaved on Mount Olympus"?

4. The poem is written from a mother's point of view. Who is the poet's audience? Do you think Jane would understand the poem her mother has written for her? Explain your answer.

*Looking at Connections:*

1. This poem is written from the perspective of a mother watching her adolescent daughter growing away, while Susan Toth is reflecting on her adolescent experiences. Do both writers find similar struggles in adolescence? What are they?

2. Contrast Maxine Kumin's perspectives on parenting an adolescent who is "growing away" with those of Michael Dorris in "Moving Out," later in this chapter. You might want to consider the particular references to imagery related to water and staying afloat.

*Suggestions for Writing:*

1. Develop an issue brought up in "For Jane at Thirteen" into an essay. Support your main ideas with examples from your own experiences to illustrate why "growing away," either as a parent or as a child, is a complex and difficult experience.

2. Write an essay exploring Jane's feelings about the journey she is about to take.

3. Write an essay about a literal journey that you took in your adolescence that also had a symbolic significance. Narrate the literal journey and then reflect on the journey's symbolic significance.

4. Write about a turning point or a growing-away experience you went through during adolescence from two points of view—your own and that of one of your parents.

**JOURNAL ENTRY**

Write about a time in your life when you felt that a parent was being too possessive of you. What did you do to create a separation, a boundary between you and your parent?

**BERNARD MALAMUD: "My Son the Murderer"**  Bernard Malamud (1914–1986) grew up in Brooklyn, where his father ran a small business. He received his B.A. from City College in New York (1936) and his M.A. from Columbia University (1942). After teaching evening school in New York, Malamud was offered a position at Oregon State College; later he became a professor of English at Bennington College. Malamud is best known for his short stories and fiction. His novel, *The Natural* (1952), was adapted into a film starring Robert Redford in 1984. *The Fixer* (1967) won the Pulitzer Prize and the National Book Award. Malamud published four collections of short stories: *The Magic Barrel* (1958) won the National Book Award. "My Son the Murderer" was originally published in *Esquire* magazine (1968) and is included in the retrospective collection *The Stories of Bernard Malamud* (1983). As you read Malamud's story notice how he captures the particular emotions and point of view of each of his characters in order to help his readers to understand and empathize with both of them.

BERNARD MALAMUD

# *My Son the Murderer*

He wakes feeling his father is in the hallway, listening. He listens to him sleep and dream. Listening to him get up and fumble for his pants. He won't put on his shoes. To him not going to the kitchen to eat. Staring with shut eyes in the mirror. Sitting an hour on the toilet. Flipping the pages of a book he can't read. To his anguish, loneliness. The father stands in the hall. The son hears him listen.

My son the stranger, he won't tell me anything.

I open the door and see my father in the hall. Why are you standing there, why don't you go to work?

On account of I took my vacation in the winter instead of the summer like I usually do.

What the hell for if you spend it in this dark smelly hallway, watching my every move? Guessing what you can't see. Why are you always spying on me?

My father goes to the bedroom and after a while sneaks out in the hallway again, listening.

I hear him sometimes in his room but he don't talk to me and I don't know what's what. It's a terrible feeling for a father. Maybe some-day he will write me a letter, my dear father. . .

My dear son Harry, open up your door. My son the prisoner.

My wife leaves in the morning to stay with my married daughter, who is expecting her fourth child. The mother cooks and cleans for her and takes care of the three children. My daughter is having a bad preg-nancy, with high blood pressure, and lays in bed most of the time. This is what the doctor advised her. My wife is gone all day. She worries something is wrong with Harry. Since he graduated college last sum-mer he is alone, nervous, in his own thoughts. If you talk to him, half the time he yells if he answers you. He reads the papers, smokes, he stays in his room. Or once in a while he goes for a walk in the street.

How was the walk, Harry?

A walk.

My wife advised him to go look for work, and a couple of times he went, but when he got some kind of an offer he didn't take the job.

It's not that I don't want to work. It's that I feel bad.

So why do you feel bad?

I feel what I feel. I feel what is.

Is it your health, sonny? Maybe you ought to go to a doctor?

I asked you not to call me by that name any more. It's not my health. Whatever it is I don't want to talk about it. The work wasn't the kind I want.

So take something temporary in the meantime, my wife said to him.

He starts to yell. Everything's temporary. Why should I add more to what's temporary? My gut feels temporary. The goddamn world is temporary. On top of that I don't want temporary work. I want the op-posite of temporary, but where is it? Where do you find it?

My father listens in the kitchen.

My temporary son.

She says I'll feel better if I work. I say I won't. I'm twenty-two since December, a college graduate, and you know where you can stick that. At night I watch the news programs. I watch the war from day to day. It's a big burning war on a small screen. It rains bombs and the flames roar higher. Sometimes I lean over and touch the war with the flat of my hand. I wait for my hand to die.

My son with the dead hand.

I expect to be drafted any day but it doesn't bother me the way it used to. I won't go. I'll go to Canada or somewhere I can go.

The way he is frightens my wife and she is glad to go to my daugh-ter's house early in the morning to take care of the three children. I stay with him in the house but he don't talk to me.

You ought to call up Harry and talk to him, my wife says to my daughter.

I will sometime but don't forget there's nine years' difference be-tween our ages. I think he thinks of me as another mother around and one is enough. I used to like him when he was a little boy but now it's hard to deal with a person who won't reciprocate to you.

She's got high blood pressure. I think she's afraid to call.

I took two weeks off from my work. I'm a clerk at the stamp window in the post office. I told the superintendent I wasn't feeling so good, which is no lie, and he said I should take sick leave. I said I wasn't that sick, I only needed a little vacation. But I told my friend Moe Berkman I was staying out because Harry has me worried.

I understand what you mean, Leo. I got my own worries and anxieties about my kids. If you got two girls growing up you got hostages to fortune. Still in all we got to live. Why don't you come to poker on this Friday night? We got a nice game going. Don't deprive yourself of a good form of relaxation.

I'll see how I feel by Friday how everything is coming along. I can't promise you.

Try to come. These things, if you give them time, all will pass away. If it looks better to you, come on over. Even if it don't look so good, come on over anyway because it might relieve your tension and worry that you're under. It's not so good for your heart at your age if you carry that much worry around.

It's the worst kind of worry. If I worry about myself I know what the worry is. What I mean, there's no mystery. I can say to myself, Leo you're a big fool, stop worrying about nothing—over what, a few bucks? Over my health that has always stood up pretty good although I have my ups and downs? Over that I'm now close to sixty and not getting any younger? Everybody that don't die by age fifty-nine gets to be sixty. You can't beat time when it runs along with you. But if the worry is about somebody else, that's the worst kind. That's the real worry because if he won't tell you, you can't get inside of the other person and find out why. You don't know where's the switch to turn off. All you do is worry more.

So I wait out in the hall.

Harry, don't worry so much about the war.

Please don't tell me what to worry about or what not to worry about.

Harry, your father loves you. When you were a little boy, every night when I came home you used to run to me. I picked you up and lifted you up to the ceiling. You liked to touch it with your small hand.

I don't want to hear about that any more. It's the very thing I don't want to hear. I don't want to hear about when I was a child.

Harry, we live like strangers. All I'm saying is I remember better days. I remember when we weren't afraid to show we loved each other.

He says nothing.

Let me cook you an egg.

An egg is the last thing in the world I want.

So what do you want?

He put his coat on. He pulled his hat off the clothes tree and went down into the street.

Harry walked along Ocean Parkway in his long overcoat and creased brown hat. His father was following him and it filled him with rage.

He walked at a fast pace up the broad avenue. In the old days there was a bridle path at the side of the walk where the concrete bicycle path is now. And there were fewer trees, their black branches cutting the sunless sky. At the corner of Avenue X, just about where you can smell Coney Island, he crossed the street and began to walk home. He pretended not to see his father cross over, though he was infuriated. The father crossed over and followed his son home. When he got to the house he figured Harry was upstairs already. He was in his room with the door shut. Whatever he did in his room he was already doing.

Leo took out his small key and opened the mailbox. There were three letters. He looked to see if one of them was, by any chance, from his son to him. My dear father, let me explain myself. The reason I act as I do . . . There was no such letter. One of the letters was from the Post Office Clerks Benevolent Society, which he slipped into his coat pocket. The other two letters were for Harry. One was from the draft board. He brought it up to his son's room, knocked on the door, and waited.

He waited for a while.

To the boy's grunt he said, There is a draft-board letter here for you. He turned the knob and entered the room. His son was lying on his bed with his eyes shut.

Leave it on the table.

Do you want me to open it for you, Harry?

No, I don't want you to open it. Leave it on the table. I know what's in it.

Did you write them another letter?

That's my goddamn business.

The father left it on the table.

The other letter to his son he took into the kitchen, shut the door, and boiled up some water in a pot. He thought he would read it quickly and seal it carefully with a little paste, then go downstairs and put it back in the mailbox. His wife would take it out with her key when she returned from their daughter's house and bring it up to Harry.

The father read the letter. It was a short letter from a girl. The girl said Harry had borrowed two of her books more than six months ago and since she valued them highly she would like him to send them back to her. Could he do that as soon as possible so that she wouldn't have to write again?

As Leo was reading the girl's letter Harry came into the kitchen and when he saw the surprised and guilty look on his father's face, he tore the letter out of his hands.

I ought to murder you the way you spy on me.

Leo turned away, looking out of the small kitchen window into the dark apartment-house courtyard. His face burned, he felt sick.

Harry read the letter at a glance and tore it up. He then tore up the envelope marked personal.

If you do this again don't be surprised if I kill you. I'm sick of you spying on me.

Harry, you are talking to your father.

He left the house.

Leo went into his room and looked around. He looked in the dresser drawers and found nothing unusual. On the desk by the window was a paper Harry had written on. It said: Dear Edith, why don't you go fuck yourself? If you write me another stupid letter I'll murder you.

The father got his hat and coat and left the house. He ran slowly for a while, running then walking until he saw Harry on the other side of the street. He followed him, half a block behind.

He followed Harry to Coney Island Avenue and was in time to see him board a trolleybus going to the Island. Leo had to wait for the next one. He thought of taking a taxi and following the trolleybus, but no taxi came by. The next bus came fifteen minutes later and he took it all the way to the Island. It was February and Coney Island was wet, cold, and deserted. There were few cars on Surf Avenue and few people on the streets. It felt like snow. Leo walked on the boardwalk amid snow flurries, looking for his son. The gray sunless beaches were empty. The hot-dog stands, shooting galleries, and bathhouses were shuttered up. The gunmetal ocean, moving like melted lead, looked freezing. A wind blew in off the water and worked its way into his clothes so that he shivered as he walked. The wind whitecapped the leaden waves and the slow surf broke on the empty beaches with a quiet roar.

He walked in the blow almost to Sea Gate, searching for his son, and then walked back again. On his way toward Brighton Beach he saw a man on the shore standing in the foaming surf. Leo hurried down the boardwalk stairs and onto the ribbed-sand beach. The man on the roaring shore was Harry, standing in water to the tops of his shoes.

Leo ran to his son. Harry, it was a mistake, excuse me, I'm sorry I opened your letter.

Harry did not move. He stood in the water, his eyes on the swelling leaden waves.

Harry, I'm frightened. Tell me what's the matter. My son, have mercy on me.

I'm frightened of the world, Harry thought. It fills me with fright.

He said nothing.

A blast of wind lifted his father's hat and carried it away over the beach. It looked as though it was going to be blown into the surf, but then the wind blew it toward the boardwalk, rolling like a wheel along the wet sand. Leo chased after his hat. He chased it one way, then another, then toward the water. The wind blew the hat against his legs and he caught it. By now he was crying. Breathless, he wiped his eyes with icy fingers and returned to his son at the edge of the water.

He is a lonely man. This is the type he is. He will always be lonely.

My son who made himself into a lonely man.

Harry, what can I say to you? All I can say to you is who says life is easy? Since when? It wasn't for me and it isn't for you. It's life, that's the way it is—what more can I say? But if a person don't want to live what can he do if he's dead? Nothing is nothing, it's better to live.

Come home, Harry, he said. It's cold here. You'll catch a cold with your feet in the water.

Harry stood motionless in the water and after a while his father left. As he was leaving, the wind plucked his hat off his head and sent it rolling along the shore. He watched it go.

My father listens in the hallway. He follows me in the street. We meet at the edge of the water.

He runs after his hat.

My son stands with his feet in the ocean.

## QUESTIONS

*Looking at Ideas:*

1. Is the father always "spying" on his son, as the son claims? Why is the father so worried about his son?

2. Why is the son troubled? Why does Harry reject his father's help? Do you think that the father and son understand one another even though they don't seem to be able to communicate directly with one another? Refer to passages in the story to support your point of view.

3. Why does the father feel that "if the worry is about somebody else that's the worst kind"? Do you agree with him? Present an example to support your point of view.

4. Did you expect a different type of story after reading the title? Why would Malamud have chosen this title? Explain the meaning of the title in the context of the story.

5. In the story's final scene Harry and Leo meet at the water's edge where Leo loses his hat. How is this moment symbolic? Would you say that their relationship is universal in that their relationship reflects problems that occur in many father-son relationships? Could you understand and/or relate to their communication problem?

*Looking at Strategies:*

1. Whose point of view can you trust as being more realistic? Why does Malamud let the reader know more about Leo's frame of mind than Harry's?

2. In what ways is Malamud's use of dialogue and dialect especially effective?

3. What do you think the letter from the draft board said? Why does Malamud leave this question for the reader to answer?

4. Malamud leaves the ending of the story ambiguous. What do you imagine will happen in the relationship between Harry and his son after the story's end?

445

*Looking at Connections:*

1. Compare and contrast the fears and dilemmas faced by the two young people engaged in the process of separating from their parents in "For Jane at Thirteen" and "My Son the Murderer."

2. Compare and contrast Leo's fears for his son Harry's future in "My Son the Murderer" with the fears Michael Dorris has for his son Adam's future in "Moving Out," the next selection.

*Suggestions for Writing:*

1. Write a conclusion to the story that explains what happens next to Leo and Harry. Then explain why you devised such a conclusion.

2. Write an essay in which you discuss why you think it can be as difficult for a parent to communicate his or her love and desire to help a son or daughter as it is for Leo. Support your assertions with examples from your own experiences, from those of siblings and friends, or from films and books with which you are familiar.

**MICHAEL DORRIS: "Moving Out"**  Michael Dorris was born in Dayton, Washington, in 1945. He completed his B.A. at Georgetown University (1967) and his M. Phil. at Yale University (1970). Michael Dorris is married to novelist Louise Erdrich; they live with their five children in rural New Hampshire. Dorris and Erdrich often collaborate on writing projects such as their recent novel, *The Crown of Columbus* (1991). Dorris is a professor of anthropology and the chairman of Native American Studies at Dartmouth College. His first work of fiction was *A Yellow Raft in Blue Water* (1987). *The Broken Cord* (1989), a *New York Times* best-seller, is the story of his adopted son's struggle to overcome the learning disabilities that are a consequence of Fetal Alcohol Syndrome. In the selected excerpt, "Moving Out," Dorris shares the emotional conflicts he has had to face and his realizations as he helps his son find a job and live independently.

MICHAEL DORRIS

# *Moving Out*

Adam moved out of our house in late spring of 1988. It was time, but the decision for him to go had not come easily. It was a choice made by default, a move we could rationalize as "for the best" but which was weighted with worry. Our farm was too remote for him to work at hours that lasted longer than the span of a school bus run. Moreover, he was in his final year at Hartford, the last period during which he would be eligible for employment training and placement assistance from the excellent staff. Adam had qualified as a client for the local social service agency, whose representative, Tony Gahn, found him a supervised boardinghouse in Hanover, near enough to public transportation that he could commute to and from a regular dishwashing job at a bowling alley. The manager liked Adam and was prepared to make allowances during what everyone rightly expected to be an erratic period of adjustment.

On a muddy Sunday in March we packed up the belongings Adam wanted to take with him to his new room. It was an odd collection of stuffed animals and paper dolls he had carefully cut out on the sly from a women's underwear catalogue and pasted on cardboard backing, a

447

stack of *Minneapolis Star and Tribune* Sunday cartoons, a suitcase of clothing, a black-and-white television set, and a collection of family photographs and old birthday cards. He took his typewriter and the ongoing "Adam Dorris Story by Adam Dorris," and he brought the voluminous lists I had prepared—times and amounts of medication, sequence of actions to be followed each morning, emergency telephone numbers and instructions for using a pay phone.

He was to be one of several boarders in the home of a couple who bred hairless cats, but he didn't notice the distinctive pheromonal tang that permeated the residence. It was within a short walk of a grocery, a pharmacy, and a movie theater and only a twenty-mile drive from our farm. We were all very, very fortunate, and yet, as Adam walked without a backward glance from the house in which he had lived for almost sixteen years, I experienced a quiet weight of sorrow.

When things are the best they can be, you have no excuse to complain, but that doesn't mean you forgo regret. I had no right to want more for Adam than it's possible for him to have, no right to impose my aspirations on his life. If I were a better person, a wise and accepting person, I would have rejoiced without qualifications that he was agreeable and competent to make this step. Certainly that attitude was the tenor of the words I spoke as we drove to town, unloaded his possessions, and said good-bye. I was hearty in my congratulations and encouragements, proud in my praisings, full of upbeat confidence to Adam that this was the first rung on the ladder of his success.

But lurking within me as we drove away was a different reaction: its arms were folded tightly, its mouth was a compressed line, its shoulders were hunched in impotent fury. It demanded better for Adam. It demanded that he not be penalized for someone else's Original Sin, for a crime committed in ignorance or wanton carelessness before he was born.

Adam's departure was in many respects liberating for Louise and me; we were no longer responsible for arranging his schedule, for getting him places on time, for picking him up when he was done with an activity. It was no longer up to us to ensure that Adam took his medication, dressed in clean clothing, made his bed, did his chores. We soon became aware of just how much of our time had been automatically absorbed by rote instruction: Adam, sit up straight. Adam, say thank-you if someone does you a favor. Adam, that's too much potato on your fork. Adam, shut the door when you go out. Adam, don't wipe your runny nose on the wall. Adam, flush the toilet after you use it. Adam, your shirt is on backward. Adam, turn off the light and the radio when you go to bed.

After years of repetition, we eventually had uttered these sentences without adding verbal justifications. Direct commands were easier on all parties than tortuous, tedious, and ultimately wasted explanations. Appeals to logic had never worked with Adam. The question "Why?" had continued to stump him, no matter what the context, from early childhood. He would mouth the words he thought we wanted to hear. As often as not he guessed wrong, which would only increase the level of our frustration. We had become so used to thinking *for* Adam that the quiet of the house after he left was eerily luxurious, the silence of a painting or a book.

It was a good while before I visited Adam at his place of employment, and when I saw him, I knew why. I walked into the almost empty restaurant of the bowling alley—The Red Rooster—and caught a glimpse of my son through the open door that led into the kitchen. It was only the most fleeting look, snatched as he passed from view in the space of a few strides, but it was enough. He was a collection of repeated admonitions left unchecked, an impression he confirmed as, a few minutes later, he sat across from me in a booth.

I had determined in advance to under no circumstances be disapproving, so it was only to myself that I said: "Adam, where are your glasses? You can't see without them." I did not mention the fact that he had not shaved or washed his face in some time. I did not criticize his choice of clothing: a torn T-shirt in frigid November, a shabby pair of sweat pants, worn obviously without underwear, the ravaged running shoes I had begged him to discard weeks before. The nails on his fingers were long and jagged, his teeth not clean, his hair unbrushed. There was a spot of fresh blood on his lower lip, the result of his tendency for chapped skin in winter dryness. All through public school, from October through March, I would apply balm to his lips as my last act before he left the house. Today I controlled my urge to remind him.

Rather, I asked about his recent injury, a burn he had sustained on his forearm when he had stumbled into a hot stove. No one, least of all Adam, seemed sure how this accident had happened, but it was probable that on one of the many days he had neglected to take his midday medicine—or skipped lunch—he had suffered a minor seizure. That one was not a major attack, but those had occurred as well. In just a few months on the job, Adam had been sent in an ambulance to the emergency room at Mary Hitchcock Hospital on three separate occasions after collapsing. He had banged his head on the floor, bruised his leg, bloodied his nose, and each time it was later discovered that the convulsions had been released because the medication level in his bloodstream was too low.

When responsible for his own care, Adam sometimes became confused about his dosage, "remembering" he had taken his Dilantin or Tegretol but warping the time frame. After seventeen years of instruction he still mixed up breakfast and lunch, lunch and dinner, the hours intervening from one meal to the other evaporating in his memory. Or, conversely, the minutes seemed to him to multiply between the event of swallowing a pill and the event of sitting at the table; at those times he overdosed and became drowsy, lethargic. Every now and then, I was convinced, his failure to take his medicine was, to the extent Adam was capable of it, intentional—a nonact rising out of anger at his need, at routine, at infirmity. He got mad at the pills and spurned them, only to pay dearly later for his defiance.

Now he held up his arm for me to examine. A long red scar shaped like the blade of a sword extended from his wrist to his elbow. The doctor on the case had complained to me that Adam had not kept the bandages clean, had removed them often to examine the wound, and that as a consequence the healing process had been neither quick nor ideal. There would be more of a lasting disfigurement than there had to be.

But I didn't bring this up. "It looks much better," I said.

Adam, like me, is astigmatic—that is, without his glasses he has a "lazy eye." While one eye focuses, the other drifts. He seemed to be looking over my shoulder, even as he opened the clear plastic bag that held the food he had brought from his boarding home.

"What happened to your lunch box?" I asked, referring to the expensive contraption Louise had purchased for him when he started the job.

"The handle is loose," he said. "So to make sure, I don't use it." He unpacked three sandwiches, three hard-boiled eggs, and a banana and methodically began to eat. The blood on his lip was wiped with every bite, then reappeared as he worked his jaws. I wanted to reach across the table with my napkin and blot it. I wanted to run next door to the drugstore and buy Vaseline. I wanted to do a lot of things, but Adam would immediately discontinue doing them when I was gone.

Instead, I though of all the school lunches I had fixed, early in the morning. There was a period of perhaps a year during which Adam consumed the entire contents of his lunch box on the school bus, minutes after he had eaten breakfast. At lunchtime he would have nothing to eat. Then there was another phase during which he didn't eat at all. One day I was looking for something in his closet and discovered a cache of decayed, moldy sandwiches, cookies, and fruit stuffed into a corner.

Today Adam's meal consisted of dry pieces of white bread framing thin slices of baloney. No mayonnaise or mustard. "I think they'd taste better if you jazzed them up a little bit," I offered. He labored to crack an egg, bending low over the table in his myopia and tapping the shell until a series of fissures appeared, then he peeled it, dropping each fragment, one at a time, into the plastic bag. When the surface of the egg was clear, he took a bite, and I couldn't stop myself. "Try just a bit of salt," I suggested. "It will bring out the flavor." He obliged me, prompting yet another memory as he virtually pressed the salt shaker against the egg skin. Years of instruction echoed in my brain: "Hold the ketchup away from the hot dog when you pour it, Adam." "Don't touch the potatoes with the pepper shaker, Adam." "Hold the milk carton above the glass, Adam."

He tried the salted egg and pronounced it an improvement, but as he progressed through the other two eggs, he forgot the salt. So did I. By all evidence Adam didn't take much notice of what he ate. Feeding, for him, seemed to be an act independent of sensation, of preference or enjoyment. He put what was before him into his mouth, chewed and swallowed it, and continued the exercise until there was nothing left. No matter what was served, one dish seemed indistinguishable from another to him. This impression had alternately irritated and depressed me; a well-prepared meal was one of life's small pleasures to which Adam was oblivious. It was a gift that a thoughtful host might serve a guest; but no matter what was offered, Adam reciprocated—unless he was prodded each time to do so—with not the slightest appreciation.

The conversation between my nearly twenty-one-year-old son and me consisted as usual of me asking questions and him answering.

"How's work going?"

"Good."

"Have you seen any movies?"

"I haven't gotten around to it yet."

I gestured to the wooden lanes visible through the interior windows. "Have you been bowling since you've worked here?"

"Not yet."

"What's your favorite program on TV these days?"

"I guess 'Mama's Family.' "

"What did you have for dinner last night?"

"A TV dinner."

"What kind?"

He paused in thought, searched his memory. "I can't say. Probably it was macaroni or turkey."

All this time he worked his way through the food he had brought like a beaver devouring a tree trunk.

"Don't you want something to drink?" I asked. "Some milk or a Coke?"

"No," he said. "I generally don't drink anything."

"You know, you've got a cracked lip. It's bleeding. Did you run out of the stuff you need this time of year?"

Adam touched his finger to the wound, then held it before him and examined the blood. "No," he said and turned his attention back to the egg.

"What's work been like today?"

This was a question he was equipped to handle, and he started with the beginning of the morning when he boarded the bus. He got off the bus at the bus stop. He came into the Red Rooster through the front door. He hung his jacket on the hook. He swept the floor with the broom. He stacked dishes from the dishwasher. He got his jacket and zipped it up. He went outside. He picked trash off the parking lot. A milk carton. A piece of newspaper. Two pop cans. Something else he couldn't remember. He came back inside. He took off his jacket and hung it on the hook.

I listened as Adam recounted, like a videocassette playback, the blow by blow of his day. The hours existed for him as a series of unrelated acts, connected neither by analysis nor by critical perspective, uncolored by like or dislike, undistinguished by incident. As I nodded, inviting him to continue, I yearned to put words in his mouth, to break through the barrier of his plodding progress, to find in him some spark of sarcasm or wit. "So Adam," I wanted to say. "Who are you going to vote for in the presidential election? What do you think of the new Soviet foreign policy? I just read this great mystery novel—you've got to try it."

This was my problem, not his. Where was the fine line between acceptance of a condition I could never change and despair or, worse, indifference? When did I stop wanting, demanding, feeling that Adam had been cheated? When did I let go, quell my passion to power his life, direct his interests, think his thoughts? I was not proud of my complaints; they had long since ceased to do Adam much good and, in fact, interfered with the rhythm of the father-son relationship that he would probably prefer. I tried to imagine this lunch through his perspective, and everything was perfectly satisfactory, better even than satisfactory: Dad had said he would come, and Dad came. No problem. No anxiety that the instructions had been remembered wrong. Adam had not forgotten his lunch. He had brought his medicine and taken it. He had not been criticized. He was on a turf with which he was familiar, at ease. He had not made a mistake. There were no questions he had to struggle to answer. There was no disruption of familiar pattern, and the rest of the day would proceed on schedule, no surprises.

I had no doubt that Adam was glad to see me, that my presence alone was for him a good thing. On an emotional level, he required no more of me than my tacit approval. He liked having the category "Dad" in his life—characters on TV had dads, and so did he. He liked having a person with whom he shared enough history to make some small talk. I confirmed his world, and that's all he wanted. The desire for more came only from me.

Adam's birthdays are, I think, the hardest anniversaries, even though as an adoptive father I was not present to hear Adam's first cry, to feel the aspirated warmth of his body meeting air for the first time. I was not present to count his fingers, to exclaim at the surprise of gender, to be comforted by the hope at the heart of his new existence.

From what I've learned, from the sum of gathered profiles divided by the tragedy of each case, the delivery of my premature son was unlikely to have been a joyous occasion. Most fetal alcohol babies emerge not in a tide, the facsimile of saline, primordial, life-granting sea, but instead enter this world tainted with stale wine. Their amniotic fluid literally reeks of Thunderbird or Ripple, and the whole operating theater stinks like the scene of a three-day party. Delivery room staff who have been witness time and again tell of undernourished babies thrown into delirium tremens when the cord that brought sustenance and poison is severed. Nurses close their eyes at the memory. An infant with the shakes, as cold turkey as a raving derelict deprived of the next fix, is hard to forget.

Compared to the ideal, Adam started far in the hole, differently from the child who began a march through the years without the scars of fetters on his ankles, with eyes and ears that worked, with nothing to carry except what he or she collected along the path.

Adam's birthdays are reminders for me. For each celebration commemorating that he was born, there is the pang, the rage, that he was not born whole. I grieve for what he might have, what he should have been. I magnify and sustain those looks of understanding or compassion or curiosity that fleet across his face, fast as a breeze, unexpected as the voice of God—the time he said to me in the car, the words arising from no context I could see, "Kansas is between Oklahoma and Texas." But when I turned in amazement, agreeing loudly, still ready after all these years to discover a buried talent or passion for geography, for anything, that possible person had disappeared.

"What made you say that?" I asked.

"Say what?" he answered. "I didn't say anything."

The sixteenth birthday, the eighteenth. The milestones. The driver's license, voting, the adult boundary-marker birthdays. The days I envisioned while watching the mails for the response to my first adoption application, the days that set forth like distant skyscrapers as I projected ahead through my years of fatherhood. I had given little specific consideration to what might come between, but of those outstanding days I had been sure. They were the pillars I followed, the oases of certainty. Alone in the cabin in Alaska or in the basement apartment near Franconia while I waited for the definition of the rest of my life to commence, I planned the elaborate cake decorations for those big birthdays, the significant presents I would save to buy. Odd as it may seem, the anticipation of the acts of letting Adam go began before I even knew his name. I looked forward to the proud days on which the world would recognize my son as progressively more his own man. Those were among the strongest hooks that bonded me to him in my imagination.

As each of these anniversaries finally came and went, nothing like I expected them to be, I doubly mourned. First, selfishly, for me, and second for Adam, because he didn't know what he was missing, what he had already missed, what he would miss. I wanted to burst through those birthdays like a speeding train blasts a weak gate, to get past them and back into the anonymous years for which I had made no models, where there were no obvious measurements, no cakes with candles that would never be lit.

It was a coincidence that Adam turned twenty-one as this book neared completion, but it seemed appropriate. On the morning of his birthday, I rose early and baked him a lemon cake, his favorite, and left the layers to cool while I drove to Hanover to pick him up. His gifts were wrapped and on the kitchen table—an electric shaver, clothes, a Garfield calendar. For his special dinner he had requested tacos, and as always I had reserved a magic candle—the kind that keeps reigniting no matter how often it is blown out—for the center of his cake.

I was greeted at Adam's house by the news that he had just had a

453

seizure, a small one this time, but it had left him groggy. I helped him on with his coat, bent to tie his shoelace, all the while talking about the fun we would have during the day. He looked out the window. Only the week before he had been laid off from his dishwashing job. December had been a bad month for seizures, some due to his body's adjustment to a change in dosage and some occurring because Adam had skipped taking medicine altogether. The bowling alley's insurance carrier was concerned and that, combined with an after-Christmas slump in business, decided the issue. Now he was back at Hartford for a few weeks while Ken Kramberg and his associates sought a new work placement. I thought perhaps Adam was depressed about this turn of events, so I tried to cheer him up as we drove south on the familiar road to Cornish.

"So, Adam," I said, making conversation, summoning the conventional words, "do you feel any older? What's good about being twenty-one?"

He turned to me and grinned. There *was* something good.

"Well," he answered, "now the guys at work say I'm old enough to drink."

His unexpected words kicked me in the stomach. They crowded every thought from my brain.

"Adam, you can't," I protested. "I've told you about your birth-mother, about your other father. Do you remember what happened to them?" I knew he did. I had told him the story several times, and we had gone over it together as he read, or I read to him, parts of this book.

Adam thought for a moment. "They were sick?" he offered finally. "That's why I have seizures?"

"No, they weren't sick. They died, Adam. They died from drinking. If you drank, it could happen to you." My memory played back all the statistics about sons of alcoholic fathers and their particular susceptibility to substance abuse. "It would not mix well with your medicine."

Adam sniffed, turned away, but not before I recognized the amused disbelief in his expression. He did not take death seriously, never had. It was an abstract concept out of his reach and therefore of no interest to him. Death was less real than Santa Claus—after all, Adam had in his album a photograph of himself seated on Santa Claus's lap. Death was no threat, no good reason to refuse his first drink.

My son will forever travel through a moonless night with only the roar of wind for company. Don't talk to him of mountains, of tropical beaches. Don't ask him to swoon at sunrises or marvel at the filter of light through leaves. He's never had time for such things, and he does not believe in them. He may pass by them close enough to touch on either side, but his hands are stretched forward, grasping for balance instead of pleasure. He doesn't wonder where he came from, where he's going. He doesn't ask who he is, or why. Questions are a luxury, the province of those at a distance from the periodic shock of rain.

Gravity presses Adam so hard against reality that he doesn't feel the points at which he touches it. A drowning man is not separated from the lust for air by a bridge of thought—he is one with it—and my son, conceived and grown in an ethanol bath, lives each day in the act of drowning. For him there is no shore.

*Chapter Eight: Growing Away*

## QUESTIONS

*Looking at Ideas:*

1. What mixed emotions about his son's future does Michael Dorris have as he drops Adam off at his new residence?
2. How was Adam's departure "liberating" for Dorris and his wife?
3. How does Dorris feel when he visits Adam at his first home away from home? How well is Adam managing his life? Based on the experiences Adam has had so far, how much independence do you think he will be able to handle? What will happen to him? Who will help him take care of himself? How does Dorris come to accept the limitations of Adam's life?
4. Why are Adam's birthdays especially difficult for Dorris? What realizations does Dorris have on Adam's twenty-first birthday?
5. Dorris's fears about Adam's thoughts of drinking are strong ones. How is his response different from that of ordinary parents who are concerned about their children's drinking? Does he handle the situation truthfully or effectively?

*Looking at Strategies:*

1. Michael Dorris uses very powerful examples and closely observed, specific details to support the major questions and decisions he must make regarding Adam's ability to care for himself. Discuss several of these detailed examples; explain why you think each one is particularly effective.
2. Dorris has several conversations with Adam in the course of the narrative. What do we learn about Adam's mental processes and his relationship with his father through these passages?
3. Adam is writing the story of his life, "The Adam Dorris Story." Based on the information given in the story, how do you imagine Adam would narrate the events covered here? How might he perceive his father differently from the way Dorris perceives himself? What emotions might he share, if any?
4. Dorris ends his essay with a series of metaphors. How effectively do these metaphors sum up for us Adam's inner life? Interpret his closing image of a drowning man in light of the chapter you have just read, with its many vivid and disheartening examples.

*Looking at Connections:*

1. Compare and contrast Adam Dorris's search for a life independent of his family with those of such "normal" adolescents as Susan Toth and Annie Dillard.

455

2. Compare Dorris's response to his son's growing-away process with that of Maxine Kumin's in "For Jane at Thirteen." How are both parents' concerns similar, despite the differences between their children's possible futures?

*Suggestions for Writing:*

1. Write a reflective essay about an experience you have had interacting with a learning-disabled sibling, friend, relative, or parent. What were the greatest challenges and rewards in the situation?

2. After reading this chapter and thinking about the many adolescents who have Fetal Alcohol Syndrome or other severe learning disabilities, write an essay about what you imagine would be the most difficult aspects of raising a son or daughter with disabilities. What rewards would such a parent have?

3. Do some research into one or two organizations in your community that support the disabled, and then write an essay exploring the challenges these community agencies face and the services they offer. You might interview workers and clients of the agencies and include excerpts from the interviews as evidence for your conclusions.

**JOURNAL ENTRY**

Write about a memorial service that you attended for a family member,
relative, or close friend.

**JAMES BALDWIN: "Notes of a Native Son" (Part III)**   James Baldwin (1924–
1987) was raised in Harlem in a fundamentalist Christian household. He was a
Young Minister at Fireside Pentecostal Assembly in New York from 1938 to
1942 and graduated from DeWitt Clinton High School in 1942. Baldwin lived
and worked in Harlem as a writer and odd-jobs man until 1948. Then he lived
in Europe until 1957, when he returned to lecture and crusade for the civil
rights movement. In 1965 he returned once again to Europe. Baldwin is well
known for the essays, novels, and short stories that reflect his experiences
growing up in Harlem and struggling with racial injustice in the United States.
Some of his works include *The Fire Next Time* (1963), *In Another Country*
(1967), and *Evidence of Things Not Seen* (1985). The following selection was
taken from one of his best-known essays, "Notes of a Native Son" (1955). As
you read Baldwin's observations about his father's funeral and his reflections
on his father's life, think about why he is considered one of the most passionate, introspective, and controversial essayists of his time.

JAMES BALDWIN

# *Notes of a Native Son (Part III)*

For my father's funeral I had nothing black to wear and this posed a
nagging problem all day long. It was one of those problems, simple, or
impossible of solution, to which the mind insanely clings in order to
avoid the mind's real trouble. I spent most of that day at the downtown
apartment of a girl I knew, celebrating my birthday with whiskey and
wondering what to wear that night. When planning a birthday celebration one naturally does not expect that it will be up against competition
from a funeral and this girl had anticipated taking me out that night,
for a big dinner and a night club afterwards. Sometime during the
course of that long day we decided that we would go out anyway, when
my father's funeral service was over. I imagine *I* decided it, since, as the
funeral hour approached, it became clearer and clearer to me that I
would not know what to do with myself when it was over. The girl, sti-
fling her very lively concern as to the possible effects of the whiskey on
one of my father's chief mourners, concentrated on being conciliatory
and practically helpful. She found a black shirt for me somewhere and
ironed it and, dressed in the darkest pants and jacket I owned, and
slightly drunk, I made my way to my father's funeral.

The chapel was full, but not packed, and very quiet. There were, mainly, my father's relatives, and his children, and here and there I saw faces I had not seen since childhood, the faces of my father's one-time friends. They were very dark and solemn now, seeming somehow to suggest that they had known all along that something like this would happen. Chief among the mourners was my aunt, who had quarreled with my father all his life; by which I do not mean to suggest that her mourning was insincere or that she had not loved him. I suppose that she was one of the few people in the world who had, and their incessant quarreling proved precisely the strength of the tie that bound them. The only other person in the world, as far as I knew, whose relationship to my father rivaled my aunt's in depth was my mother, who was not there.

It seemed to me, of course, that it was a very long funeral. But it was, if anything, a rather shorter funeral than most, nor, since there were no overwhelming uncontrollable expressions of grief, could it be called—if I dare to use the word—successful. The minister who preached my father's funeral sermon was one of the few my father had still been seeing as he neared his end. He presented to us in his sermon a man whom none of us had ever seen—a man thoughtful, patient, and forbearing, a Christian inspiration to all who knew him, and a model for his children. And no doubt the children, in their disturbed and guilty state, were almost ready to believe this; he had been remote enough to be anything and, anyway, the shock of the incontrovertible, that it was really our father lying up there in that casket, prepared the mind for anything. His sister moaned and this grief-stricken moaning was taken as corroboration. The other faces held a dark, non-committal thoughtfulness. This was not the man they had known, but they had scarcely expected to be confronted with *him;* this was, in a sense deeper than questions of fact, the man they had not known, and the man they had not known may have been the real one. The real man, whoever he had been, had suffered and now he was dead: this was all that was sure and all that mattered now. Every man in the chapel hoped that when his hour came he, too, would be eulogized, which is to say forgiven, and that all of his lapses, greeds, errors, and strayings from the truth would be invested with coherence and looked upon with charity. This was perhaps the last thing human beings could give each other and it was what they demanded, after all, of the Lord. Only the Lord saw the midnight tears, only He was present when one of His children, moaning and wringing hands, paced up and down the room. When one slapped one's child in anger the recoil in the heart reverberated through heaven and became part of the pain of the universe. And when the children were hungry and sullen and distrustful and one watched them, daily, growing wilder, and further away, and running headlong into danger, it was the Lord who knew what the charged heart endured as the strap was laid to the backside; the Lord alone who knew what one *would* have said if one had had, like the Lord, the gift of the living word. It was the Lord who knew of the impossibility every parent in that room faced: how to prepare the child for the day when the child would be despised and how to *create* in the child—by what means?—a stronger antidote to this poison than one had found for oneself. The avenues, side streets, bars, billiard halls, hospitals, police stations, and even the playgrounds of Harlem—not to mention the houses of correction, the jails, and the morgue—testified to the potency of the poison while remaining silent as to the efficacy of whatever antidote, irresistibly raising the question of whether or not such an antidote existed; raising, which was worse, the question of whether or not an antidote was desirable; perhaps poison should be fought with poison. With these several schisms in the mind and with more terrors in the heart than could be named, it was better not to judge the man who had gone down under an impossible burden. It was better to remember: *Thou knowest this man's fall; but thou knowest not his wrassling.*

While the preacher talked and I watched the children—years of changing their diapers, scrubbing them, slapping them, taking them to school, and scolding them had had the perhaps inevitable result of making me love them, though I am not sure I knew this then—my mind was busily breaking out with a rash of disconnected impressions. Snatches of popular songs, indecent jokes, bits of books I had read, movie sequences, faces, voices, political issues—I thought I was going mad; all these impressions suspended, as it were, in the solution of the faint nausea produced in me by the heat and liquor. For a moment I had the impression that my alcoholic breath, inefficiently disguised with chewing gum, filled the entire chapel. Then someone began singing one of my father's favorite songs and, abruptly, I was with him, sitting on his knee, in the hot, enormous, crowded church which was the first church we attended. It was the Abyssinia Baptist Church on 138th Street. We had not gone there long. With this image, a host of others came. I had forgotten, in the rage of my growing up, how proud my father had been of me when I was little. Apparently, I had had a voice and my father had liked to show me off before the members of the church. I had forgotten what he had looked like when he was pleased but now I remembered that he had always been grinning with pleasure when my solos ended. I even remembered certain expressions on his face when he teased my mother—had he loved her? I would never know. And when had it all begun to change? For now it seemed that he had not always been cruel. I remembered being taken for a haircut and scraping my knee on the footrest of the barber's chair and I remembered by father's face as he soothed my crying and applied the stinging iodine. Then I remembered our fights, fights which had been of the worst possible kind because my technique had been silence.

I remembered the one time in all our life together when we had really spoken to each other.

It was on a Sunday and it must have been shortly before I left home. We were walking, just the two of us, in our usual silence, to or from church. I was in high school and had been doing a lot of writing and I was, at about this time, the editor of the high school magazine.

But I had also been a Young Minister and had been preaching from the pulpit. Lately, I had been taking fewer engagements and preached as rarely as possible. It was said in the church, quite truthfully, that I was "cooling off."

My father asked me abruptly, "You'd rather write than preach, wouldn't you?"

I was astonished at his question—because it was a real question. I answered, "Yes."

That was all we said. It was awful to remember that that was all we had *ever* said.

The casket now was opened and the mourners were being led up the aisle to look for the last time on the deceased. The assumption was that the family was too overcome with grief to be allowed to make this journey alone and I watched while my aunt was led to the casket and, muffled in black, and shaking, led back to her seat. I disapproved of forcing the children to look on their dead father, considering that the shock of his death, or, more truthfully, the shock of death as a reality, was already a little more than a child could bear, but my judgment in this matter had been overruled and there they were, bewildered and frightened and very small, being led, one by one, to the casket. But there is also something very gallant about children at such moments. It has something to do with their silence and gravity and with the fact that one cannot help them. Their legs, somehow, seem *exposed,* so that it is at once incredible and terribly clear that their legs are all they have to hold them up.

I had not wanted to go to the casket myself and I certainly had not wished to be led there, but there was no way of avoiding either of these forms. One of the deacons led me up and I looked on my father's face. I cannot say that it looked like him at all. His blackness had been equivocated by powder and there was no suggestion in that casket of what his power had or could have been. He was simply an old man dead, and it was hard to believe that he had ever given anyone either joy or pain. Yet, his life filled that room. Further up the avenue his wife was holding his newborn child. Life and death so close together, and love and hatred, and right and wrong, said something to me which I did not want to hear concerning man, concerning the life of man.

After the funeral, while I was downtown desperately celebrating my birthday, a Negro soldier, in the lobby of the Hotel Braddock, got into a fight with a white policeman over a Negro girl. Negro girls, white policemen, in or out of uniform, and Negro males—in or out of uniform —were part of the furniture of the lobby of the Hotel Braddock and this was certainly not the first time such an incident had occurred. It was destined, however, to receive an unprecedented publicity, for the fight between the policeman and the soldier ended with the shooting of the soldier. Rumor, flowing immediately to the streets outside, stated that the soldier had been shot in the back, an instantaneous and revealing invention, and that the soldier had died protecting a Negro woman. The facts were somewhat different—for example, the soldier had not been shot in the back, and was not dead, and the girl seems to have been as dubious a symbol of womanhood as her white counterpart in Georgia usually is, but no one was interested in the facts. They preferred the invention because this invention expressed and corroborated their hates and fears so perfectly. It is just as well to remember that people are always doing this. Perhaps many of those legends, including Christianity, to which the world clings began their conquest of the world with just some such concerted surrender to distortion. The effect, in Harlem, of this particular legend was like the effect of a lit match in a tin of gasoline. The mob gathered before the doors of the Hotel Braddock simply began to swell and to spread in every direction, and Harlem exploded.

The mob did not cross the ghetto lines. It would have been easy, for example, to have gone over to Morningside Park on the west side or to have crossed the Grand Central railroad tracks at 125th Street on the east side, to wreak havoc in white neighborhoods. The mob seems to have been mainly interested in something more potent and real than the white face, that is, in white power, and the principal damage done during the riot of the summer of 1943 was to white business establishments in Harlem. It might have been a far bloodier story, of course, if, at the hour the riot began, these establishments had still been open. From the Hotel Braddock the mob fanned out, east and west along 125th Street, and for the entire length of Lenox, Seventh, and Eighth avenues. Along each of these avenues, and along each major side street—116th, 125th, 135th, and so on—bars, stores, pawnshops, restaurants, even little luncheonettes had been smashed open and entered and looted—looted, it might be added, with more haste than efficiency. The shelves really looked as though a bomb had struck them. Cans of beans and soup and dog food, along with toilet paper, corn flakes, sardines, and milk tumbled every which way, and abandoned cash registers and cases of beer leaned crazily out of the splintered windows and were strewn along the avenues. Sheets, blankets, and clothing of every description formed a kind of path, as though people had dropped them while running. I truly had not realized that Harlem *had* so many stores until I saw them all smashed open; the first time the word *wealth* ever entered my mind in relation to Harlem was when I saw it scattered in the streets. But one's first, incongruous impression of plenty was countered immediately by an impression of waste. None of this was doing anybody any good. It would have been better to have left the plate glass as it had been and the goods lying in the stores.

It would have been better, but it would also have been intolerable, for Harlem had needed something to smash. To smash something is the ghetto's chronic need. Most of the time it is the members of the ghetto who smash each other, and themselves. But as long as the ghetto walls are standing there will always come a moment when these outlets do not work. That summer, for example, it was not enough to get into a fight on Lenox Avenue, or curse out one's cronies in the barber shops. If ever, indeed, the violence which fills Harlem's churches, pool halls,

461

and bars erupts outward in a more direct fashion, Harlem and its citizens are likely to vanish in an apocalyptic flood. That this is not likely to happen is due to a great many reasons, most hidden and powerful among them the Negro's real relation to the white American. This relation prohibits, simply, anything as uncomplicated and satisfactory as pure hatred. In order really to hate white people, one has to blot so much out of the mind—and the heart—that this hatred itself becomes an exhausting and self-destructive pose. But this does not mean, on the other hand, that love comes easily: the white world is too powerful, too complacent, too ready with gratuitous humiliation, and, above all, too ignorant and too innocent for that. One is absolutely forced to make perpetual qualifications and one's own reactions are always canceling each other out. It is this, really, which has driven so many people mad, both white and black. One is always in the position of having to decide between amputation and gangrene. Amputation is swift but time may prove that the amputation was not necessary—or one may delay the amputation too long. Gangrene is slow, but it is impossible to be sure that one is reading one's symptoms right. The idea of going through life as a cripple is more than one can bear, and equally unbearable is the risk of swelling up slowly, in agony, with poison. And the trouble, finally, is that the risks are real even if the choices do not exist.

"But as for me and my house," my father had said, "we will serve the Lord." I wondered, as we drove him to his resting place, what this line had meant for him. I had heard him preach it many times. I had preached it once myself, proudly giving it an interpretation different from my father's. Now the whole thing came back to me, as though my father and I were on our way to Sunday school and I were memorizing the golden text: *And if it seem evil unto you to serve the Lord, choose you this day whom you will serve; whether the gods which your fathers served that were on the other side of the flood, or the gods of the Amorites, in whose land ye dwell: but as for me and my house, we will serve the Lord.* I suspected in these familiar lines a meaning which had never been there for me before. All of my father's texts and songs, which I had decided were meaningless, were arranged before me at his death like empty bottles, waiting to hold the meaning which life would give them for me. This was his legacy: nothing is ever escaped. That bleakly memorable morning I hated the unbelievable streets and the Negroes and whites who had, equally, made them that way. But I knew that it was folly, as my father would have said, this bitterness was folly. It was necessary to hold on to the things that mattered. The dead man mattered, the new life mattered; blackness and whiteness did not matter; to believe that they did was to acquiesce in one's own destruction. Hatred, which could destroy so much, never failed to destroy the man who hated and this was an immutable law.

It began to seem that one would have to hold in the mind forever two ideas which seemed to be in opposition. The first idea was acceptance, the acceptance, totally without rancor, of life as it is, and men as they are: in the light of this idea, it goes without saying that injustice is a commonplace. But this did not mean that one could be complacent, for the second idea was of equal power: that one must never, in one's own life, accept these injustices as commonplace but must fight them with all one's strength. This fight begins, however, in the heart and it now had been laid to my charge to keep my own heart free of hatred and despair. This intimation made my heart heavy and, now that my father was irrecoverable, I wished that he had been beside me so that I could have searched his face for the answers which only the future would give me now.

## QUESTIONS

*Looking at Ideas:*

1. How does Baldwin prepare himself for his father's funeral?
2. Does Baldwin believe that the mourners at his father's funeral knew the "real man"? According to Baldwin, who is in a position to judge his father's life? Why?
3. How does Baldwin feel about his father? Why does he finally remember "the one time in all our life together when we had really spoken"? What does this conversation reveal about their relationship?
4. What is the legacy Baldwin finally feels his father's death has brought him? Refer to specific passages in the text to support your answer.

*Looking at Strategies:*

1. Characterize Baldwin's language and tone. Do you think they are appropriate for the material he is discussing?
2. What events and details does Baldwin develop to create sympathy for his father?
3. Why does Baldwin describe the race riot following his father's funeral? If you see this episode as an example, what point does the example make?
4. How do Baldwin's father's religious beliefs help Baldwin see the hatred that erupted during the riot in a life-affirming perspective?
5. Baldwin's mother is not at the funeral because she has just given birth to another child. Baldwin leaves the funeral to "desperately celebrate his birthday." How do these contrasting life and death realities reflect on the meaning of Baldwin's father's death?

*Looking at Connections:*

1. Compare Baldwin's attitude toward his father with Alice Walker's attitude toward hers in her memoir, "Father" (Chapter One).
2. Contrast Baldwin's attitude toward his father to David Sherwood's attitude toward his father in "Discarded" (Chapter Two).

*Suggestions for Writing:*

1. Baldwin makes the point that a child's departure from home and a parent's death are linked, in that neither experience can be prepared for adequately. How do you understand the relationship between these two important separations or moments of growing away? In answer to this

question write a reflective essay in which you refer to your own life experiences as points of reference.

2. As parents separate from their adolescents, they may feel inadequate and helpless, being aware of the trials that life holds for their children. Baldwin suggests that parents give their children an antidote that will neutralize the "poison" of society. What form might this antidote take? Write an essay in which you explore what you feel parents can give their children to help them face adult life on their own.

3. Reflecting on his father's funeral brought Baldwin a revelation and a legacy: ". . . injustice is a commonplace. But this did not mean that one could be complacent, for the second idea was of equal power: that one must never, in one's own life, accept these injustices as commonplace but must fight them with all one's strength. This fight begins, however, in the heart free of hatred and despair." Narrate a turning point in your life that led you to a synthesis and a revelation. Focus on developing the connections between the event and the revelation. How did the event empower you to effect changes in your life?

**JOURNAL ENTRY**
Write about how you adjusted to the death of a family member
or a close friend.

*Chapter Eight:*
*Growing Away*

**ELIZABETH KÜBLER-ROSS: "The Patient's Family"**   Elizabeth Kübler-Ross was born in Zurich, Switzerland, in 1926. She married, had two children, and then completed her M.D. at the University of Zurich in 1957. Ross studied psychiatry at the University of Colorado and the University of Chicago. She has earned many honorary degrees and completed a Ph.D. at the Medical College of Pennsylvania in 1975. Elizabeth Kübler-Ross is best known for her three books about learning to accept death: *On Death and Dying* (1969), *Questions and Answers on Death and Dying* (1972), and *The Final Stage* (1974). The following selection, "The Patient's Family," was excerpted from her first book. As you read her advice, think about how it could help you adjust to the death of a family member.

ELIZABETH KÜBLER-ROSS

# The Patient's Family

## Coping with the Reality of Terminal Illness in the Family

Family members undergo different stages of adjustment similar to the ones described for our patients. At first many of them cannot believe that it is true. They may deny the fact that there is such an illness in the family or "shop around" from doctor to doctor in the vain hope of hearing that this was the wrong diagnosis. They may seek help and reassurance (that it is all not true) from fortune-tellers and faith healers. They may arrange for expensive trips to famous clinics and physicians and only gradually face up to the reality which may change their life so drastically. Greatly dependent on the patient's attitude, awareness, and ability to communicate, the family then undergoes certain changes. If they are able to share their common concerns, they can take care of important matters early and under less pressure of time and emotions. If each one tries to keep a secret from the other, they will keep an artificial barrier between them which will make it difficult for any preparatory grief for the patient or his family. The end result will be much more dramatic than for those who can talk and cry together at times.

Just as the patient goes through a stage of anger, the immediate family will experience the same emotional reaction. They will be angry alternately with the doctor who examined the patient first and did not come forth with the diagnosis and the doctor who confronted them with the sad reality. They may project their rage to the hospital personnel who never care enough, no matter how efficient the care is in reality. There is a great deal of envy in this reaction, as family members often feel cheated at not being able or allowed to be with the patient and to care for him. There is also much guilt and a wish to make up for missed past opportunities. The more we can help the relative to express these emotions before the death of a loved one, the more comfortable the family member will be.

When anger, resentment, and guilt can be worked through, the family will then go through a phase of preparatory grief, just as the dying person does. The more this grief can be expressed before death, the less unbearable it becomes afterward. We often hear relatives say proudly of themselves that they always tried to keep a smiling face when confronted with the patient, until one day they just could not keep that facade any longer. Little do they realize that genuine emotions on the part of a member of the family are much easier to take than a make-believe mask which the patient can see through anyway and which means to him a disguise rather than a sharing of a sad situation.

If members of a family can share these emotions together, they will gradually face the reality of impending separation and come to an acceptance of it together. The most heartbreaking time, perhaps, for the family is the final phase, when the patient is slowly detaching himself from his world including his family. They do not understand that a dying man who has found peace and acceptance in his death will have to separate himself, step by step, from his environment, including his most loved ones. How could he ever be ready to die if he continued to hold onto the meaningful relationships of which a man has so many? When the patient asks to be visited only by a few more friends, then by his children and finally only by his wife, it should be understood that that is the way of separating himself gradually. It is often misinterpreted by the immediate family as a rejection, and we have met several husbands and wives who have reacted dramatically to this normal and healthy detachment. I think we can be of greatest service to them if we help them understand that only patients who have worked through their dying are able to detach themselves slowly and peacefully in this manner. It should be a source of comfort and solace to them and not one of grief and resentment. It is during this time that the family needs the most support, the patient perhaps the least. I do not mean to imply by this that the patient should then be left alone. We should always be available, but a patient who has reached this stage of acceptance and decathexis usually requires little in terms of interpersonal relationship. If the meaning of this detachment is not explained to the family, problems can arise. . . .

The most tragic death is perhaps—aside from the very young—the death of the very old when we look at it from point of view of the family. Whether the generations have lived together or separately, each generation has a need and a right to live their own lives, to have their own privacy, their own needs fulfilled appropriate to their generation. The old folks have outlived their usefulness in terms of our economic system and have earned, on the other hand, a right to live out their lives in dignity and peace. As long as they are healthy in body and mind and self-supporting, this may all be quite possible. We have seen many old men and women, however, who have become disabled physically or emotionally and who require a tremendous sum of money for a dignified maintenance at a level their family desires for them. The family is then often confronted with a difficult decision, namely, to mobilize all available money, including loans and savings for their own retirement, in order to afford such final care. The tragedy of these old people is perhaps that the amount of money and often financial sacrifice does not involve any improvement of the condition but is a mere maintenance at a minimal level of existence. If medical complications occur, the expenses are manifold and the family often wishes for a quick and painless death, but rarely expresses that wish openly. That such wishes bring about feelings of guilt is obvious.

I am reminded of an old woman who had been hospitalized for several weeks and required extensive and expensive nursing care in a private hospital. Everybody expected her to die soon, but day after day she remained in an unchanged condition. Her daughter was torn between sending her to a nursing home or keeping her in the hospital, where she apparently wanted to stay. Her son-in-law was angry at her for having used up their life savings and had innumerable arguments with his wife, who felt too guilty to take her out of the hospital. When I visited the old woman she looked frightened and weary. I asked her simply what she was so afraid of. She looked at me and finally expressed what she had been unable to communicate before, because she herself realized how unrealistic her fears were. She was afraid of "being eaten up alive by the worms." While I was catching my breath and tried to understand the real meaning of this statement, her daughter blurted out, "If that's what's keeping you from dying, we can burn you," by which she naturally meant that a cremation would prevent her from having any contact with earthworms. All her suppressed anger was in this statement. I sat with the old woman alone for a while. We talked calmly about her life-long phobias and her fear of death which was presented in this fear of worms, as if she would be aware of them after her death. She felt greatly relieved for having expressed it and had nothing but understanding for her daughter's anger. I encouraged her to share some of these feelings with her daughter, so that the latter might not have to feel so bad about her outburst.

When I met the daughter outside the room I told her of her mother's understanding, and they finally got together to talk about their concerns, ending up by making arrangements for the funeral, a cremation. Instead of sitting silently in anger, they communicated and consoled each other. The mother died the next day. If I had not see the peaceful look on her face during her last day, I might have worried that this outburst of anger might have killed her.

Another aspect that is often not taken into account is what kind of a fatal illness the patient has. There are certain expectations of cancer, just as there are certain pictures associated with heart disease. The former is often viewed as a lingering, pain-producing illness while the latter can strike suddenly, painless but final. I think there is a great deal of difference if a loved one dies slowly with much time available for preparatory grief on both sides, compared to the feared phone call, "It happened, it's all over." It is easier to talk with a cancer patient about death and dying than it is with a cardiac patient, who arouses concerns in us that we might frighten him and thus provoke a coronary, i.e., his death. The relatives of a cancer patient are therefore more amenable to discussing the expected end than the family of someone with heart disease, when the end can come any moment and a discussion may provoke it, at least in the opinion of many members of families whom we have spoken with.

I remember a mother of a young man in Colorado who did not allow her son to take any exercise, not even the most minimal kind, in spite of the contrary advice on part of his doctors. In conversations this mother would often make statements like "if he does too much he will drop dead on me," as if she expected a hostile act on the part of her son to be committed against her. She was totally unaware of her own hostility even after sharing with us some of her resentment for having "such a weak son," whom she very often associated with her ineffective and unsuccessful husband. It took months of careful, patient listening to this mother before she was able to express some of her own destructive wishes toward her child. She rationalized these by the fact that he was the cause of her limited social and professional life, thus rendering her as ineffective as she regarded her husband to be. These are complicated family situations, in which a sick member of the family is rendered more incapable of functioning because of the relative's conflicts. If we can learn to respond to such family members with compassion and understanding rather than judgement and criticism, we also help the patient bear his handicap with more ease and dignity.

The following example of Mr. P. demonstrates the difficulties that can occur for the patient when he is ready to separate himself but the family is unable to accept the reality, thus contributing to the patient's conflicts. Our goal should always be to help the patient and his family face the crisis together in order to achieve acceptance of this final reality simultaneously.

Mr. P. was a man in his mid-fifties who looked about fifteen years older than his age. The doctors felt that he had only a poor chance to respond to treatment, partially because of his advanced cancer and marasmus, but mainly because of his lack of "fighting spirit." Mr. P. had his stomach removed because of cancer five years prior to this hospitalization. At first he accepted his illness quite well and was full of hope. As he grew weaker and thinner, he became increasingly depressed until the time of his readmission, when a chest X-ray revealed metastatic tumors in his lungs. The patient had not been informed of the biopsy result when I saw him. The question was raised as to the advisability of possible radiation or surgery for a man in his weak condition. Our interview proceeded in two sessions. The first visit served the purpose of introducing myself and of telling him that I was available should he wish to talk about the seriousness of his illness and the problems that this might cause. A telephone interrupted us and I left the room, asking him to think about it. I also informed him about the time of my next visit.

When I saw him the next day, Mr. P. put his arm out in welcome and signaled to the chair as an invitation to sit down. In spite of many interruptions by a change of infusion bottles, distribution of medication, and routine pulse and blood pressure measurements, we sat for over an hour. Mr. P. had sensed that he would be allowed to "open his shades" as he called it. There was no defensiveness, no evasiveness in his accounts. He was a man whose hours seemed to count, who had no precious time to lose, and who seemed to be eager to share his concerns and regrets with someone who could listen.

The day before, he made the statement, "I want to sleep, sleep, sleep and not wake up." Today he repeated the same thing, but added the word "but." I looked at him questioningly and he proceeded to tell me with a weak soft voice that his wife had come to visit him. She was convinced that he would make it. She expected him home to take care of the garden and the flowers. She also reminded him of his promise to retire soon, to move to Arizona perhaps, to have a few more good years. . . .

He talked with much warmth and affection about his daughter, twenty-one years old, who came to visit him on a leave from college, and who was shocked to see him in this condition. He mentioned all these things, as if he was to be blamed for disappointing his family, for not living up to their expectations.

I mentioned that to him and he nodded. He talked about all the regrets he had. He spent the first years of his marriage accumulating material goods for his family, trying to "make them a good home," and by doing so spent most of his time away from home and family. After the occurrence of cancer he spared every moment to be with them, but by then, it seemed to be too late. His daughter was away at school and had her own friends. When she was small and needed and wanted him, he was too busy making money.

Talking about his present condition he said, "Sleep is the only relief. Every moment of awakening is anguish, pure anguish. There is no relief. I am thinking in envy of two men I saw executed. I sat right in front of the first man. I felt nothing. Now, I think, he was a lucky guy. He deserved to die. He had no anguish, it was fast and painless. Here I lie in bed, every hour, every day is agony."

Mr. P. was not so much concerned about pain and physical discomfort as he was tortured by regrets for not being able to fulfill his family's expectations, for being "a failure." He was tortured by his tremen-

469

dous need to "let go and sleep, sleep, sleep" and the continuous flow of expectations from his environment. "The nurses come in and say I have to eat or I get too weak, the doctors come in and tell me about the new treatment they started, and expect me to be happy about it; my wife comes and tells me about the work I am supposed to do when I get out of here, and my daughter just looks at me and says 'You have to get well'—how can a man die in peace this way?"

For a brief moment he smiled and said, "I will take this treatment and go home once more. I will return to work the next day and make a bit more money. My insurance will pay for my daughter's education anyway, but she still needs a father for a while. But you know and I know, I just cannot do it. Maybe they have to learn to face it. It would make dying so much easier!"

Mr. P. showed . . . how difficult it is for patients to face impending and anticipated death when the family is not ready to "let go" and implicitly or explicitly prevents them from separating themselves from the involvements here on earth. Mrs. W.'s husband just stood at her bedside, reminding her of their happy marriage which should not end and pleading with the doctors to do everything humanly possible to prevent her from dying. Mr. P.'s wife reminded him of unfulfilled promises and undone tasks, thus communicating the same needs to him, namely, to have him around for many more years to come. I cannot say that both these partners used denial. Both of them knew the reality of the condition of their spouses. Yet both, because of their own needs, looked away from this reality. They faced it when talking with other people but denied it in front of the patients. And it was the patients who needed to hear that they too were aware of the seriousness of their condition and were able to accept this reality. Without this knowledge "every moment of awakening is pure anguish," in Mr. P.'s words. Our interview ended with the expression of hope that the important people in his environment would learn to face the reality of his dying rather than expressing hope for a prolonging of his life.

This man was ready to separate himself from this world. He was ready to enter the final stage when the end is more promising or there is not enough strength left to live. One might argue whether an all-out medical effort is appropriate in such circumstances. With enough infusions and transfusions, vitamins, energizers, and antidepressant medication, with psychotherapy and symptomatic treatment, many such patients may be given an additional "lease on life." I have heard more curses than words of appreciation for the gained time, and I repeat my conviction that a patient has a right to die in peace and dignity. He should not be used to fulfill our own needs when his own wishes are in opposition to ours. I am referring to patients who have a physical illness but who are sane and capable enough to make decisions for themselves. Their wishes and opinions should be respected, they should be listened to and consulted. If the patient's wishes are contrary to our beliefs or convictions, we should express this conflict openly and leave the decisions up to the patient in respect to further interventions or treatments. In the many terminally ill patients I have so far interviewed, I have not seen any irrational behavior or unacceptable requests, and this includes the two psychotic women earlier described, who followed through with their treatment, one of them in spite of her otherwise almost complete denial of her illness.

## *The Family After Death Has Occurred*

Once the patient dies, I find it cruel and inappropriate to speak of the love of God. When we lose someone, especially when we have had little if any time to prepare ourselves, we are enraged, angry, in despair; we should be allowed to express these feelings. The family members are often left alone as soon as they have given their consent for autopsy. Bitter, angry, or just numb, they walk through the corridors of the hospital, unable often to face the brutal reality. The first few days may be filled with busywork, with arrangements and visiting relatives. The void and emptiness is felt after the funeral, after the departure of the relatives. It is at this time that family members feel most grateful to have someone to talk to, especially if it is someone who had recent contact with the deceased and who can share anecdotes of some good moments towards the end of the deceased's life. This helps the relative over the shock and the initial grief and prepares him for a gradual acceptance.

Many relatives are preoccupied by memories and ruminate in fantasies, often even talk to the deceased as if he was still alive. They not only isolate themselves from the living but make it harder for themselves to face the reality of the person's death. For some, however, this is the only way they can cope with the loss, and it would be cruel indeed to ridicule them or to confront them daily with the unacceptable reality. It would be more helpful to understand this need and to help them separate themselves by taking them out of their isolation gradually. I have seen this behavior mainly in young widows who had lost their husbands at an early age and were rather unprepared. It may be more frequently encountered in the days of war where death of a young person occurs elsewhere, though I believe a war always makes relatives more aware of the possibility of no return. They are therefore more prepared for that death than, for example, for the unexpected death of a young man through a rapidly progressing illness.

A last word should be mentioned about the children. They are often the forgotten ones. Not so much that nobody cares; the opposite is often true. But few people feel comfortable talking to a child about death. Young children have different concepts of death, and they have to be taken into consideration in order to talk to them and to understand their communications. Up to the age of three a child is concerned only about separation, later followed by the fear of mutilation. It is at this age that the small child begins to mobilize, to take his first trips out "into the world," the sidewalk trips by tricycle. It is in this environment that he may see the first beloved pet run over by a car or a beautiful bird torn apart by a cat. This is what mutilation means to him, since it is the age when he is concerned about the integrity of his body and is threatened by anything that can destroy it.

Also, death . . . is not a permanent fact for the three-to-five-year-old. It is as temporary as burying a flower bulb in the soil in the fall to have it come up again the following spring.

After the age of five death is often regarded as a man, a bogeyman who comes to take people away; it is still attributed to an outward intervention.

Around the ages of nine to ten the realistic conception begins to show, namely, death as a permanent biological process.

Children will react differently to the death of a parent, from a silent withdrawal and isolation to a wild loud mourning which attracts attention and thus a replacement of a loved and needed object. Since children cannot yet differentiate between the wish and the deed . . . they may feel a great deal of remorse and guilt. They will feel responsible for having killed the parents and thus fear a gruesome punishment in retribution. They may, on the other hand, take the separation relatively calmly and utter such statements as "She will come back for the spring vacation" or secretly put an apple out for her—in order to assure that she has enough to eat for the temporary trip. If adults, who are upset already during this period, do not understand such children and reprimand or correct them, the children may hold inside their own way of grieving—which is often a root for later emotional disturbance.

With an adolescent, however, things are not much different than with an adult. Naturally adolescence is in itself a difficult time and added loss of a parent is often too much for such a youngster to endure. They should be listened to and allowed to ventilate their feelings, whether they be guilt, anger or plain sadness.

## Resolution of Grief and Anger

What I am saying again here is, let the relative talk, cry, or scream if necessary. Let them share and ventilate, but be available. The relative has a long time of mourning ahead of him, when the problems for the dead are solved. He needs help and assistance from the confirmation of a so-called bad diagnosis until months after the death of a member of the family.

By help I naturally do not assume that this has to be professional counseling of any form; most people neither need nor can afford this. But they need a human being, a friend, doctor, nurse, or chaplain—it matters little. The social worker may be the most meaningful one, if she has helped with arrangements for a nursing home and if the family wishes to talk more about their mother in that particular set-up, which may have been a source of guilt feelings for not having kept her at home. Such families have at times visited other old folks in the same nursing home and continued their task of caring for someone, perhaps

as a partial denial, perhaps just to do good for all the missed opportunities with Grandma. No matter what the underlying reason we should
try to understand their needs and to help relatives direct these needs
constructively to diminish guilt, shame, or fear of retribution. The most
meaningful help that we can give any relative, child or adult, is to share
his feelings before the event of death and to allow him to work through
his feelings, whether they are rational or irrational.

If we tolerate their anger, whether it is directed at us, at the deceased, or at God, we are helping them take a great step towards acceptance without guilt. If we blame them for daring to ventilate such socially poorly tolerated thoughts, we are blameworthy for prolonging
their grief, shame, and guilt which often results in physical and emotional ill health.

## QUESTIONS

*Looking at Ideas:*

1.  What stages of adjustment does a family pass through as it comes to
    accept the loss of a family member?

2.  According to Ross, what is the most heartbreaking stage for a family
    facing the death of a loved one? Has your family ever experienced such
    a separation? What helped you adjust to the death?

3.  Why does Ross believe that "the most tragic death is—aside from the
    very young—the very old when we look at it from the point of view of
    the family"? Do you agree with her? Why or why not?

4.  Ross thinks that "a patient has a right to die in peace and dignity. He
    should not be used to fulfill our own needs when his own wishes are in
    opposition to ours." Do you agree with Ross? Have you ever had to
    face this decision in your own family?

5.  Why is it especially difficult for young children to cope with the death
    of a loved family member?

6.  What final advice does Ross give to the friends and family of people
    who have lost a loved one?

*Looking at Strategies:*

1.  Discuss several of the examples Ross includes to illustrate her major
    points. Explain why the examples are effective. Would you have liked
    to see her develop more examples or other types of examples?

2.  Characterize Ross's tone. Does her tone encourage you to follow her
    advice? Does it reinforce her credibility? Why or why not?

3.  Many readers are offended by advice books, an increasingly popular
    genre, because such books sometimes simplify complex issues. On the
    other hand, many readers appreciate the information and general
    guidelines that advice books offer. How do you feel about such advice
    books? Judging from this excerpt, do you think Ross's book is a success-
    ful one? Why or why not?

*Looking at Connections:*

1. Elizabeth Kubler-Ross approaches separation and loss from a sociological rather than a personal point of view. What different kinds of insight
   did you gain from this approach as opposed to the fictional treatment of
   separation in works such as "For Jane at Thirteen" or "My Son the Murderer"?

2. Does Ross's explanation help you understand Baldwin's response to his
   father's death? Why or why not?

*Suggestions for Writing:*

1. Write about the death of someone in your family. Consider Ross's explanations and advice. Did the selection help you understand the process of mourning and adjustment that you and your family may have
   experienced? How were you and your family changed by the experience?

2. Write an essay in which you explain how and why a particular film,
   story, song, or essay helped you to understand the process of mourning
   and adjustment that a family goes through when a member dies. (For
   example, many students have been strongly affected by the film *Ordinary People.*)

J. B. Taylor grew up in the Los Angeles area. In his freshman year in college he played for his college's volleyball team; after the completion of his freshman year he began a two-year mission abroad in service of his church. On returning, Taylor plans to major in biology and hopes to attend medical school. He wrote the following essay for his composition class in response to a question that asked students to "Write about an institution or an organization that has some of the characteristics of a family. If you feel that the institution is helping you to become a strong and self-sufficient individual, try to determine what makes it work well and what you have gained from participating in it."

J. B. TAYLOR

# *Teamwork*

The morning air was warm and dry; the distinct smell of dust-covered cactus penetrated my senses. It was 6:15 A.M. and the pitch-black night was reluctantly giving way to a warm, glowing morning. I vividly recall strapping on my worn day-pack, inserting a soothing cassette into my dying Walk-man, and commencing on my morning's journey. As I sleepishly walked up the rock-lined trail, I followed the clear black silhouettes of those who had started before me. That was almost a year ago, but I still remember the overwhelming sense of belonging that I felt that morning. The boys before me were like family, like the closest of brothers; they were my teammates.

That was during Spring break of my senior year, when my high school volleyball team took a trip to Cabo San Lucas, Mexico. While the majority of my friends were at home sleeping in late, playing at the beach all day, and partying at night, the twelve of us and our fearless leader, coach Oz Simmons, had one goal in mind—conditioning. Three times a day, once at dawn, once at high noon, and once at dusk, for seven days straight, we had lengthy, excruciating workouts on the coarse-sand beaches of Mexico. Our physical capabilities were pushed to the extreme. Often, the few hours we had between workouts were utilized for one sole purpose—sleep. At night, we futilely fought off sleep knowing that once the the night was gone, it would seem like only seconds before we were running and sweating again. However, something much more important than physical strength was refined on that trip. There was the birth and creation of a family, an almost ideal family, one which is still intact and treasured by all its members. Moreover, I feel that if most families or organizations modeled themselves after our team, or at least followed some of the basic principles we followed, then then they would function more effectively.

First of all, our family had a distinct leader: our coach Oz. He is the type of coach that every athlete dreams of playing for. I don't think I ever heard him direct a harsh word at a player, but rather he has mastered the "art" of constructive criticism. Oz is one of few people I have ever encountered who simply commands respect. It is not as if he "demands" respect with orders and rules; rather he earns it through his actions and teachings. For instance, Oz made a point of suffering every workout alongside of us. It was difficult to gripe and complain of an unfair coach, when he was panting just as hard as I was and usually ten yards in the lead. Our leader was continually teaching us lessons and principles that will help us in our futures outside of volleyball. For example, following victory or defeat, we had to thank each referee and tournament director before we boarded the bus for home. All families would benefit from a leader of Oz's caliber.

I truly feel that in order for a family to become strong, its members must suffer together as well as share successes. The hardships which a family has encountered are what make it unique. As the twelve of us got on the plane and traveled to the southern tip of Baja California, I know that we were expecting a week of bathing in the intense equatorial sun, with an occasional volleyball drill thrown in. Were we surprised! An aerial observer would have seen our small troupe running backwards down the endless white beaches, swimming for miles in the warm baja waters, scaling the highest of the local mountains in an attempt to reach the peak before the sun did, and doing four thousand, two hundred push-ups and sit-ups (yes, that's six hundred a day!). On our return to Southern California, it was impossible to explain to our friends all we had suffered; in fact, few of us even tried. What we had encountered together had almost become sacred to us. It was what made our family unique and separate from other teams and our individual families within the home. Our shared experiences strengthened our respect for one another, bonded us closer and protected our team family from outsiders and strangers. No one could understand the "little things" we shared, the inside jokes we created, and again, the pain which we had only exposed to one another. This sense of belonging and protection is absolutely imperative if a family is to operate most effectively.

The third ingredient which our ideal family possesses is a silent, mutual understanding of the feelings we share about each other. After observing my own immediate family and the relationships between people outside our team, it appears that sometimes friendships are made "heavy" with displays of affection. Moms and dads will always demand hugs and thank-yous, and sometimes friends will give each other gifts in order to overtly show their friendship. However, within our team, none of this was ever needed, nor was it expected. On a team consisting of twelve players, where only six can play on the court at a time, problems arise because not everyone can compete equally well or at the same time. However, our team overcame this potential obstacle, a problem which I have seen destroy other teams through bickering and backstabbing. Without ever actually discussing the topic, the starters on our team felt a strong sense of support from those who sat on the bench, and in return those who played never really fostered feelings of superiority over those who did not. I felt very grateful to be included in a group of guys where we all assumed unconditional respect and admiration from each other; no uncomfortable "great lengths" were ever needed to display these feelings. In addition to developing this silent and mutual affection, it is imperative that members of a functioning family know, understand, and accept their roles within the team.

Finally, a family, if it is to provide an experience of meaning and value for its members, must have a purpose and a goal, a goal which is directed at serving other families and groups. If I were to make one criticism about my own immediate family, it is that we too often concentrate on what we are doing for ourselves as a family. However, the times that have brought us the closest were those activities in which we served others. I truly felt a sense of "family" the year we took a neighboring home a Christmas tree which I picked out, my mother made the ornaments for, and my sister decorated. Likewise, our volleyball team had one goal which we all worked for—winning volleyball matches. While ostensibly this might solely seem like a self-serving goal, we were in actuality representing our school. After we had left an opponent's gym, few would remember the individuals who played on our team, but many would remember if we won or lost the game that day. When we lost, people were likely to say, "That school was horrible"; when we won, the word was "Dana Hills—what a great school!" Our biggest satisfaction came from pleasing those who came to watch us play, whether they were family members, friends or just people in the community. Similarly, our biggest defeats came not from just losing volleyball matches, but from disappointing our supporters. It is vital for a family or organization to have established goals for which all of its members strive together.

I have always considered our volleyball team as the "ideal family." As a result of this, I have attempted to take some of the lessons I learned from participating in this "family," and have tried to apply them to my own immediate family. I now feel it is important to respect and value the differences between members of a family. Although volleyball was a common bond between our team, we had a diverse group including a science genius, a concert violinist, a "surf rat" and a future Air Force pilot. From this diversity, I have learned to interact with my own family more flexibly and tolerantly. Now, instead of trying to shape my sister's pursuits, I have come to respect her different interests. In addition, I have learned the value of listening. In a "family" of twelve 17-year-old boys, I did not have the same opportunity to control conversations as I did in a home of two parents and two kids.

Furthermore, I have learned to seek supportive family-like groups in other areas. This freshman year, my first "home away from home"

477

experience, I quickly found and helped create a close circle of friends. I am positive my past role in my team "family" helped make the transition year much smoother and more enjoyable. Moreover, I know I will continually be forming new "families" in my life after college; my team experience will definitely aid me in adapting to new surroundings.

I think all of us have "ideal" families which we look up to. They are important and valuable because they are the only means of seeing reasons to make constructive changes in our homes. For me, this ideal was my volleyball team. For others it might be a certain church group, their classroom, or the home of a friend. In my ideal, I saw four characteristics from which I thought all families could benefit. In order to be well functioning, I believe a family must have a distinct leader, must suffer as well as succeed together, and must have a prevailing silent understanding between members in regard to their roles and obligations. Finally, a family must bond together in establishing and conquering goals, preferably goals which serve others.

## QUESTIONS FOR DISCUSSION

1. What role did the intensive physical training and strict leadership of Taylor's team play in bringing the group together as a family? Do you think a family needs this kind of discipline to succeed?
2. Do you agree with Taylor that service to other groups and families is essential to a meaningful family life? Do you think that many of today's families incorporate such idealism into their life-styles?
3. How did Taylor's membership in the team family help him prepare for the smooth transition into life away from home at college? Do you think that participation in team and other intensive extracurricular activities in high school often has this effect of preparing students for college life?
4. How does Taylor organize his essay? Note the thesis statement and the major topic sentences and divisions of his paper. Do you consider it a well-organized and well-developed paper? What advice would you give him for a revision?
5. Working individually or in a group, write a peer critique that includes several supportive comments and several suggestions for strengthening the essay. Comment on the content and writing style.

## Reaching Out: Chapter Activities

1. Create a group of three. Then decide if you will leave off the beginning or the ending of the essay you are working on currently. Bring your essay on a computer disc to a group meeting, leaving out the essay's introduction or conclusion (but being sure to save a complete copy for yourself). Have each group member write an opening or conclusion to the essay (depending on which you've left out) for the other two papers in the group. Print up the two new versions of each essay and compare them to the original versions. When you are finished, discuss what you have learned from this activity. Will you change your introduction or conclusion?

2. Get together with your group and discuss what you see as the major transitions or stages in growing away from one's family. Have one member take notes on the discussion. Then write a collaborative paper in which you include your personal experiences and insights, referring to selections in this chapter and to research done in your library or local bookstore. Your group should decide on how it wants to divide the work of research, analysis, interpretation, and writing. Submit a log of your collaborative process along with your report.

3. Do some research into community organizations that help adolescents and others making major transitions in family life. Check with church groups, youth organizations, and service agencies. Write a short report that introduces the range of organizations in your community and then discuss the ways in which such community organizations can help people trying to adjust to a major change in family life. Would such agencies have helped you at an earlier period in your life? Do you think you might need their services later on? Why or why not? You might decide to volunteer to write for one of the agencies that you have located in your community.

4. See one of the following films either by yourself or with several of your classmates. Write an individual or collaborative review of the film that takes into account the way the film explores themes of separation from the family and the transformation of the family through time.

*Dead Poets' Society.* Dir., Peter Weir. With Robin Williams. 1989.
*Driving Miss Daisy.* Dir., Bruce Beresford. With Dan Aykroyd, Morgan Freeman, Jessica Tandy. 1990.
*The Graduate.* Dir., Mike Nichols. With Dustin Hoffman, Anne Bancroft. 1967.
*Smooth Talk.* Dir., Joyce Chopra. With Laura Derne, Treat Williams. 1985.
*Tell Me a Riddle.* Dir., Lee Grant. With Melvyn Douglas. 1980.

CHAPTER NINE

# Family and Community

*Call it a clan, call it a network, call it a tribe, call it a family. Whatever you*
*call it, whoever you are, you need one. You need one because you are human.*
—Jane Howard, "All Happy Clans are Alike"

*If allowed to become exclusive, engrossing, clannish, so as to shut out the*
*general claims of the human race, the highest end of Providence is frustrated,*
*and home, instead of being the nursery, becomes the grave of the heart.*
—William Everett Channing

*Men and women who have come to understand, in their own intimate*
*settings, the principles of "wholeness incorporating diversity," the arts of di-*
*minishing polarization, the meaning of teamwork and participation, will be*
*far better allies in the effort to build elements of community into the metrop-*
*olis, the nation, the world.* —John W. Gardner, "Building Community"

*A*s Jane Howard asserts, to be human is to seek others, to join with
others in some form of kinship, whether by chance or by choice—
to relate to others, to form, build, and nurture communities. People
seek to balance their individuality, their uniqueness, with the need to be
with others: immediate family, extended family, friends, neighbors, colleagues, and society. In the preceding chapters you have looked at the
family from many perspectives. You have considered memories that
have shaped who you are and how you think of your family and yourself. You have explored the relationships, the rituals, the tensions that
come about because you are human and need other people but are also
an individual in need of personal independence. It is this tension, between the need for individual self-assertion and the need to connect
with the rest of humankind, that drives people to create new kinds of
families and communities, to connect with others while striving to cope
with contemporary society.

The family is not only a way in which you develop and nurture
your private self. It is a way to connect to the larger community—a way
to connect the private self to the public world; a way to balance individual needs with the needs of a larger, public community that in many
ways reflects the relationships of the family. Those who learn the meaning of community close to home will be in the best position to build the
larger, more public versions of community. It is through the family that
people often become familiar with and initiated into the larger world or
community; it is the community that often, in turn, reaches back to
families to foster them and to support them in need. As members of a
community, you are in a position to develop creative solutions for
problems that affect the family and, ultimately, the community itself. In
designing creative solutions and crafting proposals that address the
needs of the family, you are working to build the kind of community
that, as John Gardner notes, exists through "wholeness incorporating
diversity."

In the first chapter reading, "All Happy Clans Are Alike: In Search of the Good Family," Jane Howard broadens the definition of family to include friends and colleagues. Becoming involved in the larger community offers a feeling of belonging and of identity. In "Christmas at Home," P.W. Alexander writes of her family's tradition of service to others during the holidays, and of her childhood frustration with, and gradual acceptance and affirmation of, their tradition. In his poem "For the Student Strikers," Richard Wilbur encourages students involved in campus protest activities to "go talk with those who are rumored to be unlike you." Service to the community is also discussed by Deborah Baldwin in her essay, "Creating Community: A Fast-Food Generation Looks for a Home-Cooked Meal."

At the same time, some aspects of traditional kinship have not only survived, but are thriving—and may hold the key to finding innovative ways to deal with some of the problems of modern American society. In "Self-Help: A Black Tradition," Dorothy Height argues for recognition of the strength in traditional extended black families, while Toni Cade Bambara's story, "My Man Bovanne," points out differing perceptions of what members of the family and community take to be the place of disabled and older people. The last two essays in the chapter are proposals for reaching out to support families in crisis. Mindy Holliday and Robin Cronin, in their article, "Families First: A Significant Step toward Family Preservation," put forth a plan to support families with abused children. In the final essay, "Families Separated by Bars," student writer Howard Libit explores ways of helping families of the incarcerated by balancing the inmate's family's needs with the community's need to punish and segregate criminal offenders.

All of these selections argue, in one way or another, for a view of community and family as being interrelated, as well as for ways in which individuals, families, and communities can work together for comfort, for survival, for the future. The readings articulate ways of exploring the balance between individualism and community—with the family at the center of this balance. As you read and discuss the works of literature, social commentary, and specific proposals for social welfare reform included in "Family and Community," consider how effectively these writers, philosophers, and social activists present ideas that may help solve some of the difficulties families and communities face in contemporary American society. Consider as well what ideas you would put forth to build your own present and future communities.

**JOURNAL ENTRY**

How do you define "family"? Whom or what do you think of when you hear the expression "extended family"?

**JANE HOWARD: "All Happy Clans Are Alike: In Search of the Good Family"**
Jane Temple Howard was born in 1935 in Springfield, Illinois, the daughter of a newspaper reporter. She received her B.A. degree from the University of Michigan in 1956 and worked as a reporter for *Life* magazine from 1958 to 1963. She served as assistant editor at the magazine from 1965 to 1967 and then became a staff writer in 1967. Howard was book critic for *Mademoiselle* from 1974 to 1983; she also has been a visiting lecturer at the University of Georgia, University of Iowa, and Yale University. Howard's work includes examining a wide range of individuals and groups. She has been particularly interested in women's potential and in how women make their own lives. Her major publications include *Please Touch: A Guided Tour of the Human Potential Movement* (1970), *Margaret Mead: A Life* (1984), and *Sunshine and Shadow* (1987). She is also the author of *Families*, published in 1978, from which the following article was excerpted. As you read the following selection, think about how Howard's study of different groups of people has contributed to her outlook on the family.

JANE HOWARD

# All Happy Clans Are Alike

## In Search of the Good Family

Call it a clan, call it a network, call it a tribe, call it a family. Whatever you call it, whoever you are, you need one. You need one because you are human. You didn't come from nowhere. Before you, around you, and presumably after you, too, there are others. Some of these others must matter a lot—to you, and if you are very lucky, to one another. Their welfare must be nearly as important to you as your own. Even if you live alone, even if your solitude is elected and ebullient, you still cannot do without a clan or a tribe.

The trouble with the clans and tribes many of us were born into is not that they consist of meddlesome ogres but that they are too far away. In emergencies we rush across continents and if need be oceans to their sides, as they do to ours. Maybe we even make a habit of seeing them, once or twice a year, for the sheer pleasure of it. But blood ties seldom dictate our addresses. Our blood kin are often too remote to ease us from our Tuesdays to our Wednesdays. For this we must rely on our families of friends. If our relatives are not, do not wish to be, or for whatever reasons cannot be our friends, then by some complex alchemy we must try to transform our friends into our relatives. If blood and roots don't do the job, then we must look to water and branches, and sort ourselves into new constellations, new families.

These new families, to borrow the terminology of an African tribe (the Bangwa of the Cameroons), may consist either of friends of the road, ascribed by chance, or friends of the heart, achieved by choice. Ascribed friends are those we happen to go to school with, work with, or live near. They know where we went last weekend and whether we still have a cold. Just being around gives them a provisional importance in our lives, and us in theirs. Maybe they will still matter to us when we or they move away; quite likely they won't. Six months or two years will probably erase us from each other's thoughts, unless by some chance they and we have become friends of the heart.

Wishing to be friends, as Aristotle wrote, is quick work, but friendship is a slowly ripening fruit. An ancient proverb he quotes in his *Ethics* had it that you cannot know a man until you and he together have eaten a peck of salt. Now a peck, a quarter of a bushel, is quite a lot of salt—more, perhaps, than most pairs of people ever have occasion to share. We must try though. We must sit together at as many tables as we can. We must steer each other through enough seasons and weathers so that sooner or later it crosses our minds that one of us, God knows which or with what sorrow, must one day mourn the other.

We must devise new ways, or revive old ones, to equip ourselves with kinfolk. Maybe such an impulse prompted whoever ordered the cake I saw in my neighborhood bakery to have it frosted to say "HAPPY BIRTHDAY SURROGATE." I like to think that this cake was decorated not for a judge but for someone's surrogate mother or surrogate brother: Loathsome jargon, but admirable sentiment. If you didn't conceive me or if we didn't grow up in the same house, we can still be related, if we decide we ought to be. It is never too late, I like to hope, to augment our families in ways nature neglected to do. It is never too late to choose new clans.

The best-chosen clans, like the best friendships and the best blood families, endure by accumulating a history solid enough to suggest a future. But clans that don't last have merit too. We can lament them but we shouldn't deride them. Better an ephemeral clan or tribe than none at all. A few of my life's most tribally joyous times, in fact, have been spent with people whom I have yet to see again. This saddens me, as it may them too, but dwelling overlong on such sadness does no good. A more fertile exercise is to think back on those times and try to figure out what made them, for all their brevity, so stirring. What can such times teach us about forming new and more lasting tribes in the future?

New tribes and clans can no more be willed into existence, of course, than any other good thing can. We keep trying, though. To try, with gritted teeth and girded loins, is after all American. That is what the two Helens and I were talking about the day we had lunch in a room up in a high-rise motel near the Kansas City airport. We had lunch there at the end of a two-day conference on families. The two Helens were social scientists, but I liked them even so, among other reasons because they both objected to that motel's coffee shop even more than I did. One of the Helens, from Virginia, disliked it so much that she had brought along homemade whole wheat bread, sesame butter, and honey from her parents' farm in South Dakota, where she had visited before the conference. Her picnic was the best thing that happened, to me at least, those whole two days.

"If you're voluntarily childless and alone," said the other Helen, who was from Pennsylvania by way of Puerto Rico, "it gets harder and harder with the passage of time. It's stressful. That's why you need support systems." I had been hearing quite a bit of talk about "support systems." The term is not among my favorites, but I can understand its currency. Whatever "support systems" may be, the need for them is clearly urgent, and not just in this country. Are there not thriving "megafamilies" of as many as three hundred people in Scandinavia? Have not the Japanese for years had an honored, enduring—if perhaps by our standards rather rigid—custom of adopting nonrelatives to fill gaps in their families? Should we not applaud and maybe imitate such ingenuity?

And consider our own Unitarians. From Santa Barbara to Boston they have been earnestly dividing their congregations into arbitrary "extended families" whose members are bound to act like each other's relatives. Kurt Vonnegut, Jr., plays with a similar train of thought in his fictional *Slapstick*. In that book every newborn baby is assigned a randomly chosen middle name, like Uranium or Daffodil or Raspberry. These middle names are connected with hyphens to numbers between one and twenty, and any two people who have the same middle name are automatically related. This is all to the good, the author thinks, because "human beings need all the relatives they can get—as possible donors or receivers not of love but of common decency." He envisions these extended families as "one of the four greatest inventions by Americans," the others being *Robert's Rules of Order,* the Bill of Rights, and the principles of Alcoholics Anonymous.

This charming notion might even work, if it weren't so arbitrary. Already each of us is born into one family not of our choosing. If we're going to devise new ones, we might as well have the luxury of picking the members ourselves. Clever picking might result in new families whose benefits would surpass or at least equal those of the old. As a member in reasonable standing of six or seven tribes in addition to the one I was born to, I have been trying to figure which characteristics are common to both kinds of families.

1. Good families have a chief, or a heroine, or a founder—someone around whom others cluster, whose achievements, as the Yiddish word has it, let them *kvell,* and whose example spurs them on to like feats.

Some blood dynasties produce such figures regularly; others languish for as many as five generations between demigods, wondering with each new pregnancy whether this, at last, might be the messianic baby who will redeem them. Look, is there not something gubernatorial about her footstep, or musical about the way he bangs with his spoon on his cup? All clans, of all kinds, need such a figure now and then. Sometimes clans based on water rather than blood harbor several such personages at one time. The Bloomsbury Group in London six decades ago was not much hampered by its lack of a temporal history.

2. Good families have a switchboard operator—someone who cannot help but keep track of what all the others are up to, who plays Houston Mission Control to everyone else's Apollo. This role is assumed rather than assigned. The person who volunteers for it often has the instincts of an archivist, and feels driven to keep scrapbooks and photograph albums up to date, so that the clan can see proof of its own continuity.

3. Good families are much to all their members, but everything to none. Good families are fortresses with many windows and doors to the outer world. The blood clans I feel most drawn to were founded by parents who are nearly as devoted to what they do outside as they are to each other and their children. Their curiosity and passion are contagious. Everybody, where they live, is busy. Paint is spattered on eyeglasses. Mud lurks under fingernails. Person-to-person calls come in the middle of the night from Tokyo and Brussels. Catcher's mitts, ballet slippers, overdue library books, and other signs of extrafamilial concerns are everywhere.

4. Good families are hospitable. Knowing that hosts need guests as much as guests need hosts, they are generous with honorary memberships for friends, whom they urge to come early and often and to stay late. Such clans exude a vivid sense of surrounding rings of relatives, neighbors, teachers, students, and godparents, any of whom at any time might break or slide into the inner circle. Inside that circle a wholesome, tacit emotional feudalism develops: you give me protection, I'll give you fealty. Such pacts begin with, but soon go far beyond, the jolly exchange of pie at Thanksgiving or cake on a birthday. They mean that you can ask me to supervise your children for the fortnight you will be in the hospital, and that however inconvenient this might be for me, I shall manage to do so. It means I can phone you on what for me is a dreary, wretched Sunday afternoon and for you is the eve of a deadline, knowing you will tell me to come right over, if only to watch you type. It means we need not dissemble. ("To yield to seeming," as Martin Buber wrote, "is man's essential cowardice, to resist it is his essential courage . . . one must at times pay dearly for life lived from the being, but it is never too dear.")

5. Good families deal squarely with direness. Pity the tribe that doesn't have, and cherish, at least one flamboyant eccentric. Pity too the one that supposes it can avoid for long the woes to which all flesh is heir. Lunacy, bankruptcy, suicide, and other unthinkable fates sooner

or later afflict the noblest of clans with an undertow of gloom. Family life is a set of givens, someone once told me, and it takes courage to see certain givens as blessings rather than as curses. It surely does. Contradictions and inconsistencies are givens, too. So is the battle against what the Oregon patriarch Kenneth Babbs calls malarkey. "There's always malarkey lurking, bubbles in the cesspool, fetid bubbles that pop and smell. But I don't put up with malarkey, between my stepkids and my natural ones or anywhere else in the family."

6. Good families prize their rituals. Nothing welds a family more than these. Rituals are vital especially for clans without histories, because they evoke a past, imply a future, and hint at continuity. No line in the seder service at Passover reassures more than the last: "Next year in Jerusalem!" A clan becomes more of a clan each time it gathers to observe a fixed ritual (Christmas, birthdays, Thanksgiving, and so on), grieves at a funeral (anyone may come to most funerals; those who do declare their tribalness), and devises a new rite of its own. Equinox breakfasts can be at least as welding as Memorial Day parades. Several of my colleagues and I used to meet for lunch every Pearl Harbor Day, preferably to eat some politically neutral fare like smorgasbord, to "forgive" our only ancestrally Japanese friend, Irene Kubota Neves. For that and other things we became, and remain, a sort of family.

"Rituals," a California friend of mine said, "aren't just externals and holidays. They are the performances of our lives. They are a kind of shorthand. They can't be decreed. My mother used to try to decree them. She'd make such a goddamn fuss over what we talked about at dinner, aiming at Topics of Common Interest, topics that celebrated our cohesion as a family. These performances were always hollow, because the phenomenology of the moment got sacrificed for the *idea* of the moment. Real rituals are discovered in retrospect. They emerge around constitutive moments, moments that only happen once, around whose memory meanings cluster. You don't choose those moments. They choose themselves." A lucky clan includes a born mythologizer, like my blood sister, who has the gift for apprehending such a moment when she sees it, and who cannot help but invent new rituals everywhere she goes.

7. Good families are affectionate. This of course is a matter of style. I know clans whose members greet each other with gingerly handshakes or, in what pass for kisses, with hurried brushes of jawbones, as if the object were to touch not the lips but the ears. I don't see how such people manage. "The tribe that does not hug," as someone who has been part of many *ad hoc* families recently wrote to me, "is no tribe at all. More and more I realize that everybody, regardless of age, needs to be hugged and comforted in a brotherly or sisterly way now and then. Preferably now."

8. Good families have a sense of place, which these days is not achieved easily. As Susanne Langer wrote in 1957, "Most people have no home that is a symbol of their childhood, not even a definite memory of one place to serve that purpose . . . all the old symbols are

gone." Once I asked a roomful of supper guests if anyone felt a strong pull to any certain spot on the face of the earth. Everyone was silent, except for a visitor from Bavaria. The rest of us seemed to know all too well what Walker Percy means in *The Moviegoer* when he tells of the "genie-soul of a place, which every place has or else is not a place [and which] wherever you go, you must meet and master or else be met and mastered." All that meeting and mastering saps plenty of strength. It also underscores our need for tribal bases of the sort which soaring real estate taxes and splintering families have made all but obsolete.

So what are we to do, those of us whose habit and pleasure and doom is our tendency, as a Georgia lady put it, to "fly off at every other whipstitch?" Think in terms of movable feasts, that's what. Live here, wherever here may be, as if we were going to belong here for the rest of our lives. Learn to hallow whatever ground we happen to stand on or land on. Like medieval knights who took their tapestries along on Crusades, like modern Afghanis with their yurts, we must pack such totems and icons as we can to make short-term quarters feel like home. Pillows, small rugs, watercolors can dispel much of the chilling anonymity of a motel room or sublet apartment. When we can, we should live in rooms with stoves or fireplaces or at least candlelight. The ancient saying is still true: Extinguished hearth, extinguished family.

Round tables help too, and as a friend of mine once put it, so do "too many comfortable chairs, with surfaces to put feet on, arranged so as to encourage a maximum of eye contact." Such rooms inspire good talk, of which good clans can never have enough.

9. Good families, not just the blood kind, find some way to connect with posterity. "To forge a link in the humble chain of being, encircling heirs to ancestors," as Michael Novak has written, "is to walk within a circle of magic as primitive as humans knew in caves." He is talking of course about babies, feeling them leap in wombs, giving them suck. Parenthood, however, is a state which some miss by chance and others by design, and a vocation to which not all are called. Some of us, like the novelist Richard P. Brickner, look on as others "name their children and their children in turn name their own lives, devising their own flags from their parents' cloth." What are we who lack children to do? Build houses? Plant trees? Write books or symphonies or laws? Perhaps, but even if we do these things, there should be children on the sidelines if not at the center of our lives.

It is a sadly impoverished tribe that does not allow access to, and make much of, some children. Not too much, of course; it has truly been said that never in history have so many educated people devoted so much attention to so few children. Attention, in excess, can turn to fawning, which isn't much better than neglect. Still, if we don't regularly see and talk to and laugh with people who can expect to outlive us by twenty years or so, we had better get busy and find some.

10. Good families also honor their elders. The wider the age range, the stronger the tribe. Jean-Paul Sartre and Margaret Mead, to name two spectacularly confident former children, have both remarked on

the central importance of grandparents in their own early lives. Grandparents are now in much more abundant supply than they were a generation or two ago, when old age was more rare. If actual grandparents are not at hand, no family should have too hard a time finding substitute ones to whom to pay unfeigned homage. The Soviet Union's enchantment with day-care centers, I have heard, stems at least in part from the state's eagerness to keep children away from their presumably subversive grandparents. Let that be a lesson to clans based on interest as well as to those based on genes.

Of course there are elders and elders. Most people in America, as David T. Bazelon has written, haven't the slightest idea of what to do with the extra thirty years they have been given to live. Few are as briskly secure as Alice Roosevelt Longworth, who once, when I visited her for tea, showed a recent photograph and asked whether I didn't think it made her look like "a malevolent Eurasian concubine—an *aged* malevolent Eurasian concubine." I admitted that it did, which was just what she wanted to hear. But those of us whose fathers weren't Presidents may not grow old, if at all, with such style.

Sad stories abound. The mother of one friend of mine languished for years, never far from a coma, in a nursing home. Only when her husband and children sang one of her favorite old songs, such as "Lord Jeffrey Amherst," would a smile fleet across her face. But a man I know of in New Jersey, who couldn't stand the state of Iowa or babies, changed his mind on both counts when his daughter, who lived in Iowa, had a baby. Suddenly he took to inventing business trips to St. Louis, by way of Cedar Rapids, phoning to say he would be at the airport there at 11:31 P.M. and "Be sure to bring Jake!" That cheers me. So did part of a talk I had with a woman in Albuquerque, whom I hadn't seen since a trip some years before to the Soviet Union.

"Honey," she said when I phoned her during a short stopover and asked how she was, "if I were any better I'd blow up and *bust!* I can't *tell* you how *neat* it is to put some age on! A lot of it, of course, has to do with going to the shrink, getting uncorked, and of course it doesn't hurt to have money—no, we *don't* have a ranch; it's only 900 acres, so we call it a farm. But every year, as far as age is concerned, I seem to get better, doing more and more stuff I love to do. The only thing I've ever wanted and don't have is a good marriage. Nothing I do ever pleases the men I marry. The only reason I'm still married now is it's too much trouble not to be. But my girls are growing up to be just *neat* humans, and the men they're sharing their lives with are too. They pick nice guys, my girls. I wish I could say the same. But I'm a lot better off than many women my age. I go to parties where sixty-year-olds with blue bouffant hairdos are still telling the same jokes they told twenty-five or thirty years ago. Complacent? No, that's not it, exactly. What they are is sad—sad as the dickens. They don't seem to be *connected*."

Some days my handwriting resembles my mother's, slanting hopefully and a bit extravagantly eastward. Other days it looks more like my father's: resolute, vertical, guardedly free of loops. Both my parents will remain in my nerves and muscles and mind until the day I die, and so will my sister, but they aren't the only ones. If I were to die tomorrow, the obituary would note that my father and sister survived me. True, but not true enough. Like most official lists of survivors, this one would be incomplete.

Several of the most affecting relationships I have ever known of, or been part of, have sprung not from genes or contracts but from serendipitous, uncanny bonds of choice. I don't think enough can be said for the fierce tenderness such bonds can generate. Maybe the best thing to say is nothing at all, or very little. Midwestern preachers used to hold that "a heavy rain doesn't seep into the ground but rolls off—when you preach to farmers, your sermon should be a drizzle instead of a downpour." So too with any cause that matters: shouting and lapel-grabbing and institutionalizing can do more harm than good. A quiet approach works better.

"I wish it would hurry up and get colder," I said one warm afternoon several Octobers ago to a black man with whom I was walking in a park.

"Don't worry," he told me. "Like my grandmother used to say when I was a boy, 'Hawk'll be here soon enough.' "

"What did she mean by 'hawk'?"

"Hawk meant winter, cold, trouble. And she was right: the hawk always came."

With regard to families, many would say that the hawk has long been here, hovering. "I'd rather put up with being lonely now than have to put up with being still more lonely in the future," says a character in Natsume Soseki's novel *Kokoro*. "We live in an age of freedom, independence, and the self, and I imagine this loneliness is the price we have to pay for it." Seven decades earlier, in *Either/Or*, Sören Kierkegaard had written, "Our age has lost all the substantial categories of family, state, and race. It must leave the individual entirely to himself, so that in a stricter sense he becomes his own creator."

If it is true that we must create ourselves, maybe while we are about it we can also devise some new kinds of families, new connections to supplement the old ones. The second verse of a hymn by James Russell Lowell says,

> New occasions bring new duties;
> Time makes ancient good uncouth.

Surely one outworn "good" is the maxim that blood relatives are the only ones who can or should greatly matter. Or look at it another way: go back six generations, and each one of us has sixty-four direct ancestors. Go back twenty—only four or five centuries, not such a big chunk of human history—and we each have more than a million. Does it not

491

stand to reason, since the world population was then so much smaller, that we all have a lot more cousins—though admittedly distant ones—than we were brought up to suspect? And don't these cousins deserve our attention?

One day after lunch at a friend's apartment I waited in his lobby while he collected his mail. Out of the elevator came two nurses supporting a wizened, staring woman who couldn't have weighed much more than seventy pounds. It was all the woman could do to make her way down the three steps to the sidewalk and the curb where a car was waiting. Those steps must have been to that woman what a steep mountain trail would be to me. The nurses guided her down them with infinite patience.

"Easy, darlin'," one nurse said to the woman.

"That's a good girl," said the other. The woman, my friend's doorman told us, was ninety. That morning she had fallen and hurt herself. On her forehead was something which, had it not been a bruise, we might have thought beautiful: a marvel of mauve and lavender and magenta. This woman, who was then being taken to a nursing home, had lived in my friend's apartment building for forty years. All her relatives were dead, and her few surviving friends no longer chose to see her.

"But how can that be?" I asked my friend. "*We* could never be that alone, could we?"

"Don't be so sure," said my friend, who knows more of such matters than I do. "Even if we were to end up in the same nursing home, if I was in markedly worse shape than you were, you might not want to see me, either."

"But I can't imagine not wanting to see you."

"It happens," my friend said.

Maybe we can keep it from happening. Maybe the hawk can be kept at bay, if we give more thought to our tribes and our clans and our several kinds of families. No aim seems to me more urgent, nor any achievement more worthy of a psalm. So *hosanna in excelsis*, and blest be the tie that binds. And please pass the salt.

## QUESTIONS

*Looking at Ideas:*

1. Do you agree that people who are not blood relatives can create a kind of family? What kinds of "family" might college students create?

2. The title of this selection echoes the opening line of Tolstoy's *Anna Karenina:* "All happy families are alike, but unhappy families are unhappy after their own fashion." Do you agree with this sentiment? How does Howard's list of qualities common among good families underscore this assertion? Do you think Howard agrees with the latter part of Tolstoy's statement?

3. What does Howard mean when she says that the best-chosen clans

"endure by accumulating a history solid enough to suggest a future"? Does her statement that transitory families or clans are also valuable necessarily contradict this assertion?

4. Do you agree with Howard's list of the qualities essential in a "happy clan"? Would you add any others?

*Looking at Strategies:*
1. Branches, constellations, and a "moveable feast" are some of the images the author uses. Give examples of other metaphors in the selection and discuss their effectiveness in supporting the author's assertions.
2. What does the author mean when she says, in Paragraph 2, "The two Helens were social scientists, but I liked them even so"? How does this comment help establish the tone of her essay? What other comments help establish tone?
3. Howard uses the term "support system" without explicitly defining it. What do you infer, from her use of the term in this essay, about its meaning? Is its meaning here consistent with your general understanding of the term?

*Looking at Connections:*
1. Howard writes that "good families prize their rituals." Compare Howard's view of myths and rituals with that presented in Bruno Bettelheim's essay, "Magic Days," in Chapter Three.
2. In "The Whispering of the Walls" (Chapter Two) Suzanne Short writes about the negative impact of poor family communication. How does Short's view compare with Howard's beliefs about the role of open communication in family life?

*Suggestions for Writing:*
1. Howard lists several qualities that are good families should have. Write an essay in which you create your own list of the qualities of a good family, clan, or tribe—whether blood relatives or not—and explain why each quality is important.
2. Consider various created families, clans, or associations in your community. Do they represent good families according to Howard's criteria? In an essay, discuss the ways in which a clan may support society as a whole as well as the clan itself.
3. Write a paper in which you discuss the role of children, or posterity, in the family or clan. Is the presence of or access to children equally important in all types of clans?

**JOURNAL ENTRY**

Write about one of your family's holiday traditions. Did the celebration or observance include anyone from outside your immediate family? In what ways did it connect you to the larger community or culture?

**P. W. ALEXANDER: "Christmas at Home"** P. W. Alexander, teacher and writer, was born in South Florida in 1951, one of ten children in a Mexican-American family. She was educated at San Francisco State University, received Montessori training at the University of California, San Diego, and is an advanced graduate student in the School of Education at Stanford University. Besides working as a teacher, she has held a number of jobs, including that of waitress in a Hell's Angels' bar in southern California. She has had a lifelong commitment to public service and has twice received Humanities and Arts Fellowships to develop her own art and that of children in her community. Alexander writes both fiction and nonfiction about love, loss, relationships, and magic. As you read the following essay, consider the ways in which this memoir explores the complex connections between family and community.

P. W. ALEXANDER

# *Christmas at Home*

*"It must have been fun growing up in a big family. I bet the holidays were great."*

I look into the face of the woman standing before me. Her expression is some combination of curiosity, affirmation, and hope. It is a question I hear from time to time and not one as easily answered as asked. I can say, "Oh it was wonderful. We had a house full of people. We laughed, we cried, we fought and we made up. I had lots of sisters to love and to tease and to tell my darkest secrets." It is the second question, I bet the holidays were great, that causes me to hesitate, to look at the asker and wonder how much she really wants to hear.

As a child I did not look forward to the holidays. We have an expectation for holidays here in America. It is family time. We have a Norman Rockwell picture of the clan gathered around a long table, in the center of a comfortably furnished dining room, draped in freshly pressed linen and festooned with candles and flowers. At the center of attention is the huge bird, glistening, beckoning us to overeat. People are smiling. Children are neat, Sunday-best-dressed. It is a hopeful image, and I admit, I too am taken by it. It is a holiday scene that would have fit our family well. We had the well-furnished dining room. We had a long cherrywood table that could seat fourteen, three more chairs

494

than our family needed. We had the yards of lace and linen and the wreaths, candles, centerpieces and china. My parents, however, had some other vision of how the holidays should be spent.

As a young child I simply accepted our family observance of holidays; I knew nothing else. It began with Halloween. In the morning we went to church and in the evening we collected for UNICEF. At first I thought little of the cup of money I brought home that was poured into a large glass jar and eventually spirited away somewhere. As I got older and greedier I began to dislike those nameless, faceless children in countries with odd names pointed out to me on the globe in the library. I wanted to take just one of those dimes and buy a full-size Snickers bar. I was glad when I became "too big" to go out trick or treating.

Thanksgiving and Christmas were equally painful. My mother would sign us all up to work at the soup kitchen. While other families watched televised parades, chased cousins under the piano and yelled at grandma because she had left her hearing aid home, we stood in line and served people from the fringe. We chopped and washed and sliced in the church kitchen. We wore old clothes because the work was messy and we didn't want to "show off." My brother and I were fascinated with the size of the ovens and the number of turkeys that they contained. We carried stacks of plates and bowls and dragged crates of vegetables across the concrete floors. My older brother had the most annoying habit of whistling or humming as he went about his kitchen chores. He was never a part of our kitchen shenanigans. We had games we played between ourselves—who could wash the most forks in one minute, how many cups of coffee could we carry on one tray without spilling. We stuck our fingers in pumpkin pies and covered the damage with whipped cream from a can.

One particularly cold Thanksgiving we were in West Virginia for the school holidays. My father found a place for us to serve. It was snowing hard. People came in long before the meal was ready. I remember them warming their hands on hot cups of coffee. I shivered in the warm church basement. They brought the icy wind inside with them. It was in their thin coats and wet shoes. The image of that red, cracked skin on their hands and faces stayed with me for a long time. I remember how much people would eat, and how quickly. I was scandalized at their table manners. Napkins were often left untouched at the side of their plates. My younger brother, Steven, relished these meals. He delighted in the piles of food and lack of rules. He announced once on the way home, "I ate mashed potatoes—with my fingers!" I had seen people surreptitiously stuffing unwrapped food into their pockets. They never left anything on the plate, not even a polite pea or a genteel stalk of asparagus.

As I got older, I began to ask more questions. Why don't they have homes? Why don't they have food? Why don't they work? And I always asked, WHY do WE have to do this? My mother's response was always the same. The same five words in the same calm, even voice. It was as if she had some perverse tape running inside her head that spewed out the same tired message time after time: "Because we have so much."

The year I was thirteen I thought we would all be saved the embarrassment, the humiliation, the torture of the slave galley. Grandmother was coming from Boston. Grandmother was a lady who always wore gloves. White gloves with little pearl buttons and lacy fingers. Grandmother would never ladle murky soup into plastic bowls or slice great slabs of turkey into scratched beige plates with little compartments. But Grandmother did. She did it with grace and humility. She hugged unwashed people with matted hair and open sores. She shook hands with their red, raw claws and she blessed them. She asked them to pray for her. She wrapped turkey legs in newspaper and openly invited people to take them home. She sat down next to a scruffy little girl and introduced herself as grandma. People smiled at her and showed her all the teeth they didn't have.

That night, my sister Katalina and I snuggled close together in my top bunk and talked long into the night. She often crept up from her bed so we could whisper together after "lights out." We had never spoken much about our service. It was a dreaded event, something to complain about, one more reason to stand by our resolve never to sell our children into indentured servitude. But that night, that Thanksgiving that Grandmother came and took off her white lacy gloves and served gravy to poor people, that night we talked of other things.

We talked about how hard it was not to stare. We knew staring was impolite. These people were so dirty, so poor, and so ugly. If they caught you looking at them they turned away quickly. There was something haunting in their eyes, something of pain and of shame and of sadness. They looked at the floor, at the plate of food heaped before them, at the crucifix on the wall over the table. "They have no dad." My sister Susana cried out in the darkness from her bed on the other side of the room. "Grandmother washed those two boys' hands in the kitchen sink and she sat by them and they told her they had no dad." I squeezed Katalina's hand. *No Dad.* Who took them to the beach, who gave them quarters for the movie, who told them stories at bedtime so they wouldn't have bad dreams?

A month later, at Christmas, Katalina and I gave away our two favorite books to the gift drive our church held. My older brother donated his bicycle and his skates. We didn't put up a tree that year but we did buy one and give it to some people we had read about in the newspaper. Their house and all their presents burned up in a fire.

I work at the homeless shelter and I stand in the serving line and ladle soup and gravy. I shake hands with people who don't bathe and I have on occasion hugged people with dried vomit on their clothing. Three years ago I came home on Thanksgiving with head lice. It is a small part of the job. It is a very small part of the experience. I am in service to my fellow human beings. I do this not out of any sense of duty or obligation, I do it because it is my family tradition. It would not be Thanksgiving or Christmas if I did not stand for a brief moment in front of my closet, gaze at my favorite party frock and feel a slight twinge of regret. It passes very quickly and then I put on my work clothes and I go to the church kitchen to do my service. I see the same hard, lined faces, the same out-of-fashion ragged clothes. I smell the same street dirt and sour alcohol. I hear the same stories of injustice and pain. The people whose eyes I avoided as a child I now seek. I search their faces for some harbinger of hope, some sign of change. If you ask me why I do it, I can only say, because I have so much.

## QUESTIONS

*Looking at Ideas:*

1. What is Alexander's attitude toward her family and toward their tradition? How does her attitude change over time?
2. What kinds of varied relationships between parents and children and between siblings are developed and discussed in the memoir?
3. Contrast the Norman Rockwell image Alexander cites in her essay with the picture you see of her family. Does one or the other image seem more genuinely "American"? How so? Contrast these images with others in the story: the two boys with "no dad," the proper grandmother from Boston.
4. Does the family's service seem based on religion or other moral issues? To what do you attribute their commitment?

*Looking at Strategies:*

1. Alexander uses abundant imagery in her memoir. Select and discuss images that seem particularly vivid to you.
2. What is the tone of the memoir? How does the author convey that tone? Cite examples from the text.
3. How does Alexander incorporate description into her narrative? Are the narrative and descriptive strategies still arguing a point?

*Looking at Connections:*

1. Do Alexander's family and Jane Howard's "clan" have much in common? Discuss both similarities and areas of difference. Would Howard approve of Alexander's family tradition?

*Suggestions for Writing:*

1. Drawing from your journal writing or working through brainstorming and freewriting activities, write a reflective essay on one of your family's traditions. Are there others in the community who share your rituals? What would be the effects of enlarging your family circle for one of your traditions and including others from the community? Would your family prosper by extending the clan, or would including people from outside the immediate family be intrusive?
2. If you live near family members, do some research into the history of your family. Write an essay that presents your family history and ana-

lyzes your family's relationship to the larger community over several generations.

3. Contact a local agency that serves people in need in your community. Find out the agency's needs for volunteers; then write a letter to the editor of your school newspaper arguing for student involvement at this particular agency or for other service organizations in the area.

**RICHARD WILBUR: "For the Student Strikers"**   Richard Wilbur was born
in New York City in 1921, the son of a portrait artist. His grandparents were
both editors and influenced his decision to write. Wilbur received his
B.A. from Amherst College in 1942 and his M.A. from Harvard in 1947. He
served in the U.S. Army Infantry from 1943 to 1945. Wilbur has been a
professor at Harvard University, Wellesley College, and Smith College. His
honors and awards are numerous: he was Poet Laureate of the United
States from 1987 to 1988, received the Pulitzer Prize and National Book
Award in 1957 for *Things of This World* and again won the Pulitzer Prize
in 1989 for *New and Collected Poems*. As you read the following
poem, written during the years of the student protest movement of the late
1960s, notice how Wilbur uses traditional verse forms to reflect on contemporary problems and to advise young people determined to change
society.

RICHARD WILBUR

# For the Student Strikers

(1970)

Go talk with those who are rumored to be unlike you,
And whom, it is said, you are so unlike.
Stand on the stoops of their houses and tell them why
You are out on strike.

It is not yet time for the rock, the bullet, the blunt
Slogan that fuddles the mind toward force.
Let the new sound in our streets be the patient sound
Of your discourse.

Doors will be shut in your faces, I do not doubt.
Yet here or there, it may be, there will start,
Much as the lights blink on in a block at evening,
Changes of heart.

They are your houses; the people are not unlike you;
Talk with them, then, and let it be done
Even for the grey wife of your nightmare sheriff
And the guardsman's son.

# QUESTIONS:

*Looking at Ideas:*

1. Why does the poem's speaker urge students to go to people unlike themselves? Are these people really different? How so?

2. What is your personal response to the poem? Do you find the poem moving or inspiring? Why or why not? Do you feel as if you are being addressed personally?

3. Who is the speaker talking about when he refers to "the grey wife of your nightmare sheriff/And the guardsman's son"? What do those images convey to you?

4. Is the sentiment expressed in the poem still applicable today? How so? Is its applicability limited to college students?

*Looking at Strategies:*

1. How would you characterize the diction in this poem? How does the diction set the tone? How do diction and tone contribute to your response to the poem?

2. Analyze the pauses, sentence lengths, and line stops in the poem; what kinds of speech do they reflect? Why, in the third stanza, is the verb phrase, "there will start/" separated from its complement, "Changes of heart"? What is the effect of delaying "Changes of heart" until the end of the stanza?

3. Why has Wilbur chosen traditional verse forms to embody the message and images in the poem? How persuasive would the poem be if it were written using the kind of free verse that was popular on campuses in the late 1960s?

4. What do you infer from the phrase, "the blunt/Slogan that fuddles the mind toward force"? What attitudes does this phrase reveal? Why is this phrase juxtaposed with "the rock, the bullet"?

*Looking at Connections:*

1. Relate the notion of making connections between students and others in the community to Gardner's quote in the chapter introduction about "wholeness incorporating diversity."

2. Compare the speaker's urging of a realistic, practical approach to effecting social change with the perspective on community organizing implied in Toni Cade Bambara's "My Man Bovanne," later in this chapter.

*Suggestions for Writing:*

1. Contact a public service agency, volunteer office on campus, or school newspaper and interview workers about the current state of student involvement and activism on your campus. Write an essay in which you try to explain why student activism has either increased or declined in recent years.

2. In a letter or article, argue for a cause or principle you believe in and urge others to join you. Explain what steps need to be taken to get people involved in your cause. You could address the campus newspaper, a local paper, the members of a campus organization, or other youth group.

3. Rewrite your argument for a cause or principle in the form of a poem. As Wilbur does, write your argument in the form of an exhortation.

**DEBORAH BALDWIN: "Creating Community: A Fast-Food Generation Looks for a Home-Cooked Meal"**   Deborah Baldwin was born in 1949 in Washington, D.C. She received her B.A. from the University of Pennsylvania in 1970 and her M.A. from the University of Oregon in 1973. She has worked as an editor since 1974, and she became editor and vice president of *Common Cause* magazine in 1987. Baldwin has written essays questioning the U.S. government and its aims and relations with other countries. She is also interested in issues of society, including what influences our involvement and how we respond to our environment. Her articles about social change include a profile of John W. Gardner which appeared in *Common Cause,* as did the following article, "Creating Community: A Fast-Food Generation Looks for a Home-Cooked Meal." As you read the article, consider how Baldwin views community in the context of social involvement and activism.

DEBORAH BALDWIN

# Creating Community

## A Fast-Food Generation Looks for a Home-Cooked Meal

Members of the so-called baby-boom generation spent the last two decades on the move, like migratory birds on a flight pattern tuned to the everchanging socio-economic winds. Now, say the pundits, an entire generation has a vague longing to settle down and be part of something—like a community.

Some symptoms of the nascent desire among baby boomers to flock together:

· Many once-mobile midlifers indicate signs of work-related burnout. Beginning to wonder what it all means, they are casting for ways to contribute to the commonweal, strengthening their ties to communities in the process. Volunteerism, which dipped in the 1980s, is back where it was and expected to rise.

· Families are beginning to stay put, presumably bound to their current roosting places by jobs and schools.

· As their offspring enter school, baby boomers feel compelled to get involved in one of the most visible of all community institutions.

501

· An absence of leadership in Washington—which turned its back on many social needs during the '80s—is forcing attention back to the community level.

· Other symptoms of America's craving for connections: Computer networks, which conquer distance and loneliness in the great tradition of the ham radio, are springing up across the country. Call-in TV and radio talk shows, which enable complete strangers to share their most intimate secrets, proliferate.

· The popular culture is beginning to reflect interest in community and self-improvement of the helping-others kind. The 1985 bestseller, *Habits of the Heart: Individualism and Commitment in American Life,* which explored personal and social values in America, is still selling well. More recent titles include *The Hunger for More: Searching for Values in an Age of Greed* and *The Brighter Side of Human Nature: Altruism and Empathy in Everyday Life.*

Because baby boomers—numbering an estimated 76 million—represent such a sizable chunk of the buying population, their perceived longing for human ties is already reflected on Madison Avenue, where ads for beer ("Miller Time") and Big Macs ("Food, Folks and Fun") feature warm images of friends and community. Television programming, too, which some media critics view as an extension of advertising, is increasingly sensitive to these themes; "Twin Peaks" got a lot of attention partly because it evoked people's fantasies about homespun small-town America and then blew them apart.

Some of the shameless sentiment being exploited on prime-time TV may be part of an inchoate nostalgia for a world that not only isn't what it used to be, but probably never was. At the same time, the imagery seems to reflect a palpable yearning for new ways of viewing the world and the individual's place in it.

The purported rebirth of the great American community poses a number of interesting questions, among them: How will community be defined in the 1990s? Are baby boomers willing to work to create and maintain communities—or will the concept remain an object of their fantasies? And if new kinds of communities are in fact springing up, what are the implications for political candidates and causes?

## *The Schmooze Factor*
The tension between individualism and community is intrinsic to American culture. More than 150 years ago, French social philosopher Alexis de Tocqueville referred to the "thousand different types" of associations in colonial America that formed a bridge between individual self-interest and the community at large; the authors of *Habits of the Heart* (a phrase borrowed from Tocqueville) cite his belief that, through associations, Americans bonded to wider political communities and developed a sense of responsibility for the public good. Periodically—actually, most of the time—these highminded impulses lose out to the equally powerful forces of entrepreneurship and personal mobility.

Given the cyclical nature of such things, it perhaps isn't surprising that after the mass group effort of World War II brought many Americans together, the advent of suburbia drove many of them apart. "Bedroom communities"—economically and racially segregated clusters of homes and schools—sprang up around the country and were communities only in the loosest sense. People moved constantly; to this day, one out of 10 homes changes hands every year.

As early as the 1950s, sociologist Robert Nisbet deplored America's changing physical and social landscape, saying it had profound ramifications for the democratic system. In his book *The Quest for Community,* first published 37 years ago and reissued this year, Nisbet asserted that the erosion of traditional family authority, neighborhoods and local community led to the citizenry's alienation and dependence on remote, centralized governmental powers.

Refugees from congested city neighborhoods and claustrophobic small towns rarely looked back, however. They focused on acquiring and maintaining their own high-quality private space—which 50s-era suburbs offered in abundance. Ensconced in roomy homes equipped with two-car garages, the middle class enjoyed a vast array of consumer products designed to make cocooning an increasingly feasible way of life.

The suburb has become a symbol of isolationism, but it occurred within cities too. At one time Chicago, Boston, New York and other cities were made up of racial and ethnic enclaves where people had at least nodding acquaintances with one another and shared some public space—if not town squares then crowded stores and sidewalks. Today the typical inner-city neighborhood is slapped with labels like "transition" or "gentrified," based on the number of yuppies who dwell there.

Starting in the '70s, dual-income couples divided their loyalties between workplace and home. By the 1980s, a period of rampant individualism, upper-income dwellers of inner cities and suburbia alike found they could enjoy all the conveniences of a fully equipped kitchen, laundromat, movie theater and rec room in the comforts of home, with only occasional forays to stock the shelves and refuel the car. With the more recent addition of a fitness center, VCR and computer-equipped office to the home environment, one could really feel alone.

Now that the pendulum is starting to swing slightly, living in style has become a symbol of loss as much as gain. As one radio commentator recently noted, we now have a society where people learn the meaning of community by sitting in front of the tube watching the neighborhood-bar comedy "Cheers." A similarly poignant image—of a lonely yuppie running on a treadmill in front of the TV set because he doesn't have the sense to don his coat and walk to a neighborhood bar or diner —was offered in a recent issue of the alternative magazine *Utne Reader* by a 40something who deplored his generation's disconnectedness.

The repressed urge to mingle has never completely disappeared and surfaces in curious ways. Gregarious individuals like to vacation in

503

quaint places like New Hope, Pa., Nantucket, Mass., and Key West, Fla., where they can practically ruin a place walking around wishing they lived there. Town planner Andres Duany goes so far as to theorize that families flock to Disneyland not for the rides but for an opportunity to rub shoulders with other human beings in a pleasant, traffic-free environment.

Duany believes suburbanites in particular are tyrannized by their long, lonely commutes, which force them to spend most of their free time—he also calls it "political time"—in hermetic capsules. "You have a certain amount of free time in the day," he explained in a radio interview earlier this year, "and in a town you might go to a corner store and discuss the issues of the day with other people like you."

Duany belongs to a school of community enthusiasts that includes Ray Oldenburg, author of a paean to the endangered community watering hole called *The Great Good Place*. Oldenburg says bars, corner stores, barbershops and the like are essential to the democratic process because they engender face-to-face grassroots involvement. "Television has obscured that need," he notes dryly, "but it has not obviated it."

The notion that the 1990s may usher in new definitions of community—to encompass extended families, friends, coworkers and even radio call-in show audiences—strikes Oldenburg as pathetic. "Can we really create a satisfactory community apart from geography?" he asks. "My answer is 'no.'"

"I'm aware of networking and how it helps careers and workplaces," he says, "but these are going in the wrong direction." Part of the problem: Professional networks shut out children, for whom community ties can be especially meaningful. In an effort to help raise his own sons' consciousness, the Pensacola, Florida-based sociology professor took them to his home town of Henderson, Minnesota, population 740, where they ordered dime phosphates at an old-fashioned drugstore.

As community meeting places go, so go town criers. More than 7,000 American cities have no daily newspaper of their own, according to media critic Ben Bagdikian's seminal book *The Media Monopoly*. He views the concomitant decentralization of America and rise of the homogenized, monopolized, consumer-driven mass media as one of the biggest threats to our political way of life. While citizens vote in 20,000 urban and rural places around the country, he points out, they are served by media "organized on the basis of 210 television 'markets,' which is the way merchandisers and media corporations sell ads."

While some small-town refugees might question the level of political discourse that typically occurs in the pages of community newspapers, few would disagree with Duany's description of how most Americans gather information about the outside world: at home, after an exhausting day at work, in front of the TV. "Politics becomes extraordinarily primitive because there is no room for discussion," he maintains, "It's what you're fed by the media."

To qualify as a community, a town or city should be able to pass the so-called "South American Revolution Test," Duany says: "When you hear that the revolution has started, do you know exactly where to go, or do you have to go to the TV set to find out where people are gathering?"

## The Community Redefined

During the 1950s and '60s, college and careers scattered young people across the country, far from immediate family and childhood friends. But, as Oldenburg suggests, the Tocquevillian urge to congregate and associate never disappeared. Definitions of "community" simply changed. Suburban-bred students formed urban and rural communes. Or they gravitated to the antiwar, women's and civil rights movements, which in a sense were communities based not on locale but shared values and goals. During the '90s, some social trendwatchers believe, the same overwhelming urge to join will drive aging yuppies off their treadmills and into the streets. Or at least so the theory goes.

The resurgence of interest in communities is often cast not only as a reaction to the Me Generation's flitting mobility and the sterility of its surroundings but also to the spiritual emptiness of the 1980s, commonly referred to as the Decade of Greed. "After a virtual orgy of individualism, Americans may finally be rejecting the idea that the best things in life come from looking out for No. 1," Suzanne Gordon, author of *Lonely in America,* wrote earlier this year.

Turn-of-the-decade commentators take hope from the statistics. The Boston-area branch of United Way attracted two and a half times more volunteers in 1989 than in 1988, according to a spokesperson. She notes a trend toward involvement in one-time, short-term projects—possibly a reflection of the hectic lives and short attention spans of many midlifers.

Perhaps as significant as trends like these are people's perceptions of them: While Gallup Poll data shows that volunteerism increased gradually during the 1980s, the level in late 1989 was about the same as it was before Bush took office amid all the fanfare about points of light. Nonetheless, the polling group reported, four in 10 Americans think the spirit of volunteerism in their communities is on the rise.

Rhetoric often precedes action, but in some cases it can replace it entirely; after all, it's a good deal easier to talk about the need for community and helping others than to do something about it. President George Bush seemed to get the words right in his inaugural speech, saying, "We cannot hope only to leave our children a bigger car, a bigger bank account. We must hope to give them a sense of what it means to be a loyal friend; a loving parent; a citizen who leaves his home, his neighborhood and town better than he found it." But for some reason those words sound hollow compared to President John Kennedy's ringing call for citizen involvement, "ask not what your country can do for you. . . ." which helped lead thousands of Americans into public service.

505

Maybe life was simpler then. Certainly, people believed they had more time and fewer obligations. "The biggest contradiction is that people would like to be active, but in most households both adults are working," says Jerry Hagstrom, author of *Beyond Reagan: The New Landscape of American Politics.* "My suspicion is that you'll see more involvement as people grow older. But you have to ask if it's in their own interest. . . . People are very active with schools because they have kids in them. Organizations through which they gain no personal benefit? I'm not so sure."

In the wry essay in *Utne Reader* mentioned earlier, writer Brad Edmondson points out that real community work means giving something up, and that's hard. He seems to capture his age group's ambivalence, noting, "We're passionate about community issues, but forever thinking about moving away to get a better job, more money or some other abstraction. The state of being in one place and thinking about another is our natural habitat."

Edmondson ends up predicting that during the '90s "more and more people will be in a position to join real communities instead of pining after imaginary ones," but not because he believes yuppies' politics will suddenly change. Rather, baby boomers are getting older, and older people don't move around so much.

## Rethinking the '80s

Meanwhile, were the '80s as bad as some people think?

At least one social interpreter, Mark Satin, the iconoclastic editor of the political newsletter *New Options,* says no. "I guess I'm not sophisticated enough to see things correctly," he wrote early this year with self-conscious irony. "I liked the 1980s. . . . In the '80s we laid the groundwork for realizing the longings that were first brought to mass consciousness in the '60s. All kinds of strains are waiting to be hot-wired, now, by a new social movement."

Satin maintains that a new cultural archetype emerged during the '80s, "the caring individual," or one who is equally committed to self-development and social change, to individual freedom and social justice. A true grassroots democracy, he argues, requires these personally and socially responsible individuals.

Satin is heartened by the fact that many potential grassroots activists are now in their 40s or older, their "public years," in the words of Virginia Hodgkinson, who tracks national trends in volunteerism and charitable giving at the Washington-based Independent Sector. The public years typically follow two decades of absorbed careerism and childrearing and can be a fertile time for personal growth and social commitment, Hodgkinson and others believe. Her latest research indicates that midlifers and seniors are increasingly active in community organizations, but not necessarily because they are nearby. Rather, they tend to pitch in at places they are attracted to ideologically. (To accommodate volunteers from outside the neighborhood, Hodgkinson suggests churches and other community centers build big parking lots.)

For many baby boomers and their younger siblings, there's an added inducement—the memory of the '60s. One opinion poll of people in their 30s that showed 61 percent viewed the '60s as a constructive period and 51 percent missed the sense of community that existed back then.

During the '70s and '80s, says Satin, "They were digging in for the long haul, by getting the degrees and establishing their careers. Now they're able to go out in the world and have an impact."

Just as he rejects the "media caricatures" of the '80s, he rejects some of the romanticization of the 1960s. An antiwar activist who fled to Canada to organize similarly disaffected Americans, Satin, now 43, recalls the era as divisive and judgmental, with too much emphasis on us-vs.-them. "I hope what we're moving toward is an integration of individualism and community with acceptance of the diversity in our society," he says.

Unlike Oldenburg and others, Satin is uninterested in bringing back small-town America, with its Main Streets lined with barbershops and bars. "I've lived in small towns," he says flatly, alluding to a childhood in small-town Minnesota and a more recent two-year stopover in tiny Winchester, Va. "It was boring."

Characterizing the notion of neighborhoods and geographical communities as "totally unrealistic," Satin says we tend to forget that the people who held together traditional communities were women. He credits the women's movement and other positive social changes for making traditional communities "impossible" and says even urban ethnic communities have been romanticized. "I suspect most of the city neighborhoods written about nostalgically were in transition. People were bound together by wanting to move up and out; their vivid, warm memories are of people similar to them, who were also eager to move on."

Others agree that it's a mistake to idealize the past. "We can never bring the traditional community back," social philosopher John Gardner wrote in the *Kettering Review* last year. "The traditional community was homogeneous. We live with heterogeneity and must design communities to handle it." The author of books on leadership, self-renewal and other topics, Gardner added, "The traditional community commonly demanded a high degree of conformity. Because of the nature of the world we live in, our communities must be pluralistic and adaptive, fostering individual freedom and responsibility within a framework of group obligation."

Many community advocates nonetheless like the idea of having some sort of physical meeting place where all these diverse individuals can assemble, if more along the lines of a town hall than a corner store. In this kind of setting, Satin argues, participatory democracy, the kind that features face-to-face communication, can begin to flourish.

### Armchair Activists

Others, however, seek society at the computer terminal. All it takes is a personal computer, special software, a telephone line and a funny little box called a modem, which enables one computer to connect to another. Viewed by some as a panacea for citizens who, by design or default, are isolated geographically, socially or politically, electronic networks enable like-minded individuals to hold "conferences," share information and organize political campaigns.

While some computer illiterates find the technology intimidating, advocates see it as a warm, user-friendly way to give anyone who wants an opportunity to participate. "I happen to think the advent of new technologies, like cable TV and electronic networks, makes grassroots democracy a lot more viable than it ever has been," says Roger Craver, a fundraising expert who communicates mostly in writing and cheerfully admits he learned the significance of the electronic media by watching how his teenagers absorb information. (One observer has dubbed this multimedia process "paraliterate osmosis.") Craver says people are getting used to communicating by leaving messages and picking up threads of conversation on their computers, hashing things out electronically instead of in person.

"The sense of community is now multi-dimensional," he believes. "While the fear is that [computers] subvert the interpersonal capacity, the fact that they are physically remote increases people's candor and willingness to share."

It's either the most exciting thing to come along since Tom Paine's printing press—or a classic couch potato's idea of getting involved. Either way, computer communities are spreading, spawning their own lingo and tribal customs. Some are tiny, while others boast so many members they can afford a professional system operator ("sysop") to manage the flow of information and edit it for usefulness.

One of the biggest and best-known grew out of the Hands Across America anti-hunger campaign, which put up $140,000 to help get it started. Apple also donated free training and $500,000 worth of computers and modems—no doubt in the hopes that such enterprises would grow and multiply.

Based in Santa Cruz, Calif., HandsNet was launched in late 1987 to help disparate anti-hunger groups learn from one another's successes and failures. Subscribers get the latest in antipoverty news and activities—all without the bother of paper and postage: "E-Mail" (electronic mail) does away with letters and telephone tag, and an "on-line" library generates data. "The main thing is the feeling of community," says network editor Susan Dormanen. "There's a national constituency [for antipoverty efforts] and it's a real empowering feeling for people, especially for small groups, to have access to all this information."

Other examples include SeniorNet, a San Francisco-based effort to break the isolation of computer-phobic senior citizens. It offers opportunities to "socialize" and classes in "electronic citizenship," or the art of applying pressure by modem.

Then there's SCARCNet, short for the Smoke Control Advocacy Resource Center Network, an anti-tobacco campaign run out of the Advocacy Institute in Washington. It comes with an international counterpart aimed at pressuring the U.S. to stop marketing cigarettes overseas. Both, says manager Nancy Stefanik, serve what she calls "the smoking control community."

No one knows how many electronic forums there are, although Tom Sherman, of the five-year-old Electronic Networking Association, guesses there are "thousands." Not surprisingly, ENA has no physical headquarters and issues its newsletter, "Netweaver," by computer.

One of the more intriguing experiments in computer communications is taking a trial run in hip Santa Monica, Calif. Its Public Electronic Network is free to all 95,000 residents, who can jump on-line to read city files, including the City Council's agenda, hold informal town meetings and accept and receive private E-mail.

The PEN system has been an overnight success, says a spokesperson, who scanned her computer files to identify the number of "accesses" during one recent month (7,095). She says residents have used PEN to debate such hot issues as rent control and the proposed construction of a new hotel. Some City Council members use it to gauge public opinion, although they are barred from using PEN to send out the electronic equivalent of franked junk mail.

Many Santa Monicans already own computers, but for those who don't, the city hopes to install terminals in the one place that might be thought of as where to go during the next revolution: the local shopping mall.

## QUESTIONS

*Looking at Ideas:*

1. How does the "tension between individualism and community" affect Americans' involvement in public life?
2. According to the article, what is the role of public meeting places in a democracy? What examples of meeting places does Baldwin mention?
3. How might "the caring individual" be described? How could that individual find a way to resolve the tension between self-interest and interest in the greater community?
4. How has the women's movement affected traditional communities? How do you think communities need to change to accommodate changes in women's lives?
5. In what ways has technology changed the way we think about community? Overall, have these changes been good or bad for society?

*Looking at Strategies:*

1. Baldwin is writing for a nonacademic audience. How does this affect her method of documenting her sources? How would you cite such sources for an academic essay?
2. How and where does Baldwin weave her cited material into the fabric of the essay? Where does she summarize? Where does she quote the speaker or author directly? How well do the quotes work to convey important points succinctly?

3. Although the author conveys a great deal of information from a number of different sources, she maintains a personal voice in the essay. Cite an example from the text where you get the sense of a real person behind the prose.

4. Baldwin did extensive research for her article. Where do you think she got most of her information? Interviews? Readings? Other sources?

5. How effective is the metaphor in the article's subtitle?

*Looking at Connections:*

1. Consider the statement quoted in this essay that, "professional networks shut out children." How does this statement relate to Jane Howard's claim that children are essential to a "happy clan"?

*Suggestions for Writing:*

1. Research the state of involvement and volunteerism in your community. Interview civic leaders, community agency directors, and others. Find out who gets involved and why. Write a documented report for an agency seeking involvement from more members of the community. Alternatively, write a letter to the editor arguing for more civic involvement.

2. Write an essay in which you argue either for or against Baldwin's thesis that the children of the baby boom are becoming more socially committed and active in their communities. Use examples drawn from your readings on the subject and from discussions and interviews with people in this age group (late thirties and forties).

3. Interview people in your age group to find out their feelings about and expectations of becoming involved in public service work. Write a research paper based on your interviews in which you try to draw some conclusions about the level of public commitment among the people you have interviewed.

<table>
<tr><td>

**JOURNAL ENTRY**

Whom do you include when you consider your own extended family?
Write about the different degrees of kinship you feel with various members
of your "clan."

</td></tr>
</table>

**DOROTHY I. HEIGHT: "Self-Help—A Black Tradition"**    Dorothy I. Height
was born in 1910 in Richmond, Virginia. She was educated at New York University, where she took her M.A., and at the New York School of Social Work.
A civil rights activist, Height worked with the New York City Welfare Department and served as Director of the Center for Racial Justice. A national president of the National Council of Negro Women, Inc., Height also served as
consultant on African Affairs to the Secretary of State and on the President's
Commission on the Status of Women. Height has received numerous awards,
including the Distinguished Service Award from the National Conference on
Social Welfare in 1971. As you read the following article, originally published
in *The Nation,* think about the ways in which the African-American tradition
of the extended family could be a useful model for other groups as well.

DOROTHY HEIGHT

# Self-Help—A Black Tradition

*It is our task to make plain to ourselves the great story of our rise in Amer-
ica from "less than dust" to the heights of sound achievement. . . . The situation we face must be defined, reflected and evaluated.*
                                        —Mary McLeod Bethune, 1937

Recent negative portrayals of the black family have made it painfully clear to most African-Americans that although much has changed
in the national life, much remains the same. The incessant emphasis on
the dysfunctioning of black people is simply one more attempt to show
that African-Americans do not really fit into the society—that we are
"overdependent" and predominantly welfare-oriented. Quite overlooked in this equation is the fact that most black Americans are, on the
contrary, overwhelmingly among the *working* poor.

Equally overlooked when the disingenuous topic of the supposed
lack of black "self-help" is conjured up, is a fundamental truth: that the
major energies of black people in America historically have had to be
directed to attaining the most elementary human freedoms (such as
owning one's own body and the fruits thereof) that our white sisters
and brothers take for granted. The civil rights movement of the 1950s
and 1960s was perhaps the most extraordinary example of a mass

511

"self-help" movement in American history: self-help mounted under grave conditions to throw off the yoke of American apartheid. Yet it was not a new event so much as the continuation of an old tradition. Since the end of the slave era black people have had to provide services for one another in every conceivable way: feeding and clothing the destitute; tending the sick; caring for orphaned children and the aged; establishing insurance companies, burial societies, travelers' accommodations when hotels were segregated—the list goes on.

In 1909, almost fifty years before the modern civil rights movement emerged, the National Association for the Advancement of Colored People (preceded by the Du Bois–organized Niagara Movement) was founded following the lynching of a black man in Springfield, Illinois. Its first major undertaking was the fight against the hundreds of such atrocities then occurring annually. The Urban League was founded the next year to advance economic self-help.

Eighteen years earlier, a fearless journalist named Ida B. Wells began a crusade against lynching, by lecturing, organizing and compiling the first documentation of the social, political and economic facts behind the atrocities. In 1895, the National Association of Colored Women's Clubs was formed to bring to bear the collective strength of women in ameliorating the desperate conditions in which our people lived.

What is clear to us in the current era of ever mounting disparagement of the black family—and the internalizing by our young people of the negativism thrust upon them daily—is that we need a movement that will retrieve and build upon the value system of the traditional extended family, the strong sense of kinship ties that goes back to the days of the trans-Atlantic slave trade, when it was up to us either to forge ties of mutual support or perish as a people. Those unbreakable bonds sent people searching for one another after the forced separations of slavery. They are still evident in our custom of calling one another brother and sister—and mother, aunt and uncle—even when there is no blood relationship. There's an entire history behind these interactions that is precious to our sense of self-worth and identity as a people. Those who attempt to supplant our conception of ourselves with their own are either ignorant of this proud history or, worse, bent on concealing or eradicating it.

The history of self-help among blacks offers models that will be useful in the search for innovative approaches to current problems. For instance, I recall that in 1939, when I worked in the Harlem Y.W.C.A., the Florence Crittendon Homes took in unmarried white mothers, but there was not a bed in the city for unwed black mothers. The only help available to them was in the limited facilities the Y.W.C.A. could provide. To supplement these we found some black women who belonged to an organization called Club Caroline and who were able to acquire a small house to shelter unwed mothers. Their example was followed by black women's clubs all over the country, whose members formed a national network of assistance, keeping registers of people who were willing to take in a young mother. Economic realities today make it impossible for black people to set up enough small homes to accommodate the large numbers of single mothers, drug addicts, the jobless and homeless, and the thousands of un-claimed black infants languishing in hospitals and foster homes.

Nevertheless, we can learn something from the methods used by the traditional black extended family in which adults possessed the authority to look out for the young, whether or not they were blood relatives. We may not be able to restore entirely the old concept of the extended family, given the present complex (and chaotic) social, political and economic conditions in the large urban centers. But enough of it survives to draw upon in encouraging more caring communities in which neighbors look around them to see what's happening and set up networks for alerting others to impending threats. It is important for our young people to know that our past holds valuable traditions. Black sociologists have not been alone in pointing out that instead of constantly focusing on the problems of black families, their white counterparts should examine its historic strengths: the respect for older people, the communal nurturing of children, the ability to feed an entire family on next to nothing, the unceasing toil of parents (often assisted by the community) to send their children through college, the black entrepreneurs who built up businesses to serve our needs after others refused to. In short, our endless coping skills.

We have always stressed the work ethic. We have never been a lazy people; hard work has killed a great number of us. A. Philip Randolph, president of the Brotherhood of Sleeping Car Porters, used to say that what black folk needed was not more work but more pay for the work that they do, and they could manage the rest. It is only recently in the cities, where higher skills are required and the quality of education has deteriorated, that unemployment and the grimmest kind of poverty have become constants and whole generations are growing up in neighborhoods where few people have jobs.

Some social analysts are correct when they say that public policies had a great deal to do with producing this state of affairs, but they refuse to acknowledge the impact of racial discrimination on education and employment. They define a "family" as a social/economic/political unit with a man at its head, and they continue to insist on this definition even at a time when divorce rates and serial marriages, resulting in merged families and increasing numbers of female-headed households, reveal how archaic it is.

For black people, this definition has never applied. Black traditions of the extended family grew out of the primary need to survive, an urgency that for the most part made gender differentials largely irrelevant. So did the grim economic realities that traditionally necessitated that both black men and women work in order to earn a decent living for their families—or, for that matter, to make their way at all. That throughout history many black women have had to accomplish these things without male partners consistently at our sides is much more the result of the racism that limits—and frequently destroys—black males than of "immorality" (as white scholars could discern, if they ever deigned to do research in this area).

513

Blacks have never said to a child, "Unless you have a mother, father, sister, brother, you don't have a family." I think that the wrongheaded emphasis on the nuclear family has led to the demoralization of young people, both white and black. Because of it, a child who is not part of a nuclear family—or whose family does not behave in the manner of the model—may well say, "I'm nobody."

## The N.C.N.W. and the Black 'Family Celebrations'

For fifty-four years the National Council of Negro Women—composed of civic, church, educational, labor, community and professional organizations uniting 4 million members—has carried on the tradition of black self-help. We at the N.C.N.W., following in the footsteps of our founder, the indefatigable educator Mary McLeod Bethune, have focused attention on the concerns of black women and their families. On behalf of young black people, the N.C.N.W. has taken counteractions aimed at restoring or bolstering collective self-esteem in order to lift the morale of the people in coping with the problems they face, whether related to drugs, education, teen-age pregnancy, employability, health problems or whatever they might be.

In recent years we at the N.C.N.W. have built on the special tradition of black "family celebrations" to bring people together. In 1986 we sponsored the first Black Family Reunion Celebration, held on the Washington Mall with almost 200,000 people in attendance. In 1987 three others followed, in Washington, Los Angeles and Detroit. In 1988 a coming-together was celebrated in Philadelphia and again on the Washington Mall in what had become a national movement.

So far, nearly 2 million African-Americans have flocked to the black family celebrations, a turnout that attests to the hunger of our people to hear something other than the constant negativism that is directed our way, to gain strength and inspiration from one another and, in many cases, to secure advice or help from someone we can trust. We have used these occasions to stress black history and the tradition of helping one another, qualified by our awareness that we now live in a society and world that is vastly different from the simpler times in which our sense of community—whatever threatened us—was intact.

In these celebrations, the N.C.N.W. stresses what we consider to be genuine family values. Coretta Scott King shared what it has meant to be a single mother for all the years since her husband's assassination. She spoke not as the wife of a martyred leader but as the mother of children whom she had to bring up alone. We regularly have Masons come to talk about their early history and how they have contributed to the building of their communities. We have celebrities galore, but we also have young people rapping about teen-age pregnancy, drugs or whatever is their most urgent concern. And we also provide allied services. In Washington, when the D.C. Drugmobile was brought to the Mall, the lines before it were as long as those before the black film festival. The impact of our offerings has been felt in the public schools, where teachers report that in the week following the reunion celebration, children flock to school eager to make reports on their activities. All because we have a children's pavilion with black history puppets and African and African-American storytelling.

The N.C.N.W. also offers health checks. At the very first celebration, 20,000 people were tested for cholesterol levels and untold numbers for high blood pressure. Many had never had checkups of any kind before. And children waited patiently in line to get their teeth examined at facilities provided by the Howard University College of Dentistry.

Long lines also formed before our education booths. A young woman taxi driver told me recently that until she and her husband attended the Black Family Reunion Celebration she did not know that someone could earn a high-school diploma without going back to the classroom. Subsequently, they decided that they were too young to be included in the numbers of unskilled blacks predicted for the year 2000. Both took extra jobs and were studying for the General Education Development test.

I was sobered by the realization that this young woman might have lived near an adult education center and never dreamed that it was meant for her. The N.C.N.W. is helping people understand that they can be active on their own behalf. At the Family Celebration in Atlanta we disseminated information from the Summer Youth Employment Training Program about jobs that were going begging for lack of applicants. When the young people in attendance discovered that the opportunities were not limited to those with special qualifications, they promptly got on the telephone to call their friends. As a result, there were applicants for almost all the jobs before the celebration ended.

There are many such stories growing out of our reunions. Of course, some may say the victories are small compared with the breadth of the problem. But activities in which a million people participate cannot be taken lightly. We at the N.C.N.W. and other black self-help organizations have no intention of spending our time lamenting the inadequacies of a society that has failed to develop the means to make every member aware that he or she belongs. The N.C.N.W. has a wide range of programs to serve African-American women and their families in the United States and an international division to assist women and their families in African countries. Currently, we are working to make a difference in all of the critical areas of human suffering enumerated here. Our first priority, as exemplified by our Black Family Reunion Celebrations, is to make clear that ours is a caring community and to inspire others, particularly our young, to press on in various ways, both to advance themselves and to further the larger struggle of our people.

One lesson is plain as we proceed: that public officials can establish all kinds of public programs thought up by people removed from the problems, and most will not work because the people for whom the programs are intended have been permitted no input in defining the problems as they actually know them to be, or in recommending the solutions. Skilled black professionals (and sensitive others) trusted by the community because they have contributed to its well-being can play a vital role in contributing to the formulation of wiser public policies—if only we can get decision-makers to listen.

## QUESTIONS

*Looking at Ideas:*
1. How did the tradition of the extended black family develop? What does Height see as the historic strength of this institution?
2. What modern social problems might be solved through using the traditional extended black family as a model?
3. How does the N.C.N.W.'s "family celebration" foster a caring community? What do they offer in place of the overwhelmingly negative assessments of the black family?
4. How does the traditional extended family help care for and support young people? In what ways does Height's proposition focus on taking care of children's needs?

*Looking at Strategies:*
1. Describe Height's tone. Who seems to be her primary audience? What is her attitude toward her subject?
2. Why does Height need to develop such an extensive introduction before stating her proposition in the fifth paragraph? What is she assuming about her audience?
3. How does Height cite authority without using footnotes or other scholarly documentation?

*Looking at Connections:*
1. How do Height's suggestions about the black extended family reinforce Baldwin's arguments about ways to create community? Cite examples.
2. Compare Height's expository treatment of the extended African-American family with Bambara's fictional treatment in "My Man Bovanne" (next selection). For example, Height notes that "we can learn something from the methods used by the traditional black extended family in which adults possessed the authority to look out for the young, whether or not they were blood relatives." How does Bambara indicate that Bovanne fulfilled this role?

*Suggestions for Writing:*
1. Do some library research into different kinds of extended families in American and other cultures. After you have done some reading on the subject, write an essay in which you discuss what seem to be the strengths and weaknesses of such models.
2. After doing some research on the subject of the extended-family reunion, which is an increasingly popular form of family celebration to-

day, write an essay in which you examine the role family reunions play in fostering a renewed sense of community among different ethnic groups in America.

3. Using the model of self-help discussed in Height's essay, focus on a social concern in your community and write a proposal for using community resources to help resolve the social problem in question.

**JOURNAL ENTRY**

What role do older people play in your extended family?

**TONI CADE BAMBARA: "My Man Bovanne"**   For a biography of Toni Cade Bambara, see the headnote to "Raymond's Run" in Chapter Two. In "My Man Bovanne," Bambara develops the theme of family and community through focusing on the role of older people in an African-American community in which the younger people are developing a sense of social activism. As you read "My Man Bovanne," consider the importance of relationships between members of a family and members of different generations in building a successful movement for social reform.

TONI CADE BAMBARA

# *My Man Bovanne*

Blind people got a hummin jones if you notice. Which is understandable completely once you been around one and notice what no eyes will force you into to see people, and you get past the first time, which seems to come out of nowhere, and it's like you in church again with fat-chest ladies and old gents gruntin a hum low in the throat to whatever the preacher be saying. Shakey Bee bottom lip all swole up with Sweet Peach and me explainin how come the sweetpotato bread was a dollar-quarter this time stead of dollar regular and he say uh hunh he understand, then he break into this *thizzin* kind of hum which is quiet, but fiercesome just the same if you ain't ready for it. Which I wasn't. But I got used to it and the onliest time I had to say somethin bout it was when he was playin checkers on the stoop one time and he commenst to hummin quite churchy seem to me. So I says. "Look here Shakey Bee, I can't beat you and Jesus too." He stop.

So that's how come I asked My Man Bovanne to dance. He ain't my man mind you, just a nice ole gent from the block that we all know cause he fixes things and the kids like him. Or used to fore Black Power got hold their minds and mess em around till they can't be civil to ole folks. So we at this benefit for my niece's cousin who's runnin for somethin with this Black party somethin or other behind her. And I press up close to dance with Bovanne who blind and I'm hummin and he hummin, chest to chest like talkin. Not jammin my breasts into the man. Wasn't bout tits. Was bout vibrations. And he dug it and asked me what color dress I had on and how my hair was fixed and how I was doin without a man, not nosy but nice-like, and who was at this affair and was the canapes dainty-stingy or healthy enough to get hold of proper. Comfy and cheery is what I'm trying to get across. Touch talkin like the heel of the hand on the tambourine or on a drum.

But right away Joe Lee come up on us and frown for dancin so close to the man. My own son who knows what kind of warm I am about; and don't grown men call me long distance and in the middle of the night for a little Mama comfort? But he frown. Which ain't right since Bovanne can't see and defend himself. Just a nice old man who fixes toasters and busted irons and bicycles and things and changes the lock on my door when my men friends get messy. Nice man. Which is not why they invited him. Grassroots you see. Me and Sister Taylor and the woman who does heads at Mamies and the man from the barber shop, we all there on account of we grassroots. And I ain't never been souther than Brooklyn Battery and no more country than the window box on my fire escape. And just yesterday my kids tellin me to take them countrified rags off my head and be cool. And now can't get Black enough to suit em. So everybody passin sayin My Man Bovanne. Big deal, keep stepping and don't even stop a minute to get the man a drink or one of them cute sandwiches or tell him what's goin on. And him standin there with a smile ready case someone do speak he want to be ready. So that's how come I pull him on the dance floor and we dance squeezin past the tables and chairs and all them coats and people standin round up in each other face talkin bout this and that but got no use for this blind man who mostly fixed skates and skooters for all these folks when they was just kids. So I'm pressed up close and we touch talkin with the hum. And here come my daughter cuttin her eye at me like she do when she tell me about my "apolitical" self like I got hoof and mouf disease and there ain't no hope at all. And I don't pay her no mind and just look up in Bovanne shadow face and tell him his stomach like a drum and he laugh. Laugh real loud. And here come my youngest, Task, with a tap on my elbow like he the third-grade monitor and I'm cuttin up on the line to assembly.

"I was just talkin on the drums," I explained when they hauled me into the kitchen. I figured drums was my best defense. They can get ready for drums what with all this heritage business. And Bovanne stomach just like that drum Task give me when he come back from Africa. You just touch it and it hum thizzim, thizzim. So I stuck to the drum story. "Just drummin that's all."

"Mama, what are you talkin about?"

"She had too much to drink," say Elo to Task cause she don't hardly say nuthin to me direct no more since that ugly argument about my wigs.

"Look here, Mama," say Task, the gentle one. "We just tryin to pull your coat. You were makin a spectacle of yourself out there dancing like that."

"Dancin like what?"

Task run a hand over his left ear like his father for the world and his father before that.

519

"Like a bitch in heat," say Elo.

"Well uhh, I was goin to say like one of them sex-starved ladies gettin on in years and not too discriminating. Know what I mean?"

I don't answer cause I'll cry. Terrible thing when your own children talk to you like that. Pullin me out the party and hustlin me into some stranger's kitchen in the back of a bar just like the damn police. And ain't like I'm old old. I can still wear me some sleeveless dresses without the meat hangin off my arm. And I keep up with some thangs through my kids. Who ain't kids no more. To hear them tell it. So I don't say nuthin.

"Dancin with that tom," say Elo to Joe Lee, who leanin on the folks' freezer. "His feet can smell a cracker a mile away and go into their shuffle number post haste. And them eyes. He could be a little considerate and put on some shades. Who wants to look into them blown-out fuses that—"

"Is this what they call the generation gap?" I say.

"Generation gap," spits Elo, like I suggested castor oil and fricassee possum in the milk shakes or somethin. "That's a white concept for a white phenomenon. There's no generation gap among Black people. We are a col—"

"Yeh, well never mind," says Joe Lee. "The point is Mama . . . well, it's pride. You embarrass yourself and us too dancin like that."

"I wasn't shame." Then nobody say nuthin. Them standin there in they pretty clothes with drinks in they hands and gangin up on me, and me in the third-degree chair and nary a olive to my name. Felt just like the police got hold to me.

"First of all," Task say, holding up his hand and tickin off the offenses, "the dress. Now that dress is too short, Mama, and too low cut for a woman your age. And Tamu's going to make a speech tonight to kick off the campaign and will be introducin you and expecting you to organize the Council of Elders—"

"Me? Didn nobody ask me nuthin. You mean Nisi? She change her name?"

"Well, Norton was supposed to tell you about it. Nisi wants to introduce you and then encourage the older folks to form a Council of the Elders to act as an advisory—"

"And you going to be standing there with your boobs out and that wig on your head and that hem up to your ass. And people'll say, 'Ain't that the horny bitch that was grindin with the blind dude?' "

"Elo, be cool a minute," say Task, gettin to the next finger. "And then there's the drinkin. Mama, you know you can't drink cause next thing you know you be laughin loud and carryin on," and he grab another finger for the loudness. "And then there's the dancin. You been tattooed on the man for four records straight and slow draggin even on the fast numbers. How you think that look for a woman your age?"

"What's my age?"

"What?"

"I'm axin you all a simple question. You keep talkin bout what's proper for a woman my age. How old am I anyhow?" And Joe Lee slams his eyes shut and squinches up his face to figure. And Task run a hand over his ear and stare into his glass like the ice cubes goin calculate for him. And Elo just starin at the top of my head like she goin rip the wig off any minute now.

"Is your hair braided up under that thing? If so, why don't you take it off? You always did do a neat cornroll."

"Uh huh," cause I'm think how she couldn't undo her hair fast enough talking bout cornroll so countrified. None of which was the subject. "How old, I say?"

"Sixtee-one or—"

"You a damn lie Joe Lee Peoples."

"And that's another thing," say Task on the fingers.

"You know what you all can kiss," I say, gettin up and brushin the wrinkles out my lap.

"Oh, Mama," Elo say, puttin a hand on my shoulder like she hasn't done since she left home and the hand landin light and not sure it supposed to be there. Which hurt me to my heart. Cause this was the child in our happiness fore Mr. Peoples die. And I carried that child strapped to my chest till she was nearly two. We was close is what I'm tryin to tell you. Cause it was more me in the child than the others. And even after Task it was the girl-child I covered in the night and wept over for no reason at all less it was she was a chub-chub like me and not very pretty, but a warm child. And how did things get to this, that she can't put a sure hand on me and say Mama we love you and care about you and you entitled to enjoy yourself cause you a good woman?

"And then there's Reverend Trent," say Task, glancin from left to right like they hatchin a plot and just now lettin me in on it. "You were suppose to be talking with him tonight, Mama, about giving us his basement for campaign headquarters and—"

"Didn nobody tell me nuthin. If grassroots mean you kept in the dark I can't use it. I really can't. And Reven Trent a fool anyway the way he tore into the widow man up there on Edgecombe cause he wouldn't take in three of them foster children and the woman not even comfy in the ground yet and the man's mind messed up and—"

"Look here," say Task. "What we need is a family conference so we can get all this stuff cleared up and laid out on the table. In the meantime I think we better get back into the other room and tend to business. And in the meantime, Mama, see if you can't get to Reverend Trent and—"

"You want me to belly rub with the Reven, that it?"

"Oh damn," Elo say and go through the swingin door.

"We'll talk about all this at dinner. How's tomorrow night, Joe Lee?"

While Joe Lee being self-important I'm wonderin who's doin the cookin and how come nobody ax me if I'm free and do I get a corsage and things like that. Then Joe nod that it's O.K. and he go through the swingin door and just a little hubbub come through from the other

521

room. Then Task smile his smile, lookin just like his daddy, and he leave. And it just me in this stranger's kitchen, which was a mess I wouldn't never let my kitchen look like. Poison you just to look at the pots. Then the door swing the other way and it's My Man Bovanne standin there saying Miss Hazel but lookin at the deep fry and then at the steam table, and most surprised when I come up on him from the other direction and take him on out of there. Pass the folks pushing up toward the stage where Nisi and some other people settin and ready to talk, and folks gettin to the last of the sandwiches and the booze fore they settle down in one spot and listen serious. And I'm thinkin bout tellin Bovanne what a lovely long dress Nisi got on and the earrings and her hair piled up in a cone and the people bout to hear how we all gettin screwed and gotta form our own party and everybody there listenin and lookin. But instead I just haul the man on out of there, and Joe Lee and his wife look at me like I'm terrible, but they ain't said boo to the man yet. Cause he blind and old and don't nobody there need him since they grown up and don't need they skates fixed no more.

"Where we goin, Miss Hazel?" Him knowin all the time.

"First we gonna buy you some dark sunglasses. Then you comin with me to the supermarket so I can pick up tomorrow's dinner, which is goin to be a grand thing proper and you invited. Then we going to my house."

"That be fine. I surely would like to rest my feet." Bein cute, but you got to let men play out they little show, blind or not. So he chat on bout how tired he is and how he appreciate me taking him in hand this way. And I'm thinkin I'll have him change the lock on my door first thing. Then I'll give the man a nice warm bath with jasmine leaves in the water and a little Epsom salt on the sponge to do his back. And then a good rubdown with rosewater and olive oil. Then a cup of lemon tea with a taste in it. And a little talcum, some of that fancy stuff Nisi mother sent over last Christmas. And then a massage, a good face massage round the forehead which is the worryin part. Cause you gots to take care of the older folks. And let them know they still needed to run the mimeo machine and keep the spark plugs clean and fix the mailboxes for folks who might help us get the breakfast program goin, and the school for the little kids and the campaign and all. Cause old folks is the nation. That what Nisi was sayin and I mean to do my part.

"I imagine you are a very pretty woman, Miss Hazel."

"I surely am," I say just like the hussy my daughter always say I was.

## QUESTIONS

*Looking at Ideas:*

1. Characterize the narrator of the story. Is she likable? What is her attitude toward her children, toward Bovanne, and toward other people in her community?

2. Discuss Bovanne's role in the community, both in earlier days and in the time frame of the story. What has changed and why?

3. Discuss the children's attitude toward their mother and toward her behavior. Are they acting in her interest, as they suggest, or in their own interest? Why do the children not want her dancing so close to Bovanne?

4. Do you agree with Elo that there is no generation gap among black people? Does the story support Elo's position in any way?

*Looking at Strategies:*

1. How does the author establish the narrator's voice? Cite examples of her use of Black vernacular. Is her speech revealing and authentic-sounding, or did it become a barrier to comprehension for you?

2. The author uses a great deal of imagery and figurative language in the story, such as "a tap on my elbow like he the third grade monitor and I'm cutting up on the line to assembly." Examine other images in the story you particularly enjoyed. What makes them effective? How do they underscore the points being made?

3. Examine the use of dialogue in the story. How does it help to illustrate character and attitude? Cite examples.

*Looking at Connections:*

1. Compare the narrator's notion of Bovanne's role with Jane Howard's perception of the place of elders in a "happy clan."

2. In what ways does Miss Hazel act on the tradition of black self-help as discussed in Height's essay?

*Suggestions for Writing:*

1. Write an essay in which you discuss the role older people have played in your childhood and youth; consider your own family, your neighborhood, your religious congregation.

2. Explain and discuss the narrator's assertion that "old folks is the nation." Do you agree? Why or why not? Write an argumentative essay supporting or refuting this idea.

3. What programs exist in your community to help care for older people without families? Consider day-care facilities, nursing homes, recreational programs, and other related programs. Use your findings to write a proposal or a letter to the editor to argue for necessary resources or programs for older people. Alternatively, propose a program that enables older people to use their skills and knowledge to support others in the community, such as children in need.

### JOURNAL ENTRY

What particular problems of families have you been thinking about as you have read through the preceding chapters? Select one that seems especially compelling, and brainstorm several creative approaches to dealing with the problem.

**MINDY HOLLIDAY AND ROBIN CRONIN: "Families First: A Significant Step toward Family Preservation"** Mindy Holliday and Robin Cronin are affiliated with Catholic Client Services in Macoomb County, Minnesota. Holiday is the director of Families First, and Cronin is vice president. The following article is an editorial that was published in *Families in Society: The Journal of Contemporary Human Services* (1990). As you read the article, think about whether this alternative approach to supporting families in need could be implemented on a large scale.

MINDY HOLLIDAY AND ROBIN CRONIN

# Families First

## A Significant Step toward Family Preservation

Child abuse and neglect permeate American society. In 1978–88, 49,352 reported cases of abuse and neglect were investigated in Michigan alone (Public Hearings, 1989). Historically, efforts to address this tremendous problem have evolved into techniques that divide families. "The child-saving and child rescue movements of the nineteenth century gradually crystallized into a system of services which emphasized placement of children as a solution to a family's problems" (Hartman & Laird, 1983). When a family experienced difficulty in caring for its members, the state tended to move in and take over completely *in loco parentis* rather than to seek to enhance the family's ability to take care of itself. Research has shown numerous weaknesses in the foster care/ child placement system (Fanshel & Shinn, 1978; Jenkins & Sauber, 1966; Jenkins, 1967), most notably that child placement has been used not only as a solution to child abuse and neglect but often as a substitute for financial and social assistance to needy families.

The Office of Children and Youth Services (OCYS) within Michigan's Department of Social Services has recognized these problems in the current system of child welfare services. The OCYS has made a substantial commitment to providing family preservation programs, thus expanding the continuum of services available to children and their families. The Families First project, which poses a striking alternative to the traditional model of intervention, is now in operation as a demonstration project statewide in Michigan. A progressive philosophical orientation is evident in OCYS's description of the model:

> A basic principle of the child welfare system in the United States is that every child is entitled to grow up in a permanent family. Inherent in this principle is the need to make all reasonable efforts to keep families together and to place children out of their homes only if their well-being cannot be protected within their families (Office of Children and Youth Services, 1988).

## Program Approach

Families First is a time-limited, intensive, home-based program. It is modeled after the Homebuilders program developed and implemented in Washington State in 1974, which provides intensive in-home crisis intervention and family education. Families First focuses on the family system as a unit, rather than on the parents or children as individual clients. Philosophically, the model is partly based on crisis intervention theory in that it seeks "to resolve the present difficulty, to rework the previous struggle, and to break the linkage between the two" (Golan, 1978, pp. 8–9). Intervention focuses on facilitating stability within the family system, on assisting the family to identify where they are "stuck," and facilitating the development of "new adaptive styles which will enable the system to cope more effectively with other situations in the future" (p. 9). In line with crisis intervention theory, the Families First model seeks to accomplish the following objectives using the family's own goals (Golan, 1978, pp. 71–72):

1. Relief of symptoms (stress on the family often results in the appearance of the symptom of abuse or neglect)
2. Restoration to precrisis level of functioning (or improvement in the level of precrisis functioning, given a family with inadequate coping or parenting skills)
3. Some understanding of the relevant precipitating events that led to the state of disequilibrium
4. Identification of remedial measures that the client or family can take or that are available through community resources (liaison, linkage, or advocacy are also functions of the Families First program)

When personality and social situations are favorable, two additional goals are added:

5. Connecting the current life stresses with past life experiences and conflicts (assisting the client to connect previous family-of-origin experiences with current stressors resulting in abuse or neglect)
6. Initiating new modes of perceiving, thinking, and feeling and de-

veloping new adaptive and coping responses that can be useful beyond the immediate crisis situation

Families First intervenes with a family when a crisis has brought the family to the attention of Children's Protective Services (CPS). The program serves for selected families as an alternative to the removal of children from the home environment due to physical, emotional, or sexual abuse; neglect; or delinquency. The goal of the program is to teach families alternative ways to communicate, interact, and develop new skills while promoting parental autonomy and family empowerment. In addition to a variety of counseling and assessment services, Families First has discretionary monies available for "hard services" such as food, utilities, clothing, and medical care.

### Referral Guidelines

Referrals for services are initiated by CPS staff. Upon substantiating a report of abuse, neglect, or delinquency, CPS staff have the option of utilizing the Families First program for families that could potentially benefit from these services in lieu of immediate removal of the children from the home. A referral to Families First is not made if the goal is solely to keep the family together until an out-of-home placement can be arranged. The OCYS staff have established specific guidelines to determine appropriate and inappropriate referrals to the program. For example, appropriate referrals have been identified as those for which

· At least one parent is available in the home to participate in Families First
· Other, less intensive services would not sufficiently reduce the risk, or are unavailable
· The CPS worker has determined that the family is willing to collaborate in goal setting and treatment, some family strengths have been identified, and parental autonomy is possible
· The child could remain in the home and would not be at risk if intensive in-home training services were made available
· The family would respond reasonably or favorably to the service and attempt to make some positive changes to reduce the risk to the minor
· No ongoing criminal activity in the home poses a risk to the Families First worker or family members

Inappropriate referrals include:

· Cases with long-term chronic neglect, in which CPS has had several different referrals unsuccessfully resolved
· Family has no home
· Family member(s) consistently threaten to hurt any worker who comes to the home or who works with the family
· A history of serious physical abuse exists, current abuse is consid-

526

ered life-threatening, and/or the parents have been unwilling or unco-operative in treatment of such serious abuse (Office of Children and Youth Services, 1988)

Although many families benefit from the Families First services, certain families do not. The latter include families who do not believe they have a problem and are unwilling to work with Families First or who appear to be seriously mentally ill and unable to meet the needs of their children. Parents who continually put their children at risk of sex-ual abuse by exposing them to perpetrators who frequent the home, who disregard a court order keeping perpetrators away, or who attempt to minimize the risks facing minor children are not eligible for services. Families in which both parents are involved in the sexual abuse or in which abusing siblings remain in the home are also ineligible for the Families First program.

## Service Delivery

The basic philosophy behind the service is that many families oper-ating under tremendous stress can improve their situation given the op-portunity and encouragement to do so. Family empowerment is the fo-cus of the program; the family is actively involved in setting its own treatment goals in collaboration with the Families First staff. The pro-gram provides the opportunities, skills, and support necessary to en-hance the family's ability to accomplish its goals. The Families First program provides an alternative intervention with multiproblem fami-lies.

The Families First staff must assess and intervene with families whose children would be removed under the traditional child welfare system. Similar to the Homebuilders program, practice methods are primarily behavioral, psychoeducational, and cognitive. In addition, Families First Program of Michigan places significant emphasis on ap-plying these intervention modes within the context of the entire family system. In operating within a brief therapy framework, Families First staff have found that even though a family's basic values and beliefs may not be significantly changed in a four- to six-week period, instilling hope and rejuvenating the family's ability to heal itself is quite possible.

In order to accomplish these goals, Families First staff respond within 24 hours of a referral—immediately if necessary. Staff members work with only two families at a time and are available 24 hours a day, seven days a week. The staff provide various services in the family's home for up to 20 hours a week. Services are scheduled at the family's convenience over a five- to six-week period. Counseling, education, al-ternative parenting techniques, and household-management skills are provided through skills-based interventions to address goals established conjointly by the Families First staff and the family. The treatment ap-proach highlights and builds on the family's strengths and targets their immediate needs. Transportation, money for concrete needs such as food or clothing, and linkage and advocacy with appropriate community resources are also provided.

Several factors make this program effective for families at risk. The small case load allows families to receive services as they experience difficulties on a daily basis. The flexible scheduling allows the family to have access to support during those times the family identifies as most difficult for them; the mere presence of a staff member in the family's home for extensive periods helps ensure the safety of the children. The availability of both counseling and concrete services allows the family to receive support for immediate needs, often encouraging them to be receptive to other forms of intervention. As a result, the family begins to function with increased autonomy and becomes more effective in utilizing community resources.

## Case Example

The following case was referred to Families First following an investigation by CPS staff. The family consisted of two members, a 28-year-old divorced mother and her 8-year-old son. The mother was threatening to harm her son and herself. She also admitted abusing marijuana for the past four years. She was depressed and had been receiving outpatient counseling. She had little family support, and the boy's father had been minimally involved with her and their child since their divorce in 1983.

The Families First staff met the mother at her home the evening of the referral. The eight-year-old son was severely mentally impaired. It was quickly determined that he functioned at the level of a 15-month-old. The mother was an Italian immigrant who had limited knowledge of her community or of how to locate services. She had stopped abusing marijuana and had been attending Narcotics Anonymous for 30 days prior to the referral.

The nature of the intervention was twofold. In-depth assessments of the child's functioning and the mother's psychological well-being were scheduled, including an evaluation that resulted in the child being placed on methylphenidate, which dramatically reduced his periods of "out of control" behavior. The mother received a psychiatric evaluation that determined she was overwhelmed by her situation and not chronically mentally ill. An in-home assessment by a qualified parent/child trainer for handicapped individuals was arranged, and the family was identified as appropriate for community mental health services.

Besides the formal assessment and advocacy for appropriate services, other services were provided to the mother on a daily basis. These included instruction on how to accomplish daily routines, mood-management techniques, child development, and techniques for building self-esteem. Recreational outings were provided for the family as well as respite care when the mother suffered a severe bout of the flu.

This case clearly demonstrates that the changes necessary for supporting this family's ability to remain together included changes in the community's response to the family. She had received few services for nearly eight years, the primary one being a special school for her son. The needs of the family had gone unnoticed to the point of near institutionalization of the child, despite repeated efforts of the client to obtain assistance. Six months following the intervention, the family continues to make significant gains, including moving to larger housing more suited to the special needs of the child. The mother is currently investigating how she might continue her college education. The child is now toilet trained, able to feed himself, and able to play independently for brief periods, all of which he was unable to do prior to the intervention.

*Chapter Nine: Family and Community*

## Implications

Families First offers an alternative to the traditional approach of removing the child from the home in cases of abuse and neglect. By virtue of the program's design, child welfare professionals are challenged to view and work with families from a family-strengths perspective as opposed to focusing on a family's deficits. Empowerment is a powerful motivator not only for the families served but also for child welfare workers, who find themselves empowered by the changes they witness.

The Families First model represents one alternative along a continuum of services that aim to discourage abuse and neglect and to support families. Based on a crisis intervention model and focusing on family empowerment and skill building, the Families First model challenges the community to recognize the limitations of the services that are currently being offered and to respond to the basic needs of people in trouble. The model works because it seeks to remove obstacles, instills hope, and reduces stresses that impede the family's ability to achieve a higher level of functioning.

## References

Fanshel, D., & Shinn, E. (1978). *Children in foster care: A longitudinal investigation.* New York: Columbia University Press.

Golan, N. (1978). *Treatment in crisis situations.* New York: Free Press.

Hartman, A., & Laird, J. (1983). *Family-centered social work practice.* New York: Free Press.

Jenkins, S. (1967). "Duration of Foster Care—Some Relevant Antecedent Variables." *Child Welfare,* 46, 450–456.

Jenkins, S., & Sauber, M. (1966). *Paths to child placement.* New York: Community Council of Greater New York.

Office of Children and Youth Services (OCYS). (1988, October). *Families First Guidelines.* Lansing, MI: Family Preservation Unit Staff of OCYS.

Public Hearings. (1989, July 24). *Testimony regarding children at risk.* Mount Clemens, MI: Michigan Department of Social Services.

*Looking at Ideas:*

1. As described in the article's introduction, what has been the traditional approach for social workers in dealing with abused and neglected children? What do the authors see as the problem with such an approach?

2. How might the Families First approach help with cases of misdiagnosed child abuse—e.g., reports of cases that turn out to be untrue or unsubstantiated?

3. How does the Families First view of the problem of child abuse differ from more traditional approaches? Does the argument that a different approach is needed seem sound? What are the goals of the Families First project?

4. Do you agree with the authors that there is an advantage to keeping the family intact if possible? Do you think any associated risks are outweighed by the advantages?

*Looking at Strategies:*

1. What is the organizational strategy of the article? What expository techniques are used to set up the argument? Do the subheadings in the article adequately guide the reader through the essay?

2. What do the documentation style and the list of references tell you about the periodical in which this article was published and the kind of audience for whom the article is intended?

3. What does the essay's introduction attempt to accomplish? Why do the authors need this kind of introduction to their proposal?

*Looking at Connections:*

1. What links do you see between Holliday and Cronin's proposal and Height's assertions about the concept of the extended family? To what extent do you think that the child abuse and neglect Holliday and Cronin write about can be countered by an extended family?

2. Does the Families First approach seem to avoid the pitfalls of social-worker intervention discussed in Dan Zegart's article, "Solomon's Choice" in Chapter Six?

*Suggestions for Writing:*

1. Write an essay in which you develop your point of view on the advantages or disadvantages of keeping intact a family in which children have been abused and neglected.

2. Write an essay in response to Holliday and Cronin's proposal indicating other, more effective ways that social workers could intervene and assist families to function effectively. Take into account some of the objections raised by Dan Zegart (in "Solomon's Choice") to social-worker intervention.

3. Write an essay in which you discuss the role of the community in helping families to resolve their internal problems. To what extent can and should the community intercede in domestic differences? To what extent is the community at large the ultimate guardian of its children?

HOWARD LIBIT: "Families Separated by Bars" Howard Libit grew up in Highland Park, Illinois, a suburb of Chicago. He has varied interests and is considering medicine or journalism after graduating from college. Libit wrote this paper because of his relationship with a friend whose father was sent to prison while the friend was in high school. Through his research and interviews, Libit hoped to gain a better understanding of the feelings of children of imprisoned parents and to examine the need for compassion within the criminal justice system.

HOWARD LIBIT

# *Families Separated by Bars*

The father of a close friend of mine was convicted of tax evasion and fraud about a year ago. My friend rarely visited his father and only occasionally spoke to him by telephone. Not yet an adult, my friend lived on his own, staying with various friends and often in his house by himself because his mother had died several years earlier. While he had no financial problems during his father's incarceration, he was emotionally fragile much of the time and his grades steadily declined. When his father was released six months later, their relationship had changed. Incarceration destroyed the sense of trust and closeness that had once been present between them.

Unfortunately, my friend is not alone in his plight and may be considered relatively fortunate compared to others. What sets my friend apart from many other children of incarcerated parents is his financial situation. Living in a wealthy suburb, he was able to survive with his father's money and investments and was able to attend college with funds set aside before his father entered prison. However, nearly half of America's prisoners live below the poverty-line. The majority do not even possess a high school education (Jorgensen 47).

Consequently, when a parent, sometimes the only one, is incarcerated, the family faces major financial difficulties. The numbers of parents incarcerated by the criminal justice system is already high and continues to grow at an alarming rate. As of December 31, 1989, the most recent statistics, America's federal and state prisons hold 663,998 men and 39,689 women (Church 20). Recent studies indicate that 60 percent of male prisoners are fathers while 80 percent of female prisoners are mothers (Church 21).

In the United States, 188 of every 100,000 people are imprisoned, representing the third-highest rate of incarceration in the world. Yet despite this already astonishing rate, the numbers keep rising as mandatory sentences, established in response to the public backlash against

531

crime, send more people to prison for longer periods of time (Jorgensen 47). Additionally, the rate of female prisoners entering prison is rising faster than the rate of male prisoners. The number of women imprisoned increased 133 percent during a ten-year period while the number of men incarcerated increased only 86 percent (Schoenbauer 579).

In addition to the higher number of female prisoners who have children than male convicts who are fathers, a key distinction between the two sexes is evident in the area of custodial responsibility for those children. Of the mothers who are prisoners, 85 percent have custody of their children. However, fewer than 50 percent of male prisoners with children actually have custody (Church 21). Consequently, although men with children do make up a significant part of the prison body, the high number of women in prison with children poses a unique set of problems (Schoenbauer 579). If current incarceration practices result in de facto punishment of innocent children and families of prisoners, then programs must be designed to alleviate, or at least lessen, any negative effects of the incarceration of a mother or father.

Experts agree that as the nation's prison system grows, more and more families will be affected (Jorgensen 47). It is important to examine the impacts of correctional policies on the family: ". . . [I]t is impractical to attempt an understanding of our laws and institutions without examining the impact of those laws and institutions on the lives and experiences of human beings they affect." (Hale 147). The importance of this issue cannot be ignored, for our criminal justice system was designed to punish only the guilty. The children and families of prisoners are not guilty of any crime and they should not be punished.

The effects of imprisonment upon the family structure can be divided into two general areas. These categories are the relationship between the prisoner and the family and, more specifically, the relationship between the prisoner and the child. Examination of both of these areas will demonstrate the profound effects of the incarceration of a parent.

In the eyes of the criminal justice system, the most important benefit of strong family ties involves rehabilitation of the prisoner. Donna C. Hale, assistant professor of criminal justice at the University of Baltimore, explained that the family is essential to a prisoner's well-being after release. "If reentry into the community is to be successful, the returning offender must be reentering a society where he/she will be supported by a family system or network which will strengthen his/her rehabilitation and prevent him/her from becoming a recidivist" (Hale 143–144). Four out of five studies have demonstrated that recidivism, the tendency of an exconvict to commit crimes, tends to decrease when family contact is maintained throughout the period of incarceration (Hairston 49). A possible explanation of this may be that the family network provides both emotional and financial support for the prisoner during and after the sentence (Hairston 50). The maintenance of the family system can enhance the possibility of rehabilitation and helps make punishment within the criminal justice system workable and humane.

Unfortunately, many aspects of current incarceration practices tend to weaken the family structure. Studies indicate that "the practical problems encountered by inmates' families in their everyday lives" weaken the family (Hale 147). These problems include stigmatization, finances and housing, loneliness, contact with and supervision of children (Hale 147). While the family drifts apart during the period of incarceration, male and female prisoners face different prospects in regard to their marriages: "[H]usbands, boyfriends and brothers usually drop a woman convict 'like a hot potato.' While wives and girlfriends line up to visit male inmates, visiting days at women's prisons are virtually all-female affairs" (Church 21). A similar reaction of the spouses of both male and female prisoners is the treatment of incarceration as death. Spouses often exhibit symptoms of grief typical of mourning (Jorgensen 47).

There are several reasons why the family, and more specifically the spouse, becomes alienated from the inmate during the period of incarceration. The criminal justice system does not provide accurate information to the family about the condition and fate of the prisoner during the entire process, from the beginning arrest to parole. Confusion surrounding the information is magnified by a minimal understanding of English by some minority families (Jorgensen 48). Difficulties during visiting also occur that decrease, or eliminate, the number of contacts between prisoners and their families. As one study indicated, families will often move immediately after a parent is incarcerated, thus cutting off the convict from all further communication (Jorgensen 49).

The effects of the incarceration on a parent are also numerous. During the actual period of imprisonment, the family will often suffer financially if the parent was the sole family provider. As a result, studies indicate that the quality of life declines for nearly one-third of the families of prisoners (Jorgensen 49). Although programs in male prisons train men for well-paying jobs after imprisonment, female prison work programs continue to concentrate on jobs that are low-paying and correspond to gender stereotypes (Church 21). When the spouse returns home from the period of imprisonment, the family has undergone significant changes. The inmate has lost contact with the day-to-day issues of the family and may find conflict in returning to a decision-making role in the household. Although the family is essential for the successful return of a convict to society, there exist many barriers in the maintenance of close contact, which can cause the family to experience difficult times during and after the sentence.

When a parent is imprisoned, the only way to maintain the parent-child bond is through visitation. Unfortunately, obstacles exist that hinder and limit visitation between parent and child in the prison setting. The distance to the prison often prohibits frequent visits, as do the high costs associated with traveling that distance (Schoenbauer 583). Because of the distance, it may be difficult for the child to find an adult to accompany him or her to the prison. The policies of particular prisons often limit the length of each visit (Hairston & Hess 106). During the visit itself, the visiting rooms of the prison are often separated by thick glass windows and are poorly furnished (Church 21). Some prisons even insist upon searching young children before they may visit their parents (Schoenbauer 583). For example, my friend, who was old enough to drive to the prison, was searched as he entered the prison and visited his father in small, dingy rooms. The prison also scheduled visiting hours at times that were not convenient, such as during the week when he had school. Consequently, he did not enjoy the visits and was often unable to see his father. These conditions intimidate children and make them afraid to visit their parents in prison.

The separation between parent and child results in a traumatic experience for the child. The child is ashamed of his parent and hides his feelings from anyone except a close friend. Studies indicate that the child, when separated from a parent due to incarceration, feels abandoned and lonely (Hale 149). In a recent study it was shown that, in families where a parent is incarcerated, "children . . . missed their parents and, not surprisingly, longed for their return. The children were observed to be more aggressive toward each other, less obedient, and more anti-social" (Jorgensen 48). These studies also conclude that the child's performance in school declines after a parent is imprisoned (48). Perhaps the most disturbing effect is a tendency for many of these children eventually to end up in prison themselves (Gauch 34). While it is unlikely that my friend will be imprisoned, his school performance did decline more than most second-semester high seniors, as he never had anyone to motivate him or even to see his report cards. He also often found himself alone in his empty house with nothing to do. He kept to himself and often refused to reveal his feelings. Although he was almost eighteen, he missed his father very much.

During the judicial process, the criminal justice system encourages a parent to relinquish his or her rights to children. Parents sometimes believe that they are only giving the state temporary custody of the child, but their rights may be terminated during the prison sentence (Schoenbauer 583–584). The other alternatives for the care of a child in a single-parent marriage are adoption, foster care, or care by other relatives (Church 21). The prevailing attitude among social workers is that children should not be placed with parents who have been convicted of a crime, particularly mothers, for "the biggest myth about women in prison is that they are bad mothers" (Gauch 33). However, with the significant damage that the separation of parent and child causes for all concerned, it would be wise for policymakers of the criminal justice system to reconsider their attitudes and actions towards the incarcerated parent.

Despite the increasing number of studies about the effects of imprisonment of a parent on a child, the situation receives little serious attention. "The idea that the criminal justice system should take any responsibility for what happens to children of offenders is totally alien to the traditional concept of police, the judiciary or corrections" (Hale 150). This traditional concept of the purpose of imprisonment is reflected in day-to-day policies. "Parent-child relationships are rarely addressed in state corrections policies. The data, furthermore, suggest that policies governing visiting are seldom developed with attention to the special needs of children, the importance of parent-child attachments, or the nature of complex family networks." (Hairston & Hess 106). Admittedly, a few programs have been developed that begin to address such issues and problems (Hairston 48). However, despite such efforts, the increasing number of parents in prison necessitates more broad-scale concerted action (Church 22).

Before examining nationwide policies that should be implemented, a brief discussion of one specific prison might help put things in perspective. One prison on the "cutting edge" of parent-child programs is the Dwight Correctional Center, the only female prison in the state of Illinois. Dwight offers many programs to parents and has a liberal visitation policy. Dwight provides play areas in which parents and children can visit comfortably (Gauch 33). Women in this prison are trained for money-making jobs that will allow them to care for their children when they are released from prison (Gauch 35). Chicago Legal Aid to Incarcerated Mothers, a volunteer legal organization, attempts to maintain the family structure even while the mother is in prison (Auster 18). In this program, mothers are taught to work with the state agencies in order to keep their children. Yet despite valiant efforts, the women's prison is vastly underfunded (Gauch 34). These "extra" programs at Dwight rely upon funding from private charities dedicated to maintaining the parent-child relationship. If even Dwight, the prison with the best available programs to-date, has problems with programs, there is no question that a system-wide solution is needed.

There exist numerous partial solutions to maintain the parent-child relationship, and combinations of different programs will likely provide a unique and adequate solution for various states. Prisons should establish liberal visitation policies for children of inmates and allow the visits to include contact (Schoenbauer 596). Funds should be made available to the families of prisoners in order to allow them to travel to the prison for visits. Family service programs, staffed by certified social workers, would help families of prisoners understand their emotions and maintain the family relationship. Community centers and self-help groups could also help prisoners during their transition from prison into society (Jorgensen 51).

For convicts who are pregnant, a prison nursery or half-way house could provide a better, more healthy environment (Schoenbauer 595). Reformation and clarification of parental rights statutes would also provide a means to prevent the involuntary split of a family (Schoenbauer 599). Judges might consider the impact of a sentence on the family, avoiding breaking up a family when possible (Bush 15). Alternatives to prison, such as electronic monitoring and house arrest programs, would allow a family to stay together in the home setting while the convict serves his or her sentence (Gauch 35).

Many states are currently experimenting with small programs designed to maintain the parent-child relationship. However, these limited efforts are simply not enough. As Dr. Creasie Hairston, Professor of Social Work at Indiana University, argues, "It would be a mistake to expect that isolated family programs can make a significant impact on recidivism without fundamental changes in corrections communications policies and practices. . . . Without basic changes, a future 'nothing works' attributed to family programs might be better phrased as 'nothing is permitted to work' " (Hairston 51). System-wide changes, both in attitude and policy, are necessary to solve the deep-seated problems of our criminal justice system.

Society will continue to feel the need to punish criminals for their crimes. Although prison is sometimes the only viable option for punishment, in the case of those convicted of drug possession and other so-called "victimless" crimes, halfway houses that rehabilitate and provide a means for families to stay together would be a better solution than prison. In my friend's case, there was no reason that his father had to serve time in jail for tax evasion and fraud when home incarceration, electronic monitoring, or some form of community service would have deterred equally well. If jail time does seem to be the only alternative, programs should be established that would best maintain the parent-child bond based upon the individual needs of the specific prison's population.

America's prison system is growing at an astounding pace, and among the nation's prisoners are many fathers and mothers. While the criminal justice system is designed to punish these convicts, it is inadvertently hurting the families of the prisoners. The effects of the incarceration of a parent can be mitigated by well-coordinated, carefully thought out programs within the prison. While some states experiment with such ideas on a limited, experimental basis, the prison system continues to damage the lives of innocent children. Only through the adoption of a comprehensive family support policy can the corrections system adequately maintain the relationship between the incarcerated parent and the family.

## Works Cited

Auster, Amy. "Mothering From Jail." *Chicago Magazine,* Nov. 1990: 18.

Bush, Eleanor L. "Not Ordinarily Relevant? Considering the Defendants' Children at Sentencing." *Federal Probation,* Mar. 1990: 15–21.

Church, George J. "The View from Behind Bars." *Time,* Fall 1990: 20–22.

Gauch, Sarah. "When Mothers Go To Prison." *Human Rights,* Summer 1989: 33–35.

Hairston, Creasie Finney. "Family Ties During Imprisonment: Do They Influence Future Criminal Activity?" *Federal Probation,* Mar. 1988: 48–52.

Hairston, Creasie Finney, and Peg McCartt Hess. "Family Ties: Maintaining Child-Parent Bonds Is Important." *Corrections Today,* Apr. 1989: 102–106.

Hale, Donna C. "The Impact of Mothers' Incarceration on the Family System: Research and Recommendations." *Marriage and Family Review,* 1987: 143–154.

Jorgensen, James D., et al. "Addressing the Social Needs of Families of Prisoners: A Tool for Inmate Rehabilitation." *Federal Probation,* Dec. 1986: 47–52.

Schoenbauer, Laura J. "Incarcerated Parents and Their Children: Forgotten Families." *Law & Inequality: A Journal of Theory and Practice,* Oct. 1986: 579–601.

## Questions on "Families Separated by Bars"

1. What is the author's proposal? How does he support that proposal? What is his overall organizational pattern? Is his evidence persuasive?

2. Who might be Libit's intended audience? Is he attempting to persuade policymakers, politicians, the general public, multiple audiences?

3. The author begins with an anecdote, or brief story. Do you find this an effective technique? Is it appropriate for the subject and for research writing generally?

4. Does Libit's evidence—his use of facts and citation of authorities— seem well-integrated into the essay? Does Libit manage to maintain his own writer's voice while presenting the "voices" of his sources?

5. Overall, do you find that Libit presents a persuasive argument for a case or just a report on a social issue?

6. If you were discussing Libit's essay in your peer group, what advice would you have for him for further revision?

1. With several members of your class, develop an oral history project. Get in touch with your local public library, historical society or museum to see if they have suggestions or can supply equipment such as tape recorders in exchange for a copy of the information you obtain. Locate older people who have lived in the area for a while or who have worked in certain fields (the arts, local commerce, government) and focus on a subject that your group agrees on such as a history of the town or stories of local ethnic communities. Pool your information from the interviews; then compile a report and publish your findings for interested groups in the community.

2. What shelters or kitchens in your community are geared toward serving families in need? Are family-oriented facilities needed? Research your community's specific needs; get in touch with social service agencies and local government people; survey workers and clients to find out more about specific needs. Then write a proposal, perhaps working with or on behalf of a local service agency, to an appropriate funding source such as a private foundation or government agency. Alternatively, send your proposal to the local newspaper to inform others of what is needed.

3. Examine the kinds of special interest groups that have their own bulletin boards and report to your class on the range of "communities" found via the computer network. If possible, participate in a computer network "community." Does it fulfill the characteristics of community as described in this chapter's readings? In what ways?

4. One community that exemplifies the "movable feast" Jane Howard speaks of is the military. Do some research on the ways in which military families and communities work, how they develop ties, what they believe constitutes "community." You could do research in *Social Science Abstracts,* social science journals, and military publications; be sure to interview someone associated with the military, including family members of long-term service personnel.

5. A number of films, both commercial and documentary, profile the lives of families within communities and issues in community involvement. Working separately or with a group of students, view one of these films and write an analysis of it in which you discuss what new insights the film brought you about the nature of family, community, and ideas for community involvement. Below is a list of related films on video.

*Do the Right Thing.* Dir., Spike Lee. With Danny Aiello, Spike Lee, Rubie Dee. 1989.
*The Milagro Beanfield War.* Dir., Robert Redford, 1988.
*Norma Rae.* Dir., Martin Ritt. With Sally Field, Ron Leibman. 1979.
*Roger and Me.* Dir., Michael Moore. 1990.

# *Glossaries*

# Glossary of Terms Related to the Family

**Abuse, Abusive Family:** Families can be categorized as abusive for a number of reasons. One or more parents may engage in the physical abuse of children, such as pushing, hitting, or some form of sexual abuse. Often abuse is more subtle, taking the form of verbal abuse and deprecation, which may lead the child to feel worthless and defeated early in life. Patterns of abuse are often passed on from generation to generation within a family. Patterns of abuse within a family are discussed in the readings contained in Chapter Two, "Relationships," Chapter Six "Tensions," and Chapter Nine, "Family and Community."

**Adolescence:** Biologically and chronologically, this generally refers to ages 12–21, with early adolescence referring to the years 12–16 and late adolescence, the years 17–21. Socially, it is the time during which young people have outgrown a child's social status but have not yet been granted the full privileges of adulthood. Chapter Eight, "Growing Away," reflects particularly on this difficult time in the lives of family members.

**Alienation:** A state of feeling isolated or separated from others. Feelings of alienation are discussed and reflected on in many of the essays and much of the fiction included in Chapter Four, "The Mass-Produced Family," and Chapter Eight, "Growing Away."

**Assimilation:** The process of becoming a part of a new society or dominant culture—usually through the adoption of the language and behavior of the mainstream culture. The reading selections in Chapter Five, "The Family in a Multicultural Society," confront issues of both social and linguistic assimilation.

**Bilingualism:** The ability to communicate equally well in two languages. Several writers represented in *Coming from Home*—among them Richard Rodriguez, Simon Ortiz, and student writer Josephine Ramos—discuss the advantages and disadvantages of growing up fully or partially bilingual.

**Blended Family:** A family composed of children from former marriages and spouses who have previously divorced or become widowed, and then remarried. Blended families can be a source of exciting interactions as well as considerable stress, both for parents and children.

**Community:** A group of people who live in close proximity, or have some kind of social organization, or share a common interest or purpose. A criticism of modern life is that there is little sense of community—that is, little sense of commonality, of mutual help and engagement. Our readings in Chapter Nine, "Family and Community," emphasize ways in which family members can be a part of the larger communities surrounding them.

**Community Service:** Working in a community or public arena, generally without financial compensation, often for nonprofit agencies or other not-for-profit organizations that serve the public interest. P. W. Alexander's essay, "Christmas at Home," in Chapter Nine is an example of community service at the level of the individual family unit.

**Cultures:** Socially transmitted behaviors, beliefs, arts, institutions, and products of human work and thought characteristic of a community or population. Cultural issues involving the family are explored in Chapter Three, "Myths and Rituals," Chapter Four, "The Mass-Produced Family," which examines the family's relationship to mass culture, and Chapter Five, "The Family in a Multicultural Society."

**Cultural Diversity:** The presence of varied cultures within a society or region. See particularly Chapter Five, "The Family in a Multicultural Society," for an exploration of cultural diversity in America and its impact on family life.

**Divorce:** The legal dissolution of a marriage. Divorce is increasingly common in modern life, and the long-term effects of divorce are felt strongly by children, as discussed in Judith Wallerstein's "On the Brow of the Hill" in Chapter Six.

**Dual-Career Family:** A family headed by a union of two people, usually parents, both of whom work outside the home or at employment in addition to rearing children. Arlie Hochschild's essay in Chapter Six explores the impact of dual careers on family life.

**Dysfunctional Family:** A disordered or poorly functioning family system, whose problems are caused by the impairment of individual members and/or by their inability to work together as a unit. Lily Collett's "Step by Step" in Chapter Six examines how a dysfunctional or abusive family can have negative long-term effects on the self-concepts of individuals who grow up in such homes.

**Ethnicity:** The characteristics or traits of cultural heritage, traditions, biology, race, or religion that indicate belonging to a particular group of people. Chapter Five, "The Family in a Multicultural Society," examines family issues relating to ethnicity.

**Extended Family:** A unit that includes not only the immediate family unit of parents and children, but also other relatives, such as grandparents, aunts, uncles, and cousins. Although many critics mourn the shrinking of the extended family, Dorothy Height's essay in Chapter Nine, "Family and Community," discusses a particular group, the African Americans, that has relied strongly for its survival in America on the extended-family support system.

**Family:** Traditionally speaking, a fundamental biological or social unit, usually consisting of parents and their offspring, or a group of people sharing ancestry. Today the term "family" is defined in increasingly broad terms, encompassing persons in living-together arrangements of various kinds, as well as the even more amorphous groupings of individuals involved as colleagues in a work or other institutional environment.

**Feminism:** A system of belief that calls for equal political, social, and sexual rights for women and for a reeducation of society as to the positive attributes and values of women. Authors such as Barbara Ehren-reich, Arlie Hochschild, and Judith Stacey speak about the family from a feminist perspective.

**Gay (as an orientation):** Homosexual; refers to sexual orientation toward members of the same gender. "Gay" is often used to refer to homosexual men, while "lesbian" is generally used to refer to homosexual women. An issue of particular concern to gay people is that of the family. Should gay relationships be legally recognized as "families," with child custody rights and rights to medical and other benefits?

**Heritage:** Cultural values and traditions passed down through the generations. Chapter Three, "Myths and Rituals," explores the ways in which family heritage expresses itself in such ritualized behavior as the honoring of special days through celebrations and the retelling of family stories.

**Ideology:** The beliefs about life, values, and politics, both conscious and unconscious, of an individual, group, or culture.

**Mass Media:** Communications systems designed for sending out messages to a large audience, either electronically, using sound and/or pictures; through print; or via a combination of words, sounds and images. The mass media are usually thought of in America as commercial entities and also function as vehicles for advertising and promoting a wide range of consumer-oriented products. Mass media give families a sense of cultural identity while controlling behavior through powerful, repeated advertising and the creation of compelling role models.

**Middle-Class Family:** In sociological terms, a family that is neither poor nor wealthy, but which has an income in between the two extremes. Middle-class families are often assumed (sometimes erroneously) to have moderate or mainstream values.

**Modern Family:** Also defined as a "traditional" family. The term usually refers to a family having a breadwinning-father, a stay-at-home, non-employed mother, and children.

**Multicultural:** Refers to both the presence of diverse ethnic and cultural groups and, increasingly, to the positive aspects of what those diverse groups bring to society.

**Myth:** A symbolic or imaginative story, often about a heroic or ancestral figure, generally not traceable to specific historical events, and dealing with recurring themes such as creation, knowledge, will, and redemption. Myths reflect the values of a culture and of particular families. Many of the readings in Chapter Three, "Myths and Rituals," explore the role of myths—both cultural myths and stories that are a unique part of each family's heritage—in sustaining family values and traditions.

**Neighborhood:** An area or district, often with distinct characteristics. Modern neighborhoods often have little sense of belonging or involvement. Many of the essays in Chapter Nine discuss the difference between a neighborhood and a genuine community.

**Network (of computers):** A system through which individuals with personal computers or workstations can communicate across distances—within a classroom or across campuses, cities, countries, or oceans.

**Network (of friends):** A group of friends, often formed at work or through social interactions, and often functioning as a support system.

**Oedipus Complex:** Refers to sexual feelings of a young (three-to-five-year-old) child toward a parent of the opposite gender, with hostility toward the parent of the same gender. (Usually refers to a male child.) When the hostility is experienced by a female child it is sometimes called an "Electra complex."

**Postmodern Family:** A family system distinguished from the so-called modern mid-twentieth-century family (which is characterized by a hierarchy of a breadwinning father, stay-at-home mother, and children). The term "postmodern family" encompasses diverse family arrangements, including step-families and single-parent families, and suggests some increased involvement of men in family care, while acknowledging that women still seem largely responsible for maintaining family ties.

**Ritual:** Behavior that is performed regularly according to a set pattern and sequence. Religious celebrations and ceremonies often involve elaborate rituals designed to emphasize a pattern of belief. In a similar way, family rituals, such as sitting down to a special meal on a holiday or other special occasion, playing games together, or going on regular family vacations, help to affirm family values. See Chapter Three, "Myths and Rituals" for further examples and discussion.

**Serial Monogamy:** Sometimes used to refer to marrying and divorcing several times, but having only one spouse at any one time.

**Sibling Rivalry:** The competition for attention that often develops between brothers, sisters, or a brother and sister. Sibling rivalry can become even more complex within the step-family or blended family environment. See essays in Chapter Two, "Relationships."

**Single-Parent Family:** A family headed by a parent who has either divorced, become widowed, or had a child out of wedlock. Single-parent families at one time were seen as transitional or as diminished family structures, but they are increasingly becoming the norm in a society with an extremely high divorce rate.

**Stereotype:** A preconceived notion of someone or something that assumes all members of a group possess certain characteristics, without considering or accounting for individual variations and difference. A traditional stereotype of the single-parent family is one headed by a woman on welfare, or a woman "unable to hold a man." The reality is that some single-parent families today are intentionally so, some are headed by males, and many are middle-class rather than poor.

**Traditional Family:** Often, what is meant by the term "modern family." Another, older meaning of "traditional family" would coincide with the definition of "extended family" above. The term "traditional family" is often used as a codeword for a return to the values of the past.

## Glossary of Rhetorical Terms and Writing Strategies

**Allusion:** A direct or indirect reference to something outside the text at hand. The effectiveness of an allusion depends on how well it supports/amplifies the point at hand and how familiar the reader is with the reference. In her essay, "The Whispering of the Walls" (Chapter Two, "Relationships") Susanne Newby Short alludes to D.H. Lawrence's "The Rocking-Horse Winner." She uses Lawrence's classic short story as a point of departure for her observations about the need for parents to understand and deal with the anxiety children feel about family stress and disagreements.

**Analogy:** A comparison of two items or situations with similar attributes in order to clarify a point or support an argument. One of the items compared is more commonplace and familiar than the other, in order to shed light on the more complex or less well-known of the two. Analogy is rarely adequate alone to support an argument. Analogies are often used to begin an essay.

**Argument:** A discussion or debate involving a presentation of evidence to support an assertion and refute contradictory evidence or claims. In expository writing, an argument is often a piece of writing in which the thesis has an "argumentative edge"; the body of the essay provides evidence supporting that thesis. Some instructors and writers believe that nearly all expository writing (and sometimes expressive writing) entails some degree of argument. In *Coming from Home,* most of the essays could be considered arguments. Some chapters focus on pro or con positions on controversial issues (as in the "Breaking the Mold" essays in Chapter Seven); some focus on arguments for a particular set of causes or effects (as with many of the essays in Chapter Six); and some focus on proposals that might help solve a particular problem or conflict (as do the problem-and-solution essays in Chapter Nine).

**Audience:** The readers of a written work or the viewers/listeners of a work in another media. One's sense of audience helps to shape one's writing and determines many of an author's crucial choices of style and content: level of language, background information, emotional appeals, extent of narrative. The audience for writing can be very specific—a particular individual, a small circle of friends, members of a certain professional group—or it can be quite broad, such as the "general reader" of popular periodicals. In reading the selections in *Coming from Home*, notice the wide range of audiences which the authors have chosen to address in their comments on the subject of the family.

**Cause and Effect:** A type of paragraph or essay organization that considers an event or situation and looks back, analyzing origins and influences, or looks forward, discussing potential future outcomes or results. Writers must take special care in analyzing distant, coincidental, or immediate causes and examining possible future effects. Most of the essays in Chapter Six, "Tensions," explore the causes and/or effects of the stresses and tensions that beset the modern family.

**Classification:** In expository writing, refers to a means of developing a piece of writing through sorting, or categorizing, items, people, or ideals by class or type. In an essay, the classification should support a thesis and increase the reader's understanding; there must also be a clearly stated purpose supported by the process of categorization. Ella Taylor's essay, "Prime-Time Families" (Chapter Four) classifies the different images of American family life presented by television situation comedies.

**Collaboration:** Working together, especially in joint intellectual activity. In composition courses, students frequently collaborate in and out of class through peer workshops and study groups, responding to each others' drafts, working on exercises, studying readings, and sometimes composing drafts together. Collaborative groups need to set guidelines for effective work, such as agreeing to come to class prepared, selecting a group leader and notetaker, preparing time schedules, and carefully considering all members' observations.

**Comparison/Contrast:** A paragraph or essay organized so as to discuss similarities and or differences between two things, places, people, or theories, in order to increase the reader's understanding of one or both and to support an assertion. Jeremy Seabrook's essay, "A Twin Is Only Half a Person," like many essays in Chapter Two, "Relationships," is organized around a comparison between two close relatives—in this case, twin brothers.

**Conclusion:** The closing part of an essay or story. The conclusion of an essay drives home the point, while often supplying a thought-provoking argument to encourage the reader to reconsider the points made in the essay or to reflect on the long-term implications of the problem under discussion. In P. W. Alexander's "Christmas at Home" (Chapter Nine), her conclusion brings her reflection on her family tradition full circle, ending with a thought-provoking phrase or "clincher" sentence: "If you ask me why I do it, I can only say, because I have so much." Conclusions in stories or poems are usually less direct than conclusions in essays, leaving readers with more room for interpretation.

**Connotation/Denotation:** Connotation refers to the nonexplicit, unspoken associations a word has for various audiences. Denotation refers to the explicit, dictionary-style definitions of a word. "Home," for example, denotes "a place where one lives, a residence," while to many people it also connotes belonging, comfort, warmth. Issues of connotation in language are particularly important when reading poetry, where almost every word must be weighed carefully for its connotations.

545

**Critique:** A critical review of a piece of writing or artistic production. Because a critique involves a judgment or evaluation, it needs to state clearly the underlying criteria or values upon which its evaluation rests, as well as provide specific references to the work under consideration. See Barbara Ehrenreich's essay on Roseanne Barr in Chapter Four, "The Wretched of the Hearth."

**Definition:** A definition categorizes, amplifies, and explains what one means by a particular term. How and to what degree one defines largely depends on the overall purpose and audience for a particular piece of writing. A definition essay can be developed using a number of different writing techniques: comparison (with other similar, easily confused meanings); classification (different varieties or types); and, of course, argumentation (that your definition is the best one or the most appropriate).

**Description:** The process of putting mental images or sense impressions into words. Description is often used to support claims or other strategies of writing. The dream sequence in Toni Cade Bambara's "Raymond's Run" (Chapter Two), for example, entails a type of description quite different from the rest of the story, conveying a different mood and making a point about the scene taking place and the story as a whole.

**Essay:** A brief piece of writing, usually several pages in length, on a single subject, expressing the writer's point of view. An essay may be developed by any number of modes and organizational strategies. See the "Students' Introduction" at the beginning of this text for a fuller discussion of the essay form and composition.

**Example:** An illustration to support or demonstrate a point; a specific representative of a group or whole. Examples are a common type of evidence used to support claims. An example should be introduced clearly, with an adequate transition and emphasis on its relevance to the main point of the paragraph in which it is found, as in the following passage from Stephen Kline's "Limits to the Imagination": Marketing and Children's Culture (Chapter Four):

> The third and most important element in tie-in marketing is the personality toy. Although Mickey Mouse showed that animal cartoons could be popular with the very young, it was Barbie—the best-selling character of all time—who during the 1950s and 1960s provided the object lesson in character marketing.

**Exposition, Expository:** In fiction, exposition refers to background explanation of events that took place before the events narrated in the story. An example would be the brief background on the economic status of the family in Lawrence's "The Rocking-Horse Winner" that begins the story. In essay writing, exposition involves a careful explanation of events or ideas for purposes of enhancing the understanding of the reader. Strategies for expository writing include definition, process, classification, comparison, and, in some cases, cause-and-effect writing.

**Figurative Language:** Nonliteral, comparative language that makes use of metaphor (direct comparisons of two items which may seem on the surface to have little in common) and simile (comparisons using "like" or "as"). Poems often communicate their primary meaning through figurative language, whereas in essays, figurative language is often used to create a mood or to add an extra, imaginative dimension to the discussion. Note the use of metaphor in the poem, "The Child," by George Keithley in Chapter One: "Each face is flame." On the other hand, essayists like Jane Howard also use metaphor, but in a more discursive, expository fashion, as in "All Happy Clans Are Alike: In Search of The Good Family," in which Howard suggests that "good families are fortresses with many windows and doors to the outer world."

**Image:** A representation or a picture in the mind, often evoked through both literal and figurative language. An image tends to make writing seem more vivid and concrete, as in the following image from Alice Walker's essay, "Father," in Chapter One: "When the black power movement came, with its emphasis on cropped natural hair, I did the job myself, filling the face bowl and bathroom floor with hair and shocking my husband when he arrived home."

**Introduction:** The first part of an essay that enables the writer and reader to get on common ground. The introduction broaches the subject and establishes the tone and direction of the essay, often terminating with a thesis statement. An introduction may try to get the reader's attention, sometimes starting off with a question, or beginning with a startling fact, image, or brief narrative, as does Melinda Blau's "Adult Children: Tied to the Past" in Chapter Six that begins with several paragraphs that explore a misunderstanding between a member of the Adult Child movment and her 75-year-old mother.

**Irony:** The use of words or events to convey the opposite of their literal meaning; an expression contrasting apparent and intended meaning, often for rhetorical, dramatic, or humorous effect. An example of effective use of irony to begin an essay can be found in the first two sentences of Alfred Lubrano's "Bricklayer's Boy" in Chapter Two:

> My father and I were college buddies back in the mid-1970s. While I was in class at Columbia, struggling with the esoterica du jour, he was on a bricklayer's scaffold not far up the street, working on a campus building.

**Memoir:** An account of the personal experiences of the author, as in an autobiography. Chapters One and Eight contain a number of examples of effective memoir writing.

**Narrative:** Generally refers to the recounting of a fictional or nonfictional event. Many of the readings in Chapters One, Two, Three, and Eight contain strong narrative elements. Narratives can be used in essays to serve as extended examples of more general points, the way the "family stories" that Elizabeth Stone narrates in her essay in Chapter

*Glossaries*

547

Three help to make her larger points about the importance of such stories in family life.

**Paragraph:** A piece of writing that begins with an indentation and generally develops one topic or one aspect of a topic. Unlike journalists, who must write short paragraphs to fill narrow columns of print for quick reading, the average paragraph in expository essays is often seven or eight sentences in length, which allows for a clear topic sentence, one or two related examples, and other developing detail and supporting facts.

**Peer Sharing:** The process of working with fellow students to share drafts and other work, usually in small groups. Often, groups working together over the length of a term at school develop ties and methods of working that parallel those described in some of the readings on family and community.

**Personification:** A type of figurative expression found in poetry, fiction, and sometimes in nonfiction in which a nonhuman object, animal, or idea is given human characteristics. Stephen Dunn's "Middle Class Poem" in Chapter Four personifies "the news of the world" as an unfaithful lover who embraces us, pulls back, and "roams the streets."

**Plot:** The main events of a story or other narrative in their causal order. Plots may move forward in a temporal sequence, or they may travel back and forth in time, revealing important past events when necessary to make sense of an evolving action. A full plot involves the exposition, the initial unfolding of events, the introduction of conflict, the rising action as suspense mounts, the climax or high point of action, and the final resolution or ending of the story.

**Poetry:** Literary works in rhythmical language or verse. Poems are very subtle and concentrated in their use of language. They usually involve a heightened use of figurative language, such as extended metaphor, and they may employ a central speaking voice or persona to convey ideas. Sometimes the persona of the poem seems to espouse the poet's own views, as in the case of Susan Griffin's "Love Should Grow Up Like a Wild Flower in the Fields," (Chapter Seven), or reflect on childhood experiences, as in Theodore Roethke's "My Papa's Waltz" (Chapter Six) and Marie Howe's "Letter to My Sister" (Chapter Two). Often, however, as in George Keithley's "The Child" (Chapter One), the poem and its imaginary world take on a life of their own and are subject to a wide range of interpretations.

**Point of View:** The perspective or vantage point from which one views or conveys action or information. Stories and poems are usually narrated either in the first-person, the third-person limited (that is, limited to the awareness of a single character), or the third-person omniscient (the all-knowing narrative voice). Essays are sometimes told using the first-person, or "I," point of view, as in the personal-experience narratives found in Chapter One. Academic or research-oriented essays frequently employ the third-person point of view. However, many researchers on the family choose to involve themselves personally in their research and share narratives based on their own first-hand observations, as in the case of Judith Wallerstein's study of divorced families, "On the Brow of the Hill," in Chapter Six.

**Process:** A mode of writing involving the analysis and discussion of some action as a series of clearly explained steps. As its title suggests, Lilly Collett's essay "Step by Step" (Chapter Six) is organized according to the unfolding phases in her relationship with her past as a survivor of an abusive family.

**Proposal:** A specific kind of argument urging that something be done to resolve a problem or issue. A proposal usually begins by stating a problem that needs to be solved and emphasizing, in a brief historical statement, what series of causes and effects helped create the problem. Then the writer develops a series of ideas which might effectively resolve some of the major difficulties raised in the first section of the essay, briefly defending each step and clarifying the reasons why other previous attempts have failed to work. A good example of a proposal is Mindy Holliday's and Robin Cronin's essay "Families First" (Chapter Nine) which presents a model program for "in-home crisis intervention and family education."

**Reading Process:** Like writing, the reading process can be seen as a series of overlapping steps, such as prereading, asking questions about main headings and topic sentences, making response entries in a reader's journal, then rereading and evaluating the selection as a whole. See the "Students' Introduction" at the start of the text for more information.

**Reflective Essay:** An essay in which authors examine aspects of their personal experience to draw some larger conclusions about themselves and the world they live in. Many of the essays in Chapter Eight, "Growing Away," reflect on the writers' experiences as they reevaluate their relationships with their families.

**Setting:** The place where a work of fiction or autobiography takes place. Setting can include any details that indicate time of day, weather conditions, historical period, etc. Joan Didion's autobiographical essay, "Going Home," in Chapter One is set in Didion's family home, to which she returns as a mother with a young child. Her emphasis on the details that distinguish her family's home, such as its rural location near a stream and graveyard in the Central Valley of California, its dustiness, and its family mementos, give her essay a powerful sense of place and underscore her thesis about the difficulty of reconciling oneself with the past.

**Short Story:** A brief fictional narrative, designed to create a strong emotional response in a reader or to make a point about a theme through skillful use of such fictional techniques as point of view, characters, plot, and setting. See the "Students' Introduction" at the start of this book for information on the differences between nonfiction reading and understanding the ideas expressed in short stories and other fictional works.

**Style:** The diction, sentence length and structure, organizational strategies, and other characteristics of a particular writer's work.

**Symbol:** An object, place, or person that, because of association, resemblance, or custom, represents something else, often something invisible or intangible. An example of a powerful literary symbol is the rocking horse in D. H. Lawrence's short story, "The Rocking-Horse Winner." The rocking horse suggests at first to us the safety and restful play of the nursery; later it takes on more ominous, worldly, and destructive overtones.

**Theme:** An idea, point of view, or perception that is amplified or discussed in a literary work or composition. Most of the works in *Coming from Home* have been chosen because they relate to the theme of the family and its impact on the individual; however, many of the works have many other themes as well. Thus it is possible to read imaginative works repeatedly as we go through life, responding to different themes with each successive reading.

**Thesis:** The central point or core assertion in a piece of writing. The rest of the writing, typically an essay, develops and supports the thesis. Judith Stacey asserts in "The Postmodern Family" (Chapter Seven), for example, that while some may long for the stereotypical traditional American family of the past, it cannot and should not be brought back.

**Tone:** The author's stance on or attitude toward a subject, expressed through ideas about the topic and the language used to express those ideas. When Jane Howard, in "All Happy Clans Are Alike: In Search of the Good Family" (Chapter Nine) comments, "Both my parents will remain in my nerves and muscles and mind until the day I die . . . but they aren't the only ones," she is expressing an emotional and intellectual perspective on the family that she maintains throughout the essay: a mixture of warm nostalgia and realistic regard for the need to compromise and grow.

**Voice:** In writing, a term that refers to the sense of an author's personal presence in a piece of writing—the style and tone of a writer that comes through in the prose, giving the reading an individual, lively quality. In the fictional story "Raymond's Run" (Chapter Two), author Toni Cade Bambara establishes the voice of the young narrator through dialogue and narration—short clauses and fragments with many coordinating conjunctions characteristic of children's speech.

**Writing Process:** The act of writing can be seen as involving a number of recursive phases consisting of prewriting/planning, drafting, and revising. Good writing tends to evolve through spending adequate time in each of these phases, going over the piece frequently, and sharing it with others to see it from different perspectives. See the "Students' Introduction" at the start of this book for a fuller explanation.

# ACKNOWLEDGMENTS

Lily Collett, "Step by Step" first appeared in *Mother Jones* magazine, July 1988. Copyright held by the author. Reprinted by permission.

Joan Didion, "On Going Home" from *Slouching Toward Bethlehem*. Copyright © 1967, 1968 by Joan Didion. Reprinted by permission of Farrar, Straus & Giroux, Inc.

Annie Dillard, "Adolescence" from *An American Childhood*. Copyright © 1987 by Annie Dillard. Reprinted by permission of HarperCollins Publishers.

Chita Divakaruni, "Indian Movie, New Jersey" is reprinted by permission of the author.

Michael Dorris, "Moving Out" from *The Broken Cord*. Copyright © 1989 by Michael Dorris. Reprinted by permission of HarperCollins Publishers.

Stephen Dunn, "Middle Class Poem" from *Not Dancing*. Reprinted by permission of Carnegie-Mellon University Press. Copyright © 1984 by Stephen Dunn.

Barbara Ehrenreich, "The Wretched of the Hearth: The Undainty Feminism of Rosanne Barr," *New Republic,* April 2, 1990. Reprinted by permission of the author.

David Elkind, "The Child Inside" from *The Hurried Child*. Copyright © 1988 by David Elkind. Reprinted by permission of Addison-Wesley Publishing Company.

Angel C. Fabian, "Sharing the Blame" is reprinted by permission of the author.

Bruce Fein, "Reserve Marriage for Heterosexuals" originally appeared in *Journal of the American Bar Association,* the lawyer's magazine, January 1990. Reprinted by permission of the author.

Susan Griffin, "Love Should Grow Up Like a Wild Iris in the Fields" from *Like the Iris of an Eye* (New York: Harper, 1976). Reprinted by permission of the author.

Dorothy Height, "Self-Help—A Black Tradition" is reprinted from *The Nation* magazine, July 24–31, 1989, The Nation Company, Inc., © 1989.

Arlie Hochschild and Ann Machung, "Stepping into Old Biographies or Making History Happen?" from *Second Shift*. Copyright © 1989 by Arlie Hochschild and Ann Machung. Used by permission of Viking Penguin, a division of Penguin Books USA, Inc.

Mindy Holliday and Robin Cronin, "Families First: A Significant Step Toward Family Preservation" from May 1990 *Families in Society*. Reprinted by permission of Family Service America, Inc.

Jane Howard, "All Happy Clans Are Alike: In Search of the Good Family" from *Families*. Copyright © 1978 by Jane Howard. Reprinted by permission of Simon & Schuster.

Marie Howe, "Letter to My Sister" from *The Good Thief*. Copyright © 1988 by Marie Howe. Reprinted by permission of Persea Books.

Alfred Kazin, "In Mother's Kitchen" excerpted from "The Kitchen" in *A Walker in the City*. Copyright 1951 and renewed © 1979 by Alfred Kazin. Reprinted by permission of Harcourt Brace Jovanovich, Inc.

*Acknowledgments*

George Keithley, "The Child," reprinted by permission of *The Iowa Review*, Volume 11, No. 2–3, Spring–Summer 1980, copyright © 1981 by The University of Iowa.

Maxine Hong Kingston, "No Name Woman" from *Woman Warrior*. Copyright © 1975, 1976 by Maxine Hong Kingston. Reprinted by permission of Alfred A. Knopf, Inc.

Stephen Kline, "Limits to the Imagination: Marketing and Children's Culture," from Ian Angus and Sut Jhally (eds.), *Culture Politics in Contemporary America*, is reprinted by permission of Routledge, Chapman & Hall, Ltd.

Elisabeth Kübler-Ross, "The Patient's Family" from *On Death and Dying*. Copyright © 1969 by Elisabeth Kübler-Ross. Reprinted by permission of Macmillan Publishing Company.

Maxine Kumin, "the journey: for jane at thirteen" reprinted by permission of Curtis Brown, Ltd.

D. H. Lawrence, "The Rocking Horse Winner" from *The Complete Short Stories of D. H. Lawrence*. Copyright 1933 by The Estate of D. H. Lawrence, renewed © 1961 by Angelo Ravagli and C. M. Weekley, Executors of the Estate of Frieda Lawrence. Used by permission of Viking Penguin, a division of Penguin Books USA, Inc.

Howard Libit, "Families Separated by Bars" is reprinted by permission of the author.

Sara Lawrence Lightfoot, "Beginnings" from *Balm in Gilead*. Reprinted with permission of Addison-Wesley Publishing Company. Copyright © 1989 by Sara Lawrence Lightfoot.

Alfred Lubrano, "Bricklayer's Boy," originally appeared in *Gentleman's Quarterly*, June 1989. Reprinted by permission of the author. Copyright © 1989 Alfred Lubrano. Alfred Lubrano is a reporter with New York Newsday.

Bernard Malamud, "My Son the Murderer" from *The Collected Stories of Bernard Malamud* (Farrar, Straus and Giraux). Copyright © 1968, 1983 by Bernard Malamud. This story was originally published in *Esquire* magazine. Reprinted by permission of Russell Volkening, Inc.

Amy Marx, "My Grandfather's Memories" is reprinted by permission of the author.

Kathryn McCamant and Charles Durrett, "Cohousing and the American Dream" from *Cohousing: A Contemporary Approach to Housing Ourselves*. Copyright © 1988 by Kathryn McCamant and Charles Durrett. Reprinted by permission of Ten Speed Press, Berkeley, California.

Toni Morrison, "A Slow Walk of Trees" originally appeared in *New York Times Magazine*, July 4, 1976. Copyright © 1976 by Toni Morrison. Reprinted by permission of International Creative Management.

Lance Morrow, "Downsizing an American Dream" from *Fishing in the Tiber* by Lance Morrow. Copyright © 1988 by Lance Morrow. Reprinted by permission of Henry Holt and Company, Inc.

Gloria Naylor, "The Two" from *The Women of Brewster Place*. Copyright © 1980, 1982 by Gloria Naylor. Reprinted by permission of Viking Penguin, a division of Penguin Books USA, Inc.

Tillie Olsen, "I Stand Here Ironing," from *Tell Me a Riddle* by Tillie Olsen. Copyright © 1956, 1957, 1960, 1961 by Tillie Olsen. Reprinted by permission of Delacourt Press/Seymour Lawrence, a division of Bantam Doubleday Dell Publishing Group, Inc.

Simon Ortiz, "The Language We Know" is reprinted from *I Tell You Now: Autobiographical Essays of Native American Writers,* edited by Brian Swann and Arnold Krupat, by permission of University of Nebraska Press. Copyright © 1987 by University of Nebraska Press.

Keenen Peck, "When 'Family' Is Not a Household Word," *The Progressive,* September 1988, is reprinted by permission of *The Progressive,* 409 East Main Street, Madison, WI 53703.

Carlos Perez, "Once Upon a Time in New England," is reprinted by permission of the author.

Josephine Ramos, "Growing Up Bilingual," is reprinted by permission of the author.

Alberto Alvaro Rios, "Nani" from *Whispering to Fool the Wind* (Bronx, New York: Sheep Meadow Press, 1982). Copyright © 1982 by Alberto Rios. Reprinted by permission of the author.

Richard Rodriguez, "Private and Public Language" from *Hunger of Memory* by Richard Rodriguez. Copyright © 1982 by Richard Rodriguez. Reprinted by permission of David R. Godine, Publisher.

Theodore Roethke, "My Papa's Waltz" from *The Collected Poems of Theodore Roethke* by Theodore Roethke. Copyright © 1942 by Hearst Magazines, Inc. Used by permission of Doubleday, a division of Bantam Doubleday Dell Publishing Group, Inc.

Javier Ruiz, "Terminator 2: A Machine that Loves," is reprinted by permission of the author.

Jeremy Seabrook, "A Twin Is Only Half a Person" from *Mother and Son.* Copyright © 1980 by Jeremy Seabrook. Reprinted by permission of Pantheon Books, a division of Random House, Inc.

Dr. Seuss, "Oh, the Places You'll Go!" Copyright © 1990 by Theodor S. Geisel and Audrey S. Geisel, trustees under trust agreement dated August 27, 1984. Reprinted by permission of Random House, Inc.

David Sherwood, "Discarded" originally appeared in the *New York Times,* February 9, 1986. Copyright © 1986 by The New York Times Company. Reprinted by permission.

Susanne Newby Short, "The Whispering of the Walls" from *Reclaiming the In-*

*ner Child,* edited by Jeremiah Abrams (Los Angeles: Tarcher Books, 1989). Copyright © 1989 by Susanne Newby Short. Reprinted by permission of the author.

Judith Stacey, "Postmodern Families, For Better and Worse" from *Brave New Families.* Copyright © 1990 by Judith Stacey. Reprinted by permission of Basic Books, a division of HarperCollins Publishers, Inc.

Shelby Steele, "Being Black and Feeling Blue," from *The Content of Our Character,* and reprinted with permission of St. Martin's Press, Inc., New York. Copyright © 1990 by Shelby Steele.

Thomas Stoddard, "Marriage Is a Fundamental Right" originally appeared in the *New York Times,* March 4, 1989. Copyright © 1989 by The New York Times Company. Reprinted by permission.

Elizabeth Stone, "Family Myths: Explanation Myths" from *Black Sheep and Kissing Cousins.* Copyright © 1988 by Elizabeth Stone. Reprinted by permission of Times Books, a division of Random House, Inc.

Amy Tan, "Scar" and "American Translation/Waverley Jong: Four Directions" from *The Joy Luck Club.* Copyright © 1989 by Amy Tan. Reprinted by permission of G. P. Putnam's Sons.

Ella Taylor, "Family Television: Then and Now" from *Prime-Time Families: Television Culture in Postwar America,* pages 157–167. Copyright © 1989 The Regents of the University of California. Reprinted by permission.

J. B. Taylor, "Teamwork" is reprinted by permission of the author.

Susan Allen Toth, "Boyfriends" from *Blooming: A Small Town Girlhood.* Copyright © 1978, 1987 by Susan Allen Toth. Reprinted by permission of Little, Brown and Company.

Klarice Tsing, "The Violin" is reprinted by permission of the author.

Alice Walker, "Father" from *Living by the Word.* Copyright © 1985 by Alice Walker. Reprinted by permission of Harcourt Brace Jovanovich, Inc.

Judith Wallerstein and Sandra Blakeslee, "On the Brow of the Hill" from *Second Changes.* Copyright © 1989 by Judith S. Wallerstein and Sandra Blakeslee. Reprinted by permission of Ticknor & Fields, a Houghton Mifflin imprint. All rights reserved.

Richard Wilbur, "For the Student Strikers" from *The Mind-Reader: New Poems.* Copyright © 1971 by Richard Wilbur. Reprinted by permission of Harcourt Brace Jovanovich, Inc.

Laura Ingalls Wilder, "Moving In" from *Little House on the Prairie.* Copyright 1935 by Laura Ingalls Wilder. Copyright renewed © 1963 by Roger L. McBride. Reprinted by permission of HarperCollins Publishers.

Marie Winn, "Television and Family Rituals" from *The Plug-in Drug.* Copyright © 1977, 1985 by Marie Winn Miller. Used by permission of Viking Penguin, a division of Penguin Books USA, Inc.

Dan Zegart, "Solomon's Choice" from *Ms. Magazine,* June 1989. Copyright © 1989. Reprinted by permission of *Ms. Magazine.*

# INDEX